ADMINISTERING
The Company Financial Function

ADMINISTERING
The Company Financial Function

Edward W. Buge

PRENTICE-HALL, INC.   Englewood Cliffs, N.J.

Prentice-Hall International, Inc., *London*
Prentice-Hall of Australia, Pty., Ltd., *Sydney*
Prentice-Hall of Canada, Ltd., *Toronto*
Prentice-Hall of India Private Ltd., *New Delhi*
Prentice-Hall of Japan, Inc., *Tokyo*
Prentice-Hall of Southeast Asia, Pte., Ltd., *Singapore*
Whitehall Books, Ltd., *Wellington, New Zealand*

© 1979, *by*

PRENTICE-HALL, INC.

Englewood Cliffs, N.J.

All rights reserved. No part of this book may be reproduced in any form or by any means, without permission in writing from the publisher.

Library of Congress Cataloging in Publication Data

Buge, Edward W
    Administering the company financial function.

    Includes index.
    1. Business enterprises--Finance.
2. Corporations--Finance. I. Title.
HG4026.B83   658.1'5   78-11768
ISBN 0-13-004879-8

Printed in the United States of America

To Louise,
whose thoughtfulness and patience
provided the long periods of time
necessary for the book's preparation.

"The Science of Today
Is the Technology of
Tomorrow."

—Edward Teller—

Acknowledgment

To my many friends who have contributed much of their time, knowledge, ideas and financial reports, I owe a deep debt of gratitude. It is a wonderful feeling to be able to call upon these individuals and have them take time to assist in a demanding project. To all, my sincere thanks!

Edward W. Buge

About the Author

Edward W. Buge is principal owner of his own C.P.A. firm in Tucson. He has a long and distinguished career as Certified Public Accountant in four states and as Controller, Treasurer, Financial Vice President and President of various industrial firms. His broad-gauged financial managerial experience covers key administrative responsibilities for mining, manufacturing, wholesale, retail, construction and service enterprises.

In addition to his duties in accountancy, the author serves as President of Task Analysis Center, a minicomputer-oriented "think tank" specializing in financial planning and control for smaller firms.

Mr. Buge organized the Planning Executives Institute in which he now serves as Director, and is an active member of the American Institute of Certified Public Accountants, and the National Association of Accountants.

The author of How to Get More Net from the Gross Sales Dollar, Mr. Buge was graduated from the University of Illinois and the Walton School of Accountancy.

FOREWORD

Financial Administration is a major aspect of today's business gamesmanship requiring a knowledge of and affecting every facet of a business whether it be large or small. While many books and articles exist covering theoretical techniques largely applicable to major or large corporations, there has existed a gap in the "how to" applications for small- or medium-sized organizations.

Recognizing that gap, E. W. Buge, a long-time practitioner of financial administration and planning, has prepared this book, setting forth practical applications based upon his personal experiences supplemented with his intimate knowledge of the experiences of his many friends occupied in all aspects of the business and financial world.

Mr. Buge has long been forward-looking in his thinking. His personal influence was instrumental in the formation of the organization which was the forerunner of today's Planning Executives Institute. The author served as the first president of the organization and has been active in its development over the years, now serving on its Advisory Board of Directors.

Buge's method of presentation should make for interesting and fascinating reading, with resultant financial rewards as the tools and procedures are applied to your company or your job.

G. M. Rayburn, President
New Mexico and Arizona Land Company

What This Book Will Do for You

This book will give you concise, concrete examples of the profitable techniques used by financial executives across the nation in administering the financial function of their firm. The techniques and methods have saved actual companies hundreds of millions of dollars, running the financial function as a profit-center, not an item of overhead.

It explores and records the magnitude of the task of confronting the twin challenges of growth and inflation through interviews and actual case studies. New techniques and methods to enhance the status and stream-of-profit contribution of the financial operation are detailed for your review and practical application.

KEY WAYS THIS BOOK WILL HELP YOU

- Recognizes that the financial administrator's function is now a major part of the corporate structure. More corporate presidents are being drafted from the ranks of financial executives than ever before. See Chapter 1.

- Tells you how to target lucrative new ways to implement efficiencies and prepare for them. Interviews reveal five major items to prepare for and at least twenty ideas for capitalizing on profit opportunities in the financial field. See Chapter 2.

- Alerts you to the tremendous potential of the management communications center and the minicomputer—what they are, their capabilities, their weaknesses and the profit potential inherent in their use. Seven practical ideas for their use are also included. See Chapter 8. This is a most interesting chapter.

- Details the financial planning and strategy utilized by numerous firms—how to plan growth, profits and financial stability; the techniques for models, simulation and "What if?" for evaluating proposed corporate strategies and actions; how to enhance your image through planning techniques and reports; a checklist for planners. See Chapter 7.

- Stresses the necessity of control. (Control techniques can be as profitable as planning. It can reduce or avoid losses.) Tells how a reduction in costs of one hundred dollars can reduce the pressure on sales and production functions by five thousand dollars. Illustrates the four-hundred-thousand dollar annual cost reduction program of a small firm and a control plan for 4.5 million dollars in cost reduction by a major firm. Techniques for speedy control data are reviewed. See Chapter 5.

- Explores the use of the Delphi technique—is it practical under day-to-day business conditions? Illustrates the results of the disaster theory in operating a business; the creative approach to unlimited growth; the reaction of financial executives to models and game theory. See Chapter 6.

- Demonstrates the huge potential the profit making tools of information storage, retrieval and use can have for your firm. Information is *power—money—profit*. The new Key-Result approach to management information is detailed to assist you in setting up or revising your system. See Chapter 8.
- Applies the new microtechnology in financial reporting through minicomputers used for up-to-the-minute cost accounting. The newest types of reports and the development of the financial profit center concept are described. Thirty do's and don'ts in financial reporting are listed. Instant alerts to deviation from plan are covered. See Chapter 9.
- Pinpoints major responsibilities in dealing with SEC and public reports; new concepts of accounting; new strategies and alerts to current and future trends. See Chapter 16.
- Explores leasing in detail—the tax benefits, increased cash flow and increased return on investment through leasing. Details "Lease or Purchase" decision models. All types of leases, forms and checklists are illustrated. See Chapter 10.
- Points out the major threat to financial executives of corporate liquidity; shows that leverage plus sweat and headaches can yield fabulous profits. Also covered are: Protecting cash flow by using variable payment debt; how to successfully restructure debt in times of crisis; production payment loans; balloon note financing; borrowing and repayment techniques; warning chart of debt versus payoffs; scheduling debt repayment; how financial administrators handle large amounts of debt. See Chapter 13.
- Explains how to sharpen your financial and economic acumen; methods used to update your financial systems, techniques and knowledge; brain-sharing with other financial administrators; the challenge of radical changes and how you cope with them. *Survival Rule:* Be alert—ready for change! (Explained throughout the entire text.)

HOW THIS BOOK IS ORGANIZED

Administering the Company Financial Function is organized into eighteen chapters with a Locatomatic reference section at the back of the book. It starts with the challenge of the future for the basic financial organization and details the many methods, techniques, theories and actual practical methods used by the financial administrators of large, medium and small firms. The ways to increase the status and profitability of the financial function are discussed and explored. The financial executive has developed into a major factor in the decision making process of the firm. The financial organization is presently one of the top profit centers of the firm.

The information contained in the book was developed by actual interviews with individuals currently serving as top financial administrators. It presents a documented insight into the day-to-day operations, the problems encountered and the practical solutions applied to those problems. Within eighteen short chapters you have over fifty ways to increase the profits of your firm. Each chapter contains actual examples of detailed methods, techniques and forms used by financial administrators.

- Chapter 2 alerts you to current trends and illustrates how to think ahead and meet the growth challenges of the future. It has a checklist which is certain to provide you with ways to increase the efficiency of your organization.
- Chapter 3 gives an insight into the latest "on line" reports with specific examples.

What This Book Will Do for You

- Chapter 8 is probably the hottest subject in financial administration today: the use of management communications centers and minicomputers has virtually limitless potential. Correctly and effectively used they can vault the financial administrator into a major factor in all business operations. *Red flag* this chapter, it deserves careful review and thought. Your success or failure in the financial world may depend on your effective use of these latest techniques.
- Now go back to Chapter 7, The Management Communications Center—The Financial Data Bank. Within this chapter you are introduced to the techniques and practical applications of financial planning. Ten Ways to Keep Your Planning on Target is a sure-fire profit increasing checklist for action.
- Skip ahead to Chapter 18, Case Studies in Successful Financial Administration. Here is an insight into actual corporate administration. Actual operations of three sizes of firms supported by data gleaned from other case studies.
- Need specific help? Look through the Locatomatic at the back of the book. Here is a catalog of forms, reports, worksheets, checklists and ideas for saving development time. At least 15 profit opportunities exist in the use of some of the material.
- The remaining pages expose you to theories, methods, thoughts and comments of successful financial administrators. There are no fewer than 46 different ideas and ways to help you administer the financial function "more profitably." Each chapter has its share of illustrations, actual "in use" forms and methods.

The preceding pages spelled out what this book will do for you and how the book is organized. Now consider these additional profitable uses of the book . . .

1. If you have a specific problem ranging from the basic organization of the financial administration function to "Should you rent, lease or buy?"—turn to the index or to the table of contents to find the chapter or page relating to that topic. Herein, are contained most of the possible options together with actual formulas and forms to use in determining the financial feasibility of each option. Read the text, use the supporting forms and appropriate formulae for a step-by-step solution to your problem.
2. If you need to design a special report form for your operations, turn to the Locatomatic at the back of the book and review the various forms to see if one will fit your requirements. Often a simple modification will fill your needs.
3. If you have many across-the-board financial administration problems, start with one point at a time, running through Chapters 1 through 12, in sequence. Compare the present method used by you with those currently in use by other financial executives. This review will doubtlessly reveal any weakness in your procedure and indicate opportunities for improvement. A careful review of your entire operational procedure will undoubtedly point out several ways to implement the effectiveness and profitability of your organization.
4. If you need actual formulas, forms, models and instructions, you will find the book well worth the cost due to the savings in time spent on research, design and debugging. You can adapt any of the items to your specific needs. The Locatomatic catalogs the reports, forms, worksheets and checklists. The checklists alone are valuable time and money savers.

Edward W. Buge

Table of Contents

Foreword 7

What This Book Will Do for You 9

1. New Techniques in Financial Administration That Meet Growth Challenges 25

What Is Financial Administration—How Did It Get Where It is?—26
Basic Point—27
New Techniques—27
Portable Data Terminals—28
On-Line Challenges—28
Interfacing Data—28
Cost Estimating—28
Case in Point—29
Flexibility—29
Microfiche—29
Facsimile—30
Cost Savings—Case in Point—30
Telefax—30
Graphics Video Display—30
International Communication Links—30
Why Use a Financial Management System?—31
Providing a Data Base—31
Economic and Financial Links—32
What Are the Reasons for Expansion or Growth?—32
Aim to Be the Very Best—A Person of Ability and Quality—33
Why Plan for Progress?—33
Those Are the Problems! What are the Solutions?—33
What Are the Tools Available?—34
Word of Warning—35
Case in Point—36
Distributing Computers—36

2. On-Line Reports: New Approaches to Daily Profit-and-Loss Reports 37

Getting on Line—37
Operating on Line—38
Case in Point—39
What Is the Language?—39
Case in Point—40
Inventories—40
Case in Point—40
Widespread Use—40
What Are the Features of an On-Line System for Inventory?—41
On-Line Daily Status Report—41
New Approaches to Daily Profit-and-Loss Reporting—43
Control Techniques for Variables—43
One Additional Feature—43
Let's Face Facts—44
Conclusions—44

3. Administering with Control Techniques: Using Corporate Profit Centers 55

Case in Point—56
Warning—56
Matrix Organizations—56
Case in Point—56
Case in Point—57
What Are the Essential Elements of Control?—57
Case in Point—57
Case in Point—58
What Are the Requirements of Control?—58
Case in Point—58
What Will a Profit Center Control System Provide?—59
The Basic Activity or Cost Centers—59
Administering with Control Techniques—63
Note—64
How the Plans Are Evolved—65
Case in Point—65
Reporting—65
Sample Type of Report—Sales—65
What Do We Accomplish?—66
Case in Point—66
Point to Note—67
Zero–Based Budgeting for Control—68
Case in Point—69
Case in Point—69
What Is Involved in ZBB?—69
What Is a Decision Package?—70
What Is Documentation?—70

Table of Contents

3. Administering with Control Techniques: Using Corporate Profit Centers (Cont'd.)

Plans, Goals and Strategies: What They Are and How They Are Set—82
The Four Basic Steps in Zero-Based Budgeting—Determining the Decision Units—The Decision Reporting Packages Illustrated—86
How the Decision Packages Are Ranked—97
Lessons Learned—101
The Planning Calendar, Allocation of Resources and What If?—105
Measuring, Analyzing and Correcting Performance—121

4. Administering Cost Reduction Programs—Creating Profits 129

Examples—129
Staffing for Cost Reduction—130
The Basic Plan—131
What to Do! The Action Checklist—132
Case in Point—132
Case in Point—133
Case in Point—133
Let's Look at Payroll and Payroll Expenses—134
Case in Point—134
Case in Point—135
Some Miscellaneous Items—135
Case in Point—135
Case in Point—135
Do not Be Deterred or Retreat Under Adverse Conditions—136
Case in Point—137
Wrap-Up—137
The Cost Equation—Components—138

5. Modern Approaches to Administering Financial Planning and Strategy 139

Planning and Strategy—139
Case in Point—139
Development of Planning—140
What Are the Forecasts?—140
Objectives in Planning: Organizational—Functional—141
Organizational Objectives—141
Objective and Function Interfacing—143
Case in Point—143
Management by Objective—143
Preparing the Plan—Annual or Long-Range—144
Monitoring a Plan—144
Offensive Plans—145
Defensive Plans—145
Let's Look at a Marketing Plan—145
What Can Planning Do for You?—146

5. Modern Approaches to Administering Financial Planning and Strategy (Cont'd.)

Five Steps in Objective Planning—147
Financial Planning—Results—147
Let's Look at Objectives—What Are the Basic Requirements?—147
The New Breed of Cats—147
Long-Range Planning—148
Strategies—149
How Do Financial Executives Develop Strategies?—149
The Mousetraps—How to Spot Them—150
Flexibility—150
Generalities—150
What Are the Strategic Factors of a Business?—151
The Delphi Theory—152
The Development of Strategic Organizations—152
Case in Point—152
Available Tools—152
Strategic Planning Is Here to Stay—153
Zero-Based Budgeting—153
Interesting Reading—154
Checklist for Keeping Planning and Strategies on Target—154

6. The Use of Financial Models by the Financial Administrator 165

Corporate Models—165
What Specific Types of Models Are Used?—166
Answers to Interviews—What Is a Model? What Does It Do?—166
What Purpose Do Models Serve?—167
Who Uses the Models?—167
What Are the Major Modeling Techniques?—168
What Is a Financial Model?—168
Model Inputs and Outputs—168
How Are the Models Varied for Conditions?—170
A Typical Model Base—171
What Does a Divestiture Model Tell You?—171
What Is "Top Down"-"Bottom Up"?—171
Best Method—172
The Strategic Model—172
Strategic Planning Model—Five-Year Basis Forecast—173
The Strategic Model Described—174
Standard Models—174
Control Models—174
Factory Control Models—174
Breakeven Point Models—175
Do's and Don'ts in Modeling—175
Game Theory—Is It Usable?—176
Models Are Practical at Every Level—177
A Defensive Cash Model—177
Basic Growth Rate Formula—178

Table of Contents

7. **The Management Communications Center—The Financial Data Bank** **191**

    Information Is Profit, Power and Success—191
    What Are the Staff Requirements?—192
    Let's Face Facts!—192
    Why It Is Important—193
    The Role of the Minicomputer—193
    Developing the Data Bank—194
    What Strategies Are Available to the Financial Administrator?—195
    Speed of Information Requirements—196
    Tact and Consideration—196
    Who Requires the Information? What Type?—196
    Types of Information to Put in the Bank—196
    Competitive Information—197
    What You Need to Know About a Specific Product—198
    Red Alert—The Failing Product—198
    Remember—Intelligence Technology Is Your Basic Strength—198
    These Are a Few Outside Sources of Data—199
    The Paperless Office—199
    The Central Data Base—199
    Coding for Instant Retrieval—200
    Sample Master Files—200
    Sources of Outside Data—201
    Do's and Don'ts for Data Bases—202
    Customer Competitive Information Report—203

8. **Computerized Accounting Yields Financial Reports— Concise and Fast!** **207**

    The Opportunity!—207
    The Organization Required—207
    What Reports Are Available?—208
    Case in Point—208
    Case in Point—209
    Who Uses Computers?—209
    Opportunity for the Financial Administrator!—209
    Easy to Learn—Easy to Use—210
    Case in Point—210
    Priorities—210
    Case in Point—Critical Decision—210
    Small Business Systems—211
    What Is Required to Utilize a Minicomputer?—211
    Case in Point—211
    What Are the Minicomputers Used for?—212
    Setting Up the System—213
    Basic Benefits Expected—213
    Do's and Don'ts—213
    Cases in Point—214
    Text Editor Terminals—214

8. Computerized Accounting Yields Financial Reports—Concise and Fast! (Cont'd.)

Summary of Equipment Utilized—214
Report Standards—226
Establishment of Report Objectives—226
Computer Reports—226
Typical Management Reports—226
Justification of Reports—227

9. Capital Investments—Lease, Rent or Buy? 229

Lease or Purchase—How to Decide!—230
Financial Reporting of Leases—234
Annual Report Comments on Leases—235
Worth Noting!—236
What Can Be Leased?—236
Types of Leases Available—236
What Are the Pitfalls?—237
Advantages of Leasing—237
A Typical Lease Document—238
Leveraged Leases—243
Basic Requirements—243
What a Leveraged Lease Covers—243
Cost of a Leveraged Lease—244
Opinions on Advantages and Disadvantages—244
Case in Point—244
Financial Model—245
Sorting It out—246
Determination and Allocation—246
Allocation Criteria—246
Determination Criteria—247
Rating Projects—247
Basic Steps—247
Control Reports—248
Should You Lease That Machine?—Truck?—Office Furniture?—250

10. Administering Financial Control of Current Assets 253

Financial Administration of Current Assets—253
Examples of Speeding Up Cash Flow—255
Cash Administration—255
Duration of Cash Cycle—256
Cash Strategy—257
Time Cycle for Idle Cash Investments—257
Basic Rule—258
Effectiveness—258
The Credit Function—A Challenge—258
Performance Rating—259
Inventories—The Largest Current Asset—259

Table of Contents

10. Administering Financial Control of Current Assets (Cont'd.)

Meeting the Challenge of Inflation and Growth—260
Reporting Techniques for Controlling Current Assets—261
Forecast Receivable Balances—262
Forecast Inventory Balances—263
Inventory by Customer—By Product—264
Maintaining an Emergency Cash Balance—264
On-Line Control of Cash, Inventory and Accounts Receivable—265
Zero Balance Accounts—265
Advantages of Zero Balance Accounts—266
Drafts—266
Conclusions—266

11. Financial Control of Current Liabilities 273

Current Liabilities—273
Plan for Progress—273
Organization of the Liability Control Function—274
Financial Administration of Current Liabilities—275
Accounts Payable—275
Case in Point—276
Case in Point—276
Contracts, Notes and Mortgages Payable—276
Accrued Items—277
Pension Costs—277
Deferred Items—277
Techniques for Stretching Payments in Time of Stress—277
Cash Flow Techniques—279
Maintaining Liquidity, Stability and Vendor Relations—279
Case in Point—280
The Role of the Minicomputer—280
Case in Point—280
Revolving Credit Agreements—281
Survival Tip—281
Financial Strain—281
Tuning In—281
Financial Strain—281
New Methods—New Techniques—282

12. Financial Administration of Debt and Equity Capital 289

Corporate Security and Survival—290
Case in Point—290
Classes of Stock Available—291
Preferred Stock—291
Case in Point—292
Warrants—292
Long-Term Financing—292
Bonds—293
Mortgage Bonds—293

12. Financial Administration of Debt and Equity Capital (Cont'd.)

Worth Noting—293
Collateral Trust—Equipment Trust Certificates—293
Income Bonds—293
Debentures—Subordinated Debentures—Convertible Debentures—294
Conditional Sales Agreements—294
Subordinated—What Is It?—294
Special Financing—294
Deep Discount Bonds—294
Overborrowed?—295
Short Term—Convertible to Longer Term—296
Other Loan Restrictions—296
Balloon Notes—296
Type of Revolving Credit—297
Special Projects—297
Income Revenue Bonds—297
Revenue Bonds—297
Eurobond Loans or Multicurrency Loans—297
What Are the Loans Used for?—297
Things to Remember About Financing—297
Methods of Payment on Loans—298
Project Financing—298
Leasing—Long-Term Financing—298
Creation of a Trust to Acquire Property—298
Case in Point—298
Eurobond Financing—299
Loan Traps—299
Latest Wrinkle in Financing—300
Ideas for or Against—300
Increasing Your Profit—300
Restructure of Debt—300
Cases in Point—300
How to Acquire Financing—301
Short-Term Financing—Coupled with Term Financing—301
Conclusion—302
Case in Point—303

13. New Techniques in Financial Administration of Taxes 305

Astute Tax Planning—Key Catalyst to Corporate Profits—305
Significant Case in Point—305
Case in Point—306
Organization and Staff for Tax Management—306
Tax Calendars, Records, Files and Sources of Information—307
The Tax Calendar—307
Case in Point—308
Note to Financial Administrators—308

Table of Contents

13. New Techniques in Financial Administration of Taxes (Cont'd.)

Working Papers—308
Files—308
Sources of Information—308
Tax Planning—309
Tax Problems Encountered—310
State and Local Taxes—310
Corporate Tax Shelter—311
Scrapping the Corporate Income Tax—311
International Taxation—311
Tax Dodges—312
Tax Strategies—313
Foreign Tax Matters—313
Tax Manuals—314
Keeping Up with Skull Sessions—314
Case in Point—314
Federal Tax Audits—315
Tax Crackdown—Key Items—316
Interesting Position—317
General—317
Tax Calendar—Two-Employee Firm Located in Arizona—318
What Does the Financial Administrator Expect of His Tax Manager?—318
Checklists—319
Handling Taxes in the Annual Report—320
Audits and IRS Procedures—321
The Simple Tax Calendar—322
Allocations on State Tax Returns—322

14. Mergers, Acquisitions, Takeovers, Divestitures 385

Mania for Growth—385
The Financial Administrator's Role in Mergers, Acquisitions, Takeovers and Divestitures—385
Evaluation of Acquisitions and Takeovers—Acquiring Information—386
Planning and Checklists for Acquisitions—387
Acquisition Checklist—388
Merger Checklist—388
Why Are Firms Acquired?—389
Tenders—390
Joint Ventures—391
Planning and Checklists for Divestitures—391
"Go" or "No Go!"—392
Checklist for Divestitures—393
Models and Means of Determining "What If?"—393
Odds and Ends—395
Castor Oil!—396
Case Study—Merger Evaluation—396
Study Number Two—397

22   Table of Contents

15. Administering and Complying with SEC Financial Reporting Requirements 399

Major Agencies—400
Key SEC Definitions—404
These Are the Questions Facing the Financial Administrator—404
Benefits and Problems of Disclosure—References—404
What Are Some of the Important Factors in Reports—405
SEC Action Can Affect Earnings—406
Word of Warning—406
Late Developments—406
Time Factor—407

16. Macroeconomics and Financial Administration 409

Major Key—409
Why Forecast?—409
Do not Underestimate!—410
Importance of Macroeconomics—410
Administrating and Staffing the Economic Function—410
Macroeconomics—411
What Is the Trend?—413
Sources of Economic Data—413
Types of Reports and Charts—416
Leading, Coincidental and Lagging Indicators—417
Business Activity—417
Stock Prices—417
The Ebb and Flow—418
Government Securities Held—418
Paperboard—Paper—418
Truck Activity and Railroad Carloadings—419
Retail Sales—419
Computer Models for Spotting Trends—419
Personal Income—420

17. Interfacing Financial Administration with Total Company Operation 425

Operation—"Control and Plan"—425
Planning—425
Case in Point—426
Control—427
Financial Control—427
Points to Emphasize—428
Growing Importance of Interfacing—428

18. Case Studies in Successful Financial Administration 429

Company A—429
Operations—429
Problems—Operational—430

Table of Contents

18. Case Studies in Successful Financial Administration (Cont'd.)

Financial Problems—430
Outside Assistance—430
Conference Results—431
Preliminary Report—Company A—431
The Basic Problems Encountered—432
Some of the Solutions—432
Conclusions—433
Company B—433
Growth—434
A New Product Line—434
Stealing a March on Industry—434
Operational Problems—435
The Financial Problem—435
Sales Problems—436
Cost Problems—436
Credit Problems—436
Purchasing Problems—436
Production Problems—437
New Product Problems—437
Solutions—437
Company C—438
Problems—439
Plan for Change—439
New Corporate Structure—440
Planning—What and How!—440
Other Results of Planning—441

Financial Administrator's Locatomatic 475

Definition—Vice President Finance and Staff—Duties, Responsibilities and Functions—477
Catalog—481

Index 489

1

New Techniques in Financial Administration That Meet Growth Challenges

In the search for better methods and approaches to financial administration it might be well to travel around the country and perhaps abroad to find out what others are doing. Over the past months visits with financial executives across the country have yielded a wealth of information. The principal factor is the major changes that are occurring in the reporting function. There is a revolution in the field, one which may swamp the financial executive with work that cannot wait or be deferred.

The challenges of growth coupled with inflation and the tremendous amount of capital it chews up is of prime concern to all financial executives. Keeping the corporation in funds presents a staggering and formidable task.

The path of success and progress is greased with money. If you are small or capitally deficient you have some basic problems. A source of credit or the ability to lease equipment and facilities is a major asset for every financial genius. The days are long gone when we could be content to grow slowly and steadily by plowing back profits. Your competition will eat you alive at that pace. The deficiency in capital is becoming more acute as firm after firm goes to the money well in periods of low interest rates. More and more you hear the common plea: "I have the products or ideas. Do you have the money?"

25

26   Techniques in Financial Administration That Meet Growth Challenges

The impact of rapid growth on capital is best illustrated by the following example presented below:

000 Omitted	OPERATING REVENUES	WORKING CAPITAL	LONG-TERM DEBT
19xx	$ 28,000	$7,212	$2,900
19xy	32,000	5,801	4,800
19yx	37,000	3,459	4,800
19yy	61,000	158	19,800
19yz	104,000	7,908	41,300

As indicated the working capital dropped to a paltry $158,000 in the first year of rapid growth. The cure was an immediate rise in long-term debt to over $41,000,000.

Under the impact of inflation the investments in fixed assets, accounts receivable and inventories have forced firms to leased financing, rentals and other means.

The prospect of the smaller firms battling the industrial giants with unlimited resources and credit to spend on marketing, advertising, promotions, research and development and internal sources of energy is a frightening one. Their assets are tremendous brainpower, ingenuity and hard work. To use Churchill's words they have only—"Blood, sweat and tears"—lubricated by lots of midnight oil.

Small industry desperately needs seasoned financial personnel to help them conquer the tasks ahead. The day of the "Hotshot Chinese Paper" financier is over. They need mature individuals who know what to do, why they do it and when it needs to be done—solid, patient, tactful persons who will not panic under adversity.

WHAT IS FINANCIAL ADMINISTRATION—HOW DID IT GET WHERE IT IS?

During periods of recession, adversity or crisis financial executives have risen in corporate position and esteem. Their ability to bail out firms and provide the necessary financial know-how to keep cash available and flowing will often provide the stability that is required to weather any crisis. Any growing business needs financial administration. It needs to anticipate, in advance, the financial requirements, resources and capital structure it will need. These requirements must be determined in advance, preferably from two to five years, and must contain options for change, dependent upon the rate of growth. A sharp financial executive will analyze the financial requirements of the business in advance. These will naturally vary by function and type of industry. In the electrical contracting field, a doubling in sales will automatically result in a doubling of accounts receivable. On the other hand, inventories may only increase by 25%. Manpower will double, but transportation equipment will only increase by 50%. The knowledgeable executive will provide this financing well in advance of the actual requirements, through short-term notes, three- to five-year notes, long-term debt or an increase in equity capital. The skill of the financial administrator is measured by his ability to avoid a financial crisis for the rapidly growing firm. As rapid growth creates liquidity and cash flow problems, he can maintain control of the situation and keep it out of serious financial problems. Not only do financial problems stunt the growth of a firm by causing it to lose profitable opportunities, they also affect relations with customers, creditors and suppliers. As your creditors pound on you for the payment of their obligations, your reaction is to pound on your customers for more prompt payment of their bills. This can at times cause serious public relations problems.

Successful financial administration, therefore, is attacking next year's financial problems today so that your firm can obtain the type of financing it needs in the right amount and at advantageous terms and conditions when it requires that financial assistance.

BASIC POINT

Continuing business growth is dependent upon excellent financial administration. The financial administrator can assure the success of most firms by providing adequate funds at the right time and place. Failure to provide adequate financing can stunt the growth of a firm, cause it to fail or to become too expensive to run and non-competitive in the market place. Administration does not cover only finances. The matter of control, supplying adequate information, data and reports or studies is also vital to proper and profitable growth. The cost of financial administration can be measured in dollars of profit or in dollars lost!

This top position, through the medium of financial acumen and computer expertise, has become one of the most interesting and important factors in continuing corporate growth and profitability. The accumulation of vital data into an effective *data base*, detailed knowledge of the business and the new financial management techniques have increased the financial administrator's importance and participation in company strategy, planning, control and policy decisions. Increased participation in these activities has required that he increase his breadth and scope of knowledge and have brought about a major responsibility for providing the accurate and timely information and material upon which major decisions are made. Since these decisions often commit large sums of money or major resources of the firm to growth and profitability, he is placed squarely in the new role of *mission controller* for the firm.

NEW TECHNIQUES

Rapid changes in financial administration technologies make it imperative that the individual learn and utilize the new techniques. Running the show with a keyboard, printer, chart maker, microfiche generator or TV console are a necessary adjunct to financial ability. There is constant pressure for faster data, higher standards of accuracy and performance and a reduction in the time involved between the presentation of a problem and the time to solve it.

In the larger firms, the challenge of multinational operations and multinational cultures must be recognized and conquered. Financial operations and controls in a fast-changing, government-controlled world economy present a constant challenge to the alert financial executive. A daily, weekly or monthly checklist of the new equipment and methods may be necessary to keep you abreast of current developments.

PORTABLE DATA TERMINALS

The development of portable data terminals weighing about 13 pounds has revolutionized the concept of centralized data processing. Now you can have computer access at any level, even in the individual's home. It is now possible to create information in the field, at outlying plants or in the customer's office. In fact, anywhere in the field where the action is occurring! This of itself will enable business to react to today's opportunities and growth challenges much faster. It also poses tough problems for the financial executive. He must provide controls based upon adequate key files, information and simple programs. Files may be questioned for information, retrieved and updated from many sources. It will require both standardization and security measures. Operating simplicity may involve decentralizing computer operations into local control units with miniprocessors.

ON-LINE CHALLENGES

The challenge of on-line interrogation, retrieval and update will require study and implementation. The ability to respond quicker to unexpected types of inquiries and to perform in minutes operations that took days will be one of several tough problems to solve.

The *data base* is the crux of the entire system. With proper material and labor data stored in the files "What if?" questions relative to a change in costs or selling prices on profits can be readily answered or estimated. The impact of this service alone is worth thousands of dollars to any alert and progressive organization. In the manufacturing area changes in production schedules, material receipts or inventory transactions can be immediately reflected in costs, shipping schedules and purchasing operations. Access to on-line data has to be company-wide in scope.

INTERFACING DATA

In the area of costs, all cost-related items must be simply stated in terms that all can understand. No matter who reads the information, manufacturing, accounting, shipping and warehousing or purchasing, it all looks the same. Terms must be interpretable to all units.

COST ESTIMATING

In many industries cost estimating is an expensive, time consuming and challenging operation. Firms can spend thousands of dollars and a great deal of clerical and executive time in estimating bids. I have often sat and watched them struggle to meet a deadline with a bid and sweated it out with them. Often, in the absence of more time someone has to run a "seat of your pants" estimate while holding his fingers crossed and hoping that if he gets the bid that he will be at least in the ballpark. In my heart I know that the computer that I have access to can do the job if we only had time to study and do the job. This is a constant problem with the smaller firms. Short on management talent, they are forced to use everyone

Techniques in Financial Administration That Meet Growth Challenges

on today's tasks, while knowing if they could spend the time that there is a better way available.

With interactive computing it has been proven that estimates are made faster, productivity is stepped up at least 25%, there is less overtime and the estimates are more accurate.

CASE IN POINT

A construction estimate which normally took two days to complete was phoned in and compiled on a computer within one hour. The computerized version was returned to the client's office while the salesperson was still there. Several changes were made over the phone and the estimate was completed, bid and accepted in one day.

FLEXIBILITY

One of the really helpful factors in computer estimating is the ability to try different sets of numbers and conditions. You can shift profit margins, overhead margins, labor or material costs. Under competitive conditions you can sharpen your bids in short order to meet prevailing forces. The ability to conduct negotiations over the phone saves both time and money.

Another major flexibility factor is the fact that you can test alternate manufacturing methods or techniques. You can determine if you have the right productive capacity available to produce the products at the right price or what the cost of present production might be as contrasted to the optimum method or timing. You have better information for costing, can eliminate excess costs such as uneconomical machinery or overtime, or even determine if it would pay to acquire a new machine or group of machines in order to fill the anticipated orders.

MICROFICHE

Every financial executive is troubled by record storage. In the smaller firms they wind up in cardboard boxes stored in a closet or dusty storage space. After someone has shuffled through them a time or two just try to find anything. Even the label on the box often does not correctly describe the contents. Record storage in smaller firms is an absolute disaster, and I have found some larger firms that could stand a little education in this area as well. In my opinion, microfiche is the answer to the record storage problem. Current equipment is not too expensive, record retrieval is relatively easy and the cost is not high considering the flexibility of the material. In fact, current records can be kept on microfiche for the cost of current filing practices. Today's magnifications range from 42X to 72X, which means that on a 72X reduction basis almost 700 pages of computer printout can be put on one microfiche. At the 16mm reduction level from 50 to 60 pages of 8½ x 11 pages will fit on one fiche. The best feature of the fiche system is that the files can be chronologically updated on the same fiche. To wit, 50 to 60 letters from one customer could be filed chronologically on the same fiche. In the report field this enables you to have available from 50 to 700 consecutive reports.

FACSIMILE

At present we have facsimile machines that will send the copy of a page every two minutes over thousands of miles. Sub-minute facsimile is under development and will open a whole new world in the field of financial reporting. You can phone someone and fill his request for a printed copy of a report, information, drawings, engineering specifications or bids in a matter of minutes. Non-priority items can be sent out at night and be available the next morning. Available also are machines which will accept digitalized data from a computer and convert them into printed reports, drawings, graphs or bids.

COST SAVINGS—CASE IN POINT

One financial firm installed FACSIMILE in order to speed up the transfer of information and to save costs. The mail was so slow—over one week—that it often sent a courier by air to deliver important information. Now the data is transmitted by FAX in minutes.

TELEFAX

The latest in information transmission is TELEFAX. This is a combination of voice and facsimile transmissions for conferences, briefings, directors' meetings, progress reports and executive sessions. The information can be transmitted simultaneously to multiple locations wherein each individual has the opportunity of hearing the same story, seeing the same reports and making his or her recommendations to all involved. If it is extremely important that all individuals know the "right now" status this is one means of providing it.

GRAPHICS VIDEO DISPLAY

Among the newest pieces of equipment is the intelligent and interactive graphics video terminal. If you want fast action showing the important "bottom line" and "summaries" this is the way to go. The details can wait and would be furnished later. The interactive terminal can be adjusted by pointer or keyboard to show what you have right now and "What will I finish with if?" as you manipulate the chart with your pointer. These terminals are currently in use in "Mission Control," "Strategy" and "Management Control" rooms.

INTERNATIONAL COMMUNICATION LINKS

If you are a multinational firm you must provide for prompt communication with foreign operations. Such communications will be computer links covering the following (not all-inclusive!) items:

Techniques in Financial Administration That Meet Growth Challenges

    a. Order entry
    b. Sales statistics
    c. Billing—prices
    d. Inventory control
    e. Costs
    f. Payrolls
    g. Information acquisition and retrieval

WHY USE A FINANCIAL MANAGEMENT SYSTEM?

1. To manage your operations and assist in the general management of the firm
2. To diagnose company problems and offer solutions
3. To interact to internal and external requests, actions and forces
4. To save money and time throughout the entire firm
5. To provide the best possible type of financial base for your firm
6. To allocate the firm's resources to the best possible use
7. To keep abreast of financial and economic changes and conditions
8. To concentrate on the job at hand and maintain control of the firm's operations

PROVIDING A DATA BASE

The financial administrator can materially assist the growth and increase the profitability of the firm by providing a sound and adequate data base. The information in the data base must go beyond the confines of an ordinary accounting system. It must provide access to what the outside world is doing and particularly about the markets and the firm's competition. It must know who are its final customers and how and why they are buying. It must recognize the true economic conditions and their effect upon the business. It must watch sales trends and the trends of raw material or purchased item prices. The financial executive must range well beyond the confines of the accounting field even if he gets his nose bloodied at times by lack of knowledge or skill in these areas. These are some of the simple data required:

1. How are sales at the ultimate customer level?
2. What are the inventory stocks of our distributors?
3. What is the current price trend of our raw materials? Have our suppliers increased wages recently which will increase our future costs? What is the current inventory status of raw materials?
4. What is the outside economic trend? How will it affect us?
5. What is the money market, interest rates, availability or trend?
6. What is the replacement status of our equipment, availability, utilization and mechanical problems?

7. What is competition's pricing policy? Hidden discounts, allowances?
8. Are we checking on market testing by competitors? If so, what are their new products?
9. Are we watching allied industries, new technologies, mergers and acquisitions which might affect us?
10. What are the new financing techniques relative to sales or to providing capital funds for the firm?
11. Are we aware of new promotional plans by competitors which might affect our sales or our accounts receivable collection periods?

Every small firm needs to be aware of and concentrate on the vital issues of new technology, new products, new markets. It must watch the movement of its merchandise closely in order not to miss sales or to tie up vital working capital in obsolete or slow-moving items. Each item of cash creation and cash flow must be carefully watched and controlled.

ECONOMIC AND FINANCIAL LINKS

The successful administrator must develop a method of forecasting cash flow, material and labor requirements, costs and profits based upon a link with the existing or projected economic and financial conditions. This involves a correlation between economic indicators, the Gross National Product and interest rates. It would then indicate when to expand, how to search for potential developing markets and the cash requirements needed. Some linkage must be developed between business conditions and the effect of government action such as the monetary policy of the FED.

WHAT ARE THE REASONS FOR EXPANSION OR GROWTH?

I once had the pleasure of visiting with a fellow financial executive. After a short discussion about mutual problems, he invited me to take a tour of a new plant that they were equipping with new plastic and rubber molding equipment. It proved to be a very interesting tour and in the process of examining the various parts of the new facility he ventured the remark that this equipment was costing them well over one million dollars. This immediately prompted the question, "Why did you decide to spend this much money?" As the firm was not too large, over one million dollars represented a substantial risk tied up in bricks, mortar and special equipment. He quickly replied, "Well, first of all we have a captive market of over one and one-half million dollars in sales. By installing our own equipment we can eliminate the profit factor which we estimate to be at least one hundred fifty thousand dollars a year." Mentally multiplying one hundred fifty by eight (an awesome task without a modern calculator!), I decided that the venture was entirely feasible from a financial standpoint. Actually he had put the problem in the hands of outside consultants whose computer had come up with a far more favorable calculation on the number of years required to pay back the facility cost than I had. In fact, the multiplier turned out to be six instead of my snap judgement of eight.

Techniques in Financial Administration That Meet Growth Challenges

AIM TO BE THE VERY BEST—A PERSON OF ABILITY AND QUALITY

To be the very best in the financial field you must start early in your career to develop sources of financing and capital. This involves knowing the right people in the banking, insurance, financial and brokerage communities. You must develop a track record of being right, aggressive and technologically ahead of the crowd. You must have patience, guts and steel nerves. The risks of committing huge amounts of capital, manpower and executive time to growth projects are tremendous. If your data is not right and the project fails one financial executive is out looking for a new place to grow in.

WHY PLAN FOR PROGRESS?

Failure to grow or change is to fail to survive! It is a simple challenge. What are the challenges ahead?

1. Inflation
2. Costs
3. Energy
4. Competition
5. Environment
6. Bureaucracy
7. Age

You must come up with a strategy for meeting social, political and economic changes caused by population growth, fluid population shifts, new products, new markets and foreign competition.

THOSE ARE THE PROBLEMS! WHAT ARE THE SOLUTIONS?

1. Develop a sound basic plan with action and optimism as a base.
2. Keep financially liquid and keep your liquidity ratio stable.
3. Secure adequate financing in advance.
4. Plan ahead even if it is only a small plan. Elaborate planning may solve fewer problems than simple ones.
5. Evaluate projects carefully—recognize the risks involved.
6. Assign priorities to all items.
7. Keep abreast of industry trends, price trends, economic trends, political trends and competitive action.
8. Develop a data base second to none and keep the pipelines open.
9. Watch your cash flow!

34 Techniques in Financial Administration That Meet Growth Challenges

10. Control your accounts receivable and credit.
11. Control your accounts payable carefully. This is your lifeline to success.
12. Control your short-term and long-term debt—the life preserver.
13. Control costs—failure is certain death!
14. Do not restrict your operating personnel by being overconservative.
15. Have a defensive plan and a *plan for survival!*
16. Watch for new ideas in the financial field—be alert to changes.
17. Watch the tax laws.
18. Constantly review all phases of your operations.
19. Have good operation manuals and keep them updated.
20. Aim to be the very best in the field!

WHAT ARE THE TOOLS AVAILABLE?

1. Facsimile units for transmitting data, drawings, memos, bids or specifications.
2. Telefax—combination facsimile and voice communications for conferences, progress reports, executive meetings.
3. Key to Disc computer units—data input over the phone lines or by mail. Portable terminal units—briefcase style—facts from where the action is!
4. Inventory tracking systems.
   A. Tracks materials through manufacturing processes and bar codes. Checks rail cars along the right of way.
   B. On-line inventory control for tighter inventory control. Helps cut down losses, overstocking and obsolescence.
   C. Studies of inventory movement to keep production in tune with sales and to see what items can be cut out of product lines.
   D. Inventory price checks and updating for accurate costs and recognition of price changes for adjustment of selling prices.
5. Computer optimization of tasks.
   A. Loading trucks—scheduling distribution or routes.
   B. Stocking warehouses.
   C. Watching production trends.
   D. Scheduling salesmen.
6. Computers—Desk top—for instant information—interfacing with other divisions and departments.
7. Complete audio-visual display for senior and middle management.
8. Corporate Financial Control Centers.
9. Graphic displays with the ability to vary the data interactively to find out what happens if some phase changes—instant results!
10. Color TV for the following techniques:
    A. Single period comparison—year-to-date comparison.

Techniques in Financial Administration That Meet Growth Challenges

      B. Historical comparison.
      C. Historical analysis and current variation analysis.
11. Document storage—instant access—video transmission to remote locations and available hard copy.
12. Microprocessor text editing units—data available right now!
13. Miniature disc units—unlimited local storage
14. Huge computer memories with answers to all types of questions—simulation programs which provide an insight to future changes.
15. On-line financial statements—daily profit and loss—no more guessing!
16. On-line accounts receivable—cash—accounts payable—individual invoice data.
17. New types of financing—dutch auctions—leasing—production prepayments—advances.
18. Endless opportunities to get better answers faster—limited only by your knowledge, intelligence and ability.
19. Use of computer techniques to increase your productivity and adaptation to change.

WORD OF WARNING

Interviews and observations of the operations of the smaller firms indicates a lack of financial control that is almost unbelievable. Naturally these firms cannot afford a great deal of top management nor expensive financial executives; however, the problem is real and needs attention. Small business usually starts with one, two or several individuals who have an idea, determination and guts to carry it through. They work hard and generally are engineers, product designers, manufacturing geniuses or good sales and promotional persons. They have ability, drive and patience to succeed. Once they grow beyond the "one man" or "family" stage they are often lost. They keep books only because Uncle Sam says they must, and financial statements are often a periodic novelty. Normally they are not endowed with too high a degree of financial sense. They need assistance and help from youthful financial aspirants who are not afraid to gamble and grow with the smaller firms. Unfortunately the compensation does not attract personnel with a high degree of competency. Somehow we need to assist them in the following areas:

1. Start with a sound financial base or plan.
2. Finance the land, buildings and equipment before you buy it—not after.
3. To grow you need money—recognize it now!
4. Do some financial planning—plan ahead for at least two years.
5. Check and adjust to changes in your plans.
6. Set up a simple data system—you need information.
7. Establish a cost system—know your costs—keep them up to date!
8. Know your customers—their strengths and weaknesses.
9. Watch your credit and accounts receivable.
10. What business are you really in?
11. Establish good banking relations.

12. Establish financial controls.
13. Control your inventories.
14. Allocate your resources and manpower to the most productive and profitable uses.
15. Conserve your resources—protect your assets.

CASE IN POINT

One firm which had eighteen trucks on the road never bothered to set up a maintenance program. They ran the trucks until they broke down. Ordinary maintenance such as oil and filter changes were left to the individual drivers. Some did and some did not maintain their vehicles. Mandatory maintenance and inspections would have increased the life of the trucks by at least 25% if not more.

Sometimes old techniques pay off!

DISTRIBUTING COMPUTERS

The latest trend is to put the processing power where it will be most useful. With the new minicomputers the cost is low enough to enable most firms to do so. *Printed words are out—video terminals and pictures are in. Control through graphics.*

2

On-Line Reports: New Approaches to Daily Profit-and-Loss Reports

GETTING ON LINE

The financial administrator now has the capability of providing instant information with an "on-line" system. This capability, if exploited to the fullest degree, can increase his stature within and outside of the organization. It puts him in the unique position of being the quarterback for the entire operating team. The system is part of the computer operation and is best handled by a "Task Analysis Team" and a "Task Analysis Center." The steps are as follows:

1. You define and set the parameters of your data base structure.
2. You enter your business data into the computer memory bank.
3. You are now in a position to make inquiries and display the information on the video terminal or print out on the printer units.

OPERATING ON LINE

1. Customers' Orders—sales orders are entered directly from the terminals. (Varies from one to many, dependent upon the size of the system.) Orders can be placed on hold file while credit is checked, inventory status is determined or delivery dates are ascertained. Credit checks, pricing, inventory reservation and total amount of the order are done automatically.
2. Detailed customer information on status of orders, past shipments or products used.
3. Order inquiries—allows the data on any order to be printed out or displayed at any terminal.
4. Invoicing—customer invoices can be printed as soon as the order is firm. Aids in reducing your outstanding accounts by getting the invoices to the customer faster.
5. Scheduling of the order is immediate—if a stock item, the pick list is generated so that the order can be filled promptly and the inventory updated immediately.
6. Quotations—you can enter and price quotations immediately. Then print and have the quotation ready for transmittal within short order.
7. Merchandise inquiry—during order processing you can search the entire product line for substitutes or alternate selections. This eliminates searching catalogs saving time.
8. Orders can be updated—changed—cancelled, including any charges such as shipping and insurance.
9. Credit memos can be issued before the invoice is prepared or at any time.
10. Create daily activity reports—as a by-product of order handling and invoicing, you can create the following reports at any stage of the cycle:

    A. Order Status Report
      a. Open unfilled orders
      b. Orders on hold
      c. Orders invoiced
      d. Orders cancelled
      e. Credit memos issued

    B. Daily Shipment Report
      a. By product or product line
      b. By customer or sales territory

    C. Daily Inventory Report
      a. By product or product line
      b. Stock shortages
      c. Stock overages
      d. Fast moving items

    D. Daily Production Reports
      a. By product or product line
      b. Order status report—quantity ready—time to complete

This is only a very short list of the capabilities of an "on line" system. Many financial administrators consider a daily profit-and-loss report an impossibility. They are overlooking

On-Line Reports: New Approaches to Daily Profit-and-Loss Reports

the tremendous potential of the computers, terminals and systems. In this era of rapid change the financial executive must keep abreast of the times. He must recognize that he is in the unique position of being able to produce reports which record the last transaction and its effect upon the entire operation. Widespread activities, constant fluctuations in prices, currencies, costs and economic factors have increased management's need for timely, vital information. Daily performance against plan has progressed from a visionary dream to an operating reality. It is here and you had better take advantage of it! With daily reports on activity versus plan, fast action can be taken on deviations. This can save the corporation money; in fact, the early recognition of trends and prompt action could save the firm's very existence in some instances. Financial administrators have always been accused of being guardians of the past, producing voluminous reports too late for action. With an on-line terminal system the action is available to all authorized parties instantly. One does not need to snow the other executives with printed reports, they can view the results on their personal desktop terminal in many instances.

The new terminals and minicomputers make it possible to present information in any form desired. Some individuals like graphs. Their needs are satisfied with graphic terminals. New simplified programming languages, like modified BASIC and others, allows the users to specify their report requirements and generate a new type of report in minutes. A call for CHART DATA X will produce a chart to specifications. MATRIX will produce a matrix type review system. Strange terms like TILT—DRAW—REVERSE and CHECK have appeared on the reporting scene.

On-line systems offer advantages to companies needing prompt, current inventory or order information in order to keep up with fast moving sales.

CASE IN POINT

A huge retail furniture operation of the warehouse type maintains thousands of items in an on-line inventory system. The salesman knows exactly how many are in stock, or if they are not in stock if they are on order, and when delivery can be expected. This service costs over $2,000 a month to maintain; however, it is felt that the system costs less than the benefits received. Manually it would be virtually impossible to maintain.

WHAT IS THE LANGUAGE?

1. On-line entry: The process of entering new data from any of the terminals served by the system.
2. On-line inquiry: Asking the computer for data from one of the terminals (printer or video); i.e., "What is the inventory status of item 3001?"
3. On-line reporting: The computer answers the terminal (prints it or displays it); i.e., "We have 5 3001's in stock and 25 on order." It could create a full report of sales in detail if requested.
4. On-line editing: Someone reviews the incoming data and corrects it if necessary prior to storage in the computer. On-line editors can be utilized to maintain accounts payable, accounts receivable, order or inventory files in some simple systems.

40   On-Line Reports: New Approaches to Daily Profit-and-Loss Reports

CASE IN POINT

You have a video terminal with a cursor editor. You maintain your inventory in a mag tape file. You search the file for item 3001. It displays the data as follows:

CODE NO.	IN INV.	ON ORDER	OTHER DATA
3001	15	25	discontinued item
3002	5	10	
3003	36	0	

You move to line 3001. The cursor looks like this 3001 under the 3. Suppose you had sold 6 of the item and wished to reduce the inventory. You move the ___ over until it is under the 15 and delete it, then the 5 and delete it. Where the 5 had been you insert a 9 and your new inventory will be

| 3001 | 9 | 25 | discontinued item |

It also works well in correcting numbers in text or wiping out portions of the file.

5. On-line update: In this instance you update the file material by deleting old items, changing items or inserting new information.
6. CRT or VIDEO TERMINAL: A modified TV system that enables you to visually examine the data inputted or outputted.

INVENTORIES

If you are contemplating installing an on-line inventory system, you could require from one to many video terminals dependent upon the size and scope of your organization.

CASE IN POINT

One system required the installation of 12 video terminals. Terminals were placed in shipping, four inventory locations, production control, manufacturing, plant manager, two sales offices, accounting and even one for the president of the firm.

WIDESPREAD USE

Most firms have recently moved toward consolidating their inventories in regional warehouses and carrying only minor stocks in retail outlets, wholesale outlets or smaller warehouses. This has made the utilization of on-line inventory control systems a necessity and a money saving device. Regional warehouses are often placed in states which have low personal property tax rates or none at all. The tax savings can pay for a substantial part of the cost of the system. Deliveries from most of these warehouses can be made overnight by truck so that few orders are lost because of out-of-stock problems. In addition, large warehouses make for more efficient grouping of orders, order picking, sequenced loading of trucks or rail cars in or out and better overall inventory control.

On-Line Reports: New Approaches to Daily Profit-and-Loss Reports   41

WHAT ARE THE FEATURES OF AN ON-LINE SYSTEM FOR INVENTORY?

1. Order entry
2. Order inquiry
3. Inventory inquiry
4. Credit check
5. Receiving system
6. Order update
7. Inventory update
8. Inventory packing list
9. Truck loading list
10. Customer invoicing
11. Low stock or out-of-stock notices

ON-LINE DAILY STATUS REPORT

For a small business it is relatively easy to create a daily status report which indicates the financial and operating condition of the firm. The operational data is standard costed to the extent that the labor operations are loaded by a percentage factor to cover overhead. Material is loaded by a percentage factor to cover waste and taxes paid on its sale. The report looks like this:

DAILY STATUS REPORT   DATE...TODAY........

DESCRIPTION	TODAY AMOUNT	
CASH	$$$$$$$	
ACCOUNTS RECEIVABLE-1	$$$$$$$	
ACCOUNTS RECEIVABLE-2	$$$$$$$	
INVENTORIES	$$$$$$$	
TOTAL QUICK ASSETS	$$$$$$$	
BANK LOAN	$$$$$$$	
ACCOUNTS PAYABLE	$$$$$$$	
TOTAL QUICK LIABILITIES	$$$$$$$	
		MONTH TO DATE
SALES—LINE 1	$$$$$	$$$$$$$
MATERIAL COSTS	$$$$	$$$$$
LABOR COSTS	$$$$	$$$$$
TOTAL COSTS	$$$$$	$$$$$$
PROFIT—LINE 1	$$$	$$$$
SALES—LINE 2	$$$$$$	$$$$$$

MATERIAL COSTS	$$$$	$$$$
LABOR COSTS	$$$$	$$$$
TOTAL COSTS	$$$$$	$$$$$$
PROFIT—LINE 2	$$$	$$$$

While the operations of any one day may or may not be significant it certainly alerts management to the relationship between merchandise shipped and costs involved on a day-to-day basis. Obviously wherever there is a long period of work involved before the billing occurs another method would have to be utilized. Daily profit and loss reports are feasible in certain industries. With computers they have moved from a visionary concept to actuality.

REPORTS—ON-LINE STATEMENT OF ACCOUNT

CUSTOMER	AR608	NAME—ADDRESS		
CUST. PO.	3967			
ORDER NO.	ESA-96322	DATE XXXX	DOC. NO. 50089	
TERMS	145	TYPE INV.	MATURITY XXXX	
AMOUNT	538.60	DAYS TO PAST DUE	45	

						121
TOTAL OWED	1-15	16-30	31-60	61-90	91-120	AND OVER
$539						

REPORTS—MACHINE EFFECTIVENESS—3 MACHINE BANK—1 OPERATOR

MACHINE	1	2	3	4	5	TOTAL
1						
UNITS	38	52	52	54	45	241
$$	76	104	104	108	90	$482
2						
UNITS	26	28	21	28	26	129
$$	52	56	42	56	52	258
3						
UNITS	54	31	44	34	36	199
$$	108	62	88	68	72	398
TOTAL						
UNITS	118	111	117	116	107	569
$$	236	222	234	232	214	1,138
LABOR	80	80	80	80	80	400
MAT'L	59	56	58	58	54	285
SETUP	27	25	27	34	33	146
OVERTIME	0	0	0	0	0	0

On-Line Reports: New Approaches to Daily Profit-and-Loss Reports

NEW APPROACHES TO DAILY PROFIT-AND-LOSS REPORTING

The advent of the *minicomputer* has made the dream of every financial executive come true.... *the daily profit-and-loss statement*. Not only can he produce a daily profit-and-loss account but with the same computer and modeling technics he can forecast trends.

This is how the system operates! With on-line video terminals instant access can be had to every phase of the business. The point of sale computer transmits sales information to the computer almost instantly. This when coupled with the other point-of-transaction recorders will give instant recording of the other items such as production, shipments, material receipts and cash disbursements. If the system is set up properly and coded correctly these items will pyramid into the apex of the triangle called the "daily net income."

The skeptics will argue—there are too many variables! This is often true! However, if the system is standardized and set up to report variables as one of its functions, this too can be overcome.

CONTROL TECHNIQUES FOR VARIABLES

Suppose we were to consider the fork lift truck operation which is a segment of material handling. This is plant A—Account 200-05—and salaries are coded 2111.

Let us assume that for some reason we had to work the fork lift truck operator overtime in order to get the customer's merchandise out that day. The charges would be recorded as follows:

CONTROL	COST CENTER	NORMAL EXPENSE	ABNORMAL ITEM
200	200-05	2111	2131
	$67.00	$51.00	$16.00

Assume that we ship material to another plant within the same organization by air freight due to time requirements. The charges would be recorded as follows:

CONTROL	COST CENTER	NORMAL EXPENSE	ABNORMAL ITEM
200	200-07	2403	2405
	$500.00	$400.00*	$100.00**

* Truckload Freight Rate
** Air Freight Premium

Once again the variance pops out immediately and can be recognized in the daily reports.

ONE ADDITIONAL FEATURE

With this type of variance reporting you have an instant awareness of abnormal operations occurring within your operations that might require executive corrective action.

LET'S FACE FACTS

The advent of the minicomputer has made it possible for the financial executive to extend his knowledge, awareness, and financial acumen to their fullest extent. It is not going to happen *tomorrow*. It is a reality that is with you *today!* If you haven't explored the techniques in use you had better get out of your chair and take a quick look around at the *new* in financial administration. You have come out of the past into the moving present. Historical records and accounting have changed to *now* and *what if* in the future.

CONCLUSIONS

In interviews with financial executives and others we have found that new techniques are evolving every day in the field of on-line reporting and accounting. Everywhere you go you find CRT terminals, microfiche readers, hard copy printers and graphic displays being used for a variety of *on-line* purposes. As of now there is no standardization of equipment, techniques or methods. Each individual has developed a reporting system to fulfill management requirements. Many of them are very reticent to talk about or discuss the projects in current use.

The era of the mini-computer has arrived. Along with simple English programming language and video displays your ability to answer problems and provide instant answers has increased a thousandfold. Your ability to utilize these modern tools and techniques is limited only by your mental awareness and ingenuity. The desktop problem solver is here! It's easy to learn how to use, flexible and versatile. If you can punch the keys of a typewriter with one finger you have access to its tremendous capabilities.

We have long awaited the day of the Daily Profit-and-Loss Statement. Now if we can use it properly to stimulate executive action, we can have financially stronger firms which will react to changing conditions faster and more effectively.

THE COMPUTER IN ACTION

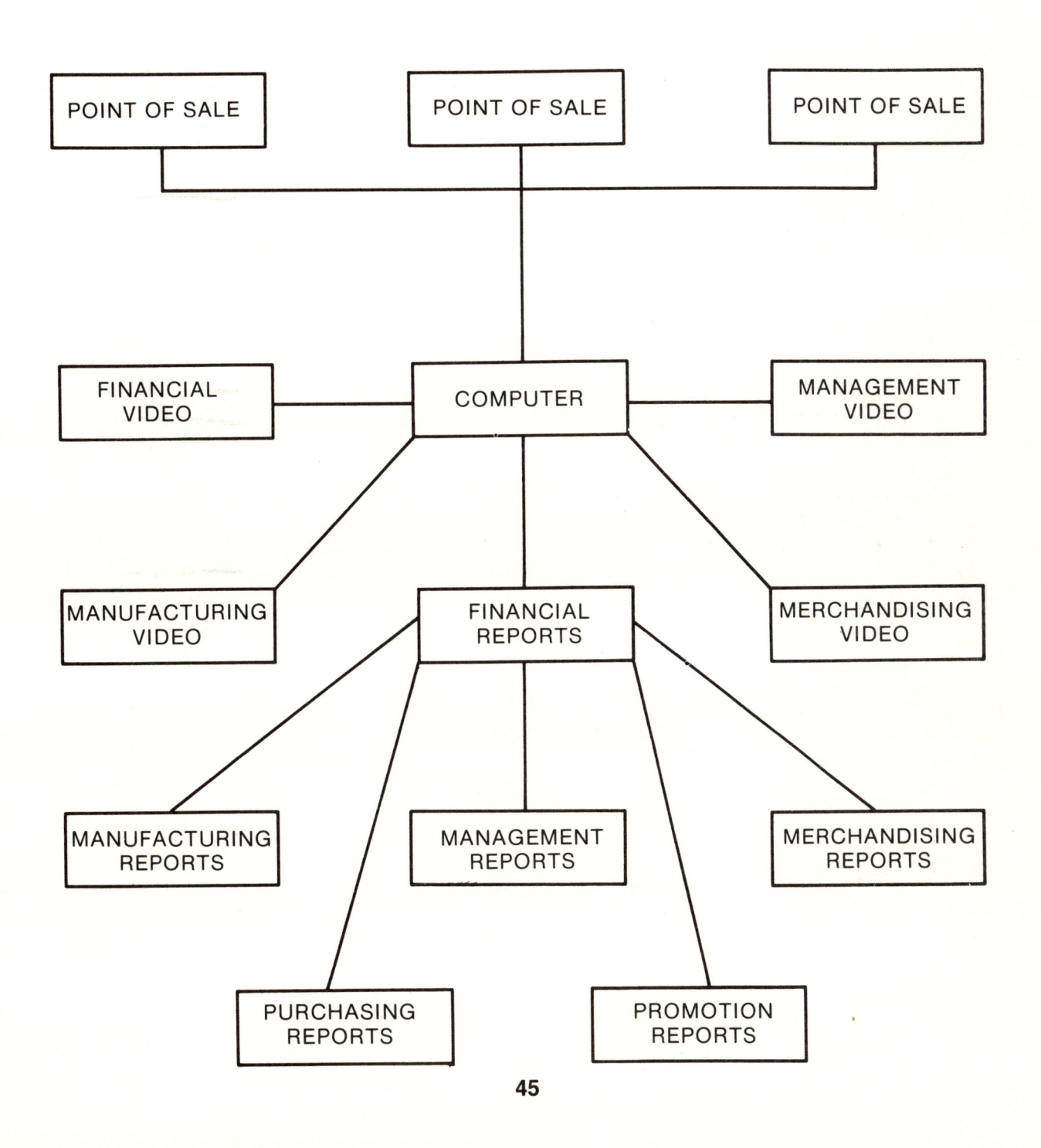

```
┌──────────────┐      ┌──────────────┐      ┌──────────────┐
│ POINT OF SALE│      │ POINT OF SALE│      │ POINT OF SALE│
└──────┬───────┘      └──────┬───────┘      └──────┬───────┘
       └─────────────────────┼─────────────────────┘
                             │
┌──────────────┐      ┌──────────────┐      ┌──────────────┐
│  FINANCIAL   ├──────┤   COMPUTER   ├──────┤  MANAGEMENT  │
│    VIDEO     │      │              │      │    VIDEO     │
└──────────────┘      └──────┬───────┘      └──────────────┘
                             │
┌──────────────┐      ┌──────────────┐      ┌──────────────┐
│MANUFACTURING │      │  FINANCIAL   │      │MERCHANDISING │
│    VIDEO     │      │   REPORTS    │      │    VIDEO     │
└──────────────┘      └──────┬───────┘      └──────────────┘
                             │
┌──────────────┐      ┌──────────────┐      ┌──────────────┐
│MANUFACTURING │      │  MANAGEMENT  │      │MERCHANDISING │
│   REPORTS    │      │   REPORTS    │      │   REPORTS    │
└──────────────┘      └──────────────┘      └──────────────┘

        ┌──────────────┐      ┌──────────────┐
        │  PURCHASING  │      │  PROMOTION   │
        │   REPORTS    │      │   REPORTS    │
        └──────────────┘      └──────────────┘
```

ON-LINE

DAILY PROFIT AND LOSS

```
DATE . . . . 03-06-XX
TIME  3:45 P.M.
```

TODAY'S SALES . . .	$30,145.67	PLANNED	$35,000.00
TODAY'S COSTS . . .	24,980.00	PLANNED	27,500.00
TODAY'S INCOME	5,165.67	PLANNED	7,500.00

MAJOR VARIATIONS

VOLUME DECLINE DUE TO PRODUCT MIX	$1,550.00
COSTS UP DUE TO INCREASED LOW MARGIN ITEM SALES	650.00
SALES EXPENSES OVER PLAN DUE TO LOW VOLUME	200.00
ANTICIPATED DECLINE IN VOLUME FOR THIS DAY—BELOW PLAN	2,500.00
ANTICIPATED INCOME DECLINE THIS DAY	
DUE TO INCREASED COSTS	300.00
SALE OF LOW MARGIN ITEMS	400.00
TOTAL	$700.00

```
DATE . . . 03-06-XX
TIME 3:45 P.M.
ON-LINE SALES REPORT
```

	ACTUAL	PLAN	VARIATION
UNIT 1	$7,654.17	$7,500.00	+ $154.17
UNIT 2	3,301.50	3,500.00	− 198.50
UNIT 3	4,190.00	4,000.00	+ 190.00
UNIT 4	5,000.00	6,550.00	− 1,550.00
UNIT 5	10,000.00	13,450.00	− 3,450.00
TOTAL	$30,145.67	$35,000.00	− $4,834.53

TASK ANALYSIS CENTER

HI.
THIS IS YOUR TAC COMPUTER. PLEASE SELECT THE TASK YOU WANT PERFORMED FROM THE FOLLOWING LIST:

1. SALES ANALYSIS
2. CREDIT INFORMATION
3. ORDER ENTRY
4. ACCOUNTS RECEIVABLE
5. INVENTORY
6. ACCOUNTS PAYABLE
7. PRICES
8. COSTS
9. BILLING
10. PAYROLL
11. GENERAL LEDGER

On-Line Reports: New Approaches to Daily Profit-and-Loss Reports 47

INVENTORY STATUS

DATE

CODE NO.	IN INV.	SHOW ROOM	ON ORDER	RESERVED FOR
3011	8	1	25-0789	5-DAVIS

INVENTORY STATUS

DATE

CODE NO. 3011   BATHROOM LIGHT-CHROME SUPPLIER—PROGRESS

ON HAND 8   ON ORDER 25 PO-0789-1/23/X DELIVERY 3 WEEKS

    RESERVED 5 DAVIS

RETAIL PRICE $23.90   WHOLESALE PRICE $18.00

COST $12.00   FREIGHT PREPAID

SALES THIS MONTH   2   YEAR TO DATE   21

INVENTORY STATUS

DATE

CODE NO.	PRICE	COST	IN INV.	ON ORDER
3011	$23.90	18.00	8	25 PO-0789

TASK ANALYSIS CENTER

ACCOUNTS RECEIVABLE INQUIRY

CUST. NO.	NAME—ADDRESS	TERR.	SALESMAN
121	M. LEMARR 4545 E. WHITMAN TUCSON, AZ. 85711 PHONE 795-3625	3	8

CR. LIMIT	CURR. BAL.	CURRENT	PAST DUE	LAST PYT DATE
3,000	2,000	1,500	500	2/03/X

SALES	THIS MO.	YEAR TD		LAST PYT AMT
	100	6,100		500

```
TASK ANALYSIS CENTER
ACCOUNTS RECEIVABLE INQUIRY
CUST. NO.          NAME—ADDRESS              TERR.      SALESMAN
121                M. L. BUGE                  3            8
                   4444 E. WHITMAN
                   TUCSON, AZ. 85711
                   PHONE   795-3625

   INV. NO.     DATE        AMOUNT      CURRENT       PAST DUE
   0456         11/12/X      500.00                    500.00
   0489         12/30/X    1,500.00    1,500.00
   0501         01/11/Y      600.00      600.00

TOTAL                       2,600.00    2,100.00        500.00

CREDIT LIMIT   $5,000

SALES   MO TD      600    YR TD    600    LAST YR TD    2,100
```

```
TASK ANALYSIS CENTER
TERRITORIAL EXPENSE INQUIRY
DATE
                     THIS MONTH                YEAR TO DATE
TERRITORY       EXPENSES    PLANNED       EXPENSES    PLANNED
NORTH             6,100       7,000         34,000     35,000
SOUTH             5,000       4,000         28,000     30,000
EAST              3,000       2,500         18,000     15,000
WEST              9,000       7,000         40,000     38,000
```

ON-LINE GRAPHIC DISPLAYS

```
                    TERRITORIAL SALES ANALYSIS

TERRITORY       PERFORMANCE AS A PERCENT OF PLAN    XXX = MTD --- = YTD

WESTERN         XXXXXXXXXX
                -------------------------
SOUTHWEST       XXXXXXXXXXXXXXX
                -------------------------
MIDWEST         XXXXX
                ----------------------
EASTERN         XXXXXXXXXXXX
                ------------------------
NORTHERN        XXX
                ------------------
SOUTHERN        XXXXXXXXXXXXXXXXXXXXX
                -----------------------------
%               0 .. 10 .. 20 .. 30 .. 40 .. 50 .. 60 .. 70 .. 80 .. 90 .. 100 .. 110 .. 120 ..
```

TASK ANALYSIS CENTER

WEEKLY REPORT ON BUSINESS ACTIVITY

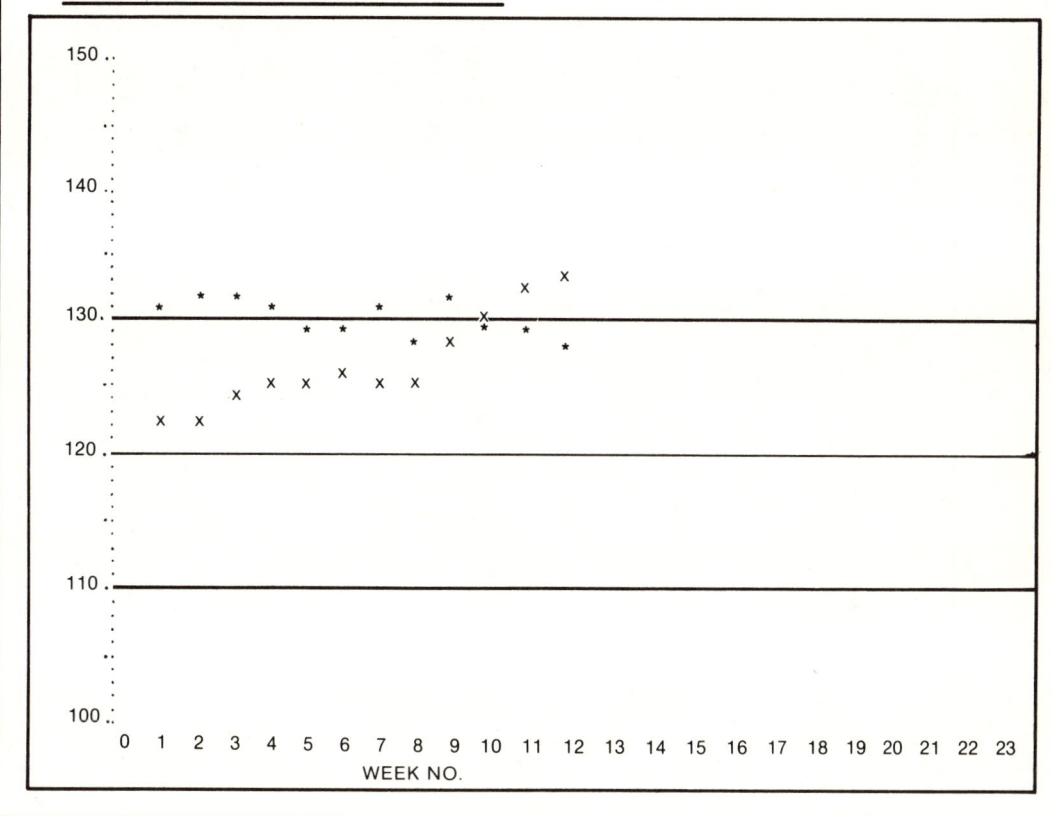

DAILY OPERATING REPORT FOR 09-20-XX

DIV. NO.	DEPT NO.	COST CENTER	ACCT NO.	DET NO.	DESCRIPTION	TODAY	MONTH TO DATE	YEAR TO DATE
09	02	2100	1000	01	SALES ITEM 1	$2,700	$12,642	$68,732
09	02	2100	1000	02	SALES ITEM 2	0	26	320**
09	02	2100	1000	03	SALES ITEM 3	16,295	138,513	1,143.976
09	02	2100	1000	04	SALES ITEM 4	3,315	26,332	279,465
					SALES 1 THROUGH 4	$22,310	$177,518	$1,492,494
09	02	2100	5600	210	DISCOUNTS GIVEN	379	2,485	31,248
09	02	2100	4300	410	DISCOUNTS TAKEN	1,313	7,583	56,638
09	02	2100	5800	100	TRAVEL EXPENSES	99	3,656	29,536

HOW WERE SALES TODAY?
WHAT IS THE PRESENT STATUS OF COST?
ARE ANY ITEMS OUT OF LINE? - ** LOW VOLUME ITEM
ARE EXPENSES IN LINE WITH REVENUES?

On-Line Reports: New Approaches to Daily Profit-and-Loss Reports

```
THIS SIMPLE PROGRAM                              YIELDS INSTANT ANALYSIS REPORTS

READY
LIST                                             RUN #1
0010  U=P+A+B+C+D                                ? 9000,500,500,500,500
0020  INPUT U,P,A,B,C,D                          TOTAL PRODUCTION REQUIRED IS    11000
0030  H=P/150                                    MACHINE #1                      9000
0040  J=A/25                                     MACH BANK #1      500   500     1000
0050  K=B/25                                     MACH BANK #2      500   500     1000
0060  L=C/30                                     TOTAL HOURS REQUIRED                    133.3
0070  M=D/30                                     TOTAL COSTS                          12,483.00
0080  T=H+J+K+L+M                                HOURS MACH #1                    60
0090  N=H*10+1000+P*.85                          HOURS BANK #1      20    20      40
0100  O=J*10+200+A*.85                           HOURS BANK #2     16.3   17    33.3
0110  P=K*10+200+B*.85                           SET UP COSTS                    825
0120  Q=L*10+200+C*.85                           PROD COST MACH #1              9000
0130  R=M*10+200+d*.85                           PROD COST BANK #1              1328
0140  X=N+O+P+Q+R                                PROD COST BANK #2              1330
0200  IF U=2001 GOTO 300
0210  PRINT "TOTAL PRODUCTION",N
0220  PRINT "MACHINE #1",P:PRINT "MACH BANK #1",A,B,A+B
0221  PRINT "MACH BANK #2",C,D,C+D,(A+B)+(C+D)
0222  PRINT "TOTAL HOURS REQUIRED",T:PRINT "TOTAL COSTS",X
0223  PRINT "SET UP COSTS",X*6.26
0224  PRINT "PROD COST MACH #1",P*1.00
0225  PRINT "PROD COST BANK #1",(A+B)*1.33
0226  PRINT "PROD COST BANK #2",(C+D)*1.33
0230  PRINT "ALTERNATE ESTIMATE ? - Y=YES N=NO"
0232  INPUT W (ANSWER)
0233  IF W=Y GOTO 20: IF W=N GOTO 300
0300  END
```

DAILY JOB COST SUMMARY

JOB #	TOTAL CONTRACT	PAYMENTS REC TO DATE	BAL ON CONTRACT	ESTIMATED COSTS	ACTUAL COSTS	PERCENTAGE OF REC	BILLED	EST	SLS PR
1230	$10,000	$100	$9,900	$7,500	$868	1.0%	25.0%	11.6%	8.7%
1231	10,000	100	9,900	8,000	868	1.0%	25.0%	10.9%	8.7%
1232	12,000	100	11,900	9,000	964	.8%	25.0%	10.7%	8.0%
1233	10,000	100	9,900	7,500	964	1.0%	25.0%	12.9%	9.6%
1234	12,000	100	11,900	9,000	1,012	.8%	35.0%	11.2%	8.4%
1235	11,000	100	10,900	7,500	1,060	.8%	25.0%	14.1%	8.4%
1236	8,000	100	7,900	6,000	868	1.3%	25.0%	14.5%	10.9%
1237	12,000	100	11,900	8,000	916	.8%	25.0%	11.5%	7.6%
1238	5,000	100	4,900	4,000	916	2.0%	25.0%	22.9%	18.3%
1239	7,500	100	7,400	5,500	916	1.3$	25.0%	16.6%	12.2%
1240	50,000	10,000	40,000	40,000	0	.0%	20.0%	.0%	.0%

REC= PAYMENTS RECEIVED

BILLED= AMOUNT BILLED

EST= ACTUAL COSTS AS A % OF ESTIMATED

SLS PR= ACTUAL COSTS AS A % OF THE SALES PRICE

On-Line Reports: New Approaches to Daily Profit-and-Loss Reports

```
                          DAILY COST SUMMARY - JOBS

       ESTIMATED  ACTUAL    ESTIMATED  ACTUAL   ESTIMATED  ACTUAL   EST    ACTUAL  UNUSED
JOB    LABOR      LABOR     MATERIAL   MAT'L    OTHER      OTHER    HOURS  HOURS   HOURS

100    4500       168       2500       200      500        500      800    40      760
101    5000       168       2500       200      500        500      900    40      860
102    6000       264       2500       200      500        500      875    40      835
103    4500       264       2500       200      500        500      550    40      510
104    5000       360       3500       200      500        500      600    40      560
105    4500       360       2500       200      500        500      500    40      460
106    3500       168       2000       200      500        500      250    40      210
107    3500       168       2000       200      500        250      250    40      210
108    25000      0         10000      0        5000       0        1250   0       1250
109    6000       216       1500       200      500        500      900    40      860
110    2500       2160      1000       800      500        300      250    210     40
111    3500       1016      2000       400      800        600      250    98      152
112    9000       4500      8000       1000     4000       1000     700    1000    -300
```

TIRE DEPT. DAILY SALES AND ALLOWANCE CONTROL REPORT

Date _____ 19 ___

Article Number	Tires	Valves	Unit Basic List Selling Price	Gross Sales	Sales Promotion	ALLOWANCES Trade-in	Adjustment Treadwear Roadhazard Adjustable	ALL OTHER Com'l. Nat'l. Acct. Emp. Disc.	Used Tire Sales	Net Sales	W/B	Sales-man No.	Sales-check No.
1	2	3	4	5	6	7	8	9	10	11	12	13	14

TOTAL TODAY
TOTAL M.T.D.

	RADIAL		BELTED		BIAS		TOTAL PASSENGER		TOTAL LIGHT TRUCK		TOTAL LARGE TRUCK		TOTAL VALVE STEMS	
	TODAY	M.T.D.	TODAY	M.T.D.	TODAY	M.T.D.	TODAY	M.T.D.	TODAY	M.T.D.	TODAY	M.T.D.	TODAY	M.T.D.
Tires Sold at Regular Price														
Tires Sold at Sale Price														
TOTAL														

31989-5   *NOTE: Include tires taken in trade which can be sold for as much or more than amount shown in "Trade-in" column.

SALES AND PROFIT SUMMARY — 15 DAY _____ MONTH _____

A GROSS SALES _____

Total Discount & Allowances
— Used Tire Sales
— Adjustment Credits

B NET DISCOUNT & ALLOW _____

C NET SALES (A–B) _____

X Previous Months M.U.I. _____ %

D GROSS PROFIT DOLLARS _____

Net Discount & Allow (B)
X Compliment of Mark Up, In. Inv.

E COST OF DISC. & ALLOW _____

F NET PROFIT DOLLARS (D–E) _____

G MGP % (F ÷ C) _____ %

3

Administering with Control Techniques: Using Corporate Profit Centers

How does a small firm with a few employees maintain control over its operations? How does a large firm that gives its plants, divisions, units or managers complete autonomy, maintain control? The answer is simple! Through a system of financial controls. Control reporting has become a vital financial administrative function. This places the responsibility for developing a system of effective controls squarely in the lap of the financial administrator and his staff.

The evolution of super-corporations with assets in excess of one billion dollars, diversified into many unrelated fields has created an unparalleled opportunity for financial executives to demonstrate their financial acumen. There is an absolute need for new techniques. The solution to the problem is best accomplished through the utilization of corporate profit centers.

Strangely enough, the methods and systems developed for the giants are very effective for the small- or medium-sized business as well. The theory of profit centers involves breaking the activity down into small component parts and utilizing planning and control to increase their profitability and to maintain tight control of the operation. This assures that the allocation of resources is directed toward company objectives and highest profitability.

CASE IN POINT

One extremely large manufacturer has as a profit center a small service operation consisting of a manager, a secretary-receptionist and three servicemen. This unit prepares its own budget of operations, receives the same type of reports as the major units and is controlled in precisely the same manner as the larger units.

WARNING

When the full attention of management is focused on growth, expansion and profits, emphasis is normally directed toward increasing sales volume and the most profitable items in the line. If costs increase in direct relation to sales the effect on profits is negligible. In addition, the trend toward promoting the higher margin items can cause neglect of other profitable markets or stable "bread and butter" items. The basic objective of profit centers is the proper allocation of resources and profitable spending for planned results.

MATRIX ORGANIZATIONS

One of the newer, more successful methods of controlling an organization of varied depth is to utilize the matrix approach. With this method you create a matrix or series of interlocking cells for tasks which are passed from one unit to another. Each cell is held responsible for its own profits and transfer prices are used to pass along the costs for the next cell.

CASE IN POINT

A successful printing firm allows each department to bid for its share of work on a job. When the final results are tabulated, if the bid is unsatisfactory it is sent back for rebidding until the order is obtained or the project is dropped. When the order is obtained each department is credited with its share of the total revenue. Charges are made for its direct costs on the job. If it is produced at a profit (costs less than the bid) the excess is put into a pool. At the end of the year 90% of the pool is distributed to the individuals as a bonus. Losses are also charged to the pool. The 10% reserve and any losses are carried forward into the following year. Losses are carried forward one year as a penalty for poor performance. The 10% reserve is accumulated for five years after which one year's accumulation is added to the bonus paid each year.

This means that each department manager is responsible for his own operating profit and that of the entire firm. The equation is as follows:

DEPT.-1 + DEPT.-2 + DEPT.-3 + DEPT.-4 = TOTAL DIRECT COSTS

REVENUES − (MATERIAL + DIRECT COSTS) = CONTRIBUTION TO CORPORATE OVERHEAD AND PROFIT.

Normally under this type of approach to profits and compensation, the internal policing of costs is rather stringent.

Administering with Control Techniques: Using Corporate Profit Centers

The development of huge corporations resulted in a massive fiasco during the middle 1970's when the recession exposed their weaknesses. The failure to control operations and expansion resulted in tremendous losses and brought many firms close to bankruptcy. This resulted in a whole new concept of corporate responsibility accounting, wherein entire plants and managers were given complete autonomy over their operations and held strictly accountable for profits, financial health and the return on the corporate investment. The overall control exercised was a financial one in that they had to come to corporate headquarters for funds with which to operate. The strict financial controls made certain that they had a good, justifiable reason for spending funds and that the expected results met or exceeded corporate objectives.

CASE IN POINT

The basic objective of one corporation is an 18% return on the stockholders' equity. This represents a 2% increase over the past year and 8% over the average of the past five years. In a period of five years they had succeeded in raising the rate of return over 5%.

WHAT ARE THE ESSENTIAL ELEMENTS OF CONTROL?

1. It must be simple and concise

    The entire system must be kept simple, concise and effective enough to react to potential problems before they become a reality.

2. It must be flexible enough to react to changing conditions.

    The system must be able to adapt quickly to sharp increases or decreases in sales, production, prices or business conditions.

3. It must spot deviations from plan early or immediately. OR SOONER.

    The managers and the financial administrator must not be deluged with bushel baskets of reports which are three weeks late and a dollar short!

CASE IN POINT

One firm knows from historical studies of its past sales and production patterns that if 26% of their shipments have been made by the tenth of the month that their sales and production goals for the month will be met. If this has not occurred by the tenth day they still have time to solve the problem within the next twenty days.

4. The costs of the system must not exceed the benefits.
5. Corrective action must result from its use.

    It is far better to react quickly than to wait too long. It is the lag in action that costs most firms money and wasted time. Action must be decisive. If it cannot be saved or made to be profitable without too much effort, *dump it!*

6. There must be positive as well as negative action.

    If sales increase or new markets develop, the plan must provide for action to take advantage of the situation. Many sales have been lost through a failure to provide sufficient goods or services.

58 Administering with Control Techniques: Using Corporate Profit Centers

CASE IN POINT

Because of continuing low stocks and slow deliveries a major account was lost by a small firm. When the customer could not get delivery in a few days, it gave the business to a competitor who had adequate stocks and could deliver immediately.

7. Controls cannot be too widespread.

    In practically every business 25% of the items are vitally important whether it be sales, production or inventories. If you watch and control the 25% you will be controlling over 75% of your operations. The remainder will generally fall in line.

    Deal primarily with the exceptions—the problems. Time can often be wasted on items that are performing alright or that have no significant bearing on the results of operations.

Controls normally consist of two basic parts—*financial and administrative* and *operational*. Each has its specific function and requires monitoring to make certain that it is in working order. A control system, in the broad sense, measures your performance against your plans and objectives and provides a formula for taking alternative or corrective action when deviations occur.

WHAT ARE THE REQUIREMENTS OF CONTROL?

1. You must have a basic plan and objectives for the business.

    Most individuals and small businesses fail because of three factors. First, they do not have a plan or objective. Secondly, many owners do not know or understand what a simple plan or budget can do for them. The word "budget" raises the specter of restraint. It has become such a nasty word in business that most firms now use the term "planning." In addition, the budget associations have changed their names to planning organizations. Thirdly, most firms lack the administrative and internal discipline to make a plan and stick to it. It is the "in" thing for awhile and then it is forgotten.

2. You must assign responsibility for each segment of the business to some individual.
3. Expenditures must be planned, regulated and controlled.
4. It must measure performance by segment or responsibility.
5. It must provide a method for predicting cash flow so that expansion or growth can be properly financed.

CASE IN POINT

A beauty salon commenced building a $40,000 addition without a prior financing commitment. Currently the addition is standing one-half finished because a verbal funds commitment fell through and the owner ran out of money. Long-term financing under these conditions is a problem.

Another small firm built a $15,000 warehouse with short-term funds. When business slowed down and cash flow dropped it became strapped for cash and had to extend the loan. Long-term financing should have been secured before the building was built.

Administering with Control Techniques: Using Corporate Profit Centers

A simple cash flow statement would have pointed out to these owners the future problems they are now encountering.

6. It rewards good performance and punishes poor performance. Sweating out a poor cash position can be sufficient punishment for a small business executive.

WHAT WILL A PROFIT CENTER CONTROL SYSTEM PROVIDE?

1. A sound basis for profitable planning. It will make the owners and managers think about the future.
2. It will force awareness of the need for profitability in each of the operations and a recognition of the part that each segment plays in the overall picture.

    "For want of a cap no drug could be bottled;
    For want of production all sales were throttled;
    For want of a sale the boss became nervous!
    It wouldn't have happened with our good service."

3. It will force review of your pricing policies.
4. It will help you plan your merchandising efforts and control them.
5. It will help control profits and costs.

    The owner or manager of every business needs to know if he is making a profit and if so, how much? Are his costs out of line? Where is his breakeven point and where does he start making money?

6. Wage determinations and employee performance will be reviewed periodically.
7. It will force assessment of expansion plans and where the funds required will come from.
8. It will provide cost controls, inventory controls, production controls, credit controls, and purchasing controls.
9. Detailing expenses and costs by function and profit center will provide an insight into how the sales dollar is spent.

Large businesses have found that by breaking themselves into smaller components they can function more effectively and efficiently. It follows, therefore, that a program which will create revenues and regulate capital expenditures for the small business will apply equally as well. Each small business has a program that can benefit all sizes and types of organizations. It is realized that each individual case will require some modifications but overall the basic problems are the same. Business requires people; people spend money to accomplish the corporate goals. In many instances it is only a difference in the amount.

With this in mind we will start at the top of a theoretical profit center control system and work our way down.

THE BASIC ACTIVITY OR COST CENTERS

1. The smaller firm
    a. Administration
    b. Selling or marketing

60 Administering with Control Techniques: Using Corporate Profit Centers

  c. Production—operations—purchasing—inventories
  d. Financial activities

    bb. Breakdown of sales—marketing

     1. Commercial activities
     2. Residential Activities

    cc. Breakdown of production—operations—purchasing—inventories

     1. Commercial
     2. Residential

 2. The larger firms

  There are three basic centers of activity

  a. Corporate headquarters—main office
  b. Individual plant or manufacturing activity
  c. Sales office—branch—regional plant—warehouse—regional or local distribution center

For control purposes the activities of the units are broken down in the following manner:

CONTROL ACCOUNT	DESCRIPTION
100	CORPORATE HEADQUARTERS—MAIN OFFICE
100-01	Administration
100-02	Marketing Research
100-03	Manufacturing Development—New Processes and Equipment
100-04	Transportation and Transportation Research—Including Material Handling
100-05	Engineering—Design—Development of New Products and Packages
100-06	Research—Basic—Long-Range
100-07	Distribution Research
100-08	Purchasing—Materials—Inventories
100-09	Planning and Policies
100-10	Financial Administration and Control
100-11	Employee Relations—Security

CONTROL ACCOUNT	DESCRIPTION—COST CONTROL OR PROFIT CENTERS
200	INDIVIDUAL PLANT
200-01	Administration
200-02	Sales—Customer Relations
200-03	Order Entry
200-04	Order Assembly—Scheduling—Production Planning
200-05	Material Handling
200-06	Warehousing—Inventories
200-07	Shipping—Receiving—Truck Operations
200-08	Inter-Plant Transfers
200-09	Purchasing
200-10	Production Operations
200-11	Maintenance
200-12	Employee Relations—Security
200-13	Financial Administration and Control

Administering with Control Techniques: Using Corporate Profit Centers

CONTROL ACCOUNT	DESCRIPTION—COST CONTROL OR PROFIT CENTERS
300	BRANCH—WAREHOUSE—SALES OFFICE—DISTRIBUTION CENTER
300-01	Administration
300-02	Sales—Customer Relations
300-03	Order Entry—Processing
300-04	Shipping—Receiving
300-05	Transportation—Local Deliveries
300-06	Material Handling
300-07	Inventories
300-08	Packaging—Repackaging
300-09	Financial Administration and Control
300-10	Building and Equipment Maintenance
300-11	Employee Relations and Security

In another instance the basic activities are broken down as follows:

CONTROL ACCOUNT	DESCRIPTION OF PROFIT CENTER
100	CORPORATE HEADQUARTERS—MAIN OFFICE
200	MANUFACTURING
300	MARKETING—SALES—ADVERTISING
400	FINANCIAL ADMINISTRATION AND CONTROL
500	EMPLOYEE RELATIONS AND SECURITY

Corporate headquarters might be broken down as follows:

CONTROL ACCOUNT	PROFIT CENTER FUNCTION
500-01	ADMINISTRATION
500-02	MANUFACTURING
500-03	MARKETING
500-04	FINANCIAL
500-05	RESEARCH AND DEVELOPMENT
500-06	EMPLOYEE RELATIONS—SECURITY
500-07	GOVERNMENT AND COMMUNITY RELATIONS
500-08	LEGAL

The expenses for all operations are functionalized in the following manner:

CONTROL ACCOUNT	
500-02-01	SALARIES
-011	ADMINISTRATIVE
-012	SUPERVISORS
-013	CLERICAL

62 Administering with Control Techniques: Using Corporate Profit Centers

	-014	HOURLY WORKERS
	-015	OTHER
500-02-02		EMPLOYEE BENEFITS
	-021	FICA
	-022	UNEMPLOYMENT
	-023	INSURANCE—HEALTH
	-024	INSURANCE—LIFE
	-025	PENSIONS
	-026	OTHER
500-02-03		EXCESS PAYROLL COSTS
	-031	SHIFT PREMIUM
	-032	OVERTIME PREMIUM
	-033	NON-PRODUCTIVE WORK
	-034	UNION OR COMMUNITY EFFORT
	-035	HOLIDAY PAY
	-036	VACATION PAY
500-02-09		INVENTORY COSTS
	-091	WAREHOUSE RENT
	-092	INSURANCE
	-093	TAXES
	-094	CARRYING COSTS
	-095	OBSOLESCENCE AND SPOILAGE LOSSES

Exhibits A and B demonstrate the type of reporting and control maintained over a small service operation of a large firm. This is indicative of the type of cost center or profit center control and reporting in this firm. It details the operating results for the period versus the plan and last year. It also shows the gross investment in the facility and the financial return on that investment. Notice the "head count" of the unit is periodically reported on.

Since these reports are standardized for units of the firm, any number can be consolidated into districts, regions and the entire firm in a very short time. When costs are automatically recorded in this manner, it is easier to discover hidden costs and to compare the cost effectiveness of one unit against another. If similar operations occur in various sections of the country comparisons are easy and performance can be rated unit by unit.

Certain firms have used the "brand manager" approach to control operations that are consumer sales oriented—cereals, cosmetics, liquors and other consumer packaged items. Under current conditions of ruthless competition, brand loyalty and product life cycles have been shortened to the point that this type of system is under close review. Currently many firms trend toward utilizing the functional or specialized job approach.

The marketing hierarchy for the brand manager approach to profit and performance control is shown in the following chart:

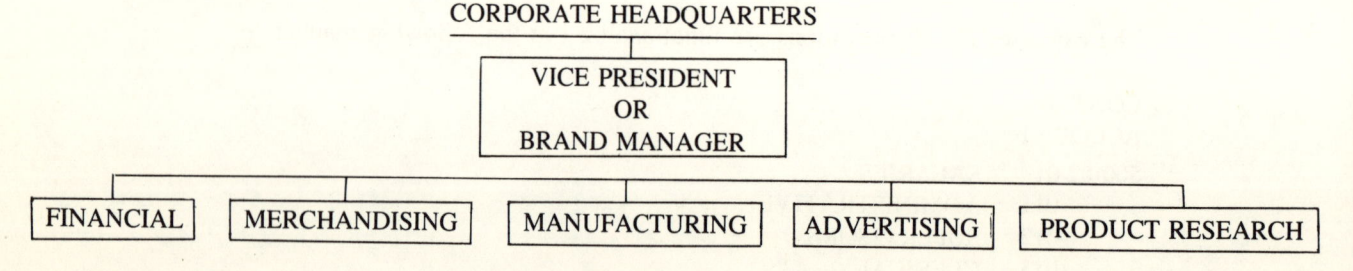

CORPORATE HEADQUARTERS

VICE PRESIDENT OR BRAND MANAGER

| FINANCIAL | MERCHANDISING | MANUFACTURING | ADVERTISING | PRODUCT RESEARCH |

Administering with Control Techniques: Using Corporate Profit Centers

Assistants are provided dependent upon the number of products handled and the total volume of sales.

ADMINISTERING WITH CONTROL TECHNIQUES

Brand managers have the responsibility of coordinating the various corporate activities to make certain that their products get an equal share of corporate action and funds. They are judged on their performance in growth, profitability, share of the market and return on investment. Other than major policy decisions, they are pretty much left alone as long as their performance meets the overall corporate requirements. One of the basic faults in this type of operation is that the managers strive for volume and high profitability and ignore complete segments of the market that may have high future potentials or long-sustained product life.

Another form of operation is the specialized or functional job approach as indicated below:

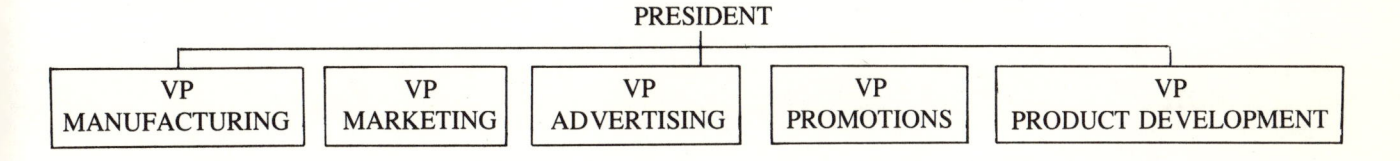

```
                          PRESIDENT
   ┌──────────┬──────────┬──────────┬──────────┐
   VP         VP         VP         VP         VP
MANUFACTURING MARKETING ADVERTISING PROMOTIONS PRODUCT DEVELOPMENT
```

or as follows:
PRESIDENT
VICE PRESIDENT—FINANCIAL ADMINISTRATION
    A. MANAGER—PLANNING AND CONTROL
    B. MANAGER—ACQUISITIONS—GROWTH
    C. MANAGER—ACCOUNTING REPORTS—OPERATIONS
    D. MANAGER—TAXES
    E. MANAGER—COORDINATION WITH OPERATIONS
VICE PRESIDENT—MARKETING
    A. MANAGER—REGION 1
    B. MANAGER—REGION 2
    C. MANAGER—REGION 3
    D. MANAGER—MARKET PLANNING
    E. MANAGER—DISTRIBUTION PLANNING
    F. MANAGER—NEW PRODUCTS—PACKAGES
VICE PRESIDENT—PRODUCTION
    A. MANAGER—OPERATIONS
    B. MANAGER—PRODUCTION PLANNING
    C. MANAGER—PURCHASING
    D. MANAGER—WAREHOUSING—SHIPPING AND RECEIVING
    E. MANAGER—MACHINERY AND EQUIPMENT
    F. MANAGER—TRANSPORTATION
VICE PRESIDENT—ADVERTISING

64 Administering with Control Techniques: Using Corporate Profit Centers

ADMINISTERING WITH CONTROL TECHNIQUES
   A. MANAGER—MEDIA ADVERTISING
   B. MANAGER—SPECIAL PROMOTIONS
VICE PRESIDENT—RESEARCH AND DEVELOPMENT
   A. MANAGER—BASIC RESEARCH
   B. MANAGER—DEVELOPMENT NEW PRODUCTS
VICE PRESIDENT—PUBLIC RELATIONS
   A. MANAGER—EMPLOYEE RELATIONS
   B. MANAGER CIVIC AND GOVERNMENT RELATIONS
   C. MANAGER—SECURITY
VICE PRESIDENT—LEGAL

Under this type of organization, the jobs are filled by individuals who have the expertise in their particular fields. You have a specialist in advertising, in special promotions, in market analysis and planning. They cover all brands and are not confined to one brand or one line. They could specialize in distribution techniques and introduce new products for any brand line.

NOTE

There is one major drawback to the system! You could have a "brand a month" specialist if you are not careful.

The use of computers in marketing has made it possible to break down markets into life styles, age groups, income groups or geographical location. This means that the individual who handled one product or one brand is gradually being replaced by a specialist who has a broad knowledge of economics, planning, merchandise promotion, distribution and financial controls.

This fluid, changing type of organization has created real problems for the financial administrator who is charged with the financial control of the entire organization. The team approach creates situations wherein if all of the members participate in the introduction and promotion of a new product, who is responsible for the costs of the operation? How do you allocate costs of the various functions to the product? When the brand or product manager was the president of his own little organization, you could design controls that showed what was happening under current conditions and who was responsible for it. The functional departments do not really pinpoint profitability accountability. Each administrator may have his or her funds to spend and budget to meet, but when a product bombs who absorbs the loss? Profits are made of bits and pieces throughout the entire organization, and the financial administrator is like a cat chasing his tail as he tries to pin profit or loss responsibility down.

In this respect, I personally feel that all operations of each segment of a business are essentially the same. People in action spend money whatever their function. Basically all that is necessary to control these expenditures is to record them properly; i.e., classifying spending and attempting to justify each expenditure by relating it to the growth and profitability of the entire enterprise.

The first and primary challenge is to find out what goes on. After this is determined you can set up a reporting system that will measure the performance. If the job is done well profits are created. If it is done poorly you are in the red, and unless you are color blind the primary determination is relatively simple.

Administering with Control Techniques: Using Corporate Profit Centers

HOW THE PLANS ARE EVOLVED

The basis for all control is planning. The company and each individual unit must have a goal or benchmark to measure performance against.

CASE IN POINT

It is assumed that each plant manager is running his or her own business!

Four months prior to the start of the next year each manager is given the following information:

1. A detailed projection for each product line and product by marketing area.
2. An economic forecast showing the projections for the various markets, inflation rate, interest rates, prices of products and purchased items.

One month prior to the start of the new year each manager must submit for review and consultation his or her forecast of individual operations. This is detailed, month by month, for the coming year and perhaps weekly in some instances. In addition, they must submit a revised long-term plan, in lesser detail, for the coming three to five years. Some firms only use a two-year projection.

Once the managers and management agree on their projections this plan then becomes the manager's commitment for the year. At the time the initial economic report is issued and at the final session, the manager is made fully aware of the corporate plan for growth and expansion by acquisition.

REPORTING

In the field of control reports we have the basic categories as follows:

1. *Sales* ....daily ....weekly ....monthly
2. *Production* ....daily ....weekly ....monthly
3. *Inventories* ....daily ....weekly ....monthly
4. *Personnel* ....daily ....weekly ....monthly
5. *Financial* ....daily ....weekly ....monthly
6. *Current Problems* .... as required ....

Issuance of reports will vary from firm to firm dependent upon requirements and deemed importance.

SAMPLE TYPE OF REPORT—SALES

PROFIT BY PRODUCT
REGION 1 TERRITORY 7

PRODUCT	UNITS	$$$$$$	GROSS PROFIT	UNITS	$$$$$$	VOLUME	PRICE	MIX
0123	5,000	10,000	2,500	0000	−1,000	000	−1,000	0
0167	1,000	5,000	2,000	− 500	−2,000	−2,500	000	+500
0170	8,000	8,000	2,000	−1,000	+ 750	+1,000	− 250	0

(VARIATION FROM PLAN)

66 Administering with Control Techniques: Using Corporate Profit Centers

PROFIT BY PRODUCT—SUMMARY

0100	56,000	112,000	22,000	−4,000	−10,000	−8,000	−2,000	0
0123	60,000	120,000	30,000	0	0	0	0	
0167	50,000	250,000	50,000	0	−4,000		−5,000	+1,000

PROFIT BY SALES REGION

GROSS
PROFIT $$$ ADVERTISING   SALARIES   SALES EXPENSES   NET CONTRIBUTION

PROFIT BY SALES REGION

VARIATION FROM PLAN

ADVERTISING $$$ SALARIES $$$ SALES EXPENSES $$$

REGION 1

REGION 2

REGIONAL PROFIT SUMMARY

This entire system of reporting consolidates into one major contribution report wherein we have a profit and loss by product starting at the individual customer level. This consolidates into a territorial summary, a regional summary and a plant summary. The individual plants are then summarized into a company total.

WHAT DO WE ACCOMPLISH?

The results of the consolidations are readily apparent. We have a profit contribution by product, by customer, by territory, by region and by plant.

Product contribution—this enables you to see precisely what each product is contributing to the territory, region or plant profit.

Plant contribution—this report enables one to determine what each plant is contributing to the entire company profitability. In the report the numbers are reported in a manner that will show the individual components and the total plant performance against planned operations.

By breaking the figures down into individual cost centers or profit contribution centers, we can analyze the costs and profit contributions of each segment of the business. The old bugaboo of unallocated expenses is not charged against the performance of the individual operations by management but is separated into an individual cost of the overall operation.

CASE IN POINT

An electrical contractor controls his operations as follows:

1. Each residence is allocated a number of hours for what is called an electrical "rough" or "trim" based upon the original job estimate. Material is allocated on the same basis. Normally two men are assigned to a crew to complete the work.

Administering with Control Techniques: Using Corporate Profit Centers 67

2. Material is issued in job packs—one rough, one trim, one for any extras. Charges are made for additional materials issued and credits are given for materials returned.
3. Hours are accumulated from the individual time tickets
4. Charges are made for tools, truck expenses and other labor costs through a labor loader. This is a set amount per hour of labor.

The control report looks like this:

CREW NO. 1
CONTRACTOR NO. 1
SUBDIVISION NO. 1

	CREW	CONT.	SUBV.	LOT	PLAN	HOURS	$$$$$	MAT'L	TOTAL COST	BILLED	+ OR −	OPERATION
E	01	01	01	103	57	24	360	450	810	1,200	+390	R
A	01	01	01	103	57	26	380	450	830	1,200	+370	R
V						+2	+20		+20		−20	

E = ESTIMATED OPERATIONS
A = ACTUAL OPERATIONS
V = VARIATION FROM PLAN

The results are tabulated for each subdivision and then converted into a summary by contractor. Each week the performance is tabulated and reported as follows:

CODE	NAME	HOURS	$$$$$$	MAT'L	TOTAL COSTS	BILLING	+ OR −	VARIATION + OR −
010	CONTRACTOR	112	1,680	2,000	3,680	4,000	320	− 110
020	CONTRACTOR	400	6,000	5,000	11,000	15,000	4,000	+1,000
030	CONTRACTOR	500	8,000	7,000	15,000	14,000	−1,000	−2,000

Each week the totals are summarized into a continuing weekly report:

WEEK ENDING	LABOR HOURS	$$$$$$	MAT'L	TOTAL COSTS	BILLING	+ OR −	SUPV. ADM	NET + OR −	VARIED + OR −
00-00-0	1,000	15,000	11,000	26,000	30,000	+4,000	2,000	+2,000	−1,000
00-00-1	900	14,000	9,000	23,000	28,000	+5,000	2,000	+3,000	+1,000

POINT TO NOTE

The percentage contribution by product is not always a true criterion of the contribution of a product. One product could carry a high profit potential but be limited by production capacity or machine speed. This type of situation often exists:

PRODUCT	DAILY PRODUCTION	% GROSS	$$$$ GROSS	MACHINE COST
A	25,000	30%	$7,500	$100,000
B	50,000	20%	10,000	$125,000

A careful analysis must be made of all factors prior to changing over to high markup products. Relations to equipment costs, speeds and market capacities are required.

In this computer economy we have noticed that all retail stores are swinging toward the promotion of fast-moving, high margin items. As a result everyone has gotten into the act and no one is covering a lucrative out-of-the-ordinary market. *Control begins* at the retail level! Sears Roebuck found this out when they taught their salesmen to upgrade the customers from medium-priced merchandise to the higher priced, higher margin items. For a period of time this was successful. Then the alert competition realized that there was a vast profitable market under the high-priced level and took advantage of it. As a result Sears has had to revise their merchandising practices. Control of sales techniques to cover existing profitable markets is as vital to success as any other type of control technique. What you do at the top line is just as important as any function of the business.

ZERO-BASED BUDGETING FOR CONTROL

The most effective means of planning and controlling the activities of any organization may well lie in the technique of *zero-based budgeting*. Under this searching process the firm must divide its activities into single *decision units* and analyze each function in order to determine its true value in the overall corporate picture.

We need to return to the very basics in business, and critically analyze every function. *Why do we do what we do?* What does it contribute to the total activity? What is its exact function? Can we get along with fewer people? Can we consolidate the activities with others and still perform efficiently? Do the functions need to be reduced, expanded?

ZBB is the technique which will provide you with some of the answers to your questions and problems. It will, if applied effectively, enable you to run a "tight ship" and an efficient, highly profitable firm. We also need it to control the continuing growth of government bureaucracy, federal, state and local. Too often, once a function is initiated it goes on eternally until the company fails, is merged into another firm or a recession forces action. The very fact that it exists justifies its existence. If it sees its function diminishing it will create ways and means of continuing to operate. One new government form can create a new department with staff. Make-work is a common practice, hard to spot and hard to eliminate.

Too often in the planning process we are inclined to allow past expenditures to stand as a base point for future plans. We have not been inclined to question changes in goals, shifting priorities or the actual need for retaining each unit as one of the vital parts of the corporate function. Just because something worked well last year does not mean that it will next year or three years down the line. We must equate external changes with organization activities and needs.

The basic idea of ZBB was proposed by Arthur Burns when he stated that a substantial amount of government expenditures could be eliminated if each agency were to request funds each year as a new entity. Peter Pyhrr then created the concept of zero-based budgeting by starting each year at zero and justifying all expenditures. While I do not agree entirely on a complete annual justification, due to practical applications, time and manpower, I do believe that it is vital for every organization to completely justify each unit every two to five years. If

Administering with Control Techniques: Using Corporate Profit Centers

possible it should be done on an annual or annual rotating basis. This offers a true means of controlling your operations by forcing you to critically review your entire organization periodically. Too often, when things are going well, we let controls slide and fat creep up on the corporate skeleton. It takes a major recession or corporate disaster to obtain a critical review in many instances. The headlines and stories telling of the elimination of personnel, functions and operations only make one wonder: "How did it happen in the first place?"

Many firms utilize zero-based budgeting with a high percentage of success and it definitely is a vital tool for every financial administrator. The control procedures and reports do not change radically, only the method of critically reviewing and justifying the existence, activities and expenditures of each function.

CASE IN POINT

One municipal organization had a high overtime cost factor. When questioned about the activity, the department head stated that it was necessary in order to complete a heavy workload without hiring additional employees. Studies indicated that the employees loafed during the day, read the newspaper and the scratch sheets. They ran across the street to place their bets in the morning and collect their winnings in the afternoon (if any). There were four bookie parlors within a block of city hall—three of them were only 200 feet away. From 5 p.m. until 8 p.m., the overtime hours, everyone was busily engaged in completing the day's work.

CASE IN POINT

A member of the Assessor's Office makes a trip home for lunch almost every day ostensibly to complete his paperwork. Actually he completes some personal chores. Normally he arrives home about 11:15 to 11:30 a.m. and leaves about 1:30 p.m. Since he drives an automobile furnished by the government agency, this means that he travels untold miles out of his way. From the time lost by this individual, and if there were three more like him, we could reduce the cost of the office by 25% for personnel alone.

CASE IN POINT

We have senators who admit that they spend little time in their home state over a long period. We have congressmen who junket around for years. Who represents the people during their absence? This also applies to corporate executives. In your review and control of executive costs, travel time and expenses are a major factor. This is an easy item for ZBB.

WHAT IS INVOLVED IN ZBB?

One of the large utilities in the Southwest embarked upon a ZBB installation in the mid-1970's. A financial administrator was imported to install and implement the program. After about eighteen months the installation was well on its way to completion. Documented

70 Administering with Control Techniques: Using Corporate Profit Centers

savings in the first year amounted to over $300,000, and it is conservatively estimated that the savings would run into millions during the first five years of operation.

In discussing the installation the financial administrator made these comments:

1. We need ZBB data—the techniques and experience of others—manuals—forms—organization of the planning function—how a ZBB team is staffed.
2. Determination of the individual decision units was agonizingly slow. Each unit had to be presented, analyzed and approved by the executive committee. This was extremely time consuming.
3. The entire organization had to be educated in the ZBB techniques, concepts, procedures and objectives. Resistance was exceedingly high in the beginning as most individuals felt their jobs or power structures might be threatened.
4. Each step had to be carefully and explicitly documented and approved.
5. In the process of reviewing the various decision units, their functions, expenditures and very existence, we must have developed at least 1,500 ideas on how we could operate on an improved basis. Many of the ideas created sufficient savings to adopt them almost immediately. Some required additional expenditures for future periods or additional investigation. Even if the ZBB program had failed, the benefits from the detailed analysis of our operations will have paid for the time and effort involved. In addition, we have a long list of alternatives for future consideration.

ZBB is not a panacea for all evils, but a carefully structured analytical plan. Its basic premise is: "You are not needed! Now justify your existence within the corporate structure!" What would happen to our operations if your function was eliminated—reduced—combined—replaced or even expanded? You can start from *zero* and work up or start from where you are and work down to *zero* by the process of elimination. You can eliminate each function and then attempt to determine what effect it would have on your sales, costs or services. What are the alternatives if the function was eliminated, if it was reduced? In the governmental area the trick is to eliminate the function that will create the most public reaction while steering away from the real sensitive items that could be eliminated. Stay away from this trap in your review and analysis.

WHAT IS A DECISION PACKAGE?

A decision package is an identifiable function ranging from one individual to many. It includes its related costs which can be segregated with the unit, documented and an independent decision made.

WHAT IS DOCUMENTATION?

Documentation of a decision package is writing out in detail its program objectives and goals. It details what the function is supposed to do, the resources required—men, women, money, machines, time. It also includes the vital factor of the unit of measurable production and how it will be measured in performance, the benefits expected of the unit and its place in the entire corporate structure. Each unit must be documented.

Administering with Control Techniques: Using Corporate Profit Centers

STEP ONE — Identify all of the decision packages within the organization.
For example:
1. Purchasing
2. Production Control
3. Personnel
4. Credit and Collections
5. Legal
6. Tax Administration

STEP TWO — Identify all the expenditures associated with each decision package.

STEP THREE — Relate the current functions, operations and costs to the entire corporate structure.

STEP FOUR — *This is where it hits the fan—the dogs start howling for your demise!* You pose the questions and alternatives:

What if?
1. We eliminated the function.
2. We cut it to a bare minimum.
3. We continue it at the present level.
4. We replace it with another function.
5. We expand the function.

STEP FIVE — Assign priorities—not all items can be acted upon immediately or at one time. The basic decisions must be made as to what to do first and which action might be the most productive. Often the low-cost items may be approached first.

This in short is ZBB—as a financial administrator if it is not now in your tool kit you had better acquire it. It is one of the most vital and productive tools available for financial control. Coupled with access to a computer and computer simulation programs, you can be a dynamic part of the management team!

Walter D. Hill, former president of the Planning Executives Institute, has furnished me with considerable material relative to the Zero-Based-Budgeting installation at GENRAD, Inc. I deeply appreciate the material and the in-depth discussions on the topic with someone who has done an outstanding job in the field.

The Planning Executives Institute published a monogram as follows:

IMPLEMENTING ZERO-BASED BUDGETING—
The Real World

A Case Study

by

Walter D. Hill,
Controller
GENRAD, Inc.

As the first president of the Institute I am delighted to see them continue in the forward echelon of planning and control. I am also deeply appreciative of their permission to utilize material from the text of the monogram by Walter.

72 Administering with Control Techniques: Using Corporate Profit Centers

In addition, the PEI has recently published a noteworthy text in the field of planning. It is as follows:

>EXPLORATORY PLANNING
>
>Briefs of Practice
>
>by
>
>W. W. Simmons
>President
>Applied Futures, Inc.

Both of these publications are available from the:

>Planning Executives Institute
>P.O. Box 70
>Oxford, Ohio   45056

To better illustrate how zero-based budgeting is used in actual practice I have presented abstracts of the material furnished by Walter D. Hill and the Planning Executives Institute. Beginning on the next page, a case study of an actual application and the various steps taken throughout is illustrated.

I. WHY SHOULD I BE INTERESTED IN ZERO-BASED BUDGETING?

There was a cry often heard in Boston over the past few years concerning the fortunes of the Red Sox "Wait 'til Next Year!"

Occasionally, "next year" arrived "this year" as it did in 1967 and 1975 and they reached for the pennant. Too often, unfortunately, the Red Sox fell short of their goals and the fans spent the following winter second guessing management for their trades, handling of players, etc.

Is this your position with *your* fans, the stockholders?

Many companies do planning by "wishful thinking" and never attain their goals and objectives. They succumb to the hockey stick syndrome of planning!

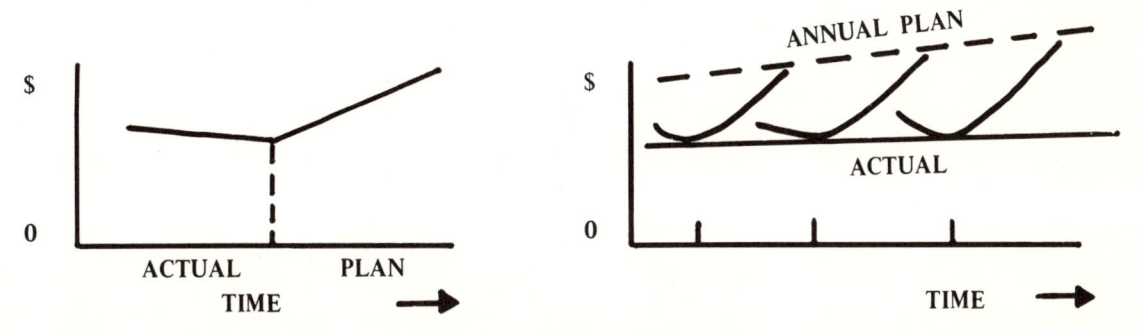

Other companies are in such fast moving industries that they must run faster and faster just to keep up with the state-of-the-art, and their competition. The electronics industry is a good example, particularly those companies in the calculator business. Or even that staid old Swiss-based industry of watch making which is being shaken to its foundation by the introduction of liquid-crystal, digital watches based upon the new technology of micro-circuits encapsulated on silicon chips. They need a tool to be able to react faster to changes in direction.

Even companies, like DuPont, with extremely sophisticated long-range planning systems, get caught by such "unforeseen" events as the recent oil crisis which affected their petroleum based plastics. So contingency planning suddenly becomes a vital piece of our whole planning-budgeting process.

The tempo of the times is one of rapid, sometimes unexpected, changes and we need to be prepared to cope with changes in either rate or direction.

Zero-based budgeting (**ZBB**) can be a useful tool to help you cope with contingency plans, changes in tempo (up or down) and changes in direction.

The traditional approach to budgeting tends to be monolithic, i.e., it assumes that whatever you are doing now is OK and is what you want to do next year. Therefore, all you need to think about is the relative efficiency of your present operations in doing the same job next year, subject to some corporate guidelines on inflation rates to be used in extrapolating present costs in terms of next year's dollars.

The **ZBB** approach requires you to segment your present operations into recognizable activities and to analyze them, along with proposed new programs, in terms of cost-benefit trade-offs which will support the goals and objectives you have set for yourself. It forces that awkward question "Is this activity necessary?"

EXHIBIT 1 shows a comparison of the traditional approach versus the **ZBB** incremental approach to budgeting during a period of inflation.

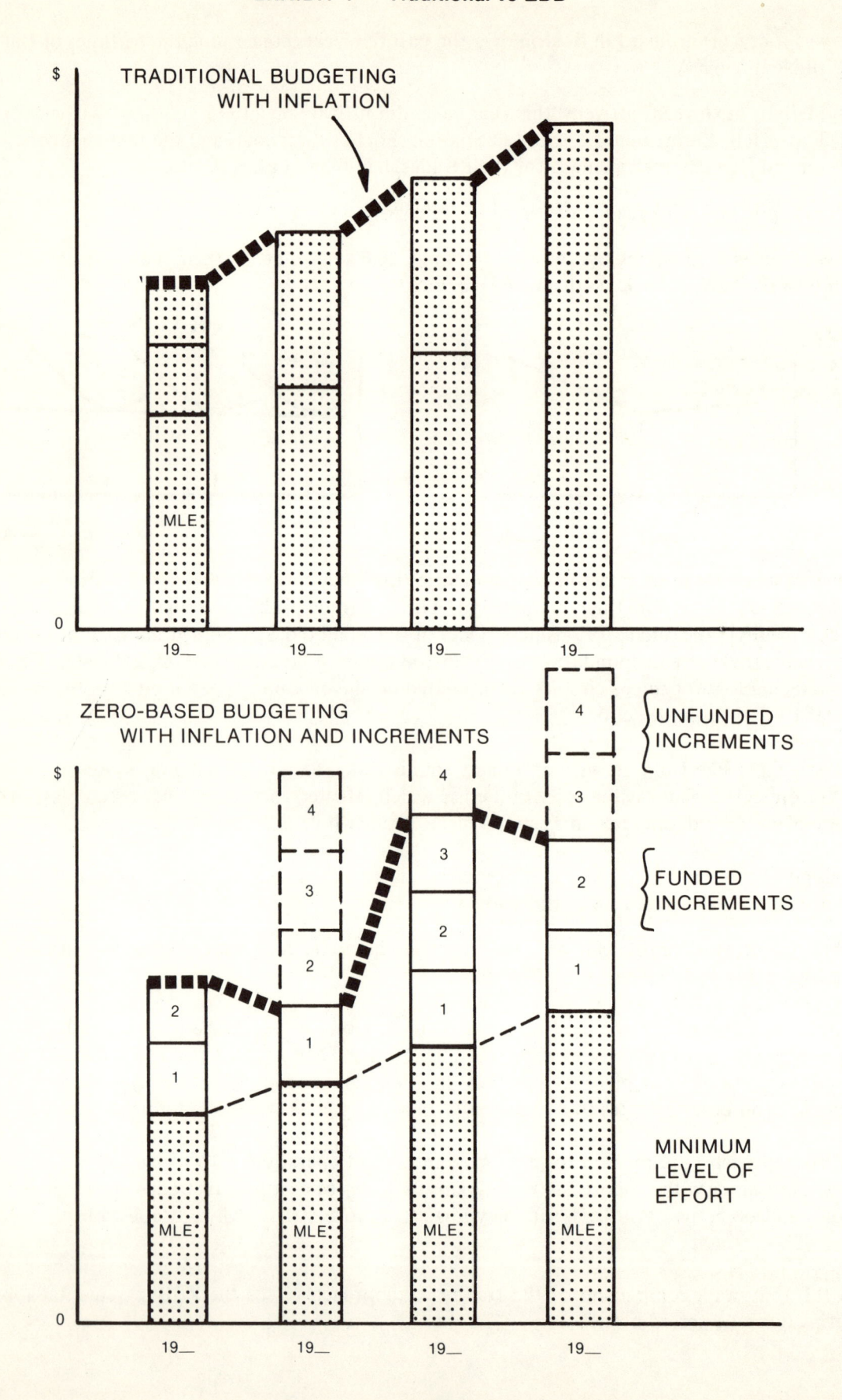

EXHIBIT 1 — Traditional *vs* ZBB

II. ZERO BASE BUDGETING - The Concept

Traditionally companies start the budgeting process using this year's expenditure rate as the base.... as the *necessary* rate of expenditure.... without questioning shifting priorities, changes in corporate plans, or even the necessity to perpetuate this particular function or operation's existence.

Peter Pyhrr created the concept of Zero-Based Budgeting when he was Manager of Staff Control at Texas Instruments in Dallas, Texas. He was inspired by a 1969 speech by Arthur Burns to the Tax Foundation in which he, Burns, suggested that "substantial savings could undoubtedly be realized if it were required that every agency .... make a case for its entire appropriation request *each year*, just as if its program or programs were entirely new."

Pyhrr asked himself why this concept of starting each year from base zero and justifying *all* expenditures could not be applied to industry .... specifically to Texas Instruments where he worked. Thus was born Zero-Based Budgeting.

Pyhrr has gone on to fame and fortune applying the concept at Texas Instruments, writing a 1970 article for the *Harvard Business Review* .... which was read by the newly elected Governor of Georgia, Jimmy Carter, who thought the process could be applied to the State of Georgia. Pyhrr became a consultant to Jimmy Carter and the concept was used to develop the entire executive budget recommendations for Fiscal Year, July 1972 - June 1973. Pyhrr wrote of his experiences and had them published by John Wiley & Sons in a 1973 book entitled *ZERO BASE BUDGETING*.

The WALL STREET JOURNAL in its "Review and Outlook" comments of October 22, 1976, noted that Jimmy Carter in the presidential debates cited his introduction of **ZBB** in Georgia as evidence of his managerial skills. The article goes on to say:

> "Predictably, things didn't go that smoothly when the idea was put into practice. Many lower level bureaucrats didn't catch on at first to the business of defining "decision packages," and those bureaus that lost funds became quite hostile to the whole idea. More than a few apparently shuffled their priorities to protect their people. Furthermore, the sheer volume of decision units drawn up, some 6,000 in all, was too great to handle at the governor's level, so the full **ZBB** review was unevenly applied. Yet the process took hold and, in a recent survey, a large majority of the state's departmental budget officials favored retaining it."

> "Whether **ZBB** did everything it was supposed to in Georgia seems to depend upon the sympathies of the person you talk to .... Mr. Pyhrr reports that in the first year of use it did in fact produce important changes, in spite of the confusion. The first **ZBB** budget, he says, faced a $57 million short-fall, and coped with it by cuts ranging from zero to 15% among the state's 65 agencies. A standard budgetary process could never have responded so flexibly."

ZBB tries to force the hard questions which sometimes never get asked by management:

> "Is this department overstaffed at its present level of operation?"

> "Does this department continue to serve a useful function?"

> "Should this program be curtailed to fund an alternative, higher priority program?"

> "Are we using available funds to promote *corporate* goals and objectives or an individual manager's whims?"

"What are the consequences of not funding this activity? and what are the available trade-offs?"

Under ZBB, top management sets priorities, establishes goals and operating guidelines and determines the available funds for the up-coming budgeting process. Then, middle and lower management set their goals and objectives within the corporate or division guidelines, evaluate their own operations, propose courses of action to achieve their goals and cost out the resources required to accomplish these goals. In addition, they recommend priorities and establish performance measures thus becoming thoroughly committed to the whole goal setting process.

Final funding levels, and allocation of resources, result from various levels of management review which establish any changes in corporate priorities. The ultimate decision rests with top management, usually the Chief Operating Officer.

III. GENRAD, INC. - WHO OR WHAT IS GENRAD?

In order to put this discussion into the proper perspective it is necessary to describe who or what is GenRad . . . . and why they chose **ZBB**.

GenRad was founded in 1915 as the General Radio Company when the word "radio" was synonymous with "communications," or as we know it now "electronics." GenRad was a pioneer in instrumentation for radio communications . . . . one of their precision air/capacitors being used as a component in the first experimental modern radio. Since then, GR has achieved an array of innovations in instruments that improve the performance of broadcast receivers and transmitters, or facilitate laboratory research.

GenRad is also involved in instruments and systems for testing electronic circuits and components; audiometric devices for dealing with speech and hearing problems; equipment for analyzing and measuring noise and vibration; and computer-controlled systems for testing high frequency integrated circuits. Product prices range from $10 to more than $100,000.

In many ways, GR was as much a family as a business. The 40-hour week and profitsharing for all employees were both introduced in 1919. During the Great Depression of the 1930's the company retained its entire work force . . . . using a management incentive program geared to orders and shipments to share the reduced corporate income with the workers who were on short time. Salaries were adjusted on a *monthly* basis using an indexing system keyed to the average of orders and shipments compared to the monthly plan.

Management's belief in a primary responsibility to both employees and existing customers was reflected in a 1942 advertisement headed . . . . "We Don't Want To Grow Too Large." Operationally, this policy was implemented in decisions such as abandoning development of the oscilloscope, which was first developed as a commercial product in GR's research labs. The oscilloscope is now an instrument with an annual market of several *hundred* million dollars.

By 1966, however, management concluded that corporate growth was a valid objective, both to keep pace with the fast moving electronics industry and to provide ample opportunities for GR's people.

The plan for growth called for concerted product and sales efforts focused on selected major markets. Other existing products would be maintained as long as they were profitable, to help finance priority product development.

At the time (19__) when we introduced MBO and **ZBB** into our planning-budgeting procedures, GR had 1,600 employees; four manufacturing locations (three in the U.S.) and worldwide sales of $50-55 million. We were experiencing an annual growth rate of about 15%, with almost 40% of our orders originating outside of the U.S.

IV. WHY DID GENRAD PICK ZBB?

Professor Edward Roberts of the Alfred P. Sloan School of Management at Massachusetts Institute of Technology, a proponent of the theory of industrial dynamics, asserts that the problems of an enterprise arise from inter-related series of causes and effects that spiral upward or downward as positive or negative feedback loops. This is similar to the multiplier theory applied to changes in the Gross National Product. **EXHIBIT 2** illustrates the spiral effect.

EXHIBIT 2 - SPIRAL EFFECT

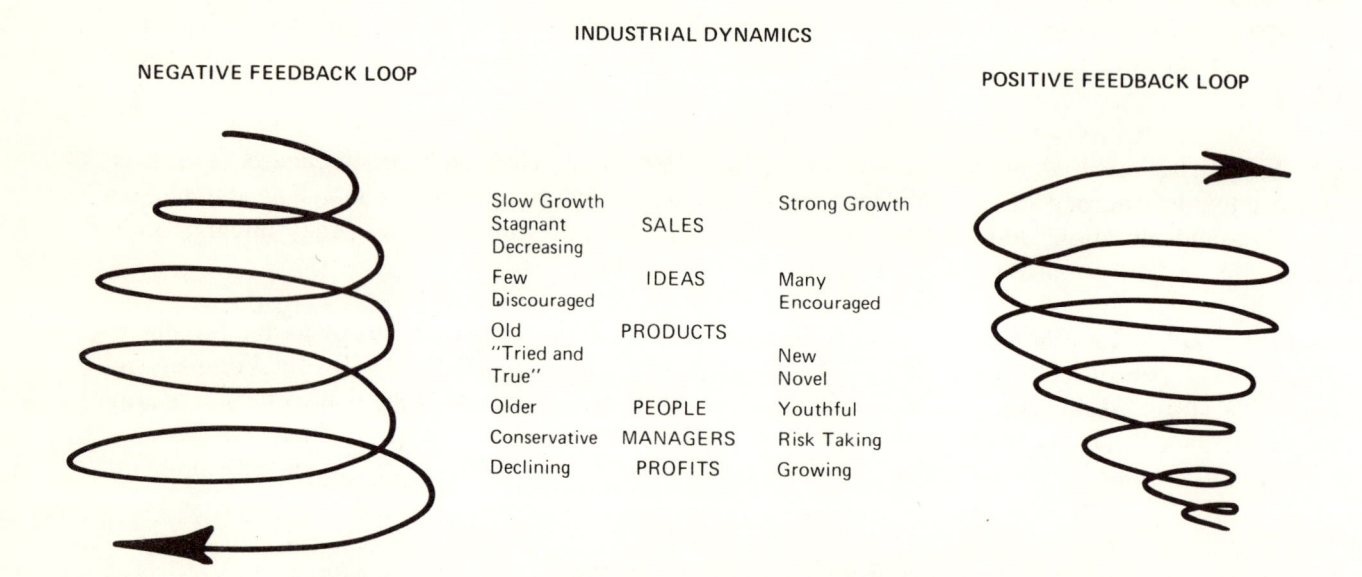

INDUSTRIAL DYNAMICS

NEGATIVE FEEDBACK LOOP			POSITIVE FEEDBACK LOOP
Slow Growth / Stagnant / Decreasing	SALES	Strong Growth	
Few / Discouraged	IDEAS	Many / Encouraged	
Old / "Tried and True"	PRODUCTS	New / Novel	
Older	PEOPLE	Youthful	
Conservative	MANAGERS	Risk Taking	
Declining	PROFITS	Growing	

In an article in *Business Horizons* (Winter, 1967 - Indiana University), he proposes that organizations which do not plan carefully to provide growth opportunities, or to weed out stagnating employees, will quickly become enmeshed in a downward spiral of declining R & D effectiveness as a result of "age-caused" problems. A rejuvenation cure for this disease is to bring in new Ph.D.'s, pump in more money, add new personnel, and give the R & D groups new assignments.

By the middle 60's, GenRad's management felt that their own efforts were being caught in one of these downward spirals and that at 50, their R & D effort, which is the life-blood of their company, was succumbing to hardening of the arteries.

We tried acquisitions, splitting our company into Business Areas which would concentrate on specific product areas, and matrix-management. It was a difficult period for GR as we tried to make a break with the past, giving up certain cherished products long associated with our company while trying to gain momentum in newer, faster moving markets.

It was not until the 70's that GenRad regained the momentum of earlier years and began to move ahead. A new management team took over the decision-making process.

> "GR's traditional decision-making structure had been based on standing committees. This form of management resulted in slow organizational response and diffused responsibility, weaknesses that can be costly in a competitive, fast paced industry. So the decision-making structure was changed.

Product development/marketing units were set up, with the responsibility for decisions and results shifted to individuals. Task forces now deal with . . . . matters that require co-ordination across lines of individual responsibility. These changes, which date from 1973, have resulted in more responsive decision making and improvement in the flow of vital management information."*

Mr. Thurston, GenRad's President, had for many years used the approach of personally analyzing programs and plans in terms of levels of activity. In 1974, when planning-budgeting for 1975, he used an "ongoing-same level," "increased level," "new activities," "functional projects" and "new product projects" approach to analyzing funding requests. He felt that **ZBB** was a logical extension of this approach, but would solve one of the flaws in the 1975 budget presentation, i.e., that the "ongoing-*same level"* nearly equalled his total budget target, allowing him very little room for *new* activities or projects.

In an August, 1975 memo to all managers and supervisors, he set the stage for **ZBB**:

"We had no effective way to examine this great big 'starting base' (ongoing-same level) in order to compare the importance of its established components with the new proposals being made. It was shortly after this experience that we heard about the zero-base concept and bought 'the book,' (by Peter Pyhrr) . . . . I believe that these techniques, new to us, will help you to make a better analysis of your operations and enable me to do a better job of allocating the corporations' funds for next year."

                                                   Bill

                                      William R. Thurston, President

The MBO/ZBB procedures were introduced to the 200 managers and supervisors of our Concord and Bolton, Massachusetts plants where 1,200 of our employees were based. These two plants included corporate headquarters and the product development-marketing teams of three of our four divisions who shared common manufacturing facilities, the latter accounting for about 90% of our total production.

---

* REPORT TO SHAREHOLDERS, William R. Thurston, President
    February 24, 1976

VIII. WHAT HAS BEEN THE EXPERIENCE OF OTHERS?

The **ZBB** process has been in use in an increasing number of diverse corporations, such as Texas Instruments (1970), Dillingham Corp., (1971), United California Bank (1973), Southern California Edison (1974) as well as Magnavox, Xerox, Combustion Engineering and Tektronix. Some comments made by managers of these and other companies follow:

"Avoid establishing inadequate or unclear goals for each decision package . . . . to avoid considerable time wasted on budget items with little probability of top-management's approval. Also, keep the process from becoming too mechanical. And, be sure to feedback to all levels of the company the final disposition and rationale of each decision package . . . . otherwise it will be demotivating." (1)

>Charles W. Kight
>Mgr. Financial Planning Analysis
>Texas Instruments

"We used **ZBB** because the inputs from the old budgeting process were inadequate to plan solidly for the year ahead and determine the best places to allocate resources . . . . we were missing out on opportunities for improving efficiency." (1)

>James Pollock
>Controller
>Dillingham Corp.

"For other managers, it's a threat that they are going to be completely dismantled or that functions they consider sacrosanct will be discarded. The fact is that many managers in many companies don't even know what really happens in their departments, or how . . . . the process consumes a great deal of extra time . . . . " (1)

>David DeWind
>V.P. Systems Engineering
>United California Bank

"The basic advantage is the vast amount of analysis **ZBB** makes available . . . . as much is disclosed about the manager as about his area of responsibilities . . . . " (2)

>Donald S. Anderson
>Budget Director
>Southern California Edison

"It is an efficient way of restraining middle management from the perpetual performance of unnecessary functions, and it exposes the tendency for expenses to grow layer after layer under conventional budgeting." (2)

>Jack Schang
>President
>Allied Van Lines

"The process is time-intensive . . . . should not be limited to paring spending . . . . biggest payback is in gathering intelligence for the best spending of the money you have at any time on the down or upside." (2)

Larry Choruby
Budget Director
Tektronix, Inc.

---

(1) DUN'S REVIEW, October, 1974

(2) INDUSTRY WEEK, January, 1976

PLANS, GOALS AND STRATEGIES: WHAT THEY ARE AND HOW THEY ARE SET

V. GENRAD'S CORPORATE PLANNING PROCESS

The Marketing Plan

Corporate Long Range Objectives & Strategies

The key to the whole planning process at GenRad was to have our Chief Executive Officer put down in writing his philosophy, where GR had been and where we were going. It put much of the ensuing effort into the proper perspective and provided common guidelines to which all managers could relate. It is an absolutely essential precursor to the whole planning-budgeting process . . . . and must be done early in the cycle.

In August, Mr. Thurston wrote a memo which delegated responsibility for each of the 39 numbered Corporate Objectives and Strategies to eleven top officers. For example, "Increase Profitability Rapidly," "Greatly Reduce Inventory," "Information for Control" and "Human Aspects of Management." Once the CEO had set the framework of corporate objectives and strategies each manager could then fit his objectives, strategies and goals within his framework.

We define an *objective* as a desired future condition, a statement of intent, something to shoot for. It is usually general and long range (two to five years) in nature, broad in focus and generally more difficult to measure than a goal. It's a "what."

A statement of *strategy* shows how resources are to be deployed to meet an objective and establishes a broad course of action having major importance and operating over a long time span. There will generally be at least one strategy statement supporting each objective. It's a "how."

A *goal* is a desired accomplishment or result. It is specific, narrower in focus than an objective, has a shorter time frame (usually a year or less). It should be expressed in quantitative, explicit terms and with a scheduled completion date. The steps to defining a goal are:

- Specify the action to be taken
- Focus on an identifiable result
- Specify the completion date
- Be sure it's measurable, tangible, or verifiable
- Be sure it's challenging
- It must be realistic and attainable
- Consistent with organization Objectives, Strategies and Policies
- And be written and kept for future reference by the relevant parties

These goals now become the key to establishing meaningful **ZBB** decision packages. They provide the reference point for justifying the continued funding of certain programs and the discontinuance of others. They help establish priorities and will provide the performance measurements which the managers will use to calibrate their levels of effort in the **ZBB** exercise.

Preliminary Orders Forecast

This look-ahead was provided by our Vice-President Marketing and helped the CEO set his short-term goals into place in the long-range objectives and strategies . . . . and helped set the stage for the Marketing Strategy Profiles.

---
* Appendix D contains excerpts from the 1976-77 Corporate Planning Manual.

Strategy Center Profiles

The various responsible product development and product marketing managers analyzed our product lines with emphasis on their strength and weaknesses compared to the competition, their growth rates, relative profitability, and capital resource requirements. They used a "strategy center profiling" concept introduced to us by Robert Wright of Arthur D. Little, Inc.

Orders Forecast
Backlog Plan
Shipment Plan

Once the profiling process is completed a more detailed orders forecast can be made as the original preliminary forecast is fine-tuned based upon later information and what is now known of the strategy plans for the various product lines.

The marketing managers work in conjunction with the manufacturing managers to determine the optimum backlog situation for each product line, taking into account the orders forecast, the competitive situation and the desired shipments plan. It is important that all three . . . . orders, backlog and shipments . . . . be tied together to insure consistency.

The Operations Plan

CEO sets Annual Goals & Objectives

Concurrent with the Marketing Plan the CEO develops his annual goals and programs in support of the corporate objectives and strategies plus the Marketing Plan. The latter will, obviously, have a major impact on the corporate level goals and programs.

The Corporate Unit Managers (Vice Presidents) develop their goals in support of the annual corporate objectives, strategies, and goals. These are presented to, and reviewed by, the CEO who evaluates, accepts, rejects and/or recommends changes to make them all supportive and cohesive.

Managers Establish Objectives, Strategies & Goals

Once approved the Corporate Unit Managers follow the same procedure with their managers . . . . at this time introducing the Management by Objectives (MBO) concepts of mutual goal setting . . . . which is the foundation of the ZBB process.

Managers divide their goals into three categories:

> Ongoing goals
> Problem-Solving Goals
> Innovative Goals

Ongoing Goals - Also called routine goals or regular goals or performance standards. These are statements of conditions that exist when the job is being performed satisfactorily. They are the "way things *should* be."

Most people have three to ten major job functions and these are the result of "boiling down" all the various activities which they perform. These can be examined for the control aspects of each function which then becomes the basis for a performance measure.

Problem-Solving Goals - These are goals designed to solve a problem. A problem exists when something is not the way it ought to be, e.g., an Ongoing Goal has slipped and the slip is not just a temporary one. It is the way things should be but are *not*.

These are identified by having the manager list all the problems which he or his unit has which are performance related. Most managers will have two to four key problems. The "key problems" are those whose solution has the greatest amount of pay off for the effort involved in solving it.

Innovative Goals - These are goals which create an opportunity to take advantage of a money making idea, cut costs, improve efficiency, etc. These are the way things *could* be (if we were more efficient, etc.).

A Problem-Solving Goal improves a sub-standard condition while an Innovative Goal builds on an already positive condition.

Once the goals have been agreed upon then the Manager is in a position to do his budgeting.

The Financial Plan

The keystone of this plan is the **ZBB** process . . . . where managers must divide their activities into decision units and analyze them accordingly:

The first question to be asked is . . . . "What is the *purpose* of this organization?"

Next, "What are the *activities* required to carry out this purpose," and

Finally, "What *dollars* do I need to carry out these activities?"

One must decide what are the alternative methods of accomplishing the organization's purpose . . . . a cost/benefit approach to analyzing one's activities . . . . *and what levels of service can be performed for different levels of funding.*

THE FOUR BASIC STEPS IN ZERO-BASED BUDGETING—
DETERMINING THE DECISION UNITS—
THE DECISION REPORTING PACKAGES ILLUSTRATED

As with many planning-budgeting processes there is a jargon that is used. See Appendix A - Glossary of Terms.

There are four steps to **Zero-Base Budgeting**:

1. **Identify "Decision Units"**

    Done by department managers who identify discrete functions, services or activities.

    Usually a cost center which may be sub-divided, or aggregated, to suit the organization making up the decision unit. For example, the Personnel Department may want to isolate the discrete functions of Benefits, Management Development and Training, Hiring and Compensation Planning.

    One must insure the unit is large enough to provide flexibility and small enough to be manageable.

2. **Analyze the "Decision Units"**

    Again done by the manager(s) involved with some assistance from Finance. They must ask the three basic questions:

    "Is the service necessary?"

    "Is there a better way to operate?"

    "What different levels of service and cost are possible?"

3. **Evaluate and Rank "Increments"**

    Successive levels of management evaluate and inter-rank the increments. Within a decision unit there can be several cost/benefit increments. As the ranking process proceeds up the management chain, the increments of different decision units become inter-ranked in order of priority; i.e., in order of the higher level management's priorities.

4. **Prepare Final Budgets**

    Once approval is obtained for decision packages, i.e., groups of increments, then the cost center budgets can be constructed from these increments. Each manager now knows which of his increments were approved and prepares his budget accordingly using regular budget worksheets for loading the computerized financial reporting system.

ZBB - Determining Decision Units

At GenRad we decided we could treat our whole budgeting process in terms of decision units, including the Project/Program (primarily R & D and M.I.S.) as well as the Manufacturing Plan (the shipments driven COGS plan). In retrospect this turned out to be a mistake because we tried to do too much too soon. Our continuing drive for significant profit improvement in each of several succeeding years caused our ambitions to outstrip our resources. This was particularly so since we were introducing MBO at the same time and our managers suffered from an information overload.

We chose a **ZBB** reporting package drawing upon the experience of our consultants, MAC Inc., but tailoring it to the requirements of our management and those managers who had to fill out the forms. We tried to keep continuity with the past, i.e., cost center budgeting, while introducing the concepts of MBO and **ZBB**. We made three versions of the package, one for the Project/Programs, one for the Manufacturing Plan and one for the Overhead packages. The cover sheets were identical as were the general format of the back-up sheets. Each package was color coded.

Once having determined what decision unit(s) (activity) it was one was to analyze one applied the basic concept of **ZBB** which is to break activities down into a *Minimum Level of Effort and Additional Levels of Effort* (increments). The usual decision unit was a cost center or a grouping of small, homogenous cost centers.

Fortunately, we were in a position to build upon our previous budgeting techniques in which we had asked managers to present their budgets in three segments:

* On going - same level of activity,
* Increased levels of activity, and
* New Projects/Programs activities

The Minimum Level of Effort was set at a guideline of 85% of 1975 expenses without an allowance for inflation. The latter was given as 7% in the corporate guidelines which meant a 1976 minimum spending level of 80% in terms of 1975 dollars.

A Project/Program Plan was defined as meeting the following criteria . . . .

1. Has a finite beginning and end,

2. Has a project manager, and

3. Involves *substantial* resources outside of the decision unit (substantial being defined as $50,000 or more) . . . . several smaller projects could be aggregated to avoid a proliferation of decision packages.

The **Manufacturing Plan** was defined as being driven by the Inventory and Shipments Plan, i.e., customer driven. The Minimum Level of Effort was re-christened the "Required Level of Effort" and the increments were in terms of capital equipment which would substantially affect the manufacturing budgets, i.e., equipment over and above that required for the normal methods of operation. This was used to establish a preliminary capital budget but did not imply a spending approval. That would come later, after the usual ROI, and be subject to a time-phased budget cut/revision involving the claimed savings so as to "make believers" of those submitting the proposal.

The **Overhead Plan Packages** were applied to "everything else," including those resource groups supporting the Projects and Manufacturing Plans, whose total requirements were not already covered in a **ZBB** package. See **EXHIBIT 3**.

The most difficult problem we faced was integrating projects, manufacturing and overhead plans into a **ZBB** format for uniform comparison of alternative funding choices. This meant using the same type of cover sheet showing cumulative positions and cumulative operating expenses by increment.

EXHIBIT 3 — Projects — Overhead

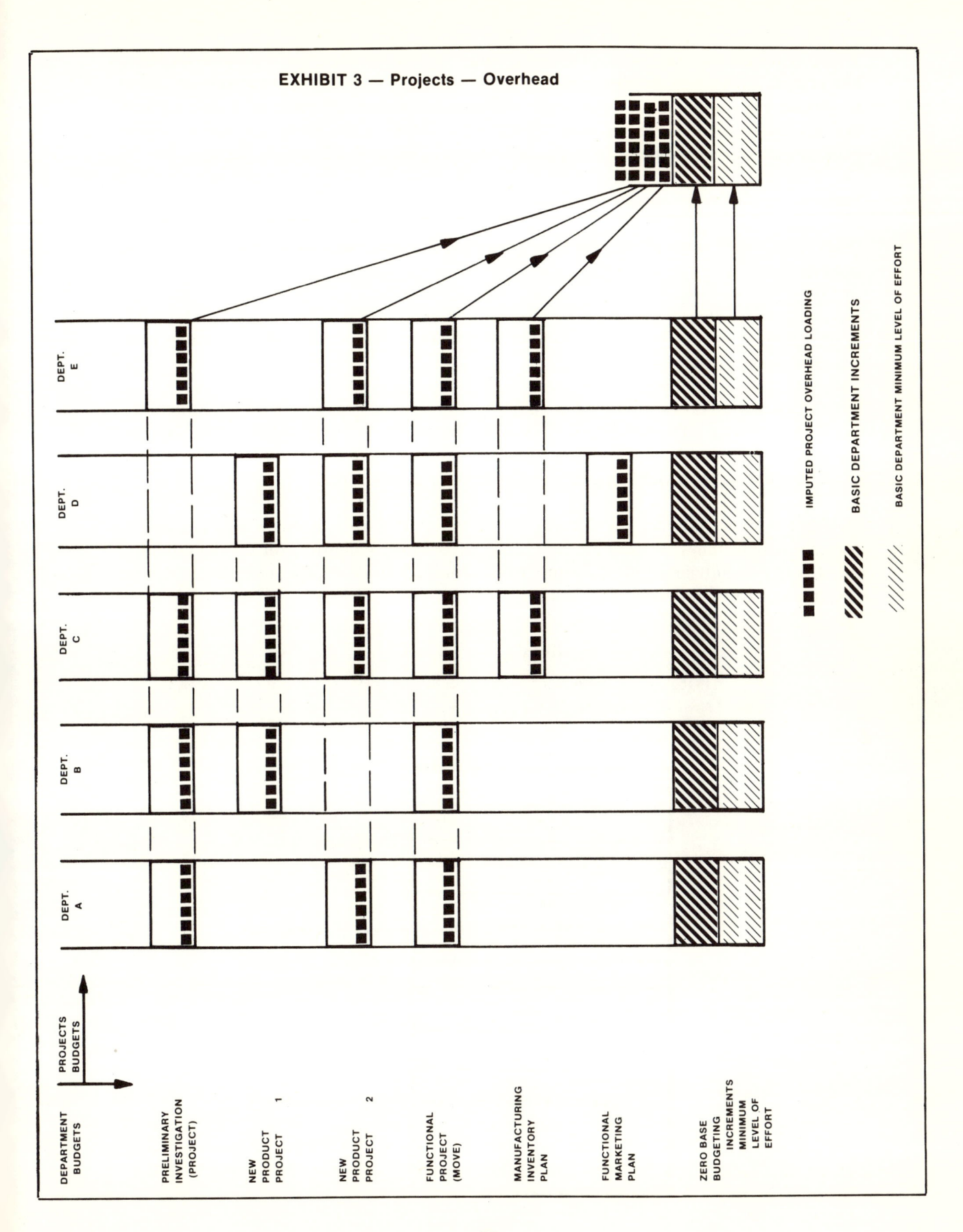

89

It was in the backup sheets that the three types of decision packages became distinctive. The project packages were prepared by project managers, rather than department managers, since their projects drew upon the resources of several departments; e.g., a central Drafting Department, a central Model Shop, etc. However, the project manager was required to consult with the resource manager(s) when preparing his project plans.

Similarly, in the manufacturing area, there were direct labor departments which drew upon the support of some other resources; e.g., Quality Control, Drafting, etc. The preparation of these packages required close cooperation of all the managers involved and absorbed a great deal of effort.

The objective of the integration efforts was to be able to judge the impact on all departments involved of funding or not funding a particular project. **EXHIBIT 3** shows how this process operated.

New Product Project #1 affects only Departments B, C and D, whereas Functional Project (Move) affects all departments. Thus, the budget for Department E is composed of segments of three projects, the Manufacturing Plan plus some minimum level of effort of its own which makes it viable regardless of externally driven forces.

EXHIBIT 4 shows this layering effect for the Drafting Department which provides layout drawings and sketches for new product projects, assembly blueprints for the manufacturing plan plus maintenance of blueprints for established products; e.g., engineering design changes, as part of its overhead activities.

EXHIBIT 4

INTEGRATION OF RESOURCE DEPARTMENT BUDGETS

(DRAFTING DEPARTMENT)

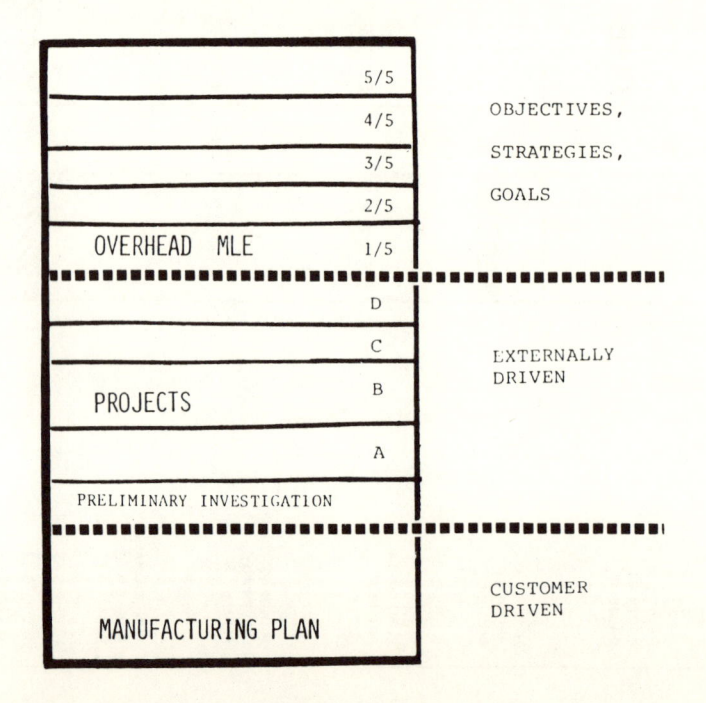

A typical decision package consisted of five (5) different forms:

1. A Cover/Summary sheet recapping all increments (**EXHIBIT 5**)

2. A Minimum Level of Effort (MLE) sheet (**EXHIBITS 6** and **7**)
   EXHIBIT 6 is for an Overhead package while **EXHIBIT 7** (Top) shows a Project/Program MLE sheet.

3. Additional Level(s) of Effort (ALE) sheet(s) were in the same format as the MLE sheet with only the title changed. **EXHIBIT 7** (Bottom) shows an ALE sheet for the Manufacturing Plan.

4. Cost Center Budget Worksheets (**EXHIBIT 8**), or Resource Planning Worksheet(s) (**EXHIBIT 9**)

5. Ongoing and Problem-Solving/Innovative Goals to support the funding requests.

One Cover Sheet, one MLE and one Cost Center Worksheet were required in each package and as many ALE's as were required to complete the package; i.e., substantiate each increment.

Appendix B shows one manager's completed decision package. He is the Credit Manager who reports to the Controller. An example like this was used in our educational sessions which were presented by the Finance Department to small groups of managers using written hand-outs and slide presentations. Some companies use video-taped presentations. It was in these sessions that our consultants were of help to our small budget staff, since we could draw upon their experience in training managers in **ZBB**.

How Do I Go About Filling Out The Forms?

The COVER SHEET is common to all packages and provides a capsule overview of the decision unit and its packages/increments. Sections 1 - 7 describe the units, its level in the organization, who prepared the package and when. Section 8 provides for a rank and numerical coding of the package and increments.

Section 9 - *"Describe the Current Services Provided, Resources Used, Direct Clients of Services, and How The Decision Unit Operates."*

Here the Manager describes the number and kinds of personnel and what they do, particular skills and equipment required and who are the main customers for these services. It is here that he lays bare his soul rationalizing his reason for existence.

Section 10 - *"Describe Desired Means of Accomplishing This Decision Unit's Goals."*

Now the Manager must tie his activities to his goals and objectives and make his plea for funding. The increments which back up the cover sheet will explain in more detail each level of funding which is being requested.

Section 11 - *"List Discarded Alternative Means of Accomplishing This Decision Unit's Goals and Reasons for Discarding Alternatives."*

This section forces the manager to think through his proposals carefully, especially since one alternative is to disband the whole unit!

EXHIBIT 5

General Radio	DECISION PACKAGE COVER SHEET ZERO-BASE BUDGETING OVERHEAD [ ][1][ ][ ][ ]	(8) RANK Increment ____ of ____ $(000)
(1) DECISION UNIT NAME:	(9) DESCRIBE CURRENT SERVICES PROVIDED, RESOURCES USED, DIRECT CLIENTS OF SERVICE, AND HOW THE DECISION UNIT OPERATES:	
(2) CORPORATE UNIT:		
(3) LEVEL A ORGANIZATION UNIT:		
(4) LEVEL B ORGANIZATION UNIT(S):		
(5) LEVEL C ORGANIZATION UNIT(S):		
(6) PREPARED BY:		
(7) DATE:		

(10) DESCRIBE DESIRED MEANS OF ACCOMPLISHING THIS DECISION UNIT'S GOALS:

(11) LIST DISCARDED ALTERNATIVE MEANS OF ACCOMPLISHING THIS DECISION UNIT'S GOALS AND REASONS FOR DISCARDING ALTERNATIVES:

(12) SUMMARY OF DECISION PACKAGE INCREMENTS:	1975 PROJECTED	POSITIONS		OPERATING EXPENSES			CAPITAL EXPENSES	INVENT. COM.
		1976 INCR.	1976 CUM.	1976 INCR.	1976 CUM.	%CUM. 76/75	CUM. 1976	CUM. 1976
1 of								
2 of								
3 of								
4 of								
5 of								
6 of								

FORM 1A

EXHIBIT 6

General Radio

Increment _____ of _____

ZERO-BASE BUDGETING—OVERHEAD
MINIMUM LEVEL OF EFFORT   INCREMENTAL ANALYSIS $(000)

(1) DECISION UNIT NAME	(13) RESOURCES REQUIRED	19__ ACT	19__ BUDG.	19__ PROJ.	19__ PROP.
	POSITIONS THIS INCREMENT				
(14) DESCRIBE OPERATIONS PERFORMED AND SERVICES PROVIDED:	POSITIONS CUMULATIVE				
	OPERATING EXPENSE THIS INCREMENT				
	OPERATING EXPENSE CUMULATIVE				
	OPERATING EXPENSE % PRIOR YEAR				
	CAPITAL EXPENSE THIS INCREMENT				
	CAPITAL EXPENSE CUMULATIVE				
	INVENTORY COMMITMENT THIS INCREMENT				
	INVENTORY COMMITMENT CUMULATIVE				

(15) DESCRIBE CHANGES FROM CURRENT OPERATIONS:

(16) DESCRIBE BENEFITS OF APPROVING THIS INCREMENT:

(17) OPERATING EXPENSES % 76/75 FOR MINIMUM LEVEL OF EFFORT _____
REASONS WHY LOWER LEVEL OF EFFORT WAS NOT CHOSEN

(18) WORKLOAD/PERFORMANCE MEASUREMENTS	19__ ACT.	19__ PROJ.	19__ THIS INCR.	19__ CUM	% CUM. OF 19__

Form 2

EXHIBIT 9

General Radio

RESOURCE PLANNING SHEET

NAME: _____ TYPE #, CATALOG DESCRIPTION _____

PROJECT MANAGER: _____
DATE: _____

DIVISION _____ PAGE _____ OF _____ YEAR _____ NEW PRODUCT PROJECT # _____
ASSIGNMENT PROJECT _____
AUXILIARY TASK _____

MILESTONE: _____

D. PERSON WEEKS

LINE		1Q	2Q	3Q	4Q	TOTAL YEAR	LOADING FACTORS	1Q	2Q	3Q	4Q	TOTAL YEAR	LINE #
1.	RES + DEV: ENGINEERS, SR.												1
2.	ENGINEERS, JR.												2
3.	ASSISTANTS												3
4.	SOFTWARE PROGRAMMING												4
5.	OTHER												5
6.	OPERATIONS ENGINEERING:												6
7.	ENGINEERING SERVICES												7
8.	Printed Circuit Shop												8
9.	Drafting, Regular												9
10.	Drafting, Etch Layout												10
11.	X-Shop												11
12.	Technical Publication												12
13.	Mfg. Documentation												13
14.	New Product MCP												14
15.	PRODUCT ENGINEERING												15
16.	Mechanical Design												16
17.	PROCESS ENGINEERING												17
18.	Standards Group												18
19.	FABRICATION ENGINEERING												19
20.	Toolroom												20
21.	INDUSTRIAL ENGINEERING												21
22.	QUALITY ENGINEERING												22
23.	MICRO ELECTRONICS												23
24.	PRODUCT MARKETING												24
25.	Service												25
26.	FUNCTIONAL MARKETING - Training												26
27.	Sales Promotion												27
28.	Exhibits												28
29.	Service												29
30.	MANUFACTURING: Learning Curve												30
31.	**TOTAL LABOR**												31

E. NONPAYROLL COSTS ($,000) — DESCRIPTION

			LINE #
1.	RES + DEV.: Project Material		1
2.	Royalties/Licenses		2
3.	Consultants		3
4.	OPERATIONAL ENGINEERING: Supplies		4
5.	Trial Lot Mat'l/Scrap		5
6.	Expensed Tooling		6
7.	Documentation		7
8.	PRODUCT MARKETING: Travel		8
9.	Exhibits/Seminars		9
10.	Spares/Scrap		10
11.	FUNCTIONAL MARKETING: Advertising		11
12.			12
13.	**TOTAL NON-PAY**		13

F. CAPITAL INVESTMENT ($,000)

			LINE #
1.	ACCOUNTS RECEIVABLE _____ Days		1
2.	INVENTORIES: Work-in-Process		2
3.	(M+L+O) Finished		3
4.	Demo/Loan		4
5.	Service/Spares		5
6.	EQUIPMENT: Test Equipment		6
7.	Machinery		7
8.	Tooling		8
9.	**TOTAL CAPITAL**		9

FORM 7

Section 12 - *"Summary of Decision Package Increments."*

This section provides for a numerical summary of the increments in terms of personnel requirements, operating expenses, capital expenditures and inventory investments. Comparative data for the present year (projected to year end) is also shown and the cumulative proposed operating expenses are shown as a percentage of the prior year.

The next sheet in the package is the MINIMUM LEVEL OF EFFORT Worksheet.

Section 13 - *"Resources Required."*

Provides numerical data for this particular increment with a comparison to current year projected expenses, current year budget and last year's actual. The summary of this data appears on the Cover Sheet in Section 12.

Section 14 - *"Describe Operations Performed and Services Provided."*

The focus of attention now shifts from a general description of the overall cost center which appeared in Section 9 to this particular increment . . . . the Minimum Level of Effort below which the unit ceases to be viable.

Section 15 - *"Describe Changes from Current Operations."*

Obviously with less staff, fewer goals can be accomplished, perhaps not even the On-Going Goals. But, the smaller funding required is the trade-off against the unaccomplished goals and missing services.

Section 16 - *"Describe Benefits of Approving This Increment."*

Reduced expenses is the most obvious benefit . . . . with some minimal service being provided.

Section 17 - *"Reasons Why Lower Level of Effort Was Not Chosen."*

The manager is again forced to explain why he made the choice of increments that he did, and why he could not go lower to reach a minimum level of effort.

Section 18 - *"Workload/Performance Measurements."*

The Manager must again quantify his goals and objectives and relate them to the increments he wants funded. The Credit Manager might say "with so much money I will hold the days sales outstanding (aging) to 75 days; with some more money I will reduce them to 60 days; with more money to 45 days," etc. Another performance measure he might use would be the value of the bad debt write-off at various levels of funding of his Collection group.

After the Minimum Level of Effort sheets there follows one or more ADDITIONAL LEVEL OF EFFORT sheets which are identical to the former except for Section 19 which replaces Section 17.

Section 19 - *"Impact of Not Funding This Increment."*

Instead of asking about why a lower level of effort was not used this question concerns itself with this particular increment, and the consequences of not funding it. Here is where the higher level manager can get some feel for the trade-offs involved in ranking one manager's increment above another's . . . . should the latter fail to pass the cut-off line in funding.

In the example shown the Credit Manager, who reports to the Controller, outlines his present staffing and other resources used, identifies his clients and sets forth some alternative courses of action. He is careful to point out the trade-off between reduced departmental operating costs and the increased potential for Bad Debts plus the interest cost involved in stretched collection of accounts receivable.

At each level of funding he establishes performance measures keyed to the resources made available to him. With a reduced staff he cannot be expected to collect his receivables in the same time frame as with a full staff; i.e., his Days Sales Outstanding (DSO) will increase.

The final sheet in the package is a Form 4 which is a detailed worksheet for recapping the cost center expenses in terms of increments by nature of expense, e.g., payroll, supplies, travel, depreciation, etc. To help managers plan we provided them with a computer print-out similar to this sheet which showed the prior year's expenses, this year's budget and a projection consisting of 8 months' actual plus the remaining 4 months' budget. We also calculated their depreciation on existing assets for a year ahead.

The Program/Project and Manufacturing Plan decision packages were similar in construction but tailored to their special requirements. For example, Forms 4 for Projects were Resource Planning Sheets for each project involved. These sheets are used in our new-product planning procedures to estimate resource requirements, cost them out and provide the basis for a discounted-cash-flow Return on Investment Analysis. Using the same form provided the project managers with a familiarity and continuity in planning.

HOW THE DECISION PACKAGES ARE RANKED

The final form to be filled out was the **DECISION PACKAGE RANKING** Sheet which is shown in **EXHIBIT 10**. On this sheet, a manager with several diverse decision units could inter-rank the various increments of his lower level managers. Remember that the lowest level of ranking is the increments *within* a decision unit's package. At the higher levels, increments become inter-ranked with those of other decision units.

EXHIBIT 10

General Radio

SUBJECT: DECISION PACKAGE REVIEW AND RANKING

Page Rev. ONLY	1	OCT 6 19__
NUMBER	REV NO.	EFF DATE SEP 12 19__
BY:		PAGE 4 OF 7

General Radio — DECISION PACKAGING RANKING ($000)

(1) RANK	(2) DECISION UNIT NAME	INCREMENT	(3) 19__ PROPOSED POS	OP EXP	(4) 19__ CUMULATIVE POS	OP EXP	(5) 19__ CAP EXPENSE INCR	CUMUL	(6) 19__ INV COMMITMENT INCR	CUMUL
1	Personnel	5 1 1 0 0 0 1 1 3	2	36	2	36	—	—	—	—
2	Concord Service Dept.	3 2 1 0 0 0 2 1 6	11	294	13	330	—	—	34	34
3	Industrial Engineering	3 1 1 0 0 0 3 1 5	3	93	16	423	—	—	—	34
4	Concord Service Dept.	3 2 1 0 0 0 4 2 6	4	80	20	503	—	—	12	46
5	Industrial Engineering	3 1 1 0 0 0 5 2 5	2	70	22	573	—	—	—	46
6	Industrial Engineering	3 1 1 0 0 0 6 3 5	2	30	24	603	—	—	—	46
7	Concord Service Dept.	3 2 1 0 0 0 7 3 6	2	41	26	644	—	—	6	52
8	Concord Service Dept.	3 2 1 0 0 0 8 4 6	1	19	27	663	—	—	3	55
9	Personnel	5 1 1 0 0 0 9 2 3	5	215	32	878	—	—	—	55
10	Concord Service Dept.	3 2 1 0 0 1 0 5 6	1	17	33	895	—	—	3	58
11	Concord Service Dept.	3 2 1 0 0 1 1 5 6	1	20	34	915	2	2	—	58
12	Industrial Engineering	3 1 1 0 0 1 2 4 5	10	130	44	1045	—	2	—	58
13	Industrial Engineering	3 1 1 0 0 1 3 5 5	2	14	46	1059	—	2	—	58
14	Personnel	5 1 1 0 0 1 4 3 3	3	43	49	1102	—	2	—	58
15										
	PRIOR YEAR'S RECAP									

ORGANIZATIONAL UNITS BEING RANKED | PREPARED BY | DATE | PAGE

Form 6

NOTE:
This ranking example is for the Personnel, Concord Service Department, and Industrial Engineering Decision Packages of General Radio.

In **EXHIBIT 11** we see a manager who has three departments reporting to him, A, B and C, each of whose manager's have established their incremental ranking in a decision package. The higher level manager breaks the incremental ranking by establishing his priorities so that increments B3, A4 and A5 fall to the bottom of the list, while A1, A2, B1 and C1 rise easily to the top. The remaining increments are where all the attention will be focussed as the three departments vie for funding priority, since no one is quite sure where the final line will be drawn.

EXHIBIT 11

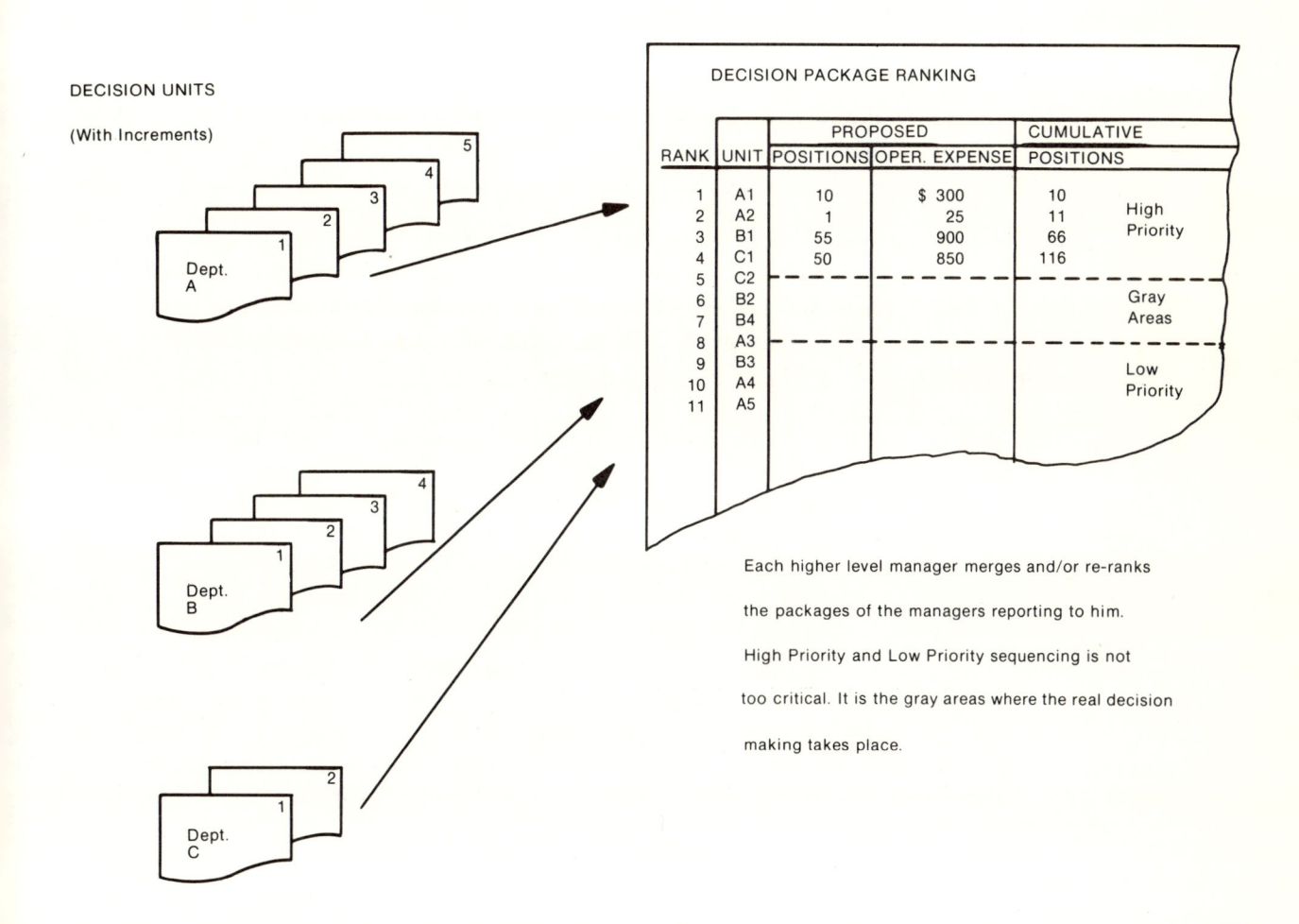

DECISION UNITS
(With Increments)

Dept. A — increments 1, 2, 3, 4, 5

Dept. B — increments 1, 2, 3, 4

Dept. C — increments 1, 2

DECISION PACKAGE RANKING

RANK	UNIT	PROPOSED POSITIONS	OPER. EXPENSE	CUMULATIVE POSITIONS	
1	A1	10	$ 300	10	High Priority
2	A2	1	25	11	
3	B1	55	900	66	
4	C1	50	850	116	
5	C2				Gray Areas
6	B2				
7	B4				
8	A3				
9	B3				Low Priority
10	A4				
11	A5				

Each higher level manager merges and/or re-ranks the packages of the managers reporting to him. High Priority and Low Priority sequencing is not too critical. It is the gray areas where the real decision making takes place.

Once the decision package/ranking process moved to higher levels of management we automated the ranking *and re-ranking* process. Each increment was coded/named and the basic summary data from Section 12 of the Cover Sheet was keypunched onto a deck of cards. The program would automatically cumulate totals by increment for each of the numerical factors . . . . positions, operating expenses, etc. To rerank and recalculate the cumulative totals one merely changed the position of the card in the deck and reran the program. Since we were ranking several hundred increments this was an important timesaver.

How Did the Chief Executive Officer Know Where to Draw the Line?

In order to determine the level of funding available to the CEO we used a "value added" approach. We took our forecast of Net Sales less Direct Material and called this the "**ZBB** Pool." Next the CEO and Chief Financial Officer determined what their target profit was to be and this plus interest charges were deducted from the **ZBB** Pool. The remainder was available for funding the various packages/increments, a bonus allocation, and profitsharing.

All minimum levels rose to the top of the list without much time wasted on ranking them. Next came most of the packages raising the funding to current levels of operation and, finally, those going beyond the current level. There were three broad bands of increments . . . . those with very high priority/ranking, those with very low priority/ranking and a middle "gray" area.

It was in the middle area that all the fireworks occurred as managers fought for ranking since it was here that a current level for one manager was being displaced by additional levels of effort going beyond the current level for someone else. Thus, although we had several hundred packages being ranked, the main thrust of attention was on those two or three dozen in the area close to the cutoff line.

After listening to all the arguments and proposals, reviewing the package descriptions and examining his profit goals, the CEO drew his line and said, "We have a Budget." The Finance area then worked with the managers to convert their approved decision packages/increments into cost center budgets for loading to our computer. The Resource Planning Sheets were keypunched and run through explosion programs which converted personweeks by quarter into project labor and project overhead budgets for each cost center involved.

LESSONS LEARNED

VI. WHAT DID WE LEARN AND WHAT ARE WE GOING TO DO DIFFERENTLY

A brand new Harvard Business School case* starts out

"It's been one hell of a lot of work, but I finally know what I'm supposed to be doing!"

This is quoted as the typical reaction of the Managers at GenRad, by Steve Stadler, our Chief Financial Officer.

Another manager makes the comment "tying the goals to the budget is important. I have already had experience with MBO in my fourteen years with _____ and my four years with _____. (Both Fortune 500 Corporation.) The problem there was that the objectives were not properly tied to the budget. More than once you would be assigned a goal without access to the dollars needed to achieve the goal. Here, you are in a position to say "either give me the money or get off my back."

Bill Thurston's reaction was favorable since he liked the logical approach of setting goals, defining programs accordingly and then giving high visibility to each of the programs with **ZBB**. Plans were made to improve on the process and continue it for our 1976-7 planning-budgeting exercise.

Information Overload

In our eagerness to break Professor Roberts' downward spiral by infusing new management concepts into GR, I feel we gave our managers a case of "information overload."

In the summer of 1975 we were running them through courses in Transactional Analysis, Management-by-Objectives *and* Zero-Based Budgeting. The result was some confusion, a dilution of efforts and a three month delay in the whole budgeting process. We tried to do too much, too soon.

We did learn that, after several years of cost cutting, we were a pretty lean organization. It was difficult, in some instances, to come up with a meaningful Minimum Level of Effort substantially below the current level of effort.

Since our project control and accounting system was also in the process of being upgraded we ran into some difficulties in reconciling the full Project/Program impact on the resource departments. Particularly in sorting out project driven overhead from that normally required to support the department's activities.

We also felt the need for better co-ordination between our project managers and the resource managers in pricing out projects and that a "reasonableness" audit by the Cost & Budget Department is essential.

---

* GENRAD, INC. (4 - 176 - 227)
Professor Francis Aguilar
Distributed by Inter-collegiate Case Clearing House

program. Good follow-up also includes a wide range of other activities, stretching from the many informal ways top-level managers use to keep in touch with what is going on to the motivations provided by appropriate formal incentive and compensation schemes for managers.

Summary

Much can be said about the virtues and shortcomings of the MBO and ZBB systems employed in Gen-Rad and of how they were introduced and used. But this kind of analysis is insufficient and unrealistic if we do not consider these systems in their real context. First we should recognize that they often serve to redefine strategies and objectives as well as to implement them. Second, we should recognize that their success will depend: (1) on clear, meaningful strategic inputs; (2) on managers' abilities to conceive effective programs; and (3) on follow-up measures to ensure the successful outcome of these programs.

It seems to me that anyone using or thinking of introducing MBO and/or ZBB in their organization will court problems if considerations fail to go beyond the narrow boundaries of the systems themselves.

EXHIBIT 12

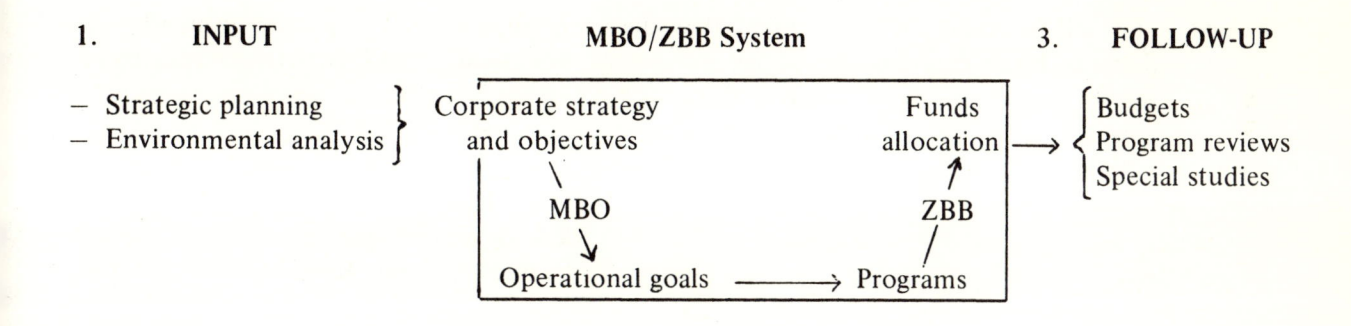

1. **INPUT**   MBO/ZBB System   3. **FOLLOW-UP**

- Strategic planning
- Environmental analysis

```
Corporate strategy              Funds
and objectives               allocation
       \                         ↗
        MBO                    ZBB
         ↘                    ↗
        Operational goals ——→ Programs
```

→ Budgets
    Program reviews
    Special studies

2. **EXPERTISE**

- Instructions about how MBO/ZBB is to work
- Developing managers' analytical and conceptual skills.

VIII. WHAT HAS BEEN THE EXPERIENCE OF OTHERS?

The **ZBB** process has been in use in an increasing number of diverse corporations, such as Texas Instruments (1970), Dillingham Corp., (1971), United California Bank (1973), Southern California Edison (1974) as well as Magnavox, Xerox, Combustion Engineering and Tektronix. Some comments made by managers of these and other companies follow:

> "Avoid establishing inadequate or unclear goals for each decision package . . . . to avoid considerable time wasted on budget items with little probability of top-management's approval. Also, keep the process from becoming too mechanical. And, be sure to feedback to all levels of the company the final disposition and rationale of each decision package . . . . otherwise it will be demotivating." (1)

> > Charles W. Kight
> > Mgr. Financial Planning Analysis
> > Texas Instruments

> "We used **ZBB** because the inputs from the old budgeting process were inadequate to plan solidly for the year ahead and determine the best places to allocate resources . . . . we were missing out on opportunities for improving efficiency." (1)

> > James Pollock
> > Controller
> > Dillingham Corp.

> "For other managers, it's a threat that they are going to be completely dismantled or that functions they consider sacrosanct will be discarded. The fact is that many managers in many companies don't even know what really happens in their departments, or how . . . . the process consumes a great deal of extra time . . . . " (1)

> > David DeWind
> > V.P. Systems Engineering
> > United California Bank

> "The basic advantage is the vast amount of analysis **ZBB** makes available . . . . as much is disclosed about the manager as about his area of responsibilities . . . . " (2)

> > Donald S. Anderson
> > Budget Director
> > Southern California Edison

> "It is an efficient way of restraining middle management from the perpetual performance of unnecessary functions, and it exposes the tendency for expenses to grow layer after layer under conventional budgeting." (2)

> > Jack Schang
> > President
> > Allied Van Lines

> THE PLANNING CALENDAR,
> ALLOCATION OF RESOURCES
> AND
> WHAT IF?

"The process is time-intensive . . . . should not be limited to paring spending . . . . biggest payback is in gathering intelligence for the best spending of the money you have at any time on the down or upside." (2)

> Larry Choruby
> Budget Director
> Tektronix, Inc.

---

(1) DUN'S REVIEW, October, 1974

(2) INDUSTRY WEEK, January, 1976

IX. SELECTED REFERENCES

Aguilar, Frances
GenRad, Inc.
A Case Study, #4-176-227
Harvard Business School, 1976
Boston, Massachusetts

Anderson, Donald N.
Management Review
"Zero-Base Budgeting: How to Get Rid of Corporate Crabgrass"
A.G.A. - EEI Accounting Conference
AMACOM

"The Tough Job of Zero Budgeting"
Dun's Review
October, 1974

"Zero-Based Budgets Offer Data, Spending Control"
Industry Week
January 12, 1976

Pyhrr, Peter A.
"Zero-Base Budgeting"
Harvard Business Review
May - June, 1970

Pyhrr, Peter A.
Zero-Base Budgeting
John Wiley and Sons, N.Y., 1973

Stonich, Paul J.
"Zero Base Planning - A Management Tool"
Managerial Planning
July/August, 1976
Planning Executives Institute

Pyhrr, Peter A.
"Zero-Base Budgeting: A Management Tool to Evaluate and Control Expenses"
Budgeting for Profit
Planning Executives Institute, 1975

APPENDIX D — Planning Calendar — 1

GenRad

SUBJECT: PLANNING CALENDAR

NUMBER	REV NO.	EFF. DATE
1.2		SEP 8 19
BY:		PAGE
		1 of 1

Approved: *W. R. Thurston*

Title: Chief Executive Officer

SCOPE: All Corporate Units.

GENERAL:

The normal planning process will procede as follows:

MONTH	EVENT	MONTHS UNTIL PLAN IN EFFECT
November	Preparation for Strategic Planning	14
December	Background research and data collection	13
January	for Strategic Planning	12
February	Preparation of Strategic Plans	11
March		10
April	Review of Strategic Plans	9
May		8
June	Project Planning	7
July	Objectives and Goals	6
August		5
September	Budgeting	4
October	Final Corporate Unit Plans	3
November	Preparation of Corporate Plans	2
December	Review and presentation of Corporate Plans	1
January	Implementation of Plans	0

A specific events schedule will be issued for each year's planning process.

APPENDIX D — Incremental Funding Policy — 2

GenRad

SUBJECT: INCREMENTAL FUNDING POLICY

NUMBER	REV NO.	EFF. DATE
6.1		JUN 6 19

BY:

PAGE: 1 of 1

Approved: W. R. Thurston

Title: Chief Executive Officer

SCOPE: Corporate wide

GENERAL:

One of the fundamental pieces of the Corporate Planning Process is the allocation of company resources to the various operating units. This allocation is made possible by breaking the Unit's operations down into increments. Each increment consists of a combination of goals and the expenses required to accomplish those goals. These goal and expense increments are ranked in terms of their importance and economic return to the company. The actual analysis of the goal and expense increments is accomplished with a planning document set known as the Incremental Funding Package (IF Package).

POLICY:

1. The Corporate Unit Manager, upon acceptance of his Unit Objectives, Strategies and Goals, directs and coordinates the efforts required to develop the unit's IF Packages. IF Packages are prepared for the three types of expense; project expense (see Procedure 6.1-1), manufacturing expense (see Procedure 6.1-2) and overhead expense (see Procedure 6.1-3).

   The Corporate Financial Staff provides support to the Corporate Unit Manager during this effort to ensure that A, B, & C level managers receive proper instruction in IF Package development.

2. IF Packages are presented (with appropriate explanations) to the Chief Executive Officer by each Corporate Unit Manager. (Reference Procedure 6.1-14, 6.1-24, 6.1-34)

   The Chief Executive Officer, in concert with the Chief Financial Officer, in order to allocate the available resources, will:

   A. Rank all IF Packages on a corporate wide basis.

   B. Strike an approval line indicating which IF Packages can be funded in 1977.

   C. Return all IF Packages to the appropriate Corporate Unit Manager.

3. Upon completion of the allocation effort, the Chief Financial Officer directs the efforts to assemble the approved IF Packages for inclusion into the final Corporate Planning Package and the subsequent development of the final presentation to the CEO and the Board of Directors (Reference Procedure 7.1).

APPENDIX D — Project IF Packages — 3

GenRad

SUBJECT: PROJECT IF PACKAGES

NUMBER	REV NO.	EFF. DATE
6.1-1		JUN 6 19

BY:

PAGE 1 of 1

Approved: *W. R. Thurston*

Title: Chief Executive Officer

REFERENCE:	
RESPONSIBILITY	**ACTION**
Corporate Unit Manager	1. Provides direction for his staff in determining Project Incremental Funding (IF) Packages which conform to his Corporate Unit's strategic business plans and/or functional and support strategies. 2. Assigns temporary Project Managers for project proposals which do not have a manager. 3. Directs Project Managers in the completion of Resource Planning Sheets. (Reference Procedure 6.1-11)
Project Managers	4. Complete the Project Resource Planning Sheet(s) in accordance with instructions.

Corporate Unit Manager	5. Reviews Resource Planning Sheet(s) with Project Manager.
	
	APPROVES → NO → RETURN TO STEP 4
	↓
	YES — PROCEED WITH STEP 6.
	
	6. Ranks each project in terms of its importance.
	
	7. Prepares a Project Schedule and Ranking Sheet. (See Procedure 6.1-12) Note: In this process the ranked projects are organized into IF Packages.
	
	8. Prepares an IF Package Cover Sheet Form for each IF Package (see Procedure 6.1-13).
	
	9 Makes up a full set of Project IF Packages for presentation to the CEO and CFO. Each completed Project IF Package will consist of:
	  (a) The IF Package Cover Sheet
	  (b) The Project Schedule & Ranking Form
	  (c) A Project Resource Planning Sheet for every project included in this IF Package.
	Note: This is event M-5 in the planning process.

APPENDIX D — Manufacturing IF Packages — 4

GenRad

SUBJECT: MANUFACTURING IF PACKAGES

NUMBER	REV NO.	EFF. DATE
6.1-2		SEP 3 19
BY:		PAGE 1 of 1

Approved: W. R. Thurston

Title: Chief Executive Officer

REFERENCE:

RESPONSIBILITY	ACTION
Corporate Unit Manager	1. Provides direction for his staff in determining Manufacturing Incremental Funding (IF) Packages which conform to his Corporate Unit's Objectives & Goals.
	2. Directs Manufacturing Unit Supervisors and Managers in the completion of Resource Planning Sheets. (Reference Procedure 6.1-21)
Manufacturing Unit Supervisors & Managers Manager of next higher unit.	3. Complete the Resource Planning Sheet(s) in accordance with instructions.
	4. Reviews the Goals and Resource Planning Sheets of each of his lower level manufacturing units.
	Approves → No: Return to Step 3. / Yes: Proceed with Step 5.
	5. Combines each into his own set of Goals and fills out a Resource Planning Sheet which combines the funding requirements of each lower level unit as specified in Procedure 6.1-4.

APPENDIX D — Current Level of Expenditure Calculation — 7

GenRad

NUMBER 6.3	REV NO.	EFF. DATE SEP 8 19
BY:		PAGE 1 of 2
Approved: W.R. Thurston		
Title: Chief Executive Officer		

SUBJECT: CURRENT LEVEL OF EXPENDITURE CALCULATION

SCOPE: Corporate Wide

GENERAL:

The corporate planning process utilizes an incremental funding concept. The funding requirements for the annual plan are built up with increments in which the first increment is defined as being the current level. Current level is defined so that it represents the way the company is operating at the time the planning process is carried out. It is used as a tool to aid the CEO and Corporate Unit Managers to comprehend more easily the implications of funding incremental programs. Since the current mode of operation can be accurately measured and quantified by the corporate accounting system, the way in which the company's resources are currently allocated can be accurately determined, and the implications of this allocation can be comprehended and forecast.

With the current level established, additional funding requests can be analyzed as changes from the known current mode of operations. This makes the incremental improvements and benefits expected to be more easily weighed against the incremental costs thereby facilitating ranking an prioritizing.

PROCEDURE:

1. Calculation of Current Level
   Corporate Finance is responsible for measuring and defining current level each year as an input to the planning process. Current level will be determined as follows:

   A. Current level is essentially the sum of all the company's actual expenditures in the first six months multiplied by two. Therefore the first step is to calculate the actual expenditure level for each Corporate Unit for the first six months and multiply by two.

   B. This number is then modified to correct payroll to the latest approved personnel levels. Actual payroll is subtracted and an aproved payroll amount is added. The approved payroll is provided by the Personnel Development Department. It is the annual payroll for all the personnel actually on board on July 31 plus any open, approved requisitions.

   C. Current level is further modified by subtracting occupancy and fringe benefit allocations.

   D. For Corporate Units containing direct labor departments, inventory and project labor absorption is separated out to allow analysis of current expense levels.

   E. Also, to the extent that Corporate Units contain manufacturing units, an adjustment is made to compensate for forecasted changes in shipment volume. This is done by determining the variable portion of manufacturing expense. The variable expense is arbitrarily defined as (1) weekly labor payroll, overtime and incentive, (2) manufacturing supplies, and (3) scrap. The variable portion of current level is then increased or decreased as a percent of the change in turn-in's between the first six months of 1976 and the forecast level of turn-in's in 1977.

   F. The end result should be a list of current level amounts for each Corporate Unit, the sum of which can be expressed as the expense portion of the Corporate and Divisional Profit and Loss Statements.

   G. Current Level will not be adjusted for inflation, raises, and other anticipated increases in expense levels in the second half of 1976. However, adjustments will be made for large and significant discontinuities which depress or inflate a single Corporate Unit's current level **relative** to other Corporate Units.

APPENDIX D — Current Level of Expenditure Calculation — 8

GenRad

SUBJECT: CURRENT LEVEL OF EXPENDITURE CALCULATION

NUMBER	REV NO.	EFF. DATE
6.3		SEP 8 19
BY:		PAGE 2 of 2

2. Use of the Current Level of Expenditure Calculations

The current level amount defines exactly the maximum amount of funding which each Corporate Unit Manager can have to fund his first level IF Package. Additions to the current level must then be the subject of higher level IF Packages and submitted to the CEO for approval.

APPENDIX D — The Project Resource Planning Sheet — 9

GenRad

NUMBER 6.1-11	REV NO.	EFF. DATE JUN 21 19
BY:		PAGE 1 of 7
Approved: W. R. Thurston		
Title: Chief Executive Officer		

SUBJECT: THE PROJECT RESOURCE PLANNING SHEET

SCOPE: All Corporate Units

GENERAL:

The Project Resource Planning Sheet (Exhibit A) is designed to be used as a check-off list, worksheet and/or summarization sheet for planning time-phased project resource requirements. Both new product and functional projects can be planned on this form.

When filled out, the Project Resource Planning Sheet must provide enough data to:

- inform the CEO of what the estimated total cost of a specific project is so that company resources can be correctly allocated,
- inform resource managers of the demands expected of them for project work, and
- allow computation of specific budgets, estimates of R&D expenditure level, and construction of detail P&L statements.

When complete, the Project Resource Planning Sheet is just a summary of the best estimate of the Project Manager and the effected Resource Managers. Project Managers are responsible for being able to provide the back-up material of appropriate accuracy to justify the estimate. In the case of on-going new product projects or projects which are fully specified, this would be a detailed estimate by phase, organization code, and function or the equivalent. For projects which are still unspecified or only roughly identified, the detail and accuracy can be reasonably reduced.

Cognizant financial units will assist Project Managers in the development of budgetary and other financial requirements.

PROCEDURE:

NOTE: These instructions are keyed to the headings on the Project Resource Planning Sheet. (Exhibit A).

1. **Sheet headings**

   These sheets are used for planning and/or budgeting project resource requirements by quarter. The quarters are referred to as periods to prevent confusing them with calendar quarters. They refer only to the quarters during which the project is being carried out. The space marked 1st Prd. is for whatever quarter the project is started, the 2nd Prd. for the next and so forth, independent of the calendar. For projects already in progress, the 1st Prd. will be the first for which planning will be required, i.e., the third calendar quarter of 1976.

   If no project number is issued, a temporary identifier must be used in the absence of an assigned project number.

   A. *Project Name*
   The name or basic descriptor of the product or project for which the Resource Planning Sheet is being prepared.

   Example:

1722	Screening Otoadmittance Meter
TYPE No.,	CATALOG DESCRIPTION

APPENDIX D — The Project Resource Planning Sheet — 10

GenRad

NUMBER	REV NO.	EFF. DATE
6.1-11		JUN 21 19
BY:		PAGE 2 of 7

SUBJECT: THE PROJECT RESOURCE PLANNING SHEET

B. *Project Number*
The numerical four digit project number or temporary identifier which uniquely describes this project. For assignment of temporary identifier see Procedure 1.1.

C. *Page*
For projects which extend more than 2 years, use one page for each sequential eight quarters. Therefore Page 1 will cover the first eight quarters and Page 2 will cover quarters 9 through 16, etc.

D. *Project Manager*
The manager who is responsible for this project. For new product projects this is usually a product marketing or product engineering person.

E. *Corporate Unit*
The Product Division or Support Unit responsible for the project, e.g., Environmedics Division, Electronic Instrument Division, Test Systems Division, Time/Data Division, Corporate Marketing, Mass. Operations, etc.

F. *Strategy Center & Strategy*
The strategy center, specific strategy, and strategy identification number which resulted in the requirement for this project, for example:

Strategy Number: 5306
Strategy Center: Hearing measurement/middle-ear segment
Strategy: To increase market share in medium price middle-ear market by designing a new automatic instrument.

G. *Finance*
Name of the accounting representative assinged to support the Project Manager.

2. **Section A, Labor Resource**

A. *Labor Resource Description*
Name of the basic labor type required, e.g., drafting, model shop, etc. (See Exhibit B for typical categories.)

B. *Legal Entity Code (Accounting-System Code)*
Enter the Legal Entity Code in order to allow correct accounting treatment of each resource item. The Legal Entity Codes required are:

01 — GR/Mass. (Concord & Bolton, except EMD)
02 — Canada
03 — Environmedics Division
04 — Time/Data Division

See example following D.

NOTE: The *name* of this code is no longer a correct name since EMD & TDD are no longer separate *legal entities*. Their accounting systems are still separate, however, and this code now identifies which accounting system is involved.

C. *O/C, Department*
This is the organization code or department number which defines in accounting terms where this line of labor resource originates. See Example following D.

APPENDIX D — The Project Resource Planning Sheet — 15

GenRad

SUBJECT: THE PROJECT RESOURCE PLANNING SHEET

NUMBER	REV NO.	EFF. DATE
6.1-11		JUN 21 19
BY:		PAGE 7 of 7

Exhibit B

Labor Resource descriptions may include, but are not limited to the listing below:

1. R&D: Engineers, Sr.
2.   Engineers, Jr.
3.   Assistants
4. Software Programming
5. Engineering Services
6.   Printed Circuit Shop
7.   Drafting, Regular
8.   Drafting, Etch Layout
9.   X-Shop
10.   Technical Publications
11.   Mfg. Documentation
12.   New Product MCP
13. Product Enginering
14.   Mechanical Design
15. Process Engineering
16.   Standard Group
17. Fabrication Engineering
18.   Toolroom
19. Industrial Engineering
20. Quality Engineering
21. Micro-Electronics
22. Product Marketing
23.   Service
24. Functional Marketing
25.   Training
26.   Sales Promotion
27.   Exhibits
28.   Service
29. Manufacturing: Learning Curve

APPENDIX D — The Manufacturing Resource Planning Sheet — 16

GenRad

NUMBER 6.1-21	REV NO.	EFF. DATE SEP 8 19
SUBJECT: THE MANUFACTURING RESOURCE PLANNING SHEET	BY:	PAGE 1 of 3
	Approved: W. R. Thurston	
	Title: Chief Executive Officer	

SCOPE: Corporate Wide.

GENERAL:

The Resource Planning Sheet (Exhibit A) is designed to plan the next year's operations for a manufacturing department. A manufacturing department is one which produces COGS or Inventory Direct Labor for the company's products.

When filled out, the manufacturing Resource Planning Sheet must provide data for a line-by-line budget for 1977. This budget must provide the amount and type of expenses which, for a given shipments forecast, will be needed in 1977. It is to be arranged in funding increments ranked in order of priority.

PROCEDURE:

Note: These instructions are keyed to the headings on the Resource Planning Sheet (Exhibit A).

1. **SHEET HEADINGS**

    A. **Corporate Unit**
       The Corporate Unit within which this Budget Center belongs.

    B. **Budget Center**
       This is the name and accounting number of the Unit preparing the Resource Planning Sheet.

    C. **Budget Center Manager**
       The manager or supervisor who is responsible for this Budget Center.

    D. **Date**
       The date prepared by the Budget Center Manager.

2. **COLUMN HEADINGS**

    A. **N/E Name and No.**
       This is the account name and number for each line in the budget. Enter the expense items below exactly as they appear in the operating budget for this Unit.

       A few overhead departments will have labor absorption in addition to expenses. Absorption items for New Product Projects, Functional Projects, or Inventory Labor, should be separated out and listed below Total Expense and should be listed without overhead.

    B. **1975 Actual**
       This is the actual amount spent in these budget categories in 1975.

    C. **1976 Budget**
       This is the amount budgeted in these budget categories for 1976.

    D. **1976 Projected**
       This is the projected expenditure for each of these budget categories in 1976.

    E. **1977 Increment 1 to 4**
       This is the budget proposed for 1977. For Corporate Units Increment 1 should be current level and Increments 2 and above are for spending levels beyond current level. At lower organization levels, some shifting of resources is possible.

APPENDIX D — The Overhead Resource Planning Sheet — 23

GenRad

NUMBER 6.1-31	REV NO.	EFF. DATE SEP 8 19
BY:		PAGE 1 of 3
Approved:		
Title: Chief Executive Officer		

SUBJECT: THE OVERHEAD RESOURCE PLANNING SHEET

SCOPE: Corporate Wide

GENERAL:

The Resource Planning Sheet (Exhibit A) is designed to plan the next year's operations for an overhead department.

When filled out, the overhead Resource Planning Sheet must provide data for a line-by-line budget for 1977. This budget must provide the amount and types of expenses which will be needed in 1977. It is to be arranged in funding increments which are ranked in order of priority.

PROCEDURE:

Note: These instructions are keyed to the headings on the Resource Planning Sheet (Exhibit A).

1. **SHEET HEADINGS**

    A. **Corporate Unit**
    The Corporate Unit within which this Budget Center belongs.

    B. **Budget Center**
    This is the name and accounting number of the Unit preparing the Resource Planning Sheet.

    C. **Budget Center Manager**
    The manager or supervisor who is responsible for this Budget Center.

    D. **Date**
    The date prepared by the Budget Center Manager.

2. **COLUMN HEADINGS**

    A. **N/E Name and No.**
    This is the account name and number for each line in the budget. Enter the expense items below exactly as they appear in the operating budget for this Unit.

    A few overhead departments will have labor absorption in addition to expenses. Absorption items for New Product Projects, Functional Projects, or Inventory Labor, should be separated out and listed below Total Expense and should be listed without overhead.

    B. **1975 Actual**
    This is the actual amount spent in these budget categories in 1975.

    C. **1976 Budget**
    This is the amount budgeted in these budget categories for 1976.

    D. **1976 Projected**
    This is the projected expenditure for each of these budget categories in 1976.

    E. **1977 Increment 1 to 4**
    This is the budget proposed for 1977. For Corporate Units Increment 1 should be current level and Increments 2 and above are for spending levels beyond current level. At lower organization levels, some shifting of resources is possible.

APPENDIX D — The Overhead Resource Planning Sheet — 24

GenRad

SUBJECT: THE OVERHEAD RESOURCE PLANNING SHEET

NUMBER	REV NO.	EFF. DATE
6.1-31		SEP 8 19
BY:		PAGE 2 of 3

3. **SUMMARIES**

   A. **Total Expense**
   This is the total of all budget items except for Labor Absorbed.

   NOTE: Normally Overhead Departments will have no Labor Absorbed and will therefore not have to fill out Sections B and C.

   B. **Total Direct Labor**
   This is the unloaded total of any budgeted Direct Labor Absorbed. It includes both inventory and project labor each of which must be separately listed.

   C. **Ratio — DL ÷ Total Labor**
   This is the ratio of B, Direct Labor Absorbed divided by the total of **all** weekly and monthly payrolls, overtimes, incentives, etc.

   D. **Positions**
   This is the total number of full-time people employed by the Unit at year end.

   E. **Capital Expense**
   This item provides for listing any capital expenditures required during 1977 by this Unit.

APPENDIX D — Overhead IF Package Cover Sheet — 29

Gen Rad

SUBJECT: OVERHEAD IF PACKAGE COVER SHEET

NUMBER 6.1-33	REV NO.	EFF. DATE SEP 8 19__
BY:		PAGE 4 of 4

EXHIBIT A

GenRad — Exhibit A

INCREMENTAL FUNDING PACKAGE COVER SHEET

☐ Product Project ☐ Manufacturing
☐ Functional Project ☐ Overhead

Package Number	Increment Of	Rank

Unit Name	Prepared By
Unit O/C or Dept No. _____ Level Corp Unit ☐ A ☐ B ☐ C ☐	Date

Describe the Unit and its operations including resources used and services provided

Summary of Package Increments (Expense in $000's) — 1976 Budgeted

	Positions		Operating Expenses			Capital Equipment	
	1977 Incr.	1977 Cum.	1977 Incr.	1977 Cum.	% Cum.	1977 Incr.	1977 Cum.
1 of — Current Level							
2 of							
3 of							
4 of							
5 of							
6 of							

Incremental analysis of goals addressed

Goal No.	Goal Summary	Increment Number
		1	2	3	4	5	6

MEASURING, ANALYZING AND CORRECTING PERFORMANCE

APPENDIX D — Performance Measurement, Analysis and Corrective Action — 30

GenRad

SUBJECT: PERFORMANCE MEASUREMENT, ANALYSIS AND CORRECTIVE ACTION

NUMBER 8.0	REV NO.	EFF. DATE AUG 3 19
BY:		PAGE 1 of 12
Approved: W. R. Thurston		
Title: Chief Executive Officer		

SCOPE: Corporate Wide

GENERAL:
Successful execution of the Short Range Plan requires that GR managers at all levels participate in a continuing formalized performance evaluation and reporting program.

POLICY:

1. Every manager, within the GR Organization Structure, is responsible for knowing and understanding the Goals, Objectives, and Strategies of his/her organizational unit and of the larger unit of which he/she is a part.

2. Every manager is required to develop control systems to measure performance against On-Going goals and program plans to aid in measuring progress towards Problem-Solving and Innovative Goals. Refer to Exhibits B and C.

3. Managers at all levels are responsible for audit, evaluation and reporting of their organizations' performance against approved goals and measurement criteria using the control systems and program plans.

4. When an organizational unit's performance falls below the acceptable levels established by the annual plan and the associated criteria, the cognizant manager must develop a corrective action plan and:

    A. Implement the plan if all factors involved fall within his/her scope of authority.

    B. Present the plan to the next higher level of management for review, modification, and/or approval if the plan involves actions outside his/her scope of authority.

5. Reporting frequency is established by management level in accordance with the following table:

MANAGEMENT LEVEL	REPORTING FREQUENCY*
B & C Level Managers	Once each month (dates set by A Level Managers)
A Level Managers	Once each month (dates set by Corporate Unit Managers)
Corporate Unit	Once each quarter (dates set by Chief Executive Officer)

*This refers to a formal periodic review. Informal reporting should be done as often as required.

APPENDIX D — Performance Measurement, Analysis and Corrective Action — 31

GenRad

SUBJECT: PERFORMANCE MEASUREMENT, ANALYSIS AND CORRECTIVE ACTION

NUMBER	REV NO.	EFF. DATE
8.0		AUG 3 19
BY:		PAGE 2 of 12

6. Reports are prepared in accordance with the following standard (8½" x 11") format:
   - Unit Name
   - Date
   - Cognizant Manager's Name
   - Reports to
   - Established Goals and Measurement Criteria
   - Activity Highlights
     - Items on Target
     - Items Requiring Corrective Action
       - Corrective Action Taken
       - Corrective Action Suggested
     - Recommended Changes in Goals

APPENDIX D — Performance Measurement, Analysis and Corrective Action — 32

GenRad

NUMBER 8.0	REV NO.	EFF. DATE AUG 3 19
BY:		PAGE 3 of 12

SUBJECT: PERFORMANCE MEASUREMENT, ANALYSIS AND CORRECTIVE ACTION

REFERENCE:

RESPONSIBILITY	ACTION
Cognizant Manager	NOTE: This procedure is a model outlining the actions taken when the "Cognizant Manager" is at the B or C Level of the management structure. When the Cognizant Manager is at the A Level or above, the same approach holds true with fewer management levels participating. The flow chart (Reference: Exhibit A) depicts the sequence of events associated with performance measuring and reporting and additionally, corrective action development and implementation. 1. Measures organizational performance against the goals and measurement criteria relevant to his/her operation as contained in the Short Range Plan by using the control systems and program plans previously developed. 2. Determines if performance meets plan requirements. [Flow chart: Performance on Target — NO → Corrective Action Taken — NO; YES → (Enter in Report Highlights) ← YES, Continue with Step 3.] 3. Develops definition (scope) of problem(s). 4. Develops suggested course of action to correct the problem as defined, including definite goals, cost limits, impacts on person power, capital expenditures, inventory, schedule and reporting milestones for significant steps. 5. Contacts the next higher level of management and enters into verbal discussion re: problem and solution.
Next Higher Level of Management	6. Obtains understanding of problem and the proposed Corrective Program Plan.

124

APPENDIX D — Performance Measurement, Analysis and Corrective Action — 33

GenRad

	NUMBER	REV NO.	EFF. DATE
	8.0		AUG 3 19
	BY:		PAGE
			4 of 12

SUBJECT: PERFORMANCE MEASUREMENT, ANALYSIS AND CORRECTIVE ACTION

REFERENCE:

RESPONSIBILITY	ACTION
Corporate Unit Manager and/or Chief Executive Officer **Cognizant Manager**	7. Determines if actions required fall within his/her management level scope of authority. *[Flowchart: Authority to Initiate Corrective Action — YES → Move to Step 10; NO → Continue with Step 8]* 8. Routes the problem definition and suggested action plan up the organizational ladder through the various managerial levels until an authority level commensurate with the nature and scope of the problem is reached. 9. Obtains understanding of problem and the proposed Corrective Program Plan. 10. Reviews and amends proposed Corrective Program Plan as required. 11. Approves Cognizant Manager's Corrective Program Plan as modified. 12. Implements approved Corrective Program Plan and reports progress in established reporting framework.

APPENDIX D — Performance Measurement, Analysis and Corrective Action — 34

GenRad

SUBJECT: PERFORMANCE MEASUREMENT, ANALYSIS AND CORRECTIVE ACTION

NUMBER	REV NO.	EFF. DATE
8.0		AUG 3 19__
BY:		PAGE
		5 of 12

EXHIBIT A

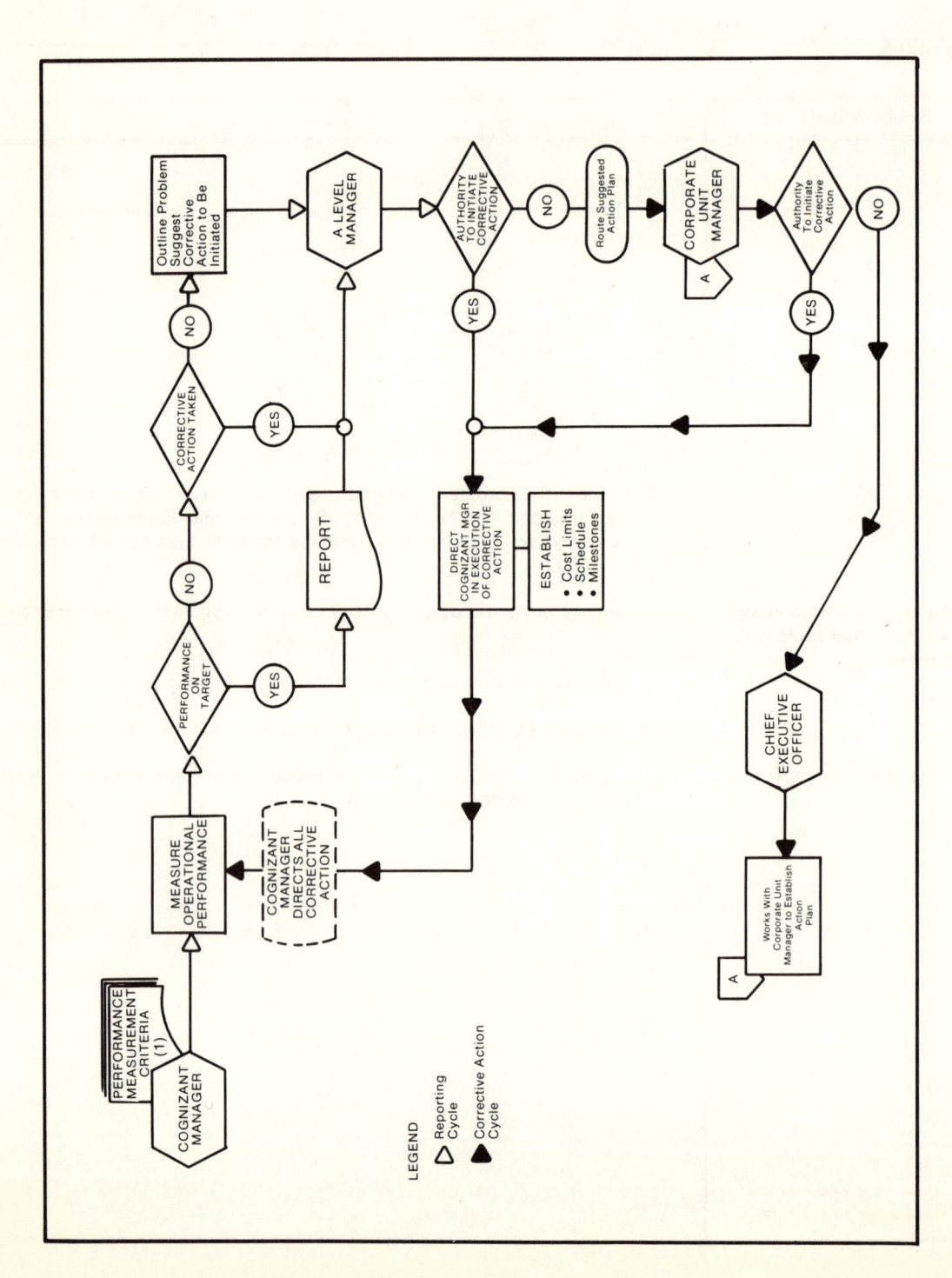

APPENDIX D — Performance Measurement, Analysis and Corrective Action — 41

GenRad

NUMBER 8.0	REV NO.	EFF. DATE AUG 3 19
BY:		PAGE 12 of 12

SUBJECT: PERFORMANCE MEASUREMENT ANALYSIS AND CORRECTIVE ACTION

EXHIBIT D

Periodic progress reviews are held between a manager or supervisor and his/her higher level manager, according to the frequency shown in Policy 8.0, and more often if desirable. Such reviews are designed to assess progress, identify problem areas and obstacles and agree upon solutions. These review sessions should be seen as a time for summing up; the manager will be meeting with his/her superior as urgent problems or questions arise. Involved in the progress review are a written report prepared by the manager and submitted to his/her reviewer beforehand and a discussion and progress review/problem-solving session between the two parties.

In a one-on-one progress review session the reviewer will play a number of different rules: coach, consultant, sounding board. He may help the subordinate recognize potential problems and may offer help and support in solving them. In addition, he may have the authority to make decisions or take action which the subordinate cannot, or will be in a position to refer the problem *and proposed solution* to the appropriate higher level of management.

Reporting Progress

Policy 8.0 provides a suggested format for preparing a progress report. Essentially, the manager ought to report on those items which are on target or have been completed since the last review; also, he should note those goals or projects or activities requiring corrective action. If corrective action is or was required, the manager should report on the action he has taken or plans to take if such action is within the scope of his authority. If the necessary corrective action is beyond the scope of his authority, he should present a recommended course of action. The report should also present any changes, deletions, or modifications in his On-Going Problem Solving, or Innovative Goals which the manager wishes to recommend.

It may be useful to attach to the report any documents or reports or graphs, etc. which are part of the control systems for monitoring On-Going Goals, as well as attaching any updated program plan charts.

Conducting the Periodic Progress Review

Having studied the report and attachments prepared by the manager, the reviewer next meets with the manager to discuss progress. Part of the discussion will center around those items which are on target or have been completed. On those items which require corrective action the manager will have proposed a plan to the reviewer (if corrective action has not already been taken) and two individuals will work together to accomplish the following activities.

1. **Remove obstacles.** The action required to correct a problem will probably have been suggested by the manager prior to the session, so the session serves as a means of reviewing the proposed plan, identifying, and planning to remove obstacles and deciding how and when to present the plan to higher management, if required.

2. **Identify problems.** There may be instances where the manager has not been able to identify the causes of a problem — all he knows is that progress towards a goal is off target. The review session provides a opportunity to combine the information of the reviewer and the manager and makes it easier to distinguish between causes and symptoms.

3. **Priority problems.** The recommended solution provided by the manager may be reviewed to see if it ought to be done at all — other problems may be more pressing or it may be too costly to solve this one.

4. **Revise existing goals.** A proposed plan or a plan developed during the session may require a modification in the level of a goal, in the schedule for achieving it, or in its place in the priority of goals. It may be necessary that a goal be dropped altogether, at least for the current year. It may also be advisable to add a new goal in the same or a different results area to take care of a problem or to respond to a new opportunity or innovative idea which has surfaced during the session. Any changes to or additions to goals ought to be indicated on the manager's and reviewer's copies of the goals.

5. **Summarize the session.** The last action during the session should be a summary of action steps and activities agreed upon.

4

Administering Cost Reduction Programs— Creating Profits

Cost reduction is most effectively described by Thomas A. Edison: "There is a better way to do anything—find it."

Squeezing profits from a business is a matter of financial control! This places the financial administrator in the enviable position of being able to create profits through creative, non-restrictive cost reduction programs. His role in this area is a vital, continuing factor in maintaining corporate profitability.

Too often the approach to cost reduction is conducted in the following manner: "Dump the losers!"—"Fire the secretaries and the janitors!" There are some concrete approaches to cost control that will yield practical, profitable results.

EXAMPLES

The morning paper has an article stating that the local government is overstaffed by 11% according to a study made by a "Big Eight" accounting firm. Not only is government overstaffed, but in my personal opinion practically every firm in the country could cut its staff by 10% without seriously affecting either quality or quantity of production, work or sales.

One firm, under pressure to reduce costs, cut its headquarters staff in half within six months. By the end of a year it had reduced the remaining personnel by one-third. Efficiency and effectiveness increased. Costs were reduced over seven million dollars.

Turning the lights off and the thermometer down yielded over eight million dollars in savings for another firm. No large task, just a simple elimination of waste!

Installation of solar panels for heating reduces power consumption from 15% to 50% dependent upon your location.

The utilization of surge control units in plants, stores, golf courses and homes reduces the electrical consumption by a minimum of 10%.

$25,000 was saved by eliminating one entrance to the plant—reduced security and manning costs.

Water used to cool production equipment was cycled through the plant and office heating systems instead of dumping it down the sewer. It was then recycled through the machinery. Savings in power and water usage totaled 25% on the previous annual bills.

The local newspaper reviewed its entire power consumption plan. It soon found that it could use the lights for heating in the winter. In addition, it found that practically every one of its motors was overrated for the job. By replacing the major motors immediately it reduced its power bill by 10%.

Every firm should review its copying costs! These have gotten out of hand. One small firm reduced its copying costs $650 per year by cutting copying procedures.

One firm spent $25,000 modifying its lighting system in order to reduce current consumption. Less heat from the lights reduced the air conditioning bill. Annual savings was $55,000.

Individuals and businesses can save by using electrical, room-by-room heating. The average savings ranges from 15% to 45% annually. The use of new low energy ballasts in fluorescent fixtures will save a minimum of five dollars per unit per year.

STAFFING FOR COST REDUCTION

How does one approach cost reduction on a logical and effective basis? First of all, someone must assume the responsibility, and it must be a continuing, planned operation. Dependent upon the size of your organization, your cost reduction staff can vary from one part-time individual to several task forces ranging over the entire spectrum of operations. Whether it be one individual or many, the effort must be continuous, periodically reported on and the expenditures compared with the results.

Staffing for cost reduction should include wherever possible individuals from all segments of the business. The clerks, machine operators, lift truck operators and others who are on the firing line day after day can contribute ideas with merit for cost reduction. If they are not included in the task force group they at least should be interviewed and listened to. Your individuals or task forces should exude talent. They must be innovative, coldly analytical and have a sharp mind. In addition, they must not easily be deterred by resistance to change or comments that ideas will not work.

Most firms utilize the task force approach to solve problems. When the problem is solved, the force is disbanded and a new one formed to attack another problem. One must remember, the smaller the unit the more effective it can be!

Administering Cost Reduction Programs—Creating Profits

THE BASIC PLAN

The basic plan for cost reduction is the realization that sales are important to business survival only if they produce a profit. In order to convert the sales dollar into a bottom line profit dollar one must keep the costs below the revenues. A decrease in costs can take much of the pressure off of your sales and productive organizations while it creates additional funds for ultimate growth. The leverage in reducing costs is greater than that obtained from increasing sales. Many firms spend huge sums on sales training and sales promotions and not a solitary dollar on cost reduction training or analysis. If you have a 10% profit margin on your sales dollar the leverage of a ten-dollar reduction in costs over a one-hundred-dollar increase in sales is ten to one.

The first step in cost reduction is to analyze your business. Draw up a chart setting out the various segments of your business and each of its operations. These are the items that you are going to review, carefully and in depth. Each item must be questioned and forced to defend its existence in the overall corporate activity.

The next task is to set up a timetable for the work and to assign the personnel to the tasks or problems. Priority will have to be assigned to each problem based upon the dollar return anticipated. Dependent upon size, personnel and time factors, this can range from one individual (yourself!) to multipersonnel task forces and time spans from a day to many months. My personal recommendation is that one person can accomplish a great deal if given time and supporting help. I still refer to the Texas Ranger statue in the Dallas airport: "ONE RIOT, ONE RANGER." Too often, everyone wants to get into the act. In the larger firms, task forces might range from three to five individuals.

There is a lot to be gained from the orderly approach in which you systematically take your operations apart piece by piece, see what makes them function and justify their existence. Strangely enough, despite the best talent, the larger the firm the less efficient it is. In fact, one often wonders if the legendary American efficiency is a fairy story or another American dream lost to huge enterprises and mass production. In the smaller firm someone cares what happens every day. Someone watches the daily invoices and the daily expenditures and attempts to keep the latter from exceeding the daily outflow of goods and services. When one reads stories of huge writeoffs, wholesale divestitures of losing operations or of individuals who have saved firms by laying off thousands of employees and closing numerous plants, one wonders how did it ever get in that shape in the first place. Somewhere these individual parts lost momentum and became classic examples of dead-end operations, full of duplication, obsolete equipment and techniques, living retirees, useless effort and lack of brains. They are monuments to slovenly methods, procedures, products and no plans, goals or objectives. Their obvious efficiency is often 50 to 60%, if that high. Surely they didn't start out that way. So where did they fail? In your systematic approach to an analysis of things presently happening you must keep this in mind. You must be fair, tough-minded and adopt a "no nonsense" approach to each operation. Either it performs profitably and has some future potential for a profit or it gets washed out at the earliest opportunity.

Once the plan is established—follow it! Your financial division can contribute at least 10% to any firm's growth by properly planning, carrying on and expediting a sound cost reduction program on a continuing basis.

WHAT TO DO! THE ACTION CHECKLIST

Start at the top line—*sales*:

1. Are production problems hindering sales?
2. Check your sales per employee against your competitor. Can it be improved?
3. What is the ratio, man by man, versus your competition? One firm's ratio of sales per employee was one-half of that of its major competitor.
4. Can you increase sales by dropping some product lines and increasing your effort on the bread and butter items?
5. Analyze the profit by product line and individual products if possible.
6. Analyze the profit by individual customer. Can marginal customers be eliminated? Are sufficient efforts being put on developing potential large customers?
7. Duplication of sales efforts—Can one man handle more of your lines? Often acquisitions result in duplication of effort.
8. Can you increase your inventory turnover with fewer products?
9. Can you cut sales efforts on low margin and low turnover items?
10. Analyze and determine the future potential and product life of each item in your line. What is its profit potential five years from now?
11. Discover and evaluate sales problems.
12. Project for one to five years the potential sales and profits for each product. Change the projections to reflect a 10% increase in sales, a 10% increase in costs and a 10% decrease in sales and costs. What is the projected profit potential for each product? Can the sales, promotion or manufacturing expenses be cut?

Then—analyze sales expenses:

1. Can travel expenses be cut—Is each trip really necessary?
2. What are your sales expenses per dollar of sales? Do they compare favorably with those of your competitors? What are your costs by product? Are some products more expensive to sell than others? Analyze your sales costs by customer. Is each customer as profitable as you think he is?
3. Is your sales training effective? Is it too costly? Is it adequate?

CASE IN POINT

Many small firms send salesmen out to sell and install products with little or no knowledge of their job or installation procedures. The result is a great deal of misdirected and lost effort. Tricky installations often result in additional time being spent on the job, bad customer relations and lost jobs or returns due to improper installations. Check on the men in the field and whether the customer is satisfied. It pays off!

4. What do your sales personnel think of your products? What do they think of your sales promotions?

Administering Cost Reduction Programs—Creating Profits

5. Are salesmen rewarded for good efforts and punished for bad? Lack of punishment can be fatal to your firm!
6. Can your sales promotions and conference activities be less plush and still do an effective job at less cost? Sales and advertising people love to spend money lavishly.
7. Are you using computer methods to direct sales personnel and to measure the effectiveness of sales calls. Is your sales routing planned or haphazard?
8. Are you using the latest in videotape presentations to keep your sales personnel informed? This method can reduce sales meeting and travel costs.
9. Do you rate sales personnel? Do you keep a running check on their performance? Are you constantly upgrading your personnel or are you conducting a living retirement program?
10. Advertising—is it effective? Can you prove it? Can some of it be cut without hurting sales?

CASE IN POINT

One firm cut magazine ads from twelve to six without a loss of effectiveness. Another firm eliminated TV advertising and doubled sales by employing a full-time outside salesman at 50% of the cost of the TV ads.

11. Is the sales headquarters overstaffed? Too many vice presidents or possibly too few? Too few indians—too many chiefs!
12. Do your salesmen report economic and competitive events to some central intelligence center? This is one of the least expensive means of acquiring economic and competitive knowledge.
13. Do you analyze and check on your competitors' sales and marketing efforts?

Next—work on production costs:

1. How does your production per employee compare with that of your competition?
2. How does your dollar investment in plant compare with that of your competitors?
3. Do you use value analysis to continually look for new ideas, techniques, processes and materials?
4. Do you analyze your competitors' products, jobs, methods or techniques for new ideas?
5. Do you break your product lines down into individual items and review the costs and production processes for each one? How profitable is it? Can the costs be reduced?
6. Are there production bugs which are increasing costs or hurting sales?
7. Do you review your inventory cycle? Is the material moving through the plant in a steady flow? What is your cost turnover and can it be reduced?
8. Can inventory costs be reduced and space requirements eased by dumping slow-moving items at a discount?
9. Are there new processes or new machinery which will reduce costs?

CASE IN POINT

Paper making firms report reducing energy and water costs appreciably by using new processes. In addition, production was speeded up. The resulting savings amounted to millions of dollars.

10. Do you have a planned program for discovering production problems and working on them? Remember the finest equipment in the world is only as good as the people operating it.
11. Do you inventory skills and maintain a performance file on your employees?
12. Do you rotate jobs wherever possible to eliminate boredom and lack of alertness?
13. Do you talk to the people about production problems?
14. Do you realize that increasing the quality of your production will lower costs by decreasing product liability claims, recalls and warranty costs?
15. Do you check and classify your defective merchandise reports, returns, allowances and warranty adjustments?
16. Are you operating at capacity? Does lack of machinery or space hamper your production and performance?
17. Are you using your materials handling equipment efficiently? Can you rent equipment for short periods for less than owning or long-term leasing?
18. Is your basic objective to be the low cost producer in everything you make? If not, do you have a valid reason why?

LET'S LOOK AT PAYROLL AND PAYROLL EXPENSES

1. Overtime can be an additional cost or it can be a means of greater production at a lesser overall cost.

CASE IN POINT

The Ford Motor Company opts for increased production (to a point) by increased overtime due to the high cost of hiring and maintaining additional workers on the payroll. Overall costs are less.

Overtime can be cut by carefully reviewing each request and determining its absolute necessity. It can be cut by staggering working hours or by the use of temporary or part-time employees.

There are additional maneuvers such as compensatory time off (used in the accounting profession) and the use of supervisory personnel for extra work.

2. Compensation Insurance—in some operations this is a very high cost. You should review your coverages carefully and take advantage of all classifications with favorable rates. Utilize pre-employment physicals to discover past injuries or possible disability claims. The cost of a permanently disabled individual can increase costs tremendously. Utilize the services of the insurance firm to the fullest to point out hazards, and conduct safety courses and inspections.
3. Tax Benefits—By reporting sick pay separately you can save on FICA and other payroll taxes. Utilize independent contractors to save FICA and payroll taxes. Avoid unnecessary layoffs which will increase your unemployment tax rates. Hiring of temporary employees from an agency may be less expensive in the long run.

Administering Cost Reduction Programs—Creating Profits

CASE IN POINT

Contrast the cost of increasing your unemployment rate from .1% to 1.0% versus the cost of personnel from an agency for a short period of time, not to mention the clerical costs of adding people to the payroll and processing the separation information.

With many large firms the directive is to hold down the "head count" at all costs. A sales representative of a large firm does 2.5 million dollars in sales a year at the present time. His costs are 2.6% of these sales. He is denied the right to hire a permanent secretary but can hire all of the temporary help from an outside agency that he requires.

SOME MISCELLANEOUS ITEMS

1. Cut continuing costs by dumping obsolete or slow-moving inventory.
2. Adopt an aggressive approach toward speeding up cash collections. It can increase your cash flow, cut down on your interest costs and result in fewer bad debts.
3. Spend some money in promoting purchases. Let your requirements be known to a larger group of suppliers. It could result in lower prices.
4. Utilize discounts whenever you can. 1% for ten days equates to 18% a year. 2% for ten days doubles the discount to 36%.
5. Many firms charge interest on delinquent accounts. 1% on accounts over 30 days old is common practice. At 1% per month or a portion thereof your collections will pick up.
6. Order in the proper quantities. Utilize requirement contracts and bulk orders with quantities to be drawn out as required.

CASE IN POINT

One small firm lost the freight allowance on several shipments by ordering a smaller dollar amount than the supplier would allow freight on. In one instance freight was prepaid on all shipments over $350. In another instance a freight allowance of 5% was allowed on all shipments over $500. During a price check the higher prices involved turned up the fact that the items ordered were 10% higher than anticipated. Two $200 orders issued within ten days could have been combined for a 10% savings in cost.

7. Periodically check invoice prices. Many small firms do not do this on a regular or continuing basis. Checking invoice prices accomplishes at least two things. One, you ascertain that the quoted price and the invoice price are the same—errors do occur! Two, if you are estimating costs and quoting jobs you are aware of the recent price changes and your estimating file can be kept up-to-date. The use of current or current projected costs is worth many dollars to most firms.

CASE IN POINT

A small firm using outdated costs was underquoting its jobs by six dollars a unit. In six weeks' time the loss was over six thousand dollars.

8. Provide your customers with free surveys—During the 1970's with the emphasis on electrical energy conservation the electrical contractors could provide free surveys on how power costs could be reduced. This developed increased business for them and lowered their costs. The surveys, while requiring plant or equipment investments, turned up cost saving possibilities for their customers. In addition, the surveys developed many new types of business for the electrical contractors. Customers' problems gave them a new insight on their market potential at a very low cost.

9. Use of manufactured parts—In many instances parts can be utilized in assemblies cheaper than manufacturing the same items. When one studies the cost of raw materials, storage, handling and fabrication, it is often possible to purchase these items at the same or lesser costs. The auto manufacturers import many parts for assembly into their units because of the cost factor.

10. Energy savings have been increased through the use of time clocks. Heat and light are only turned on when required. During cleanup, the area being worked on is the only one lighted.

11. Use of existing circuits for control—By utilizing bursts of high voltage current over existing circuits equipment can be turned on or off.

12. Utilizing a shorter work week can cut costs—cut one hour off of each day.

13. Burning an emulsion of oil and water in place of oil saved over $250,000 a year for one firm.

14. Move into smaller plants in smaller towns—This resulted in lower labor rates of about 50% of those previously paid. In addition, fringes such as medical and pensions were eliminated. The smaller units were more efficient and turned out better quality products.

15. Phase out full-time jobs—Hire part-time workers for more flexible schedules and a three-day work week.

16. Under energy and mileage restrictions the auto makers have dropped weight a minimum of 15% and will continue to substitute lighter materials as the price of oil rises.

Remember: The addition or reduction of people in your work force will have a direct bearing upon costs. Always remember that people spend money, people require funds to operate and the more you have, the more money you will spend. Reduction in personnel will reduce other costs. Under any cost reduction program the justification of people on the payroll is a prime consideration.

DO NOT BE DETERRED OR RETREAT UNDER ADVERSE CONDITIONS

Most people are conservative. Most machines are conservatively rated. Most manufacturing processes are susceptible to improvements. Sometimes you have to take a chance! People will not accept responsibility, and when they say: "We can't do that!" they are not really certain but merely afraid to exceed the limits of the past. If a machine is turning up at 300 strokes a minute and you wish to push it to 400 they will object. If you stay with them while you push it up and are willing to accept the price of failure, they will go along with you. Such are the changes made in industry to speed up production, to lower costs, to increase profits and to continue growth. Most people will react negatively to change. The more radical the change the greater the opposition! Sometimes you may have to embark upon

Administering Cost Reduction Programs—Creating Profits   137

a project secretly. If you succeed you are a hero, if not you are a bum—perhaps an ex-employee!

The possibilities for cost reduction in every business are endless. Every function, every activity, every material may be a target for cost reduction or elimination. Under the energy crisis push for reduced costs National Can Company reduced its consumption of natural gas by 42% in one year without cutting production or materially increasing costs. In most instances it takes a crisis, a war or a recession to activate cost reduction or material substitution programs.

The primary target of cost reduction should be the elimination of waste. This single item is a major factor in increased costs. Most waste is readily apparent in that it appears as a spoiled or worthless product. Some waste is the normal product of a manufacturing process such as the webbing formed by the punching of bottle caps out of a sheet of tin plate. Those used on soft drink bottles produced a webbing that was sold to the manufacturer of air conditioner and furnace filters. For years they used two on each filter. Under the pressure of inflation they now use only one. This probably saves .002 cents per unit and produces a flimsy but workable filter. On sales of a billion or more filters a year the savings is quite large. It looked small and insignificant but look at the total money involved!

Waste can involve equipment, time, materials, supplies and effort. Much of it is hard to ascertain. Some of it is quite simple, occurs every day as a normal item and yet is exceedingly hard to ascertain. Some of it requires diligence and creative thinking to discover and much of it is just hard to recognize or locate.

The cost of not doing something is the most difficult to ascertain. One needs to check and recheck to make certain that directives are carried out properly and consistently.

CASE IN POINT

An operator of a small fleet of trucks wondered why his repair costs were so high. In checking it was found that no maintenance schedule was set up and most of the trucks were driven until they simply refused to run. No one was in charge of checking the oil, the tires or other items. Consequently nothing was done on schedule and the repair costs gradually mounted until they became unbearable. A fixed schedule of maintenance under the control of one individual decreased maintenance 40% the first year and increased the life of the equipment by 25% over a three-year period.

WRAP-UP

To control costs effectively so that they can be reduced or eliminated:

You need .... a staff or responsible individual
                .... a plan or program
                .... a time cycle
                .... a priority system
                .... a continuing, determined effort

138 Administering Cost Reduction Programs—Creating Profits

.... innovation and ingenuity

.... perseverance

.... a cost control system that points out trouble spots before they become a major disaster

.... a series of reports showing the dollar results of cost reduction programs.

.... the ability to disband an operation when the problem is solved

Remember . . . Your investment in cost reduction and control can be quite small. The returns in increased profits can be quite high. The leverage factor is enormous!

THE COST EQUATION—COMPONENTS

In the final analysis costs must be reduced to their simplest form. The proper procedure for analysis is product by product and customer by customer as follows:

	PRODUCT	% OF TOTAL	CUSTOMER	% OF TOTAL
SALES	$	%	$	%
ALLOWANCES—RETURNS				
NET SALES				
COSTS INVOLVED				
MANUFACTURING				
MATERIAL				
DIRECT LABOR				
TRANSPORTATION IN				
TRANSPORTATION OUT				
TOTAL DIRECT COSTS				
OVERHEAD ABSORBED				
FIXED CHARGES ABSORBED				
MANUFACTURING PROFIT				
SALES COSTS				
ADVERTISING—PROMOTION				
SALES SALARIES				
SALES EXPENSES				
SALES ADMINISTRATION				
TOTAL SALES COSTS				
COMMISSIONS				
TOTAL SELLING COSTS				
ADMINISTRATIVE COSTS ABSORBED				
TOTAL SALES AND ADMINISTRATIVE COSTS				
PROFIT PER CUSTOMER OR PER INDIVIDUAL PRODUCT	$	%	$	%

5

Modern Approaches to Administering Financial Planning and Strategy

PLANNING AND STRATEGY

The need for sound, effective and aggressive corporate planning has never been greater. In a business world very likely to continue to be beset by inflation, rising costs and rapidly changing technology, the planning and strategy function has become a major corporate activity. Large or small, every firm must plan, must have well-defined objectives and strategies, to remain viable in the competitive struggle.

Practically every top financial executive that I have known or interviewed admits that planning and strategy formulation is a fascinating process. The thrill of seeing a well-formulated plan or strategy being developed and producing profitable results is the realization of a dream for all financial planners. Now and then one also suffers the agonies of defeat as plans go astray and financial losses occur.

CASE IN POINT

The development of one financial plan resulted in a seven-million dollar increase in profit for one paper manufacturer by pointing out areas for cost reduction, markets where prices could be increased and the lack of sufficient capacity to meet demand in another area.

140 Modern Approaches to Administering Financial Planning and Strategy

DEVELOPMENT OF PLANNING

Throughout modern history, the function of planning has always been carried on. It started to formalize in the great depression of the 30's when hard-pressed businesses started developing budgets. The success of these budgetary forecasting and control techniques then led to the development of modern techniques. The computer revolution, with its rapid ability to cope with change brought planning and strategy operations into a major corporate function. It is an exciting, intriguing phase of financial administration that all of us thoroughly enjoy. Planning is developing into a systematic science and despite skepticism about long-range planning it has become a major function in practically all of the larger and medium-sized firms. There exists a serious deficiency in the art of planning in most of the smaller firms.

So rapidly is the field expanding that many firms are now engaged in futuristic planning and strategies wherein environmental analyses and forecasts are utilized to determine the opportunities and threats inherent in future environments. Some major firms have put some of their brightest young minds on the task of determining or forecasting what the firm's activities will consist of 20 to 25 years from now. These studies have led to some interesting projections of technological advances, social, economic and environmental changes and often to radical forecasts of what the individual firms will be like in the future. The synthesis of business, science, technology and economics will exert powerful influences upon all of our lives in the future. The energy crisis alone will develop a new thermoelectric revolution in heating and cooling structures.

Thus, in a span of less than 50 years, we have seen planning and strategy develop from simple budgets to forecast and control operations (helping firms to survive the effects of a depression) to a major force in analyzing, forecasting and enabling all of mankind to cope with developing energy and material shortages. Alert firms are already moving into areas which will protect their resources and profits and enable them to dominate certain areas of the economy, which will increase their competitive importance in the future.

WHAT ARE THE FORECASTS?

1. Increasingly better communications—worldwide; radical changes in data and document transmission.
2. Greater reliance upon business forecasting and offensive and defensive strategies.
3. Decentralized national and international management—control will be placed where the action is. Complete changes in the corporate hierarchy.
4. An explosion in the field of minicomputers for personal use, education and smaller firms.
5. Radical changes in home construction design—portable, disposable, perhaps underground.
6. Radical changes in heating and cooling of buildings through solar energy, thermoelectric modules and the development of new insulation products.
7. A move toward an electric type economy and the gradual conversion of the gasoline engine to electric.

Modern Approaches to Administering Financial Planning and Strategy

8. A move from the conservative logic of saving for a rainy day to a complete corporate or government support system—lifetime job guarantees or salaries.
9. A complete rental economy wherein no one owns anything anymore.
10. Increasing control of business by government—witness the current SEC action and the movement into accounting controls.
11. Controlled atmosphere—water and sewage disposal in our cities; concentrated efforts to end pollution.
12. Instant accounting—computerized manufacturing operations providing on-line information at any stage; dynamic cost and production controls.
13. Shorter work weeks and rotating of employees—longer vacations; increasing elimination of jobs.
14. Critical energy and food shortages.
15. Proliferation of a nuclear economy—its benefits and threats to civilization.

These are only a few of the things which are forecast for the future. They represent some of the opportunities and problems which you must plan for and develop adequate strategies to cope with. They pose a real challenge to every farsighted financial executive.

The problems of today and those developing for the future make planning an essential corporate activity. It gives you the ability to select the means of coping with these problems to achieve solid growth and profitability. These are your targets, objectives, goals.

OBJECTIVES IN PLANNING: ORGANIZATIONAL—FUNCTIONAL

A short definition of corporate planning might be stated as: "the systematic approach to establish objectives, policies, and strategies and the detailed processes to achieve these objectives." There is, of course, no pat answer or formula to apply to all firms. Each financial executive must consider his own situation and develop whatever is required for his firm.

ORGANIZATIONAL OBJECTIVES

Organizational objectives are spelled out by many firms in their publicity releases or annual reports. Basically these cover the following items:

1. Type of organization and its options.
2. Type of business and what they intend to do.
3. The resources of the firm and how they will be allocated.
4. An analysis of the risks involved and the expected returns.
5. Target for growth and how to achieve it.
6. Anticipated ROI.

This is a release by Boise Cascade:

STRATEGY NUMBER 1. —We plan to concentrate on our two basic businesses—building materials and paper products. We plan to invest $1.1 billion in them between 1974 and 1978 while holding to our target debt to equity ratio of 0.6 to 1. We plan to generate an average annual return on investment of *at least 12% after taxes* on each project within the $850 million we're using to improve and expand our businesses.

STRATEGY NUMBER 2. —We plan to invest 27% of our capital dollars in our converting and distributing operations in order to maximize the earning power of our forest-oriented products.

STRATEGY NUMBER 3. —We plan to divide our capital investment about equally between our paper and building materials operations in order to maintain our relatively equal balance between the two.

GEORGIA PACIFIC—FIVE-YEAR PLAN

BASIC PHILOSOPHY—Never enter a market unless you can expect $50 million to $100 million in sales.

OBJECTIVES —Management for growth—resources—new products and a constantly expanding distribution system.

STRATEGY —Investment of $200 million a year in capital expenditures.

FUNCTIONAL OBJECTIVES

FINANCIAL —Planned debt to equity ratios
Financial statement structure
Earnings per share—dividends per share
Return on investment %
Target profitability on sales %
Cost controls or reduction
Cash flow
Capital expenditures

PERSONNEL —Personnel costs as a % of sales
Employees per dollar of sales
Ratio of line to staff
Personnel acquisitions or reductions

MANUFACTURING —Plant expansion
Plant capacity and utilization
Quality levels on production
Inventory requirements
Operating cost ratios—labor, material overhead

MARKETING —Major markets and customers—potential
sales force productivity
Sales and profit objectives by product line
Sources of new markets—new products

Modern Approaches to Administering Financial Planning and Strategy

	Promotional activity objectives
	Distribution channels—sales—inventories—customer service
	Out-of-stock requirements
	Complaints—returns—allowances
RESEARCH	—Basic research
	New products
	Quality control and product improvement

OBJECTIVE AND FUNCTION INTERFACING

Often one finds that objectives sound wonderful on paper or in the planning stage but when it comes to implementation you have some real problems. Let us examine one instance:

CASE IN POINT

This firm projected a fifteen-million dollar increase in sales volume. In comparing the unit production required under the plan it was found that capacity (present and contemplated) would fall eight-million dollars short of the target. Even with additional capacity that level of sales was unattainable due to the time factor for increasing productive capacity.

MANPOWER	—Do we have the skills and productivity required?
FINANCIAL	—Can we borrow enough money to cover the growth in plant, accounts receivables, inventories and personnel costs? Will our cash flow be adequate?
MANUFACTURING	—Do we have the plant capacity in the right places? Can we warehouse the required inventories in the right places?
MARKETING	—Will promotion produce the anticipated sales volume? Is our sales force and distributive organization large enough? What happens if competition cuts prices—introduces new products?
GENERAL	—Do we have a flexible system that will enable us to adapt to changing conditions? Do we have a defensive plan for back-up? Are all of the phases of the business coordinated and interfaced properly so that each knows the objectives of the other units? Do we have communication to make certain that the feedback of essential data will be available to all units?

MANAGEMENT BY OBJECTIVE

Management by objective is the "in" concept today. The majority of the larger firms are using it successfully. There are some programs that are failing miserably primarily because the managers fail to understand the underlying concept of objectives. They accept it as a normal "top management" toy and go along for the ride without really understanding why it is successful. The major problem is to make the managers look objectively at what they are doing! It also brings out a meaningful interpretation of what the figures mean and their relationship with the other units of the organization. Frankly speaking: "It spells it out!"

144 Modern Approaches to Administering Financial Planning and Strategy

Most managers resent the management-by-objective approach simply because they have to go on record with an objective and a plan. They feel that they cannot win or that they will be severely punished if they fail to meet the objective targets. They feel that it hampers their freedom to operate under difficult conditions.

PREPARING THE PLAN—ANNUAL OR LONG-RANGE

1. You must standardize by having a manual that gives both procedures and standard format.
2. You must have a planning timetable—preliminary review, adjustments, finalizing and presentation.
3. You should have forms available for each phase of the business.
    a. Financial
    b. Executive—Directors
    c. Manufacturing
    d. Marketing
    e. Personnel
    f. Research and Development
    g. Other
4. Bench marks for evaluating plans and objectives.
5. Is it optimistic or pessimistic? Does it conform with market and economic conditions?
6. Is it fair? Are we trying to stretch it too far?
7. Timetable for reports, responsibility for preparation and review.
8. Detail of the required items by phase or division.
9. One-on-one or team approach—spell it out!
10. How interdepartmental interfacing will be accomplished.
11. What the final plan is to be.

MONITORING A PLAN

In order to make any plan effective and operational you must develop ways and means for monitoring performance and reporting deviations to all affected parties. Perhaps the best way to do this is to start with the marketing division:

1. Monitor sales—volume by days, weeks, months.
2. Monitor sales by market—by customer, by product line, by individual product.
3. Production by sales force—territory, individual salesman.

Next in line would be the monitoring of production facilities. These are only representative items and not all-inclusive:

1. Plant utilization—percent of performance, unusual breakdowns.
2. Is anticipated additional capacity on schedule?
3. Are costs in line with projections?
4. Do we have adequate personnel—are turnover rates, absenteeism normal?

Modern Approaches to Administering Financial Planning and Strategy 145

Financing probably would be next in line for monitoring. Here we have the following items:

1. Are we creating sufficient cash flow? Are we having problems financing receivables, inventories or servicing debt? Are we handling our accounts payables properly so that our creditors will continue to service us as a valued customer?
2. How is the ROI, percent profit to sales? Are costs being kept current? Are the reports coming out on time?

OFFENSIVE PLANS

1. What do we do to meet demand if sales exceed targets? Do we have a plan of action?
2. Do we have a plan to shift markets if unexpected profit potentials develop?

DEFENSIVE PLANS

1. What happens if sales fall below targets? What action do we take?
2. What happens if some of our facilities are damaged by fire? Closed by strikes within or without the firm?
3. What happens if there is a rail or truck strike?
4. What happens if parts supplies or raw materials do not arrive on schedule?
5. What happens if we run out of money?
6. What happens if competition drops the price below our costs?
7. What happens if our productivity falls or costs increase?
8. Suppose key executives leave or die?
9. Who decides when to "trigger" the alternate plans? Who implements them?

LET'S LOOK AT A MARKETING PLAN

First off, the plan must tell us all about our sales program—who the customers are, where they are and how much we anticipate selling them. This must be implemented by data on who will sell them and the distributive functions involved in those sales.

1. Who are our customers?
2. What do they need? How can we supply these needs?
3. Is the market static, growing or declining?
4. What are the prospects for each customer for the next five years?
5. What prices are they paying? What are the prospects for price increases over the next five years?
6. What is our vulnerability to competition?
7. What influences this customer's sales?
8. Do we have a profit and loss for each product and for each customer?

9. Is the account profitable? Has it always been?
10. Historical sales data by product—by customer—five years.
11. Possibility of selling new products. Are we overlooking any customer needs or opportunities?

In planning sales and possible marketing strategies, the sales manager must have a clear picture of the current sales volume and the rate at which it is changing. He must take into consideration seasonal patterns and marketing trends. It is in this area that the computer and minicomputer can be of greatest assistance. With this type of a tool he can apply statistical techniques and with the new graphic terminals project or graph the rate at which the trend is changing. This will enable him to better utilize his manpower and alert the production division to changes in requirements for merchandise and inventory stocks.

Through the use of models he can relate his future sales demands to easily predictable factors and project financial, manpower, distribution and inventory requirements for all levels of activity. Models make it increasingly easy to change any factor, price, cost, shortage, inventory and come up with the anticipated reaction to such change.

Too often we have great swings in demand wherein customers fearing shortages have overordered or overbought. When the markets collapsed we had a great deal of distressed merchandise on hand. Inventories were written down as prices fell under the pressure to liquidate for cash. Often what you sell in one period can affect your sales at a later date. *Every marketing plan needs a monitoring system that reaches down to the final customer level.* This type of sampling can keep you out of trouble and save a great deal of money.

Every marketing plan must include an analysis of its basic function to see if anything has happened or is about to happen which has changed it. Failure to adapt to change is a serious marketing error.

WHAT CAN PLANNING DO FOR YOU?

In one instance it produced profits to liquidate a staggering debt load. It enabled the firm to survive a two-hundred-fifty-million dollar decline in pre-tax income.

In another instance it sharpened management techniques to the point that it enabled them to cut two full-time purchasing departments into one. The one only operates during certain hours of the day and not every day during the week.

In the majority of cases management by objective and planning has either produced increased profitable operations, enabled them to take advantage of profitable opportunities or cut costs dramatically. Something happens when you plan. One firm instituted a crash course in planning for its managers. The results were dramatic. Within one year the ROI had increased from 8% to 20%. Other firms have been able to reduce personnel and costs from 20% to 50%. Firms are becoming more sophisticated in allocating resources and increasing their ROI.

Planning has developed from a mere system of putting numbers together to a dynamic science of analyzing and running a business. When you finish the annual plan you have a "consensus" opinion and objectivity in running the firm. This type of teamwork is bound to have a dramatic effect on your operations.

Modern Approaches to Administering Financial Planning and Strategy

FIVE STEPS IN OBJECTIVE PLANNING

1. Improve profit margins to create the capital to operate with.
2. Then start to grow—secure your financing for long-term growth.
3. Improve your use of materials.
4. Improve your personnel productivity.
5. Improve your ROI.

FINANCIAL PLANNING—RESULTS

"Financial planning has resulted in a major strengthening of Signal's balance sheet, including a substantial reduction in future debt retirement obligations. The safety, liquidity and high returns obtained in 1974 from the proceeds of the sale of our oil and gas operations are other examples of coordinated financial planning."

Financial planning enabled one firm's profits to grow 30% annually. Thinking things over resulted in upgrading commodity items into sophisticated intermediate products producing a vastly higher profit margin.

Another instance indicated that a joint venture with another firm would enable both of them to secure needed raw materials. Neither could afford an individual plant. This type of planning secures a steady source of supply without relying on outside suppliers and has the added benefit of lower raw material costs.

LET'S LOOK AT OBJECTIVES—WHAT ARE THE BASIC REQUIREMENTS?

1. They must be explicit.
2. They must have a timetable for achievement.
3. Naturally they must be objective and specific.
4. They must relate to the other phases of the business.
5. *They are the very basics of management*. Without objectives you are lost!
6. Those who establish them should have the authority and responsibility to achieve them.
7. Policies are the guidelines for objectives.
8. Monitors and reports are the scorecards.

THE NEW BREED OF CATS

Operating within the corporate structure today we have a new breed of intelligent young chargers called "knowledge specialists." One firm has over 300 individuals in this classification with over 90 of them residing in the financial administrator's domain. This group makes extensive use of computers and a computer model specialist. We have the following classifications:

1. Senior Knowledge Specialist.
2. Middle Management Knowledge Specialist.

148 Modern Approaches to Administering Financial Planning and Strategy

    3. Financial Knowledge Specialist.

    4. Computer Knowledge Specialist.

    5. Tax Knowledge Specialist.

Somehow they seemed to have expanded like bacteria on a culture plate as they delve into international economics, parametric growth curves, political implications of elections in India or Israel, and algebraic relationships with the environment. Like most "think tanks" they range way out. The financial knowledge specialists produce an annual business plan in binders one inch thick and quarterly revisions one-half inch thick. They not only project the profits and ROI required right now but also what they are seeking five years hence. This business is segmented into about twenty separate units and each unit has its complete and complex plan. They raise one point which is worthy of consideration: "How much of your business is actually under management control?" It appears that there are only four or five major options available to you.

LONG-RANGE PLANNING

During the past five to ten years the growth in long-range planning among most firms has been phenomenal. The use of computers and their ability to react quickly to changes that would have taken innumerable man hours to digest previously has raised both the acceptance and use of planning into a major corporate financial function. While it undoubtedly has had a major effect on profits, there is a great deal of difficulty in measuring the exact amount of the profit contribution. This has given its opponents somewhat of a wedge in fighting it as a "gimmick."

Basically we can define and spell out the *long-range plan* as follows:

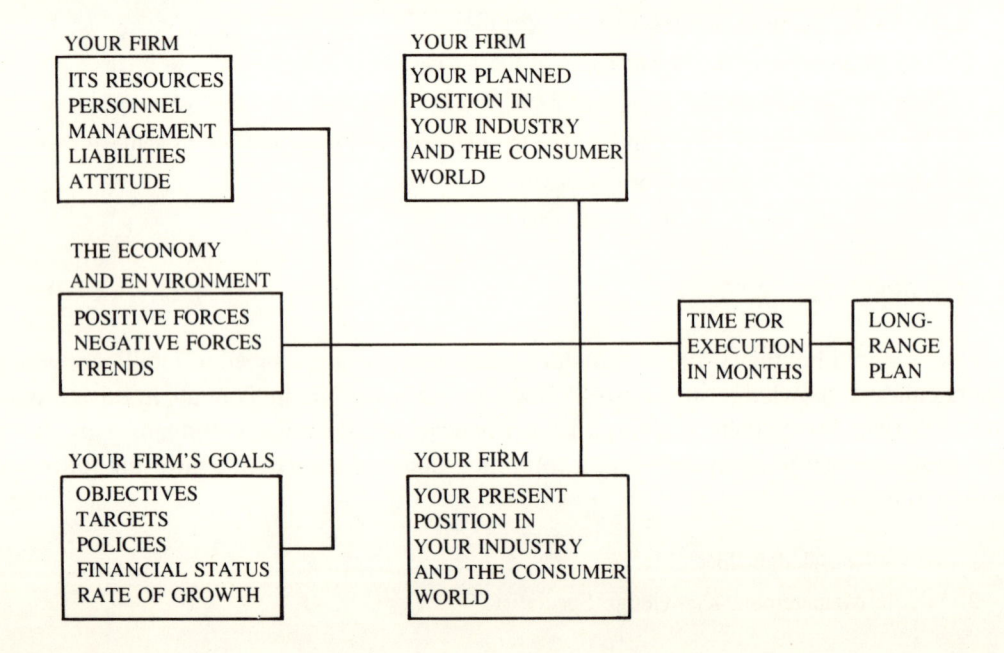

```
YOUR FIRM                           YOUR FIRM
┌─────────────────┐                 ┌──────────────────┐
│ ITS RESOURCES   │                 │ YOUR PLANNED     │
│ PERSONNEL       │                 │ POSITION IN      │
│ MANAGEMENT      │─────────┐       │ YOUR INDUSTRY    │
│ LIABILITIES     │         │       │ AND THE CONSUMER │
│ ATTITUDE        │         │       │ WORLD            │
└─────────────────┘         │       └──────────────────┘
                            │                │
THE ECONOMY                 │                │
AND ENVIRONMENT             │                │
┌─────────────────┐         │                │       ┌──────────┐   ┌────────┐
│ POSITIVE FORCES │         │                │       │ TIME FOR │   │ LONG-  │
│ NEGATIVE FORCES │─────────┼────────────────┼───────│ EXECUTION│───│ RANGE  │
│ TRENDS          │         │                │       │ IN MONTHS│   │ PLAN   │
└─────────────────┘         │                │       └──────────┘   └────────┘
                            │                │
YOUR FIRM'S GOALS           │       YOUR FIRM
┌─────────────────┐         │       ┌──────────────────┐
│ OBJECTIVES      │         │       │ YOUR PRESENT     │
│ TARGETS         │         │       │ POSITION IN      │
│ POLICIES        │─────────┘       │ YOUR INDUSTRY    │
│ FINANCIAL STATUS│                 │ AND THE CONSUMER │
│ RATE OF GROWTH  │                 │ WORLD            │
└─────────────────┘                 └──────────────────┘
```

Modern Approaches to Administering Financial Planning and Strategy 149

STRATEGIES

It is in the area of strategy that most plans fail. This is without a doubt the most difficult and intriguing part of the entire planning process. It is analogous to a war or a chess game—as the enemy moves you must counter immediately. Strategy calls for attack, holding or retreat. Change is ever present and the ability to meet these changes with strategies that are acceptable and profitable is a constant challenge to your planning and monitoring group. In most instances strategy will concern external forces developing outside of your firm; however, the application of these forces upon the resources or manpower of the firm can create the need for dealing with internal forces, and strategy plans must be formulated for this type of crisis. In my humble opinion, shared by many financial administrators, the formulation of successful strategies, implementing them and seeing them work is one of the most interesting and fascinating parts of financial tasks. The thrill of success is hard to beat and that sinking feeling that occurs when strategies fail is beyond expression. If the failure is a major one the old adage applies: "Here today—gone tomorrow!" Your track record had better be *good!*

HOW DO FINANCIAL EXECUTIVES DEVELOP STRATEGIES?

1. First, you determine what your current strategies are, if any.
2. Screen the present strategies, keep the best, discard the poorer ones.
3. Develop an intelligence unit within your operation. Let it be fairly broad based with all phases of the operation represented. The size of the unit will depend upon the size of the organization.
4. Set this "task analysis" or "intelligence" group to work identifying and classifying your current problems.
5. The group should attempt to forecast future problems which may be encountered in a time span of one to five years ahead.
6. Examine current performance against plans and attempt to analyze and record any problems or opportunities which are developing.
7. If serious problems are encountered make a thorough analysis and study of their causes and recommend immediate remedial action.
8. Set up "What if?" alternate strategies under the following categories:
   O—Optimistic—aggressive
   N—Normal, proceeding according to plan
   C—Conservative—holding stage
   E—Exodus—get out fast!
   S—*Shrink*, the future looks tough!
9. Evaluate each of the alternate strategies and develop plans for implementing them. Determine what effect each will have upon your future stability, financial position and growth.
10. Prepare a *disaster* alternative
11. Look forward into the future and set up new strategies for the years ahead.

The crux of the entire planning process is in its ability to spot developing problems and provide alternate solutions for them. Taking your business apart piece by piece as you

150 Modern Approaches to Administering Financial Planning and Strategy

develop the plans and strategies will give you an insight into the very basics of your operations. It is here that the problems are created. To counter these problems you must have an effective method of solving strategic problems. You must know the effect of these items upon your firm's resources and manpower. You must be able to develop a competitive advantage from the solution to these problems. Last but not least, the solutions should not create greater problems than existed prior to the solution. This is one fallacy inherent in government planning: "The solutions create greater problems than we had before we applied the solution!"

THE MOUSETRAPS—HOW TO SPOT THEM

1. Absence of top management support—this is almost always fatal.
2. Resistance—there are those who like to plan for the other guy, but no one is going to plan for me.
3. No manuals, standardized procedures or guidelines.
4. Failure to communicate or interface—everyone must be on the team and the team must have a common objective. You cannot sell it if production does not have the capacity to produce it.
5. Too elaborate plans—start off simple and grow into a good planning and strategy system.
6. Lack of knowledge—it takes time and effort to teach everyone what it is all about. A clear understanding of what the process is will reduce the friction and resistance. Use simple terms.
7. The plan may not be possible of achievement—strategies may be wrong or too elaborate. Set up critical reviews by top management and make certain that all elements mesh into a workable strategy or plan.
8. Resistance to change—there is a latent hostility in everyone; this can result in crucial confrontations or actual sabotage of strategies and plans.
9. Just plain errors—one firm predicted sales would rise 10%; actually, they fell 7%. Another firm forecast interest rates of 8%; actually, they went to 12%.

FLEXIBILITY

Above all you must stress flexibility in planning to cope with changes and contingencies. The world is a constantly changing place with external forces well beyond the control of any group or industry. To survive and be successful you must have a *game plan*. You must learn to react quickly. If you miss your objectives or targets at least *react!*

GENERALITIES

Plans and strategies provide information on the following topics:

1. What goes on now.
2. What possibilities exist—now—in the future.
3. What obstacles you have to overcome—now—in the future.

Modern Approaches to Administering Financial Planning and Strategy

Plans provide the following:

1. Well-thought-out objectives, targets, policies for initiating performance. They provide performance measures and information sources. They provide a descriptive, concise statement of the existing objectives and plans for the operation of each cost or profit center and each organizational unit of the entire corporate entity.
2. Good planning prevents hostility among corporate entities.

When measuring the performance of or analyzing a corporation one finds vast differences in personnel, allocation of vital resources or performance, he can be certain that something is wrong with the strategy and planning function of that firm.

WHAT ARE THE STRATEGIC FACTORS OF A BUSINESS?

Interviews with several financial administrators brought out a list of over 100 strategic factors that they felt were of importance in the planning and operations of their firms. We have streamlined this to 20 of what we felt were the most important items. They are not necessarily listed in the order of importance in the strategic field:

1. Top management—have it or secure it.
2. Sound, stable organization—efficient operating personnel.
3. Middle management talent—intelligence—have it or secure it.
4. A good short-term and long-term planning process.
5. Computerized forecasting and control.
6. A high-caliber intelligence or "task analysis" group.
7. A constant flow of new products and new processes.
8. The ability to take risks—an aggressive organization.
9. Operations profitable—ROI high.
10. Thorough knowledge of markets and customers.
11. Good communications—excellent interfacing.
12. Low costs—quality products.
13. Adequate capital—available credit. Financially sound.
14. Adequate or controlled material sources.
15. Ability to meet changing conditions—flexible.
16. Efficient plant—ability to produce on time.
17. Ability to sell and service customers.
18. Ingenuity in advertising and promotion.
19. Technologically alert.
20. Ability to make and implement decisions.

THE DELPHI THEORY

To avoid the effects of one individual or a group of individuals dominating the planning process Dr. Olaf Helmer developed what is known as the Delphi Technique or method. It is now widely used by industry in its long-range or futuristic planning processes. A series of questions are fed to a group of experts who may be located within one firm or spread across the world as the case may be. The results of the query are then analyzed by computer and fed back to the experts. Each is then requested to restate his position and to explain why it varies from the majority opinion. Again the data is fed back and results reanalyzed until a consensus is apparently reached. Although the process is not infallible it is far more accurate and reliable than the opinions or judgements of one or two individuals. It will be applied to the problems or plans of the individual firms in setting up their strategies, objectives and plans. It is undoubtedly one of the best ways for industry to keep abreast of the future in economics and technological advances. Great strides have already been made in the technology and environmental fields by futuristic planners.

THE DEVELOPMENT OF STRATEGIC ORGANIZATIONS

The financial administrator with his access to data, business knowledge and computer techniques has a golden opportunity to become the strategic "king pin" in the new strategic organizations that are developing. There is a trend because of the success of strategic planning to develop an entire organization dedicated to making it work. The success of some firms in using the process has begun to filter down throughout industry. The financial fiasco of 1975 and 1976 hastened the development and adoption of the concept. Every firm must concentrate on allocating its resources to the best advantage and must tightly control and measure the results of such allocation. This is *strategic planning!* Profit centers, departments, divisions and personnel of all types must have their performance measured and their compensation based upon the assets they manage and their success in achieving the corporate goals.

CASE IN POINT

Quoted from the annual report of one of the banks: "During 1976 a sophisticated financial planning modeling system was installed. It makes possible the quick determination of the future impact of a multitude of variables that can affect the bank's financial condition and profitability. The model was used extensively during the year and enabled management to anticipate rather than react to significant internal and external changes. It is proving an invaluable tool in refining our profit planning process and in enhancing asset and liability management techniques."

AVAILABLE TOOLS

You have available computerized planning and strategy systems that will enable you to:

Modern Approaches to Administering Financial Planning and Strategy 153

1. Run summary or detailed projections.
2. Change plans—summary items or detailed.
3. Maximize options—point out alternatives.
4. Reproject—summary or in detail—within a limited time span.
5. Perform exhaustive and detailed analyses by function.
6. Time span analysis
   1 to 6 months—daily
   1 to 24 months—by month
   1 to 60 months—quarterly
   any number of years—annually
7. You can adjust for price level changes, demand changes and shifts in the economy.
8. These are the techniques:
   a. Delphi
   b. Historical analysis of items and comparable products
   c. Management judgments
   d. Input/output relationships
   e. Priority basis
   f. Available resource basis
   g. Time series analysis
   h. Econometric models
   i. Simulation models
   j. Strategic models

Through the use of computer techniques you can determine product life cycles, product design, facilities to produce given quantities of products—adequate, new or expansion. You can determine the size of markets, determine the effect of advertising and promotion, specials new product tests and prices. You can test various packaging sizes, shapes or colors. Most of all you can determine sales trends and inventory requirements, when and where.

STRATEGIC PLANNING IS HERE TO STAY

As an alert financial administrator you must consider a shift in emphasis from strictly financial operations to a strategic planning posture. In a world of variables—economic, political, energy and government—the emphasis is upon strategic planning for profits, growth and even survival. You have the basic knowledge, the ability, the equipment and the technology available. Do you have the courage and aggressiveness to make the change and become head of the new strategic organization? The risks are high! The rewards immense! Perhaps due to our financial conservatism we will be unable to adjust to the aggressive strategic planning of tomorrow. *I hope not!*

ZERO-BASED BUDGETING

Peter Pyhrr created the concept of Zero-Based Budgeting based upon a comment by Arthur Burns, Chairman of the Federal Reserve Board that government expenditures could be reduced if each agency was required to justify its request for its entire appropriation each year. The concept while radical in nature has tremendous merit. Its strict application can force answers to tough questions about every departmental function and the personnel required to staff it. It forces a critical review of the allocation of resources and the priorities involved. It precludes continuation of the activity just because it existed in the prior year. While I personally am not thoroughly convinced that an annual dissection is required for every phase of the operation, I am convinced that a complete justification of each activity should be made every third to fifth year. Assigning of priorities might occur at two- to three-year intervals.

INTERESTING READING

IMPLEMENTING ZERO-BASED BUDGETING
THE REAL WORLD

A Case Study

by Walter D. Hill, Controller
GENRAD, Inc.

Published by: The Planning Executives Institute
5500 College Corner Pike
Oxford, Ohio 45056

It was my privilege to be the founder and first president of the Institute.

CHECKLIST FOR KEEPING PLANNING AND STRATEGIES ON TARGET

1. Focus on the future—decisions are today—planning is for tomorrow and beyond.
2. Beware of underestimating in bad times and overestimating in good times. Salesmen are optimists, production executives pessimists.
3. Take into account the inflationary effect on large capital expenditures this year, next year and beyond. Make certain that future expenditures are realistic.
4. Consider the effects of inflation upon future operating costs and prices.
5. Keep top management involved and interested in the program.
6. Let everyone participate in the strategy and planning. It will give you better balance and realistic planning.
7. Do not overreact to economic trends, changes in the business cycle or competitive pressures. During good times prepare for a downturn and in slow periods get set to take full advantage of the upswing.
8. Set long-range goals first, then reduce them to shorten plans. Don't shoot the works for immediate profits and sacrifice the long-range objectives.
9. Keep it simple and flexible.
10. Go after the major items first, put your time in where the action and the profits are. Make certain that you are only dealing with vital data.

11. Check and recheck your assumptions. Make certain your data is as valid as possible under the circumstances.
12. Listen to dissent. In our eagerness to produce good tidings we often overlook the criticism or wisdom of the dissenter. Not everything will be good.
13. Listen to the experiences of the "other guy"; sometimes he can tip you off to newer methods or pitfalls in planning.
14. Occasionally look back—there may be some lessons in the past.

Without Intelligent Long-Range Planning
a Business Can Remain Static or Perish!

The Key to Sound Growth

Is

the Ability to Plan Ahead.

THE MANAGEMENT BOX

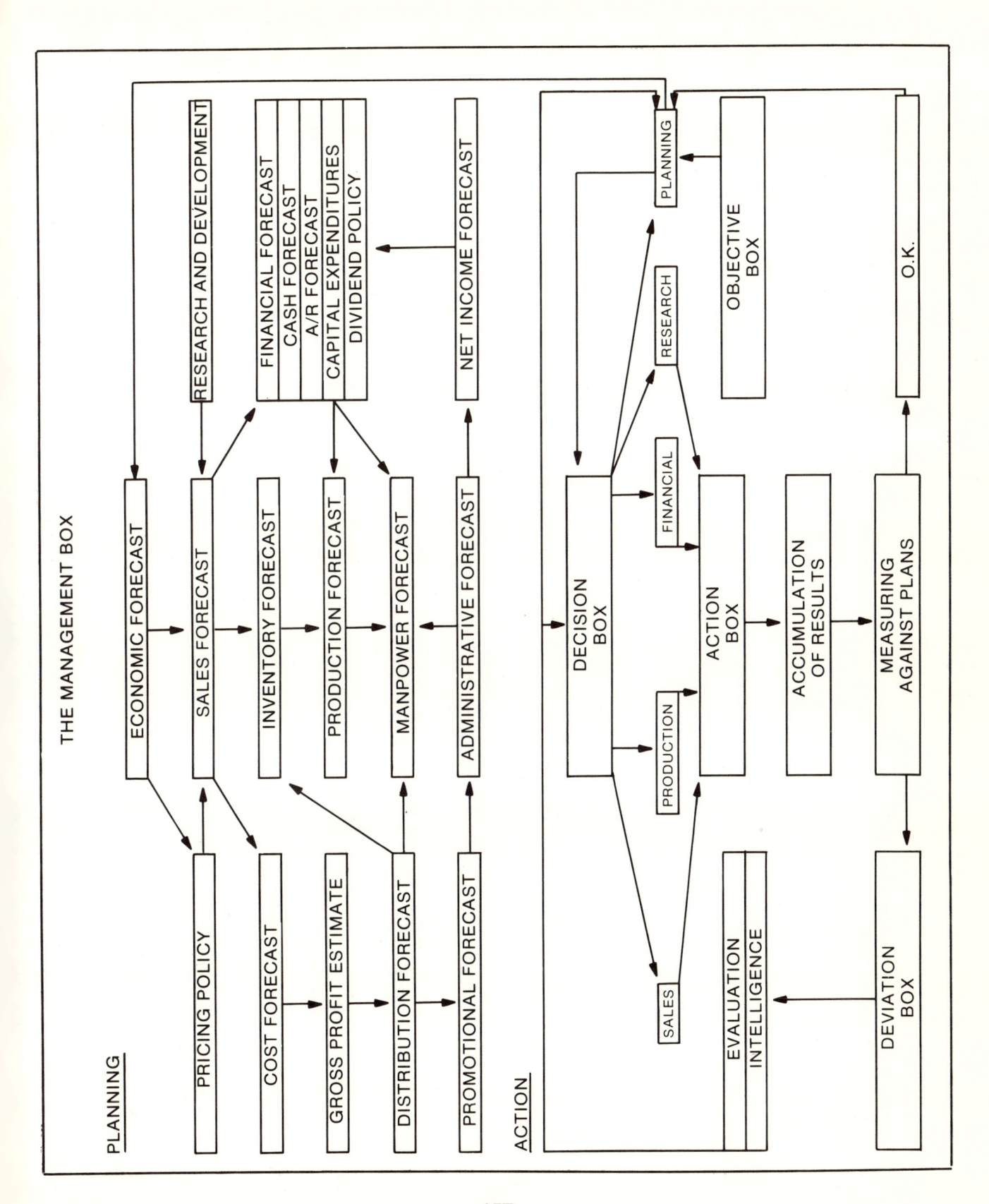

PLANNING

- ECONOMIC FORECAST
- RESEARCH AND DEVELOPMENT
- SALES FORECAST
- FINANCIAL FORECAST / CASH FORECAST / A/R FORECAST / CAPITAL EXPENDITURES / DIVIDEND POLICY
- INVENTORY FORECAST
- PRODUCTION FORECAST
- MANPOWER FORECAST
- ADMINISTRATIVE FORECAST
- NET INCOME FORECAST
- PRICING POLICY
- COST FORECAST
- GROSS PROFIT ESTIMATE
- DISTRIBUTION FORECAST
- PROMOTIONAL FORECAST

ACTION

- DECISION BOX
  - RESEARCH
  - FINANCIAL
  - PRODUCTION
  - SALES
- PLANNING
- OBJECTIVE BOX
- ACTION BOX
- ACCUMULATION OF RESULTS
- MEASURING AGAINST PLANS
- O.K.
- EVALUATION INTELLIGENCE
- DEVIATION BOX

157

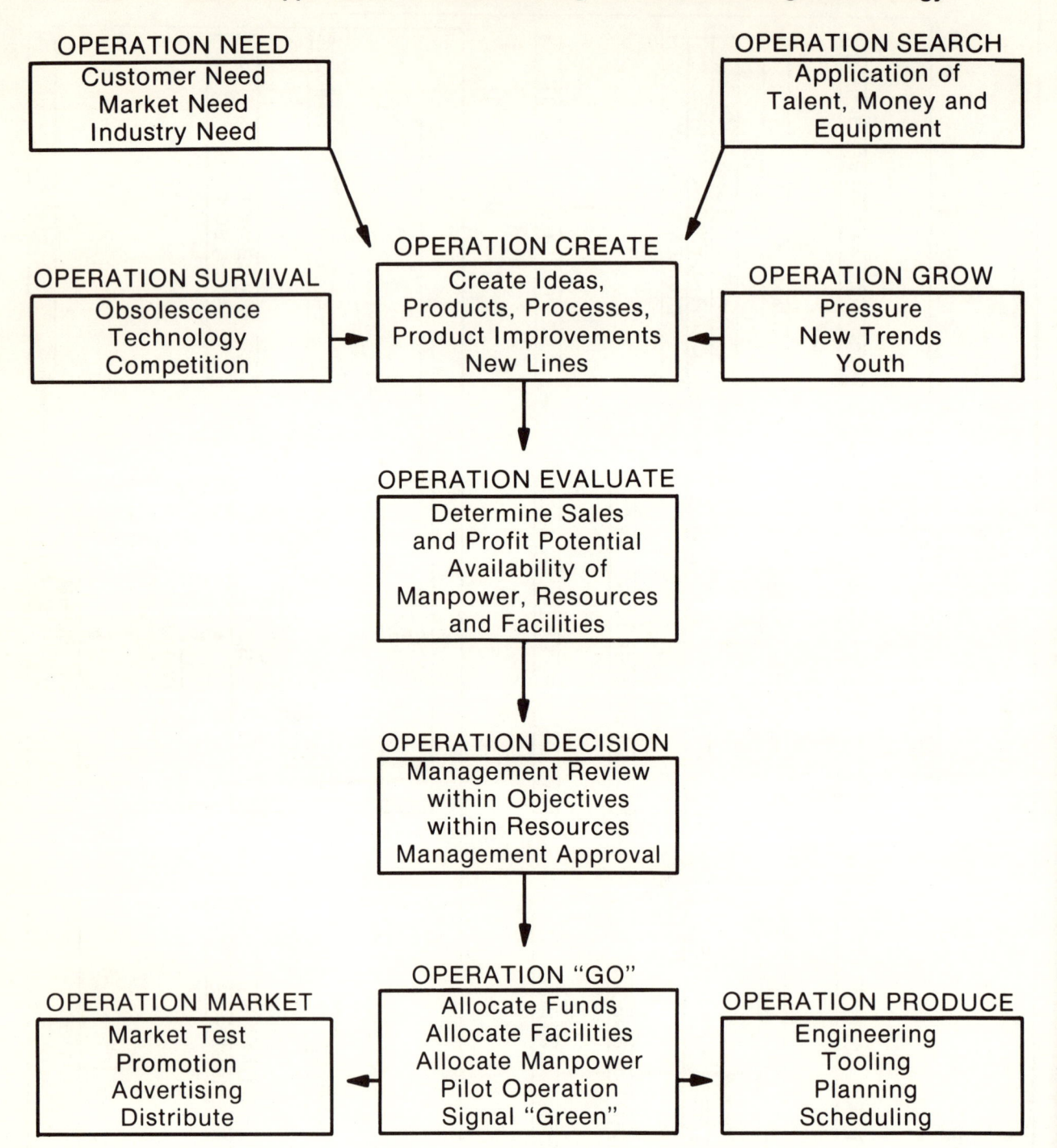

OPERATION NEED
- Customer Need
- Market Need
- Industry Need

OPERATION SEARCH
- Application of Talent, Money and Equipment

OPERATION SURVIVAL
- Obsolescence
- Technology
- Competition

OPERATION CREATE
- Create Ideas, Products, Processes, Product Improvements New Lines

OPERATION GROW
- Pressure
- New Trends
- Youth

OPERATION EVALUATE
- Determine Sales and Profit Potential Availability of Manpower, Resources and Facilities

OPERATION DECISION
- Management Review within Objectives within Resources Management Approval

OPERATION MARKET
- Market Test
- Promotion
- Advertising
- Distribute

OPERATION "GO"
- Allocate Funds
- Allocate Facilities
- Allocate Manpower
- Pilot Operation
- Signal "Green"

OPERATION PRODUCE
- Engineering
- Tooling
- Planning
- Scheduling

Modern Approaches to Administering Financial Planning and Strategy

Proper planning and strategic action emphasize the firm's strong points, and protect its weak spots and neutralize competitive strengths. It matches resources, markets, capabilities and manpower with strategy and economic conditions.

STRATEGY BOX

OPERATION PRESENT	OPERATION CAPABILITY	OPERATION FUTURE
Activity Economy Competition Technology Opportunity Problems	Potential Capacity Performance Efficiency Problems Capability	Potential Market Competitive Strength Advantages Disadvantages Rate of Growth Consumer Acceptance

Present Activity ⟶ Strategy To Move Forward

Present Objectives ⟶ New Objectives

Present Economy ⟶ Future Economy

Benchmark Now ⟶ Measuring Progress

Problems ⟶ Alternates

Troubles ⟶ Plan Revisions

Strategy For ⟶ Attack

⟶ Defense

⟶ Status Quo

160   Modern Approaches to Administering Financial Planning and Strategy

PROJECTING MANAGEMENT STRATEGY

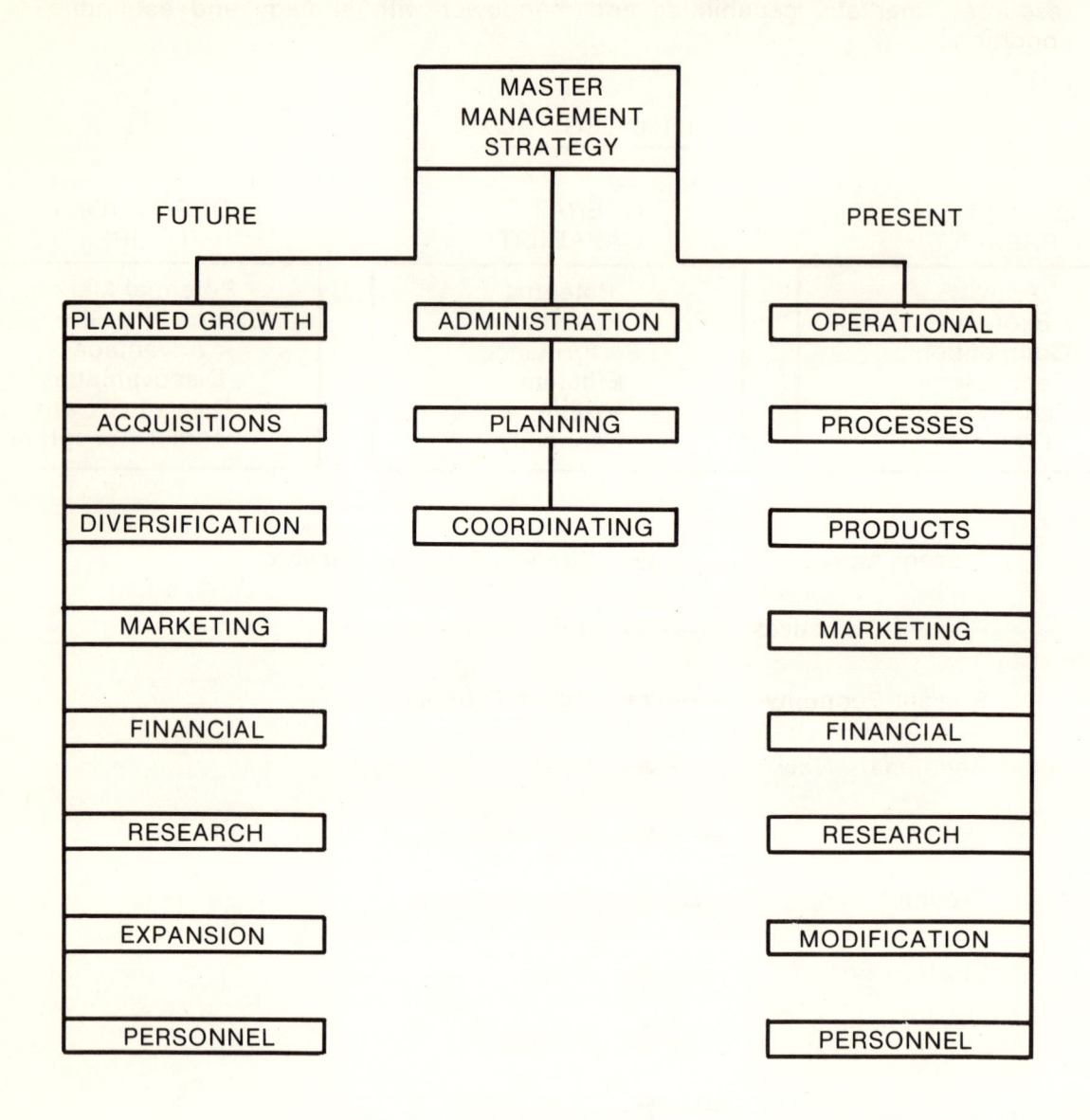

```
                        ┌─────────────┐
                        │   MASTER    │
                        │ MANAGEMENT  │
                        │  STRATEGY   │
                        └─────────────┘
      FUTURE                                       PRESENT

  ┌─────────────────┐  ┌─────────────────┐  ┌─────────────────┐
  │ PLANNED GROWTH  │  │ ADMINISTRATION  │  │   OPERATIONAL   │
  └─────────────────┘  └─────────────────┘  └─────────────────┘

  ┌─────────────────┐  ┌─────────────────┐  ┌─────────────────┐
  │   ACQUISITIONS  │  │    PLANNING     │  │    PROCESSES    │
  └─────────────────┘  └─────────────────┘  └─────────────────┘

  ┌─────────────────┐  ┌─────────────────┐  ┌─────────────────┐
  │ DIVERSIFICATION │  │   COORDINATING  │  │    PRODUCTS     │
  └─────────────────┘  └─────────────────┘  └─────────────────┘

  ┌─────────────────┐                       ┌─────────────────┐
  │    MARKETING    │                       │    MARKETING    │
  └─────────────────┘                       └─────────────────┘

  ┌─────────────────┐                       ┌─────────────────┐
  │    FINANCIAL    │                       │    FINANCIAL    │
  └─────────────────┘                       └─────────────────┘

  ┌─────────────────┐                       ┌─────────────────┐
  │    RESEARCH     │                       │    RESEARCH     │
  └─────────────────┘                       └─────────────────┘

  ┌─────────────────┐                       ┌─────────────────┐
  │    EXPANSION    │                       │  MODIFICATION   │
  └─────────────────┘                       └─────────────────┘

  ┌─────────────────┐                       ┌─────────────────┐
  │    PERSONNEL    │                       │    PERSONNEL    │
  └─────────────────┘                       └─────────────────┘
```

Modern Approaches to Administering Financial Planning and Strategy

PROJECTING RESEARCH STRATEGY

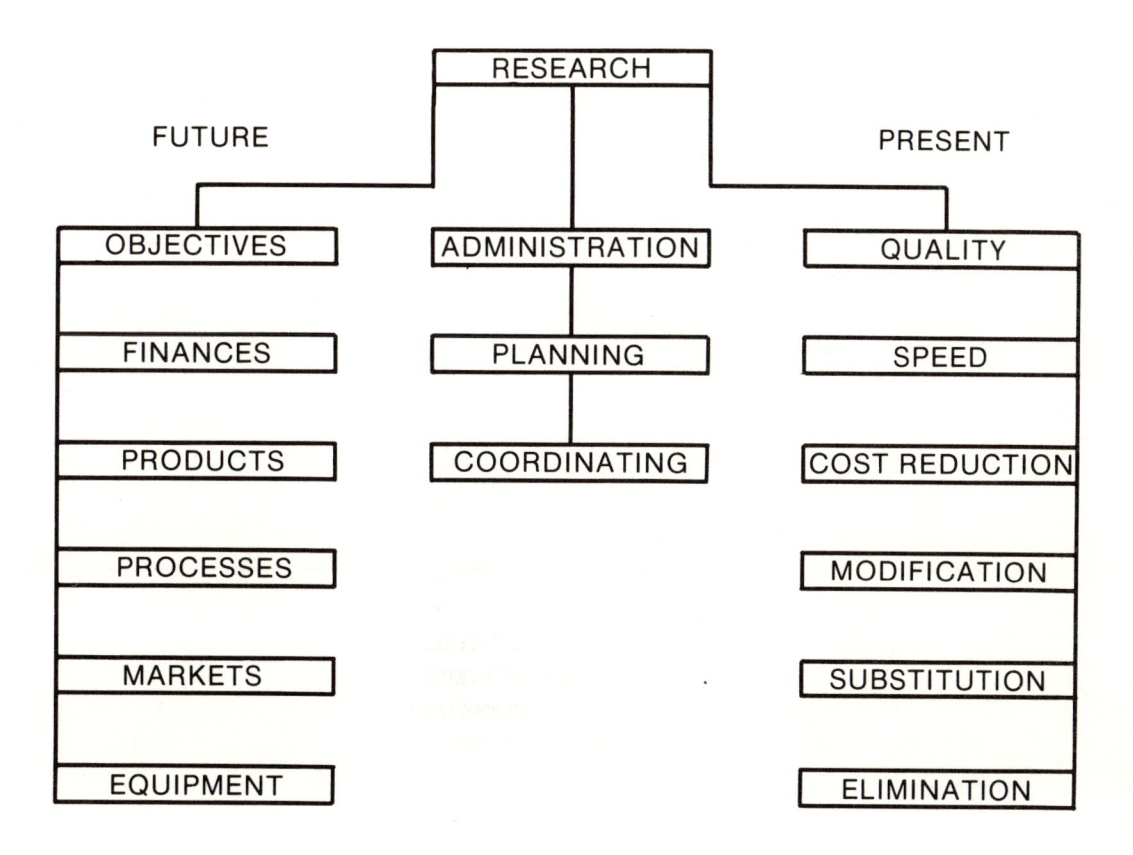

```
                        RESEARCH
          FUTURE           |            PRESENT
    ┌───────────────┬──────────────┬───────────────┐
    │  OBJECTIVES   │ ADMINISTRATION│    QUALITY    │

    │   FINANCES    │   PLANNING    │     SPEED     │

    │   PRODUCTS    │  COORDINATING │ COST REDUCTION│

    │   PROCESSES   │               │  MODIFICATION │

    │    MARKETS    │               │  SUBSTITUTION │

    │   EQUIPMENT   │               │  ELIMINATION  │
```

162 Modern Approaches to Administering Financial Planning and Strategy

Changing Strategy And Plans

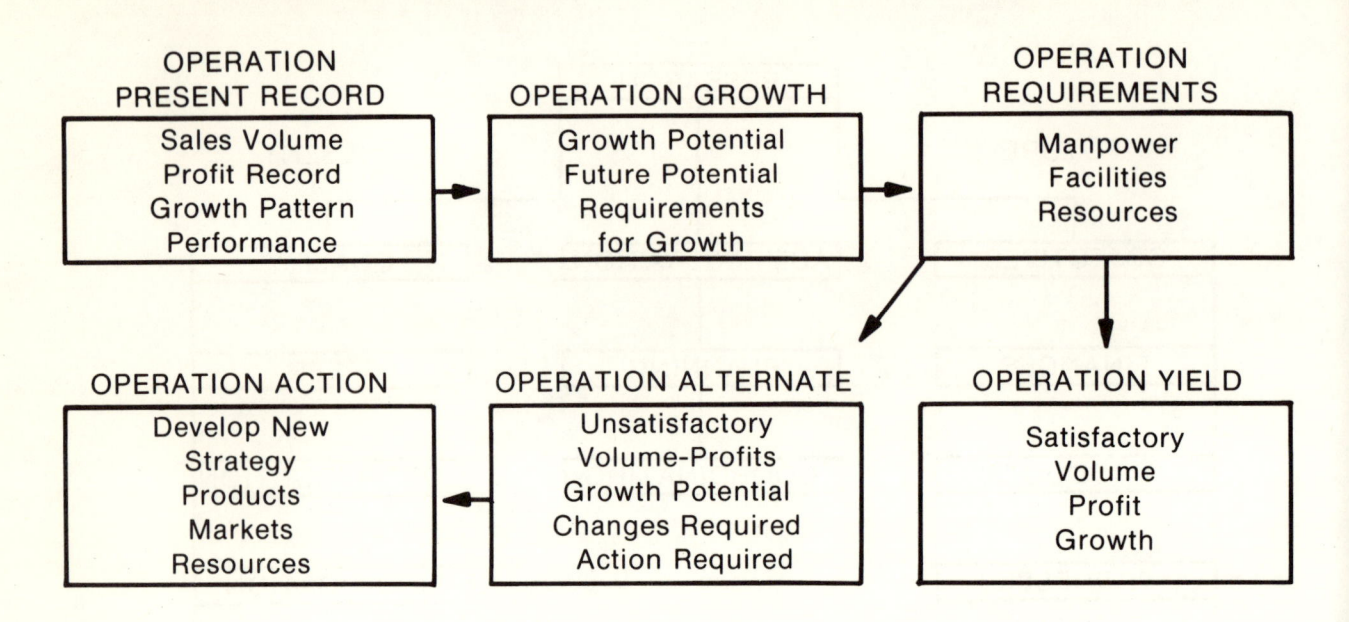

OPERATION PRESENT RECORD
- Sales Volume
- Profit Record
- Growth Pattern
- Performance

→

OPERATION GROWTH
- Growth Potential
- Future Potential
- Requirements for Growth

→

OPERATION REQUIREMENTS
- Manpower
- Facilities
- Resources

OPERATION ACTION
- Develop New
- Strategy
- Products
- Markets
- Resources

←

OPERATION ALTERNATE
- Unsatisfactory
- Volume-Profits
- Growth Potential
- Changes Required
- Action Required

OPERATION YIELD
- Satisfactory
- Volume
- Profit
- Growth

Alternate No. 1

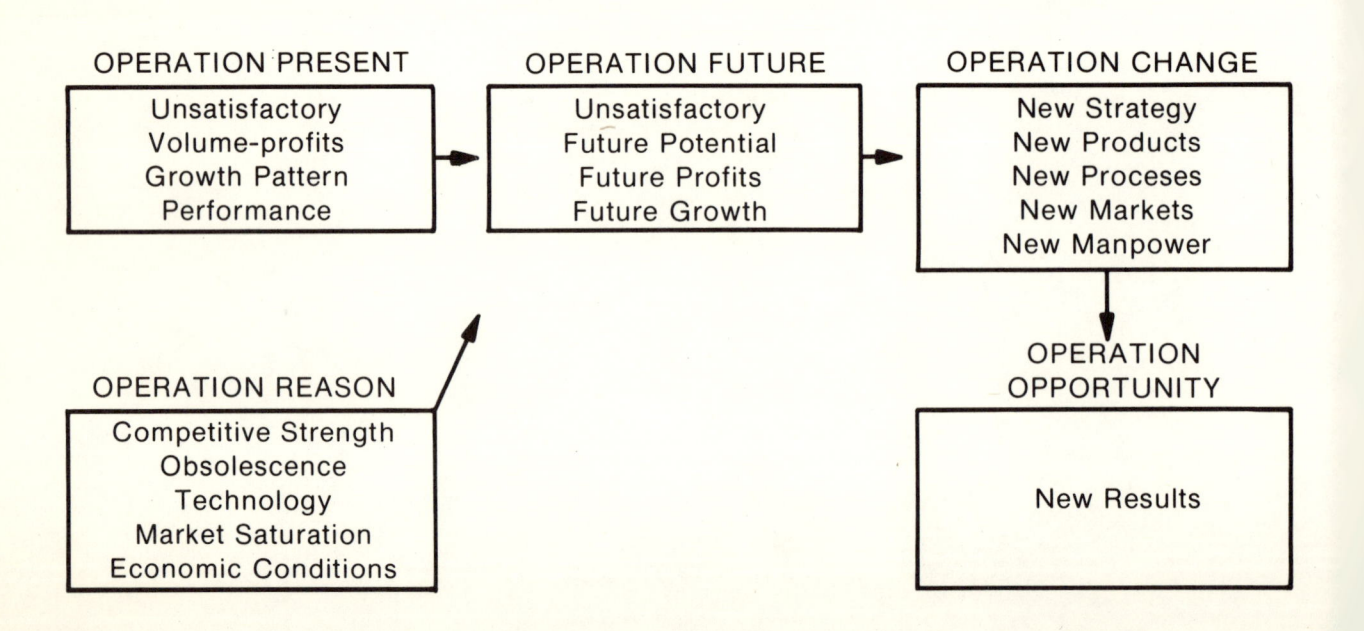

OPERATION PRESENT
- Unsatisfactory
- Volume-profits
- Growth Pattern
- Performance

→

OPERATION FUTURE
- Unsatisfactory
- Future Potential
- Future Profits
- Future Growth

→

OPERATION CHANGE
- New Strategy
- New Products
- New Processes
- New Markets
- New Manpower

OPERATION REASON
- Competitive Strength
- Obsolescence
- Technology
- Market Saturation
- Economic Conditions

OPERATION OPPORTUNITY

New Results

Modern Approaches to Administering Financial Planning and Strategy

Plan for Strategic Plant Location

N = Need
S = Start
A = Act
T = Time
C = Complete

N—Four Strategically Located Plants.

T 1—Year 1.	a - S —	Initiate market, cost and strategic location survey.
	b - A —	Present results of survey to Board of Directors for approval.
	c - S —	Directors request plant cost and feasibility report.
	d - A —	Reports furnished Directors.
	e - C —	Project approved—green light.
	f - S —	Appoint plant planning team.
	g - A —	Plant sites inspected and approved.
	h - A —	Property purchased—architects hired—plans approved—contracts let.
T 2—Year 2.	i - S —	Break up planning into major functions—each location. Equipment—personnel—purchasing—community relations—transportation—trouble-shooters.
	j - A —	Appoint individuals in charge of functions.
	k - C —	Progress reports for each site, each function.
	l - S —	Planning for production start-up in completed plants.
	m - C —	Construction completions.
T 3—Year 3.	n - A —	Trial runs on production lines.
	o - A —	Hire employees.
	p - A —	Shift personnel from old plants.
	q - A —	Switch over management and accounting functions.
	r - C —	Start production and shipments.

6

The Use of Financial Models by the Financial Administrator

Today we all live in a world of computers and computer models. A short time ago if you wished to utilize a computer model you had to develop your own. The financial administrator of today has an easier task. In this day and age, simple to sophisticated models, systems and modeling assistance are readily available. From that point on he can exercise his own ingenuity.

Basically models fall into about five major classifications:

1. *Strategic*—covering basic strategic planning.
2. *Operational*—covering operational results or changes.
3. *Analytical*—covering all types of problems—providing the answers to "What if?" questions.
4. *Forecasting*—covering the projections of the economy, financial forecasts, operational forecasts and capital expenditure projections.
5. *Long Range/Short Range*—varying time cycles.

CORPORATE MODELS

One might well ask the question: "Why should I as a financial administrator be interested in models"? The answer is relatively simple! With the widespread and growing use of computers, modeling has become the "in thing" in the financial world. Thousands of firms are using them as their managements begin to realize the effectiveness and flexibility of the models to provide fast answers to changes in policy, economic conditions, strategy, manpower, costs, competition or operations. They have become a life saver for corporate executives struggling with the huge and terrifying problems of economic uncertainty, changing monetary policies, price instability, material or energy shortages, environmental regulations and a rapidly changing business world.

Our interviews indicate that financial executives are the top users of models. This is due in part because the basic data originate in the financial sector. The demand for the information originates at the top or laterally from the heads of other sectors and it becomes the prime responsibility of the financial executive to provide ready answers. In fact, your survival as a financial administrator may well depend upon your knowledge and ability to develop models which will answer the ever present queries of top management.

Financial executives can use models to achieve success (or failure!). The modeling field represents an opportunity to solve real business problems without committing funds or excessive time. Models also should provide a method for indicating the various alternate courses or options available.

We found that among the larger firms six out of ten were utilizing models in some form or other. In the medium-sized firms the percentage dropped to 25%, and in the smaller firms the use of models was as low as 2%.

WHAT SPECIFIC TYPES OF MODELS ARE USED?

1. Corporate Financial Model
2. Planning or Strategy Models
3. Sales Forecasting
4. Production Forecasting
5. Manpower Scheduling
6. Cash Flow Projections
7. Macro-Economic Forecasting
8. Lease/Buy Analysis
9. "What if?" Situations
10. ROI Projections and Studies
11. System Design Models
12. Optimum Business Type Models

ANSWERS TO INTERVIEWS—WHAT IS A MODEL? WHAT DOES IT DO?

The model creates an awareness of the interlocking relationship of each part of the organization and its part in creating profits and achieving corporate goals.

It is a mathematical and scientific approach to the solution of real world business problems. It enables the financial executive to project any portion of his business into the future. By manipulating, substituting or changing the various factors he can then simulate the reaction of our effect on his firm to the various anticipated changes.

The Use of Financial Models by the Financial Administrator

The computer is merely a tool which extends man's mind and experience a thousandfold in assisting his mental model to sort, arrange and classify the many factors involved in modeling and to retain these factors in an orderly, logical way or manner until the solution of the problem is obtained.

Intuition and experience are inadequate to deal with the complex problems being encountered today. By using computers and models to simulate response to problems, you can produce realistic solutions for management policy making and action.

Business is a series of ever recurring problems. They start with the initial plan to start a business, buy, lease or build a plant, equip it with the proper equipment (also buy, lease or build) and obtain the manpower to staff it. The cycle starts with the first order and continues until payment is made on the goods shipped to the customer. Problems arise in the areas of pricing, costs, deliveries, too much or too little inventory, cash, orders, competitive pressures, customer service and so on in an endless procession. The Lord willing and with a lot of elbow grease and luck, the computer may help solve the financial and operating executive's dilemma of matching volume, prices and costs into a smooth-running, profitable organization.

WHAT PURPOSE DO MODELS SERVE?

1. They generate a picture of the financial position of the firm over a short-and long-term basis. They project the operating results and the need for capital to expand and still maintain the proper relationship between assets and liabilities.
2. Evaluate the impact of corporate goals, objectives and strategies upon the financial resources of the firm.
3. Project corporate capacity requirements needed to meet sales objectives.
4. Test alternate strategies and options.
5. Forecast the results of business volume or price changes.
6. Budget and control operations.
7. Schedule equipment, materials and manpower most effectively.
8. Forecast sales volumes.
9. Forecast cash flow.
10. Prepare or modify long-range forecasts as changes occur.

WHO USES THE MODELS?

1.	Accounting/Finance	35%
2.	Scientific	19%
3.	Economic Forecasting	20%
4.	Engineering and Design—R and D	20%
5.	Miscellaneous Uses	6%
		100%

WHAT ARE THE MAJOR MODELING TECHNIQUES?

1. *Discounting Technique*— Lease/Buy—Cash Flow—Risk Analysis—ROI.
2. *Simulation*— Corporate Financial Forecasting—Sales and Production Forecasting—Pricing—Budgeting, Planning and Control—Project or Venture Analysis.

WHAT IS A FINANCIAL MODEL?

It is a model which utilizes one or more financial items such as sales, production or capital investment for planning, strategy, analysis or comparison. It may cover the entire firm or any portion thereof.

The model enables the user to alter any one of the variable factors in order to provide data for strategic decisions, alternate courses of action, options available or an analysis of the potential results.

These models usually yield descriptive results in which any given input will yield certain outputs. They may be either single project models or continuing short-term or long-term models. The term "long term" usually designates periods of over one year in length.

The model may combine various inputs to find and report the optimum output under varying conditions.

This type of model generally helps the financial administrator allocate resources to the most effective and profitable use by comparing and reporting the results of alternate choices.

MODEL INPUTS AND OUTPUTS

In order to give you a better understanding of the various inputs to the models and the resulting outputs, we have summarized the various factors inputted and the resulting outputs.

MONTHLY INPUT—FINANCIAL OPERATIONS

1. Starting Balance Sheet items.
2. Actual income and expenses—daily, weekly or monthly.

MONTHLY OUTPUT

1. Ending Balance Sheet items.
2. Comparison of actual income and expenses versus plan and/or the previous year.

PLANNING INPUTS

1. Estimated sales and direct costs by product or product line.
2. Manufacturing overhead—fixed and variable.

The Use of Financial Models by the Financial Administrator 169

    3. Selling and administrative expenses.

    4. Federal and state tax rates.

PLANNING OUTPUTS

    1. Estimated gross profit by product and/or product line.

    2. Operating profit by product line and by product.

    3. Net income by product or product line.

    4. Net income after taxes.

Note . . . Planning outputs are inputted into the model to yield the contrast between the planned and actual results. The resulting variation analysis indicates major deviations from plan.

SALES FORECASTING INPUTS

    1. Estimated unit sales by product.

    2. Product prices.

    3. Promotion expenditures and timing.

    4. Share of market data—territory by territory.

    5. Test market results.

    6. Competitive price and promotion factors.

    7. Past year's growth rates.

    8. Seasonal sales patterns.

    9. Prior new product performance.

SALES FORECAST OUTPUTS

    1. Product sales and profit forecasts by customer, territory and region.

    2. Production requirements by time cycle.

    3. Promotion requirements by time cycle.

PROJECT ANALYSIS INPUTS

    1. Product units and prices.

    2. Capital investment required.

    3. Operating costs.

    4. Product life expectancy.

    5. Time cycle.

PROJECT ANALYSIS OUTPUTS

1. Projected income.
2. Cash flow.
3. Rate of return on investment (ROI). Present value or discounted.
4. Alternates and options.

ECONOMIC FORECASTS INPUT

1. Matrix analysis data on GNP, DI, CE and industry production.
2. Estimated money supply, consumer prices and inflation rates.

ECONOMIC FORECASTS OUTPUT

1. Anticipated economic and business conditions.
2. Data for product pricing and costs
3. Territorial sales expectations.

LEASE/RENT/BUY ANALYSIS INPUTS

1. Project data—costs—time period.
2. Anticipated return.
3. Availability of capital and price.

LEASE/RENT/BUY ANALYSIS OUTPUTS

1. Attractiveness and costs of alternate decisions.
2. Project ROI.

HOW ARE THE MODELS VARIED FOR CONDITIONS?

In most business situations there are a number of variables. Experience shows that not all of these items vary or change at the same time or to the same degree. Sometimes they will only vary one at a time, sometimes several at once. This complicates model building and if not properly handled could produce distorted results. For example in forecasting costs:

1. C = Price of material per unit
   V = Volume used
2. At Volume 1 C = $2.00 per unit
       Volume 2 C = 1.75 per unit
       Volume 3 C = 1.50 per unit
       Volume 4 C = 1.25 per unit
       Volume 5 C = 1.00 per unit

The Use of Financial Models by the Financial Administrator

Conversely we might have the following sales relationship:

1. C = Price of product sold
   V = Volume of product sold
2. At Price 1   V = 100,000 units
       Price 2   V = 90,000 units
       Price 3   V = 75,000 units
       Price 4   V = 50,000 units
       Price 5   V = 25,000 units

Obviously in modeling we cannot use a straightline relationship for the various factors. We must consider the interaction between factors and the interdependence of costs, prices and volumes.

A TYPICAL MODEL BASE

500 Products—15 product lines.
10 Plants—6 produce all items—2 produce 75% of items—2 produce 50% of items.
55 Warehouses—hold a full line of merchandise or may hold only a small supply of each—larger supply of fast moving items.
10 Regional Warehouses—reserve stocks—all warehouses on rail facilities—capacity six cars of merchandise.
12,000 Customers—major accounts in 100 cities.
        Customer service within three days on all orders.

Production costs by plant vary due to age, size and location.
Source of raw materials and component parts a factor in costs.

NEEDED—Optimum locations of warehouses and Regional distribution centers. Costs by product and product line at the distribution center level.

WHAT DOES A DIVESTITURE MODEL TELL YOU?

It answers the questions:

1. What happens to the total picture when the divestiture is made?
2. What is the expected effect on volume, fixed costs, expenses and profits?

WHAT IS "TOP DOWN"—"BOTTOM UP?"

Top down is probably the simplest and easiest way to start your modeling career. You start with the following items:

GROSS REVENUES		$$$$$$
MATERIAL COSTS	$$$$$	
LABOR COSTS	$$$$$	
FIXED OVERHEAD	$$$$$	

VARIABLE OVERHEAD	$$$$$	
TOTAL MANUFACTURING COSTS		$$$$$$
GROSS PROFIT		$$$$$$
SELLING EXPENSES	$$$$$	
PROMOTIONAL EXPENSES	$$$$$	
ADMINISTRATIVE EXPENSE	$$$$$	
TOTAL SELLING AND ADMINISTRATIVE		$$$$$$
OTHER INCOME		$$$$
OTHER DEDUCTIONS		$$$$
NET INCOME BEFORE TAXES		$$$$$$
PROVISION FOR TAXES		$$$$$
NET INCOME		$$$$

This yields the broad, overall picture wherein you can substitute values for each one of the items and test the various alternates. As you gain competence you can disassemble the various components for a more detailed approach. In this manner, you start modeling almost immediately and have a working model at all times. This eliminates many frustrations and the embarrassing question "When?"

Bottom up is the tough approach used only when you have a high degree of technical ability or help and plenty of time and money. With this type of development you start at the lowest point and work upward operation by operation, product by product, sales territory by sales territory, customer by customer, and man by man. You could develop an excellent model on the effective use of fork trucks while the firm is going bankrupt!

BEST METHOD

Interviews have yielded the opinion that the best way to approach modeling is from the "top down" with a wee bit of "bottom up" analysis and data in order to meet developing requests as the system grows.

THE STRATEGIC MODEL

Normally one would consider the strategic model as a long-range model dealing with the hundred or so strategic factors that concern every firm in order that it may achieve its long-range goals. This is particularly true in the case of AT&T, the utilities and the energy firms. In their planning they have taken the long-range view of the situation in communications developments, energy requirements and expansion. The oil firms started in the early 1960's to acquire coal and uranium deposits. The utilities and manufacturing firms followed suit by beginning to acquire oil, gas and coal supplies in order to have a source of fuel or raw material. A decade later they continued this trend by moving into the other natural resources such as copper, iron, sulphur, potash and aluminum. Recognition of the growing importance of solar energy has led to many joint ventures in this field financed by oil, coal or other money sources. As energy and the natural resources become scarcer they will have achieved their long-range goal of being in control of these resources. This is also true in the agriculture, forestry and food production areas. *Long-range forecasting pays off in dollars today and in the future!*

The Use of Financial Models by the Financial Administrator

In reviewing financial practices we found that strategic modeling is also utilized on a short-range basis. This is indicated by the "Strategic Profit Model" in Exhibit A. In this model the various major factors contributing to the firm's profit for any period can be manipulated or changed to see what the effect of changes in any one or several factors would have upon the entire or final results.

STRATEGIC PLANNING MODEL—FIVE-YEAR BASIS FORECAST

YEAR   XXXX XXXX XXXX XXXX XXXX

ASSETS
CURRENT
  CASH
  ACCOUNTS RECEIVABLE
  INVENTORIES
  OTHER ITEMS
    TOTAL CURRENT ASSETS

PLANT—NET

OTHER ASSETS
  TOTAL ASSETS

LIABILITIES
CURRENT
  ACCOUNTS PAYABLE
  NOTES PAYABLE
  ACCRUED ITEMS
  PROVISION FOR INCOME TAXES
    TOTAL CURRENT LIABILITIES

LONG TERM DEBT

SHAREHOLDERS EQUITY
  COMMON STOCK
  PREFERRED STOCK
  RETAINED EARNINGS
    TOTAL SHAREHOLDERS' EQUITY

FINANCIAL RATIO FORECAST
LIQUIDITY
  QUICK RATIO
  CURRENT RATIO
ACTIVITY
  DAY'S SALES IN A/R
  % PAST DUE
  INVENTORY TURNOVER
  DAY'S SALES IN INVENTORY
  SALES PER $ OF PLANT
  SALES PER EMPLOYEE

PROFITABILITY
   % TO NET SALES
   % TO NET WORTH
   RETURN ON ASSETS EMPLOYED
   RETURN ON CAPITAL EMPLOYED
LEVERAGE
   DEBT TO ASSETS
   DEBT TO CAPITAL

THE STRATEGIC MODEL DESCRIBED

1. A long-range plan.
2. Sets objectives and goals.
3. Utilizes long-range economic and marketing projections.
4. Is a broad brush approach—no finite details.
5. Indicates long-range financing and capacity plans.
6. Used for mergers and acquisitions.
7. Prints out as shown above the projections resulting from this type of data input.

STANDARD MODELS

1. Generally a short-term plan.
2. Utilizes the financial statement, income account data.
3. Short-term allocation of resources.
4. Covers current economic, marketing and corporate activities.
5. Covers all products, product lines, customers and sales force.
6. Utilized for current lease/buy decisions.
7. Cash flow projections and analysis.
8. Special studies—emergency situations.

CONTROL MODELS

1. Utilizes internal operating or transaction data.
2. Monitors operations versus plan.
3. Project, analyze or compare individual income or balance sheet accounts.
4. Immediate resource allocation—changes in capacity or manpower.

FACTORY CONTROL MODELS

1. Machine tool control—scheduling.
2. In process control—work in process status hourly or daily.

The Use of Financial Models by the Financial Administrator 175

   3. Quality control—periodic or constant checks.

   4. Adaptive control—adjust to conditions and reschedule.

   5. Inventory control—raw material—work in process—components or finished goods.

   6. CHOICES .... Machine No. XXX   Alternates   YYY   ZZZ   CCC
                        Tool No.   XXX   Alternates   YYY   ZZZ   CCC   RRR

   7. STATUS .... Promised delivery date   XXXX .... On schedule
                   or New delivery date   YYYY .... days early
                                                    ZZZZ .... days late

BREAKEVEN POINT MODELS

Let us assume that you wish to determine your breakeven point. Here is the model formula that will do it.

    BE   = BREAKEVEN POINT
    GS   = GROSS SALES
    DCF = DAILY COSTS FIXED
    DCV = DAILY COSTS VARIABLE
    U   = UNITS SOLD
    P   = PRICE
    GS 1 = U 1 × P 1   (unit level 1—price level 1)
    BE   = GS 1—DCF—DCV

Or possibly we might use the following:
    P   = Price
    V   = Variable cost per unit—manufacturing
    N   = No. of units
    F   = Fixed costs—manufacturing
    I   = Profits

$$I = (P-V)N - F$$

There are over 1,000 variables available. If you know the selling and administrative costs involved you can determine the profits required to liquidate these costs in a given time period.

DO'S AND DON'TS IN MODELING

Do select the right type of model.

Do you really need a model for the problem?

Do define the purpose and parameters of the model.

Do decide who does the modeling.

Do decide who uses the model and gets the results.

Don't start until the model has been tested or the users educated.

Do modify the model for changes and keep everyone informed of the changes.

Don't let everyone use it. A real need must be established. It is not a toy!

Do decide who provides the data and how much.

Don't assume that it will replace human intuition or "horse sense!"

Do keep it simple—at least at first. Nothing turns people off faster than a group of symbols or an equation such as this:

$$\Sigma = \frac{\phi(1-i)\Delta 9}{\Sigma \zeta(\Delta - 9)^n}$$

They might ask, "Σ, what the heck is it?" Σ is a calculus term. It is Greek for S. It is called the summation sign.

$$\begin{array}{ll} n & \text{Top upper limits of summation} \\ \Sigma & \\ i & \text{Bottom lower limits of summation} \end{array}$$

Incidentally the equation is for the determination of a weighted average.

Do resist a massive model. Start small and work up in size and scope.

Don't let the technical experts run the show.

Don't create a bad impression by promising too much—time cycle or model performance.

Do learn how to use the model yourself and punch the right keys.

Do beware of management bias.

Do beware of operational bias.

GAME THEORY—IS IT USABLE?

In the early days of computers you were introduced to business games wherein you simulated business action through a series of events and a choice of numbers to represent management decisions. From this approach in the lofty world of computers, statistics and mathematics there evolved the theory that "game theory" could be applied to the real and immensely practical world of business. Despite the highly sophisticated approaches developed in the business schools and computer manuals there still appears to be a niche for the practice within the realm of the financial administrator. In calling the roster from supercorporations to the "dad and lad" type of operation one can dream up all types of applications. For the multinational it might range from "What happens if we should be expropriated tomorrow?" or "What to do about foreign currency devaluations?" to the simple routing of a fork truck in factory X. In the smaller firm it could perhaps provide the answer to the question "What do we do now?" when dad comes home and finds that lad has just burned up the specialized machine they had just developed. While the computer will never completely replace management or human intuition business can be simulated on a computer and the

The Use of Financial Models by the Financial Administrator

game theory used to good advantage. The truly professional financial administrator is not doing his job effectively if he does not utilize to the fullest extent the techniques of game theory, risk analysis and simulation.

MODELS ARE PRACTICAL AT EVERY LEVEL

In a relatively small town in the center of Indiana there is a grain operation which includes among other things production of chicken feed. Since the price of grains varies daily the owner often has a problem in determining the price of feed. With a minicomputer and a simple model he can get an instant answer. Here are the factors used:

Daily Variables.... cost of wheat, corn, oats, beans, sunflower seeds and meat scraps.
Weekly or Monthly Variables.... cost of sacks and labor.
Irregular Variables.... cost of power, equipment maintenance, depreciation.

THE FORMULA

1000 lbs	Wheat
1300 lbs	Corn
500 lbs	Oats
50 lbs	Sunflower Seeds
100 lbs	Soybeans
50 lbs	Meat Scraps
3000 lbs	Batch

OPERATIONS

Mixing in mill	— 30 minutes 1-man crew.		
Sacking	— 25-lb sacks)		120 per hour
	50-lb sacks)	2-man crew	250 per hour
	100-lb sacks)		500 per hour
Bulk	— 1-man crew		¼ hour per batch

The owner has a simple model which will take into account all of the variables and give him the daily price. If he wishes to maintain a steady price another model will give him the answer by varying the amounts of the various ingredients providing the price is still maintainable. The savings in time previously used to make the computations have recovered the cost of the minicomputer within one year.

A DEFENSIVE CASH MODEL

Let us assume a tight cash position and we want to determine the effect of sales fluctuations on our cash position. These are the numbers:

a. Cash at start of period—$10,000
b. Expected cash collections—2,000 (varies with sales and collection days)
c. Expected cash expenses—variable—25% of sales

d. Expected cash expenses—fixed—$1,000 a day
e. Ending cash balance anticipated
f. Interest—short-term debt @ 8% of $60,000
g. Taxes—rate 22%
h. Daily sales collection period—30 days
Anticipated change in sales volume—defensive model
—10% —15% —20% —30% —40% —50%

The formula for the model is:

$$E = A + B - C - D - F - T$$

Inputting the various factors will give you the anticipated ending cash balance under any assumed circumstance.

BASIC GROWTH RATE FORMULA

One of the basic formulas used by financial executives is that used in determining growth rate.

A = An amount at the end of (n) compounding periods
P = Principal amount involved
I = Interest rate per annum
n = Number of years. It is equal to n−1

If you invested $10,000 today how long would it take to increase to $20,000 with an interest rate of 8%?

$$P = \frac{A}{(1 + I)^n}$$

$$\$10,000 = \frac{\$20,000}{(1 + 08)^n}$$

$$n = \frac{\$20,000}{\$10,000 \times (1.08)^n}$$

n = 9 +   Your money will double in slightly over nine years.

It also answers the question: "How much will I have to invest to have $100,000 in 10 years at a rate of 8%?"

Probably the most used equations in the financial dynasty are those showing the present value and the annual rate of return for investments.

$$P = \frac{R((1 + i)^n - 1)}{i(1 + i)^n}$$

P = Present value
R = Rate of return
i = Interest rate
n = Time period in years

The Use of Financial Models by the Financial Administrator

Discounted cash flow is used in many instances by financial executives under the theory that the near term dollar is worth more than the dollar of the future due to inflation and other forces outside of their control.

If you intend to be a top financial administrator of the future and do not currently know anything about models, you owe it to yourself to upgrade this gap in your knowledge. They are in use today, will be in the future and are a vital tool of financial management. Models can save you time and money! Simulated business situations, fed into the proper computer model, can aid or actually determine corporate financial decisions. There is a natural reluctance to relinquish authority to the models and the machines. It is a recognized fact that models and simulation provide the financial executive with a means of dealing immediately with the uncertainty involved in business decisions and in pulling together the numerous figures created by a viable, rapidly changing, aggressive organization. You can keep one step ahead!

CHECK LIST FOR EFFECTIVE MODELS

- ☐ STATE OBJECTIVES
- ☐ SELECT GOALS
- ☐ IDENTIFY PROBLEMS
- ☐ SET BASIC MODEL
- ☐ MODEL INPUTS
- ☐ MODEL OUTPUTS
- ☐ DEBUG & TEST
- ☐ TRIAL RUNS
- ☐ MANAGEMENT O.K.
- ☐ EXTEND & REVISE

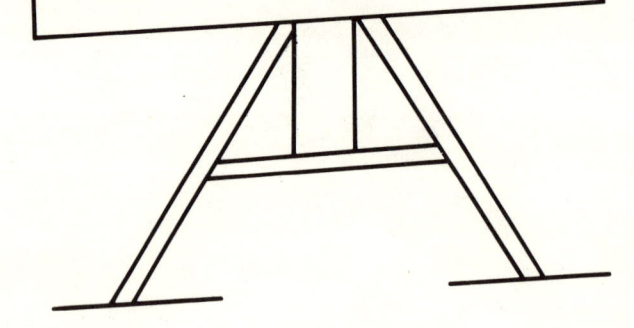

The Use of Financial Models by the Financial Administrator

PLANNING CYCLE

PRELIMINARY PLANNING INFORMATION

EXPLORATION OF CORPORATE GOALS AND OBJECTIVES

ANALYSIS OF PROBLEM SITUATIONS

SELECTION OF CORPORATE GOALS AND OBJECTIVES

STATEMENT OF FUNCTIONAL OBJECTIVES

CONTROL AND FEEDBACK

AREAS FOR DISCUSSION

1. PURPOSE OF THE MODEL
2. USES OF THE MODEL
3. DEVELOPMENT OF THE MODEL
4. DESCRIPTION OF THE MODEL
5. HIGHLIGHTS OF THE COMPUTER PROGRAM
6. THE USE OF THE MODEL IN PLANNING AND BUDGETING

PURPOSE OF MODEL

- TO PROVIDE A FAST, RELIABLE METHOD FOR FORECASTING THE FUTURE FINANCIAL POSITION OF THE COMPANY.
- TO DO THIS THE MODEL SIMULATES THE ACTUAL OPERATING PROCEDURES FOLLOWED AND THE ACCOUNTING SYSTEM.
- DOING THIS BY COMPUTER, THE PROCESS IS A RAPID ONE AND LITTLE MANPOWER IS REQUIRED.

USES OF THE MODEL

PLANNING

- AIDS IN SETTING CORPORATE GOALS AND OBJECTIVES
- IDENTIFIES PROBLEMS AND OPPORTUNITIES
- PERMITS BROAD STUDIES—INVESTMENT ALLOCATION, TAX PLANNING
- ANSWERS "WHAT IF?..." TYPE QUESTIONS

BUDGETING

- EVALUATES VALIDITY OF SHORT-TERM PROFIT PLAN
- ADDS A NEW DIMENSION TO CAPITAL INVESTMENT EVALUATIONS

MANAGEMENT INFORMATION

- IDENTIFIES KEY VARIABLES

DEVELOPMENT OF THE MODEL

- FEASIBILITY STUDY
- DETERMINATION OF BASIC MODEL STRUCTURE
- COMPUTER CODING, TESTING AND DEBUGGING
- ACCURACY TESTING
- MANAGEMENT REVIEW
- CONTINUED MODEL EXTENSIONS AND REVISIONS

DETERMINATION OF BASIC MODEL STRUCTURE

BASIC FOCAL POINT: DETAILED ANALYSIS OF INCOME STATEMENT

- WHAT INFORMATION IS PRESENTED?

- WHAT IS THE SOURCE OF THIS INFORMATION?

- CAN MEANINGFUL RELATIONSHIPS BE DEVELOPED BETWEEN REVENUES, COSTS AND LEVELS OF ACTIVITY?

BASED ON THIS ANALYSIS, A COMPLETE SYSTEM OF SIMPLE ALGEBRAIC EQUATIONS WAS DEVELOPED TO BRING TOGETHER ALL COSTS AND REVENUES.

EXTENSIVE USE WAS MADE OF REGRESSION ANALYSIS.

HIGHLIGHTS OF THE COMPUTER PROGRAM

- PROGRAMMED IN FORTRAN

- CAN BE USED FOR MULTIPLE 5-YEAR PROJECTIONS OR SENSITIVITY ANALYSES

- APPROXIMATELY 50 CRITICAL INPUTS FOR EACH RUN. TOTAL INPUTS APPROACH 650 IN NUMBER

- MODEL CONTAINS APPROXIMATELY 1,000 EQUATIONS

- ABOUT 3,600 ITEMS OF DATA ARE STORED FOR EACH YEAR

- RUNNING TIME VERY FAST

- REPORT WRITER ALLOWS READY ACCESS TO ALL DATA ITEMS

OIL COMPANY
FINANCIAL MODEL FLOW CHART

184

STRATEGIC PROFIT MODEL

LEVERAGE FACTORS

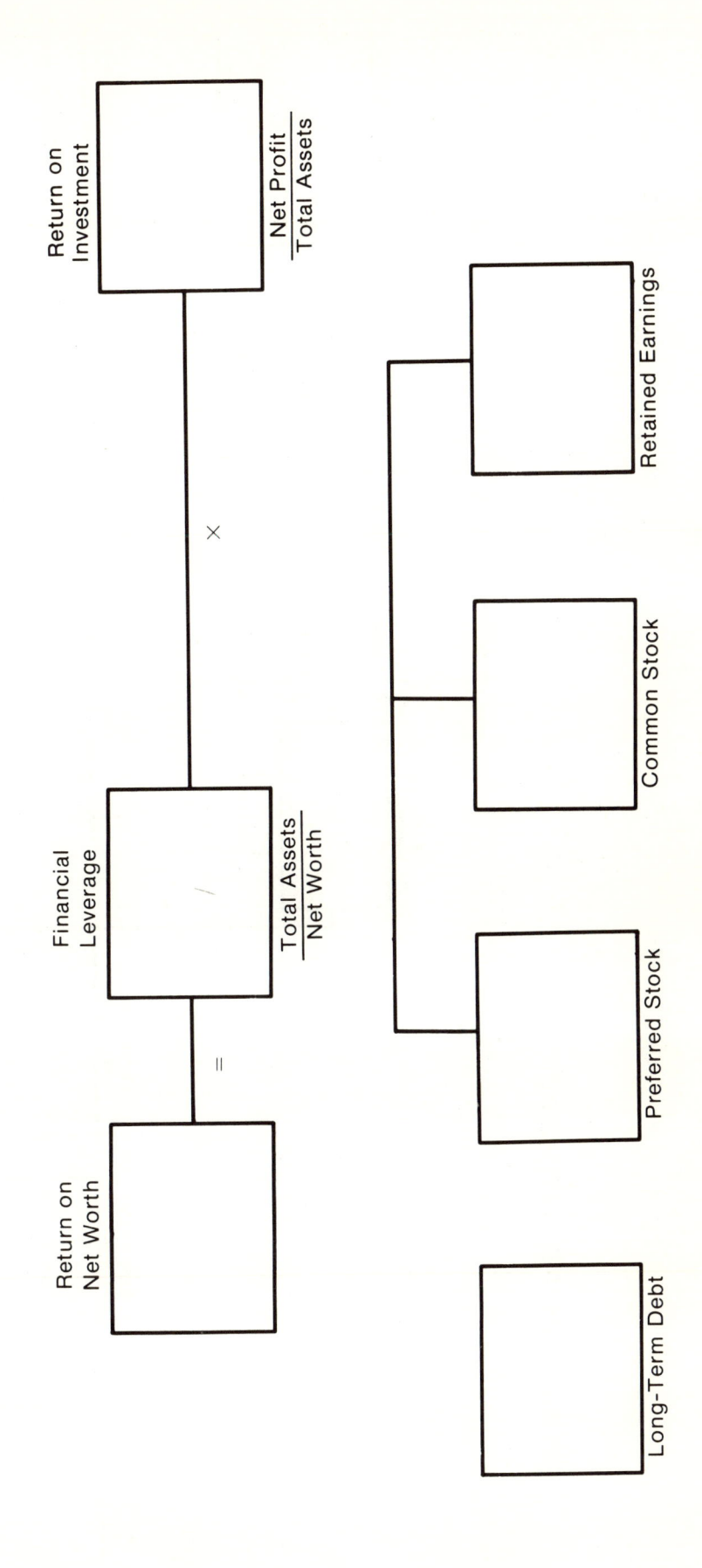

```
Return on Net Worth = Financial Leverage × Return on Investment

Financial Leverage = Total Assets / Net Worth
Return on Investment = Net Profit / Total Assets
```

Net Worth components:
- Retained Earnings
- Common Stock
- Preferred Stock

Long-Term Debt

STRATEGIC PROFIT MODEL

SALES	$ 300,000	INVENTORY	$ 64,800
−		+	
COST OF GOODS SOLD	$ 192,000	ACCOUNTS RECEIVABLE	$ 44,000
		+	
VARIABLE EXPENSES	$	OTHER CURRENT ASSETS	$ 6,243
+			
FIXED EXPENSES	$		

GROSS MARGIN
$ 108,000 + 0 = 108,000

TOTAL EXPENSES
$ 99,300 + 1,500 + 1,800 = 102,600

CURRENT ASSETS $ 115,043
+
FIXED ASSETS $ 25,926

NET PROFIT $ 5,400 ÷ SALES $ 300,000

SALES $ 300,000 ÷ TOTAL ASSETS $ 140,969

NET PROFIT MARGIN 1.8 % $\left(\dfrac{\text{net profit}}{\text{net sales}}\right)$

TIMES

ASSET TURNOVER 2.1 $\left(\dfrac{\text{net sales}}{\text{total assets}}\right)$

RETURN ON ASSETS 3.8 % $\left(\dfrac{\text{net profit}}{\text{total assets}}\right)$

×

FINANCIAL LEVERAGE 1.4 $\left(\dfrac{\text{total assets}}{\text{net worth}}\right)$

=

RETURN ON NETWORTH 4.8% $\left(\dfrac{\text{net profit}}{\text{net worth}}\right)$

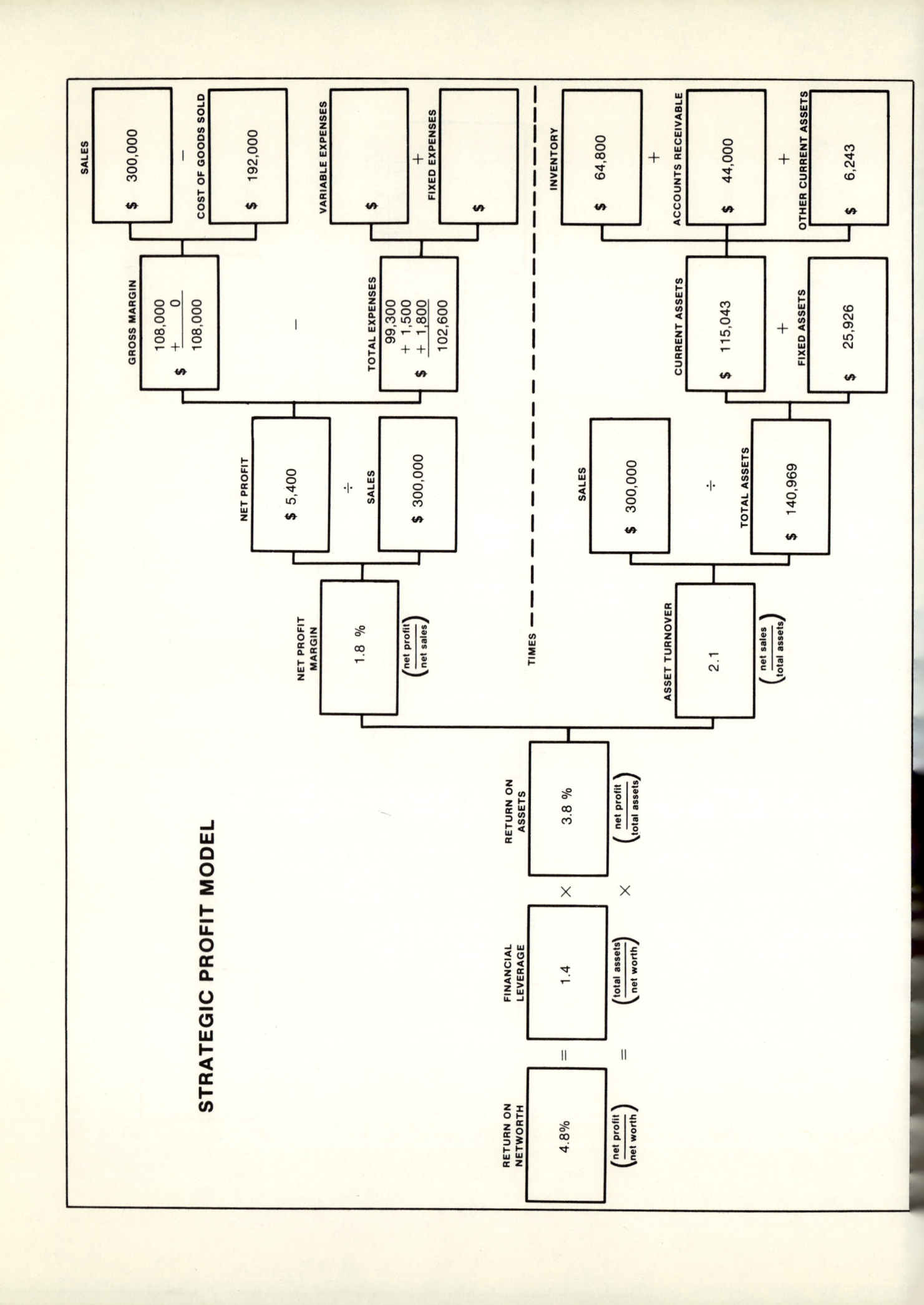

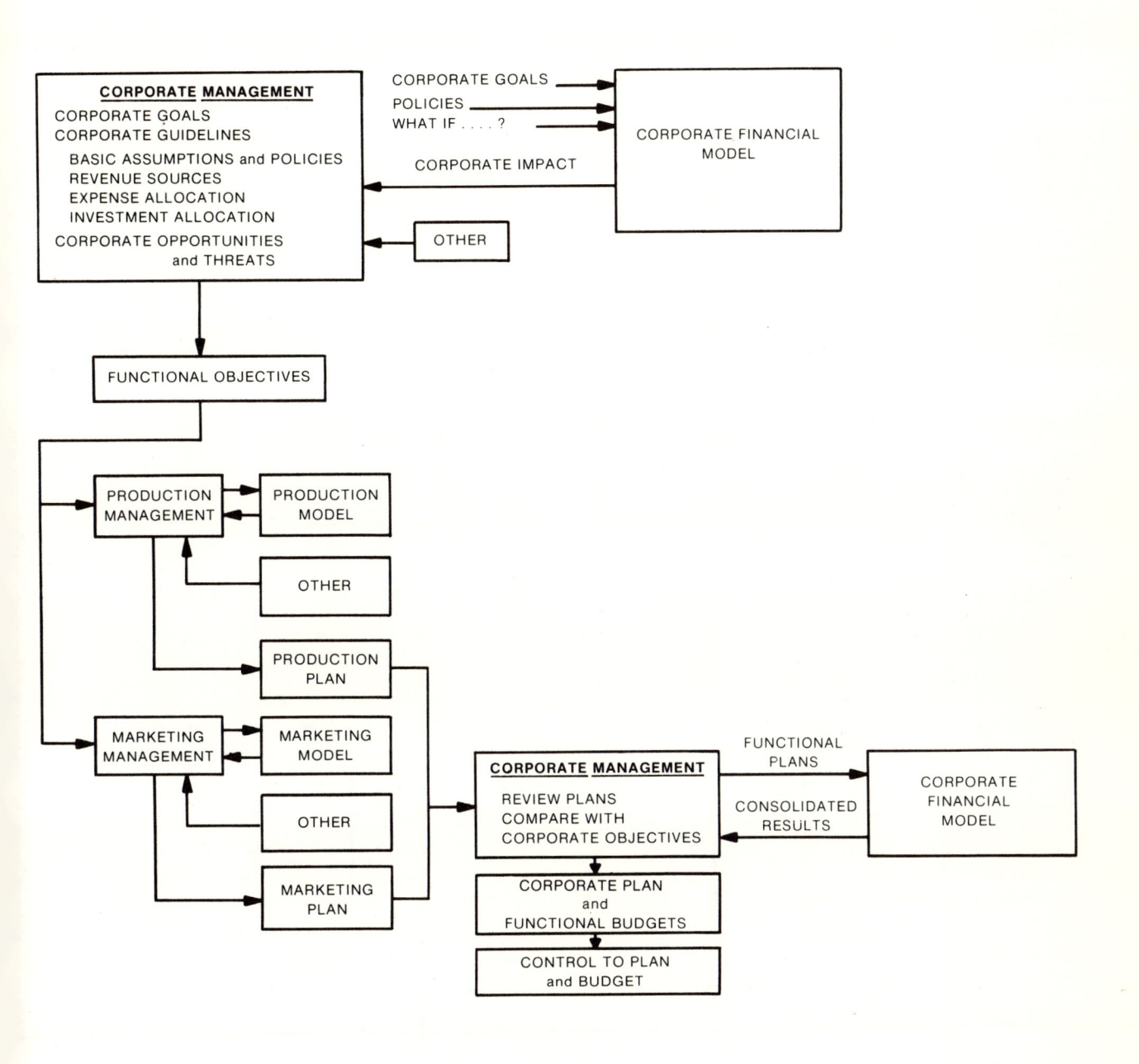

```
┌─────────────────────────────┐         CORPORATE GOALS      ┌──────────────────┐
│    CORPORATE MANAGEMENT     │         POLICIES    ────────▶│                  │
│   CORPORATE GOALS           │────────▶WHAT IF . . . . ?    │ CORPORATE FINANCIAL│
│   CORPORATE GUIDELINES      │                              │      MODEL       │
│     BASIC ASSUMPTIONS and POLICIES                         │                  │
│     REVENUE SOURCES         │◀──────  CORPORATE IMPACT     │                  │
│     EXPENSE ALLOCATION      │                              └──────────────────┘
│     INVESTMENT ALLOCATION   │         ┌────────┐
│   CORPORATE OPPORTUNITIES   │◀────────│ OTHER  │
│          and THREATS        │         └────────┘
└─────────────────────────────┘
              │
              ▼
   ┌─────────────────────┐
   │ FUNCTIONAL OBJECTIVES│
   └─────────────────────┘
     │
     │   ┌────────────┐       ┌────────────┐
     ├──▶│ PRODUCTION │──────▶│ PRODUCTION │
     │   │ MANAGEMENT │◀──────│   MODEL    │
     │   └────────────┘       └────────────┘
     │         │              ┌────────────┐
     │         │              │   OTHER    │
     │         │              └────────────┘
     │         │              ┌────────────┐
     │         └─────────────▶│ PRODUCTION │
     │                        │    PLAN    │──────┐
     │                        └────────────┘      │
     │   ┌────────────┐       ┌────────────┐      │
     └──▶│ MARKETING  │──────▶│ MARKETING  │      │
         │ MANAGEMENT │◀──────│   MODEL    │      │
         └────────────┘       └────────────┘      │
               │              ┌────────────┐      │
               │              │   OTHER    │      │
               │              └────────────┘      │
               │              ┌────────────┐      │
               └─────────────▶│ MARKETING  │──────┤
                              │    PLAN    │      │
                              └────────────┘      │
                                                  ▼
                           ┌──────────────────────────┐   FUNCTIONAL    ┌──────────────┐
                           │  CORPORATE MANAGEMENT    │   PLANS         │  CORPORATE   │
                           │  REVIEW PLANS            │────────────────▶│  FINANCIAL   │
                           │  COMPARE WITH            │  CONSOLIDATED   │    MODEL     │
                           │  CORPORATE OBJECTIVES    │◀────RESULTS─────│              │
                           └──────────────────────────┘                 └──────────────┘
                                        │
                                        ▼
                           ┌──────────────────────────┐
                           │    CORPORATE PLAN        │
                           │         and              │
                           │   FUNCTIONAL BUDGETS     │
                           └──────────────────────────┘
                                        │
                                        ▼
                           ┌──────────────────────────┐
                           │    CONTROL TO PLAN       │
                           │       and BUDGET         │
                           └──────────────────────────┘
```

187

THE HIERARCHY OF CORPORATE FINANCIAL MODELS INDEX

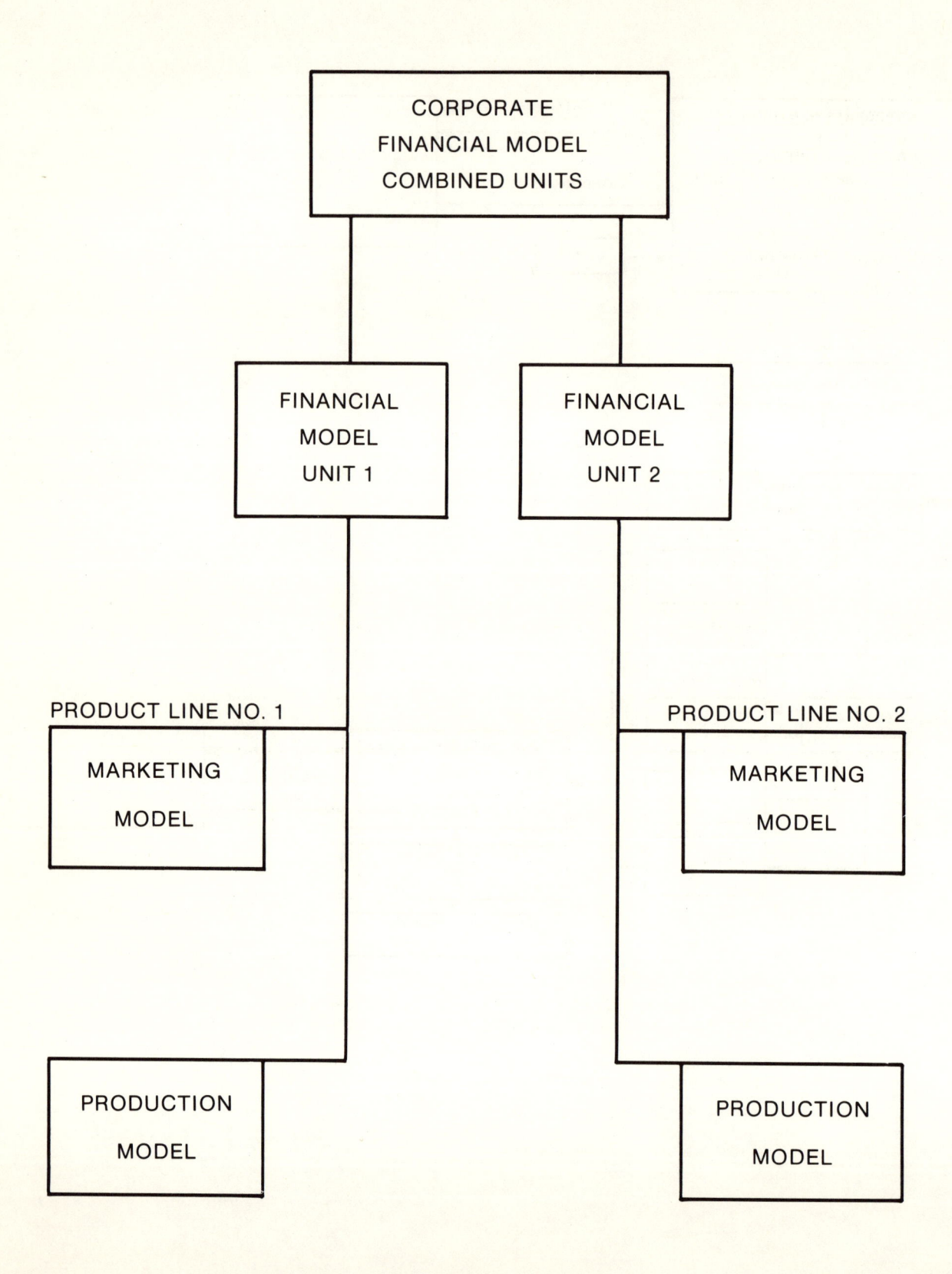

```
                    ┌─────────────────────┐
                    │      CORPORATE      │
                    │   FINANCIAL MODEL   │
                    │   COMBINED UNITS    │
                    └──────────┬──────────┘
                   ┌───────────┴───────────┐
          ┌────────┴────────┐     ┌────────┴────────┐
          │    FINANCIAL    │     │    FINANCIAL    │
          │      MODEL      │     │      MODEL      │
          │     UNIT 1      │     │     UNIT 2      │
          └────────┬────────┘     └────────┬────────┘
                   │                       │
   PRODUCT LINE NO. 1                PRODUCT LINE NO. 2
   ┌─────────────┐                        ┌─────────────┐
   │  MARKETING  │                        │  MARKETING  │
   │    MODEL    │                        │    MODEL    │
   └─────────────┘                        └─────────────┘

   ┌─────────────┐                        ┌─────────────┐
   │  PRODUCTION │                        │  PRODUCTION │
   │    MODEL    │                        │    MODEL    │
   └─────────────┘                        └─────────────┘
```

MODIFIED duPont return-on-investment model

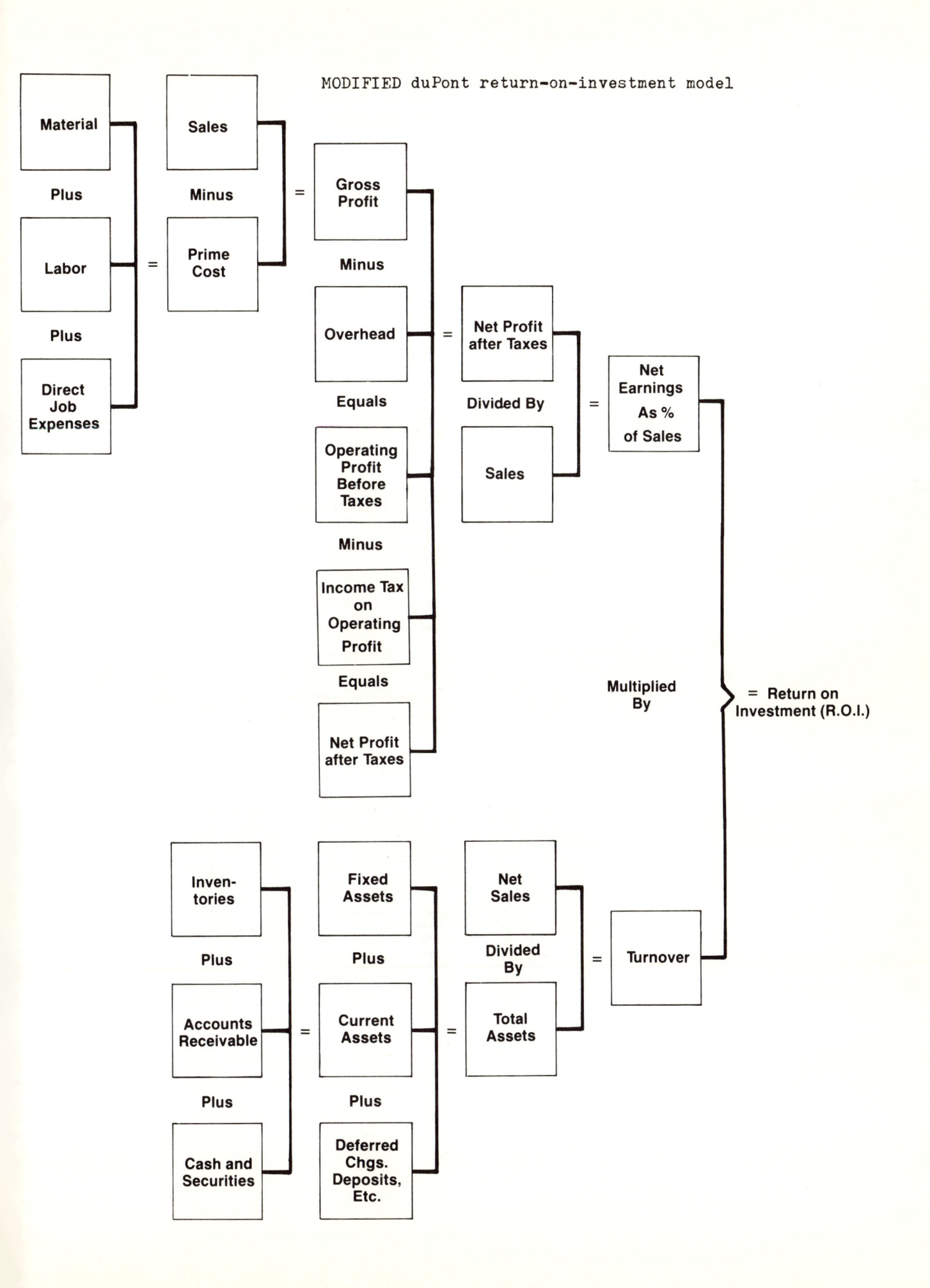

Material Plus **Labor** Plus **Direct Job Expenses** = **Prime Cost**

Sales Minus **Prime Cost** = **Gross Profit**

Gross Profit Minus **Overhead** Equals **Operating Profit Before Taxes**

Operating Profit Before Taxes Minus **Income Tax on Operating Profit** Equals **Net Profit after Taxes**

Net Profit after Taxes Divided By **Sales** = **Net Earnings As % of Sales**

Inventories Plus **Accounts Receivable** Plus **Cash and Securities** = **Current Assets**

Current Assets Plus **Fixed Assets** Plus **Deferred Chgs. Deposits, Etc.** = **Total Assets**

Net Sales Divided By **Total Assets** = **Turnover**

Net Earnings As % of Sales Multiplied By **Turnover** = **Return on Investment (R.O.I.)**

MILITARY MODEL TECHNIQUES

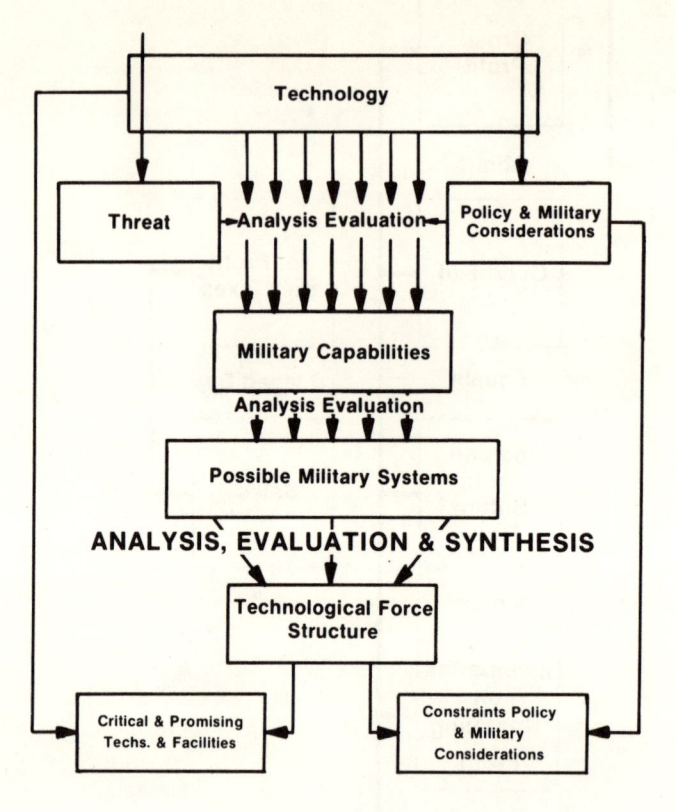

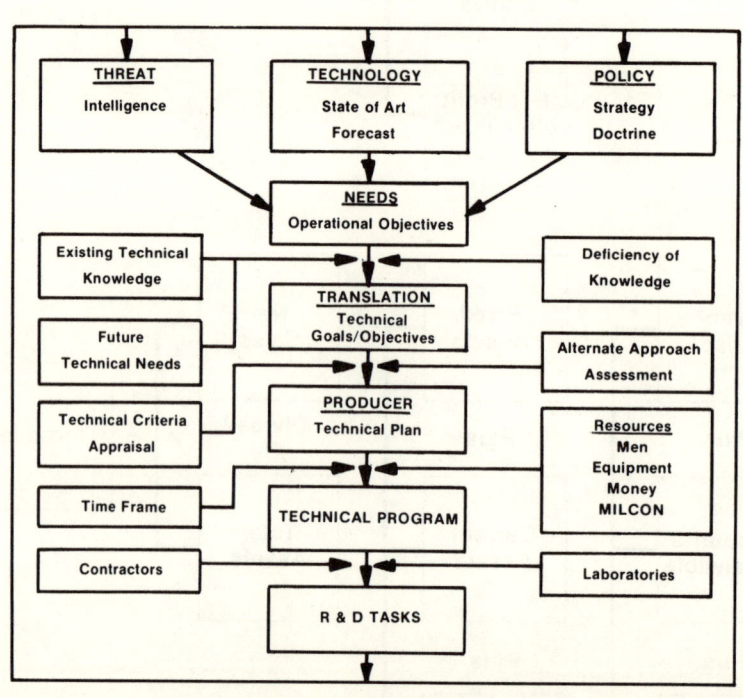

7

The Management Communications Center— The Financial Data Bank

INFORMATION IS PROFIT, POWER AND SUCCESS

The financial administrator has at his command one of the most important tools in the world. The new computers make available vast memories which if properly utilized can provide information on virtually any subject. He is installed at the very hub of communications for the entire firm. He must analyze and answer the question: "Who in this organization depends on me for information?" This is followed quickly by the queries: "What information and in what form?" He is periodically called upon to provide instant facts, which must be readily available and in such form that they can be readily analyzed or interpreted.

In order to maintain his effectiveness and solve the problem he must develop an "Intelligence" or "Task Analysis Center" within his organization in order to keep all segments of his firm alerted to all matters which might either be advantageous or adverse to the firm's strategies or plans.

Too often financial executives consider "data" or "facts" to be related to cold statistics about balance sheet items, financial ratios, sales, costs, inventories or productive facilities. Most of the information available to business is raw, undigested data, and if presented to top management personnel in this form would merely waste their valuable time trying to make it usable. A data bank needs all types of vital, living information converted into information that will meet the requirements of the recipients. It is the purpose and the use of the data that is most important. Information can cover the wide range of hobbies, fashions, package colors and sizes, trends in research, economic conditions or changes in competitive firms' strategies or personnel.

A searching analysis of your competitors' reaction to competitive pressures can be just as enlightening as a review of your sales or cost figures.

The current terminology calls the systems MIS or Management Information Systems. We prefer the term "Task Analysis Center" wherein all information is collected on a "one time" basis or on regular schedule for the ultimate task of analyzing problems in order to provide the basic material for executive decisions, corporate strategy, action or reaction. Practically every financial executive we discussed the matter with indicated that his firm had or was developing an "MIS" system or unit. The larger firms have sophisticated "Communications" or "Intelligence" centers, elaborately equipped, wherein all the latest material is available and can be displayed in the most effective manner.

WHAT ARE THE STAFF REQUIREMENTS?

Staffs for the function range from a high of over one-hundred individuals to one clerk keeping indexed records. Data was contained on simple 4 × 5 filing cards, edge-punched cards to mammoth computer memories. Equipment ranged from a small metal box for the cards to large computers with printers, CRT terminals, large screens, video displays or microfiche readers. One of the most sophisticated systems is a laser data recorder. This unit was developed by the University of Toronto and while it is still experimental it has tremendous capabilities. Vast amounts of data are inscribed on a plastic disc by means of an argon laser. If it is successful commercially it will replace the magnetic tapes and discs currently in use for data storage. This method has the ultimate capacity of storing over 500 million words on a disc the size of a large stereo record.

Whatever your budget can afford in the way of personnel your best bet is to put the best minds available in the "Task Analysis Center." These are the people who can make or break you and your organization.

LET'S FACE FACTS!

Profits, progress and growth are based upon sound business decisions supported by adequate and realistic facts. The guts of your organization is its data bank! From the data in these files more money can be made than through any other single item in the firm. When you have at your fingertips the facts for decisive action on sales, costs, profits, competitive action or strategies you have it made. The health and welfare of your firm is dependent upon the intelligence stored in this bank of information ready to be drawn out at will. Your assets in this bank are dependent not only upon what is stored there but in the manner in which it is utilized. The effectiveness of your top executives is enhanced by what is stored there and its accessibility in time of need. If they get the information they require in the form in which it is required, you can have a super-effective group of managers. As a top financial executive you

The Management Communications Center—The Financial Data Bank

control the action, reaction and ultimate profits of your firm. Therefore the quality of the job you do on setting up a data bank or communications center is vital to your continuing success.

WHY IT IS IMPORTANT

Throughout industry, from the president, through research and on down to the office messenger, 40 to 80% of the effective time of the individual is lost searching for things instead of performing that action task that they are paid for. The higher up the ladder time is lost in this manner the greater loss to your firm.

THE ROLE OF THE MINICOMPUTER

To supply up-to-the-minute information on your firm's activities requires a great deal of computer memory and incurs a great deal of cost. With the current trend toward instant facts the job becomes a stern task for the financial executive. His salvation came via the minicomputer which in its simplest form is a desktop piece of equipment with mini-floppy discs each of which will store some 256,000 bytes of information. With three discs available on-line each individual has a massive file of information at his fingertips. If properly handled and coordinated it can add to the intelligence of your entire organization.

While many financial executives will insist that decision making cannot be automated or left to computers (at times they have a point!) they must recognize the fundamental changes occurring in their field and take full advantage of the latest techniques.

The First National Bank of Chicago was one of the pioneers in the data bank field and in the development of a management communications center. It followed the basic Chinese proverb theory that "one picture is worth a thousand words." The center provides instant access to large amounts of well-formatted data through a variety of methods. It utilizes video tape and sound, film, pictures and computer-created graphs to provide instantaneous access to all required data. As the system developed from a display of actual performance versus plan, it provided a complete analysis of the underlying detail and the reasons for variations if any. Business decisions were removed from the confines and pressures of the operating level to an environment more favorable to major decision making.

Another pioneer in the management data bank center is the Dana Corporation. Overwhelmed by computer printouts and interoffice memos, they developed a closed circuit TV system for daily progress reporting. Terminals were placed in executive offices and conference rooms. The data displayed cover sales, comparative reports, cash balances and even a market report on the firm's stock. (This could be depressing at times!) The data is preformatted for historical purposes—the past—now—and the future—one day or more ahead—up to several months. Comparisons are available on performance versus last year and with planned operations. In addition to the closed circuit TV system there is an elaborate Chart Room wherein the vital statistics are displayed in color. These cover corporate operations and the current economic situation.

The change to video presentation and the use of charts has reduced their dependence upon the computer. This, plus a reduction in paperwork has saved considerable money. The availability of data instantly called up via video terminal or a CRT certainly can be economical. In one instance forty-seven reports were condensed into *one*!

DEVELOPING THE DATA BANK

Let us take the following functions and attempt to determine what data might be required for Data Bank utilization. These are the specific items:

1. *Strategic Planning*
   Set up corporate policies and objectives
   Revisions or changes in policies and objectives—updated
   Resource requirements needed to carry out these policies and objectives

2. *Financial Control*
   Break plans into logical units and determine funds required
   Provide the funds after determining the priority rank
   Personnel requirements and assignments by logical function
   Material and expense requirements by logical function
   Controls—reporting and control versus objectives
   Modification of plans to meet existing conditions

3. *Marketing Management*
   Plans for the development of new products
   Redesign of older products
   Advertising policies and strategies
   Location of distribution units
   Location of marketing units and size of staffs
   Pricing strategies
   Defensive or offensive strategies

The approach to developing the data bank and maintaining it is a continuous process once it is started. The people involved become specialists in the area or field and tend to become segregated from the day-to-day operations of the firm. Due to this fact information which should be made available to certain parts of the organization is lost in a bureaucratic shuffle. To prevent this you must utilize both a horizontal and a vertical approach in setting up the basic data base. It should flow horizontally through the entire organization with sufficient vertical integration to provide all units with the information necessary to fulfill their requirements.

Information is composed of four different types. Each requires different handling, abstracting, filing and processing. The first concerns financial information and the flow of money throughout the firm. The second covers external factors such as the general economy, political developments and competitive forces which affect your operations. The third covers the movement of physical goods throughout your operation and the equipment required for such movement. Last but not least we have the personnel factor and the required information in that area.

Interfacing these systems into one homogeneous data bank is a herculean task. It requires in many instances a redefinition of organizational structures and authority. Businesses are composed of people, tightly knit into small power structures. The development and

The Management Communications Center—The Financial Data Bank

control of the data bank can represent a major threat to some of these dynasties. Once again we cannot emphasize too highly that *knowledge is power* both within and outside of the corporate structure. Knowledge and intelligence are human attributes varying with the quality and character of the people involved. Knowledge in the data bank information enables your personnel to apply their acumen to the solution of specific problems, improves their performance and provides you with a sound base for intelligent, profitable decisions.

There is an old saying "Business needs intelligence, not data" that is a basic truth. Many firms have all types of information; however, they do not have the quality personnel, the inclination or the ability to convert this information into knowledge. Often small segments of the firm will excel but the overall performance will be poor due to a failure to interface properly or update and maintain the quality of the information and knowledge available within the firm. Intelligence is a very perishable commodity. If unused, it can deteriorate quickly. The firm and the individuals must constantly ask themselves: "Is this what we need to know?" "Has it become obsolete?" "How can we improve our information, our interpretations and our distribution of the end results?" "What have we missed and if so where do we find it?" "Have we integrated all of the facts, skills and knowledge within our firm?"

The design of the data bank must start with the basic analysis of the business. You have to understand the corporate function, see what makes it tick, who directs its various parts and diagnose any weak spots or ills. This awesome task is normally divided into about six basic factors:

1. The basic objective of the business. What is our business?
2. A searching analysis of the organization personnel.
3. An analysis of corporate resources and facilities.
4. A detailed analysis of revenues and products which create them.
5. An analysis of product costs and corporate cost centers.
6. Preparation of a list of corporate skills, intelligence and knowledge factors. What is in your current data bank?

WHAT STRATEGIES ARE AVAILABLE TO THE FINANCIAL ADMINISTRATOR?

In developing the data bank there are several approaches available to the financial executive. These normally are:

A. *The broom approach*—sweep it all up—code it—analyze it—revise and restate it or dump it in the trash can.
B. *Wait* until someone requests the information and then develop it.
C. *Steal it* from the files of the other units within the organization and use it whenever necessary.
D. *Hire outside sources* to do it. This only applies to external data in most instances.
E. *Focus*—hit only the high priority items. This can develop into a technique known as *sailboating*—whichever way the wind blows, tacking when necessary.

SPEED OF INFORMATION REQUIREMENTS

Probably the safest way to develop your data bank is to start in the *strategic planning* area. This is relatively easy to sell, has no immediate effect on the power structure and has a low data requirement speed. While the amounts of data may be large most of it will come from outside sources. Next in line would be the *management control* type of development. This requires basic top level data and begins to intrude upon the power structure of the firm in that you are now beginning to compare actual performance with planned results. It has a medium speed factor requirement and is not too critical for deadline dates. Volume of data required can vary from small to medium amounts. Last and most critical is *operational control*. Information speed requirements are high and critical. The intrusion upon the domain of the power structure is readily apparent and can result in nose-to-nose confrontations. It requires large amounts of data and covers such constantly recurring problems as the effect of machine breakdowns on production scheduling, rescheduling to meet favored customers' demands and other irritants to operating personnel.

TACT AND CONSIDERATION

Sometimes when the power structure is exceedingly strong and difficult to penetrate, the *key-result* approach will surmount the obstacles. The data bank is created slowly and carefully starting with the following statements: "We are planning to design and operate a management intelligence center for your knowledge and convenience. Tell us what data you require most, when you need the data and the priority to assign to the items." If you run into someone who wants the answers to today's problems, dollars and cents including the fractions, you may have a problem! Another one arises when the individual asks "Why?"

WHO REQUIRES THE INFORMATION? WHAT TYPE?

1. Board of Directors—strategic—economic
2. President—strategic—management control—economic
3. Vice Presidents—management control
4. Plant Managers—operational control
5. Sales Managers—operational control
6. Production Scheduling—operational control
7. Distribution and Inventory Managers—operational control

TYPES OF INFORMATION TO PUT IN THE BANK

1. Sales, gross dollar volume, type of product, units, sizes, packages and costs. Production cycle—minimum and maximum stocks—seasonal patterns.
2. Plant. All phases relative to plant and equipment, location, type, size, capacity, cost and costs of operation. Location relative to markets and raw materials.
3. Personnel. Physical characteristics, skills, intelligence, knowledge and capabilities.

The Management Communications Center—The Financial Data Bank 197

4. Operating processes, technologies, formulas, techniques.
5. Finance. Present and future requirements, strengths, weaknesses, stocks, bond issues, short-and long-term financing, leases and risk exposure.
6. Strategic plans, objectives, short-range and long-range plans, past performance.
7. Futuristic outlook, available and required future knowledge.

COMPETITIVE INFORMATION

1. All activities relative to competitive personnel, labor contracts, changes, promotions, local and national news reports.
2. Processes and production. Reports may give clues to technology, capacity, successes or failures. New items or research activities.
3. Plants. Location, type, size, cost, capacity and projected future expansion. If expanding or contracting—why?
4. A complete catalog of products and packaging, sales volume, unit pricing and methods of distribution.
5. Finance, stocks, bonds, loans, mortgages, new financing. New methods of financing. Joint ventures, partnerships or other activities. Trends in expansion. Annual reports, profit by product lines, costs, magazine and newspaper articles.
6. Miscellaneous items of possible interest.

The basic purpose of the competitive data bank is to keep your top executives and their staffs alerted to all matters which might affect your operations. Most large firms now have large intelligence or command headquarters where the latest information is displayed or is on call at your request.

A great deal of outside information can be obtained through government sources or from *The Wall Street Journal*. Copies are available on microfilm or microfiche for a reasonable sum. Through proper indexing all items relative to sensitive subjects can be collected and interpreted. The large newspapers have excellent fiche or microfilm files, and some of them are now making these available in indexed form on an annual subscription basis.

A team of investigative reporters who covered Arizona piled up an impressive total of 40,000 index cards during their investigation. The data in the files came from tips, informants, newspapers, county and state records and from court files. As they stated, it is all in the records! The success, intelligence and knowledge of your firm is there—*in the records*. In many instances we find that firms are so wrapped up in their daily activities that they neglect to collect and evaluate vital information about their own internal operations. If they are to make decisions which are sound and feasible they must be aware of all of the facts about their own organization. You must know what mistakes were made in the past and how they occurred. You need to know all about the creative and producing individuals in your firm who are responsible for its success. It is essential that you recognize the profit producing potential of each individual, each machine and each cost center. You need to know just how much money you can spend to make a profit and where to spend it. The allocation of human, physical and financial resources to best advantage is a vital function of each financial administrator. The smooth operation of the order, billing or complaint department can contribute as much to the success of your operation as quality production and excellent salesmanship.

WHAT YOU NEED TO KNOW ABOUT A SPECIFIC PRODUCT

Information in your data bank relative to specific products should include the following:

1. Total sales revenues produced.
2. Products in competition—An estimate of their sales or your share of the market. Units and dollars.
3. Costs of production and marketing. Variable expenses absorbed.
4. Required inventories and inventory turnover.
5. Capital investment required and current and historical return on investment.
6. Total development costs of the product and what percentage of these costs has been recovered.
7. List prices and discount policies for the product—current and past. Relation to competitive product pricing.
8. Percentage of total company sales and profits of each product—past—present—anticipated future contribution.
9. Projection of future sales for a minimum period of five years.

RED ALERT—THE FAILING PRODUCT

1. Declining volume in dollars or a decreasing share of the market.
2. Declining sales dollars while units sold are stable or rising. Prices must be constantly lowered to maintain or increase sales.
3. Present and future sales expectations falling below original estimates by a wide margin.
4. Return on investment well below expectations or below the minimum acceptable figure.
5. Constantly increasing costs which cannot be recovered through price adjustments.
6. Failure to contribute to overhead at the normal rate.
7. Investments in future capacity to maintain sales beyond that which will produce a satisfactory rate of return.
8. Changes in technology obsoleting the product.

REMEMBER—INTELLIGENCE TECHNOLOGY IS YOUR BASIC STRENGTH

It must utilize ingenuity and common sense. It requires skill, knowledge and patience. With the proper system you have the ability to make financial management an ANTICIPATORY process wherein you will perceive the future risks and opportunities in time to do something about them. It will enable you to analyze and make financial decisions

The Management Communications Center—The Financial Data Bank

(through the use of models and simulation) on an *after we tried them* basis. The *toughest problem* you will have to face will be *breaking old work habits*. You will have to accelerate your number acuity, abbreviate your control reports, communicate only the very essential information in a concentrated and meaningful manner.

One of the greatest drawbacks to larger industries is their inability to act fast. They suffer from inertia. In fighting this lag, the financial administrator must develop a data bank system that will predict changes well in advance of their actual happening. This will enable his firm to act within the effective time limit in order to take advantage of the data and knowledge.

THESE ARE A FEW OUTSIDE SOURCES OF DATA

New York Times Information Bank—Estimated one billion abstracts of articles from 1969 to present from their files and over 50 other publications.

A law service—Searches in as few as five minutes—Less than the time required for your personnel to go to the library and pick out a book.

Wall Street Journal—Microfilm and microfiche files beyond your requirements.

Often through *time sharing computers* all you have to do is type in the industry name—company name—government agency and the type of information, and it will print out or be displayed on a video terminal.

THE PAPERLESS OFFICE

As we move into more sophisticated data banks and electronic mail facilities we will solve one of the current problems of paperwork. Instead of paper memos we will type up the information on a video terminal, text edit it and send it on its way anywhere in the world. The major drawback will be to change the office workers' habits to use the video terminal. As the information comes over the terminal one can look at the memo—interpret it—and press a button to put it in an electronic file or to print hard copy. If the material does not require filing you scrub it. Calling up information from an electronic file is incredibly fast—printing a copy is available at the touch of the *print* button.

THE CENTRAL DATA BASE

Many firms have moved toward developing an overall company data file. All the data created throughout the firm is stored in one location for all of the information systems. This makes an economical, well-planned system which is fully integrated, and makes it possible to provide management with information it did not know existed or was not practical to obtain. In some large firms it is possible to dial up on the teletype or video screen anywhere in the world and request data on a particular subject. I stood in one office the other Saturday and watched the branch manager dial in his code numbers, the type of report desired and his location. Within seconds, his financial reports for the month were being typed out on the

200   The Management Communications Center—The Financial Data Bank

teletype. The month ended on Friday—his report was ready in detail on Saturday from a location over a thousand miles away. Somewhere in a giant honeycomb file were the combined financial results of a vast organization with thousands of units each tied together by an electronic circuit which makes the exchange of information and data easy, uncomplicated and fast.

CODING FOR INSTANT RETRIEVAL

Since there are thousands of articles published every year the task of information retrieval becomes gigantic without the use of a computer. Whether it be internal or external data the search techniques are very similar. Let us assume that we are looking for some external economic information. If we are searching one of the papers we would use a broad *key word* such as *industry sales*. This would then be refined down to *electrical contractors*. From here we can drop down to firms that are approximately the same size in *total volume* or if we want to we can go into a particular geographical location *southwest* or *mountain*. In the event we have competitors we could even use their corporate name. Once the newspapers, government bureaus, associations and libraries fully automate their facilities and utilize magnetic tape, microfilm, microfiche or the newer electronic files, computer-based retrieval systems will be an absolute necessity.

SAMPLE MASTER FILES

Personnel—   Complete information about each employee which contains one-hundred twenty-five separate items. Key reference words—Payroll—Personnel.

Inventory—   Complete information about all forms of inventory. Has over ninety classifications—code numbers—control values—sizes—styles—sales trends—costs—prices—discounts—open orders—inventory balances—minimum and maximum balance requirements.

Products—   Detailed specifications—bill of materials—set-up time—equipment utilized and production rates—tooling—description of the product—packaging requirements.

Customers—   Name, address, code number—credit limits—current outstanding balance—open orders—delivery dates—sales trend—business prospects for the future—financial stability—vulnerability to competitive action.

By the skillful application of number acuity and financial acumen control of the firm's data bank and communications control room, the financial administrator has everything he needs in intelligence, knowledge and information to turn the financial division into one of the top profit centers of the firm. *Profits and success are created by knowledge and intelligence! Intelligence is the result of a well-organized data bank.*

The look-ahead financial administrator will make his unit the headquarters for everything in the information field. As a specialist in cutting right to the heart of the matter, he will provide the latest and best information on everything of value to his corporate associates.

The Management Communications Center—The Financial Data Bank

DATA BASE SYSTEM INFORMATION FLOW

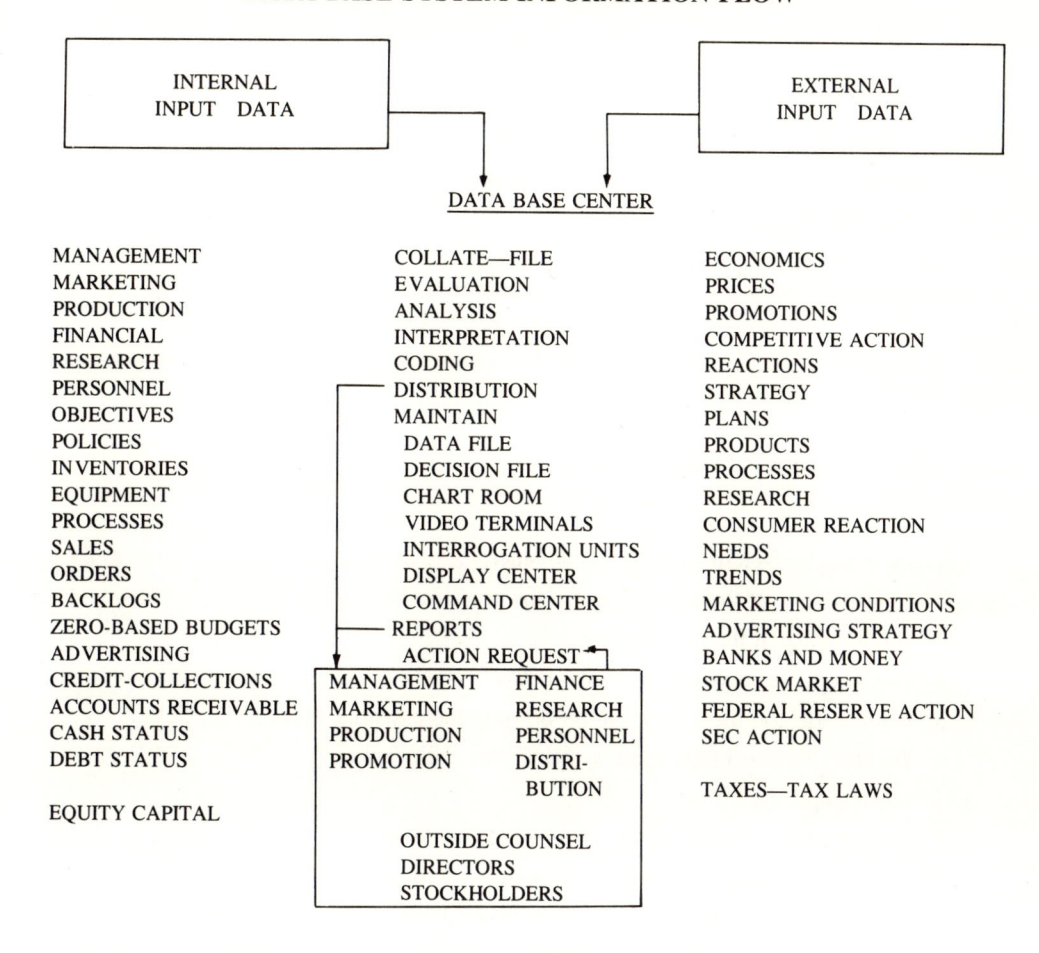

```
┌──────────────┐                    ┌──────────────┐
│   INTERNAL   │                    │   EXTERNAL   │
│  INPUT DATA  │                    │  INPUT DATA  │
└──────┬───────┘                    └──────┬───────┘
       └──────────────┬────────────────────┘
                      ▼
               DATA BASE CENTER
```

MANAGEMENT	COLLATE—FILE	ECONOMICS
MARKETING	EVALUATION	PRICES
PRODUCTION	ANALYSIS	PROMOTIONS
FINANCIAL	INTERPRETATION	COMPETITIVE ACTION
RESEARCH	CODING	REACTIONS
PERSONNEL	DISTRIBUTION	STRATEGY
OBJECTIVES	MAINTAIN	PLANS
POLICIES	DATA FILE	PRODUCTS
INVENTORIES	DECISION FILE	PROCESSES
EQUIPMENT	CHART ROOM	RESEARCH
PROCESSES	VIDEO TERMINALS	CONSUMER REACTION
SALES	INTERROGATION UNITS	NEEDS
ORDERS	DISPLAY CENTER	TRENDS
BACKLOGS	COMMAND CENTER	MARKETING CONDITIONS
ZERO-BASED BUDGETS	REPORTS	ADVERTISING STRATEGY
ADVERTISING	ACTION REQUEST	BANKS AND MONEY
CREDIT-COLLECTIONS		STOCK MARKET
ACCOUNTS RECEIVABLE	MANAGEMENT FINANCE	FEDERAL RESERVE ACTION
CASH STATUS	MARKETING RESEARCH	SEC ACTION
DEBT STATUS	PRODUCTION PERSONNEL	
	PROMOTION DISTRI-	TAXES—TAX LAWS
EQUITY CAPITAL	BUTION	
	OUTSIDE COUNSEL	
	DIRECTORS	
	STOCKHOLDERS	

SOURCES OF OUTSIDE DATA

Government Agencies .... Civil Aeronautics Board
                                              Commerce Department
                                              Congressional Proceedings
                                              HUD—DOD—EPA—FCC—FMC
                                              FPC—FTC—FDA—HEW—ICC
                                              IRS—ICC—NLRB—SEC—FRB

State Agencies .... Corporate Commission
                                              Legislative Proceedings
                                              Department of Revenue–Taxation

City Government .... City Council Proceedings
                                              Department of Revenue

202 The Management Communications Center—The Financial Data Bank

Publications	*Wall Street Journal*
	Barrons
	Daily and Sunday Newspapers
	Weekly Business Magazines
	Trade Publications
	Newsletters
Libraries	Local, national and specialized
Special Information Services	
National Technical Information Services	Access to over one million technical reports on various subjects.

DO'S AND DON'TS FOR DATA BASES

1. Do plan the system carefully in advance.
2. Do start slow at the top and work down.
3. Don't approach the task haphazardly.
4. Don't run before you walk—take it easy.
5. Do provide complete information on only the essential items.
6. Do insist on *one* information system—one data bank.
7. Don't duplicate efforts.
8. Do decide on a basic coding system familiar to all.
9. Don't waste your time on non-productive items.
10. Don't waste the specialized administrative talents of your executives on unnecessary tasks.
11. Get outside assistance if you need it.
12. Don't be arbitrary in allocating items.
13. Don't let the information system disintegrate through bad information. A small amount of good information or data is much better than a lot of data containing errors.
14. Do decide on what information your data bank will contain.
15. Do revise, review and evaluate methods periodically.
16. Do evaluate information thoroughly.
17. Do discard unnecessary items or out-of-date data periodically.
18. Do provide for permanent hard copy records of vital information.
19. Do provide adequate security for your records.
20. Don't compound errors into chaos!
21. Don't make the data bank headquarters for everything.

The Management Communications Center—The Financial Data Bank

CUSTOMER COMPETITIVE INFORMATION REPORT

ORIGINAL TO PRODUCT SALES MGR.	FROM SALESMAN
COPY TO PRICE AND CONTRACT	LOCATION OF SALESMAN
COPY TO DATA BASE	DATE
CUSTOMER NAME—ADDRESS	PLANT AFFECTED
INFORMATION SUPPLIED BY	POSITION OR TITLE
INFORMATION RECEIVED VERBALLY	IN WRITING

COMPLETE DESCRIPTION OF PRODUCTS INVOLVED

ANNUAL SALES VOLUME ALL SUPPLIERS	MINIMUM MFGR. ORDER	PRICES QUOTED	COMPETITOR	REPORTED COMPETITORS' PRICES

REMARKS

REVIEWED SALES MANAGER	REVIEWED DATA BASE
ANTICIPATED EFFECT	REQUIRED REACTION

(ENTER THIS FORM IMMEDIATELY AS THE COMPETITIVE SITUATION ARISES. REPORT ONLY ONE CUSTOMER TO A SHEET AND SHOW ALL ITEMS INVOLVED. STATE IF BUSINESS IS LOST AND THE REASON WHY, IF PRICE WAS A FACTOR. IF THE INFORMATION WAS SUPPLIED BY A CUSTOMER, SHOW COMPETITOR AND COMPETITOR'S REPORTED PRICES.)

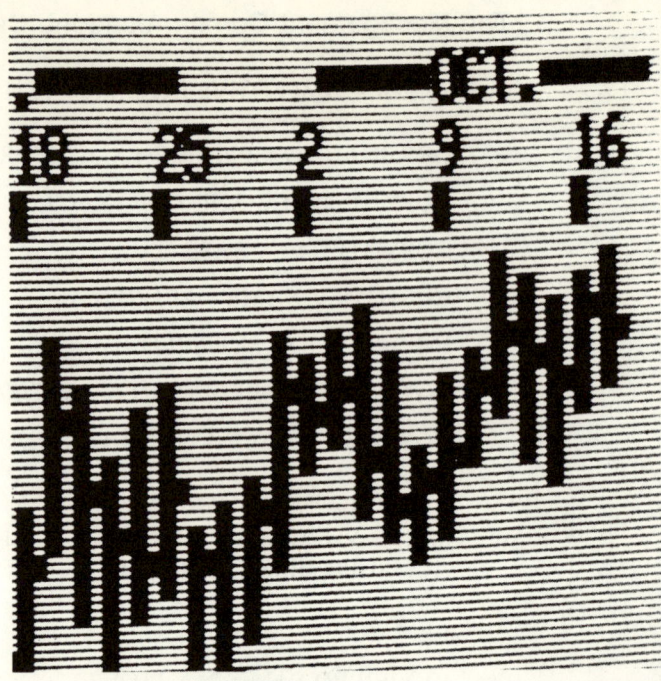

ADDS
Applied Digital
Data Systems Inc.

The Consul 980 is designed to appeal to a broad cross-section of the computer industry. This Teletype compatible series allows a user to take full advantage of the inherent flexibility of a buffered CRT Terminal. The 980 displays 24 lines of data with 80 characters per line and provides such features as block transmission, editing, protected formatting, upper/lower case display and graphics.

**Graphic Display Terminal, Consul 980.
(Courtesy of Applied Digital Data Systems, Inc.)**

```
130*      FIRST, DEFINE ALL CODES AS STRI
140*
150 STRING SO,SI,RS,US,CAN,ETB
160 STRING SOH,STX,ETX,EOT,ACK,LF,VT,F
170 FILENAME BEXEC
180 BEXEC = "BEXEC"
190*     CURSOR HOME -SOH
200 SOH = STRCHA(1,1)
```

ADDS

Applied Digital Data Systems Inc.

The Consul 580 is a low cost, teletype compatible CRT display terminal. It is designed for users who wish to take advantage of a CRT's quiet operation, fast transmission speed and inherent reliability.

The 580 displays a total of 1920 highly legible characters arranged in 24 lines with 80 characters per line. Communication with the data processing system or minicomputer takes place a character at a time on a conversational basis via a standard EIA RS232C interface or a 20 milliampere current loop interface. Transmission rates of 110, 300, 1200, 2400 or 9600 baud are available (switch selectively) on the 580's rear panel.

Text Display Terminal, Consul 580.
(Courtesy of Applied Digital Data Systems, Inc.)

8

Computerized Accounting Yields Financial Reports— Concise and Fast!

THE OPPORTUNITY!

The financial administrator has a unique opportunity to enhance ability and performance through the use of the computer. The computer is normally located in the finance division primarily because it is the central clearing house for data and because this organization serves all phases of the business. Its primary purpose is to create information which can increase profits. Due to this fact other divisions may have priority in its use. If used effectively the operating executives of the other divisions will utilize it fully. The ability to interface with other divisions will provide the financial executive with the opportunity to increase his importance and stature in the corporate structure.

THE ORGANIZATION REQUIRED

Dependent upon the size of the firm the computer operation may require a staff of one individual to several hundred. Basically the system is organized along the following lines:

1. Data Processing Management
2. Systems Planning and Revision

3. Computer Programming
4. Computer Operations
5. Computer Report Distribution and Communications

The smaller firm may have one individual who programs and operates the computer whereas the larger firms may have one or more individuals in each of the above functions. Programming is an essential part of the entire operation as it requires technical skill and an ability to transform the individual division's needs into a machine language that will produce the required reports in short order. Communications is equally vital in a large organization with widely scattered plants, sales offices or warehouses. Data must be moved rapidly and accurately and the cooperation and coordination of the various parts of the firm are vital to the success of the entire system.

WHAT REPORTS ARE AVAILABLE?

The computer is now a vital operating tool for most management employees. It can provide a constant inflow of information on expenses, revenues and profits. It starts at the lowest profit center and gives in-depth information on its performance and analyzes the reason for any detriment to its profits. It consolidates these figures by department, division, plant or firm until it reaches the apex of the business institution. You can monitor budget performance on a day-to-day basis and spot the major exceptions immediately! Absolute inventory control is a reality.

CASE IN POINT

The use of point-of-sale recorders by retail firms can provide hourly records of sales by department, inventory movement by item and the relationship of stocks on hand to sales. Through the utilization of either actual or standard costs one can have an hourly, daily, weekly or monthly profit report on each phase of the enterprise.

Through the use of computer graphics and color video terminals, one can display charts, show trends and highlight favorable (green) or unfavorable (red) items for management action.

Some firms are currently setting up communications centers and information rooms through their operations with video displays. These remind one of the airport terminal where one watches to see when his or her late plane will arrive.

Financial decisions are greatly simplified through the use of cleverly designed reports. Actual operations versus the plan can be reported or displayed on printers, teletypes or video terminals. These new techniques provide instant analysis upon demand. In the event of a problem your system may have the capability of offering alternate choices for executive action. Reams of paper can be eliminated.

One of the most useful techniques involves the logging of significant items and storing them in computer memory. This provides a wealth of research information for future action. Strangely enough the major items pop up and get immediate executive action; however, it is the small ones that kill you. Incidents of sloppy work, missed shipping dates, lack of information, late raw material receipts or missing parts can be the cause of larger problems somewhere along the line. If logged and accumulated their frequency will indicate trouble spots in your operations.

If your computer memory is limited in size the files can be placed on microfiche. The microfiche process utilizes a 4 × 5 film card which can be added to periodically or chronologically. Each card stores the equivalent of forty-five to fifty-five eight and one-half by eleven printed pages. A 4 × 5 metal card file will store the equivalent of eight thousand pages of data. An ordinary, special file cabinet will store from ten to twenty years of data depending upon the size of the firm and the number of records created.

CASE IN POINT

One firm uses microfiche to chronologically log their fixed assets with all of the pertinent data on specifications, costs and major repairs.

Instant comparative reporting is accomplished by one firm through the use of two microfiche cards and two or more projectors. It enables them to compare visually the data for last month, last year, planned forecasts or whatever they require.

One firm uses computer-prepared reports on microfiche for credit review and the instant spotting of past due accounts. The accounts are scanned visually and whenever a past due account is encountered it is fed into a reader printer unit and a past due notice is printed on a statement the exact size for a window mailing envelope. The advantage of visual scanning is that it prevents sending out a past-due notice on accounts with special terms.

With the new equipment and display terminals reporting, techniques depend only on the ingenuity of the financial executive.

WHO USES COMPUTERS?

Our survey of computer users showed the following results:

TYPE OF BUSINESS	NUMBER	USING COMPUTERS
Small	15	1
Medium-Sized	24	5
Large	30	30

This indicates the tremendous advantage the larger firms have over the smaller-sized firms in the utilization of computer technology. This is largely due to cost, lack of knowledge and trained personnel required to operate the systems. With the advent of the minicomputers and very simple programming languages, everyone can become a computer programmer and operator in ten easy lessons.

OPPORTUNITY FOR THE FINANCIAL ADMINISTRATOR!

The financial administrator has today, at his fingertips, one of the most powerful tools known to man. *It is the minicomputer!*

210 Computerized Accounting Yields Financial Reports—Concise and Fast!

EASY TO LEARN—EASY TO USE

If the financial executive has the talent and the acumen he can weld together within his company a network of small computers that will give his firm a useful, total management information system. If they have a larger computer it may be replaced. The smaller units can communicate with the larger ones.

As in all firms, management information systems are not new. They grew up as small units within the firm. Each was developed to meet the specific needs of the individuals involved. The financial administrator is in the unique position, through the utilization of minicomputers, to integrate these isolated units into one complete, compatible system. Strangely enough, the techniques are not tough and the expenses can be minimal. Each executive can have his own desk unit for problem solving completely under his control and yet be able to interface with other similar units throughout the entire organization.

CASE IN POINT

As one operating executive said: "At last I have my own computer on my desk! One which I can program and control myself!"

PRIORITIES

What are the priorities of the computer system? First off, it must serve all units of the business with valid and reliable information within the parameters of importance, time and conciseness. Only the essential facts for the important decisions should be accumulated. The checklist of important decisions involved is determined by the parameters of time, practicability and the various technology, skills and disciplines that exist within your firm. Naturally cost is also a factor. It must be justified by the contribution made to profitability, growth and company objectives.

CASE IN POINT—CRITICAL DECISION

This firm has a large share of its sales volume in a seasonal item. What are its inventory requirements for the coming year? How much financing will be required? All sales from January 1 through May 31 are due for payment on a discount basis on June 10, and on a net basis by June 30. In addition to the sales made during this period it must load up fifty-five warehouses prior to the selling season. There are three classes of product, each having its own market and percentage contribution within all markets. The weather has a direct bearing upon sales as the product is tied to the growing season which advances from South to North, the size of the crop and the last killing frost. The end of the season is marked by the first killing frost advancing from North to South. To make the critical decisions to start production in the fall the firm needs more precise information on how much inventory will be required in order to maintain acceptable levels of customer service. What should be the basic stocks in each of the fifty-five warehouses? In what form do we maintain the inventory: raw materials—work in process—finished goods? What is the availability of raw materials?

Computerized Accounting Yields Financial Reports—Concise and Fast!

What is the production and shipping cycle? The information required is utilized to optimize the use of inventory at every level of investment. Due to the high cost of money the information must give management all of the options for committing the inventory investment as late as possible in the production, distribution and selling cycle. In addition it must consider the weather, as after the first killing frost sales drop to zero. The carryover of large stocks of merchandise can be very unprofitable.

The solution to this situation was the development of a simulation model which indicated the various alternatives under specific conditions. As the season developed the factors could be inputted and the desired changes made.

SMALL BUSINESS SYSTEMS

All of the computer firms are now solidly into the minicomputer market which means that a small business firm or the financial executive can now afford one to handle any phase of his operations. This is one area that will provide thousands of new customers every year.

WHAT IS REQUIRED TO UTILIZE A MINICOMPUTER?

Programs are currently available which will enable you as the owner, financial executive, accountant or clerk to operate the units on normal, not too complex tasks. For example, let us assume that you own a wholesale and retail lighting fixture outlet and wish to place your inventory on line.

CASE IN POINT

The computer costs $1,000 with 16K of memory
A Teletype Machine—New $1,200, Used $700
A Video Terminal—New $1,000
Supplies $50
Initial Program $50 to $150

It also rents for $100 to $150 per month.

You physically count the inventory.

You input the items into the file as follows:

CODE NO.	IN INV.	SHOW ROOM	ON ORDER
P-7	5	1	12 PO-3576 12/6/X
P-34	18	2	26 PO-3571 1/7/X -21 for DAVIS
100 AB	3	1	
123 BR	25	2	
131	0	1	5 PO-3800 1/9/X -1 DAVIS del 6 wks
150	8	2	

You leave the computer on twenty-four hours a day after running off a mag tape or paper tape of the initial inventory. You also run a printed report of the inventory on hand.

Suppose DAVIS calls and wants to know if his order is in.

For Teletype—Type in DAVIS.

It will come back with this message:

| P-34 | 18 | 1 | 26 PO-3571 1/7/X-21 for DAVIS |
| 131 | 0 | 1 | 5 PO-3800 1/9/X-1 DAVIS del 6 wks |

Based upon the current data you have all the information on DAVIS.

For Video Terminal—Type in DAVIS and it will display the same information on the screen.

You can search for the code number—PO number, or the individual.

If the information is not in the file it will come back with a "?"

Should you wish to list all the items for one supplier you would request:

050-EAGLE LIGHTING

It will list any or all of the items as requested.

WHAT ARE THE MINICOMPUTERS USED FOR?

The list of jobs they will handle:

Payroll	Accounts Receivable	Accounts Payable
Estimating	Manpower Control	Job Cost Analysis
Cash Flow	Inventory Control	Job Bidding
Reports	Financial Statements	Equipment Control
Scheduling	Profit Center Analysis	Tool Control
Budgeting	Lease Versus Purchase	General Ledgers
ROI Analysis	Expense Analysis	Resource Projection

With a little more sophisticated programming they can handle more complex problems:

Linear Programming	Matrix Problems	Differentiation
Time Series Analysis	Smoothing	Multivariant Analysis
Interpolation	Modeling	Machine Control
Simulation	Market Analysis	
Tool Control	Integration	

Most small businesses require a minimum system in order to effect financial control. If you run a list of the cash receipts, the invoices issued, the invoices received, the checks issued and perhaps a few adjusting journal entries, you can have the complete financial story posted in a general ledger file and in prepared printed reports. Add to this the hours worked by job, the purchase orders issued, the material receipts and merchandise shipped and you can have control of most of the operations of a small- to medium-sized business. The computer will sort out the items, tuck them in the right files and with an appropriate input-output program it will spit out any facts you need to know. Timing and effectiveness are subject only to your ability to input the correct data on time.

Computerized Accounting Yields Financial Reports—Concise and Fast!

SETTING UP THE SYSTEM

Whether it be a mini or maxi the requirements are about the same. The basic checklist follows:

1. Analyze your system
2. State the goals and features desired
3. Compare the benefits versus costs
4. Organize the system—chart or document it
5. Determine the input-output requirements
6. Set up the coding system (leave room for expansion)
7. Forms required
8. Reports anticipated
9. Time schedules
10. Installation—development—debugging
11. The lucky number—review and revision

BASIC BENEFITS EXPECTED

1. No change in current personnel—ability to grow without adding people
2. Financial stability
3. A better run business
4. Greater profitability

DO'S AND DONT'S

Do keep it simple and concise

Do start off slowly

Don't move too fast

Do leave payroll until the last—it has a tight time schedule

Do it neatly—some installations are sloppy

Do direct your attention to important items first

Don't let projects die while analyzing them—data must be precise

Don't paralyze your executives with paperwork

Don't let controls become an obsession

Do try out things—if they do not work you can drop them

Don't overcentralize management—permit flexibility at the local level

Don't bog down with minutiae

Don't make a production out of reporting—fancy covers—bindings—reams of printed data

Do—if it is not used—drop it!

214 Computerized Accounting Yields Financial Reports—Concise and Fast!

CASES IN POINT

- A seventy-page report on the purchase of a fifty-thousand dollar machine—full of trivia.
- A one-inch thick sheaf of reports listing every invoice the manager of a two-hundred-fifty thousand dollar service center had issued during the year—he could care less!
- A two-inch thick stack of monthly reports for an operation grossing two-hundred-fifty thousand dollars a year. The manager is primarily interested in two things: How much did he bill and how much money did he make? A two-line to a two-page report would have sufficed.
- An organization that eliminates printed reports altogether except on an annual basis. Each month they receive their reports by video coupled with a one-hour conference. Good items are shown in green. Alert or bad items have a red arrow pointing to them and the possible problems are coded in yellow.

TEXT EDITOR TERMINALS

One of the newest wrinkles is the text editor terminal wherein the data is stored on magnetic tape. You type in your data—it is displayed on the screen—you edit it with a stylus, light pencil or cursor keyboard. The adjusted, corrected copy is stored in memory or printed out. The potential uses are for inventories—accounts receivable—accounts payable—job costs—purchase order files—private files.

Communications between terminals can result in no more departmental mail.

This type of unit can be used for Production Control and Planning. It can quickly answer the following questions when coupled to a minicomputer on the production line:

1. How are we?
2. Where are we?
3. What delivery can we quote?
4. Can we make it?

The utilization of minicomputers on the production lines will not only aid in generating better financial data but will also improve the control of job costs and job progress. It will result in better cost estimating and better production forecasting. It will provide a higher utilization of workers with less clerical effort.

SUMMARY OF EQUIPMENT UTILIZED

1. Maxicomputer
2. Medium Computer
3. Minicomputer
4. Input Equipment
   a. Keyboard
   b. Teletype
   c. Video terminal
   d. Modem—Radio
   e. Computer terminal

Computerized Accounting Yields Financial Reports—Concise and Fast!

5. Output Equipment
   a. Printer
   b. Teletype
   c. Video terminal
   d. Microfilm or microfiche
   e. Graphic terminal
   f. Radio

Types of reports and displays are illustrated in the following text beginning on the next page.

216 Computerized Accounting Yields Financial Reports—Concise and Fast!

WHAT THE COMPUTER CAN DO FOR YOU!

Analysis Reports   *Routine Functions*

Market Analysis

Sales Distribution
  Analysis

Cash Flow

Profit Center Analysis

Budgetary Planning

Manpower Requirements
  and Forecasts

Production Planning

Change Order Analysis

Payroll

Labor Job Costs and
  Analysis

Job Costs

Financial Reports

Accounts Receivable/
  Payable

Preventative Maintenance
  Scheduling

Tool and Equipment
  Cost Analysis

Tool and Equipment
  Control

Purchasing and
  Inventory Control

Planned Overhead

Estimating

PERIOD — 12
SALES — OPERATING PROFIT

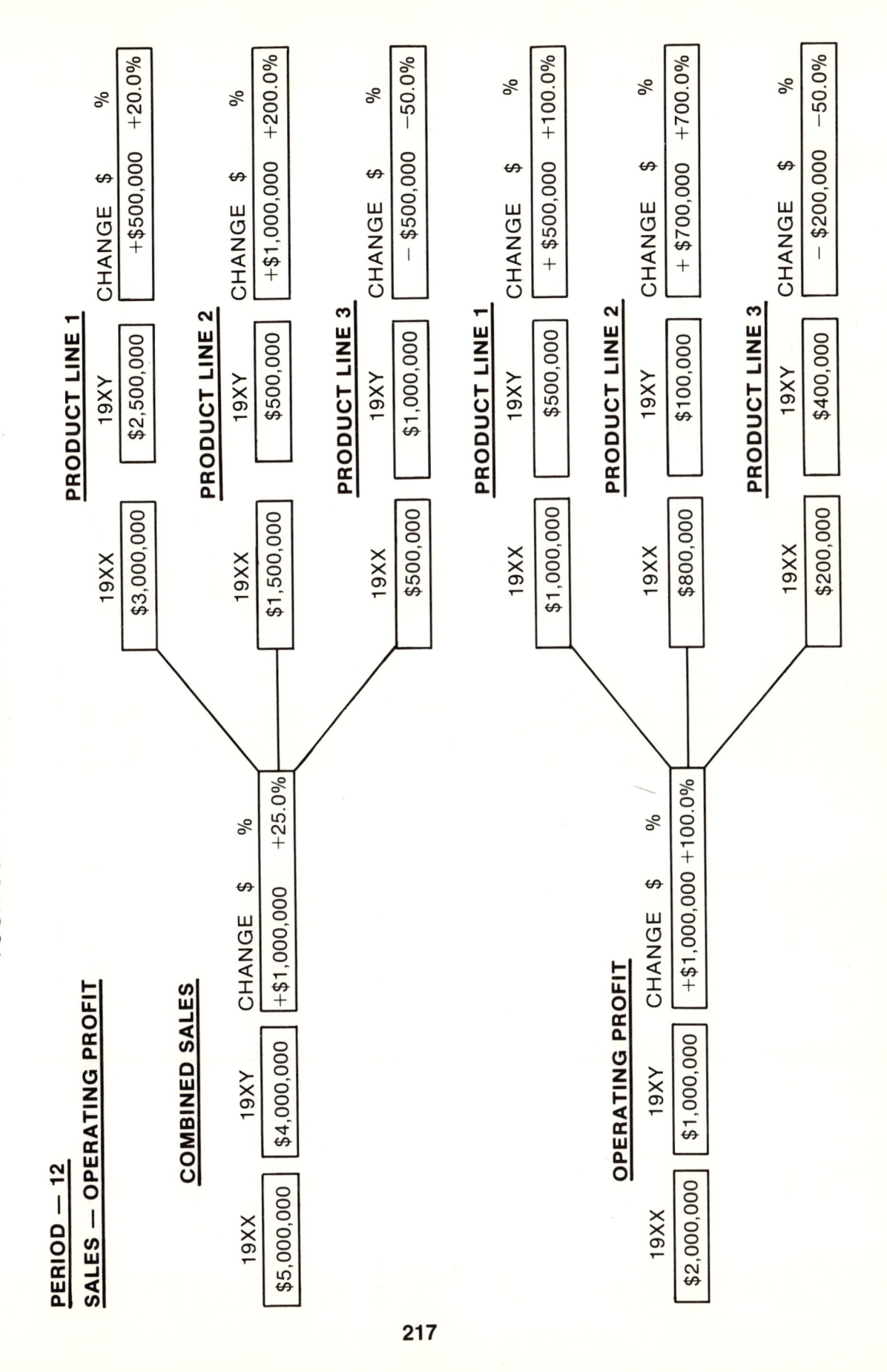

YOUR COMPANY — OPERATION XX

COMBINED SALES

	19XX	19XY	CHANGE $	%
	$5,000,000	$4,000,000	+$1,000,000	+25.0%

PRODUCT LINE 1

19XX	19XY	CHANGE $	%
$3,000,000	$2,500,000	+$500,000	+20.0%

PRODUCT LINE 2

19XX	19XY	CHANGE $	%
$1,500,000	$500,000	+$1,000,000	+200.0%

PRODUCT LINE 3

19XX	19XY	CHANGE $	%
$500,000	$1,000,000	−$500,000	−50.0%

OPERATING PROFIT

19XX	19XY	CHANGE $	%
$2,000,000	$1,000,000	+$1,000,000	+100.0%

PRODUCT LINE 1

19XX	19XY	CHANGE $	%
$1,000,000	$500,000	+$500,000	+100.0%

PRODUCT LINE 2

19XX	19XY	CHANGE $	%
$800,000	$100,000	+$700,000	+700.0%

PRODUCT LINE 3

19XX	19XY	CHANGE $	%
$200,000	$400,000	−$200,000	−50.0%

```
                              BALANCE SHEET FER    09/20/

                                         CURRENT YEAR              PREVIOUS YEAR
        ACCOUNT              CURRENT MONTH  YEAR-TO-DATE    CURRENT MONTH  YEAR-TO-DATE

1100  CASH ON HAND              2,460.95      16,794.35        1,976.38      12,554.73
1101  CASH IN BANK              10,895.41     57,465.77        7,411.19      41,368.52

        TOTAL CASH              13,356.36     74,260.12        9,387.57      53,923.25

1301  ACCOUNTS RECEIVABLE       19,758.46    116,240.97       16,132.16      97,638.15
1309  NOTES RECEIVABLE           3,120.00     29,450.00        4,200.00      32,773.19

        TOTAL RECEIVABLES       22,878.46    145,690.97       20,332.16     130,411.34

1421  INVENTORY                 16,452.09     89,674.57       18,641.37      92,117.35
1500  FIXED ASSETS              11,734.71     68,832.16        9,887.60      55,486.67

**********  TOTAL ASSETS......  64,421.62    378,457.82       58,248.70     331,938.61

2100  ACCOUNTS PAYABLE          13,126.51     41,210.30       15,007.32      38,268.53
2300  WITHHOLDING TAX           12,753.00     61,145.00       11,339.64      54,297.00
2350  OTHER LIABILITIES         21,850.50     39,126.50       22,790.35      45,498.70

        TOTAL LIABILITIES..     47,730.01    141,481.80       49,137.31     138,064.23

2911  CAPITAL STOCK                   .00    100,000.00             .00     100,000.00
2919  RETAINED EARNINGS         14,941.47    119,087.40        7,697.51      81,274.65
2925  SURPLUS - UNDIVIDED PROFITS 1,749.99    17,888.62        1,413.83      12,599.73

        TOTAL NET WORTH         16,691.46    236,976.02        9,111.39     193,874.38

****  TOTAL LIABILITIES & NET WORTH... 64,421.62  378,457.82  58,248.70     331,938.61
```

```
                           INCOME STATEMENT PER    09/20/                                          PAGE  1

    ACCOUNT                CURRENT MONTH   CURRENT BUDGET   PERCENT    YEAR TO DATE    YEAR TO DATE   PERCENT
                                                                                          BUDGET
SALES CATEGORY 1              43,000.00       42,250.00      101.78      453,900.00      448,600.00    101.18
OTHER INCOME ACCOUNTS          8,000.00        6,400.00      125.00       70,800.00       59,600.00    118.79

    TOTAL REVENUE.....        51,000.00       48,650.00      104.83      524,700.00      508,200.00    103.25

OFFICE EXPENSES                5,000.00        6,800.00       73.53       47,350.00       55,600.00     85.16
OTHER EXPENSE ACCOUNTS        39,000.00       35,200.00      110.80      421,250.00      406,300.00    103.68

    TOTAL EXPENSES.....       44,000.00       42,000.00      104.76      468,600.00      461,900.00    101.45

    NET OPERATING MARGIN       7,000.00        6,650.00      105.26       56,100.00       46,300.00    121.17

CASH DISCOUNTS ALLOWED           200.00          250.00       80.00        3,000.00        2,400.00    125.00

    NET PROFIT OR LOSS         6,800.00        6,400.00      106.25       53,100.00       43,900.00    120.96


              PRINTED   BY COMPANY        OR
                        BY DIVISION       OR
                        BY DEPARTMENT     OR
                        BY COST CENTER

              SHOWING   CURRENT MONTH OR CURRENT YEAR BALANCE
                    OR  -SAME WITH PER CENT
                    OR  CURRENT MONTH AND YEAR TO DATE
                    OR  -SAME WITH PER CENT
                    OR  CURRENT MONTH AND YTD THIS YEAR AND LAST YEAR
                    OR  -SAME WITH PER CENT
                    OR  CURRENT MONTH WITH BUDGET OR YTD WITH BUDGET
                    OR  -SAME WITH PER CENT
                    OR  CURRENT MONTH WITH BUDGET AND YTD WITH BUDGET
                    OR  -SAME WITH PER CENT
```

INCOME ACCOUNT   DATE..................

SALES	100.00		$68,924
COST OF SALES			
OPENING INVENTORY			184,628
MERCHANDISE PURCHASED			2,589
TOTAL			187,217
LESS:CLOSING INVENTORY			149,741
COST OF SALES - MATERIAL	54.24	37,383	
COST OF MARKDOWNS	.13	93	
COST OF MERCHANDISE SOLD	54.37		37,476
0800 PLUS IN FREIGHT	.05		34
GROSS PROFIT	45.58		
OPERATING EXPENSES			
0808 EMPLOYEE DISCOUNTS	.02		19
0825 SALARIES OFFICERS	6.42		4,427
0826 WAGES OTHER	8.47		5,840
0827 ADVERTISING	2.28		1,574
0828 TAXES	.36		246
0829 SUPPLIES	.24		166
0830 SERVICES PURCHASED	.81		556
0832 TRAVEL-ENTERTAINMENT	1.11		763
0834 COMMUNICATIONS	.29		201
0835 INSURANCE	.29		197
0836 DEPRECIATION	.29		202
0837 DONATIONS	.39		270
0838 BAD DEBTS	.43		295
0839 RENT	2.85		1,967
0840 UTILITIES	.29		197
0842 EQUIPMENT	.50		344
0843 CASH SHORTAGES	.01		5
0844 MISCELLANEOUS	.07		49
TOTAL OPERATING EXPENSES	25.12		
NET PROFIT	20.46		
OTHER INCOME			
0804 ALTERATIONS	.03		22
0807 SERVICE CHARGE	.87		600
0809 POSTAGE	.00		3
0854 RENTAL & MISC.	.12		85
TOTAL OTHER INCOME	1.03		710
NET PROFIT	21.49		14,810
0994 ESTIMATED FED INC TAX	5.59		3,851
NET PROFIT AFTER INCOME TAX	15.90		10,959

MONTHLY RETAIL INVENTORY MANAGEMENT REPORT (STOCK LEDGER) — MENS STORE

METHOD 1
DATE
PAGE NO. 1

SALES AT RETAIL	% OF SALES	GROSS PROFIT	% CUM MARKON	MOS INV ON HAND	PURCHASES AT COST	ADDITIONS AT RETAIL	MARK-DOWNS	END INV AT COST	END INV AT RETAIL	% INV TO TOT
3,040.19	4.41	1,298.47	42.71	3.92	.00	.00	.00	6,830.39	11,922.41	4.34
790.65	1.15	419.12	53.01	5.99	.00	.00	.00	2,223.41	4,732.18	1.72
1,439.95	2.09	793.99	55.14	1.61	.00	.00	.00	1,040.51	2,319.46	.84
4,700.50	6.82	2,330.51	49.58	6.31	.00	.00	.00	14,958.70	29,666.35	10.80
1,035.25	1.50	502.61	48.55	2.89	.00	.00	.00	1,538.44	2,990.36	1.09
2,295.77	3.33	1,111.61	48.42	2.48	.00	.00	.00	2,937.21	5,694.18	2.07
4,220.35	6.12	1,708.82	40.49	2.51	1,030.75	1,703.50	.00	6,296.29	10,579.79	3.85
705.92	1.02	372.16	52.72	1.30	.00	.00	.00	433.46	916.82	.33
659.75	.96	310.48	47.06	5.19	.00	.00	.00	1,797.22	3,395.13	1.24
351.45	.51	166.52	47.38	18.46	.00	.00	.00	3,414.34	6,488.49	2.36
995.00	1.44	504.56	50.71	6.62	.00	.00	.00	3,247.51	6,588.22	2.40
110.00	.16	56.78	51.62	66.20	.00	.00	.00	3,522.98	7,282.18	2.65
159.50	.23	66.22	41.52	23.00	.00	.00	.00	2,145.86	3,669.17	1.34
20,504.28	29.75	9,641.85	47.02	4.69	1,030.75	1,703.50	.00	50,386.32	56,244.74	35.04
3,097.05	4.49	1,386.55	44.77	1.55	.00	.00	.00	2,649.43	4,797.69	1.75
560.34	.81	293.77	58.37	1.35	.00	.00	80.00	315.99	759.16	.28
592.76	.86	322.28	54.37	4.75	.00	.00	.00	1,285.25	2,817.00	1.03
4,250.15	6.17	2,002.60	47.90	1.97	.00	.00	80.00	4,250.67	8,373.85	3.05
2,245.93	3.26	992.48	44.19	3.35	.00	.00	.00	4,201.65	7,527.66	2.74
2,230.45	3.24	898.19	40.18	.52	.00	.00	.00	699.88	1,170.00	.43
675.24	.98	337.69	50.01	.52	.00	.00	.00	175.90	351.81	.13
349.75	.51	187.50	53.61	.75	.00	.00	.00	122.28	263.65	.10
5,501.37	7.98	2,413.86	43.88	1.69	.00	.00	.00	5,199.71	9,313.12	3.39

CUSTOMER CONTRIBUTION

CUST NO	PROD CODE	UNITS	$ VALUE	MATL	LABOR	BURDEN	GROSS PROFIT	%	CONTRIBUTION $	%
02003	53100	2,000	16,260	8,380	400	1,740	5,740	35.3	7,480	46.0
	CUSTOMER TOTAL		16,260	8,380	400	1,740	5,740	35.3	7,480	46.0
02006	53101	500	4,125	2,100	110	475	1,440	34.9	1,915	46.4
02006	53105	1,500	12,379	6,210	330	1,425	4,414	35.6	5,839	47.1
	CUSTOMER TOTAL		16,504	8,310	440	1,900	5,854	35.4	7,754	46.9
02009	53136	600	3,978	1,776	162	504	1,536	38.6	2,040	51.2
	CUSTOMER TOTAL		3,978	1,776	162	504	1,536	38.6	2,040	51.2
	GRAND TOTAL		36,742	18,466	1,002	4,144	13,130	35.7	17,274	47.0

PERIODIC LIABILITY FORECAST-SCHEDULED DATES 15-9 / 22-9

FORECAST PERIOD IS 7 DAYS

	INVOICE AMOUNT	DISCOUNT AMOUNT	PAYABLE AMOUNT
TOTAL CURRENT	$13,586	$215	$13,371
TOTAL FUTURE	34,193	548	33,645
TOTAL ACCOUNTS PAYABLE	$47,778	$763	$47,015

PAST	--0--	--1--	--2--	--3--	--4--	--5--	--6--	--7--	--8--	--9--	--10--	BALANCE
3725	9122	583	1695	8637	2764	2991	495	0	4164	0	0	12,835

ANSWERS THESE QUESTIONS

HOW MUCH DO WE OWE OUR VENDORS? - HOW MUCH IS DUE FOR PAYMENT?

- HOW MUCH IS FUTURE?

HOW MUCH OF THE FUTURE LIABILITY IS DUE WITHIN....000DAYS?

IF WE CAN PAY A MAXIMUM OF $000,000 (ESTIMATED) WHERE DO WE SET OUR PAYMENT DATES TO TAKE ADVANTAGE OF THE MAXIMUM DISCOUNTS?

SHOULD WE RETURN THE REPORT TO SEE WHAT IT WOULD LOOK LIKE WITH ANOTHER OR REVISED FORECAST PERIOD?

DETAILED AGE ANALYSIS 09/20/ PAGE 1

CUSTOMER NO.	TELEPHONE NO.	DATE LAST PAYMENT	ACCOUNT BALANCE	SALES YTD	UNAPPLIED CASH
136542	643-9234	05/11/7-	16,432.26	26,289	.00

INVOICE NO.	INVOICE DATE	CURRENT BALANCE	30 DAY BALANCE	60 DAY BALANCE	90 DAY BALANCE
12345	05/25/7-				2,237.41
13749	07/18/7-			2,981.74	
13963	08/11/7-		3,682.94		
15327	09/04/7-	1,946.21			
15419	09/09/7-	3,216.84			
15732	09/16/7-	2,367.12			
TOTAL		7,530.17	3,682.94	2,981.74	2,237.41

CUSTOMER NO.	TELEPHONE NO.	DATE LAST PAYMENT	ACCOUNT BALANCE	SALES YTD	UNAPPLIED CASH
164916	646-2663	08/24/7-	3,245.90	21,297	4,975.45

INVOICE NO.	INVOICE DATE	CURRENT BALANCE	30 DAY BALANCE	60 DAY BALANCE	90 DAY BALANCE
13821	07/22/7-			4,975.45	
15432	09/09/7-	3,245.90			
TOTAL		3,245.90		4,975.45	
GRAND TOTAL		19,678.16	10,776.07	3,682.94	7,957.19	2,237.41

TOP MANAGEMENT REPORT
DETAILED CUSTOMER AGING ANALYSIS

NUMBER	CUSTOMER NAME	PHONE NO.	DATE LAST PAYMENT	ACCOUNT BALANCE	SALES YTD	UNAPPLIED FUNDS
P123	NAVAJO DRUGS	689-3625	01-07-XX	$16,432	26,289	00

	INVOICE	DATE	CURRENT	30-DAYS	60-DAYS	90-DAYS
	1111	05/23/X				2,237
	1234	07/09/X			2,982	
	1324	08/07/X		3,683		
	1423	09/08/X	1,946			
	1429	09/09/X	3,217			
	1500	09/30/X	2,367			
	TOTAL		$7,530	$3,683	$2,982	$2,237

P167	NORVILLE CENTER	W89-5678	08-08/XX	3 $3,246	21,297	$4,975

	INVOICE	DATE	CURRENT	30-DAYS	60-DAYS	90-DAYS
	1420	07/12/X	3,246		4,975	
	1501	09/30/X				
	TOTAL		3,246		4,975	

| TOTAL RECEIVABLES | $19,678 | | $10,776 | $3,682 | $7,957 | $2,237 |

REPORT STANDARDS

Make it accurate—make it complete. The preparation of the report must be preceded by an analysis of the pertinent data. This, of itself, requires an orderly method to accumulate and classify the information to be used. Results must be interpreted in a manner that will reveal the problem clearly and in detail. It should indicate, whenever possible, the desired action. The presentation of the report must be carefully considered in advance. In this era of fast reporting, the financial executive is under considerable stress in making certain that the information and presentation are accurate and unbiased. Follow-up is essential to see that adequate recognition has been given to the problem and to make certain that proper action has been taken.

ESTABLISHMENT OF REPORT OBJECTIVES

1. Current and prospective economic conditions.
2. Current sales and cost trends.
3. Contemplated expansion or contraction of products, facilities and organization.
4. Estimated continued growth pattern in sales and profits.
5. Estimated sales and profits for each division for the current year contrasted with a tentative objective for the next year.
6. Current trends of sales, costs and profits for each division.
7. Estimated rate of return on assets employed and the current rate of return.
8. Analysis of factors accounting for the difference between current performance versus plan and how it may affect the performance next year.
9. Changes in policy required or major problems which must be solved if the corporate objectives are to be met this year and the next.

COMPUTER REPORTS

Computer reports keep management informed immediately on:

1. New orders received and current backlog.
2. Total revenues—cash inflow versus cash outflow.
3. Sales value of production relative to orders received.
4. Inventory status.
5. Gross profit rates.
6. Summary of operating expenses.
7. Net income before taxes and funds generated by operations.

TYPICAL MANAGEMENT REPORTS

1. *Summarized Reports*.
    a. Weekly or daily activity.

b. Weekly or daily report of actual results versus planned results in the development and merchandising of new products.

c. Daily, weekly or monthly expenses as compared to plan.

d. Daily, weekly or monthly analysis of inventory position.

e. Daily, weekly or monthly comparison of the financial position versus the forecast.

f. Daily, weekly or monthly comparison of payables and receivables against planned amounts—detailed analysis of account status by major items.

f. Reports of variances from standard costs (if used) separated into labor, materials and controllable expenses.

g. Head count by function, division, department or other classification.

2. *Issued Raw—Often On-Line.*

a. Weekly summary of field staff and geographical reports on the economic conditions.

b. Daily or weekly report of orders booked.

c. Daily or weekly report of items shipped—quantities-dollars.

d. Daily or weekly report of inventory status.

e. Weekly report of capital expenditure and other major appropriations.

f. Weekly or monthly report of business prospects by area, territory or customers.

g. Daily head count—added—attrition.

h. Daily report of financial condition.

3. *Specifically Prepared for the Directors.*

a. Sales volumes—analysis of variations from plan.

b. Major differences in actual or standard costs.

c. Profit margins—reasons for variations.

d. Expenses—reasons for major variations from plan.

JUSTIFICATION OF REPORTS

Every now and then one must clean up the number of reports issued. Reports have a habit of growing, and when one hears of a single institution requiring over one million copies of reports a year one has to wonder: "Are they all really necessary?" At least once a year many firms send out a questionnaire in order to determine if the reports are really required. It looks something like this:

REPORT NO. .... TITLE ....

ISSUED   DAILY____WEEKLY____MONTHLY____QUARTERLY____

ANNUALLY _____

1. IS THIS REPORT NECESSARY TO YOUR OPERATIONS?   YES ___ NO _____
2. HOW OFTEN IS IT USED?   DAILY_____ OTHER _____

3. WHAT IS ITS IMPORTANCE TO YOU?
    100- VITAL _____
    75-IMPORTANT _____
    50-USEFUL _____
    25-REFERENCE _____
    0-SOME VALUE _____

4. IS THE REPORT RECEIVED ON TIME?
    100-ALWAYS _____
    75-MOST ALWAYS _____
    50-SOMETIMES _____
    25-NEVER _____

5. SHOULD THE FREQUENCY BE CHANGED?
    MORE OFTEN _____
    LESS OFTEN _____

6. DO OTHERS USE THE REPORT? YES _____ NO _____

7. WHAT USE DO THEY MAKE OF THE REPORT?
    INFORMATION _____
    ACTION _____

8. DOES IT NEED REVISION? YES _____ NO _____
HOW WOULD YOU REVISE IT?

9. IF OTHERS FEEL THEY NO LONGER NEED THE REPORT WOULD YOU STILL REQUIRE IT? YES _____ NO _____

10. DO YOU RECEIVE TOO MANY REPORTS? YES _____ NO _____

11. YOUR FURTHER COMMENTS WOULD BE APPRECIATED!

INDIVIDUAL _____
DIVISION _____
DEPARTMENT _____

(Always keep in mind we are trying to keep down the size and number of reports issued in order to furnish you the vital information as fast as possible.)

9

Capital Investments— Lease, Rent or Buy?

Keeping up with the corporate "Joneses" is no problem these days where you pay as you use for the very latest in plant, equipment, automobiles, trucks or jet planes. One firm highlights the gold seat belt buckles and gold faucets on its fleet of jets for lease or sale to corporate executives or their firms in order that they may live in ostentation these days. In fact if you are so inclined and your profits will stand the gaff you can embark upon a program of trading in the "old" every year. This applies to jet planes, typewriters, desks, computers or even the suits, uniforms or other accoutrements worn by your personnel.

No longer is the lack of funds a restraining factor when you consider the various ways to improve the competitive position of your business. Your strategy for acquiring new productive machinery, replacing a rapidly obsolescing sector of your plant or a major expansion in order to gain a competitive edge on your competition, is now available through leasing.

Leasing is a rapidly growing financial tool that is providing financial administrators with a convenient, simple and highly successful answer to the pressing problem of raising sufficient capital to finance rapid growth plans. By leasing everything, including office equipment, or by converting currently owned assets into cash through sale and lease-back, the modern financial executive can unlock the long-term funds invested in a plant and create working capital that can be directed into more effective profit generation, at a larger rate of return. Larger profits can be obtained through the *use* of plant and equipment than are obtained through the ownership of it!

One of the leasing firms advertises that it leases over fifty-thousand pieces of equipment to more than forty thousand businesses. Among the unusual items listed by them are flagpoles, gorilla cages, janitorial gear, noise generators, quick-deposit boxes, spaghetti makers, walk-up windows, yachts and zipper bags. You name it, they will find a way to lease it!

The financial executive must face up to many important decisions relative to capital investments as his firm grows. Capital expenditures can make or break the firm that employs him. No single item has as important a role in the future of your firm and your job as does the acquisition of capital assets, whether they be bought, leased or rented. The cost of capital and the effective use of it is the least understood and least used concept in financial management; yet it is the most effective way to evaluate the risks and potential profit payoffs.

The current name of the game is "earnings and return on investment." You must be ready to go to bat with new ideas, new methods, forms and modeling or computer techniques.

LEASE OR PURCHASE—HOW TO DECIDE!

Many owners and financial executives refuse to lease plant and equipment because of a built-in bias toward capital items. Owners of businesses and their financial executives feel that owning capital assets is essential to their security and success in running the operations. They feel that if they own the plant and equipment they can weather any recession or period of depressed sales and profits. From a conservative standpoint this opinion has merit and cannot be disregarded. Many firms retreat from leasing simply because they are unable to accurately compute the costs of leasing versus buying outright or on long-term financing. The younger breed of entrepreneurs and financiers have been raised in a "rental" type economy and all they ask is: "How much are the monthly payments?" Somewhere between these two approaches is the cold, logical analysis of the true results of each method of financing expansion.

The first decision that each firm must make is whether the investment is really essential and that the profits attained will more than offset the risk. Once this decision is made the comparison between the options is made in the following fashion:

THE BASIC PARAMETERS

COST OF THE EQUIPMENT		$110,000
LIFE OF EQUIPMENT		10 YEARS
COST OF BORROWED FUNDS		8%
TYPE OF DEPRECIATION	OPTION 1	STRAIGHT LINE 10% (A)
	OPTION 2	DECLINING BALANCE 20%
	OPTION 3	SUM OF THE YEAR'S DIGITS
AVERAGE ANNUAL INCOME CREATED BY THE EQUIPMENT		$ 40,000

Capital Investments—Lease, Rent or Buy?

COST OF PURCHASING—CASH

The decision to purchase requires that the firm have sufficient funds available to make the purchase. It must also establish that it can tie up the funds over the life of the asset. Once this test is made you can proceed.

COSTS INVOLVED $110,000

This could be reduced by a cash discount or the use of the funds for 30 to 60 days dependent upon the manufacturer's terms.

COST OF PURCHASE—BORROWED FUNDS

This decision requires that you have available credit at 8% in order to finance the purchase.

COSTS INVOLVED $154,000

This method assumes a 10% down payment and financing for the remaining $100,000.

COST OF UTILIZATION—LEASING CONTRACT

This decision assumes a rental cost of approximately $15.45 per $1,000 of rental value per month. It also calls for a deposit of the last month's rental in advance and no security deposit. The lease will be for eight years with an option to renew for two or more years at $5,100 per year.

COSTS INVOLVED $173,400

HOW THE COSTS ARE DETERMINED

CASH PURCHASE

YEAR	CASH FLOW IN	CASH FLOW OUT	DEPRECIATION	TAX SAVING	NET CASH FLOW	NET INCOME
1	+$40,000	−$110,000	$20,000	+$9,600	−$61,400	$20,000
2	+ 40,000		18,000	+ 8,640	+ 48,640	22,000
3	+ 40,000		16,000	+ 7,680	+ 47,680	24,000
4	+ 40,000		14,000	+ 6,720	+ 46,720	26,000
5	+ 40,000		12,000	+ 5,760	+ 45,760	28,000
6	+ 40,000		10,000	+ 4,800	+ 44,800	30,000
7	+ 40,000		8,000	+ 3,840	+ 43,840	32,000
8	+ 40,000		6,000	+ 2,880	+ 42,880	34,000
9	+ 40,000		4,000	+ 1,920	+ 41,920	36,000
10	+ 40,000		2,000	+ 960	+ 40,960	38,000
	$400,000	−110,000	110,000	+52,800	+342,800	290,000

Capital Investments—Lease, Rent or Buy?

LEASED EQUIPMENT

YEAR	CASH FLOW IN	CASH FLOW OUT	TAX SAVING	NET CASH FLOW	NET INCOME
1	+$40,000	−$22,100	+$10,608	+$28,508	$17,900
2	+ 40,000	− 20,400	+ 9,792	+ 29,392	19,600
3	+ 40,000	− 20,400	+ 9,792	+ 29,392	19,600
4	+ 40,000	− 20,400	+ 9,792	+ 29,392	19,600
5	+ 40,000	− 20,400	+ 9,792	+ 29,392	19,600
6	+ 40,000	− 20,400	+ 9,792	+ 29,392	19,600
7	+ 40,000	− 20,400	+ 9,792	+ 29,392	19,600
8	+ 40,000	− 18,700	+ 8,975	+ 30,275	21,300
9	+ 40,000	− 5,100	+ 2,448	+ 37,348	34,900
10	+ 40,000	− 5,100	+ 2,448	+ 37,348	34,900
	$400,000	−173,400	+ 83,231	+309,831	226,600

PURCHASED EQUIPMENT—BORROWED FUNDS

YEAR	CASH FLOW IN	CASH FLOW OUT	INTEREST AND DEPRECIATION	TAX SAVING	NET CASH FLOW	NET INCOME
1		−$10,000	(A)		−$10,000	
1	+$40,000	− 18,000	$28,000	+13,440	+ 35,440	$12,000
2	+ 40,000	− 17,200	25,200	+12,096	+ 34,096	14,800
3	+ 40,000	− 16,400	22,400	+10,160	+ 33,760	17,600
4	+ 40,000	− 15,600	19,600	+ 9,408	+ 33,808	20,400
5	+ 40,000	− 14,800	16,800	+ 8,064	+ 33,064	23,200
6	+ 40,000	− 14,000	14,000	+ 6,720	+ 32,720	26,000
7	+ 40,000	− 13,200	11,200	+ 5,376	+ 32,176	28,800
8	+ 40,000	− 12,400	8,400	+ 4,032	+ 30,032	31,600
9	+ 40,000	− 11,600	5,600	+ 2,688	+ 31,088	34,400
10	+ 40,000	− 10,800	2,800	+ 1,344	+ 30,344	37,200
	400,000	−154,000	154,000	73,920	316,528	246,000

(A) Down payment

NET CASH FLOW COMPARISONS

YEAR	PURCHASE (A)	PURCHASE (B)	LEASING
1	−61,400	+25,440	+28,508
2	+48,640	+34,096	+29,392
3	+47,680	+33,760	+29,392
4	+46,720	+33,808	+29,392
5	+45,760	+33,064	+29,392
6	+44,800	+32,720	+29,392
7	+43,840	+32,176	+29,392
8	+42,880	+30,032	+30,275
9	+41,920	+31,088	+37,348
10	+40,960	+30,344	+37,348
	$342,800	$316,528	$309,831

Capital Investments—Lease, Rent or Buy?

Some financial executives apply a present value figure to each year's cash flow in order to determine the true costs of the different methods. Tables are readily available or the formula for Present Value is expressed as:

$$PV = \frac{C(1 - (1 + R)^{-N})}{R}$$

PV = Present Value   C = Cash Payment by years C1, C2, C3, C4, etc.
N = Lease Period   R = Interest Rate

There are three principal methods of depreciation available in determining the cost comparisons between leasing and purchasing. These methods are as follows:

YEAR	STRAIGHT LINE	DECLINING BALANCE TO (20%)	SUM OF THE YEAR'S DIGITS
1	$11,000	$22,000	$20,000
2	11,000	17,600	18,000
3	11,000	14,080	16,000
4	11,000	11,264	14,000
5	11,000	9,021	12,000
6	11,000	7,217	10,000
7	11,000	5,774	8,000
8	11,000	4,619	6,000
9	11,000	3,695	4,000
10	11,000	2,956	2,000
TOTAL	$110,000	$98,226	$110,000

The obvious disadvantage to the declining balance method is that it leaves a balance in the asset account which could become a loss in the final year.

STRAIGHT LINE—   Divide cost by the estimated life or cost less salvage value by the estimated life.

DECLINING BALANCE—200%—   Divide the cost by the number of years life and multiply it by 2—in the example this would give 20%. Subtract the first year's depreciation from the cost and take 20% of this figure for the next year, until you reach the anticipated life.

SUM OF THE YEAR'S DIGITS—   Divide the cost by the sum of the digits for the total life years. In the example this is 10 years. The sum of the digits from 1 to 10 is 55. The first year's depreciation is 10/55, the next year is 9/55, then 8/55 and the last is 1/55.

There is no simple solution to the lease or purchase question. Each firm must resolve its problems case by case. The decision to lease or purchase must be based upon the expected total cost, which in turn is associated with the firm's objectives and the probabilities involved. If your situation is stable and the possibility of your disposing of the asset exceeds five years, the decision might be to swing toward purchase. This applies particularly to equipment which has a long life and not too fast an obsolescence factor. In the plant area the tendency today is to lease the land and buildings or perhaps build, sell and lease back facilities. A growing, profitable firm can pay the leasing penalty in exchange for rapid growth.

Certainly the condition of the money market at any one point in time will have a tremendous influence upon your decisions.

FINANCIAL REPORTING OF LEASES

The wide extent of leasing is revealed in a review of many corporate annual reports. Very few firms fail to show some lease commitments in the footnotes to their reports. The following examples show how these items are currently reported:

YEAR	REAL ESTATE	MACHINERY-EQUIPMENT	TOTAL
XXXX	$4,117	$10,825	$14,942
XXXY	6,742	6,414	13,156
XXXZ	5,925	4,173	10,098
XXYX	5,716	2,018	7,754
XXYY	5,411	1,195	6,606
Next 15 yrs	98,240	2,220	100,460
TOTAL	$126,151	$26,865	$153,016

These are minimum rental commitments on non-cancellable leases expressed in thousands of dollars. Included in the above totals were $133,989,000 of financing leases.

Another firm shows its leases as follows:

YEAR	FINANCING	NON-FINANCING	TOTAL
XXXX	$150,130	$141,289	$291,429
XXXY	150,130	148,345	298,475
TOTAL	$2,500,000	$750,000	$3,250,000

The firm and two of its subsidiaries lease three buildings under non-cancellable leases expiring within ten years and one non-capitalized financing lease expiring in seventeen years. The above rentals are minimum rentals. The leases provide that the firm must pay the real estate taxes on these properties. Last year these taxes were $685,000 and the prior year they were $508,000. The present value of the non-capitalized lease based upon the interest rate in effect at the time the lease was executed is approximately $1,597,000. Had the lease been capitalized the effect on net income for the current year would have been less than 3% of the average net income for the past three years.

Another firm has these comments: Commitments under leases for facilities aggregated approximately $1,850,000 due as follows:

Capital Investments—Lease, Rent or Buy?

Year X	$550,000
Year X + 1	500,000
Year X + 2	350,000
Year X + 3	200,000
Year X + 4	80,000
Year X + 5	170,000

Included in these commitments is a building leased from certain principal stockholders under a six-year lease with options to renew for an additional five years.

ANNUAL REPORT COMMENTS ON LEASES

Several of the Company's office buildings are situated on leased land. Certain of the leases require the payment of a minimum rent plus additional rents based upon a percentage of sales and also provide for the payment of real estate taxes by the lessee.

For disclosure purposes lease arrangements have been classified as either "finance" or "operating" leases. A "finance" lease is defined as one which during the noncancellable lease period, either (i) covers 75% or more of the economic life of the property or (ii) has terms which assure the lessor a full recovery of the fair value of the property at the inception of the lease, plus a reasonable return on the use of the asset invested.

Total rent expense from long-term leases is summarized as follows:

Year Ending 12-31-	Finance*	Operating	Total
XXXX	$2,678,000	$851,000	$3,529,000
XXXY	2,759,000	741,000	3,500,000

*Includes variable rentals of $1,398,000 in XXXX and $1,293,000 in XXXY.

A summary of the present value of "finance" lease commitments follows:

	Interest Rates Used			Present Value of Lease Commitments	
	Range	XXXX	XXXY	XXXX	XXXY
Land and Buildings	6-10%	8.2%	8.5%	$10,327,000	$11,671,000
Furniture and Equipment	12%	12.0%	12.0%	455,000	748,000
				$10,782,000	$12,419,000

"If all non-capitalized "finance" leases were capitalized the impact upon net earnings in XXXX and XXXY would be less than 3% of the average net earnings of the most recent three years.

"The corporation leases certain of its plants, warehouses and general offices. Some of these leases are with corporations, the common shares of which are held or owned by the

236   **Capital Investments—Lease, Rent or Buy?**

XXXX Retirement Trust. . . . Real estate leases include a 30-year lease commitment starting in VVVV for the Corporate Headquarters.

"The present value of minimum lease commitments for non-capitalized equipment financing leases is $15,813,000 at December 31,XXXX based on the discounted present value of net lease payments, at interest rates ranging from 8.5% to 9.25% with a weighted average interest rate of 8.86%. If the non-capitalized equipment financing leases had been capitalized, there would have been no significant effect on net income for XXXX and XXXY."

WORTH NOTING!

As indicated in the above comments on company reports, leasing appears to be an excellent vehicle for providing stable income for majority stockholders and pension funds. It has been common practice in the past for individuals to incorporate a leasing firm and lease the assets to the corporation for which they work so long as good business practices are followed. It was one way of surmounting restrictive agreements or covenants in long-term financing arrangements.

WHAT CAN BE LEASED?

As indicated previously most anything can be leased for a price. Among the major items available are:

1. Plant and production equipment of all types.
2. Railroad cars of all types—Leases include maintenance, insurance, taxes, risk of obsolescence, mileage auditing, regulatory changes.
3. Highway trailers and tractors—Earth moving equipment—material handling equipment—construction and maintenance items.
4. Computers and peripheral equipment—Complete office equipment—copiers, business machines, desks, typewriters, etc.
5. Uniforms—Formal wear for a tux rental business.
6. Bulk storage equipment for grain and chemicals.

These represent only a few of the items. Others include stores, offices, autos, trucks, golf carts, production facilities, airplanes and airlines.

TYPES OF LEASES AVAILABLE

The current leasing picture includes three basic types of leases:

1. *Operating Leases*—The lessee acquires the use of an asset for a portion of its useful life. There is no option to purchase the item at the end of the lease.
2. *Finance Leases*—The lessee acquires use of the asset for most of its useful life—may acquire title to the item at the end of the lease.

Capital Investments—Lease, Rent or Buy?

3. *Full-Service Leases*—Either operating or finance leases with the lessor assuming all obligations for maintenance, insurance, taxes, etc.

These leases are then broken down further into the following categories:

a. Short-term operating leases.
b. Long-term finance leases—Long-term net financing leases.
c. Secured loans—Conditional sales.
d. Leveraged leases—Arranged on behalf of the lessee, using the technique of exchanging tax benefits for a lower effective interest rate.

WHAT ARE THE PITFALLS?

These are the items that you will have to watch out for in leasing or financing plants and equipment:

1. Negative covenants that tie your hands and your future financing.
2. Compensating balances that must be kept on deposit.
3. Up front payments, one or more months' rent in advance, high settlement costs, security deposits, termination penalties.
4. Closing costs, prepayment penalties, excessive paperwork and reporting.
5. Is the equipment right for the job?
6. Is the cost of the equipment right and firm?
7. Are the operating costs high? Is there an extra charge for over eight hours utilization, six or seven days use?
8. Will you be using the equipment fully—underutilization is very costly?
9. Will substitute machinery be available when breakdowns occur? If maintenance is provided in the lease what is the lessor's track record on service?
10. Can you take advantage of the 10% investment credit under the lease?

Remember that a lease is a capital asset if: title passes at the end of the lease—there is an option to purchase at a bargain price—the lease term exceeds 75% of the life of the property or the property is a special purpose machine or plant with no other use.

ADVANTAGES OF LEASING

The financial administrator has the awesome task of providing the corporation or business with adequate funds to mesh manpower, machinery, sales, promotion, production and administration. The effective utilization of all of these resources is the result of careful planning and effectively carrying out a capital expenditure of some magnitude. The financial part of the plan is the most important since it links all of the operations together. Capital expenditures must precede production and sales. Due to the fact that these expenditures are often quite large and complicated they must be well thought out and financed. They can alter a firm's ability to produce and sell at reasonable prices and costs for a considerable period of time.

Capital expenditures are time consuming. Planning is often long-term and contruction or acquisition can cover an indeterminate time period. The long process makes the payout period lengthy and subject to many variables which could adversely affect the firm. Leasing provides an interim means of testing without risking the entire amount of capital or the entire operation. These are some of the advantages:

1. Finding capital during a tight-money period can be solved by leasing.
2. It may give you a tax advantage in certain instances.
3. It can be a hedge against inflation by paying for today's equipment with tomorrow's less valuable dollar.
4. Since equipment lease payments are spread out evenly over the term of the lease virtually every lease has certain cash-flow advantages over outright purchases.
5. The conservation of working capital could make a crucial difference in your capital expansion plans.
6. Leasing offers protection from obsolescence.
7. In our opinion, the short-term tax dollars saved by leasing are of more value to the corporation than the long-term dollars provided by depreciation.
8. During periods of working capital shortages you can conserve your capital by selling your assets and leasing them back. In this manner you can convert a capital expenditure into operating expenses and provide some cash flow.
9. Leasing permits "off balance sheet" financing.
10. It must have some concrete advantages since all of the larger firms use it to good advantage.

A TYPICAL LEASE DOCUMENT

Samples of Equilease Forms follow on the next page.

EQUILEASE CORPORATION
Subsidiary of **ELTRA** *Corporation*
LESSOR

387 PARK AVENUE SOUTH
New York, N. Y. 10016

LESSEE
Name
Address _____ County
City _____ State _____ Zip Code
PERSON TO CONTACT
TELEPHONE NO. →

SUPPLIER of EQUIPMENT
Name
Address
City _____ State _____ Zip Code
SALESMAN
TELEPHONE NO. →

QUANTITY	ITEM	MODEL NO.	SERIAL NO.	PRICE
				$

☐ I WANT CREDIT LIFE INSURANCE
NAME OF INSURED
SIGNED
See instructions regarding inclusion of SALES or USE TAX here.

FEDERAL EXCISE TAX $
(LESS TRADE IN, IF ANY) $
OTHER $
SALES TAX $
TOTAL COST TO LESSOR → $

EQUIPMENT LOCATION, IF OTHER THAN ABOVE ADDRESS OF APPLICANT.

NO. OF MONTHS	NO. OF RENTAL PAYMENTS	RENTAL PAYMENTS WILL BE MADE	RENTAL PAYMENT AMOUNT:
		☐ MON. ☐ QUAR.	___ Payments of $_____ Plus Sales Tax $_____ Total $_____

FIRST PAYMENT
Check For This Amount Must Accompany Lease Application.
$ _____
1st ☐ Mo. ☐ Quar., and
Last _____ ☐ Mo. ☐ Quar.
or ☐ Purchase Option
OR AS PROVIDED IN PARAGRAPH 1

☐ CORPORATION
☐ PARTNERSHIP
☐ PROPRIETORSHIP

NATURE OF BUSINESS:
IF PARTNERSHIP OR PROPRIETORSHIP, GIVE NAMES AND HOME ADDRESSES OF PARTNERS OR OWNERS:
HOW LONG IN BUSINESS: _____ YEARS

REFERENCES: (PREVIOUS OR SECOND BANK REQUIRED IF APPLICANT HAS BEEN AT PRESENT BANK LESS THAN ONE YEAR)

PRESENT BANK OF APPLICANT:
BRANCH: _____ PHONE:
NAME OF BANK OFFICER:

PREVIOUS OR SECOND BANK OF APPLICANT:
BRANCH: _____ PHONE:
NAME OF BANK OFFICER:

DOES APPLICANT WISH PURCHASE OPTION LETTER?
YES ☐ NO ☐

DOES APPLICANT NOW LEASE FROM EQUILEASE?
YES ☐ NO ☐

Please Circle Preferred Payment Date
1 2 3 4 5 6 7 8 9 10 11 12 13 14 15
16 17 18 19 20 21 22 23 24 25 26 27 28 29 30

DO NOT WRITE BELOW - FOR OFFICE USE ONLY

BRANCH P.O. # _____
DEPOSIT SLIP # _____
DATE _____
AMOUNT $ _____

CODE NO. _____
RATE _____
P/O _____
RENEWAL _____

APPLICATION

1

239

EQUILEASE CORPORATION
Subsidiary of ELTRA Corporation
LESSOR

387 PARK AVENUE SOUTH
New York, N.Y. 10016

LESSEE

Name _____

Address _____ County _____

City _____ State _____ Zip Code _____

PERSON TO CONTACT _____ TELEPHONE NO. →_____

SUPPLIER of EQUIPMENT

Name _____

Address _____

City _____ State _____ Zip Code _____

SALESMAN _____ TELEPHONE NO. →_____

QUANTITY	ITEM	MODEL NO.	SERIAL NO.	PRICE

I WANT CREDIT LIFE INSURANCE
NAME OF INSURED _____
SIGNED _____

EQUIPMENT LOCATION, IF OTHER THAN ABOVE ADDRESS OF APPLICANT.

NO. OF MONTHS	NO. OF RENTAL PAYMENTS	RENTAL PAYMENTS WILL BE MADE	RENTAL PAYMENT AMOUNT:
		MON. ☐ QUAR. ☐	___ Payments of $_____ Plus Sales Tax $_____ Total $_____

FIRST PAYMENT
Check For This Amount Must Accompany Lease Application.
$ _____
1st ☐ Mo. ☐ Quar., and
Last ____ ☐ Mo. ☐ Quar.
or ☐ Purchase Option
OR AS PROVIDED IN PARAGRAPH 1

1. Lessor leases to Lessee and Lessee rents from Lessor the equipment listed above or, if separately scheduled, in the schedule hereto annexed, marked Schedule "A" and made a part hereof. Said equipment will be located at the above address and will not be moved to a new location without written permission first given by Lessor. Lessor acknowledges receipt of the first payment referred to above from Lessee. Any part of this payment not applied by Lessor as rental for the first month or quarter of the lease, shall be held as security for the performance of the terms of this lease. If Lessee is not in default hereunder, or under any other lease between the parties hereto, at the end of the term of this lease said security shall be refunded to the Lessee upon return of the leased equipment as provided in Paragraph 5 or, solely at the Lessor's option, applied toward the payment of rent due and to become due hereunder in the inverse order of their maturities. This lease shall commence on the date accepted by Lessor and Lessee shall make his next rental payment hereunder no later than 30 days (if rentals are payable monthly) or 90 days (if rentals are payable quarterly) from the commencement date, at the sole discretion of Lessor.
2. (A) LESSEE HAS SELECTED BOTH (1) THE EQUIPMENT AND (2) THE ABOVE SUPPLIER FROM WHOM LESSOR IS TO PURCHASE THE EQUIPMENT. LESSOR MAKES NO WARRANTY EXPRESS OR IMPLIED AS TO ANY MATTER WHATSOEVER, INCLUDING THE CONDITION OF THE EQUIPMENT, ITS MERCHANTABILITY OR ITS FITNESS FOR ANY PARTICULAR PURPOSE, AND AS TO LESSOR, LESSEE LEASES THE EQUIPMENT "AS IS."
   (B) IF THE EQUIPMENT IS NOT PROPERLY INSTALLED, DOES NOT OPERATE AS REPRESENTED OR WARRANTED BY SUPPLIER OR IS UNSATISFACTORY FOR ANY REASON, LESSEE SHALL MAKE ANY CLAIM ON ACCOUNT THEREOF SOLELY AGAINST SUPPLIER AND SHALL, NEVERTHELESS, PAY LESSOR ALL RENT PAYABLE UNDER THIS LEASE, LESSEE HEREBY WAIVING ANY SUCH CLAIMS AS AGAINST LESSOR. LESSOR MAY INCLUDE, AS A CONDITION OF ITS PURCHASE ORDER, THAT SUPPLIER AGREE THAT ALL WARRANTIES, AGREEMENTS AND REPRESENTATIONS, IF ANY, WHICH MAY BE MADE BY SUPPLIER TO LESSEE OR LESSOR MAY BE ENFORCED BY LESSEE IN ITS OWN NAME. LESSOR HEREBY AGREES TO ASSIGN TO LESSEE, SOLELY FOR THE PURPOSE OF MAKING AND PROSECUTING ANY SAID CLAIM, ALL OF THE RIGHTS WHICH LESSOR HAS AGAINST SUPPLIER FOR BREACH OF WARRANTY OR OTHER REPRESENTATION RESPECTING THE EQUIPMENT. LESSOR SHALL HAVE NO RESPONSIBILITY FOR DELAY OR FAILURE TO FILL THE ORDER.
   (C) LESSEE UNDERSTANDS AND AGREES THAT NEITHER THE SUPPLIER NOR ANY SALESMAN OR OTHER AGENT OF THE SUPPLIER, IS AN AGENT OF LESSOR. NO SALESMAN OR AGENT OF SUPPLIER IS AUTHORIZED TO WAIVE OR ALTER ANY TERM OR CONDITION OF THIS LEASE, AND NO REPRESENTATION AS TO THE EQUIPMENT OR ANY OTHER MATTER BY THE SUPPLIER, SHALL IN ANY WAY AFFECT LESSEE'S DUTY TO PAY THE RENT AND PERFORM ITS OTHER OBLIGATIONS AS SET FORTH IN THIS LEASE.
   (D) LESSEE HEREBY ACKNOWLEDGES THAT HE HAS RECEIVED A COPY OF THIS LEASE.
   (E) LESSOR AGREES TO ORDER THE EQUIPMENT FROM SUPPLIER UPON THE TERMS AND CONDITIONS OF THE PURCHASE ORDER INITIALLY ATTACHED HERETO. LESSEE HEREBY AUTHORIZES LESSOR TO INSERT IN THIS LEASE THE SERIAL NUMBERS, AND OTHER IDENTIFICATION DATA, OF THE EQUIPMENT WHEN DETERMINED BY LESSOR.

THIS LEASE IS SUBJECT TO THE TERMS AND CONDITIONS PRINTED ON THE REVERSE SIDE WHICH ARE MADE A PART HEREOF AND WHICH LESSEE ACKNOWLEDGES THAT HE HAS READ.

ACCEPTED:

_____, 19____
EQUILEASE CORPORATION, Lessor

By _____
AUTHORIZED SIGNATURE

THIS IS A NON-CANCELLABLE LEASE FOR THE TERM INDICATED ABOVE

DATE _____, 19____

LESSEE _____

THE UNDERSIGNED AFFIRMS THAT HE IS A DULY AUTHORIZED CORPORATE OFFICER, PARTNER OR PROPRIETOR OF THE ABOVE NAMED LESSEE, AND HAS THE AUTHORITY TO EXECUTE THIS LEASE ON ITS BEHALF.

By(X) _____ TITLE _____

LEASE ORIGINAL

LESSEE'S SIGNATURE IN INK IS REQUIRED ON LEASE COPIES (Pages 2, 3, & 4)

2

EQUILEASE CORPORATION
Subsidiary of ELTRA *Corporation*
LESSOR

387 PARK AVENUE SOUTH
New York, N. Y. 10016

LESSEE		SUPPLIER of EQUIPMENT	
Name		Name	
Address _____ County _____		Address	
City ____ State ____ Zip Code		City ____ State ____ Zip Code	
PERSON TO CONTACT	TELEPHONE NO. →	SALESMAN	TELEPHONE NO. →

QUANTITY	ITEM	MODEL NO.	SERIAL NO.	PRICE
				$

I WANT CREDIT LIFE INSURANCE
NAME OF INSURED _____
SIGNED _____

See instructions regarding inclusion of SALES or USE TAX here.

FEDERAL EXCISE TAX	$
(LESS TRADE IN, IF ANY)	$
OTHER	$
SALES TAX	$
TOTAL COST TO LESSOR →	$

EQUIPMENT LOCATION, IF OTHER THAN ABOVE ADDRESS OF APPLICANT.

INSTRUCTIONS TO VENDOR — READ CAREFULLY

Special delivery instructions or other special terms or conditions, if any:

1. Unless otherwise specified herein this purchase order is for new equipment only.

2. Invoices in triplicate and bill of lading should be mailed on date of shipment to the Equilease branch office to which this lease application originally had been submitted.

> INVOICES CANNOT BE HONORED UNLESS FULL EQUIPMENT DESCRIPTION INCLUDING SERIAL NUMBERS, APPEAR THEREON.

3. Show our purchase order number on all crates, items, packages, invoices, and packing lists. If terms are F.O.B., ship collect to Lessee shown above who has agreed to pay all transportation charges.

4. Vendor is required to affix the attached decals to the equipment before delivery.

5. Unless otherwise provided, this PURCHASE ORDER is valid only for a period of 30 days from the date shown below and will be deemed to be cancelled if the equipment covered by this order is not delivered to and accepted by the LESSEE on an EQUILEASE ACCEPTANCE NOTICE within the aforesaid 30 days.

THIS PURCHASE ORDER IS SUBJECT TO THE TERMS AND CONDITIONS
ON REVERSE SIDE WHICH ARE MADE A PART HEREOF.

Please enter our order as above.

PURCHASE ORDER NO. _____

EQUILEASE CORPORATION, Buyer

DATE _____

By _____
AUTHORIZED SIGNATURE

PURCHASE ORDER

5

EQUILEASE CORPORATION
Subsidiary of ELTRA Corporation
LESSOR

387 PARK AVENUE SOUTH
New York, N. Y. 10016

LESSEE

Name_____

Address_____ County _____

City_____ State_____ Zip Code_____

PERSON TO CONTACT_____ TELEPHONE NO. →_____

SUPPLIER of EQUIPMENT

Name_____

Address_____

City_____ State_____ Zip Code_____

SALESMAN_____ TELEPHONE NO. →_____

QUANTITY	ITEM	MODEL NO.	SERIAL NO.

I WANT CREDIT LIFE INSURANCE

NAME OF INSURED _____

SIGNED _____

See instructions regarding inclusion of SALES or USE TAX here.

EQUIPMENT LOCATION, IF OTHER THAN ABOVE ADDRESS OF APPLICANT.

NO. OF MONTHS	NO. OF RENTAL PAYMENTS	RENTAL PAYMENTS WILL BE MADE	RENTAL PAYMENT AMOUNT:
		MON. ☐ QUAR. ☐	_____ Payments of $_____ Plus Sales Tax $_____ Total $_____

FIRST PAYMENT
Check For This Amount Must Accompany Lease Application.
$_____
1st ☐ Mo. ☐ Quar., and
Last _____ ☐ Mo. ☐ Quar.
or ☐ Purchase Option
OR AS PROVIDED IN PARAGRAPH 1

Gentlemen:

All of the item(s) referred to above were received by us and were in good order and condition and acceptable to us. The decals have been affixed to the equipment.

_____
Name of Lessee

By _____ (TITLE)

Date _____

┌─ TO LESSEE: ─────────────────────────────────┐
│ Do not sign this receipt until you have actually received the above described │
│ property. │
└──┘

TO VENDOR ▷ THIS ACCEPTANCE MUST BE SIGNED BY LESSEE AND RETURNED TO US BEFORE YOUR INVOICE CAN BE PROCESSED FOR PAYMENT.

EQUIPMENT ACCEPTANCE

6

Capital Investments—Lease, Rent or Buy?

LEVERAGED LEASES

Everyone really needs to know what is required when you apply for a lease. In this instance we will run through the requirements covering a leveraged lease of a considerable amount of property.

BASIC REQUIREMENTS

1. Annual audit reports or audited financial statements for the last three full years with appropriate monthly or quarterly reports to bring the financial information up to date.
2. Term of lease desired.
3. A detailed description of the capital equipment to be leased. Some information about the equipment and if available, the "IRS Guideline Life" of the equipment.
4. The names of the suppliers or manufacturers of the equipment.
5. When will the equipment be required?
6. Name, title and phone number of the individual negotiating the lease.
7. Any other pertinent information.

Once this information is furnished the leasing firm will prepare a preliminary bid based upon the current money market rates. Once this bid is submitted the leasing firm will ask for a letter of intent authorizing it to formalize the transaction into a firm, detailed proposal. The time schedule for the entire transaction is as follows:

a. Preliminary bid—one to three days.
b. Firm proposal—three weeks.
c. Documentation and preparation for settlement—two to three months.

WHAT A LEVERAGED LEASE COVERS

A leveraged lease will generally cover any new capital equipment and some real estate providing the value of the real estate is small compared to the entire leasing program. A minimum of one million dollars in equipment is essential in most cases. The term of the lease will run from five years to twenty-five years depending on the needs of the lessee and the useful life of the equipment to be leased.

Each lease is individually negotiated and documented and the lease must be construed as a "true lease," and it may require acknowledgment by the IRS. The lessee may have fair rental value renewal privileges and/or the right of first refusal to purchase the leased equipment at the end of the leased term for its then "fair market value." The lease will normally be a "net" lease. The lessee will be responsible for all taxes, insurance, both casualty and liability, and maintenance.

This type of major lease is available to firms with a net worth in excess of five million dollars, a bond rating of Baa or better and having a profitable past three years.

A "true lease" is defined as one in which the lessee does not build equity in the equipment during the life of the lease.

COST OF A LEVERAGED LEASE

In most instances the rates will be lower than if the lessee borrowed the money through a "private placement" and in some instances lower than the cost of borrowing from the public. The general rate for new equipment leases will be 1 to 2% less than the private placement rate, the long-term borrowing rate and sometimes below the public borrowing rate. If your present source for long-term loans is 9% from a "private" source, the probable lease rate would be between 7% and 8% simple interest.

OPINIONS ON ADVANTAGES AND DISADVANTAGES

The reactions to questions on the advantages and disadvantages of leasing were interesting. The younger financial administrators were overwhelmingly in favor of leasing whereas the older individuals tended toward borrowing the funds on a long-term basis or outright purchase on smaller items. Reasons were cited as follows:

Disadvantages

1. Increases fixed costs—possibility of heavy cancellations penalties.
2. Generally higher cost and loss of residual value in the items leased.
3. Tax disadvantages.
4. Restriction on utilization of items and other objectionable limitations in leases.
5. Restrictions on modification of leased items and difficulty in financing major improvements.
6. Some maintenance problems.

Advantages

1. Tax advantages in many instances.
2. Encourages change and trial of new equipment.
3. Increase in flexibility of use. Equipment can be leased for short periods at distant locations whenever needed. This could result in overall lower costs.
4. Avoids loss through obsolescence and eliminates problem of what to do with old items.
5. Maintains credit lines and can be used to get around restrictive bank covenants.
6. Can be used to eliminate permanent maintenance crews.
7. Conserves working capital.

CASE IN POINT

In a recent press release by a medium-sized listed firm the Chairman of the Board stated: "The firm is considering leasing another plant to replace a plant whose lease expires soon. Leasing instead of acquiring would keep capital spending down to about 1.3 million dollars. Purchasing a building could add one million dollars to the budget."

Capital Investments—Lease, Rent or Buy?

FINANCIAL MODEL

Included in the chapter on financial models are two specific models which illustrate the model techniques for comparing the various purchase or leasing options. These examples show how the various risk factors are incorporated in the calculations in order to provide answers to the "What if?" questions that arise.

Over the years there have been many theories and practical methods developed for the most effective allocation of capital. Since capital investment is a major item for most firms the trend has been toward assessing the profitability of each investment. Generally financial administrators have used the following methods (the methods apply whether you contemplate purchase, lease or rentals):

1. *Payback Method*—This is a simple estimate of the time required to recoup the amount of the capital expenditure. Some firms refine the method by using the more complex discounted rate of return. This method does not take into consideration the true profitability of the investment.
2. *Present Value Method*—This is a more complex estimate involving computing the present value of the cash expenditure for the assets and the present value of the anticipated cash receipts over a period of time. The rate used can be the current one or an average as indicated in previous present value computations. From this method the Discounted Rate of Return (DROI) can be obtained.

Interviews indicate that these two methods are most frequently used by the majority of firms.

No matter how you determine the profitability and effectiveness of your capital expenditures there is a high element of risk in all decisions. Most of the firms indicated that they took into consideration the risks and possible future uncertainties when making major fixed asset commitments. The use of financial models to quickly assess the risk factors was apparent in many instances. The logical approach in preparing your model is that based upon the element of risk involved, the rate of return fluctuates, the DROI is larger or smaller and the payout period will vary. Normally the amount of the initial payout is reasonably certain; however, in the case of some acquisitions this would not be true, but the amount of future receipts from the investment can vary widely from the estimates. This is taken into account by varying the amount of receipts in your modeling techniques and using the resulting computations in your decisions.

There is also the possibility that some capital investments may not be immediately profitable. Acquisitions are made in depressed situations in contemplation of future growth, future markets or a return to normal economic conditions. These decisions are normally made by financially secure firms such as AT&T, oil and energy firms (witness the acquisition of coal and uranium leases in the 1960's and early 1970's) or utilities and many of the large retail chains.

The major uncertainties in any decision are basically as follows:

1. The economic life of the item. Obsolescence and technology changes.
2. Product changes—Economic life of the products produced.

3. Price situation—Stability of prices over the life of either the product or the equipment.
4. Cost of capital over the life of the project.
5. Cost factors and profitability of the products.
6. Does this project represent the best use of the funds for the time period involved?

SORTING IT OUT

Capital projects are generally evaluated upon the following bases:

1. Expansion—To meet growth, enter new markets, offset competition, major changes in operations and technologies.
2. Replacement of existing facilities—Every firm should have a firm plan for replacing their facilities. This accomplishes two purposes. One, your equipment and plant do not become obsolescent or wear out all at the same time. Secondly, often by the addition of new equipment annually you become aware of improvements which can be made to the older equipment and keep it competitive. In addition, by periodically adding new equipment your costs and depreciation charges are kept up-to-date.
3. Cost reduction—Projects required to keep you competitive or to reduce costs and increase profits. Part of the replacement factors would apply in this category.
4. Mandatory—Under current laws many acquisitions are required to meet federal and state safety regulations, pollution control, union requirements or social responsibility to the community.

DETERMINATION AND ALLOCATION

As you sit down annually, or more often as the case requires, you have the responsibility of determining what funds are available for capital expansion or other projects and how to allocate these resources for the utmost in profitability. If the funds are not adequate to meet the minimum requirements the financial executive then has a financing job on his hands. Pressure is exerted from all segments of the business for funds for their projects and the sorting becomes hectic in the planning sessions. Your allocation of funds must be objective, hard-nosed and considerate of all elements of growth, profitability, costs and available funds.

ALLOCATION CRITERIA

1. Mandatory items—Absolute requirements cash flow.
2. Amount of investment required—Cash flow in and out for each project.
3. Profitability of the project.
4. Time cycle for the project—Short-range (under one year) or long-range (over one year). What investment is needed at what time? What return on the investment will be received and when?
4. The risk factors involved.
5. Is this the best use of the funds and what are the alternatives?

Capital Investments—Lease, Rent or Buy?

DETERMINATION CRITERIA

Critical to the allocation of funds is the determination of the profitability of each project. This is generally done as follows:

a. Percent return on investment (ROI) or discounted return on investment (DROI). This will give you the time and non-time value of the project expressed as a percentage return on your initial investment.
b. Payout period—How long will it take to pay off the original investment and how long will the payoff continue after this period?
c. Percentage of total funds available allocated to this project.
d. Risk factor for the project. Possible negative factor on profits or loss of investment funds.
e. Anticipated revenues in relation to total revenues and its effect on fixed costs.
f. Benefits anticipated from cost reduction. Amount of cost reduction involved relative to the total costs.

Due to the availability of computer models it is now possible to utilize most of the methods for the evaluation of major projects.

RATING PROJECTS

Projects would normally be rated in at least two categories:

1. ANNUAL CASH FLOW—CURRENT YEAR AND THREE TO FIVE YEARS

YEAR	W	X	Y	Z
Invest	($50,000)	($35,000)	($25,000)	($10,000)
1.	(20,000)	15,000	15,000	10,000
2.	15,000	15,000	20,000	8,000
3.	40,000	15,000	20,000	6,000
4.	60,000	20,000	10,000	4,000

2. OTHER FACTORS INVOLVED

Payback-Years	4.25	2.3+	1.5	1.0
Plus Factors				
Expansion	1	2	3	NF
Costs	2	4	3	1
ROI 5 Years	6.2%	4.9%	6.0%	6.4%
ROI 10 Years	9.1%	5.3%	5.0%	4.8%

The example assumes that in the fifth year the benefits would be the same as those of the fourth year and that this situation would continue for the next five years.

BASIC STEPS

The basic steps for the financial administrator in setting up his capital expenditure

248 Capital Investments—Lease, Rent or Buy?

control system, in order to allocate the firm's resources in the best possible manner, is summarized as indicated:

1. *Initiation of Projects*—What projects are to be considered? Obtain the requests from the various divisions for normal requirements. Emergency items will have to be considered as they occur.
2. *Projections*—Sales volumes, prices and markets. Availability of equipment—time cycle to acquire and install—run-in period—unusual costs. Costs involved. Funds required.
3. *Economic Climate—Money Market*—Current availability of funds and the interest rate. What is the economic projection?
4. *Presentation*—Preparation of the projects summarized by the major factors—profitability—payback period—ROI and DROI. Comparison of the projects and recommendations.
5. *Decision*—Once the management decision is made the funds must be obtained or allocated as required subject to appropriate approvals.
6. *Control and Checkup*—Preparation of control reports showing the progress being made, if it is on schedule and within the funds allotment. Reports of subsequent performance to show the variations from estimates on costs, revenues and other items. What happened and why?

CONTROL REPORTS

The methods of controlling vary with the various firms and individuals. We will only show a few simple ones in this chapter and include the more complex ones later. Since the advent of leasing we now have an additional factor in capital investment control reporting. We must take into account the amount of leases entered into under this classification.

APPROPRIATION CONTROL REPORT

APPROVED	APPROVED EXPENDED	APPROVED LEASED	REMAINING BALANCE
Project 1. $100,000	$ 50,000	$ 25,000	$ 25,000
Project 2. $500,000	300,000		200,000
Project 3. $75,000	—	75,000	—
Project 4. 200,000	100,000	100,000	—
Project 5. 25,000	5,000		20,000
TOTALS $900,000	$455,000	$200,000	$245,000

Capital Investments—Lease, Rent or Buy?

PROJECT CONTROL REPORT

EXPENDITURE PORTION

NO.	AMOUNT APPROVED	AMOUNT SPENT	VARIATION	TIME ALLOTTED	TAKEN
3.	$ 75,000	$ 74,600	− $400	6 weeks	8 weeks

Favorable variations in cost due to miscellaneous items costing less than anticipated. Time delay due to slowness in obtaining some parts. Take into consideration on any items due from this supplier in the future!

| 14. | $700,000 | $756,000 | + 56,000 | 8 months | 11 months |

See the detailed report on this project for explanations of overruns.

PERFORMANCE PORTION

PROJECT NO.	UNITS	REVENUES	PRICE	COSTS	PROFIT
3.					
Actual	10,000	$50,000	$5.00	$3.75	$1.25
Estimated	15,000	75,000	5.00	3.10	1.90
Variation	5,000	−25,000	—	+.65	−.65

Loss of unit production due to late start-up of equipment. Two weeks behind schedule. Costs adversely affected by late start and unusual start-up costs. New projected cost within two weeks is $3.25. Material cost increase has altered original estimate. Check with the sales division to see if price can be increased to offset the permanent price increase in material. Purchasing is checking for an alternate raw material source.

PROJECT CONTROL REPORT

PROJECTION REPORT
THREE MONTHS—

| | | GAIN OR LOSS DUE TO | | |
PROJECT	PRODUCTION GAIN-LOSS	PRICE VARIATION	COST VARIATION	OTHER VARIATIONS
3.	− 25,000	0	− $6,500	NONE
14.	− 100,000	0	0	− $56,000 (1)

Project 14. No production due to late start-up. Project costs exceeded estimates by $56,000. Production to start within the next two weeks. Current price and cost estimates appear to be on target. There is a possibility of increased production over the estimated daily amount.

SHOULD YOU LEASE THAT MACHINE?—TRUCK?—OFFICE FURNITURE?

PARAMETERS

No down payment—cost is $10,000
Interest rate is 10%
Depreciation 20% declining balance
Tax rate is 48%
Present value calculated at 9%

YOU BOUGHT IT—YOUR CASH

YEAR	CASH FLOW	INTEREST	DEPRECIATION	TAX SAVED	NET OUTLAY
1.	−$10,000	—	$2,000	$960	−$9,040
2.			1,600	768	+ 768
3.			1,280	614	+ 614
4.			1,024	492	+ 492
5.			819	393	+ 393

YOU BOUGHT IT—WITH BORROWED FUNDS

YEAR	CASH FLOW PRINCIPAL	INTEREST	DEPRECIATION	TAX SAVED	NET OUTLAY
1.	−$2,000	$1,000	$2,000	$1,440	−$1,560
2.	− 2,000	800	1,600	1,152	− 1,648
3.	− 2,000	600	1,280	902	− 1,698
4.	− 2,000	400	1,024	684	− 1,716
5.	− 2,000	200	819	489	− 1,711

YOU LEASED IT—AT $260 A MONTH—LAST MONTH'S RENT IN ADVANCE

YEAR	CASH FLOW —RENT	TAX SAVED	NET OUTLAY
1.	−$3,380	$1,622	−$1,758
2.	− 3,120	1,498	− 1,622
3.	− 3,120	1,498	− 1,622
4.	− 3,120	1,498	− 1,622
5.	− 2,860	1,373	− 1,487

THE COSTS WERE

	YOU BOUGHT IT	BOUGHT AND BORROWED	LEASED
Gross Cash Outlay	$10,000	$13,000	$15,600
Net Cash Outlay	6,773	8,333	8,111
Net Income Before Tax			
Based upon $10,000 Year	43,277	40,277	34,400
Income Tax	20,773	19,332	16,512
Net Income	22,504	20,945	17,888
Present Value of Net Outlay	6,574	6,458	6,347

Capital Investments—Lease, Rent or Buy?

ASSUMPTIONS:
- Equipment cost: $100,000
- Economic life: 10 years
- Bank loan: 8.5% per annum—10% down payment—payments and interest are based on loan of $90,000.
- 8 year lease: It is assumed that the fair market value is 5% at lease termination.
- Present value factor: 10% per annum return on working capital
- 50% tax bracket
- Depreciation method: double declining converting to straight line
- Installment purchase: 10% down payment, balanced financed—$90,000.

CASH PURCHASE					INSTALLMENT PURCHASE (8 YEARS) 10% down payment*				
equipment cost	depreci-ation	tax savings	cash flow present value of cash flow		annual payments	interest	depreci-ation	tax savings	cash flow present value of cash flow
$100,000			($100,000) (100,000)						*($10,000) (10,000)
	$20,000	$10,000	10,000 9,091		$17,489	$9,900	$20,000	$14,950	(2,539) (2,308)
	16,000	8,000	8,000 6,612		17,489	9,065	16,000	12,533	(4,956) (4,096)
	12,800	6,400	6,400 4,808		17,489	8,140	12,800	10,470	(7,019) (5,273)
	10,240	5,120	5,120 3,497		17,489	7,110	10,240	8,675	(8,814) (6,020)
	8,192	4,096	4,096 2,543		17,489	5,968	8,192	7,080	(10,409) (6,463)
	6,554	3,277	3,277 1,850		17,489	4,701	6,554	5,628	(11,861) (6,695)
	6,554	3,277	3,277 1,682		17,489	3,294	6,554	4,924	(12,565) (6,448)
	6,554	3,277	3,277 1,529		17,489	1,734	6,554	4,144	(13,345) (6,226)
	6,554	3,277	3,277 1,390				6,554	3,277	3,277 1,390
	6,552	3,276	3,276 1,263				6,552	3,276	3,276 1,263
100,000	100,000	50,000	(50,000) (65,735)		139,912	49,912	100,000	74,957	(74,955) (50,876)
Comparative Cash Flow			**$50,000**		**Comparative Cash Flow**				**$74,955**
Comparative Cost			**$65,735**		**Comparative Cost**				**$50,876**

251

Capital Investments—Lease, Rent or Buy?

| year | 8 YEAR LEASE ||||| BANK LOAN AT 8.5% (5 YEARS) 10% down payment* |||||
	annual rentals	exercise purchase option	depreci- ation	tax savings	cash flow present value of cash flow	annual payments	interest	depreci- ation	tax savings	cash flow present value of cash flow
0										*($10,000) (10,000)
1	$19,010			$9,505	($9,505) (8,641)	$22,839	$7,650	$20,000	$13,825	(9,014) (8,195)
2	19,010			9,505	(9,505) (7,855)	22,839	6,360	16,000	11,180	(11,660) (9,636)
3	19,010			9,505	(9,505) (7,141)	22,839	4,958	12,800	8,879	(13,960) (10,488)
4	19,010			9,505	(9,505) (6,492)	22,839	3,438	10,240	6,839	(16,000) (10,928)
5	19,010			9,505	(9,505) (5,902)	22,839	1,789	8,192	4,990	(17,848) (11,082)
6	19,010			9,505	(9,505) (5,365)			6,554	3,277	3,277 1,850
7	19,010			9,505	(9,505) (4,878)			6,554	3,277	3,277 1,682
8	19,010	$5,000		9,505	(14,505) (6,767)			6,554	3,277	3,277 1,529
9			$2,500	1,250	1,250 530			6,554	3,277	3,277 1,390
10			2,500	1,250	1,250 482			6,552	3,276	3,276 1,263
Total	152,080	5,000	5,000	78,540	(78,540) (52,029)	114,195	24,195	100,000	62,097	(62,098) (52,615)
	Comparative Cash Flow **$78,540**			**Comparative Cost**	**$52,029**	**Comparative Cash Flow** **$62,098**			**Comparative Cost**	**$52,615**

10

Administering Financial Control of Current Assets

Watching a business crank up for the day in order to produce the revenues is a delightful and intriguing process. As each individual turns to his or her allotted task the wheels begin to turn and the operation is under way. From the opening of the morning mail with its orders, remittances, complaints and other correspondence to the ringing of the phones and interoffice, interdivisional contacts, things run smoothly or are otherwise dependent upon the organization, the people and the day.

Throughout the entire operation there is a slim thread of discipline administered by the financial administrator which controls the handling of the orders, invoices, remittances, credit requests and complaints. This is the control function which can make or break any organization.

FINANCIAL ADMINISTRATION OF CURRENT ASSETS

Examining the balance sheet of most corporations you will find that current assets are divided into four primary parts. These are:

1. Cash in bank and cash equivalents
2. Accounts and notes receivable

3. Inventories

4. Prepaid expenses

Dependent upon the firm involved these items represent from 25% to 75% of a firm's assets. The financial executive has the major responsibility to properly handle, protect and report on each of the items in the current asset category. If you feel that protection is not a vital task you have never had the gut feeling of being awakened at 2 a.m. in the morning by a phone call telling you that your warehouse is on fire and will be a total loss. This is the day you break out the insurance policies, read the fine print and find out if your coverage was adequate and how good your insurance firm is.

The prompt and efficient handling of all current asset transactions and the rapid conversion of these items into cash involves the following:

CASH

1. Cash flow forecasting

2. Handling cash flow efficiently

3. Prompt investment of surplus cash

4. Good banking relations

5. Excellent and prompt cash reports

ACCOUNTS RECEIVABLE

1. Receivables flow forecasting

2. Handling accounts receivable transactions promptly and efficiently

3. Disciplined collection procedures

4. Fast, effective credit granting or denial—action on special terms

5. Good accounts receivable reporting

INVENTORIES

1. Inventory flow forecasting

2. Meshing raw materials, work in process and finished goods items—maintaining adequate stocks and eliminating obsolete items

3. Speedy and efficient handling of inventory transactions

4. Strategic placement of inventories

5. Prompt, effective inventory reports

The sole purpose of a current asset administration system is to obtain the most efficient use of the corporate resources.

The flow of cash through a business is an interesting financial process. First of all, it takes money to grease the wheels and make the business run. If you have ever had "the shorts" and had a supplier call up and tell you he was holding up delivery until he received and cashed your check, you can appreciate this statement. Providing a steady, adequate flow of funds is the number one task for every financial administrator. The ability to streamline

Administering Financial Control of Current Assets

the cash reaping process and correlate it with the cash disbursing system is the final mark of excellence for the financial executive.

EXAMPLES OF SPEEDING UP CASH FLOW

1. Simply by having its men turn in their work orders daily for billing enabled an electrical contractor to cut a week to ten days from his billing cycle. The lag was discovered through the use of an "Effectiveness Report" which disclosed that billing was lagging from one to two weeks behind the date that the time cards showed the work had been completed.
2. Computerized billing—One firm found that by computerizing its billings it saved approximately four days in the billing cycle. The development of computerized files forced them to pre-determine many of the troublesome factors in manual billing.
3. A lighting fixture firm would hold up billing when as few as one item was out of stock and had to be back-ordered. Some orders, complete except for a minor item, would be held up for as long as three weeks. By billing immediately for the items shipped they stepped up their cash flow by an amount equal to 20% of their monthly billings. In addition, since inventory records were not adjusted until the items were billed, sales were lost and overstocking resulted from lack of confidence in the inventory records.
4. One firm cut at least one day from its cycle by billing early in the morning and sending out the bills in the morning mail.
5. The treasurer of one city earned an extra million dollars by investing excess funds on Thursday night and pulling them back on Tuesday morning. Disbursements were held to the remaining three days.

CASH ADMINISTRATION

The administration of cash is a disciplined approach to all phases of the system. One must consider the forecasting of cash flow, both in and out of the firm, how to manage the cash flow, banking transactions and what disposition to make of surplus funds. Proper management of the cash function involves these objectives:

1. To move the creation of cash throughout your business as rapidly as possible, each expenditure for labor or materials must be converted into a final sale as soon as possible. Also, remember, no sale is complete until the cash is in your hands.
2. The system must be simple, not require too much administration and must return a profit.
3. Care must be exercised to make certain that customer and banking relations are not harmed by the actions taken.
4. The funds created by the better management of cash must be invested wisely.

The entire concept under which you are operating is to decrease the float on incoming cash items and increase the float on outgoing items. Your firm is subject to float from the day that the salesman receives the order until the day that the funds are deposited in your account. In order to properly review all of the steps involved you must start with the salesman who takes the order and follow it through your entire operation. First, how long does it take to get the order into your office from the salesperson? Second, once it is received how long does it take to get it processed, credit checked and into the hands of the operating departments for collation, scheduling, production and shipping? Third, is the order held up in operations through faulty procedures, incomplete records, items out of stock or other factors? Fourth, is it packaged right and shipped via the fastest carrier? Fifth, is the invoicing done quickly and efficiently? Sixth, what is the mail float on invoice delivery? Does the invoice arrive coincident to the delivery of the merchandise or is it late? Seventh, what are your credit terms and are they enforced? Finally, when a check arrives is it handled quickly and efficiently and deposited as soon as possible? Could a "lock box" be used to speed up collections?

The financial executive is the guardian of the cash resources of the firm. His job is to conserve and provide cash for the other elements of the operation which require cash expenditures for their existence. He has to plan to acquire cash to meet these needs, when it will be acquired, when it will be disbursed and how much is needed at various times in the cycle. Cash control and needs begin when you open the doors in the morning and start spending money for labor, materials and other items. It ends when the funds are received for sales and are safely deposited in the bank account. The cycle has at least nine component parts:

1. Handling of cash remittances
2. Taking the initial order
3. Entering the order in the records and transmitting it into an operation action
4. Production of the order—filling it from inventories—securing the materials on time
5. Proper shipping of orders
6. Control of inventories
7. Effective control of invoicing and transmitting invoices to customers
8. Control of disbursements—correlation of disbursements with receipts
9. Providing operations with funds and investing idle funds

DURATION OF CASH CYCLE

TIME FACTOR IN DAYS

1. Send salesperson out for orders—advertising and promote	5	5	5
2. Salesperson takes order	1	1	1
3. Transmits order to office	1	1	1
4. Order is credit rated	½	½	½
5. Order is processed	1	1	1
6. Order transmitted to production unit	½	½	½
7. Acquisition of materials	5	5	5
8. Raw material inventory	1	0	0
9. Production cycle	10	5	0
10. Work-in-process inventory	1	1	
11. Finished goods inventory	1	1	1

Administering Financial Control of Current Assets

12.	Shipment of merchandise	½	½	½
13.	Invoicing shipment	½	½	½
14.	Mail transmission time	3	3	3
15.	Credit terms 2/10 N/30	30	30	30
16.	Handling incoming cash	1	1	1
17.	Deposit and withdrawal from banks	1½	1½	1½
18.	Credit terms on accounts payable 2/10 N/30	−30	−30	−30
	Percentage of cost factor .40	12	12	12
19.	Liquidity requirements			
20.	Decision process—short term—long term			
21.	Investment of funds			

CASH STRATEGY

Our interviews indicate that approximately 50% of the larger firms have excess funds to invest. About 25% of the medium-sized firms have this problem and only a very small percentage of the small firms need to make a decision of this type. Their problem is primarily how to acquire sufficient funds to meet this week's payroll or government tax deposit.

Where do financial executives invest their idle funds? Despite the demands of inflation, growth and expansion chewing up cash balances, some individuals will have excess funds to invest. Here are the markets for the funds:

a. Treasury Bills—When it comes to investing funds for a short period of time these are the preferred items. These are the most liquid of items to invest in.

b. Commercial Paper—This is the major market for excess funds. The paper is issued by finance firms or non-financial firms. The appealing feature of paper is its high yield. While there have been a few painful experiences in this area the "big name" obligations backed by top-notch credit ratings represent very little risk.

c. Certificates of Deposit—With high rates on CD's available at certain times many firms put their excess funds in this area. These are usually issued by banks for periods of from thirty days to two years. When federal funds are excessively high banks are very accommodating in this area.

d. Repurchase Agreements—In this instance a firm purchases stocks or bonds from a dealer in securities who agrees to repurchase them in a period that ranges from one to ten days. The dealer uses these funds to carry his stock or bond inventory and is willing to pay a high price for the privilege. The bond market is an excellent vehicle for this type of financing.

e. Eurodollars—Eurobonds—A real tricky endeavor used principally by multinational firms.

TIME CYCLE FOR IDLE CASH INVESTMENTS

1. Repo Agreements—one to five days
2. Commercial Paper—five to ten days—can be used for longer periods
3. Treasury Bills—two to thirty days—can be used for longer periods
4. CD's—thirty days or longer

BASIC RULE

Remain in short-term items and minimize the risks involved with top quality investments.

EFFECTIVENESS

Cash management effectiveness can be determined by a very simple formula. If your annual sales are $24,000,000 and you have an average collection time of 10 days you have an annual float of $240,000,000 and an average monthly float of $20,000,000 on the monthly sales of $2,000,000. The opportunity to invest your funds has a maximum potential of X. This amount is determined by multiplying the monthly sales float for 10 days times the normal interest rate at the present period of time. $20,000,000 invested for 10 days at 10% would yield as determined by the formula:

$$\frac{\$2,000,000 \times 10 \times 10}{365} = X \ (\$54,795)$$

Every single dollar in the process of collection represents one dollar per day of float. When determined on the larger operational float chart rather than on a simple cash float chart this can be a substantial amount of money.

THE CREDIT FUNCTION—A CHALLENGE

Managing the credit function is a prime responsibility of the financial administrator. Fortunes have been lost and firms have gotten into serious trouble because of writeoffs totaling billions of dollars. Some of our largest institutions and banks have suffered losses which in view of subsequent events made one wonder why the credit was granted or the loans were made in the first place. Presidents, financial vice presidents and other high ranking officers toppled under the credit fiasco of 1972, 1973 and 1974. The era of the early 70's had no peer in the granting of excessive and unwise credit. It very nearly brought the entire country down in a credit collapse.

The financial executive has the unhappy position of granting sufficient credit to keep the firm growing while protecting the firm's prosperity and liquidity. It is a tough job. Both the customers and the salesforce will put on a show that rivals all but the one put on by company officials trying to convince a set of bankers that they need short- or long-term financing in huge amounts. There is a great deal of money to be made in the judicial granting of credit and taking calculated risks. There is also a great deal of loss which can occur if excessive risks are taken and the account defaults.

These are the prime factors in credit consideration:

1. A disciplined approach to credit—Set the ground rules and authority limits; make everyone aware of them.
2. Secure adequate credit information on your accounts and keep it up-to-date! Credit information is available through the following organizations:

Administering Financial Control of Current Assets

      a. Dun & Bradstreet—Credit Interchange—Industry Credit Groups—Banks—Credit Associations—Special Reporting Services—Your Own Sales Organization Through Its Customer and Competitor Contacts.
3. Maintain adequate credit files showing:
   a. Most important—current payment record
   b. Company data—all the information you can find on your customer, its personnel, prospects and business. Rate the positive and negative factors.
   c. Type and condition of account—marginal?—weigh the risks against the potential profits
   d. The cost of carrying the account—receivables, inventory, time factor versus profitability of individual products sold, how much it contributes to overhead and profit
4. How to handle the desirable account that is slow paying. How to handle other delinquent accounts. Do you need special treatment or terms?
5. Organized collection procedures. Who is responsible for the collections? In smaller firms accounts are often delinquent because no one bothers to try and collect. Some firms never even send out monthly statements. One small firm stepped up its collections and cut its accounts receivable one-third by merely assigning one person to follow up on all past due items.
6. Did the sales division grant special terms? Often salespersons make deals which never appear on the records until the normal credit terms run out.
7. Adequate accounts receivable reports for prompt notice and follow-up action.

PERFORMANCE RATING

The performance of the credit function can be rated in several ways:

    a. Bad debt losses as a percentage of sales.
    b. Profitable volume losses through negative decisions.
    c. Profits gained through the cultivation of marginal accounts or small, growing firms.
    d. Has the credit function helped in obtaining new business?
    e. Operational performance rating—efficiency, time in handling credit requests. Ability to assume risks.
    f. The scoreboard—risks taken, successes, losses.

INVENTORIES—THE LARGEST CURRENT ASSET

Interviews and studies show that inventories represent most firms' largest current asset. Accordingly they also represent the single toughest problem for the financial administrator. Every firm with expanding sales must build an inventory capable of satisfying customer demand without seriously impairing its liquidity or credit position. The factors involved in matching customer demand to the basic economics of manufacturing at the most effective cost are tough to solve. In establishing selling prices these items are critical and a factor must be included in the price to cover warehousing the inventory for a reasonable period. Despite the utilization of highly sophisticated computer systems, inventories often go astray because of the failure to observe a change in consumer demand or to recognize what the computer is telling you about your sales and inventories.

The primary application of minicomputers is inventory control. Their ability to handle huge volumes of data matching sales with stocks on hand or in the process of manufacture is most useful in inventory control. There are extremely complex systems in use which start at the master bill of materials, run through the complete manufacturing process, controlling and reporting on raw materials, work-in-process and finished goods. There are models in use which go through this complete forecasting function and can tell you what the results will be of a change in any point in the operation.

In my opinion, the simplest method of control is one that matches three factors: orders on hand, sales for the current period (day, week, month or quarter), inventory on hand and a time schedule for replacing that particular inventory item. Years ago, we utilized very simple three color bar charts showing orders on hand, sales for the past month and the current inventory. All of these items were in units. A twelve-month or fifty-two week chart would give you the current trend in all of the items, and if inventories exceeded sales expectations based upon the orders on hand and the trend you cut back on production or increased your promotional activities to move the merchandise. Today with the colored CRT these same charts are available as computer output on an instantaneous basis.

The importance of inventories to company profits can be best illustrated by a recent news article which states that XYZ Corporation was going to have to write down inventories in the amount of one million dollars prior to the end of the year. Stories of inventory writeoffs are common and range from thousands of dollars to many millions. It would therefore appear that one of the prime objectives in the control of inventories is the elimination of obsolete and slow moving items. The computer makes it possible to review your inventory status quickly. The next step is to take positive action. One of the major weaknesses of smaller firms is the accumulation of obsolete or slow moving items which chews up a large portion of their working capital and harms their potential for future growth. By keeping raw materials receipts in correlation with targeted cash receipts you can maintain your liquidity. By ruthlessly eliminating unusable inventory items you can provide faster and greater cash flow.

Periodic meetings should be scheduled between Sales, Production, Purchasing, Warehousing and Finance so that all of these activities can be coordinated on inventory control. As a result of these meetings, problems can be discussed and through a disciplined approach, inventories can be worked down to realistic levels.

MEETING THE CHALLENGE OF INFLATION AND GROWTH

The financial administrator is caught upon the twin horns of a modern dilemma. Inflation and growth have increased corporate demands for both cash and credit to carry larger receivables and inventories. He must devise ways and means to meet these needs without endangering the financial stability of the firm. Credit has been stretched to a twin point with even the largest firms leaning on their suppliers for low-cost financing. The practice has become so widespread that most firms institute a 1% to 1½% or more financing charge on all accounts over thirty days old. What are the answers to the challenge? A rigid

Administering Financial Control of Current Assets

cash and commitment control process, speed up receivable collections, eliminate unprofitable products, work down inventories to reasonable levels and avoid and unload slow moving inventories fast. Also, enforce your disciplines, utilize decision rules, coordinate your interfunctional operations and make everyone aware of the basic problems.

REPORTING TECHNIQUES FOR CONTROLLING CURRENT ASSETS

These are the types of reports utilized in controlling the various current assets:

1. FORECAST CASH FLOW

    DAILY CASH RECEIPTS   1.   2.   3.   4................TOTAL
        ESTIMATED
        ACTUAL
        VARIANCE + or −
    DAILY CASH DISBURSEMENTS
        ESTIMATED
        ACTUAL
        VARIANCE ± or −
        CUMULATIVE VARIANCE
        UNUSUAL ITEMS WHICH WILL REQUIRE SHORT-TERM FINANCING
        EXCESS CASH RESERVES TO BE INVESTED
    DAILY CASH BALANCE
         ESTIMATED
         ACTUAL

2. DAILY CASH REPORT

DAY	RECEIPTS	DISBURSEMENTS	BALANCE
			$XXXX.XX
1.	$$$$$$$$	$$$$$$$$	$YYYY.YY
2.	$$$$$$$$	$$$$$$$$	$ZZZZ.ZZ

3. FORECAST CASH FLOW

    WEEKLY RECEIPTS   WEEK 1.   WEEK 2.   WEEK 3.   WEEK 4.
    COLLECTIONS
    OTHER
    TOTAL
    DISBURSEMENTS
    SUPPLIERS
    PAYROLL
    EXPENSES
    PROMOTIONS
    CAPITAL ITEMS
    PREPAID ITEMS
    DIVIDENDS
    OTHER
    NET FUNDS AVAILABLE

```
            BUFFER BALANCE
            EXCESS CASH FUNDS
            REQUIRED BORROWINGS
            MATURING LOANS
      4.    FORECAST CASH FLOW
                                  10-DAY         NET         DELINQUENT
            SALES                DISCOUNT      30 DAYS    30 DAYS   60 DAYS

            DAY 1 OR WEEK 1     $XXXXX.XX    $XXXX.XX    $XXX.XX   $XX.XX
            PAYROLLS—ACCRUAL
            TAX DEPOSITS—ACCRUAL
            SUPPLIERS' INVOICES
               RECEIPTS BY DUE DATE
```

In this type of forecast each day's or each week's sales are forecast for a collection date based upon past experience. This gives you the estimated future receipts as each day's sales are recorded. The payroll and payroll taxes are accrued as disbursements against these receipts. In addition, suppliers' invoices are forecast for payment based upon normal credit terms in order to ascertain if sufficient cash is available for discounts. Based upon these forecasts, balances which exceed buffer cash requirements can be ascertained, and also the approximate period for which they will be available. In the event the buffer balances are depleted investment drawdowns or short-term borrowings can be utilized to fill your needs.

FORECAST RECEIVABLE BALANCES

Based upon the above cash forecasts an Accounts Receivable forecast is a by-product of the calculations. Collections are based upon experience and also upon statements which show the condition of each customer's account as follows:

CUSTOMER	INV. DATE	AMOUNT	MATURITY DATE	DAYS PAST DUE
3456	09/06/XX	$ 542.22	10/21/XX	71
3456	09/06/XX	809.03	10/21/XX	71
3456	01/21/XY	1,466.94	02/23/XY	23 −
		$2,818.19		

```
                                       PAST DUE
   TOTAL
   OWING      1–15    16–30    31–60    61–90    91–120    121 AND OVER
   $2,818                                1,351
   TOTAL CURRENT      1,467      TOTAL PAST DUE       1,351
```

Administering Financial Control of Current Assets

A complete summary is made by product line, division, branch and/or by customer. This gives you an instant run-down on the condition of your accounts receivable. Sometimes when there are only a small number of accounts a report of this type is used:

	CUSTOMER 1	CUSTOMER 2	CUSTOMER 3	CUSTOMER 4	CUSTOMER 5
BALANCE	0000000	00000	12345	34341	2100
+	90000	100	00000	4444	1000
−			2345	2222	500
BALANCE	90000	100	10000	36563	2600
+		500	10000		1000
−					2600
BALANCE	90000	600	20000	36563	1000
+		1000	10000	16563	1000
−		600	20000	36563	
BALANCE	90000	1000	10000	16563	2000

On a weekly basis this gives you a quick running review of the various customers' account activity and whether the balance is current, growing or declining. It gives clues as to your sales volume, payment activity and slow paying customers.

FORECAST INVENTORY BALANCES

The forecasting of inventory balances on the gross basis is based entirely on the type of firm involved. If orders are filled from stock the process is relatively simple, although not always easy to control. If there is a complicated production process involved you have a more complex problem. One of the simplest ways to watch an inventory is to record the inventory purchases, add them to your starting balance and deduct the cost of the items sold. If the total dollar volume starts to grow and your sales are level or declining you have a problem which requires investigation. In the more complex situations you can detail out the inventory item by item as indicated:

ITEM	ON HAND	ON ORDER	WITHDRAWN	ADDED	BALANCE
3011	76	24	45	50	81
3045	90		100	10	0
3089	56	100			56

This is a weekly report which gives you the current activity, on-order status and what stock is presently available. It can be summarized monthly, quarterly or annually. For operational purposes the report is generally shorted up as follows:

ITEM	ON ORDER	ON HAND	COMMENTS	DELIVERY DATE
3011	24	81		16 days
3045	00	0	PLACE ORDER	SLOW DELIVERY—WATCH
3089	100	56	POSSIBLE OVERSTOCK	21 days
3120	50	75	SPECIAL ORDER TO ONE CUSTOMER	7 days

INVENTORY BY CUSTOMER—BY PRODUCT

CUSTOMER—ITEM		ON HAND	IN PRODUCTION	MONTHLY USE	COMMENTS
2345	5670	567	2,000	1,500	IN BALANCE
	5671	35	0	10	SLOW MOVER. CAN WE ELIMINATE?
	5672	7,689	5,000	6,000	OK
	5673	8,000	0	2,000	OVERSTOCK. CAN WE MOVE?

Inventory control starts with the top line forecast of anticipated sales and works its way down to the issuing of purchase orders for raw materials. You must plan inventories, watch them closely, convert them into receivables as soon as possible and eliminate obsolete and slow moving items as rapidly as possible. During difficult times management is reluctant to write off items that might decrease profits or increase losses. During boom times you have an excellent opportunity to clear the decks—use it. Your target must be to reduce inventories from 10 to 50%.

MAINTAINING AN EMERGENCY CASH BALANCE

One of the financial administrator's prime responsibilities is to provide cash for emergencies. This is one of the tricks of the trade that most individuals will not discuss or divulge information on. Formal or informal, every financial executive has a few sources of cash that he protects from the inroads of the spenders. Sometimes it consists of a slow account that only needs a phone call to collect. Sometimes it is assets that can be disposed of, or suppliers that can be leaned on. Last, but not least important, it is the banker whom you have carefully cultivated for a short-term loan outside of your regular line of credit. The minicomputer is an excellent instrument for working out these problems. If you have a model which shows you, "What if?" when sales drop, collections fall off, a note comes due unexpectedly or your suppliers tighten up, you can crank in the problem and see what

Administering Financial Control of Current Assets 265

alternatives are displayed. Alert financial executives always protect themselves with an emergency cash fund.

ON-LINE CONTROL OF CASH, INVENTORY AND ACCOUNTS RECEIVABLE

The sophistication of the computer has enabled most firms to keep instantly up-to-date by placing all of their transactions on-line. The recording of the cash receipts and the writing of checks instantly updates the cash balances, the accounts receivable and other items. The recording of sales automatically decreases the inventory and the recording of the accounts payable invoice automatically decreases it. Point-of-sale recorders give you instant inventory control and access to inventory movement trends. In complicated manufacturing operations the system is more sophisticated, but by the installation of minicomputers at various stages along the way the recording and control of inventories can be achieved. With CRT displays it is possible to check the cash balance at any time, to review the status of the accounts receivable in detail and to check the status of the inventory items in short order. Minicomputers make it possible to go on-line throughout your entire operation at a very reasonable cost. Systems are now available which allow you to call up a customer's account, age it and check the collection record for as long as you desire. In your hunt for available cash, the spotting of accounts which have just exceeded the credit terms or are about to come due can be a valuable tool. Collections can be speeded up by on-line checking before shipping an order and holding it up if funds are due.

Even the smaller firms can enjoy the luxury of on-line inventory records with the new minicomputers and CRT terminals. For a cost factor in the range of two to three thousand dollars they can have a system which displays the current number on hand and on order by merely punching in the code number of the item. Another feature of on-line operations is the use of microfiche files. These files are so compact that thousands of records can be stored in a 4 x 5 card file. Through the use of codes this information is instantly available. The data can be individualized by date and can be used to store an immense amount of data on customers, materials, processes, machinery and financial data. With microfiche you can update the file chronologically whenever required without too much trouble. Doctors use it for patients' histories, firms employ it for long-range credit history, manufacturing processes, current inventory price lists, catalogs and other items. These files are readily available, and if required a hard copy can be prepared from the film within a short time.

ZERO BALANCE ACCOUNTS

The utilization of zero balance accounts came into being during the early 1970's. The system involves multiple individual accounts within the same bank for each particular activity. A firm's authorized payment agent writes checks drawn on these accounts in payment of bills for their operations. The firm maintains a central account within the same bank. The checks written on the zero balance accounts clear through the bank in normal fashion, and at the end of the day the central account is charged with all the items cleared and the individual account is cleared back to zero. The bank reports these transactions each day to the financial executive. This provides him with the basis for his cash decisions for the next day. If there are excess funds he can invest them for a day or longer dependent upon the situation.

We used this type of account for payrolls for many years. We maintained a balance of one-hundred dollars in the account and as each payroll was issued we deposited an amount equal to it in the account. The balance in the account less one-hundred dollars gave us the amount of our outstanding checks at each reconciliation date.

ADVANTAGES OF ZERO BALANCE ACCOUNTS

Disbursements activity can be maintained at the functional level while the control function is maintained by the financial administrator. Funds are concentrated at one bank, eliminating carrying compensating balances in local or outlying banks. This could hurt your banking relations in the smaller towns! The zero balance account can increase your float time which is a vital factor in cash management.

DRAFTS

Drafts have been used for trade transactions for centuries. During the depression of the 30's the shortage of cash caused firms to utilize drafts for all payments. One Midwestern firm of considerable size made all of its payments including payroll by draft. Each morning the bank would call and notify the treasurer of the amount of drafts that had cleared and he would walk down to the bank with a check to cover them. Since the operations were spread over eight states, the mail time delay in clearing the drafts created considerable float. Not only were the firm's cash requirements held to a minimum but in the event there were excess funds they were invested in treasury bills for the short time involved.

Drafts, while appearing to be checks are actually instruments drawn on the issuing firm, not on the bank, and as such they are made payable through the firm's drawee bank. The Fed processes them the same as checks and they are presented to the payable-through bank. The bank accepts little or no responsibility for the validity of the instrument's signatures, dates and other items. Any drafts which the firm does not choose to honor must be returned to the bank within twenty-four hours otherwise settlement is made immediately by check or authorized charge against the firm's demand account. Insurance firms use drafts in settlement of claims. The number of days float on a draft means that they can retain their funds for investment for a period of from one to fifteen days longer. Based upon the size of some of the operations you can readily see that this is a vital factor in cash management.

CONCLUSIONS

Discussions with financial executives indicate that while meeting obligations on time is one of their prime jobs, the management of working capital is a measuring stick of their financial acumen and ability. The goal is to increase the turnover of inventories into receivables and receivables into cash. Basically their goals are to reduce receivables by 10 to 20% and reduce inventories by 20 to 50%. The toughest problem they have is with the control of inventories and timing cash flow. Alert firms are moving into minicomputers on both items.

One very interesting report was issued by a small business. It involves reporting on the status of current assets weekly, along with payables and operating information.

Administering Financial Control of Current Assets

Some interesting comparisons were developed in comparing various-sized firms and their investment in cash, accounts receivable, inventories, accounts payable and net plant. For the basis of the study we used two hundred fifty-two working days as a base.

REVENUES	FIRM 1	PER DAY	FIRM 2	PER DAY	FIRM 3	PER DAY
IN $1,000	$4,406	$17.48	$1,896	$7.52	$3,878	$15.39
WORKING CAPITAL		No. Days		No. Days		No. Days
CASH	174	9.95	207	27.53	201	13.06
A/R	1,062	60.76	270	35.90	743	48.28
INVENTORY	750	42.91	602	80.05	912	59.26
OTHER	32	1.83	11	1.46	90	5.85
TOTAL	2,018	105.50	1,089	144.94	1,946	113.39
CURRENT LIABILITIES	1,390	79.52	218	28.99	904	58.74
NET W/C	628	25.98	817	115.95	1,042	54.65
SALES PER $ OF NET PLANT	$6.25		$4.40		$6.09	
REVENUES						
IN $1,000	$54,454	216.09	$129,426	$513.60	$409,551	$1,625.20
WORKING CAPITAL						
CASH	305	1.41	5,030	9.79	4,743	2.92
INVESTMENTS	1,400	6.48	2,533	4.93	49,273	30.32
A/R	7,554	34.96	18,143	35.33	82,380	50.69
INVENTORY	11,121	51.46	20,607	40.12	108,308	66.64
OTHER	1,094	5.06	491	.96	8,007	4.93
TOTAL	21,475	99.37	46,804	91.13	252,711	155.50
CURRENT LIABILITIES	7,725	35.75	18,497	36.01	102,242	62.91
NET W/C	13,750	63.62	28,307	55.12	150,469	92.59
SALES PER $ OF NET PLANT	$2.77		$5.29		$2.59	

It is quite apparent that surplus cash funds do not appear on the financial statements until a level of about $50,000,000 in revenues is reached. There are exceptions, however most smaller firms are generally strapped for cash instead of worrying about where to invest it. An interesting summary can be prepared from this study:

VOLUME	CASH ITEMS	RECEIVABLES	INVENTORIES	PAYABLES	NET W/C	SALES PER PLANT $
1,896	27.53	35.90	80.05	28.99	115.95	$4.40
3,878	13.06	48.28	59.26	58.74	54.65	6.09
4,406	9.95	60.76	42.91	79.52	25.28	6.25
54,454	7.89	34.96	51.46	35.75	63.62	2.77
129,426	14.72	35.33	40.12	36.01	55.12	5.29
409,551	33.24	50.69	66.64	62.91	92.59	2.59
843,051	11.35	27.67	63.88	43.98	61.20	4.49
1,944,979	7.48	21.69	37.00	29.99	38.19	6.09

268 Administering Financial Control of Current Assets

The summary points out the weaknesses of the various firms in the high amount of receivables and inventories carried. As one approaches a higher volume of sales it is also apparent that a better measure of control is exercised over both receivables and inventory. The last item on the summary shows the results of an effective control program wherein only 59-day sales are tied up in receivables and inventory. The firm with volume in the $400,000,000 range offsets a sloppy control program by leaning on its suppliers in order to carry almost 50% of its year's sales in inventory and receivables.

The firm in the $4,000,000 revenue bracket has a receivable problem. The slow conversion of these items has also caused it to lean heavily on its suppliers for financing. This is a situation which will not be tolerated too long. Strangely enough it has a low inventory position.

The most critical problem for the financial administrator is to maintain a steady flow through his current assets. The conversion of inventory into receivables and finally into cash must be maintained on an orderly, predictable basis. Continuing corporate liquidity is essential to growth and profitability. Discipline is the clue to success.

MAJOR STOCK INVENTORY REPORT—RAW MATERIALS

Item No.	Consumption Past 90	Past 30	Days This Month	Used	Current Stock	Reorder Point	Requirements—Future Next 60	Next 30	This 30
3011	457	211	14	167	500	300	500	250	83
3045	1,000	800	14	700	400	500	1000	500	0
3112	12,000	4000	14	3000	5000	4000	8000	4000	1000

MAJOR STOCK INVENTORY REPORT—FINISHED GOODS

Item No.	Sales Past 90	Past 60	Past 30	This Month	Current Stock	On Order	Requirements—Future Next 60	Next 30	Now
3500	150	100	50	50	300	0	100	50	0
4000	1200	800	100	50	2000	0	800	400	400
5000	3000	1000	0	0	5000	0	1000	0	0
6000	3000	2000	1000	1000	1000	5000	3000	1000	1000

MATERIAL CONSUMPTION REPORT—RAW MATERIALS

Item No.	Month Current	Month Last	Month 1	Month 2	Month 3	Month 4	Month 5	Month 6	Average 6 Months	Year
3011	167	211	157	89	50	100	0	200	101	145
3045	700	800	200	0	0	0	0	0	35	17
3112	3000	4000	4000	4000	3000	3000	4000	6000	4000	4000

STOCK SALES—FINISHED GOODS

3500	50	50	50	50	50	50	50	50	50	50
4000	50	100	700	400	400	500	600	700	616	800
5000	0	1000	2000	2000	3000	4000	5000	6000	3333	4567
6000	1000	1000	1000	1000	900	800	700	600	433	500

Administering Financial Control of Current Assets

STOCK STATUS—FINISHED GOODS

Item No.	Available Units	Available Dollars	Forecast Units	Forecast Dollars	Variance Units	Variance Dollars
7890	600	$600	1000	$1000	−400	+$400
7891	1000	2000	800	1600	+200	+ 400
7892	5000	10,000	5000	7500	0	+2500*

*Price Increase.

RECEIVABLES STATUS INTERROGATION—ON LINE

Customer	Balance	Current	30-60	61-90	Over 90 Days
0103	$ 5,670	$ 5,607			
0509	2,700	500	1,000	1,200	
7098	500				500 143 Days
9001	12,000	12,000			
2309	60,000		60,000		Special Terms—90
2400	600	500	100		

INVENTORY STATUS INTERROGATION—ON LINE

Stock No.	On Hand	On Order	
3011	567	100	
3023	500	0	Delivery Slow
3045	51	500	
3067	20	0	
3120	8	0	
3200	897	0	
3421	0	500	In Transit

FACTOR 1   ASSUMING MATERIAL COST IS 40% OF COST OF PRODUCT.

LIMIT CASH EXPENDITURES FOR MATERIAL TO

40 PERCENT OF A/R COLLECTIONS
40 PERCENT OF NEXT MONTH'S ESTIMATED SALES
THE LESSER OF THE TWO

FACTOR 2   ASSUMING LABOR COST IS 30% OF COST OF PRODUCT

LIMIT CASH EXPENDITURES TO

30 PERCENT OF A/R COLLECTIONS
30 PERCENT OF NEXT MONTH'S ESTIMATED SALES
THE LESSER OF THE TWO

FACTOR 3   ASSUMING CASH OVERHEAD COSTS ARE 10% OF COST OF PRODUCT

LIMIT CASH EXPENDITURES TO

10 PERCENT OF A/R COLLECTIONS
10 PERCENT OF THE NEXT MONTH'S ESTIMATED SALES
THE LESSER OF THE TWO

FACTOR 4   ASSUMING THAT CASH SELLING AND ADMINISTRATIVE ITEMS ARE 8% OF THE PRODUCT COST

LIMIT CASH EXPENDITURES TO

8 PERCENT OF THE A/R COLLECTIONS
8 PERCENT OF THE NEXT MONTH'S ESTIMATED SALES
THE LESSER OF THE TWO

FACTOR 5   LIMIT RECEIPTS OF MATERIALS TO PERCENTAGES UTILIZED IN FACTOR 1

FACTOR 6   LIMIT COMMITMENTS OR ORDERS FOR MATERIALS TO THE PERCENTAGE OF COLLECTIONS ON A/R UTILIZED IN FACTOR 1

COMPUTER PROGRAM

INPUT A IS ACTUAL COLLECTIONS ON A/R
INPUT B IS ESTIMATED SALES FOR NET PERIOD
INPUT C IS CASH EXPENDITURE FOR MATERIALS
INPUT D IS CASH EXPENDITURE FOR LABOR
INPUT E IS CASH EXPENDITURE FOR OVERHEAD
INPUT F IS CASH EXPENDITURE FOR SELLING AND ADMINISTRATIVE EXPENSES
INPUT G IS VALUE OF MATERIAL RECEIPTS
INPUT H IS VALUE OF MATERIAL COMMITMENTS OR OPEN PURCHASE ORDERS

```
10  INPUT A,B,C,D,E,F,G,H
20  IF A > B GOTO  40
30  IF A < B GOTO
40  IF C > ,40 B GOTO
50  IF D > ,30 B GOTO
60  IF E > ,10 B GOTO
70  IF F > ,08 B GOTO
80  IF G > ,40 B GOTO
90  IF C > ,40 A GOTO
100 IF D > ,30 A GOTO
110 IF E > ,10 A GOTO
120 IF F > ,08 A GOTO
130 IF G > ,40 A GOTO
140 PRINT "INVENTORY CONTROL STATUS"
150 PRINT "MATERIAL EXCEEDS ALLOWANCE BY" C-.40*B
160 PRINT "LABOR EXCEEDS ALLOWANCE BY" D-.30*B
170 PRINT "OVERHEAD EXCEEDS ALLOWANCE BY" E-.10*B
180 PRINT "ADMINISTRATIVE EXCEEDS ALLOWANCE BY" F-.08*B
190 PRINT "MATERIAL EXCEEDS ALLOWANCE BY" C-.40*A
200 PRINT "LABOR EXCEEDS ALLOWANCE BY" D-.30*A
210 PRINT "OVERHEAD EXCEEDS ALLOWANCE BY" E-.10*A
220 PRINT "ADMINISTRATIVE EXCEEDS ALLOWANCE BY" F-.08*A
230 PRINT "PURCHASE ORDERS EXCEED ALLOWANCE BY" G-.40*A
```

Administering Financial Control of Current Assets

```
240 PRINT
250 PRINT "DECISION IS REQUIRED"
260 PRINT ""  A,B:
270 PRINT ""  C,D:
280 PRINT ""  E,F:
290 PRINT "COSTS EXCEED COLLECTIONS BY" C+D+E+F−A
300 PRINT "COSTS EXCEED ESTIMATED SALES BY" C+D+E+F−B
```

WEEKLY STATUS REPORT

MONTH _____
WEEK ENDING _____

DESCRIPTION   AMOUNT

CASH IN BANK $ _____
ACCOUNTS RECEIVABLE $ _____
INVENTORY   THIS WEEK   TO DATE
   PURCHASED $ _____ $ _____
   SOLD $ _____ $ _____
TOTAL CURRENT ASSETS $ _____
ACCOUNTS PAYABLE $ _____
RATIO CURRENT ASSETS TO PAYABLES   % _____

OPERATIONS

	THIS WEEK	MONTH	YEAR TO DATE
BILLING	$_____	$_____	$_____
LABOR COSTS	$_____	$_____	$_____
MATERIAL	$_____	$_____	$_____
FREIGHT	$_____	$_____	$_____
OTHER(EXCEPT P/R TAXES)	$_____	$_____	$_____
TOTAL COSTS	$_____	$_____	
PROFIT OR (LOSS)	$_____	$_____	$_____

WEEKLY STATUS REPORT

MONTH _____
WEEK ENDING _____

DESCRIPTION   AMOUNT

CASH IN BANK $ _____
ACCOUNTS RECEIVABLE
   RESIDENTIAL $ _____
   COMMERCIAL $ _____
   INVENTORIES $ _____

TOTAL CURRENT ASSETS $ _____

BANK LOAN $ _____
ACCOUNTS PAYABLE $ _____
RATIO $ _____
OPERATIONS   THIS WEEK   MONTH TO DATE

RESIDENTIAL BILLING $ _____ $ _____
RESIDENTIAL COSTS
   LABOR $ _____ $ _____
   MATERIAL $ _____ $ _____
   TOTAL $ _____ $ _____

COMMERCIAL BILLING $ _____ $ _____
COMMERCIAL COSTS
   LABOR $ _____ $ _____
   MATERIAL $ _____ $ _____
   TOTAL $ _____ $ _____

11

Financial Control of Current Liabilities

CURRENT LIABILITIES

Inflation brought about a new era in financial administration. It is aptly termed the "era of liability management." Prior to this development much stress was placed upon the management and control of assets, operations and operating costs. Now we have the necessity of scheduling of liability payment dates in order to mesh them with our incoming receipts.

If you are finding that your cash headaches are increasing because your firm lacks sufficient funds you are a normal financial executive. If you spend and pay out until it hurts you have a common major problem. There is no way that you can avoid the paying out process and as your firm grows and expands rapidly the situation could become critical. There are ways to ease the pain of cash shortages. First of all, before your expansion starts, plan your financing needs. After you complete the plan add 20% for underestimation, inflation and rising costs. No matter how you approach it growth is stimulated by adequate financing. The proper management of current liabilities is one way of handling this problem.

PLAN FOR PROGRESS

Your plan for progress requires both timely and adequate financing. This is accomplished through two basic approaches. First, we have the "short-term" financing and then we have the more complex "long-term" obligations. Short-term obligations are normally evidenced by ninety-day notes and are generally used for seasonal purposes. They are used for increasing inventories and receivables which when liquidated provide the funds for the repayment of the loans. This type of loan is essential where you have a seasonal type of business. It is not used to stay in business or to keep your creditors happy.

Short-term financing has a definite function in assisting firms whose initial capital is low in relation to their total sales potential in maintaining a high level of business. It is used in the seasonal production of farm crops, farm equipment, textiles, toys and other items. As long as you can borrow funds at reasonable interest rates to make sales having a profitable markup far in excess of the interests costs, you are justified in making short-term loans. In the glass and cap industries they are used for a period of nine months to provide year-round production, high inventories and dated or term receivables. In this manner a steady level of production can be maintained all year with the excess production absorbed in inventory. It would require enormous amounts of capital for only a short period to carry these inventories and receivables. In order to meet payrolls and pay their suppliers, the firms turn to the banks for short-term funds. The profit return is ten to twenty times the interest cost. In addition, the interest is a tax deductible expense.

If you are a financial executive whose firm requires a line of credit which provides open-note, short-term borrowings there is a word of caution. Use it well and protect it carefully. Be certain that you only use it to finance items which can be liquidated in less than one year. Many firms fall into the trap of purchasing buildings or long-life equipment with short-term funds. Interviews indicate that most small firms are guilty of this practice. One small firm with limited capital and an open-note line of credit of one-hundred thousand dollars spent almost fifteen thousand dollars on a warehouse. Even if their markup was unusually high the practice is still a "no-no." Protect your bank credit! It is one of the most valuable growth tools available to you. Even though it shows as a liability on your balance sheet or financial statements it is a valuable asset in times of need.

ORGANIZATION OF THE LIABILITY CONTROL FUNCTION

Interviews with financial administrators indicate a wide range of organizations to handle and control the liability functions. In the very small firms one girl can handle practically the entire operation; whereas, in the larger firms, the complexity of the system is enormous. Most financial executives fail to recognize the importance of organizing the current liability control function. It is essential that tight control be exercised in this area and also in the area of the creation of current liabilities. To do this one must create a disciplined approach to the handling, recording, justification and payment of liabilities. Dependent upon the size of the firm and the magnitude and complexity of its operations, organization breaks down into about four significant factors.

1. Receipt, control and recording of incoming invoices and liabilities of all types.
2. Justification of liabilities
3. Scheduling liabilities by date of maturity. This includes the scheduling of irregular payments or payments which only occur from one to four times a year.

Financial Control of Current Liabilities

4. Contacts with operating divisions in order to keep abreast of corporate activities which will create liabilities.

The size of your staff will necessarily depend upon the volume of items handled, the amount of detailed reporting required, the size of your firm and whether you are using large or small computers. Functions will normally include the following:

1. Mail handling
2. Recording of accounts payable and other liabilities
3. Justification of liabilities—matching with supporting items
4. Price and extension testing
5. Scheduling of liabilities by maturity
6. Preparation of payment documents
7. Preparation of cash flow and liability reports
8. Filing of executed documents

FINANCIAL ADMINISTRATION OF CURRENT LIABILITIES

Included under this classification are liabilities which are due for payment within one year. Since many important financial reports are dependent upon the separation of current and long-term obligations extreme care must be exercised in this function. Current liabilities normally fall into about five major classifications:

1. Accounts Payable—normally the amounts due suppliers for materials, supplies and services. May include credit balances on accounts receivable.
2. Contracts, Notes and Mortgages Payable—the portion due within one year
3. Accrued Items—payrolls, rents, interest, lease payments, taxes, pensions, union dues and benefits—payroll deductions for FICA, federal and state income taxes.
4. Provision for Income Taxes
5. Other Items—customer deposits, deferred income, unearned royalties, subscription and unpaid declared dividends.

The importance of good recording and excellent records cannot be overemphasized in each of the five categories. Super financial administration requires that the financial administrator have at his fingertips the exact status of each of the above items. Data must be available which indicate the amount of the liability, the due date and the required type of payment. This includes full details about the correct address of the recipient.

ACCOUNTS PAYABLE

In the administration and control of accounts payable the important factors are:

1. *Justification of the invoice*—Is it supported by a receiving ticket or packing slip signed by a responsible individual? Are there any items which are missing or back-ordered? Is the

shipment in good condition or must a claim be filed? Was the original expenditure authorized by a responsible representative of the firm? Does it have a supporting purchase order?

CASE IN POINT

One smaller firm was lax in controlling its purchase orders. It was found that the pad was being used by a warehouseman to order items which were subsequently converted to his own use. Result, a loss totaling over twenty-five thousand dollars.

While riding to work on a commuter train each morning an auditor noticed that a certain address on invoices which he was checking appeared to be a vacant lot. Upon further checking he found that invoices were being submitted to the firm by a fictitious firm located at this address. The remittances were being mailed to a post office box and being cashed by a member of the audited firm.

2. *Verification of prices and extensions*—Although most invoices are priced and extended by computer these days there can be errors involved. A slipped decimal point resulted in an overcharge of over three thousand dollars on one invoice alone. Sometimes the invoices are overpriced only a few cents. Verification techniques and scope are a matter of individual preference. Efforts must be equated with results.

CASE IN POINT

Often on large jobs the material is quoted as a lot with special price quotations. Checking individual prices and totaling the amounts of the individual invoices saved an electrical contractor over fifteen thousand dollars. The prices used on the invoices were the normal ones and not the special quotations covering the entire job.

CONTRACTS, NOTES AND MORTGAGES PAYABLE

1. Contracts Payable—Auto, truck or equipment purchase contracts—could include long-term lease payments due within one year. The prepaid interest should be segregated from the asset side of the contracts. The portion due in one year is a current liability.
2. Notes Payable—Banks—others—short term.
3. Mortgages Payable—Current portion of real estate or other type mortgages.

Each of the above items should be properly scheduled with the amount and date of payment. The number of times short-term notes have been renewed is important. It is also important to know if they can be renewed again. These items must be correlated with the cash flow in order to ascertain if sufficient funds will be available to liquidate them. These are obligations which contain a legal promise to pay a specified amount at a specified date and location. If the loans are secured by collateral or specified assets these assets should be scheduled along with the obligation.

Financial Control of Current Liabilities

ACCRUED ITEMS

This field of liabilities includes such items as the interest on the firm's notes, contracts or mortgages. It can cover real estate and personal property taxes which are generally paid once or twice yearly. It can include rents or lease payments. Some of the more unusual items which pop up are anticipated warranty expenses by construction firms, and, in this day and age of product inperfections, the anticipated liability on product warranties and recall costs.

One of the major components of the accrued classification is the amount of accrued payroll, payroll taxes and union benefits. Due to the stringent requirements for the deposit of payroll taxes and union benefits one must have available cash to fund these liabilities on time. The drain upon cash resources to cover these deposits is a major headache of the financial executives of the smaller firms. They represent an immediate withdrawal of funds from the bank account. Some unions require that the check to cover the union benefits be in the hands of the depositary bank by the seventh day of the following month or you lose your union status. Penalties incurred for late payment of tax deposits represent non-deductible expenses which further add to the severity of the charge.

PENSION COSTS

The current set of rules covering pensions has become a nightmare for most financial administrators. Dependent upon the size of the firm, the provisions of the plan and the age of the plan, the current liability for accrued pension costs will vary. Normally this is a major computation prior to the annual report or publicly issued interim reports. The liability must represent the amount payable to the pension trust as of the date of the report.

DEFERRED ITEMS

Deferred items arise from income which has been received prior to the incurring of the costs involved to produce the article or service. Under this classification you could find unearned subscriptions to periodicals, production payments for coal, iron ore, limestone, oil or other raw materials. One would also include advance payments on maintenance contracts, or certain finance contracts where interest is paid in advance. The major problem encountered in this area is the prompt recording of the liability and the scheduling of its amortization over the next twelve months or longer. These items do not represent cash outlays and should be excluded from your cash flow computations.

TECHNIQUES FOR STRETCHING PAYMENTS IN TIME OF STRESS

All of us in the financial world have encountered the unhappy position of being out of funds at some time or another and in need of some way to produce cash in short order. This is your time of stress and here are a few ideas to solve the problem. While some of the ideas presented under this heading are frowned upon by bankers and respectable financial executives, there are times when one needs to maneuver liabilities about to gain time and cash for pressing problems in the current liability field.

I am reminded of an incident which occurred when I started on a new job as financial executive for a small- to medium-sized firm. The general manager took me into his office, closed the door and said, "This is my last day on this job!" After this he proceeded to open his desk drawer and display a mountain of unpaid invoices. He then stated, "This is your legacy and problem. Good luck!" The desk drawer contained over one million dollars in unpaid bills plus numerous less-than-complimentary requests for prompt payment.

Fortunately the firm had a recent financial statement showing a brand new plant financed by a six-year bank loan which required prepayments based upon a percentage of each year's profits. They had already prepaid 20% of the loan by the time they had been in the new plant for only thirty days. After scheduling the liabilities and their maturities I started flying around the country talking to the credit executives of each of our major suppliers. I explained that we had a brand new plant, lots of finished goods inventories and a very profitable operation. What we needed was some long-term financing and some equity capital. My proposal to them was simple. If they would continue to supply us with merchandise and give us extended credit on the current debt until our selling season started, we could work our way out of the bind. I sincerely feel that any firm that has a profitable operation can work its way out of any difficulty. Eighty percent of the suppliers went along with us including one major supplier who held over 50% of the unpaid debt. To this day, no one has ever replaced this supplier.

In the interim period we burned a lot of midnight oil, worked down our inventories and applied pressure on our slow paying customers. We successfully negotiated a fifteen-year mortgage on the plant and equipment. Most of the equipment had been purchased with short-term funds! In addition, we were able to negotiate a larger line of unsecured credit and managed to sell some additional preferred stock to our current stockholders. Within twelve months we had completely reversed the situation.

Preparation for stretching payments in time of stress actually begins long before the need arises. It is done through developing good relations with your suppliers and their credit executives. Visit them occasionally when your bills are paid up. Cement your relationship by building a bank of goodwill that you can draw on in the future. It helps!

The first steps involved in stretching payments is to review your current position with each supplier and the amount of business you do with him. Short-term financing can be obtained through your accounts payable. While most of us have resorted to the time-honored practice of leaning on indulgent suppliers for additional time there are other ways in which they can help you. The methods available are extended dating—deliver in January—pay in June; liberalized credit terms—one-third in ninety days, one third in one-hundred eighty days and the balance by the end of the year.

You can offer to pay them interest on the unpaid balance over thirty or sixty days. Consignments can be utilized—buy now, pay when you sell it. The availability of this type of credit depends upon the type of item sold, the toughness of the competition and the current economic and credit situation. If you do not believe it try it out on your suppliers!

Another way to gain time is to stretch out your payments to all of your suppliers. Be certain to forward some funds to each of them as an inactive account draws immediate

Financial Control of Current Liabilities

attention. Some firms only check up on your account at the end of the month or when the monthly statement is sent out. A payment sent to arrive just prior to this event will help dress up the account. Next, rotate suppliers by paying one up within its credit terms and ride another. Reverse the procedure as often as possible.

Secondly, restrict purchases and commitments for a period of time to absolutely essential items. Stress material items that are more profitable and those that have a rapid turnover. Keep purchases and commitments below the level of incoming cash. Service your best accounts and fastest paying ones first. Let the slow payers and less profitable ones wait. Offer additional discounts for early payment. Review your inventories for saleable items which can be disposed of without further or minimum processing. Try to persuade some customers to pay in advance or to give you deposits for a preferred status.

In many instances you can restructure your long-term debt so that a portion of it can be paid at a later date.

Always remember, in order to properly pay and discount your bills you must have a continuing input of data relative to the amount, discount date and maturity date of each type of liability. Interviews with smaller firms indicate that this is one of their major weaknesses. No one worries about the current liabilities until it is time to pay them. If the till is empty, it then becomes a fiasco!

CASH FLOW TECHNIQUES

The preparation of complete cash flow schedules matching income receipts with disbursements will aid materially in controlling current liabilities. By restricting commitments for materials to less than the percentage of your material costs or by limiting expenditures to 90% of your incoming receipts, you can build up your cash reserve. The cash flow technique forces you to recognize that there are periods of low cash income and keeps you aware of the problems prior to their actuality. Purchases need to be scheduled just as tightly as production operations.

For example, it was found in analyzing the incoming cash of a small firm that most of its customers were paying their bills on a sixty-day basis. In addition, most of these payments were arriving during the week of the tenth. By rescheduling their purchases they were able to avoid an overdue situation with their suppliers.

MAINTAINING LIQUIDITY, STABILITY AND VENDOR RELATIONS

The proper control of current liabilities is vitally important in the overall planning of your firm. By means of proper planning you can be assured of liquidity and stability. An organization that is constantly "out of stock" because a vendor failed to ship due to credit problems can hamper your entire operation. People who are concerned with selling, handling and shipping customer's orders are perturbed by constant problems that are beyond their control. Finance has an important part in the smooth operation of any business.

Vendor relations are important! Delinquent accounts will get poor service because of the attitude of the credit department in becoming overly protective once a default has occurred. They will often hold up shipment until your check has cleared the bank. This could result in a delay of from one to ten days.

CASE IN POINT

A small firm secured a ten-thousand dollar, sixty-day credit agreement with one of its suppliers. By failing to keep its account within these limits during the first six months it lost its credit rating and is now held down to three thousand dollars and thirty days. For a rapidly growing small firm this was a real fiasco.

Often, in the smaller firms, bills do not get paid simply because they are short-handed and no one pays attention to the bills until the monthly statements arise. By paying once a month or less often they create doubts in the minds of their suppliers. The same amount of money sent in two to four times a month would make the account look better.

The same practice should be followed with the bank's revolving line of credit. Instead of letting it remain stable at one figure, take any excess deposits and use them to reduce the loan. Even if it's only for three or four days it shows that you are concerned with your bank loan.

THE ROLE OF THE MINICOMPUTER

For all firms and particularly the smaller ones, the minicomputer is a valuable tool. It enables the firm to handle a large volume of detail in relatively short periods of time. Through sharp programming, the simple recording of invoices can produce the following results:

1. A schedule of invoices by supplier, discount date and final maturity date.
2. A schedule of liability maturity dates with a matching schedule of anticipated cash receipts.
3. Comparison of receipts and disbursements showing the danger points and the need for additional funds.
4. A schedule of discounts available, taken or lost.

In handling accounts payable many valuable additional tasks can be accomplished.

CASE IN POINT

In checking incoming invoices for prices and extensions they can be compared with inventory and cost estimating records. As each item is recorded and extended it is posted to the inventory records. At this point it is checked against the prevailing inventory price. Unless you are using an average inventory price method, any exceptions are immediately listed for further price checking to ascertain why the exception occurred. In addition, the items are run against the prices for cost estimating and any price exceptions are printed out. By keeping current on inventory pricing and cost estimate pricing one firm saved over one-hundred thousand dollars a year in revised cost estimates which reflected immediate cost changes. A small firm saved two-thousand eight hundred dollars on a job which would have been bid for approximately forty thousand dollars if the system it used had not reflected the new costs.

Financial Control of Current Liabilities

REVOLVING CREDIT AGREEMENTS

One of the methods used in financing phenomenal growth is through a revolving credit agreement with one or more banks. These agreements call for optional term loans after their expiration. This type of loan makes available a maximum amount of credit over an extended period. Some of these agreements will appear as short-term liabilities and some as long-term.

SURVIVAL TIP

Protect your sources of credit! They are a financial administrator's most valuable asset.

FINANCIAL STRAIN

The remarkable fact that most financial administrators run up against is the fact that a profitable, rapidly growing business can come under financial strain. Every business that expands or grows rapidly will at some time or another suffer from a severe case of financial stress. It is brought about through a combination of factors. First of all, any firm, after its initial capitalization, which experiences rapid growth, finds that all of its time has been spent on production, engineering or sales and very little upon the financial aspects of the business. Instead of distributing its funds equally so that all parts of the business could grow at the same pace, it finds that one part or another is out of balance. You have lots of production and inventory and no sales, or you have lots of sales and no production. Finally, these problems are solved and suddenly the impact of increased inventories, accounts receivable, equipment purchases or taxes causes the wheels to squeek. The firm has run out of the all-purpose grease called money. Now it is time for financing; however, the damage is done.

Once this happens you trot down to the bank to visit your friendly banker. You had previously assumed that you could increase your loan automatically. Suddenly the banker wants to know where all the money is going and why? What is the exact reason for the lack of cash? The embarrassing questions come thick and fast. How are collections? Have you paid your bills? Are profits increasing? Do you have a budget to show why you need the extra funds and when they will be repaid. Had you stopped to think of finances long ago many of these questions could have been avoided.

Shrewd management thinks first about finances and skillfully uses borrowed funds to keep its working capital high. Available capital makes profits easier to increase, aids in expansion, sound growth, lowered costs and increases the competitiveness of your firm. Available credit is the factor that insures success and enables you to purchase things out of earnings and not use up your important equity capital.

TUNING IN

The financial administrator must be tuned into the activities of all phases of the operations. Spending is determined by people and unless you are aware of what is going on you can be sandbagged by substantial expenditures. Your first realization that these exist comes when the morning mail is opened and up pops the invoice. At this point in time you have approximately thirty days to raise the funds to cover the expenditure. Every action involving the issuance of a purchase order or a commitment to spend money must be recorded and incorporated into your cash flow cycle. If you miss major items you are in trouble! A summary of issued purchase orders or a commitment report is an excellent means of alerting you to all types of expenditures.

NEW METHODS—NEW TECHNIQUES

These are some of the items being tested for the future:

1. Controlled purchasing—limited to a percentage of incoming orders or shipments.
2. CRT displays used for instant analysis of vendors' invoices.
3. Dynamic balancing of current assets versus current liabilities.
4. Daily reporting of quick assets versus quick liabilities.
5. Operational scheduling of cash requirements as related to the entire production cycle. Balancing the relationship between raw materials, work-in-process and finished goods.
6. Borrowing plant, equipment and inventories instead of money.
7. Standardization of invoice sizes and data content.
8. Utilization of minicomputers at all phases of the current liability operation.

6-5-00

ACCOUNTS PAYABLE MATURITY

DAY JUNE	OLD BALANCE	INVOICED	PAID	NEW BALANCE	
1	$1,000	—	—	$1,000	(dispute)
2	—	—	—	—	
3	5,600	—	$5,600	—	
4	1,200	—	1,200	—	
5	23,000	$5,000	21,000	7,000	
8	41,000	—	—	41,000	
9	4,000	500	4,500	—	
10	34,000	—	—	34,000	
11	7,000	—	500	6,500	
12	29,000	—	—	29,000	
15	—	1,000	—	1,000	
16	—	—	—	—	
17	1,800	—	—	1,800	
18	—	23,000	—	23,000	
19	—	—	—	—	
22	61,000	—	1,000	60,000	
23	6,000	11,000	—	17,000	
24	60	—	—	60	
25	100,000	25,000	—	125,000	
26	3,000	—	—	3,000	
29	1,000	—	—	1,000	
30	56,000	1,000	—	57,000	
JULY					
1	102,000	—	—	102,000	
2	11,000	5,000	1,000	15,000	
3	1,500	—	—	1,500	
6	—	93,000	—	93,000	
7	—	8,900	—	8,900	
8					
9					
10					
13					
14					
15					
16					
17					
20					
21					
22					

			Day or Week	W/E 10/17/-	

ACCOUNTS PAYABLE ANALYSIS

SUPPLIER CODE NO.	PREVIOUS BALANCE	INVOICED	PAID	NEW BALANCE	
0101	$ 37,000	$ 5,000	$ 10,000	$ 32,000	
0203	123,000	—	23,000	100,000	(1)
0908	6,750	10,000	—	16,750	
1412	236,090	1,000	37,090	200,000	
1801	3,000	—	3,000	—	
2303	15,600	5,000	10,600	10,000	
2406	1,000	25,000	—	26,000	
2609	175,000	25,000	150,000	50,000	
2617	8,500	300	8,500	300	
TOTAL	$605,940	$71,300	$242,190	$435,050	

(1) Extended terms of 120 days.

Financial Control of Current Liabilities 285

CASH FLOW RUN
WEEK ENDING 9-17-

DATE	REVENUES	PAYABLES DISCOUNT	PAYABLES NET	ACCRUED	SHORT TERM	TOTAL EX- PENDITURES

CASH FLOW RUN
WEEK ENDING 9-21-

DATE	REVENUES	PAYABLES DISCOUNT	PAYABLES NET	ACCRUED	SHORT TERM	TOTAL EX- PENDITURES
17	$56,000	$8,000	$23,000	$7,500	0	$38,500
18	23,000	11,000	17,000	0	0	28,000
19	10,000	3,000	26,000	1,000	0	30,000
20	67,000	9,000	58,000	0	0	67,000
21	5,000	10,000	24,000	1,000	0	35,000
TOTAL	159,000	41,000	148,000	9,500	0	198,500

NET CASH DEFICIENCY THIS WEEK $39,500
BEGINNING CASH BALANCE   59,023
EXCESS FUNDS   19,523

CASH FLOW RUN
WEEK ENDING 9-28-

DATE	REVENUES	PAYABLES DISCOUNT	PAYABLES NET	ACCRUED	SHORT TERM	TOTAL EX- PENDITURES
24	$34,000	$5,000	$6,000	0	0	$11,000
25	6,000	1,000	8,000	$7,500	0	16,500
26	21,000	8,000	22,000	0	0	30,000
27	12,000	4,000	19,000	1,000	0	24,000
28	50,000	6,000	14,000	1,000	$150,000	171,000
TOTAL	123,000	24,000	69,000	9,500	150,000	252,500

NET CASH DEFICIENCY THIS WEEK $119,500−
BEGINNING CASH BALANCE   19,523
NET DEFICIENCY   99,977−
OPTIONS—RENEW SHORT-TERM LOAN OF $150,000
LIQUIDATE TREASURY BILLS—CURRENTLY AVAILABLE $250,000

SHORT-TERM LOAN MATURITY RECORD

DATE	AMOUNT	MATURITY	RATE	RENEWED?
6-28-	$150,000	9-28-	8.5%	0
7-1-	200,000	9-30-	8.25%	0
8-1-	250,000	11-1-	8.5%	0

ACCOUNTS PAYABLE
DATE RECORDED..........9/20/00

VENDOR	DATE	INV. NO.	AMOUNT	ACCOUNT #	MATURITY	TERMS	DISCOUNT
0203	9/17	00345	10,000	200-01	10/05	D/05 FM	200
0617	9/20	10980	5,000	200-03	10/15	D/15 FM	100
0823	9/15	00897	1,000	400-06	10/15	N/30	
1601	9/18	11234	1,234	600-08	10/18	N/30	
1805	9/14	00098	50,000	200-01	10/05	D/05 FM	250
1805	9/15	00099	45,000	200-01	10/05	D/05 FM	225
2301	9/10	45001	6,987	200-01	10/30	SPECIAL TERMS	
2603	9/11	11223	546	900-06	10/10	P/10	

TOTAL RUN $119,767

ACCOUNTS PAYABLE LISTING

MONTH..............
WEEK..............

DATE	INVOICE NUMBER	VENDOR CODE	ACCOUNT NO.	$ AMOUNT	MATURITY	DISCOUNT

12

Financial Administration of Debt and Equity Capital

During the next ten years and perhaps for a long time to come the capital shortage of U.S. Corporations will represent an incredible sum. Estimates range from seven-hundred billion to five trillion dollars, and despite low current demand the number of firms trying to obtain capital funds keeps growing. This represents a gigantic task confronting the financial administrators of many firms. It will take all of their financial acumen to keep the coffers well-filled to meet their financial needs. There may not be a capital shortage for some firms but others will suffer, and in some instances it will become a capital crisis. The lower tier of firms will be forced out of business if and when the capital crisis becomes intense.

There is a definite limit to the extent these firms can continue to grow by piling debt on top of debt. Many firms already have a debt-to-equity ratio that is frightening. Should the financial executives fail in their task of providing capital, the effect upon their firms and the economy as a whole will be devastating.

Capital shortages are signaled by a gradual rise in interest rates as more firms come to the well to refresh their sagging finances. What and where the financial executives borrow during the interim period is the tip-off signal. Every time the interest rates decline corporations begin to borrow for long periods of time in order to beat the higher rates which will become effective as the funds market tightens. Many firms will begin to exchange common stock for long-term debentures in order to have shares available for future acquisitions or to tighten their control of the company.

Your firm could have its growth stunted if in the periods of future growth it does not have sufficient funds to increase capacity, carry higher inventories and receivables and secure adequate materials and equipment to meet growing demand.

CORPORATE SECURITY AND SURVIVAL

If you are a good financial administrator you will actively cultivate the goodwill of those who furnish capital funds for business. It is a public relations job and is as vital as any other function of the financial division. You must spend some time with the lenders, not when you need funds but in the off periods when your requirements are down. Go out of your way to visit them, have lunch or dinner with them, remember birthdays of their families. Send them a postcard when you are on vacation. In a nice quiet way keep your name in the pot for future needs.

If you wish to survive in the future you must become one of the small group of firms that can raise either equity or debt capital. Failure to do your homework, to do an excellent financial job, will jeopardize the survival of your position and the future of your firm. In addition, current action can prevent the nerve-wracking experience of having the bankers or the lenders suggest that you take your financing needs elsewhere. I have personally experienced that "sinking feeling" or "gut reaction" to the quiet words of the banker telling me that no funds were available.

Financial administrators must face the fact that there is too much debt relative to internally generated cash flow and too much debt relative to equity. We are overborrowed and must restructure our equity debt positions for corporate strength and longevity.

CASE IN POINT

Moody lowers bond rating from BBB to BBB− with this explanation: "Low level of cash flow to debt. Weak fixed charge coverage. Increased proportion of total debt to common stock."

Basically the best way to provide capital for your firm over the long run is through the issuance of capital stock. Normally this is considered to be the least expensive type of financing available. It has a singular advantage in that dividends can be deferred until considerable growth has been achieved or they are needed in times of stress. It is superior to debt on which fixed interest has to be paid as well as annual installments on the principal. Most growth firms have consistently held their dividend payouts to a minimum in order to conserve cash and working capital. As long as the investor has a stock that is increasing in value over the years he is normally satisfied with a low dividend yield. Then too, there are the operations that lose money or just break even year after year and never pay a dividend. As long as management controls enough stock there is little that the outside stockholder can do except talk about it and sell.

One of the failings of newly incorporated firms is that they fail to provide a sufficient amount of initial shares to provide for growth. Often you will find that they authorize and issue a small number of shares. They issue one thousand, two thousand, five thousand or ten thousand shares and have to go back and amend their charter in order to issue additional shares. Not only does this hinder their growth but it penalizes the originators. They should

Financial Administration of Debt and Equity Capital

have warrants to buy additional shares over a five-year-period at least, at nominal or first issue prices. If the firm is successful this enables them to participate in the growth through exercise of the warrants and makes available capital gains treatment upon sale of the stock.

We will not discuss the varied legal aspects of stock issues and covenants to be included in the stock certificates. Sufficient to say that if you are contemplating issuance of stock in order to protect your firm fully, your plans and actions should be thoroughly reviewed by your attorneys and accountants.

CLASSES OF STOCK AVAILABLE

Several classes of common stock are available for issuance. The exchanges frown upon non-voting stock; however, it is available.

1. *Common*—Voting
2. *Common*—Non-Voting
3. *Common*—Class A and Class B
4. *Common Stock*—Restricted

Often common stock is segregated into voting or non-voting by classification as Class A or Class B. Over the years when privately held firms wished to go public, they would issue a non-voting common stock which paid a set or variable dividend prior to any declaration for the voting issue. Often it would have a set dividend; i.e., fifty cents a share plus an amount equal to that paid on the voting issue. In the event of a number of defaults in the dividend on the non-voting stock it could become voting stock.

The restricted version of common stock often was a privately placed issue of common stock which could not be sold to the public or others for a period of time or until it was registered with the SEC. This stock is often held by mutual funds or venture capital firms in hopes of achieving large capital gains.

The market for capital stock among small firms is quite limited and as one president complained: "You have the ideas—do the work—and all they want is 52% of the firm!"

It is also noted that in many of the corporate annual reports wherein long-term debts were disclosed, the lenders had received warrants to purchase common stock at the market price prevailing at the time of the loan. Over a seven- to fifteen-year period this could boost the lenders' interest rate up considerably. It would also tend to dilute either the control or the equity of the other common stockholders.

PREFERRED STOCK

1. *Preferred*— *Preferred as to Assets in the Event of Liquidation*—Usually in a stated amount such as $100, etc.
2. *Preferred*— *Preferred as to Assets and Dividends*—No payment on the common shares until preferred dividends are paid. The preferred dividend is usually at a set rate such as $1.20 per share, etc.

3. *Preferred—* *Cumulative—Dividends Accumulate When Unpaid—*All dividends must be paid before any payments on common.
4. *Preferred—* *Convertible—Convertible into a Set Number of Shares of Common.*

The preferred issues can be any combination of the above. Normally preferred stock is non-voting; however, there are preferred issues which if the dividends are unpaid for a period of time become voting stock.

CASE IN POINT

One listed firm shows the following preferred stock issues in its annual report:

*Preferred A—*Dividend 45c ¼ of 1 vote
*Preferred B—*Dividend 55c no vote
Cumulative Convertible
   Preferred—$10 a share preference on dissolution.

The issuance of both common and preferred stocks is subject to both state and federal regulation. For the smaller corporation with a limited issue the limitations might be quite simple, such as applying to the Secretary of State or the Corporation Commission for a charter. As you move up the ladder you will become subject to more stringent regulations including registration with the SEC or listing on the exchanges. This is best handled by the experts and underwriters. Stock is sold as follows:

   a. Private placement with a financial institution, mutual fund or pension fund.
   b. Over-the-counter market—normally handled by underwriters or brokerage firms.
   c. Listing on the exchanges—local, American or New York Stock Exchange.

WARRANTS

Warrants to purchase common stock at a set price within a definite time are often issued with the original issue of stock or can be issued in conjunction with a debt issue. Often this is the only way you can acquire a long-term loan by sweetening up the terms with warrants to purchase some of your common stock at a set price. This price could or could not be adjusted by stock dividends and stock splits. As I write this I hold in my hand a warrant issued in conjunction with a bond issue that gives me the right until May 5th, three years from now, to purchase one hundred shares of corporation X at fifty dollars per share. Since it is currently selling (the stock) for $5.75 and the warrant for fifty cents my appreciation on the warrant is not too large. Many other instances have proven or will prove to be more profitable.

LONG-TERM FINANCING

There are numerous ways to secure long-term financing. The financial executive must review his firm's long-term objectives, the state of the money market and the individual situation prior to recommending a course of action. These are the instruments involved:

Financial Administration of Debt and Equity Capital

BONDS

There are many classes or types of bonds available. They range from ordinary bonds to mortgage bonds, collateral trust bonds, equipment trust certificates, debentures, subordinated debentures, income bonds, convertible bonds, sinking fund bonds, non-callable bonds to term callable bonds. Each has its advantages and disadvantages and its specific job to perform.

MORTGAGE BONDS

These are the most prevalent way of financing plant and equipment. With this type of bond the assets are pledged as security to the loan. In most instances it will cover land and buildings. It may just cover a single item, building or all of the assets. It represents a prior lien on the assets in the event of dissolution. The use of mortgage bonds is a clean type of financing which maintains flexibility and keeps open other lines of credit such as debentures or subordinated debentures. They are relatively easy to place with insurance firms, pension funds or other private sources of capital. When the assets involved are widely scattered they could be troublesome if the lawyers insist upon recording the liens locally.

WORTH NOTING

Whenever possible you should opt for an open-ended mortgage to allow for future growth. This will make it possible to add items to your mortgage without a great deal of red tape.

COLLATERAL TRUST—EQUIPMENT TRUST CERTIFICATES

In this type of financing title passes to a trustee who can sell the bonds or certificates in the open market. Because of the excellent collateral they are easy to sell and preferred by many investors. Since they have a short life they are only good for relatively short financing. In most cases the life of the equipment determines the life of the loan. This type of financing is utilized primarily for railroad equipment and other large, specialized items. If you will examine a railroad locomotive carefully you will generally find some bank is the trustee owner of the item. The placard states that it is collateral for a loan by the bank or insurance firm. While researching such loans I visited a newspaper plant and found that the large offset press printing the papers was collateral for equipment trust certificates.

INCOME BONDS

In most instances these are floated by municipalities for water or sewer issues and by utilities. The payment of interest and principal is guaranteed by setting aside a portion of the revenue from the facility.

DEBENTURES—SUBORDINATED DEBENTURES—CONVERTIBLE DEBENTURES

The term debenture is just another name for a bond. Normally a debenture constitutes a mortgage. Usually debentures are utilized where sinking funds are set up for their retirement, or where warrants are issued along with the bonds, or a conversion privilege to exchange it for common stock at some future date is part of the package.

CONDITIONAL SALES AGREEMENTS

A conditional sales agreement can often serve as a medium-term financing tool. In this instance title does not pass to the purchaser until the final payment is made.

SUBORDINATED—WHAT IS IT?

In the recent issue of some subordinated debentures for common stock by a listed firm, the debentures were subordinated or would not be repaid in the event of dissolution until an existing debt of one-hundred three million dollars was paid off. It ranked prior to the claims of the common and preferred stockholders.

SPECIAL FINANCING

The utilities are utilizing a special means of financing power plants. In this type of financing they set up a capital trust with the vice president of one of the banks as head of the trust. This trust builds the plant, in this instance costing fifty-three million dollars. When the plant is completed the trust sells it to the utility in a "turnkey" operation. In the interim period the utility has time to float bonds, issue common or preferred stock or obtain other long-term financing. Since the utility cannot use the interest involved in the construction process in its current rates, it provides a means for capitalizing this interest during construction and keeping it out of the current cash flow.

DEEP DISCOUNT BONDS

A new and novel financing arrangement involves the use of deep discount bonds for financing long-term projects. They have an immediate appeal for some investors from the tax standpoint as they offer a lower interest rate in exchange for a better than normal long-term capital gain. The issue must have some limitations on its call provisions in order to be attractive. Naturally there are some objections to this type of financing. First off, it is new and not too well-known. The combined charges of interest and discount could affect current earnings and the reaction or effect on other lenders or bond issues is not determinable. The call provision should be set up in five-year intervals or increments so that investors could determine their return for any set period. This would make it possible to calculate the yield to each call date.

Financial Administration of Debt and Equity Capital

OVERBORROWED?

This is what some firms look like on their financial statements:

LONG-TERM DEBT

NOTES PAYABLE—	COLLATERAL DEEDS OF TRUST ON LAND AND BUILDINGS	$7,083,000
NOTES PAYABLE—	UNSECURED—MINIMUM LOAN: $2,000,000 MAXIMUM IN 3 YEARS—$4,000,000 AT PRIME PLUS ½% CONVERTIBLE TO A 5-YEAR TERM LOAN AFTER 3 YEARS AT PRIME PLUS ¾%	2,650,000

FINANCIAL STATUS

CURRENT LIABILITIES	$2,989,000
LONG-TERM DEBT (AS ABOVE)	9,733,000
OTHER ITEMS	252,000
TOTAL DEBT	12,974,000
STOCKHOLDERS' EQUITY	13,815,000
RATIO EQUITY TO DEBT	1.42
% LTD TO EQUITY AND DEBT	41.3%

LONG-TERM DEBT—FIRM B

CONVERTIBLE DEBENTURES	62,552	(000) omitted
SUBORDINATED DEBENTURES	33,709	
7 DEBENTURE ISSUES	315,293	
2 NOTES PAYABLE	134,500	
2 NOTES PAYABLE	100,000	
MORTGAGES	35,930	
TOTAL	$681,944	

MATURITIES RANGE FROM ANNUALLY TO 25 YEARS

LONG-TERM DEBT—FIRM C

$200 MILLION REVOLVING CREDIT	120,000	(000) omitted
5 SINKING FUND DEBENTURE ISSUES	301,000	
SERIAL DEBENTURES	77,000	
NOTE PAYABLE	8,000	

THIS FIRM HAS IN ADDITION

7 CONVERTIBLE PREFERRED ISSUES
4 NON-CONVERTIBLE PREFERRED ISSUES
COMMON STOCK

LONG-TERM DEBT—FIRM D		
SINKING FUND DEBENTURES	19,260	(000) omitted
SENIOR NOTES ANNUAL PAYMENTS	5,000	
INDUSTRIAL REVENUE BONDS	4,172	

LONG-TERM DEBT—FIRM E		
NOTES DUE SEMI-ANNUALLY 3 YEARS TO 25 YEARS	14,761	(000) omitted
5-YEAR NOTES DUE BANK	1,831	
MORTGAGE NOTES 20 YEARS	3,137	
INSTALLMENT NOTES 20 YEARS	5,020	
INCOME DEBENTURES 4.1 to 6.5% ANNUALLY FOR 5 YEARS	600	

SHORT TERM—CONVERTIBLE TO LONGER TERM

Most firms report that they have "revolving credit" agreements which can after three to seven years convert to term loans. The term loans are normally five years in length. This makes financing available for a period of from five to twelve years. These loans are generally unsecured and carry a rate of from ¼% to ½% over the prime rate. In addition, you pay a commitment fee of ½% on the daily average unused balance. The additional kicker is that you must maintain (on a strictly informal basis!) compensating balances equally to 10% of the available commitment and 10% of the average daily outstanding loan.

OTHER LOAN RESTRICTIONS

Most loans carry certain standard restrictions. These are some of the items:

1. Maintain working capital at a set figure
2. Maintain tangible net worth
3. Restrict the incurrence of liens and funded debt
4. Restriction on the amount of dividends
5. Must maintain stockholders' equity
6. Restrict purchase of own stock

BALLOON NOTES

Probably some of the worst financing possible was brought out during a recent property tax case. The group in question had built four or five motels. They had financed them with 10% down and only the interest to pay for the next ten years. Even with this type of financing their attorney was pleading that the real estate taxes should be reduced as the motels were not profitable. Further investigation indicated that the entire equipment was rented or leased. The entire venture was put under way with a minimum investment. Despite this it still was not profitable. I wonder which insurance firm is currently holding the golden wallpaper?

Financial Administration of Debt and Equity Capital 297

TYPE OF REVOLVING CREDIT

3-Bank Syndicate—$30 million for 2 years with the right to convert to a 4-year term loan at maturity. Sweetener—warrants to purchase 626,667 shares of common at $16.50 if exercised within 18 months.

Financial Group— $10 million for seven years.
Sweetener—warrants to purchase 438,244 shares at $3.09.

SPECIAL PROJECTS

A petroleum firm borrows one-hundred forty dollars on a ten-year loan for its share of a $1.5 billion dollar project which will start up in three years. It combined with a chemical firm and a gas company to finance the joint venture.

INCOME REVENUE BONDS

Municipally owned plant leased. It was financed by industrial revenue bonds. The lease payments were equal to the bond maturities.

REVENUE BONDS

Cover facilities or pollution control equipment. Leases or installment purchase agreements are covered.

EUROBOND LOANS OR MULTICURRENCY LOANS

Utilized for operations in foreign countries. Interest rates are normally set at ½% to 1% over the London best rate. They are used for facilities, equipment or short-term financing.

WHAT ARE THE LOANS USED FOR?

1. Build a plant
2. Working capital
3. Pay off short-term loans
4. Buy own stock
5. Acquisition of another firm

THINGS TO REMEMBER ABOUT FINANCING

- *There is money available*—However, if you are looking for one-hundred thousand to two-hundred thousand dollars you are too small for the venture capital firms and most insurance firms.
- *Public issues under five million dollars* are considered too small for most brokerage firms or underwriters.

- *Large firms* will only help small firms that may tie in with their business. You generally must be a supplier or potential supplier.
- *Most financial firms want fast results*—They expect you to reach twenty-five million dollars in five years or less and one-hundred million dollars in about ten years.
- *It's a competitive world*—If you come up with something startling you only have a short time to exploit it. Competition will learn of your success fast and in no time at all your profits will start to erode. Technology changes rapidly and obsolescence is a big factor.
- *Know your potential!*—*know your markets*—Make your projections as accurate and conservative as possible.

METHODS OF PAYMENT ON LOANS

Both the mining and the oil industry use production payments as a way of financing projects. The oil or ore in the ground is collateral for the loan. Some financial administrators consider this a non-debt type of financing that does not restrict other financing.

PROJECT FINANCING

As indicated by the joint financing of a project by three firms, oil, chemical and gas, project financing is popular in some fields. It fits special situations. Considerations are risk involved, property life, where it is located, payout period and venture partners.

LEASING—LONG-TERM FINANCING

Multiple pieces of huge equipment are leased for periods from 15 to 20 years by insurance firms. A lease now enables you to utilize a piece of major equipment that is escalating in value through increased production costs. Payments are made from revenues created by the equipment.

CREATION OF A TRUST TO ACQUIRE PROPERTY

Very often trusts are created to purchase property for future use or development. In states where blind trusts are permitted this effectively conceals the true owners of the trusts.

CASE IN POINT

PROPOSED FORMATION OF A TRUST TO PURCHASE PROPERTY X.

PURCHASE BY TRUST:

Sales Price of Land at $1.45 per Foot	$221,000
Cash Down Payment	56,000
CONDITIONAL SALES CONTRACT	
	$165,000

Closing costs with the trust costs will run approximately $600.

Financial Administration of Debt and Equity Capital

With 20 beneficiaries taking part in the transaction, the contribution of each will be $2,830, with a monthly installment each of approximately $75.

SALE OF PROPERTY:

Sales Price at $1.62 per Foot	$246,000	
CONDITIONAL SALES CONTRACT BALANCE	163,000	
Sales Proceeds		$82,900
Expenses:		
Payments	12,000	
Closing Costs	120	
Trust Expenses	400	
Total Costs		12,520
Sales Proceeds		70,380
Less: Initial Investment		56,000
Net Sales Proceeds		$14,380

ANALYSIS OF PROFIT ON TRUST:

Initial Investment	$56,000
Expenses for Eight Months	12,520
Total Investment	$68,520
RETURN ON INVESTMENT:	$14,380/$68,520 = 21.0%

EUROBOND FINANCING

Firms utilizing Eurobond financing are among the best known in America: Amax, Ashland Oil, Beatrice Foods, Corning Glass, Ford, General Mills, General Motors, Honeywell, Monsanto, Rockwell, Scott Paper, Textron and U.S. Rubber. Rates are comparable to the normal rates of interest in the U.S.A.

LOAN TRAPS

There are a few items to watch for in committing yourself to loan agreements. These are:

1. *Commitment Fee*—Usually ½% of the principal amount.
2. *Audit Fee*—You can be forced to pay for the audit prior to the issuance of the loan and as often as quarterly thereafter. At present C.P.A. rates this could be very expensive.
3. *Compensating Balance*—Up to 20% of the commitment.
4. *Full Term Interest in Advance*—You receive the net proceeds after the interest is deducted.
5. *Float Costs*—Your payments are not deducted until your check clears. An additional one to five days' interest.
6. *Security Blanket*—The lender wants everything including the cafeteria sink as collateral.

LATEST WRINKLE IN FINANCING

One of the large oil firms has bypassed the underwriters by soliciting competitive bids on a recent security issue. It tends to auction its bonds to all financial institutions and retail customers. This could prove disastrous to the smaller firms attempting to place future bond issues. It is an adaptation of the auction process used by the U.S. Treasury.

IDEAS FOR OR AGAINST

a. The best financing—up to a point—is a long-term mortgage or bond in that the interest costs are deductible expenses. In time of stress this can become a burden.
b. Preferred Stock—The second best type of additional financing although the dividends could be cumulative or costly to the firm. It gives you an opportunity to enhance the balance sheet at no cost to the common shareholders. High yielding preferreds are very attractive to investors. The additional funds raised can improve the balance sheet to a point where additional financing by bonds or other debt is possible.
c. Common Stock—As with the preferred the dividends are not a deductible expense. When you sell additional common you are often putting good assets on the auction block at a discount.
d. Warrants—All the strength of a Continental Peso. A promise to pay out at some future date used to sweeten stock or debt issues. In times of rising markets they could be a good thing. The failure rate on warrants is relatively high.

INCREASING YOUR PROFIT

The exchange or retirement of debt and stock issues can result in profits accruing to your firm. In return you incur an increase in your fixed interest charges against a doubtful reduction in your capital liability. In the financial field it is termed the Hohokam revenge. If you go for it you may well get it. When and where is the vital question.

RESTRUCTURE OF DEBT

The rapidity with which your firm's lenders can shut off the cash tap at the first signs of trouble is a wonderful thing to behold. As you sit across from the banker or the insurance executive while he tells you that this is the end of the trail you are receiving a very sobering lesson in finance. Many individuals who have participated in the free and easy credit era and have been trapped by recession, tight money and overenthusiastic expansion plans suddenly have the gut reaction that they might have made a few financial errors in the past. At this point in time the financial maneuvering starts. What do you do to raise cash, to restructure debt, to cut down on the huge interest charges that keep accruing month by month?

Financial Administration of Debt and Equity Capital

CASES IN POINT

Company A—Exchanged cash and preferred stock for fifty-eight million dollars of subordinated debentures.

Company B—Pledged assets for a long-term agreement in exchange for short-term debt.

Company C—Exchanged assets for debt.

Company D—Restructured debt into one hundred thirty-nine million dollars of senior debt at reduced interest rates. Sold assets for cash. Cured a technical default with the cash.

Company E—Sought a merger with a financially strong firm and was successful in the attempt.

Company F—Partial liquidation—managed to outlive crisis by selling over 60% of its business.

Company G—Sold preferred stock—cancelled debt for common and preferred stock—secured additional capital through leasing assets.

HOW TO ACQUIRE FINANCING

Basically financing is secured through banks, insurance firms, venture capital organizations, underwriters, private placement specialists or other financial institutions. The requirements are similar to those required in leasing except that they will be more stringent, in greater detail and for a longer period of time. Dependent upon the type of financing required the requirements for your presentation will vary. In addition, your past experience with the individual or group of lenders will vary the amount of information to be submitted. Accordingly we will run through three typical loan request situations:

SHORT-TERM FINANCING—COUPLED WITH TERM FINANCING

If you are seeking short-term financing with the potential of converting it into a term agreement loan after two or three years, you will need the following data:

1. YOUR PROFILE

    a. Balance sheets and income accounts demonstrating a sound and profitable operation.

    b. That you have a background of good management.

    c. That you have an aggressive research and development program with good product development.

    d. That your "bread and butter" operations are stable.

2. FORECAST

    a. A short-term forecast showing the need for the funds and the time and method of repayment.

b. A long-term forecast—three to five years showing the need for longer term financing and the time and method of repayment.

c. Company objectives and plans for future growth.

d. What you will do if you do not get the loan!

3. EXHIBITS—MODELS—OTHER PRESENTATIONS

a. Charts—supporting information showing growth trends, profitability of products. Promotional efforts and their results on sales.

b. Videotape or Teletalk (slides and tape) describing the project and its potential.

c. Models—planning models are used to demonstrate through the various options available, the results of the financing requested.

CASE IN POINT

One firm used a planning model to secure more favorable line of credit from a bank. Result—a substantial savings in interest payments.

ROI models—used to illustrate the effect of the financing upon the project or projects being financed.

The procedure is essentially the same with long-term debt issues such as mortgage bonds and debentures. The principal variation is that the detail of the assets being mortgaged must be furnished, an opinion as to the title to the property obtained and other legal ramifications. For long-term debentures you may have sinking fund requirements which must be spelled out and a trustee appointed. Dependent upon the amount and complexity of the issues the financial executive, the firm's attorney and the financial institution can work out the details.

In the area of stock issues we enter a field of greater regulation and control. Once again, this is perhaps better left within the domain of the experts with financial data furnished by the financial administrator.

CONCLUSION

In the area of debt and equity capital the corporate planning model is perhaps the financial administrator's best tool and most useful servant. In my opinion, the use of these models in the financing area is vital to the individual's actual survival. The need for rapid evaluation of alternate strategies under varying conditions is essential. Uses range from the determination of asset allocations to balance sheet projections, pro-forma financial reports, ROI studies, to "What happens if we cannot secure the additional funds to finance inventories, plant or equipment?"

The computer and the minicomputer has placed these techniques within the reach of even the smallest firms.

Financial Administration of Debt and Equity Capital

CASE IN POINT

A beauty shop wishing to expand by borrowing forty thousand dollars utilized a minicomputer to show the increased revenues available, the monthly repayments of the loan and its ability to service the debt under two or more optional sets of conditions.

13

New Techniques in Financial Administration of Taxes

ASTUTE TAX PLANNING—KEY CATALYST TO CORPORATE PROFITS

Every financial administrator must recognize that *tax planning* is a very important area of corporate profit improvement. It is vitally essential that he set up pipelines of information which will keep him informed of all actions which might be affected by proper tax planning. This is an everyday, bread-and-butter type of operation that must not be neglected. In addition, it can provide a dollars-and-cents measure of his contribution to the overall corporate profits.

SIGNIFICANT CASE IN POINT

One firm had a plant nearing the end of its useful life. It had not operated at a sufficiently profitable level to enable it to take full advantage of the percentage depletion allowance for tax purposes. It availed itself of a method used by the oil industry—production payments. It sold the material in the ground during one year and repurchased it for production in the next. This bit of tax planning added some fifteen cents a share to its earnings for the year. It was a significant contribution to profit.

CASE IN POINT

One of the gas pipeline firms made advance payments of about forty million dollars to an oil firm to aid in the exploration, development and production of natural gas. In return it got preferential rights to purchase gas plus substantial tax benefits.

The area of tax planning can be a fertile field for all types of corporations.

The financial administrator of today has to contend with increasingly complex government tax regulations both at home and abroad. Tax management and planning involve a wide range of activities from income taxes to sales taxes, duties, restrictive levies and other items. Dependent upon the size of the firm and the extent of its operations the amount of technical knowledge can range from simple terms to colossal. One has the choice of staffing with specialists, employing outside professionals, shirtsleeving it or a combination of all three.

ORGANIZATION AND STAFF FOR TAX MANAGEMENT

Once again, the size of the firm and the complexity of its operations determines both the organization and size of the staff for the tax department. The tax function must be centrally controlled; however, where the firm is spread countrywide or internationally, some of the responsibility will have to be delegated locally. The tax manager cannot be arguing in Hong Kong about taxes and conducting the affairs of his department at the same time. The routine sales and use taxes, payroll tax returns and local tax schedules can be prepared by the field offices under the supervision and control of the centrally located tax department. Properly controlled, this should only require some planning, periodic review and an annual review or study of the local tax laws to ascertain the correctness of the forms filed. These units may maintain a library of the local tax laws to complement the central library.

The financial executive should hire qualified individuals to manage the tax functions. Normal sources for these individuals include members of other corporations, legal firms or C.P.A.'s.

Interviews relative to staffing tax departments range from reliance on their local accounting firm to staffs of up to one hundred individuals. Normally the smaller firms have a tax manager and a secretary. The average group appears to range from three to five individuals. One firm with sales in the fifty-million dollar range, having subsidiaries in both Canada and Mexico, had a staff of five individuals broken down into the following responsibilities:

Tax Manager —Policies—Tax Planning—Controversies—Research and Planning.

Assistant
 Tax Manager—Accounting Policies—Return Preparation and Review—General Supervision. (This individual was in line to succeed the Tax Manager within two years upon his retirement.)

Assistant 1. —Foreign Income Taxes and Duties—Exports—Imports.

Assistant 2. —Guidelines for Local Offices—Personal Property and Real Estate Taxes—Sales and Use Taxes—Payroll Taxes.

Secretary —Maintenance of Tax Calendars—Typing Returns—Filing Updating Services—Letters—Etc.

New Techniques in Financial Administration of Taxes 307

Assistants should normally have an accounting background so that they can readily obtain and check the data utilized in preparing the tax returns.

One firm with sales in the billion-dollar-plus range and multinational in character had a staff of thirty-five employees in the tax division. The corporate hierarchy was as follows:

VICE PRESIDENT FINANCE

DIRECTOR OF TAXES

MANAGER FEDERAL INCOME TAXES	MANAGER INTERNATIONAL TAXES	MANAGER STATE AND LOCAL TAXES
ASSISTANTS	ASSISTANTS	ASSISTANTS
WASHINGTON REPRESENTATIVE	FOREIGN REPRESENTATIVES	REGIONAL STAFFS

The federal income tax return of this firm represented almost two man-years of work—four volumes and at least a ream of paper.

Perhaps the smallest tax unit encountered was for a construction firm. Despite a volume of business in excess of 2.5 million dollars they relied on a clerical employee to compute and file everything but the Federal and State Income tax returns. The work was supervised by a local C.P.A. who handles the federal and state tax matters.

TAX CALENDARS, RECORDS, FILES AND SOURCES OF INFORMATION

Every executive who handles taxes must have a tax calendar, a checklist and a means of reviewing periodically, the administrative procedures. The tax dollar remitted to the federal government or local entities is the final division of an entire year's work. A dollar saved in this area is doubly rewarding.

THE TAX CALENDAR

The tax calendar lists all the returns which have to be filed in chronological order showing the due dates and the payment dates. It should show the location of the taxing authority and the type of tax. Some individuals refine it even further and show the taxes by jurisdiction and type of tax. In this manner you can determine the amount of sales taxes, real estate taxes or any other category. Accompanying the tax calendar should be another checklist which shows the normal time required for preparation, the date each return was filed, any extensions requested, hearings or controversies, audits and their results and the date the tax return was filed. One firm utilizes a tax calendar to make certain that it receives the appropriate tax forms on time and that they are handled prior to the due date. It also maintains a complete record by state and location of the pertinent data. Federal items are recorded separately. One cannot stress the importance of adequate records in this area.

CASE IN POINT

One firm was assessed a penalty of over $1,800 for filing its tax return late. It had paid the tax in two installments and the state taxing authority had no record of receiving either installment. In fact, on checking back it was found that the first installment check was still shown as outstanding on the bank reconciliation. The state had cashed the second installment check but had never raised the question of delinquency until the firm wanted to know why its first check had never been deposited. Adequate records resulted in an abatement of the penalty and interest.

NOTE TO FINANCIAL ADMINISTRATORS

It might be well to review why certain of your checks are outstanding each month!

WORKING PAPERS

Working paper forms should be developed to insure uniformity of material or data preparation. These must be in a standardized format so that the information accumulated throughout the firm is consistent and will require a minimum of reworking or contacting the originating source of the data. Adequate working papers are a vital necessity to the successful administration of any tax department.

FILES

Adequate and complete files should be maintained on all tax matters. After the statute of limitations has expired it is suggested that they be put on microfiche and filed. One advantage of this is that it will enable you to keep chronological tax records in a minimum of space. Data on capital investments often requires a longer file maintenance period. In the event of controversy it is satisfying to know that you still have the information available for reference.

SOURCES OF INFORMATION

Requirements for information will naturally vary with the size of the operation and the complexity of their tax problems. A minimum tax library would normally include the following:

1. Current Revenue Code and Regulations

    A looseleaf version is available from the Government Printing Office on an annual subscription basis.

2. A Complete Prentice-Hall Tax Service

    Covering income taxes—social security and payroll taxes—excise taxes. Whatever state taxes are required.

New Techniques in Financial Administration of Taxes 309

3. Internal Revenue Bulletin

   Available on an annual subscription basis—Government Printing Office.

4. Tax Magazines

5. Tax Reference Books on Various Subjects Which May Be Pertinent to Your Firm

6. Tax Court Cases—TDC's

   A file for at least the past ten years.

The tax information ranging in importance is best summarized as follows:

1. *Internal Revenue Code.*
2. *Treasury Regulations*—Interpretation of the Code. Available in the Federal Register and loose-leaf services.
3. *Revenue Rulings*—Interpretation of facts submitted to the IRS. Available as Letter Rulings which enable you to start action. Weekly looseleaf service.
4. *Supreme Court—The Final Decision*—Available in the Supreme Court Reporter.
5. *Court of Appeals—Decisions Above the District Courts.*
6. *Federal District Court—Decisions Only in Their District—Majority of Cases.*
7. *U.S. Tax Court—Majority of Smaller Cases*—Available from the Government Printing Office—Monthly case decisions.
8. *U.S. Court of Claims—Suits for Refunds of Taxes Paid.*
9. *Acquiescence or Non-Acquiescence by the IRS*—Reported in the Internal Revenue Bulletin—Cumulative Bulletin.

Tax Court Reports are available from Prentice-Hall, Inc., including the Memo Decisions. Others are in the federal supplement—Federal Reporter. *Writ of Certiorari*—What does it mean? *It is important enough to be reviewed by the supreme court.*

There are additional sources of information available such as the New York Institute on Federal Taxation—Annual Seminar, published in annual volumes. If an individual lives in a university town they usually have a very good tax library.

TAX PLANNING

As the tax laws change the importance of tax planning has increased the stature of the Financial Administrator. The effective minimization of federal taxes can contribute significantly to company progress, profits and growth. Any corporate strategy that does not consider the importance of tax planning can result in disastrous tax costs. The financial executive is the key in the planning process. He can point out courses of action which minimize taxes or avoid costly tax consequences. He can in many instances have the final decision in corporate strategy. Constant compliance with changing tax laws can be a major factor in determining corporate strategies. When you have a situation in which there are over 300 Code changes, 2500 TD's and over 20,000 Revenue Rulings the ability to keep up with the current law requires time, patience and ingenuity.

New Techniques in Financial Administration of Taxes

The object of many tax plans is to determine and be able to decide how much of the firm's operations are subject to external economic, political or taxation influences.

One of the basic reasons that the tax planning and management function is such a key item is readily apparent when you look at a few annual reports. This is where you publicize how you divided the results of all your corporate ingenuity, hard work and effort with Uncle Sam. Somehow the results are different for each firm despite equivalent tax rates.

Net Sales	$2,359,000,000	$83,395,000	$34,239,000	$3,500,000
Net Income	231,520,000	6,000,000	957,000	350,000
Income Taxes	83,520,000	None	373,000	155,000
Retained Earnings	148,000,000	6,000,000	584,000	195,000
% of Earnings Retained	63.9%	100.0%	61.0%	55.7%
% of Income Tax to Net Sales	3.54%	0.0%	1.09%	4.43%

TAX PROBLEMS ENCOUNTERED

In the field of taxation the tax executive has many problems to solve. These naturally vary with the size and complexity of the business. Here are a few of the items:

1. Purchase or Liquidation of a Corporation.
2. Stock Options and Deferred Compensation Plans.
3. Stock or Bond Redemptions.
4. Tax Problems of Closely Held Firms.
5. Businesses Owned and Run by the Same Family.
6. Accumulated Earnings Taxes.
7. Consolidated Returns and Affiliated Corporations, Ventures or Partnerships.
8. Tax-Free Reorganizations.
9. Real Estate and Lease Problems.
10. Individual Tax Problems of Officers, Families, Directors.
11. Tax Shelters.

STATE AND LOCAL TAXES

Normally one dismisses the state and local tax picture as a small, annoying task to be turned over to a subordinate for handling. *On the contrary!* Inflation is eating state and local governments alive and their tax bills are rising rapidly. Every firm which owns property in other states, real or personal, has a growing tax bill to contend with. Due to this fact, tax planning can result in major savings to your firm. For example, the recent case wherein out-of-state shipments were ruled to be subject to sales taxes has closed up one avenue of escaping the filing of state tax returns for many firms. If sustained this will mean sales tax returns in every state in which you sell merchandise.

New Techniques in Financial Administration of Taxes

In the field of inventory management it is often advantageous to have low inventories on the assessment date and thus reduce your personal property tax bill. Many states use the January 1 or March 1 assessment dates. Since Arizona does not have an inventory tax many firms have shifted regional inventory stocks to Arizona for servicing surrounding states. With an effective overnight delivery range of 500 miles servicing customers is not a major problem. Often there are quirks in the common practice of assessment values in the various locations. Once when I moved from one state to another the assessor called me up and said: "you don't want to declare all of this. Your tax bill will be enormous! How about using a figure of $$$?" In my professional practice I have filed schedules based upon the federal depreciation schedule and had the assessor call me up and tell me that it was too high and would I agree to a lesser figure! It appears there is gold to be mined in the local tax mines although the vein may run out soon under the impact of inflation. It is common knowledge, however, that states and local governments seeking industry are more lenient with their tax assessments than would appear on the surface. 27% of fair cash value seems to vary slightly from location to location.

CORPORATE TAX SHELTER

One of the reasons that closely held corporations are scrutinized for excessive retained earnings is that the corporation income tax actually constitutes a tax shelter for the stockholders. If all of the profits of the corporation were passed on to the stockholders the combined tax bill of the individual on the income would now be greater than the amount of tax paid. In addition, the many fringe benefits available through the corporate form of organization make it possible for an individual to benefit at the rate of 10 to 50% of his income each year. As with the unions, more and more is finding its way into the freebie pot.

SCRAPPING THE CORPORATE INCOME TAX

There is a constant growing movement to scrap the corporate income tax and replace it with a *value added* or *consumption tax*. A *national sales tax* might well be in the offing.

INTERNATIONAL TAXATION

While the subject of international taxation would require a book unto itself there is need for a few words because of the multinational aspects of our corporations. These are some of the current topics under discussion in this field:

1. Section 482—Intercompany pricing.
2. Tax treaties with other nations.
3. Puerto Rico—Taxes involved.
4. Problems of U.S. withholding agents.
5. Payments to foreign firms and individuals.
6. Compensation of expatriate executives.
7. Foreign tax credit.

8. Domestic international sales corporations.
9. Controlled foreign corporations.

One of the recent trends in this area is the U.S. Revenue Ruling 76-508. In 1976 the IRS announced the text of Revenue Ruling 76-508. This ruling holds that, where income is allocated from a foreign subsidiary corporation to a domestic parent company under section 482, the IRS may reduce the credit for foreign taxes paid by the subsidiary when dividends are received by the parent, to the extent that the subsidiary has not exhausted "all effective and practicable administrative remedies in seeking a refund of its foreign income tax liability" and the parent has not exhausted its rights to competent authority consideration under an applicable tax convention and Revenue Procedure 70-18.

TAX DODGES

In the field of *tax dodges* is the use of silver tax straddles by a firm to defer payments on capital gains for one or more years, enabling it to use the money during this period. While the method has been under fire by the IRS it is still effective. The IRS has taken the position that a commodity futures straddle must have some economic substance. In the silver straddle, the contention is that the straddle has economic substance in that a profit or loss can actually occur if the spread price changes before its liquidation.

The straddle works in this manner:

CORPORATE TAX RATES	1st	$25,000	20%
	2nd	$25,000	22%
	Over	$50,000	48%

Up to $50,000 there is no advantage on either short-term or long-term capital gains. Above $50,000 a short-term gain is taxed at 48% and a long-term gain at 30%. Therefore, if a short-term capital gain is converted into a long-term gain in the same year the corporation can save about 37% of the tax on the gain. If the short-term gain is moved into the next year as a long-term capital gain you have saved 37% and deferred payment of the tax for one year. This gives it the use of the 37% for one year.

RISING MARKET

JUNE, 19XX   Buy May Silver $4.25   Sell September Silver $4.35
DECEMBER, 19XX Buy September Silver   Sell July, 19XY Silver $4.70
                @ $4.75   (1)
Capital Loss $.40 ×5,000 = $2,000
JANUARY, 19XY   Sell May Silver @ $4.65   Buy July Silver @ $4.70
     (1)   (2)   (3)

Long-Term Capital Gain
            $.40 × 5,000 = $2,000   (3) No Gain or Loss

New Techniques in Financial Administration of Taxes 313

      NET EFFECT—19XX Short-Term Capital Loss After Commission $2,028

      19XY Long-Term Capital Gain After Commission $1,944

This maneuver yields better than 50% savings in taxes.

TAX STRATEGIES

NET SHORT-TERM CAPITAL GAIN—CONVERT TO LONG-TERM—STRADDLE
DEFER SHORT-TERM GAIN ONE YEAR—GENERATE SHORT-TERM LOSS IN CURRENT YEAR—GAIN IN NEXT—STRADDLE
DEFER TAX ON LONG-TERM CAPITAL GAIN ONE YEAR—GENERATE CAPITAL LOSS IN CURRENT YEAR AND LONG-TERM CAPITAL GAIN IN NEXT YEAR—COMMODITY STRADDLE NET CAPITAL LOSS—CONVERT CAPITAL LOSS TO ORDINARY DEDUCTION—CASH AND CARRY PURCHASE EXPIRING CARRYFORWARD CAPITAL LOSSES—CREATE CAPITAL GAIN—COMMODITY STRADDLE EXPIRING CARRYFORWARD NET OPERATING LOSS—CONVERT TO CAPITAL LOSS—STRADDLE

These are only a few of the options available.

FOREIGN TAX MATTERS

A majority of the larger firms are involved in multinational operations. Without proper tax planning and guidance one can create problems beyond comprehension. A knowledge of U.S. tax law is essential, as well as the law of the foreign country. Due to the U.S. regulations of such firms one has to be extremely careful and consider the foreign and U.S. laws applicable in each case. All sorts of factors enter into the equation—duties, tariffs, quotas, tax treaties and special U.S. regulations. A thorough knowledge of Section 482 is a basic requirement in this field.

In addition, each foreign return must be carefully reviewed before submission simply because its filing affects the U.S. tax bill and tax return. Most firms rely on foreign accountants to prepare these returns coupled with conferences and reviews by the Tax Manager. Expanding U.S. activity in the field of foreign operations has increased the responsibility of the tax executive in this area. The Treasury has set up task forces to handle all phases of foreign taxation and has conducted extensive reviews of transactions between the firms. Especially watched are loans between the firms, including interest payments, intercompany pricing on merchandise and pricing on transfers of equipment between affiliates. The attack in the pricing area has been unusually severe. Loans between units need to be put on a formal basis with all terms carefully spelled out in order to avoid controversy.

Foreign governments are particularly watchful when assets are transferred to foreign subsidiaries or affiliates. Pricing of used equipment is subject to careful review by the Customs executives and employees.

Decisions made by foreign tax officials can have a direct bearing upon your U.S. tax return and tax bill.

The current flack over illegal payments and other evasive practices has created some real problems for the tax administrator. The IRS has prepared a list of eleven rather nasty questions which can put him squarely in the *box*. Activity in this area will not subside for a number of years and will have a profound and extensive effect on all foreign operations, tax returns and reports.

TAX MANUALS

Every well-organized tax department, no matter what its size, will have a Tax Manual. Not only will it have a manual but it will see that it is updated periodically. The tax manual will designate who prepares the various returns, how they are to be prepared, the required supporting schedules and the responsibility for review and filing. One of the major items which should be prescribed is a thorough review of the prior year's return and its supporting schedules. The manner in which the returns are prepared is vital in the event of a tax audit or tax controversy which may move to higher than *revenue agent* review. The manual must contain detailed instructions about dealing with the IRS and its various divisions.

KEEPING UP WITH SKULL SESSIONS

Efficient and effective management of any tax department requires that a constant free flow of information be maintained among the departments and divisions of the firm on all matters which might have tax consequences. Tax dollars saved can be the result of such action.

CASE IN POINT

Sale of equipment—sometimes the deferring of the sale of equipment—may result in a tax saving due to the amount of the *investment tax credit retained*. With the amount of the tax credit ranging from 10% to 12% the disposal of an asset too soon can result in the loss of tax funds.

Not only must communications be maintained throughout the entire organization but also within the tax function. There must be a free flow of current information, tax bulletins, interesting decisions and other materials. A weekly, semi-monthly or even monthly staff *skull session* is a necessity. This will give all of the members a chance to present, analyze and discuss the various tax problems. One tax manager devotes a half day each week to this type of session and establishes his pipelines to vital information. Local, state and federal legislation are reviewed and discussed with the primary aim of determining their effect on the firm's operations.

Regular attendance at seminars, association meetings and tax conferences and membership in tax organizations will provide interesting clues to current actions and trends. Strangely enough attending sessions hosted by investment advisors and brokerage firms will keep you informed on the latest tax dodges in current use.

New Techniques in Financial Administration of Taxes

FEDERAL TAX AUDITS

Each of us finally reaches that dreaded day when the IRS agent calls or walks in and requests the books and records for an audit. No matter how well you think you have done your job in preparing the return you are now subject to scrutiny and appraisal by an expert.

Make no mistake about it, if one may generalize, the field agent can be a tough adversary. He is not an individual who merely checks a supporting document on an item of income or expense. The tax person is instead, in most instances, an intelligent, conscientious individual with a job to perform. It is his job to carefully audit your return, examine in detail the books and records, ascertain that all income has been reported and that all expenses, deductions and credits are properly allowable.

Handling the field agent may be properly divided into areas as follows:

1. Be extremely tactful, courteous and careful in your meetings and discussions with the agent. (We no longer can say "him"—in fact, the preferred way to address the agent is "tax person" according to a recent IRS seminar.)

2. First of all, when the agent calls, arrives or writes requesting an appointment you should determine the proper place and time that is convenient for both of you. Part of his job is to visit the business premises and examine the type of operation in order to determine what type of activities are occurring. When the agent presents himself, it is absolutely essential that you request that he identify himself and the purpose of his visit. The principal reason for this caution is to ascertain if he is a special agent. Every agent has an identity card which he generally presents but may not unless you request it. A special agent is so designated on his identity card. The obvious distinction is when a special agent arrives you have trouble and an investigation that might involve prosecution for fraud. If he is a special agent refer him to the firm's attorney immediately. There is no guaranty or certainty that a normal field agent cannot carry on a similar type of investigation. You will have to be guided by the manner in which the examination is conducted, the questions asked and the type of records involved. An unusually high amount of copying and photostating of records could be indicative of trouble.

3. Review carefully the procedures used by the agent. Since the tax law is a constantly changing factor these items will change. *The Wall Street Journal* and tax magazines can keep you abreast of current developments.

4. As the audit progresses you will have some idea of the issues in question. It is vitally important that you do not negotiate or attempt to settle any issue prior to the time that the agent has completed his examination and has all of the items ready for consideration. This policy will insure that you have a reasonably certain understanding of the entire situation and know the options you may have in conducting negotiations with the agent. It also prevents the possibility of your being *sandbagged* by some settled issue which might affect a major point of contention later on. At this time certain decisions have to be made:

    a. Are the proposed adjustments definitely required under the Revenue Code, Rulings, or Regulations? Is the agent's interpretation of the law correct in your opinion?

    b. Is the agent's determination of the facts involved a correct one? If you can point out errors he may concede the issue.

316   New Techniques in Financial Administration of Taxes

    c. Is the issue controversial? Has the government lost cases on similar issues in the courts? Are there case decisions on it?

    d. In the event any of the issues are questionable, the effect and possibility of trading off should be explored.

    e. If you are clearly at fault don't argue! Forget it!

    f. Technical issues sometimes arise that may require appealing to higher levels or even to Washington for advice or rulings.

    g. Technical rulings should be acquired during the year prior to the action whenever possible.

5. Settling with the field agent is the easiest and most advantageous approach. The majority of the agents are practical individuals who depend less on technicalities and more on practical substantiation of proof. A reasonable settlement at this level is to your advantage. In appealing issues to a higher level you run the risk of a much tighter interpretation of the Code, Rulings or Regulations. A further point to consider is the higher level of intelligence encountered, additional points which may be raised, and the expense in time and money involved may negate the potential monetary gains if you should win.

The handling and basis of negotiation with agents of the IRS on behalf of your corporation provides an excellent opportunity to sharpen your acumen in the tax field. It is an exercise in patience, good judgment and common sense. Above all it is a lesson in keeping your mouth shut! Do not volunteer information unless asked and try to think ahead. What are the questions leading to? One thing is certain, you are dealing with individuals who may be seasoned by a broad range of exposure to all types of taxpayers. It is a battle of wits and skills of each individual. The successful conclusion of a tax audit can reinforce your ego tremendously.

The methods of dealing with the revenue agent naturally differ with each firm and the size of the firm involved. Some firms are extremely formal and technical, requiring that the agent request the items in writing prior to their furnishing the records. Others are informal and furnish the data orally or upon demand without a written request. *One word of caution . . . keep a record of what is requested!*

The revenue agent of today is highly educated, often a member of a team of specialists and backed by the latest computer technology. The IRS currently has under installation a computer system which will put five years of taxpayers' records on-line for instant access by its agents. The system will cost over one billion dollars and will be the "largest data processing project ever undertaken by the federal government." This should set aside any doubts that taxes are important both to the government and to the taxpayer.

TAX CRACKDOWN—KEY ITEMS

1. Padded expense accounts. Failure to keep adequate and complete T & E records may cost your firm money.

2. Personal use of company autos—results in imputing income to the individuals of twelve cents per mile.

3. Kickbacks—bribes—illegal payoffs—suppliers' rebates. The SEC opened up this corporate bag of worms and the IRS has followed up with its famous "11 Questions."

New Techniques in Financial Administration of Taxes

4. Overbilling and overpricing—subsidiaries—affiliates—foreign firms and others.
5. Inflating costs—the result of overpricing by others.
6. Corporate lobbying—the costs of publications for the lobby.
7. Political contributions—questionable charitable contributions.
8. Deferral of income or expenses to subsequent years.
9. Intercompany costs and selling prices.
10. Inflation of new equipment purchases to take advantage of the investment credit or accelerated depreciation. Claims for depreciation of non-existing assets, patents, etc. The agents will request computer printouts of the depreciation schedules and actually make a physical attempt to verify the assets involved.
11. Costs of items purchased—valid costs—fictitious invoices.
12. Inventory valuations—manipulation of inventories to influence profits.
13. Transactions with officers and employees. Revenue agents often closely scrutinize payments between closely held firms and their stockholders for compensation and rentals. They may disallow the deductions to the corporation although the receipts may still be taxable to the individual. *Proposed remedy* . . . a binding agreement between the parties under which the payee agrees to repay the firm any amounts received which are disallowed as a deduction by the IRS. This will correct the double taxation effect of the disallowance.
14. Professional fees—justification for.

The agents now have access to data throughout the entire USA as to the types of items currently being disallowed, the frequency of use, how to find them and other data. A computer printout of operating expense comparisons with prior years or the normal expenditures for comparable items in the industry or other industries.

There are, due to the complex nature of the tax law, many gray areas where one can take a proper deduction position. In the event these items are picked up as questionable the agents will definitely disallow them or require very complete and positive verification.

INTERESTING POSITION

One liquor firm making payments to wholesale liquor dealers to handle their brands charged the items directly to *retained earnings*. Since it did not take the items as a deduction it contended that the IRS was not entitled to the details of the items. Payments were made in cash naturally!

GENERAL

So it develops into a serious game. Before each agent goes on his audit he develops his *game plan*. It consists of dissecting the tax return piece by piece, bit by bit to determine what items need thorough investigation. He has a computer printout telling him what needs verification or investigation. He knows the records required and generally what they should contain. The *audit game plan* may already include the items he intends challenging on legal or Code grounds.

TAX CALENDAR—TWO-EMPLOYEE FIRM LOCATED IN ARIZONA

JANUARY

1-10   Deposit FICA and WITHHOLDING TAXES
1-31   FILE FINAL QUARTER, W-2's and annual reconciliation for FICA, WITHHOLDING TAXES STATE AND FEDERAL RETURNS.
FILE STATE UNEMPLOYMENT TAX RETURN FINAL QUARTER
PREPARE AND FILE FEDERAL FUTA RETURN.
PREPARE AND FILE STATE SALES TAX RETURNS—CITY SALES TAXES

FEBRUARY

1-20   FILE PERSONAL PROPERTY TAX ASSESSMENT FORM—EQUIPMENT-FIXTURES-LEASED PROPERTY OWNED OR USED.
1-10   DEPOSIT FICA AND WITHHOLDING TAXES—JANUARY
2-28   STATE AND CITY SALES TAXES

MARCH

1-10   DEPOSIT OF WITHHOLDING AND FICA FOR FEBRUARY
1-15   PREPARE AND FILE FEDERAL AND STATE INCOME TAX RETURNS
1-31   FILE CITY AND STATE SALES TAX RETURNS

APRIL

1-10   DEPOSIT OF WITHHOLDING AND FICA FOR FINAL FIRST QUARTER
1-15   FILE CITY AND STATE SALES TAX RETURNS
1-15   DEPOSIT FIRST QUARTER CORPORATE INCOME TAX
1-30   PREPARE AND FILE FIRST QUARTER RETURNS
FICA AND WITHHOLDING
STATE WITHHOLDING
STATE UNEMPLOYMENT TAX RETURN
1-20   PAY FIRST INSTALLMENT REAL ESTATE AND PERSONAL PROPERTY TAXES
1-20   RENEW TRUCK LICENSE—GET EMISSIONS TEST CHECK

One does not need to stretch the imagination for the tax calendar for a large multinational firm.

WHAT DOES THE FINANCIAL ADMINISTRATOR EXPECT OF HIS TAX MANAGER?

According to the advertisements for tax personnel these are the current requirements:

DIRECTOR OF TAXES   **Tax Planning Manager**

Corporate Tax Specialist

1. The individual will report directly to the Vice President—Financial Administration.

New Techniques in Financial Administration of Taxes

2. He shall be well based in federal and state tax planning and shall provide expert counsel to top management on the tax implications relating to capital expenditures, mergers and acquisitions and other items. He will provide technical research for division or corporate personnel. He must demonstrate an ability and capability to recognize planning opportunities and follow them through from conception to final operation.
3. He shall undertake a systematic review of all planning opportunity areas and develop a follow-up system to periodically explore new areas.
4. He must be strongly oriented toward maximizing the potential tax savings.
5. He must prepare a checklist of tax strategies for all levels of management with the objective of reducing overall tax costs.
6. He will interface with all levels of management, U.S. subsidiaries and foreign firms.
7. He must interface and maintain good relations with the IRS.
8. In the area of federal and state tax compliance he will prepare and file all tax returns—federal—state—franchise—property taxes—sales and use taxes.
9. He will conduct contract reviews and review all special projects for tax liabilities.
10. He will provide executive and employee counsel on personal tax matters covering pensions, stock options, deferred compensation, estate planning or other matters. (Optional based upon corporate policy.)
11. He will supervise and review the IRS audit procedures.
12. He shall prepare and keep updated the following manuals:
    a. Payroll tax manual—state and federal.
    b. Sales and use taxes—cities and states.
    c. Real estate and personal property tax manuals.
    d. Federal income taxes.
    e. State income taxes—allocation formulas and worksheets.
    f. Tax strategies and planning.
    g. Tax accounting manual—reconciliation of tax accounting with general accounting.
    h. Interfacing and communications manual.
    i. State returns. The statutory difference should be planned for in the preparation of the federal return—means of reconciling the difference.

CHECKLISTS

In the area of taxation the possibilities for errors are enormous and as a result the checklists are normally broad and cover every phase of the data gathering and return preparation steps. A few of the examples are noted below:

1. Bad debts—charge-off or reserve, basis, prior years' recoveries.
2. Inventories—location, pricing structure, LIFO schedules.
3. Depreciation—schedule reconciled to the reserve?
4. Is there a net operating carryover loss?
5. Do charitable contributions exceed the allowance? Is there a carryover?
6. Schedule of foreign tax credits—basis.
7. Foreign stock ownership—schedule.

8. Have payments of royalties, dividends, rents, commission to others such as non-resident aliens, partnerships, domestic or foreign corporations been reported?
9. Were the accruals at the end of the year paid within the time limits?
10. Have you checked rentals and leases?
11. Sinking fund payments.
12. Securities—bought, sold, basis, gain or loss.
13. Is there bond amortization to consider?
14. Have sales been properly allocated to states?
15. Have you checked for sales of real estate, machinery and equipment, intangibles?
16. Were any returns examined during the year? What were the results? Should they be incorporated into this year's return?

A checklist might take this form:

1. *Sales*

   Check intracompany sales for deductions
   Sales to regular customers
   Sales to affiliates
   Sales to subsidiaries
   Sales to joint ventures

2. *Adjustments to Sales*

   Allowances
   Discounts
   Disputes
   Freight
   Other items

3. *Disposal of Capital Investments or Fixed Assets*

   Description
   Cost
   Remaining life
   Depreciation sustained
   Accelerated depreciation
   Investment credit
   Net book value
   Gain or loss

HANDLING TAXES IN THE ANNUAL REPORT

The differences in general accounting practices are sharply emphasized in many of the corporate annual reports as follows:

New Techniques in Financial Administration of Taxes

"Income reported for federal and foreign tax purposes differs from pretax accounting due to various requirements of internal revenue codes and the company's accounting practices. Timing differences are attributable principally to practices applied to long-term contracts, undistributed earnings of foreign subsidiaries, warranty reserves, depreciation, pension costs, and inventory valuation adjustments. The net credit balances of deferred taxes included in the balance sheet caption "Federal and foreign income taxes" was estimated to be $12,400,000 at December 31, 19XX. The provisions for federal and foreign income taxes consist of the following for the years ending December 31,

	19XX	*19XY*
Current federal income tax expense	$37,209,000	$36,396,000
Current foreign income tax expense	2,720,000	3,940,000
Deferred income tax expense	6,200,000	(900,000)
TOTAL	$46,129,000	$39,436,000

The effective income tax rates for 19XX and 19XY were 44% and 46% respectively. The effective income tax rates for 19XX and 19XY vary from the statutory rate of 48% by reason principally of investment tax credits ($2,561,000 and $1,273,000 respectively) and reduced tax rates applicable to DISC income ($2,899,000 and $792,000 respectively). The deferred income tax expense in 19XX is attributable principally to timing differences in income recognition under long-term contracts ($11,300,000) reduced by differences in depreciation ($950,000), inventory valuation adjustments ($2,420,000) and compensation costs ($1,270,000).

"The Corporation files a consolidated tax return. No taxes are currently payable inasmuch as certain items are treated differently for financial reporting and tax purposes. The principal differences are: items deducted for tax purposes which include income from debenture exchange, accelerated depreciation, interest and social security taxes and employee benefits charged to construction, and the treatment of certain severance costs."

As you may surmise, the preparation of the federal, state and foreign tax returns can require considerable additional accounting records and reconciliation schedules.

AUDITS AND IRS PROCEDURES

The following pages detail the *IRS income tax audit procedures and the normal appeal procedures*. Sample pages from the IRS audit guides are included. These are the basic references:

1. Audit Technique Handbook for Internal Revenue Agents—IRM-4231
2. Techniques Handbook for In-Depth Audit Investigations—IRM-4235
3. Handbook for Special Agents—IRM-9900

While most of the confidential and sensitive material has been removed from the manuals and they are out of date, the remaining material can provide an interesting insight into the operations of the IRS field agents.

THE SIMPLE TAX CALENDAR

This makes certain that you are making all of your tax payments. (Twelve sheets—one for each month.):

MONTH

DUE DATES   TAX RETURN   DATA REQUIRED   WHERE FILED

MAJOR MONTHS—JANUARY
                APRIL
                JULY   on different-colored paper to emphasize
                OCTOBER   major filing dates.

It acts as a "hot shot" reminder two days before each filing date. It can be kept on a computer file—prints out as many copies as required.

ALLOCATIONS ON STATE TAX RETURNS

The following allocation schedules (see next page) give an idea of the types of allocation information required for Arizona corporate income taxes. The allocations are reasonably constant throughout the various states.

Form 120

Schedule Q.—PROFIT (OR LOSS) FROM SALE OF CAPITAL ASSETS, ETC.
Include only non-depreciable assets and assets which are not connected with unitary business carried on partly within and partly without the State

DESCRIPTION OF PROPERTY SOLD – SITUS OF PROPERTIES	REAL ESTATE & TANGIBLE ASSETS		INTANGIBLE ASSETS	
	Arizona (a-1)	Everywhere (a-2)	Arizona (b-1)	Everywhere (b-2)
Total (see instructions)				

Schedule R.—ADJUSTMENTS FROM FEDERAL TO ARIZONA TAX BASIS (See Instructions)
(To Be used by Corporations Engaged in Activities Within and Without Arizona)

1. Net income before State adjustments (from line 30, page 1)
2. Add: Deduction for State, including Arizona, and Foreign government income taxes
3.   Interest on obligations of other States, foreign countries, or political subdivisions thereof
4.   Special deductions claimed by Schedule I
5.   Other additions required by law (submit schedule)
6. Total of lines 1 to 5
7. Less: (a) Dividends received from Corporation doing more than 50% of their business in Arizona
       (b) Dividends received from controlled corporations
8.   Interest on obligations of the United States, etc. from line 5, page 1
9.   Other deductions authorized by law (submit schedule)
10.   Total of lines 7 to 9
11. Total net income adjusted to Arizona tax basis (line 6 less line 11) (see instructions)

Schedule S.—ALLOCATION OF INCOME—APPORTIONMENT METHOD
This schedule must be filled in by Corporations engaged in activities within and without the State

1. Net income before apportionment (from line 11, Schedule R)
2. Deduct: Dividends included on line 4, page 1 and not deducted on line 7, Schedule R, reduced by interest expense, etc. (from Schedule O)
3.   Interest for sources not connected with unitary business reduced by interest expense, etc. (from Schedule O)
4.   Royalties other than from unitary assets (from Schedule P)
5.   Net income from rental of property not connected with unitary business (from Schedule P)
6.   Net gain (or loss) from sale of assets not connected with unitary business (from Schedule Q)
7.   Total of lines 2 to 6
8. Unitary Business income subject to apportionment. Deduct line 7 from line 1
9. Allocate ▶ .... % (from Schedule N, line 5, page 5), as income from business attributable to the State

ITEMS WHOLLY ATTRIBUTABLE TO ARIZONA

10. Gain (or loss) from sale of real estate and other tangible assets not connected with the unitary business located in this State (from Schedule Q)
11. Net income (or loss) from rental of property not connected with the unitary business located in this State (from Schedule P)
12. Royalties from property not used in the unitary business, located in this State (from Schedule P)
13. Net income (or loss) from intangible property specifically allocable to Arizona (from Schedule O)
14. Net income attributable to Arizona (total of lines 9 to 13)
15. Deduct: Capital losses (limit $1000) not deducted on line 9, page 1 (see instructions)
16.   Federal income tax on income taxed by Arizona (from separate schedule)
17.   Arizona income tax
18.   Total deductions (lines 15, 16 and 17)
19. Net taxable income (line 14 less line 18) (enter on line 31, page 1)

Schedule T.—ALLOCATION OF INCOME—SEPARATE ACCOUNTING METHOD
This schedule must be filled in by Corporations engaged in activities within and without the State and allocating net income to Arizona under the separate accounting method

1. Net business income under separate accounting method (attach detailed schedules including profit and loss statement in support of this method)
2. Deduct: Federal income tax on income taxed by Arizona (from separate schedule)
3.   Arizona income tax
4.   Total income taxes deductible (line 2 plus line 3)
5. Net income under separate accounting method (if this line is not less than line 19, Schedule S, enter on line 31, page 1)

Form 120　　Page 5

Schedule N. — APPORTIONMENT FORMULA

The following information must be submitted by all corporations having income from sources both within and without the State, regardless of method of allocation used.	Total Within Arizona (a)	Total Everywhere (b)	Percent Within Arizona (a) ÷ (b)
1 Average yearly value of real and tangible personal property:			
Inventory			
Depreciable assets less reserves			
Other (describe)			
Annual rental paid for leased real property multiplied by 8			
Annual rental paid for leased tangible personal property multiplied by 4			
Total			
Deduct: property not connected with unitary business			
Total tangible property used			
2 Wages, salaries, commissions and other compensation of employees as shown on Page 1 in:			
Line 2, cost of goods and/or operations			
Line 12, compensation of officers			
Line 13, miscellaneous			
Line 26, other deductions			
Total wages and salaries			
3 Gross Sales, less returns and allowances			
4 Total percent (sum of the percentage above)			
5 Average percentage (enter here and on line 9, Schedule S)			

Schedule O. — NET INCOME FROM INTANGIBLE PROPERTY NOT CONNECTED WITH UNITARY BUSINESS

This schedule must be filled in by corporations engaging in activities both within and without the State	INTEREST		DIVIDENDS	
	Arizona (a-1)	Everywhere (a-2)	Arizona (b-1)	Everywhere (b-2)
1 Income (see instructions)				
2 Deduct: Interest expense (see instructions)				
3 Related expense (describe) (a)				
(b)				
4 Total of lines 2, 3 (a) and 3 (b)				
5 Nonapportionable income (or loss) line 1, less line 4 (see instructions)				

Schedule P. — NET INCOME (OR LOSS) FROM RENTS AND ROYALTIES

This schedule must be filled in by corporations engaging in activities both within and without the State.	RENTS		ROYALTIES	
	Arizona (a-1)	Everywhere (a-2)	Arizona (b-1)	Everywhere (b-2)
1 Gross income (see instructions)				
2 Deduct: Depreciation and depletion				
3 Amortization of Patents, etc.				
4 Taxes				
5 Insurance				
6 Interest				
7 Repairs and Maintenance				
8 Other (describe)				
9 Total of lines 2 to 8				
10 Net income (or loss) line 1 minus line 9 see instructions				

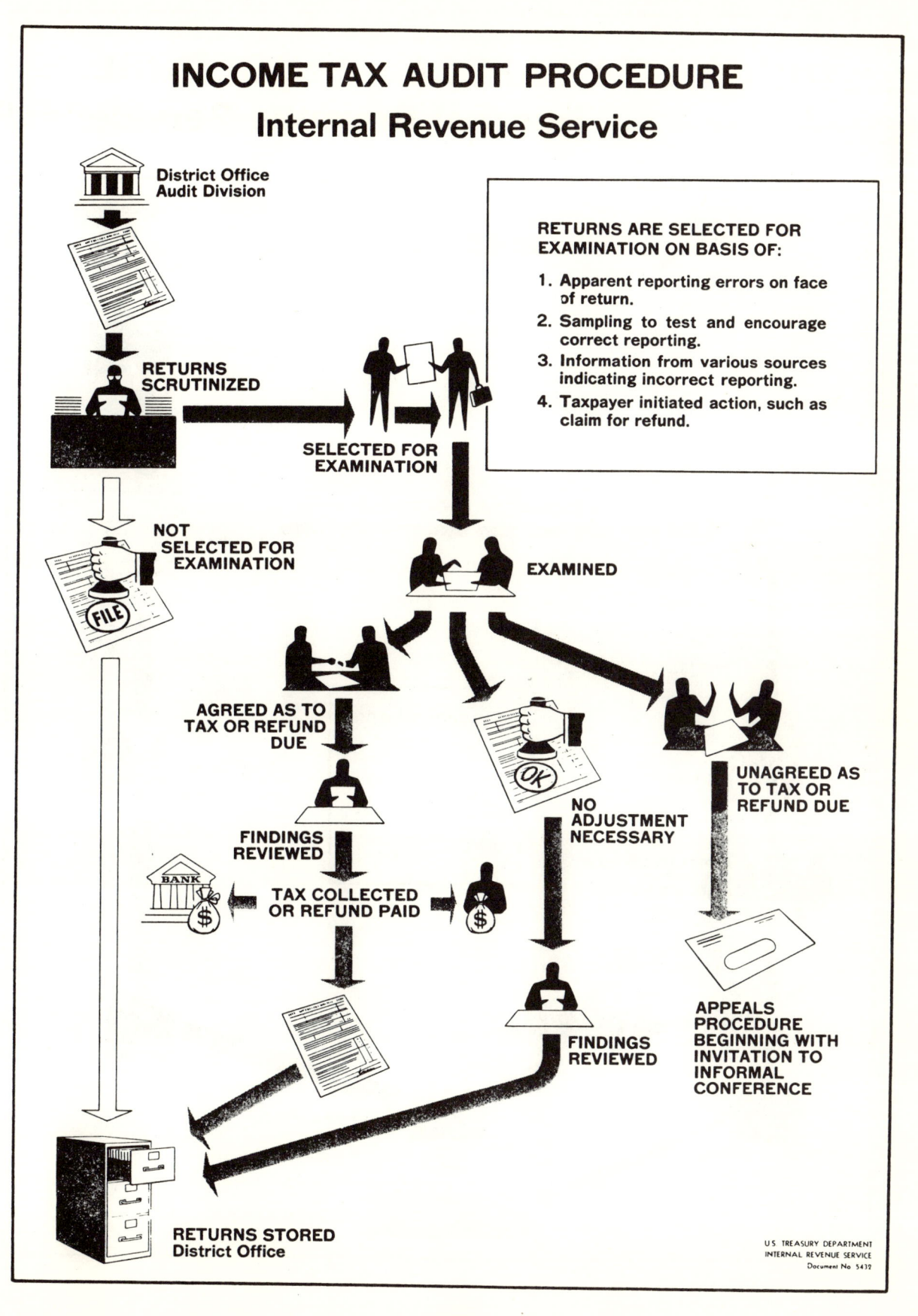

INCOME TAX AUDIT PROCEDURE
Internal Revenue Service

District Office Audit Division

RETURNS SCRUTINIZED

SELECTED FOR EXAMINATION

NOT SELECTED FOR EXAMINATION

RETURNS ARE SELECTED FOR EXAMINATION ON BASIS OF:

1. Apparent reporting errors on face of return.
2. Sampling to test and encourage correct reporting.
3. Information from various sources indicating incorrect reporting.
4. Taxpayer initiated action, such as claim for refund.

EXAMINED

AGREED AS TO TAX OR REFUND DUE

FINDINGS REVIEWED

TAX COLLECTED OR REFUND PAID

NO ADJUSTMENT NECESSARY

FINDINGS REVIEWED

UNAGREED AS TO TAX OR REFUND DUE

APPEALS PROCEDURE BEGINNING WITH INVITATION TO INFORMAL CONFERENCE

RETURNS STORED District Office

U.S. TREASURY DEPARTMENT
INTERNAL REVENUE SERVICE
Document No. 5432

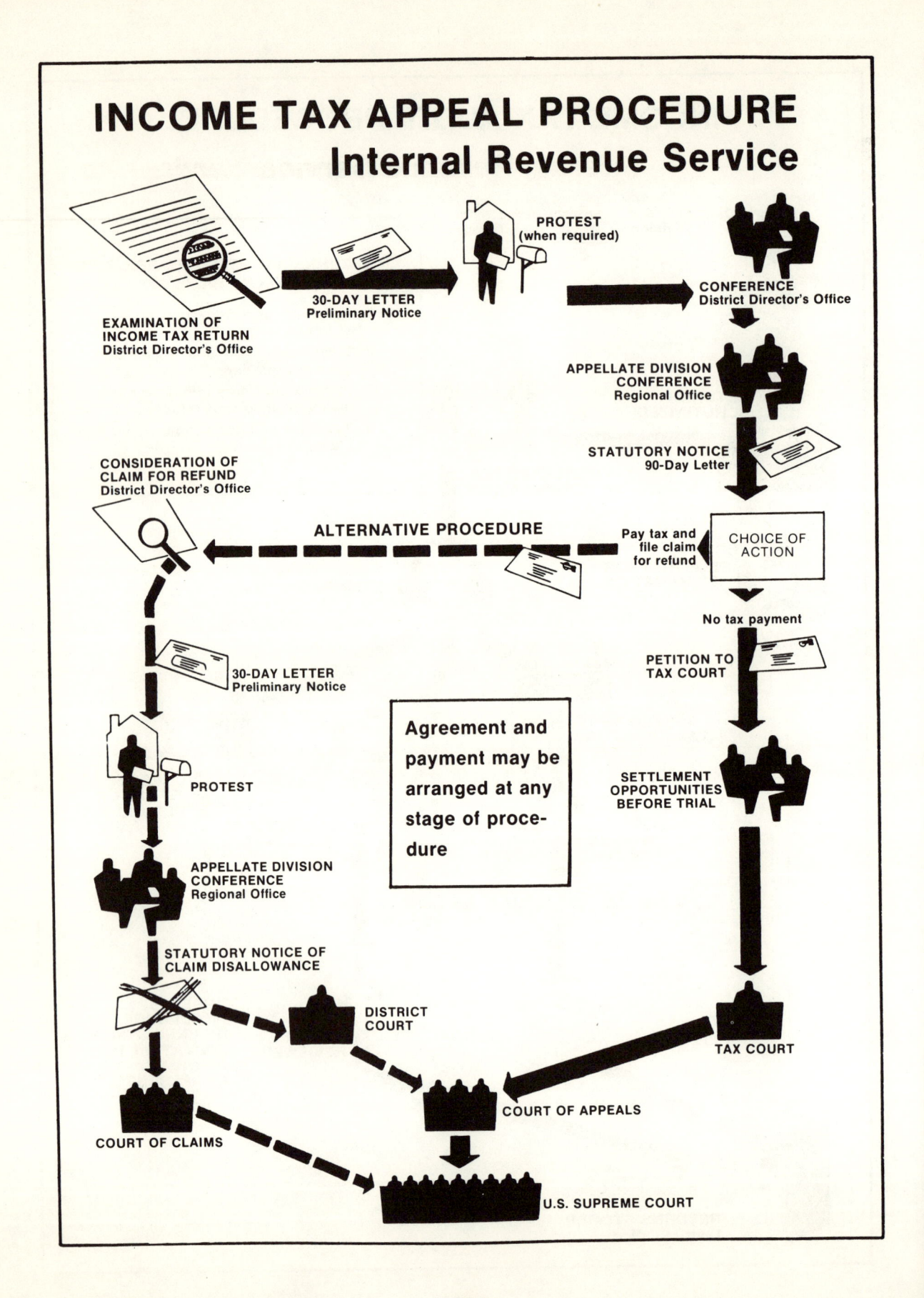

INCOME TAX APPEAL PROCEDURE
Internal Revenue Service

EXAMINATION OF INCOME TAX RETURN
District Director's Office

30-DAY LETTER
Preliminary Notice

PROTEST (when required)

CONFERENCE
District Director's Office

APPELLATE DIVISION CONFERENCE
Regional Office

STATUTORY NOTICE
90-Day Letter

CHOICE OF ACTION

ALTERNATIVE PROCEDURE — Pay tax and file claim for refund

CONSIDERATION OF CLAIM FOR REFUND
District Director's Office

30-DAY LETTER
Preliminary Notice

PROTEST

APPELLATE DIVISION CONFERENCE
Regional Office

STATUTORY NOTICE OF CLAIM DISALLOWANCE

No tax payment

PETITION TO TAX COURT

SETTLEMENT OPPORTUNITIES BEFORE TRIAL

Agreement and payment may be arranged at any stage of procedure

DISTRICT COURT

TAX COURT

COURT OF CLAIMS

COURT OF APPEALS

U.S. SUPREME COURT

500 Initial Contact

510 INTRODUCTION

During the initial contact, the taxpayer must be allowed to discuss himself, family, business, successes, failures, hobbies, financial history and sources of income including that of members of his family. The agent should guide the interview to enable him to secure as much information as possible.

520 INTERVIEW WITH TAXPAYER

(1) During the interview the agent should attempt to secure sufficient facts to enable him to survey the taxpayer's entire financial picture, such as his mode of living, insurance program, unusual expenditures, and sources of income including the receipt of any nontaxable income.

(2) If the casual conversation method is not effective, the agent may use a memorandum of interview similar to the one in Exhibit 500–1. This sample memorandum is designed to enable the agent to ask pertinent questions and record the answers immediately. If during the interview the taxpayer becomes uncooperative or adamant regarding a particular question the agent should request that the taxpayer submit an affidavit of any statements to which he is willing to attest. This should go a long way in resolving pertinent issues at an early date.

(3) The agent should not hesitate to request any information bearing on the determination of the correct tax liability. This includes requesting permission to inspect the taxpayer's safety deposit box. If the request is granted, the agent must be accompanied by another Service employee as a witness and the inspection should be accomplished at the earliest possible moment after permission is received.

530 AVAILABILITY OF BOOKS FOR CIVIL PURPOSES ONLY

(1) When requesting books and records the examining officer should be courteous, tactful, and considerate of any problems in producing records which may be several years old. A reasonable but firm approach may enable the examining officer to gain the taxpayer's confidence and cooperation, and may expedite disposition of the case.

(2) Examining officers shall not assure taxpayers that their books and records will be used solely for civil purposes. If a taxpayer insists upon such assurances, or asks the examining officer to sign a statement that the books and records are only being made available for limited purposes, the examining officer should refuse to grant any assurances and further discuss the matter with the taxpayer to determine the taxpayer's reasons for refusing to furnish his records without restriction. The agent will discontinue his examination at this point and report the matter to his supervisor. The supervisor and the examining officer should then discuss the matter with the Intelligence Division (IRM 4241.2:(5)). That office will study any available information concerning the taxpayer and will advise on further steps to be taken. The Intelligence Division may decide that, in view of all known factors including taxpayer's refusal to furnish records unconditionally, there is a possible indication that fraud exists. When appropriate, a referral to the Intelligence Division will be made in accordance with procedures in IRM 4567. Advice should be sought from the Regional Counsel whenever necessary.

MT 4235–1 (12–13–71) IR Manual

530

INITIAL CONTACT

EXHIBIT 500-1

MEMORANDUM OF INTERVIEW WITH TAXPAYER

Name of taxpayer _____

Interviewer _____

Date _____ Place _____

Persons present _____

Was taxpayer sworn? _____

QUESTIONS AND ANSWERS GIVEN THERETO BY TAXPAYER

1. What is your full name? _____

1a. What is your Social Security number? _____

2. Have you ever used any other name(s)? _____

3. Where have you resided during the past 5 years? _____
_____
_____

4. Have you used any other addresses, for business or other purposes, during the past 5 years? _____
_____

5. Give the date and place of your birth _____

6. Are you a citizen of the U. S.? _____

7. State date, place, and name of court, if naturalized _____
_____

8. What is your marital status (*single, married, divorced or separated*) _____
_____

9. State your wife's maiden name, date and place of marriage _____
_____

10. State names and dates of birth of your children _____
_____
_____

MT 4235–1 (12–13–71) IR Manual

TECHNIQUES HANDBOOK FOR IN-DEPTH AUDIT INVESTIGATIONS

EXHIBIT 500–1—Cont. (1)

11. Name all dependents, relationship and extent of support provided by you during the years _____ to _____, inclusive. _____

_____

_____

_____

_____

12. What is the extent of your education? (*State year of graduation from High School and College*): _____

_____

13. State your occupation and the amount or estimated amount of your income for each of the years since you were first employed. (Give, if possible, names and addresses of employers): _____

_____

_____

_____

_____

_____

_____

_____

_____

14. Did you file Federal income tax returns for each of the years 19____ to _____, inclusive?

   (a) If so, where? _____

   (b) If not, explain? _____

15. Did your wife file separate returns for any of the years 19__ to 19__, inclusive? _____

   (a) If so, state years for which filed, name and address shown on return, and place of filing: _____

_____

_____

MT 4235–1 (12–13–71) IR Manual

INITIAL CONTACT

EXHIBIT 500-1—Cont. (2)

16. Give the following information with respect to the Federal income tax returns filed by you as an individual or jointly by you and your wife for the years 19___ to 19___, inclusive:

   (a) Examine the following original Federal income tax returns and state whether they are returns which you filed:

Form No.	Year	Serial No.	Name(s) of Taxpayer(s)	Answer (Yes or No)

   (b) Did you sign each of these returns? _____

   (c) Which, if any, of these returns were also signed by your wife? _____

   (d) Who prepared these returns? _____

   (e) What was the source of the information as to your income and deductions contained in these returns? _____

   (f) Is all the information appearing in these returns true and correct? _____

   (g) Do these returns show all the income received by you during the years 19___ to 19___, inclusive? _____

MT 4235-1 (12-13-71) IR Manual

TECHNIQUES HANDBOOK FOR IN-DEPTH AUDIT INVESTIGATIONS

EXHIBIT 500–1—Cont. (3)

(h) Do these returns (*if joint returns*) show all the income received by your wife during the years 19___ to 19___, inclusive? _____

(i) Do you know of any business costs or expenses or deductible personal expenses which you paid or incurred which are not shown on these returns? _____

_____

17. Did you file any Federal income tax returns for any partnership, joint venture, corporation or fiduciary for the years 19___ to 19___, inclusive? _____

    If so explain: _____

    _____

18. Can you identify the following Federal income tax returns?

Form No.	Period Covered	Serial No.	Name of Taxpayer	Answer (Yes or No)

(a) Did you sign each of these returns? _____

(b) Are these the returns you filed? _____

(c) Who prepared these returns? _____

(d) What was the source of the information contained in these returns?

_____

_____

(e) Is all the information contained in these returns true and correct?

_____

19. Give the following information regarding the person who prepared the Federal income tax returns filed by you:

    (a) Name: _____

INITIAL CONTACT

EXHIBIT 500-1—Cont. (4)

(b) Address: _____

(c) His business or profession: _____

(d) Nature and extent of the services performed by him _____

_____

_____

(e) Did he prepare the returns solely from information obtained by him from books and records?
_____

If not, explain: _____

_____

(f) What was the amount of the fee which you paid him for his services?
_____

(g) What was the nature of the discussions with the person who prepared your return?
_____

_____

20. Have you ever engaged in business as a sole proprietor? _____

   If so, state:

   (a) Name under which operated: _____

   (b) Employer's identification number: _____

   (c) Principal place of business: _____

   (d) Kind of business: _____

   (e) Date commenced: _____

   (f) Is business active? _____

   (g) Where are the books and records located? _____

21. Have you ever owned any interest in any partnership? _____

   If so, give the folowing information with respect thereto:

   (a) Trade name: _____

   (b) Employer's identification number: _____

   (c) Principal place of business: _____

   (d) Kind of business: _____

   (e) Date partnership was formed: _____

MT 4235-1 (12-13-71) IR Manual

TECHNIQUES HANDBOOK FOR IN-DEPTH AUDIT INVESTIGATIONS

EXHIBIT 500-1—Cont. (5)

(f) Is partnership active? _____

(g) Name and addresses of all partners: _____
_____
_____

(h) Terms of partnership agreement: _____
_____
_____
_____

(i) Where are the books and records of the partnership? _____
_____

(j) Where were the partnership Federal income returns filed for the years 19___ to 19___, inclusive? _____
_____

22. Have you ever owned any interest in any corporation? _____

   If so, give the following information with respect thereto:

   (a) Name of corporation: _____

   (b) Employer's identification number: _____

   (c) Principal place of business: _____

   (d) When and where incorporated: _____

   (e) Kind of business: _____

   (f) Names and addresses of all officers: _____
   _____
   _____
   _____

   (g) Total number shares of each class of stock issued and outstanding:
   _____

   (h) Names and addresses of stockholders and number of shares owned by each:
   _____
   _____
   _____

MT 4235-1 (12-13-71) IR Manual

INITIAL CONTACT

EXHIBIT 500-1—Cont. (6)

(i) Does corporation file Form 1120's? _____

(j) What consideration did you give for the shares of capital stock owned by you? _____
_____

(k) Where are the corporate books and records? _____

(l) Where were Federal income tax returns of the corporation filed for the years 19___ to 19___, inclusive? _____

23. Have you engaged in any other business or in any joint venture since January 1, 19___? _____

    If so, describe: _____

24. What books and records were kept with respect to each business in which you owned an interest during the years 19___ to 19___, inclusive _____
_____
_____
_____

25. State names and addresses of principal bookkeepers employed by _____
    (Name of firm)
    during the years 19___ to 19___, inclusive: _____
_____
_____

26. Give the names and addresses of all public accountants who performed any services for you and _____
    _____ during the years 19___ to 19___, inclusive:
    (Name of firm)
_____
_____
_____

27. At what banks were business accounts maintained by you and _____ during the years 19___ to 19___, inclusive? _____
_____
_____
_____

MT 4235-1 (12-13-71) IR Manual

TECHNIQUES HANDBOOK FOR IN-DEPTH AUDIT INVESTIGATIONS

EXHIBIT 500–1—Cont. (7)

28. Were all business receipts deposited in these accounts? _____

    If not, explain _____

    _____

    _____

29. Do all deposits in these accounts represent receipts from sales? _____

    If not, explain: _____

    _____

30. Do any deposits in your business banking account(s) during the years 19___ to 19___, inclusive, represent loans or exchanges? _____

    If so, explain: _____

31. Were all business expenses paid by check? _____

    If not, explain: _____

32. Were all receipts from sales, commissions, fees, and any other sources recorded on the books and records of
    _____?
    (Name of firm)

33. What records were made of sales? _____

    _____

34. How were cash sales handled? _____

    _____

35. Give the following information with respect to all bank accounts, savings and loan, credit unions maintained by you, your wife and dependent children since January 1, 19___: *(in addition to accounts listed under Question No. 27)*:

Name of Bank	*Name of Account*	*Type of Account*

MT 4235–1 (12–13–71) IR Manual

INITIAL CONTACT

EXHIBIT 500-1—Cont. (8)

36. What was the source of the funds deposited in the bank accounts in the names of your wife and dependent children? _____
_____

37. Did your wife or dependent children receive any income during the years 19___ to 19___, inclusive? _____
If so, from whom and how much? _____
_____

38. Have you or your wife ever maintained any bank accounts or held any property for your children or for any other persons? _____

39. Have you or your wife ever maintained any bank accounts or held any property as attorney or agent for anyone? _____

40. Have you or your wife rented or had access to any safe deposit box since January 1, 19___? _____
If so, give particulars: _____
_____

41. What do you have in any safe deposit box or boxes now: _____
_____
_____

42. Have you, at any time, kept any currency in a safe deposit box? _____
_____

43. What is the largest amount of cash or currency which you have had at any time at your home, in a safe deposit box, or at any place other than on deposit in a bank? _____

44. How much cash or currency did you have, other than monies on deposit, as at:

Jan. 1, 19___? _____ Jan. 1, 19___? _____
Jan. 1, 19___? _____ Jan. 1, 19___? _____
Jan. 1, 19___? _____ Jan. 1, 19___? _____

45. How much cash or currency did your wife have, other than monies on deposit, as at:

Jan. 1, 19___? _____ Jan. 1, 19___? _____
Jan. 1, 19___? _____ Jan. 1, 19___? _____
Jan. 1, 19___? _____ Jan. 1, 19___? _____

MT 4235–1 (12–13–71) IR Manual

TECHNIQUES HANDBOOK FOR IN-DEPTH AUDIT INVESTIGATIONS

EXHIBIT 500–1—Cont. (9)

46. Did anyone else ever keep or hold for you, cash, currency or any money belonging to you? _____

47. Will you consent to an immediate inventory of your safe deposit box in the presence of representatives of the Internal Revenue Service? _____

48. Have you or your wife ever maintained any brokerage accounts? _____

    If so, give names of all firms where accounts were maintained: _____
    _____
    _____

49. Have you or your wife purchased securities through a bank? _____

50. Have you or your wife purchased or sold or redeemed any stocks or bonds *(including U. S. Government bonds)* since Jan. 1, 19___? _____

    If so, give details:

Description	Date Acquired	Cost	Date Sold	Selling Price

51. Have you or your wife ever owned any real estate? _____

    If so, state:

Description	Date Acquired	Cost	Date Sold	Selling Price

MT 4235–1 (12–13–71) IR Manual

INITIAL CONTACT

EXHIBIT 500–1—Cont. (10)

52. Give details regarding all purchases and sales of real estate, including: (a) Name(s) in which held; (b) name of other party to each transaction; (c) and names of all attorneys or title companies who participated in each settlement. _____
_____
_____
_____

53. Did you or your wife receive any income from rents or royalties during the years 19___ to 19___, inclusive?
_____
_____
_____

54. Have you ever given any mortgages on any real estate or chattels owned by you? _____
_____ If so, state:

Property Mortgaged	Mortgagee	Date Given	Original Amount	Present Balance	Rate of Interest
_____	_____	_____	_____	_____	_____
_____	_____	_____	_____	_____	_____
_____	_____	_____	_____	_____	_____

55. Have you or your wife borrowed any money from any bank, individual or firm since Jan. 1, 19___? _____
_____

If so, give details:
_____
_____

56. Have you ever submitted a statement of your assets and liabilities any bank, concern or individual? _____
If so, to whom and when? _____

57. Have you or your wife loaned any money to any person or firm since Jan 1, 19___? _____
If so, give details: _____
_____
_____
_____

MT 4235–1 (12–13–71) IR Manual

TECHNIQUES HANDBOOK FOR IN-DEPTH AUDIT INVESTIGATIONS

EXHIBIT 500–1—Cont. (11)

58. Give the following information regarding all annuity contracts and life insurance policies issued at any time in the names of or on the lives of yourself, your wife and your dependent children:

Name of Company	Insured	Face Value	Annual Premium	Type Policy	Date Issued
_____	_____	_____	_____	_____	_____
_____	_____	_____	_____	_____	_____
_____	_____	_____	_____	_____	_____
_____	_____	_____	_____	_____	_____
_____	_____	_____	_____	_____	_____

59. Have you, your wife or children ever received any inheritance? _____

    If so, give details: _____
    _____
    _____

60. What gifts have been received by yourself, your wife and dependent children since Jan. 1, 19—?
    _____
    _____

61. Have you, your wife or dependent children ever received any monies from any trust fund? _____
    _____

62. Did your wife or any other person supply, lend or make any contribution to the funds used to purchase any of the assets acquired by you or acquired jointly by you and your wife during the period from January 1, 19___ to January 1, 19___, inclusive? _____

    If so, give full details: _____
    _____
    _____
    _____

63. Have you ever purchased any cashier's or treasurer's checks from any bank? _____
    _____

MT 4235–1 (12–13–71) IR Manual

INITIAL CONTACT

EXHIBIT 500-1—Cont. (12)

64. Have you or your wife made any investments or acquired any assets since January 1, 19___ which have not been discussed during this interview? _____
_____

65. Have you or your wife received any income from any source during the years 19___ to 19___, inclusive, which have not been discussed during this interview? _____
_____

66. Has anyone as a straw party or nominee or as a favor to you, or in any way, held for you any real property, personal property, cash, currency, or anything of value? _____
_____
_____

67. Do you or your wife maintain any charge accounts? _____
    If so, give names of firms: _____
    _____

68. Has any petition in bankruptcy ever been filed by or against you? _____
    If so, give details: _____
    _____

69. Will your personal books and records and the books and records of _____
    (Name of firm)
    be made available for examination by representatives of the Internal Revenue Service? _____
    _____

70. Will all cancelled checks pertaining to all banking accounts maintained by you, your wife, and _____
    _____ be made available for examination by representatives of the Internal Revenue
    (Name of firm)
    Service? _____

71. Will you agree to submit a statement of your assets and liabilities as at _____
    _____
    _____ ? _____

MT 4235–1 (12–13–71) IR Manual

EXHIBIT 500–1—Cont. (13)

72. Will you agree to submit a statement of your estimated personal and family living expenditures for the year(s) _____? _____ _____

73. Do you wish to make any further statement regarding any of the matters discussed during this interview?

_____
_____
_____
_____
_____
_____
_____
_____
_____
_____
_____
_____
_____
_____

INTERVIEWER	DATE

MT 4235–1 (12-13-71) IR Manual

SPECIAL EXAMINATION PROCEDURES

EXHIBIT 600–1

STATEMENT OF NET WORTH

Of:_ _____

	1/1	12/31	12/31

ASSETS:

    Cash on hand

    Checking accounts

    Savings accounts

    Real estate

    Automobiles

    Stocks and bonds

    Loans receivable

    Other investments

    Jewelry

    Boats

    Other Assets

      Total Assets

LIABILITIES:

    Loans payable

    Mortgage payable

    Notes payable

    Accounts payable

    Other liabilities

    Reserve for depreciation

      Total Liabilities

      Net Worth

      Increase in Net Worth

MT 4235–1 (12–13–71) IR Manual

TECHNIQUES HANDBOOK FOR IN-DEPTH AUDIT INVESTIGATIONS

EXHIBIT 600–1—*Cont. (1)*

COMPARISON—NET WORTH TO REPORTED INCOME

	19____	19____	19____

Increase in net worth

Less: Non-taxable income

   Non-taxable capital gains

   Tax exempt interest

   Gifts received

   Excludable sick pay

   Dividend exclusions

   Insurance proceeds

   Other non-taxable income

     Total Non-taxable Income

      Net

Plus: Expenditures

   Living expenses

   Gifts made

   Non-deductible capital losses

   Non-deductible capital losses

   Other expenditures

     Total Expenditures

     Corrected Adjusted Gross Income

       Reported Adjusted Gross Income

         Unreported Gross Income

MT 4235–1 (12–13–71) IR Manual

SPECIAL EXAMINATION PROCEDURES

EXHIBIT 600–2

STATEMENT OF ESTIMATED LIVING EXPENSES

of _____ for year ending _____

	Weekly	*Monthly*	*Yearly*
Food (groceries, etc.)			
Outside meals			
Clothing			
Medical & dental expenses			
Rent or mortgage payments			
Repairs (home)			
Improvements (home)			
Home furnishings			
Utilities (gas, electricity, fuel, etc.)			
Telephone			
Laundry, dry cleaning			
Domestic help, FICA tax			
Auto expense			
Commuting expense			
Recreation—entertainment			
Vacation—travel			
Education			
Insurance (Life, Medical, Auto, etc.)			
Dues (club, lodge, union, etc.)			
Taxes (federal, state, local)			
Contributions			
Gifts			
Personal (beauty shop, liquor, tobacco, etc.)			
Miscellaneous			
Total			

MT 4235–1 (12–13–71) IR Manual

SPECIAL EXAMINATION PROCEDURES

EXHIBIT 600-3

SOURCE AND APPLICATION OF FUNDS

         19___   19___

Funds Applied

 Increase in cash on hand
 Increase in accounts receivable
 Increase in loans receivable
 Increase in stocks and bonds
 Increase in real estate
 Increase in other investments
 Increase in savings accounts, etc.
 Increase in other assets
 Decrease in accounts payable
 Decrease in notes payable
 Decrease in mortgage payable
 Decrease in other liabilities
 Decrease in depreciation reserves
 Personal living
 Income tax paid
 Nondeductible losses
  Total

Sources of Funds
 Decrease in cash on hand
 Increase in notes payable
 Increase in mortgage payable
 Increase in other liabilities
 Increase in depreciation reserves

Nontaxable capital gains

Tax exempt interest

Gifts received

Insurance proceeds

Other nontaxable income
  Total

Adjusted Gross Income as corrected

Adjusted Gross Income per return
 Additional gross income

MT 4235-1 (12-13-71) IR Manual

700 Audit Investigative Techniques

710 INTRODUCTION

(1) The audit investigative techniques that an internal revenue agent uses will depend upon the circumstances and alleged enterprises of the specific taxpayer being investigated. Imaginative agents are constantly developing new techniques as their knowledge and awareness of tax avoidance schemes increases.

(2) Within this chapter are techniques which are, or may prove to be, frequently used.

(3) The investigating agent should consider the use of these techniques when applicable but should not consider them all-inclusive. The number of techniques that can be used are endless and grow larger with each examination.

720 PAYROLL PADDING

721 Introduction

Payrolls may be padded for numerous reasons; however, the purpose is invariably the same: getting funds out of a business in the form of a deduction without the recipient paying income tax on the income. This method is used mostly where the paying enterprise is in the type of business which does not sell for cash and money can only be taken out by check. This method could be used merely as a tax evasion scheme in order to pay gambling losses or debt to loan sharks or extortion.

730 SALARY HAVEN

731 Introduction

There are some prominent figures in organized crime who have no legitimate source of income. Their only means of livelihood is from income realized through illegal activities. Therefore, in order to be able to prove how he supports himself and his family he has to have a source of legitimate income which he reports for income tax purposes. He accomplishes this by finding a business which is willing to put him on the payroll and issue him regular payroll checks. These payments are made even though the employee performs no services. The employer normally is a retail outlet owned by or associated with some other member of organized crime. In most cases these payroll payments are returned to the payer in cash and diverted.

740 SHIFTING OF INCOME AND LOSSES

741 Introduction

Some taxpayers think nothing of shifting income and losses, to reduce tax or to eliminate tax altogether. They are continually devising new ways of using their businesses as conduits to transfer income to themselves or to their nominees. The criminal element is known to resort to fictitious corporations and to corporations in foreign countries. This is a big aid to them in tax evasion, because the financial transactions there are cloaked by the secrecy afforded by foreign law. Also in certain foreign countries, if the corporation or individual has a bank account, the fruits of the crime are readily hidden, because of the strict bank secrecy rules. The problem is not confined to Switzerland, as similar secrecy prevails in Lichtenstein, Panama, and the Bahamas.

742 Examples

(1) One of the most common ways to reduce the income tax in a profitable business is to create additional corporations, either foreign or domestic. While some may have no legitimate business purpose, they do provide an-

MT 4235–1 (12–13–71) IR Manual

742

TECHNIQUES HANDBOOK FOR IN-DEPTH AUDIT INVESTIGATIONS

(742 EXAMPLES—CONT. (1))

other surtax exemption. The one common characteristic of such entities is that they are really shells, which have form on paper only, and have no substance in fact. They may or may not have an office. They usually will have a post office box. They have one employee or in many cases, none at all. The billing, mailing, planning, correspondence, and all other work will normally be handled out of the parent office. The examining agent should determine where all the paper work is done, whether the entity really exists and is in fact active in a business, and whether or not the entity is acting as a conduit for the flow of funds back to the parent or to some individuals.

(2) Another method used to shift income has been the use of false or fictitious sales or purchase prices between a parent and its affiliates, or between corporations by a controlling stockholder. As an example, in one instance the parent corporation arranged for an affiliate to purchase its product at cost, plus 10 percent. This price was less than 10 percent of the parent's regular list price for its product. In effect this resulted in a commission of over 90 percent to the affiliate. This was not an arm's-length transaction, and did not clearly reflect true income. Of course, if evidence is found of billing of goods on paper, but where no purchases were actually made and no merchandise delivered, this would constitute out-right fraud. The padding of the Cost of Sales Account by a parent through overpayments or premium payments to an affiliate has the same effect.

(3) Some parent companies do all of the buying of supplies, pay for all of the advertising, insurance, and other expenses of its affiliates, but they fail to allocate the proper shares of the expenses to the affiliates. They thus reduce their taxes by claiming additional expenses which are not really theirs. Of course the affiliate is probably already in a negative taxable position, and the additional expenses would not help it. The examining agent can best spot this condition by inspecting invoices to see where the merchandise was delivered, or where or for whom the services were performed. If the invoices are not made available, the agent can determine this condition by checking with the suppliers or vendors.

(4) Another method of shifting income occurs where materials are delivered to an affiliate, but the entire billing is made to the parent. The parent firm pays the bill, charging its purchases, but does not bill the affiliate, even though the latter received the materials. This situation can best be detected by inspection of invoices, preferably at the taxpayer's office, but if not, at the office of the supplier.

(5) A method used by some firms to reduce their taxes is to pay huge interest expense on sham notes. Was the loan necessary and did it in fact exist? This is pure out and out shifting of income from a profitable entity to one not as profitable. Was the rate of interest comparable to prevailing rates? The examining agent should determine whether loans were actually made, whether they were necessary, and ascertain the source of the funds. He should also examine the notes, and verify to see whether payments were actually made, or whether they were merely entries.

(6) Taxpayers have been using yet another method with great success. First they acquire a business here, which sells products in Europe. Then they obtain a secret bank account, either in their own name, or in the name of the business. After sales are made, they submit two invoices to the customer. They ask the foreign customer to pay the lower amount directly to the business and the balance to the secret bank account. They thus effectively shift the income from the local business to the foreign depository. This scheme has been used quite well in the opposite direction also. When buying products abroad, the seller is asked to submit an overstated invoice, with the understanding that when it is paid, the difference over the true cost will be transmitted to the secret bank account.

(7) Another method used to shift income was through the creation of a foreign corporation. The officers who controlled the corporation directed that commissions and fees which they earned here, were to be sent to their corporation, on the pretext that the foreign corporation had earned the income. Another variation of this scheme is to direct commissions or fees to a Lichtenstein trust. The trust deposits the funds in the account of the taxpayer. The same results are obtained when a controlling stockholder of a closely held corporation, causes the corporation to pay commissions or amounts said to represent business expenses to a foreign national. The foreign national then forwards the money to a foreign bank account to the credit of the controlling stockholder, or his nominee. The investigating agent should examine all foreign payments and invoices in a highly inquisitive and detailed fashion.

(8) An example of shifting a loss occurred where a company that purchased a profitable business, altered the books of the business it bought, to show a loss for the current year. It then absorbed the loss and merged it with its own operations. It thus effectively shifted a "loss" to itself to reduce its tax. How was this accomplished? Who ordered it? The agent's documentation of the alteration of the books and pertinent excerpts from correspondence or memos concerning the alteration, could provide evidence necessary to arrive at correct income and tax.

(9) Some corporations have been found to shift income and losses by the devices of having officers and stockholders improperly filing partnership returns. The business of the "partnership" is really that of the corporation. The corporate officers or its principal stockholders thus shift the corporate loss to reduce their own income or its profit to evade the corporate tax. This method is frequently resorted to by the criminal element. How can this sort of shifting be uncovered? Was the partnership legal? The examining agent should verify the authenticity of the part-

MT 4235-1 (12-13-71) IR Manual

AUDIT INVESTIGATIVE TECHNIQUES

(742 EXAMPLES—Cont. (2))

nership, its office, its business, its name, its number of years in business, and its actual transactions by tracing them through third parties, if necessary.

(10) The simplest and most expedient method of shifting losses to profitable affiliates is by book entries, usually at the end of a year. Allocations are made of expenses, materials, supplies, or overhead, whether appropriate or not. This can best be spotted by full inspection of all entries, their explanations, the basis for allocation, the reasons for, and at whose instigation were such entries made, and comparison to see if the entries are consistent with prior years' practices and the facts.

750 NOMINEE OWNERSHIPS

751 Introduction

The real and controlling ownership of funds, deeds, properties, businesses, bank accounts, options, contracts, stocks, or partnership interests, etc., will quite often be someone other than the owner of record. There are many different types of nominee ownerships and reasons for them, some obvious, and some not so obvious, some legitimate, and some illegitimate. Organized crime frequently resorts to nominee ownerships to conceal its interests. For example, convicted felons are prohibited by law from holding a liquor license in most jurisdictions, so they use nominees. This presents a real challenge to investigating agents to be able to ferret out the true owners. There follows below a description of some of the types of nominee ownerships, their purposes, and some suggestions on how to look for them.

752 Types

(1) There are many different forms the nominee ownership may take. In its most expedient and trusted form, the title of a property or an asset might be placed in the name of a close relative. Many racketeers have been known to secrete assets in the name of a trusted girl friend, or paramour. Others have used the maiden name of their wife or of their daughter-in-law.

(2) The underworld businessmen frequently set up operations under a fictitious name. Or they may place the business in an employee's name or in the name of a close associate. Many known criminals place their financial operations in the name and address of their attorney. Contractors have been found to use fictitious sub-contractors to hide branches of their operations. There have been many fictitious partnerships used to disguise true ownership. A common ploy is to adopt an alias.

(3) Past experience has shown that commercial and savings bank accounts have often been set up under false names, or under someone else's name. However, actual control of the account will be exercised by the true owner, whether by himself, or through the nominee. Bank accounts in fictitious business names, are quite common, as are U.S. citizens' accounts in foreign banks. Of course, some racketeers have used U.S. depositories for transfers of funds from foreign banks, under assumed names.

(4) U. S. taxpayers who deposit in foreign banks frequently have that bank transfer their funds back to this country to buy real estate in the name of the foreign bank. Ownership of the "transferred assets" then appears in the bank's name. In this manner the foreign depositors have recaptured the use of their secret cash, and have sheltered from U. S. taxation the income from the real estate, and any eventual gain on its sale.

753 Purposes

(1) There are in fact many reasons for nominee ownerships. Some of the more obvious are to reduce taxes or eliminate them entirely, to divert funds illegally, to skim cash, to pay off gambling debts, to claim losses, or to deceive the public and particularly the tax collector. Thus two or more businesses can be owned by one person but falsely represented as being owned by others. The profits after payment of minimal taxes by the nominee owners will then be turned over to the true owner.

(2) Some other reasons for nominee ownerships might be simply to hide the true owner, to lend an aura of respectability to the business actually operated by an underworld character, or to make it possible for a racketeer to acquire an interest in a legitimate business, which he would not have been able to do under his true identity.

(3) Nominee ownerships have been known to be set up for bribery, for political payoffs, for kickbacks, to extract a better price, to use as a conduit for illegal payments, to conceal the real buyer of a property or a business, or just to have someone else take the rap for illegal acts.

(4) Quite often individuals will secrete their assets in another's name in event of law suits to prevent attachment, in cases of divorce, at times of impending bankruptcy, or just to reduce the real net worth where the subject is under investigation.

(5) Secret foreign bank accounts figured in the takeover of some corporate ownerships through dummy nominees. Criminal elements have used foreign banks to

MT 4235-1 (12-13-71) IR Manual

TECHNIQUES HANDBOOK FOR IN-DEPTH AUDIT INVESTIGATIONS

(753 PURPOSE—CONT.)

buy stocks in the banks' names. They would then accumulate the stocks prior to a tender offer to avoid the reporting requirements of securities laws. In some of these instances millions of dollars worth of securities were acquired through secret bank accounts and then were used in subsequent corporate takeovers through dummy nominees.

760 FALSE DOCUMENTS AND STATEMENTS

761 General

Agents should be constantly alert to the probability of encountering false documents and statements. During the course of an investigation, an agent may find that such documents have been submitted as part of the taxpayer's income tax return. Upon discovery of such documents the revenue agent should immediately refer the matter to Intelligence Division in accordance with IRM 4567.31.

762 Applicable IRC Penalties

(1) Criminal penalties are provided for the submission of a false document in connection with tax matters. Some of these provisions are:

(a) IRC 7204, Fraudulent Statement—See (10) 20:(4)(d).

(b) IRC 7205—See (10)20:(4)(e).

(c) IRC 7206—See (10)20:(4)(f).

1 Statutory provisions IRC 7206(1)

a The elements of a criminal violation under IRC 7206(1) are: making and subscribing to a return, statement or other document under penalty of perjury; knowledge that it is not true and correct as to every material matter; and willfulness.

b This Code section imposes the penalty upon a person who willfully falsifies a return as to a material matter, whether or not his purpose was to evade or defeat the payment of taxes. Prosecution is appropriate when the Government is able to prove falsity of a partnership return, the issue being falsity rather than evasion. The test of materiality is whether the false statement was material to the contents of the return. It is not necessary that the government actually rely on the statement.

c It is sufficient that it be made with the intention of inducing such reliance. Prosecutions under this Code section should involve only false returns or statements presented to or filed with the Internal Revenue Service. This sanction is appropriate when it is possible to prove falsity of a return but difficult to establish evasion of an ascertainable amount of tax, or, when the falsification results in a relatively small amount of tax evasion.

d If an individual files a false and fraudulent return, it is possible for him to incur criminal liability for attempting to defeat and evade the tax and for making a false and fraudulent statement under penalty of perjury even though both offenses relate to the same return and the making of the false statement is an incidental step in consummation of the completed offense of attempting to defeat and evade taxes.

2 Statutory Provisions IRC 7206(2)

a The elements of a criminal violation under IRC 7206(2) are: aid, assist, counsel, advise or procure the preparation or presentation of a false or fraudulent document; a matter under, or in connection with any material matter arising under, the Internal Revenue laws; and willfulness.

b Generally, income tax returns or partnership information returns are involved but any document required or authorized to be filed can give rise to this offense.

c If two partners are responsible for a false and fraudulent return, they have each committed a criminal offense, but if there is evidence that only one of the partners is responsible then only he could be held liable. The choice of 26 USC 7206(1) or 26 USC 7206(2) depends upon whether the responsible partner signed the return or caused the entries that produced the false return.

d The aiding and assisting in the preparation of a false return and the subscribing of a false return are two separate offenses.

e It is sufficient to establish that the defendant wilfully and knowingly prepared or caused to be prepared false and fraudulent income tax returns for another although the fraud involved was without the knowledge and consent of the person required to make the return.

763 False, Fictitious, or Fraudulent Claims (18 USC 287)

(1) During third party investigations, agents may examine documents submitted to financial institutions, governmental agencies, customers, suppliers, etc. A false document or statement could constitute a criminal violation of a non-IRS violation. Where such a situation is encountered, the matter should be referred in accordance

MT 4235-1 (12-13-71) IR Manual

AUDIT INVESTIGATIVE TECHNIQUES

(763 FALSE, FICTITIOUS, OR FRAUDULENT CLAIMS (18 USC 287)—Cont.)

with 412.5 of this Handbook and IRM 4097. However, when the false claim is a refund return, then it is an IRS violation and should be referred to Intelligence in accordance with established procedures.

(2) The elements of a criminal violation under 18 USC 287 are:

(a) Making or presenting a claim upon or against the United States; and

(b) Knowledge that the claim is false, fictitious or fraudulent.

(3) Whether the claim is false, fictitious, or fraudulent must be determined in view of all of the facts and circumstances surrounding it and it is not essential that the bill, voucher, or other things used as the basis for the claim should in and of itself contain fraudulent or fictitious statements or entries.

764 False Statements Generally (18 USC 1001)

In connection with any matter within the jurisdiction of any department or agency of the United States, it is a criminal offense to wilfully falsify, conceal or cover up by trick, scheme, or device a material fact or to make any false, fictitious, or fraudulent statements or representations or to make or use any false writing or document knowing the same to contain any false, fictitious or fraudulent statement or entry.

765 Elements of Offense

(1) The term "jurisdiction" means the power to deal with a subject matter and the term "department" includes the United States Treasury Department.

(2) It is not necessary that the statement be required to be made by some regulation or law.

(3) The weight of authority requires proof of materiality in any prosecution under 18 USC 1001.

(4) The violation may involve formal or informal records, forms and instruments, and even oral statements. It is not essential that the statements be under oath, and the perjury corroboration rule does not apply.

(5) Knowledge cannot be imputed to a corporate officer merely because he appears to be active in corporate affairs.

(6) The statute is concerned with false statements which might impede the exercise of Federal authority. Pecuniary loss to the Government is not necessary. Any impairment of administration of its governmental functions is sufficient and the commission of the crime is not dependent upon the success of the fraudulent intent.

766 Specific Examples of False Documents and Statements

(1) A false statement in a tax return (also a violation of 26 USC 7206(1)).

(2) Concealed part ownership of individuals with felony records, whose ownership of liquor establishments may be prohibited by State law, may be designed to avoid State laws. Therefore, when Alcohol, Tobacco and Firearms Division requires that the actual owners of liquor establishments be listed on applications for Federal liquor tax stamps, the names of racketeer owners are omitted intentionally (26 USC 7206—Aiding and Abetting).

(3) Deliberate misrepresentation of material facts at administrative hearings by Federal agencies such as SEC.

(4) False representations in a protest to a proposed income tax determination. (18 USC 1001)

(5) Submission of a false net worth statement to a Federal Savings and Loan Association. (18 USC 1014)

(6) Falsification of FHA application. (18 USC 1010)

(7) False statements relative to highway projects under Federal-Aid Road Act. (18 USC 1020)

(8) In addition, violations may occur in connection with applications for credit submitted to any agency disbursing Federal funds such as the Home Loan Bank Board or Small Business Administration. Inaccurate financial statements submitted to a commercial bank may also constitute a "false statement."

770 KICKBACKS AND PAYOFFS

771 Introduction

(1) The receipt of income from "kickbacks" can occur in nearly every segment of business, large or small.

(2) The payment of kickbacks can take the form of cash, goods, or services to or for others for some kind of preferential treatment or to influence another party for such treatment.

(3) Because of the difficulty involved in tracing the receipt or payment of kickbacks, it has become a favorite source of revenue to organized crime. Kickbacks can be difficult to trace through records as they could be hidden in a maze of bookkeeping entries and buried in any number of accounts such as cost of sales, sales returns, advertising, repairs, travel and entertainment, loans and exchanges, promotional expenses, miscellaneous expenses or practically any other account. Additional difficulty occurs where the kickbacks do not appear on the books and records of the business at all, e.g. an individual will pay a kickback from his personal account or from personal cash on hand. Further, if such a payment is uncovered, there is the additional problem of determining who actually received the payment as the payor will often refuse to identify the payee.

772 Income and Deduction Features

(1) In dealing with kickbacks that are discovered, it is generally agreed that:

(a) Kickbacks are always taxable to the recipient.

(b) If the name of recipient is not disclosed, no deduction will be allowed to the payor.

(c) Kickbacks are not deductible unless they are both ordinary and necessary business expenses.

MT 4235–1 (12–13–71) IR Manual

TECHNIQUES HANDBOOK FOR IN-DEPTH AUDIT INVESTIGATIONS

780 PAYMENTS TO OR FOR PUBLIC OFFICIALS

781 Introduction

Corruption of public officials has long been a necessary prerequisite to the successful operation of organized criminal activities. It is frequently found in the area of public works and contracting. Over the years such payments have assumed many guises. The suitcase full of cash has now given way to more sophisticated methods. The methods used, today, will vary to meet the specific circumstances of the individuals who can, or will, be corrupted.

782 Types of Payments

Payments to public officials will take varied shapes. Public officials involved in the investigative or lower-level management strata may receive an offer of cash in hand.

AUDIT INVESTIGATIVE TECHNIQUES

(782 TYPES OF PAYMENTS—Cont.)

Higher level public officials might also be approached with promises of further promotion or higher appointed offices. Elected public officials could be approached through the offer of large political contributions, large blocks of votes at election time or even, for the minor elective official, the offer of loudspeaker sound trucks to broadcast his message in the local streets.

790 PENSION AND PROFIT SHARING PLANS

(1) The revenue agent should be alert to the fact that in pension and profit sharing plans there is the possibility of tax avoidance or evasion through diversion of profits. This is usually accomplished by a corporation transferring an asset such as a tract of land to the tax-exempt entity at book value which is usually substantially below the fair market value and will indicate that the transfer was made at book value resulting in no gain or loss.

(2) In a case of this type the agent discovered that the corporation, at the time the asset was transferred, had actually been negotiating for the sale of this land to a real estate developer at a price far in excess of the book value reflected on the books of the corporation. Records of the tax-exempt entity indicated that the sale resulted in a profit in excess of a quarter of a million dollars. The method employed here caused the profit on the sale of the tract of land to be diverted from a taxable corporation to a tax-exempt entity with a substantial loss in tax revenue.

(3) IRM 4288 provides instructions for preparing Form 2371 (Pension Plan Deduction Computation) and Form 2372 (Deduction of Contributions Under Profit Sharing or Stock Bonus Plan). Also see IRM 45(10)0 regarding Pension Trust Program.

(4) In an in-depth audit the revenue agent must first determine if the deduction for the contribution to the pension or profit sharing plan is allowable in accordance with the provisions of the Internal Revenue Code.

(5) A review of the plan itself should be made so that the revenue agent will become thoroughly familiar with the working provisions of the plan with particular emphasis on the operations as reflected in the receipts and disbursements.

(6) The examination by the revenue agent, in addition to the regular items covered, will entail a detailed analysis of all receipts as to source, nature and purpose regardless of the amount involved. The use of this technique may result in uncovering prohibited transactions as defined by IRC 503(f) and may also provide leads in uncovering diversions of profits through manipulation. All unusual transactions encountered during the investigations should receive close attention with respect to other taxpayers involved. Returns of related entities should be requested to compare with the known information and follow-up action pursued to the ultimate conclusion. Third party inquiries should be made and investigation undertaken, where deemed necessary.

(7) In many cases the agent will not be competent to make decisions in the pension and profit sharing areas and, therefore, should consider the advisability of requesting the services of a specialist revenue agent.

MT 4235-1 (12-13-71) IR Manual

AUDIT INVESTIGATIVE TECHNIQUES

7(12)3 Failure To Withhold or Pay Over

(1) The employer is liable for the correct amount of F.I.C.A. tax and income tax withholding required to be withheld from wages, whether or not the taxes are collected from the employee. If the employer fails to deduct the tax he is nevertheless liable for the correct amount of tax that should have been withheld. The employee also is liable for the correct amount of tax until it is collected from him.

(2) Manual Supplement 47G–82, CR42G–235, establishes the procedure and provides sample reports for use in an employment tax investigation.

7(12)5 Industry Areas of Noncompliance

(1) Experience in the examination of employment tax returns has proven that the following industries are susceptible to noncompliance:

 (a) Contractors and subcontractors (roofers, carpenters, painters, etc.)

 (b) Fishing Industry (captains and crews)

 (c) Household employees (maids, chauffeurs, gardeners)

 (d) Manufacturing Industry (employees moving expense)

 (e) Orchestras (leaders and members)

 (f) Personal services (barbers, beauticians, nurses, etc.)

 (g) Professional Services (physicians, lawyers, accountants hired on a regular or periodic basis)

 (h) Race Track ("hot walkers," pony boys, exercise boys, etc.)

 (i) Restaurants (tips, casual workers)

 (j) Retail Stores (bonuses, commissions paid in cash.)

 (k) Sales Organizations (trip awards, commissions)

 (l) Taxi Cab Companies (driver wages, tips, etc)

 (m) Trucking Industry (casual drivers, lease vs truck operation, etc.)

 (n) Union Contracts (fringe benefits)

7(13)0 BANKRUPTCY FRAUDS

7(13)1 Introduction

(1) Businesses are sometimes disposed of through illegal bankruptcy frauds. A common method of such fraudulent disposal is known as the "bust out" or "scam."

(2) The purpose of this section is to alert examining officers of the tax consequences that may result in a bust out or scam. The individual perpetrating bankruptcy fraud may be converting merchandise inventory, cash or other assets to personal use and for personal gain.

(3) The examining agent should be alert, too, to the purchases of merchandise inventory and other assets in a suspected bankruptcy fraud since the acquisition of such merchandise inventory and other assets for cash at usually near or below suppliers cost may be a potential opportunity for a "skimming" case. A "skimming" case is one in which the individual or corporation skims off the top by understating sales or revenues. He correspondingly understates purchases and cost of sales to keep the markup percentage in line with the understated sales or revenues.

(4) Agents examining bankrupt corporations should become familiar with the methods used in perpetrating bankruptcy frauds and to recognize these illegal acts.

7(13)2 Method of Operation

(1) The normal sequence of events in one type of bankruptcy fraud is the concealment of the transfer of ownership of a business which is acquired either legally or illegally. The creditors, not knowing of the change in ownership, permit the new owners to operate on the former proprietor's credit rating. After acquiring a business, frequently a number of large bank deposits are made in order to establish a more favorable credit rating. Then large amounts of merchandise are purchased from a number of suppliers. First, purchases are made for cash, then on fifteen day credit, then on thirty day credit, and finally on whatever the creditors will bear. Favoring merchandise that is troublesome to trace, easy to transport and simple to market, such as appliances, furniture and office equipment, payment for all goods is made regularly and on time. The orders are steadily increased but payments now tend to decline as to the percentage of what is due. Then, usually just before a busy season or on some specific event, huge orders are placed. Once the goods arrive the

MT 4235–1 (12–13–71) IR Manual

7(13)2

TECHNIQUES HANDBOOK FOR IN-DEPTH AUDIT INVESTIGATIONS

(7(13)2 METHOD OF OPERATION—CONT.)

"bust out" occurs. The merchandise is sold for cash, sometimes at less than wholesale prices to organized crime figures or to other businessmen who are willing to buy at cut-rate prices without asking too many questions. The creditors are left with substantial claims and a bankrupt business with no assets.

(2) Another scheme is to give the "selected" company a name almost identical to that of a well known and highly creditworthy corporation. The address given may even be on the same street as that of the reputable concern. Capitalizing on the favorable credit rating of the well known firm, "the selected company" proceeds to order goods from misled suppliers, except in this case the "bust out" can proceed faster because there is a pre-established credit rating and financial statements are often unnecessary.

(3) A third form of planned bankruptcy is similar to the first one listed above. Only in this case orders are placed for merchandise unrelated to the regular line of business (a furniture store ordering jewelry as door prizes) during the supplier's busy season and sometimes on a rush basis during the supplier's slack season, in the hope that creditors will omit a credit check in their haste to cash in on rush or off season business.

(4) Still another scheme exists whereby an individual acquires a profitable business by surreptitiously acquiring control of the outstanding stock of a corporation. Once in control of the stock, he quickly moves in and takes control of the business. All assets of the corporation are then quickly sold for whatever price they will bring leaving the remaining shareholders with a bankrupt corporation.

7(13)5 Assessment of Deficiencies

(1) Agents examining returns involving bankrupt entities are reminded of IRC 6871 which provides in effect that upon adjudication of bankruptcy, the filing of a petition, or the appointment of a receiver, any deficiency determined to be due will be subject to immediate assessment. IRM 4583.5 provides that Waiver Form 870 cannot be accepted in bankruptcy cases and IRM 4584.1: (3) prescribes that any deficiences found to be due in these cases will be subject to the quick assessment procedure.

(2) IRM 4580 through 4585.2 prescribe procedures to be followed in bankruptcy cases, jeopardy assessments and concealment or transfer of asset cases.

7(14)0 THE GRAND JURY

7(14)1 Duties of a Grand Jury

(1) It is the duty of any Federal grand dury to inquire into alleged offenses against the *criminal* laws of the States.

(2) The question has been asked as to whether a revenue agent in the conduct of his examination for purpose of determining a civil liability may utilize the service of a grand jury in order to compel a recalcitrant witness to furnish information, since a grand jury can, through the Court, compel a witness to give testimony.

AUDIT INVESTIGATIVE TECHNIQUES

(7(14)1 DUTIES OF A GRAND JURY—Cont.)

(3) The answer is no. The powers of a Federal Grand Jury are restricted to inquiries into offenses against the *criminal* laws of the United States.

7(14)2 Use of Grand Jury Information To Establish A Civil Liability

(1) If there has been a Court order directing release of the records subpoenaed by a Grand Jury and the minutes of the Jury to the Service for the purpose of establishing civil liabilities, then and only then can the revenue agent review the records and minutes in his tax audit. The Court's order, if granted, would be applied for under Rule 6(e), Federal Rules of Criminal Procedure.

(2) If records are in the possession of the Grand Jury and no Rule 6(e) order has been obtained, an attempt should be made to secure the owner's approval for the Service to examine them while in the Grand Jury's possession. Since the documents produced pursuant to a Grand Jury subpoena remain the property of the person producing them (Bendix Aviation Corp., 58 F Supp. 953 (SDNY 1965)) the consent of the owner should be sufficient for the records to be made available to the Service.

(3) In the event the above procedure does not prove workable, then the Service's summons procedure should be utilized. In this regard, prior arrangements with the United States Attorney's office will result in the Service being advised as to the time when the books and records have served the purposes of the Grand Jury and are being returned to the respective owner.

7(15)0 ORGANIZED CRIME CONTROL ACT OF 1970 (PUBLIC LAW 91-452)

7(15)1 Introduction

The Organized Crime Control Act of 1970 became law on October 15, 1970. The Act generally relates to titles of the United States Code other than to Title 26 (relating to Internal Revenue matters) but its provisions are so broad and relate so directly to subjects under IRS examination, it is deemed advisable for agents to be made knowledgeable of some of its major provisions.

7(15)2 Purpose of the Act

It is the purpose of the Act to seek the eradication of organized crime by strengthening the legal tools in the evidence gathering process, by establishing new penal prohibitions and new remedies to deal with those engaged in organized crime.

7(15)3 Definitions

(1) The Act provides specific definitions of the activities involved in order to provide guidelines in the administration of the law. Some of these definitions can be stated as follows:

(a) Racketeering Activity

1 Means any act or threat involving murder, kidnapping, gambling, arson, robbery, bribery, extortion, dealing in narcotics or dangerous drugs;

2 Any indictable act, under Title 18, relating to bribery, sports bribery, counterfeiting, thefts from interstate shipment, embezzlement from pension and welfare funds, extortionate credit transactions, transmitting gambling information, mail fraud, etc.

3 Any indictable act relating to restrictions on payments and loans to labor organizations or relating to embezzlement from union funds;

4 Any offense involving bankruptcy fraud, fraud in the sale of securities and dealings in narcotics and dangerous drugs.

(b) Pattern of racketeering activity requires at least two acts of racketeering activity, the last of which occurred within ten years after the commission of a prior act of racketeering activity.

(c) Unlawful Debt—Means a debt contracted in an illegal gambling activity or a debt the collection of which is not enforceable under State or Federal law by reason of usury.

7(15)4 Pertinent Titles of The Act

(1) Some of the more important titles of this Act that an examining agent should be acquainted with are listed below. While these titles do not directly relate to Internal Revenue matters, an investigation by a revenue agent might bring to light some matter relating to these issues. In that event it should be brought to the attention of the agent's supervisor for dissemination to the proper authority.

(a) Title III—Recalcitrant Witnesses: This title provides that whenever a witness before any court or grand jury of the United States refuses to comply with an order to testify he may summarily be confined until he is willing to testify. The period of confinement is not to exceed the life of the court proceeding or the term of the grand jury. During this period the witness cannot be admitted to bail.

(b) Title VIII—Syndicated Gambling: Congress found that illegal gambling frequently operated through the connivance and corruption of public officials. In an attempt to bear heavily upon the corrupt official Congress added this title to the Act. It makes it unlawful for two or more persons to facilitate an illegal gambling business, if one or more of them is an official or employee, elected, appointed or otherwise, of a State or political subdivision; and one or more of such persons conducts, finances, manages, supervises, directs or owns all or a part of an illegal gambling business. In this case an illegal gambling business is one in which the operation is a violation of the law of a State or political subdivision; involves five or more persons; remains in business for a period in excess of thirty days or has a gross revenue of over $2,000 a day. It includes pool-selling, bookmaking, maintaining slot machines, roulette wheels, or dice tables and conducting lotteries, policy, bolita or numbers games. This section does not apply to any bingo game, lottery or similar game

MT 4235-1 (12-13-71) IR Manual

7(15)4

TECHNIQUES HANDBOOK FOR IN-DEPTH AUDIT INVESTIGATIONS

(7(15)4 PERTINENT TITLES OF THE ACT—CONT.)

of chance conducted by an organization exempt from tax under IRC 501(c)(3).

(c) Title IX—Racketeer Influenced and Corrupt Organizations:

1 This title while relating to Title 18, a non-income tax title, may be of particular interest to an agent conducting an income tax investigation because it relates to income derived from illegal sources being diverted into legal enterprises. Tracing funds as to source and disposition is within the realm of an agent's activity and presents a challenge to his ingenuity. It is conceivable therefore that an agent in the pursuit of his investigation could uncover a violation of this provision of the Act.

2 Title IX in effect provides that it shall be unlawful for any person who has received any income derived from a pattern of racketeering activity or through collection of an unlawful debt in which such person has participated, to use or invest, directly or indirectly any part of such income or the proceeds of such income, in acquisition of any interest in, or the establishment or operation of any enterprise which is engaged in or which affects interstate or foreign commerce. The Act further provides that the purchase of securities would also be considered unlawful if after the acquisition of the stock the person controls one percent or more of the outstanding securities of any one class and if it confers the power to elect one or more directors of the issues. It shall also be unlawful for any such person to acquire or maintain any interest or control of any enterprise which is engaged in or affects interstate or foreign commerce. Further, the law provides that it shall be unlawful for any person employed by or associated with any enterprise, to conduct or participate in the conduct of any enterprise through a pattern of racketeering. Finally, it shall be unlawful to conspire to violate any provisions of this section of the Act.

7(16)0 SWISS BANK FEATURES

7(16)1 Introduction

(1) In recent years American business activities abroad have increased enormously. Paralleling this, there has been a very great increase in the use of banks in countries (such as Switzerland, Bahamas, Panama, Lichtenstein) having bank secrecy laws by U.S. taxpayers, some of whom may be using this route to evade U.S. taxes. Secrecy banks provide an excellent vehicle for tax evasion both with respect to the funds deposited (for example "skim" in the case of gamblers, unreported fees in the case of professionals) and also the income generated by the investment of these funds (capital gains, dividends and interest).

(2) Heretofore our enforcement efforts in this area were frequently aborted when taxpayers with Swiss bank accounts would not cooperate. Although these cases still remain a challenge to the agent's ingenuity and professional skill it is believed that there are tools and expertise to enable the agent to bring at least some of them to establish a correct tax liability.

(3) It must be remembered that bank secrecy applies only to requests by third parties (in this instance, the Internal Revenue Service) and not to requests by the depositor or his successor in interest such as an executor of his estate. Generally, the taxpayer or executor can obtain transcripts, copies of advices and other documents if he requests the bank to furnish them.

(4) Although much of the following will apply to banks in other secrecy countries, the focus will be on Swiss banks because they are by far the most frequently used by sophisticated taxpayers. Switzerland is politically stable, has a hard currency and its large banks operate world-wide, offering a wide array of services especially acting as stockbroker. Further, Swiss law provides criminal sanctions for those who violate the bank secrecy law.

(5) The "numbered" account has received a great deal of publicity and achieved a certain glamor in the public mind. However, all Swiss bank accounts have a number and all Swiss bank accounts are secret. "Numbered" accounts have an additional security feature in that only a few officials of the bank can identify the name of the account owner with the number of the account.

7(16)2 Method of Operation

(1) Swiss bank accounts can be opened in many ways: can be opened in person in Switzerland; through an attorney or agent in Switzerland; by mail, either directly or indirectly to Switzerland; either through the branch of a Swiss bank in a foreign country (other than the U.S.) or through a transfer from a bank in a foreign country; and, through the New York, Los Angeles and San Francisco branches of Swiss Bank Corporation and Swiss Credit Bank for transfer to a branch in Switzerland. It is believed possible to make arrangements for opening an account through a local agent or intermediary.

(2) Funds (for initial as well as subsequent deposits) may be transferred by cash. Couriers carrying such funds normally charge a two to five percent commission. Absent knowledge of an unreported bank account on which a personal check may have been drawn, or specific information as to name, date, bank and account with respect to the other instruments, the trail is not easy to find and trace.

(3) Checks drawn on domestic banks and deposited in a Swiss bank frequently go through many hands in the process. This is especially true of transactions in the diamond industry and among taxpayers involved in the export-import trade with Brazil and other South American countries. The checks may be initially written with the payee omitted, later to be stamped or typed in, or drawn to cash. There is a brisk trade between individuals who wish to circumvent the TCR regulations and others who have checks they wish to convert to cash.

MT 4235-1 (12-13-71) IR Manual
7(15)4

AUDIT INVESTIGATIVE TECHNIQUES

(7(16)2 METHOD OF OPERATION—Cont.)

(4) The more frequently encountered Swiss accounts are:

(a) Current—also known as a demand account and is similar to a U.S. checking account in that it usually earns no interest. Some Swiss banks do issue checkbooks but checks are not as popular abroad as they are in this country. A current account may be carried in Swiss francs, U.S. dollars, Canadian dollars, German marks and others.

(b) Savings—also known as deposit account, private account, investment account. These accounts are usually carried in Swiss francs and pay interest at from 3 percent to 5 percent per annum depending on the bank and on restrictions as to amount and notice on withdrawals.

(c) Time Deposits—this category would include fixed term deposits, certificates of deposit and short term bank bonds. These may be in Swiss francs or U.S. dollars and the interest rate depends on market conditions. Recently the interest rate has varied from $5\frac{1}{4}$ percent to $6\frac{1}{4}$ percent depending on the bank, the term and the market.

(d) Securities—also known as a custody account and used for stock market transactions. Swiss banks are also brokers and will buy and sell listed securities on almost any stock exchange in the world. In most recent years the biggest play has been in the U.S. exchanges. The account may be discretionary or the customer may instruct the bank as to what trades to make.

(e) Loan—this may arise from margin purchases of securities, silver, etc., or from a collateralized loan.

(f) Trust—similar to those in the United States.

(g) Safekeeping—Art, Antiques, Jewelry, Coins, Stamps.

(h) Precious Metals—Gold, Silver, Platinum, etc.

(5) Taxpayers may at the same time have several types of the accounts shown above. For example, they may have a dollar account, a Swiss franc account and a silver account or securities account. A securities account is almost always accompanied by either a current or a deposit account. A credit of dividends or coupon interest to a current or deposit account is a clue that the bank is holding securities for the taxpayer. Many banks use the same basic number for the various accounts held by a customer, merely adding a decimal point and a one or two-digit number or a letter to denote different types.

(6) Bank statements are usually sent semi-annually but may, at the request of the customer, be sent more frequently, or alternatively, not sent at all but kept until called for. However, confirmation notices for securities and precious metals transactions are sent as they occur. If the security is held in street name, the confirmation is sent to the nominee.

(7) Account holders may ask the bank to send all correspondence to another individual who may be an attorney, agent, relative, friend, etc. If the taxpayer acknowledges the existence of an account but alleges that it belongs to another (usually a nonresident alien), the examiner should insist on complete documentation and proof that the account truly belongs to someone other than the taxpayer.

(8) A Swiss bank's stock transactions on the New York and American Stock Exhanges are made in the name of the bank and usually it is not possible to ascertain the name(s) of the beneficial owners of the securities being traded. In some cases it was learned of a Swiss bank authorizing a registered representative or a stock brokerage firm to accept orders from an American. The resulting buy or sell will be for the Swiss bank and will be so reflected on the books and records of the stock brokerage firm. However, there are usually good grounds to believe that the trading is actually for the American involved. In another case, a Swiss bank maintained subaccounts for its omnibus account at a particular stock brokerage firm. Information was obtained enabling an agent to identify particular U.S. taxpayers with specific subaccounts. In the foregoing examples the key figure and the source of information as to the identity of the beneficial owner is the registered representative who is receiving commissions for these transactions.

(9) Swiss bank statements generally are more detailed since they do not as a rule return cancelled checks. The statements frequently include useful information concerning the nature of deposits, checks drawn, miscellaneous charges and credits, and sometimes give the names of payees. Although the statements may be in English they are more apt to be in German, French or Italian. When a foreign language is used the taxpayer should be asked to furnish a translation or a translation may be obtained through Service channels.

MT 4235-1 (12-13-71) IR Manual

7(16)4 Sources of Information-Miscellaneous

(5) The recently passed Foreign Bank Accounts Act (Public Law 91–508) will have a tremendous impact once it is fully implemented. It provides, among other things, for:

(a) Retention of records by banks and other financial institutions;

(b) Reports of domestic currency transactions;

(c) Reports of exports and imports of monetary instruments in excess of $5,000 at any one time;

(d) Reports of foreign transactions; and

(e) Extension of margin requirements to foreign loans to the purchasers of stock, as well as to brokers, dealers, and financial institutions who lend money for this purpose.

(6) All 1970 income tax returns include the following question: "Did you, at any time during the taxable year, have any interest in or signature or other authority over a bank, securities, or other financial account in a foreign country?" An affirmative answer will require the filing of a Form 4683.

New Techniques in Financial Administration of Taxes

520 DETAILED TECHNIQUES

520.1 INCOME AND EXPENSE ACCOUNTS

520.1-1 SALES AND CONSIGNMENTS

(1) Review the cut-off. Determine if year end sales have been included in the proper accounting period. Determine if the accounting method is acceptable and consistent with prior years.

(2) Review and inquire into entries in the account which appear to be unusual in source, nature, or amount.

(3) Determine whether merchandise is being withdrawn for personal use by corporate officer, etc., and make appropriate adjustment.

(4) Determine if income is being split-up through the use of multiple corporations both domestic and foreign, selling at abnormal prices to affiliates, etc.

(5) In the case of a cash basis taxpayer, test check the collections as recorded in the accounts receivable subsidiary records with the sales entries to determine that they have been properly recorded.

(6) In connection with an installment basis taxpayer, ascertain that collections have been properly segregated as to the year of sale and that the proper gross profit ratios have been applied. Review the unearned or deferred income account to determine if there are any uncollected balances which have been outstanding for an unreasonable period of time. This may provide a lead to diverted collections.

(7) If possible, make tests of quantities of the principal product sold with production or purchases (automobile dealers, builders, etc.).

(8) Test the recording procedures regarding returned merchandise, discounts, claims, rebates, etc. They could disclose pocketing of funds, offset of personal items, etc.

(9) Analyze the nature of income where it appears that a corporation might qualify for special tax treatment (personal holding company, Subchapter S Corporation, Western Hemisphere Trade Corporation, etc.).

(10) Inquire into the handling of miscellaneous income for items such as by-products, scrap materials, supplies, damaged or reclaimed merchandise, sales tax refunds, etc.

(11) Make a test of the footings and totals in the sales journal and trace to the general ledger account. This could disclose diversion of funds, etc.

(12) Inquire as to whether any sales were made or services rendered in exchange for other goods and services. If so, make appropriate adjustments.

(13) Ascertain whether income from consignment sales is picked up at time of sale by consignee.

(14) Review consignment agreements to insure that consigned goods are actually on consignment.

(15) Determine whether profits on consigned goods are taken up at time of shipment, as income is not realized until time of sale.

(16) Where records appear unreliable or are inadequate, consider the possibility of approaching the audit from another standpoint (bank deposit method, net worth method, etc.).

520.1-2 INTEREST AND DIVIDEND INCOME

(1) Be alert to income related to items which may not appear on the records (interest on income tax refund, interest on notes or accounts receivable dividends on investments, share of undistributed foreign personal holding company income, etc.).

(2) Determine if an accrual basis taxpayer has properly included year-end accruals.

(3) Where it is claimed that interest or dividend income is either fully or partially tax-exempt, or non-taxable, determine the

propriety thereof. Be aware also of duplication of credits (foreign dividends received and recorded net of foreign tax paid, and a further credit being taken on the return, etc.).

(4) Ascertain that proper distinction is maintained between dividends from domestic and foreign corporations and interest income. This is especially significant since either type of income may be subject to its own specific exclusion or credit.

520.1-3 RENTAL AND ROYALTY INCOME

(1) Scrutinize transactions with related taxpayers and controlled foreign entities. Look for such features as: shifting income, renting for an inadequate consideration, etc.

(2) Determine if an accrual basis taxpayer has properly accrued income of this type at year end.

(3) Determine whether there may have been income from sources which have no corresponding asset recorded. This is especially true with regard to royalty income and sub-leases.

(4) Be alert to ostensible rental contracts which may be a conditional sale.

(5) Be alert to prepaid rent or lease deposit items that may constitute income when received.

(6) Ascertain whether any nonproductive leases have been terminated where depletion has been claimed in prior years.

520.1-4 SALE OF ASSETS

(1) Reconcile gains or losses shown by books with return. Determine that proper segregation into short-term, long-term, property other than capital assets, etc., has been made.

(2) Consider and verify as necessary, the various factors involved in arriving at the gains or losses reported (i.e., holding period, basis, selling price, expense of sale, etc.).

(3) Determine the propriety of capital loss carry-overs to the year under audit. Also check limitations.

(4) Determine whether income from the sale of assets should be taxed as ordinary income rather than as capital gains in cases such as:

  (a) Dealings in a manner which would constitute a trade or business (real estate developers, building contractors, auto and truck rental business, etc.).

  (b) Dealings with related individuals or controlled foreign entities (substance vs. form).

  (c) Sale of a going business (inventory, etc.).

  (d) Security dealers transferring stocks from inventory to investment account, and treating subsequent sales as sales of capital assets.

  (e) Receivables acquired in a business transaction in exchange for inventories or services.

(5) Ascertain whether sales which reflected no gain or loss are bona fide. Sales to related taxpayers or employees below fair market value could result in ordinary income to the purchaser.

(6) Determine if any trade-ins were reported as sales of capital assets.

(7) Verify sales of property reported on the installment basis and determine if all requirements pertaining thereto have been complied with.

(8) Be alert to sales of contracts between related parties, which may transfer unrealized profits, etc.

(9) Check for excessive depreciation on items sold or exchanged. Rev. Rul. 62–92.

(10) Determine if proper accounting treatment and income reporting were given to salvage value where composite asset accounts are used and individual detail on assets is not maintained.

(11) Be alert to wash sales.

520.1-5 BLOCKED INCOME

(1) If taxpayer has made an election to defer income received in foreign countries due to currency and exchange restrictions, determine that the income is in fact deferrable.

New Techniques in Financial Administration of Taxes

(2) Ascertain that all pertinent information relative to income, deductions and credits has been reported in the required separate return or returns and verify the accuracy.

(3) Be alert to expenditures made by the home office in unblocked currency which are attributable to the production of income received in blocked currency.

520.1-6 OTHER INCOME

Scrutinize transactions with related taxpayers and controlled foreign entities. Look for such features as: shifting income, rendering of managerial and technical services without adequate consideration, etc.

520.1-7 PURCHASES

(1) Review the cut-off. Determine if year-end purchases have been recorded in the proper accounting period (see Inventory Techniques, 520.1-8).

(2) Review entries in the general ledger control account. Note and verify entries which originate from other than usual sources.

(3) Scan purchases column in the cash disbursements journal, voucher register, etc., and look for items unusual in amount and to payees or vendors not generally associated with the products or services handled by the taxpayer.

(4) Determine if the officer-stockholder consumes or withdraws for personal use such items as, food, clothing, appliances, building material, etc. If so, proper reductions should be made to purchases or cost of sales. Also, consider the possible tax effect of such withdrawals to the recipients.

(5) Test check the recorded purchases for a representative period with vendor's invoices and cancelled checks. Be alert to such items as:

    a. Personal expenses (clothing, boats, furniture, etc.)

    b. Capital expenditures

    c. Fictitious or duplicate invoices, etc.

Note—One of the best places to cover up personal and capital items is the purchases account.

(6) If purchases are made from related taxpayers, review a representative number of such transactions to determine if the following are present:

    a. Prices in excess of fair market value.

    b. Excessive rebates and allowances.

    c. Goods or services not received (this would be a good device to improperly withdraw funds and receive a resultant tax deduction).

520.1-8 INVENTORY

(1) Compare inventory balances in the return under examination with the balances for the prior and subsequent year. Verify these with the records.

(2) Determine if the method of valuing inventory is acceptable and has been consistently applied.

(3) Check for significant gross profit percentage variations.

(4) Determine meaning and significance of any notes or qualifying statements in financial reports prepared by independent accounting firms.

(5) Test check accuracy of inventory sheets and other records and trace totals to taxpayer's books and returns (extensions, pricing, unusual write-downs, etc.).

(6) Determine if inventories include the appropriate share of materials, labor, overhead expenses, and non-merchandise items such as supplies, trading stamps, etc., where applicable.

(7) Analyze unusual entries to cost of sales and inventory accounts.

(8) Determine that year-end purchases and goods not on the premises were included in closing inventory (goods on consignment, goods in public warehouses, etc.).

(9) Where a standard cost system is used, analyze the cost of goods sold account

to determine whether the variances from standard cost are substantial, and, if so, whether a proper proportion of such variances are allocated to inventories.

(10) In LIFO cases, determine if proper election has been made for items valued under this method, and verify base stock computations.

(11) Reconcile any difference between inventories shown on balance sheet and inventories shown in cost of goods sold schedule on the return.

520.1-9 OFFICERS' SALARIES

(1) Determine total compensation paid or accrued to principal officers, taking into consideration any compensation claimed under headings other than officers' salaries, such as manufacturing salaries, supervisory salaries, labor, etc., contributions to pension plans for the officers, payments of personal expenses, year-end or other bonuses, etc.

(2) Determine if and to what extent each principal officer's compensation is unreasonable, taking into account such factors as: nature of duties, background and experience, knowledge of the business, size of the business, individual's contribution to profit making, time devoted, economic conditions in general, and locally, character and amount of responsibility, time of year compensation is determined, relationship of stockholder-officer's compensation to stockholdings, whether alleged compensation is in reality, in whole or in part, payment for a business or assets acquired, the amount paid by similar size businesses in the same area to equally qualified employees for similar services, etc.

(3) Be alert to closely held multiple corporation situations in which compensation may be split between two or more related corporations, and which in the aggregate, may be considered excessive to the officer-stockholder.

(4) In closely held corporations, determine that accruals payable to controlling stockholders are paid within the prescribed time limit.

520.1-10 OTHER SALARIES AND WAGES

(1) Through examination of payroll records, retained copies of employment tax returns, inquiry, etc., determine if the wife, children, other close relatives, or servants of officer-stockholders or employees of controlled foreign entities, are on the payroll. If so, determine whether services are actually rendered to the business and the reasonableness of the compensation, taking into account the items under officers' salaries above.

(2) Where internal controls are weak, or in closely held corporations, spot check payroll checks bearing endorsements of an officer, payroll clerk, accounting officer, etc. This may reveal a padded payroll.

520.1-11 REPAIRS AND MAINTENANCE

(1) Make a representative test check of all repair and maintenance expense accounts, job orders, or work orders, to determine if capital expenditures, installation and acquisition costs, personal items, etc., have been deducted. Be alert to duplicate invoices and transactions with related taxpayers.

(2) Compare deductions claimed with that of prior years. If there is a substantial increase, ascertain the reason therefor.

(3) Inquire as to whether any new construction, etc., was done by the taxpayer's employees. If so, determine if the direct costs and appropriate amount of overhead have been capitalized.

(4) Refer to notes taken on inspection of plant which relate to apparent new construction, equipment, etc., and determine if such items have been properly capitalized.

520.1-12 BAD DEBTS

(1) Determine if the method of deducting bad debts is acceptable and consistent with the preceding year. Any change in method should be carefully considered.

(2) Obtain list of accounts charged off. Review to determine if any of the following are present:

    (a) Charge-off of accounts due from officers, stockholders, related taxpayers, controlled foreign entities, etc.

    (b) Charge-off of accounts due from police, politicians, etc.

    (c) Large and unusual items. These should be fully verified.

    (d) Premature charge-offs.

(3) Determine if accounts charged off have previously been included in income.

(4) Where a reserve method of deducting bad debts is used, these additional techniques should be followed:

    (a) Independently compute the additions to the reserve.

    (b) Verify correctness of rate used, making certain that bad debt charge-offs were actual bad debts, and do not include discounts, rebates, etc.

    (c) Determine if the additions to and the balance of the reserve are reasonable.

    (d) Ascertain if reserve has been restored to income on final return or cessation of business.

(5) If accounts charged off were created through installment sales, determine if repossessions, if any, have been properly handled, and if the amount charged off represents only unrecovered cost.

(6) Determine if recoveries are properly handled. Absence of bad debt recoveries may indicate diversion of funds, etc.

(7) Test check accounts charged off with subsidiary ledger accounts. Note any activity subsequent to charge-off. This may indicate that a premature write-off was made.

520.1-13   RENT AND ROYALTY EXPENSE

(1) Where property is rented, leased or licensed from a related taxpayer, or controlled foreign entity, consideration should be given as to whether the amounts paid are reasonable.

(2) Determine if there are any capital expenditures included in the accounts.

(3) Ascertain whether payments in advance have been deducted as expenses. Only such part as pertains to the taxable year is deductible regardless of the accounting method.

(4) Where the recipient is a nonresident alien or other foreign entity, determine if proper amount of tax has been withheld.

(5) Be alert to ostensible rental contracts that may be conditional purchases.

520.1-14   TAXES

(1) Determine that taxes paid or accrued relate to the business of the taxpayer. Be alert to such items as Federal and State income taxes improperly claimed, taxes on domestic employees, taxes on property owned by officer-stockholders, etc.

(2) Determine if deductions include any items of an unsettled or contested nature.

(3) Check year-end accruals of significant items to determine the propriety thereof.

(4) Determine if there are any taxes paid on the purchase of capital assets that should be capitalized.

(5) Determine if any taxes deducted relate to the acquisition or disposition of real property. If so, a proration may be required.

(6) Determine if a deduction has been taken for foreign income taxes and also the foreign tax credit.

520.1-15   INTEREST EXPENSE

(1) Determine if interest paid or accrued applies to obligations due to related taxpayers or controlled foreign entities, if so, be alert to such items as:

    (a) Equity capital vs. debt (thin capital structure).

    (b) Arms length features—
      1. Bona fide obligations.
      2. Interest in excess of the prevailing rates.

(c) Accrual of items payable to related taxpayers which are not paid within the prescribed time limit.

(2) Review interest accruals. Determine if the accruals are based on existing obligations.

(3) Test deductions to ascertain if interest is included on obligations not related to the business (debt of officer-stockholder, etc.).

(4) Determine if the interest deduction includes any principal amounts.

(5) Determine if deductions claimed relate to interest incurred in carrying tax-free obligations.

(6) Where the recipient is a nonresident alien or other foreign entity, determine if the proper amount of tax was withheld.

520.1-16 CONTRIBUTIONS

(1) Ascertain that the organization is one to which contributions made are deductible.

(2) Determine if contributions claimed are the nondeductible personal expense of an individual, such as payments to schools, hospitals, nursing homes, etc.

(3) Determine that limitations have not been exceeded.

(4) Trace entries covering contributions of inventory or stock in trade to ascertain that a double deduction has not been claimed; once as a contribution and again as a direct or indirect part of cost of goods sold. Also consider reasonableness of fair market value claimed on contributions made in kind.

(5) In checking other expense accounts, such as advertising, etc., be alert to contributions which have been included therein to avoid disallowance under percentage limitations, especially in loss years or where listed contributions are near the maximum allowable.

(6) If a deduction has been claimed for accrued contributions, determine if the item was properly authorized by the Board of Directors in the year deducted and paid within the time prescribed. Be alert to possible accrual in one year and duplication of the deduction when paid in the subsequent year.

(7) Verify correctness of any contribution carryover.

520.1-17 CASUALTY AND THEFT LOSSES

(1) Ascertain that a loss has actually occurred. Property may have been fully depreciated, non-existent, sold, previously expensed, lost, etc.

(2) Ascertain that the loss is claimed in the proper year—casualty losses generally in the year incurred—theft in the year discovered.

(3) Ascertain that insurance proceeds or claims, salvage proceeds, or salvage value have been properly taken into account.

(4) Ascertain that the adjusted basis has been properly computed. Where a loss is claimed based on partial destruction, using fair market value before and after the casualty, consider reasonableness of values used in the computation, and ascertain that the loss claimed does not exceed the adjusted basis.

(5) Ascertain that rules as to the manner of deductibility have been complied with (type of asset, whether insured or not, time held, etc.).

(6) In cash basis cases, be alert to the possibility that cash stolen may not have been included in income.

(7) Trace handling of losses involving inventory or stock in trade to ascertain that a double deduction is not claimed.

(8) Analyze any losses claimed for assets located in a foreign country.

520.1-18 ABANDONMENT AND DEMOLITION LOSSES

(1) Determine if an abandonment or demolition has actually occurred.

(2) Investigate any loss claimed due to threat of seizure by a foreign government.

(3) Verify the basis of the asset and the related reserves.

(4) Ascertain the period to which such loss is applicable

(5) Determine if salvage value has been taken into account in computing net loss.

(6) Ascertain if the abandonment or demolition was related to the acquisition or construction of new property, incurred for the purpose of securing a lease, etc. If so, consideration should be given to capitalizing the remaining basis and cost of removal.

(7) Determine if the retirement or abandonment loss is specifically allowable under the taxpayer's method of accounting for depreciable property.

(8) If the property was used in or relates to the operation of a mineral property where percentage depletion is claimed, determine if such loss has been included as an operating cost.

520.1-19   DEPLETION—GENERAL

(1) Utilize special depletion forms such as Form M (mines), Form O (oil and gas), or Form T (timber) where applicable and available. If such forms have not been filed currently, or filed in prior years and not brought up to date currently, and if considered essential in the case, the taxpayer should be requested to submit the form or equivalent information.

(2) If considered necessary, request engineering advice or assistance in the case.

520.1-20   COST DEPLETION

(1) Determine that any prior elections binding on subsequent years have been complied with.

(2) Determine that any aggregation or separation of mineral interests are proper.

(3) Determine that recoverable units are based on the latest geological or engineering surveys applicable to the property and that recoverable units with respect to all mineral interests included in each aggregation are taken into account.

(4) Be aware of the various types of expenditures which are recoverable only through depletion with regard to the type of operation on which depletion is claimed or allowable, and ascertain that no such expenditures paid or incurred in the period under review have been expensed, or capitalized as a depreciable or amortizable item.

(5) Ascertain that the adjusted basis of the property has been properly computed, giving particular attention to prior percentage or discovery depletion taken which may not be recorded on the books (review retained copies of prior year returns and RAR's where available). Also, consider allocation of lump-sum purchases between land, mineral, timber, etc.

(6) If a March 1, 1913, valuation is used as a basis for cost depletion, be especially alert to the possibility that the original rate per unit is being improperly used without adjustment for additions to or subtractions from the property and redeterminations of recoverable units after the original valuation.

(7) In regard to timber depletion, determine whether growth of timber has been properly taken into account in determining recoverable units.

(8) Determine that depletion is claimed only on minerals and not on land used for other purposes.

520.1-21   PERCENTAGE DEPLETION

(1) Ascertain that the taxpayer has an economic interest in the mineral in place.

(2) Determine that any aggregation of mineral interests are proper.

(3) Ascertain that the sales reported in regard to each property do not include sales applicable to another property, sales of purchased minerals, nonmineral sales, or other income items.

(4) Ascertain, where applicable, that mineral sales have been adjusted to "gross

income from the property" by reduction for such factors as unallowable treatment costs, unallowable transportation costs, rents and royalties, including a proportionate part of lease bonuses, amounts paid to others in contract mining or similar operations where the other party has acquired an economic interest and is entitled to depletion, certain ad valorem property taxes, trade discounts allowed, etc.

(5) In situations in which the basis for percentage depletion is not the actual sales price of a finished product, but a value of the mineral at the point at which it has passed through the last allowable treatment process applicable thereto, determine if the value used is the correct representative market or field price.

(6) Ascertain that mineral sales made to a business controlled by the taxpayer are not inflated to gain a tax advantage through depletion.

(7) Ascertain that all expenses applicable to a property have been charged to that property, including intangible development costs and a proper allocation of general, administrative, and overhead expenses. Be alert to shifting of expenses from a profit year to a loss year by overaccruals, underaccruals, or prepayments. Also, casualty, demolition, or abandonment losses applicable to the property should be included in cost of operations.

(8) Be alert to possible reduction of expenses by improper offsets such as income from scrap sales, cash discounts earned, sales of assets, etc.

(9) Consider whether nonproductive activities involving the furnishing of goods or services to employees at prices or amounts which consistently result in losses on that activity should be held to constitute a cost of operating the mineral property (housing furnished employees, merchandise sold at or below cost, etc.).

(10) Ascertain that the proper rates of depletion and the statutory limitations have been complied with.

520.1-22 DEPRECIATION AND AMORTIZATION

(1) Compare total depreciation as shown by the depreciation schedule with the deduction claimed on the return. Reconcile any differences. Be alert for duplication of deductions.

(2) Determine if the method and basis used for computing depreciation or amortization is acceptable and applied in accordance with applicable laws, rulings, and regulations.

(3) Review the rates to determine if they are reasonable.

(4) Determine if an appropriate amount of salvage value has been taken into account.

(5) In the case of items on which amortization is claimed or is applicable, review leases, franchises, certificates of necessity, etc., to verify if the period and amount used is correct. Also determine if accelerated depreciation is being claimed on items which should be amortized.

(6) Test check a representative number of items listed on the depreciation schedule, to determine if the depreciation reserve at the end of the accounting period exceeds the depreciable basis of the asset, taking into account salvage value where applicable.

(7) Test check some extensions and prove footings to determine if current depreciation has been correctly computed.

(8) Determine if there is any personal use of assets by officer-stockholders.

(9) Ascertain if proper allocation has been made on bulk purchase of depreciable and nondepreciable assets.

(10) Determine that proper election has been made for accelerated first-year allowances.

(11) If necessary, request engineering advice or assistance.

(12) *Revenue Procedure 62-21*

This Procedure is to be used in connection with income tax returns filed on or after

July 12, 1962 (without regard to extensions of time).

(a) *Class Lives*

1. Ascertain that all assets have been included in the correct guideline class.

2. Determine whether taxpayer has included any fully depreciated assets in determining class life.

3. Insure that taxpayer has computed the straight-line depreciation on all assets in determining the class life when other methods were used in claiming depreciation.

(b) *Reserve Ratio Test*

1. Insure that fully depreciated assets have been included in the basis of the assets in computing the reserve ratio.

2. Determine whether the taxpayer properly qualifies under the "transitional rule" applicable for the first three taxable years to which the Revenue Procedure applies.

3. Determine whether a taxpayer, using two or more methods of depreciation with respect to assets falling within a guideline class, computed the correct weighted average of the separate reserve ratio ranges determined for the different methods of depreciation.

4. Where a taxpayer wishes to use the Reserve Ratio Table to demonstrate that his retirement and replacement practices support the life used or a proposed change in the life used for prior years, a determination should be made as to whether the taxpayer meets the conditions set forth in Part II of the Procedure.

520.1-23   PENSION, ANNUITY AND PROFIT SHARING PLANS

(1) Where pensions are paid directly to stockholders or close relatives, ascertain that the recipient was an employee and that the pension paid is reasonable in relation to prior service, etc.

(2) Ascertain whether the employee trust or plan giving rise to a deduction is a qualified trust or plan. In this connection, consideration must be given to the provisions of the original trust instrument or plan, whether exemption or approval of the trust or plan has been secured, subsequent changes if any, and actual operation of the plan or trust.

(3) Consider the requirements and limitations applicable to the type of plan or trust in question and to deductions related thereto, and determine if the deductions claimed are allowable in the light of such requirements and limitations. Verify payments to determine if they were paid within the prescribed time and are correct in amount.

(4) In the case of plan termination or other taxable distributions, be alert to whether information returns were properly filed.

(5) Ascertain whether stock option plan meets the qualifications for a restricted stock option.

(6) Follow District procedures for any special reports or other requirements covering this type deduction.

520.1-24   LEGAL AND PROFESSIONAL

(1) The broad classification of "legal and professional" embraces many types of services. In considering such expenses, it should be kept in mind that account classifications vary widely among taxpayers, and may be grouped in a single account, or separate accounts. Typical account classifications are: legal, accounting, engineering, appraisals, surveys, etc.

(a) Verify expenses claimed in regard to the acquisition or sale of property, lease arrangements, etc. Such items may be capital expenditures.

(b) Ascertain if criminal defense or lobbying expenses have been claimed.

(c) Determine if any expenses relate to exempt or partially exempt income.

(d) Insure that legal fees are not applicable to the personal affairs of the taxpayer.

(e) If the expense deductions are based on retainer fees, determine whether the professional services received cover items of a capital or nondeductible nature. Consider the propriety of allocating an appropriate share to such items.

(f) Fees paid for professional services rendered on behalf of a related foreign entity should be analyzed.

(g) Verify expenses relating to the issuance of bonds, stock, reorganizations, liquidations, proxy contests, etc.

520.1-25 INSURANCE

(1) Be alert to personal insurance premiums claimed as a business expense.

(2) Check life insurance premiums claimed as an expense to ascertain that the employer is not the beneficiary, either directly or indirectly. Inquire as to whether premiums taxable to employees are included in wage statements or in other information documents.

(3) Check for the expensing of premiums covering periods subsequent to the year under review.

(4) If there has been a fire or other casualty, ascertain that insurance proceeds received or claims pending have been properly accounted for, including use and occupancy, business interruption, and similar types of insurance. If a fire or other casualty occurred in a prior period, inquire as to proper handling in the prior and current period.

(5) Be alert to policies cancelled and ascertain that any rebates of premiums are properly accounted for.

(6) Where life insurance premiums have been paid by a corporation but not deducted as an expense, determine if officer-stockholders, etc. are the owners or beneficiaries. If so, this would constitute dividends or additional compensation.

(7) In corporate cases where cash value of officer's life insurance does not appear as an asset or the premiums cleared through Schedule "M," be alert to the possibility that premiums are being improperly expensed.

(8) Where a life insurance policy is transferred from the corporation to an employee, it may result in taxable income to the employee. Furthermore there may be unearned premium transferred without adequate consideration.

520.1-26 TRAVEL AND ENTERTAINMENT

(1) *General*

(a) Many T and E items are not identified as such on returns filed by taxpayers, being earmarked instead under the functional activities which generate the expense, for example, a T and E item might be listed as "advertising," "promotion," "selling," "miscellaneous," etc., expense.

(b) The amounts spent for T and E items are deductible if they are ordinary and necessary business expenses. The records with respect to these expenditures should be checked to ascertain that the taxpayer uses acceptable accounting procedures in requiring an accounting from employees. The records should be in sufficient detail to establish the following:

1. The relationship of the expenditure to the business.

2. The payee and place of expenditure.

3. The amount of the expenditure.

4. The identity of the persons involved, including parties entertained, if any.

(2) *Techniques*

(a) Determine the corporation's policy with respect to reimbursing or giv-

New Techniques in Financial Administration of Taxes

ing allowances to officers and employees for T and E expenses.

(b) Ascertain the specific accounts in which T and E items are recorded.

(c) Prepare a summary of the totals posted to the accounts containing T and E items, and identify same with the deduction for T and E expenses claimed on the tax return.

(d) Select a representative test period (or periods). All T and E items within said period (or periods) must be broken down and classified in the suggested broad categories shown in the sample workpapers.

(e) Examine selected items within each of the aforesaid suggested categories. This is necessary in order to establish the reliability of the records and to afford a reasonable basis for determining which categories should be further examined in depth, which categories should be further test-checked, and which categories do not warrant further examination.

1. Ascertain from the foregoing tests whether the corporate officers and employees have properly accounted for the expenditures claimed to have been made by them for which they received reimbursement or an expense allowance.

2. Ascertain whether expenses accounted for by officers and employees include items of a personal or nonbusiness nature which should be charged to them as additional income.

3. Particular attention should be given to such items as company-owned or rented automobiles, hunting lodges, fishing camps, resort property, pleasure boats or yachts, airplanes, apartments and hotel suites; families at conventions or business meetings; expense-paid vacations of officers or employees, or members of their families, not reported on Form W-2.

4. Cash expenditures and checks payable to corporate officers, stockholders, and employees closely related by blood or marriage to them, should be closely examined as to the actual making of the expenditures and the corporate business purpose thereof.

(f) If the questions on the return pertaining to hunting lodges, resort property, etc., are not answered, inquiry should be made in regard thereto.

(g) Consider whether the facts of the case warrant fraud referral, or the application of the civil fraud or negligence penalty.

(h) If the records with respect to these expenditures are inadequate, consideration should be given to the issuance of an inadequate records letter.

520.1-27 MISCELLANEOUS EXPENSES

(1) Require adequate substantiation for deductions claimed.

(2) Determine whether the deduction contains any personal items. Consider the possibility of treating such amount as dividends or additional compensation to the recipients.

520.2 BALANCE SHEET ACCOUNTS

520.2-1 CASH ON HAND AND IN BANK

(1) Review cash disbursements journal for a representative period. Note any missing check numbers, checks drawn to order of cash, bearer, etc.; large or unusual items; and determine propriety thereof through a comparison with vouchers, journal entries, etc.

(a) In the case of a cash basis taxpayer, ascertain if checks were written and recorded which were issued after the close of the year under examination.

(b) Give special consideration to checks issued for cashier's checks, sight drafts, etc., where the payee and nature are not clearly shown.

(2) Obtain bank statements and cancelled checks for cash bank account for one or more months, including the last month of the period under examination.

   (a) Compare deposits shown by bank statement against entries in cash receipts book.

   (b) Note year-end bank overdrafts in case of cash basis taxpayer. This may indicate expenses which are unallowable since funds were not available for payment.

   (c) Determine if any checks have remained outstanding for an unreasonable time. This may indicate an improper deduction or duplication of disbursements. Old outstanding checks possibly could be restored to income.

   (d) Determine whether voided checks have been properly handled.

   (e) For a test period, check endorsements to see if they are the same as payee, noting any endorsements by owner, or questionable endorsements.

(3) Review cash receipts journal for items not identified with ordinary business sales, being alert to such items as sales of assets, prepaid income, income received under claim of right, etc.

(4) If records appear unreliable, tests of footings and postings should be made for a representative period.

(5) Investigate entries in general ledger cash account. Look for unusual items which do not originate from cash receipts or disbursements journals. These entries may indicate unauthorized withdrawals or expenditures, sales of capital assets, omitted sales, etc.

(6) Test check some cash sales with cash book to ascertain if they have been correctly recorded. Also check cash sales made at the beginning and end of the period under examination to determine if year-end sales have been recorded in the proper accounting period.

(7) Test check disbursements from petty cash to determine if there are any unallowable items included.

(8) Question any unusual or apparently exorbitant sales discounts or allowances.

(9) Scrutinize cash overages and shortages, being alert to irregularities which may have cleared through these accounts.

(10) Review cash on hand account to determine if there are any credit balances during the period under examination. This may indicate unrecorded receipts.

520.2-2 NOTES AND ACCOUNTS RECEIVABLE

(1) Check entries in general ledger control accounts. Look for unusual items, especially those which do not originate from the sales or cash receipts journals.

(2) Segregate amounts due from officer-stockholders, directors, domestic and foreign affiliates, etc., for consideration of less than arms length features, disguised compensation, dividends, etc.

(3) Determine if subsidiary ledgers are in agreement with control accounts, and, if not, ascertain the reasons for any differences.

(4) Note any credit balances in the general ledger or subsidary accounts. This may indicate deposits or overpayments which could be considered as additional income, or unrecorded sales.

(5) Some credit sales invoices and postings should be test checked from the sale journal to the subsidiary and control account.

(6) Determine whether accrued income on interest bearing notes or accounts has been included in income.

(7) Where taxpayer reflects an accrual method by subtracting beginning receivables and adding ending receivables to cash collected, consider checking the detailed listing of receivables at the beginning of the period to the cash receipts book. This may disclose diverting of funds, etc. Determine if begin-

ning receivables used in the computation are the same as the ending receivables of the preceding year.

(8) Insure that return conforms to books in terms of method of accounting.

520.2-3   INVESTMENTS

(1) Analyze sales and other credit entries with regard to the following:

(a) Gains or losses (basis, wash sales, interest included in sales price, etc.).

(b) Other (exchanges, write-down, write-offs, transactions with related taxpayers, controlled foreign entities or entities organized in "tax haven" countries).

(2) Review debit entries. Consider such items as:

(a) Non-taxable securities acquired with borrowed funds.

(b) Other acquisitions (transactions with related taxpayers, noncash acquisitions, creation, organization, or reorganization of a foreign corporation, etc.).

(3) Become familiar with the nature of investments, utilizing any records maintained by the taxpayer. Make necessary test checks to determine if related income has been properly reported (dividends, interest, etc.).

(4) If shares of stock are held in a foreign corporation, determine whether it is a foreign personal holding company.

520.2-4   DEPRECIABLE ASSETS

(1) Determine whether assets shown on the depreciation schedule which have a prior year acquisition date, are the same as shown on the tax return for the immediate preceding period. If not, this would point up depreciation being taken on assets which have previously been expensed or fully depreciated, etc.

(2) Review additions during the period. Test by reference to invoices, contracts, etc., giving consideration to the following:

(a) Note items which appear to have originated from unusual resources such as appraisal increases, transfers, exchanges, etc., and determine propriety thereof.

(b) Determine if costs relating to the acquisition and installation of assets, leasehold improvements, etc., have been capitalized.

(c) Ascertain if assets include items of a personal nature.

(d) Where construction or any other work of a capital nature is performed with the taxpayer's own equipment, labor, etc., for its own use, be certain that the basis of such asset includes the proper elements of material, labor and overhead, including depreciation.

(e) With regard to the basis of assets, consider such items as trade-ins, acquisitions from related taxpayers, allocations of cost between land and building, etc.

(3) Decreases in the asset accounts during the year should be noted. Gains or losses resulting therefrom should be verified.

(a) Ascertain if taxpayer has transferred assets to a controlled domestic or foreign corporation for less than fair consideration.

520.2-5   VALUATION RESERVES

(1) Review nature and source of all accounts and ascertain whether they are being used as a means of diverting or understating income, or claiming unallowable deductions.

(2) *Bad Debts Reserve*

(See techniques for bad debt expense 520.1-12).

(3) *Depreciation, Amortization, and Depletion Reserves*

Determine whether any of these are contingent reserves. Check for reasonableness of any addition.

520.2-6 INTANGIBLE ASSETS

(1) Test check current additions to determine if the basis includes the proper elements of cost, such as legal fees, application fees, etc.

(2) Determine if there have been any transactions with related taxpayers or controlled foreign entities. If so, consider arms length features.

(3) Determine if income applicable to intangibles has been included in income. In this connection be aware that it is not necessary for an intangible to have a basis or to appear on the records (e.g., subleases, overriding royalties, franchises, etc.).

(4) Be alert to any situation or transaction which logically could have given rise to an intangible which may have been expensed through inventories, fixed assets, expenses, etc. (e.g., purchase of a going business—which could involve good will, convenant not to compete, etc.).

(5) Analyze any transaction involving transfer of foreign rights to a foreign entity for an equity interest or for a nominal consideration.

520.2-7 PREPAID EXPENSES AND DEFERRED CHARGES

Make at least a cursory check as to the nature and source of these assets, and the manner in which they are charged off to expense. Prepaid expenses are generally present in all businesses. The absence of such items should be considered, since a distortion of income may be involved.

520.2-8 OTHER ASSETS

The nature and classification of other asset accounts should be considered to determine if they have a bearing on tax liability.

520.2-9 EXCHANGE, CLEARING OR SUSPENSE ACCOUNT

Determine nature and purpose of the account. Test check debit and credit entries, being aware of the possibility that such account may be used as a means for diverting sales, padding expenses, etc.

520.2-10 CURRENT AND ACCRUED LIABILITIES, INCLUDING NOTES PAYABLE

(1) Note any debit balances in the general ledger or subsidiary accounts. This may indicate diversion of funds, etc. Also note accounts which have long overdue balances. This may indicate contested liabilities and liabilities which no longer exist such as unclaimed wages, unclaimed deposits, items set up twice, etc.

(2) Review computation of year-end accruals with respect to their allowability as expenses or purchases. Also see that accruals set up at the end of the preceding year were either reversed in the current year or that the actual expenses were charged against them when paid. Be alert to large year-end items which have been shifted between years for the taxpayer's advantage.

(3) Determine if subsidiary ledgers are in agreement with controls, and, if not, ascertain the reasons of any differences.

(4) Determine if accrued items payable to related taxpayers, were paid within the time limit prescribed.

(5) Investigate entries in the general ledger control accounts. Look for unusual items, especially those which do not originate from the voucher register or cash disbursements journals. This may disclose unreported income, improper or overstated expense.

(6) Analyze amounts due to officer-stockholders, directors, domestic and foreign affiliates, etc., for consideration of arms-length features, thin capitalization, diversion of funds, constructive receipts of income, etc.

520.2-11 FIXED LIABILITIES

(1) Financing arrangements such as bonds, mortgages, debentures, certificates of indebtedness, etc., are areas in which substantial adjustments are quite often found.

New Techniques in Financial Administration of Taxes

The examiner, therefore, should acquaint himself with pertinent details with regard to such financing arrangements and consider possible adjustment areas as follows:

    (a) Legal, professional and other expenses of issuance.

    (b) Discounts and premiums on issuance or redemption.

    (c) Basis of assets received in exchange for bonds, etc.

    (d) Refunding of debt.

    (e) Transactions with related taxpayers and controlled foreign entities.

    (f) Ratio of debt to equity capital.

    (g) Related expense accounts (interest and amortization).

(2) Scrutinize any long-term outstanding liability to a controlled foreign corporation, as this may represent an equity interest rather than a creditor interest.

520.2-12 OTHER LIABILITIES

The nature and classification of other liability accounts should be considered to determine if they have any bearing on tax liability.

520.2-13 CAPITAL STOCK

(1) Review all capital stock accounts—give adequate consideration to the following:

    (a) *No changes during period*—Even though no changes in the total outstanding stock appear on the balance sheet or in the general ledger control accounts, consideration should be given to such features as:

        1. Subchapter S Corporations. Is there a valid election, number and changes in stockholders, limitation on losses, etc.

        2. Dealings in stock between shareholders. Check gains or losses to the individuals concerned, where the corporation ultimately becomes involved in such transactions and consider the possibility of distributions being essentially equivalent to a taxable dividend.

        3. Closely held companies should receive special consideration throughout the examination for such items as arms-length features, disguised dividends, etc.

    (b) *New issues and additions during the period*

        1. Compare data obtained from the corporate minute book and charter with items recorded on books to determine if proper entries have been made.

        2. Verify all credit entries. Give consideration to such features as: stock issued for services or properties, stock dividends, employee stock options, stock issued at less than fair market value, re-organizations, taxable and non-taxable exchanges, etc.

        3. Determine if expenses relating to the issuance of stock have been properly handled (legal fees, registration fees, etc.).

        4. Determine if documentary stamps have been acquired and properly affixed, and cost correctly reflected.

    (c) *Reductions and cancellations during the period*

        1. Compare data obtained from the corporate charter and minute book with items recorded on books to determine if proper entries have been made.

        2. Verify all debit entries. Give consideration to such features as partial or complete redemptions, cancellations, or liquidations; write-offs; distributions essentially equivalent to dividends; etc.

    (d) *Treasury stock*

If treasury stock transactions have occurred, consider such possibilities as acquisitions being essentially equivalent to dividends, etc.

520.2-14 SURPLUS

(1) Analyze and reconcile the surplus accounts. Verify correctness of all items, both increases and decreases, appearing on the books or return.

(2) Consider whether the surplus has been improperly accumulated beyond the reasonable needs of the business.

520.2-15 SURPLUS RESERVES

Review nature and sources of all accounts and ascertain whether they are being used as a means of diverting or understating income, or claiming unallowable deductions.

520.3 MISCELLANEOUS

520.3-1 LIQUIDATIONS AND REORGANIZATIONS

(1) Liquidations and reorganizations are highly technical areas which must be carefully considered. Specific audit steps must be determined in the light of the facts in each case, but the following steps are considered essential:

(a) Obtain a copy of the plan and refer to notes taken from the minute books in regard thereto.

(b) Determine the section or sections of law and regulations applicable and ascertain that each party involved has complied therewith. Where a foreign corporation is a party, determine that proper clearance has been secured.

(c) Determine taxability or nontaxability with regard to each party involved.

(d) Review entries made to record the transaction and ascertain propriety thereof.

(e) Be alert to special provisions of law and regulations governing basis of property in the hands of the transferee in certain liquidations and reorganizations, and those governing carryovers in reorganizations. Ascertain that such provisions have been complied with.

(f) Determine if expenses applicable to liquidations and reorganizations have been properly handled (legal and professional fees, certain taxes paid to a state where a tax-free transaction occurs, etc.).

520.3-2 FOREIGN BRANCH ACCOUNT

(1) Analyze the account.

(2) Determine if the branch profit has been included in taxable income.

(3) Have taxpayer submit a trial balance of branch operations and an analysis of unusual and substantial items.

(4) Determine if there has been duplication of deductions, elimination of income, or claiming of unallowable deductions.

(5) Check exchange rates used and computation of conversion.

(a) Have exchange gains and losses been actually realized?

520.4 FOREIGN CORPORATIONS

The additional techniques outlined below were devised for use in examinations involving foreign corporations. They are equally applicable in cases involving Western Hemisphere Trade Corporations. Certain of the techniques are also applicable in examinations involving allocation of income and deductions between related domestic entities.

520.4-1 RECOGNITION OF THE CORPORATE ENTITY

(1) Secure statement from the appropriate officer of the domestic parent corporation giving reasons for the formation of the foreign subsidiary and the selection of the foreign country in which it was organized.

(2) Scrutinize the minute book of the domestic parent corporation to determine whether it contains a record of any discussion or other information concerning the decision to form the subsidiary.

(3) Prepare a schedule comparing the capital invested with the subsequent sales and earnings and show ratios.

(4) Determine if there was a significant change in the operating results of the parent after the creation of the subsidiary.

(5) Request copies of the parent's procedural manuals covering operations before and after the creation of the subsidiary. Compare and determine if there has been any substantive change in the method of operations.

(6) Determine whether the subsidiary has assets commensurate with the scope and volume of business.

(7) Analyze payroll records of the subsidiary to determine the number, type and function of the employees and officers.

(8) Prepare schedule of officers and directors of both the parent and subsidiary.

(9) Determine whether the subsidiary operates on the credit and goodwill of the parent.

(10) Determine whether the subsidiary is absorbing its own bad debt losses or is shifting them to the parent.

(11) Determine whether the subsidiary's liquid assets are being appropriated by the parent. From the subsidiary's financial statements, prepare a statement of source and application of funds.

(12) Determine whether the subsidiary is still in existence and operating. If it was liquidated within a short period after its creation, ascertain the reason. If it is dormant, ascertain what disposition was made of its assets.

(13) If the subsidiary is allegedly a sales or purchasing organization, determine the following:

    (a) Whether the sales or purchases are directly or indirectly negotiated by the parent.

    (b) Whether it took actual possession of the goods.

    (c) Whether it maintains an inventory of goods, exclusive of goods in transit.

    (d) If an inventory is maintained abroad, determine what portion of the sales or purchases are filled from the foreign warehouse.

(e) Whether new business or sources of supply are being developed through the efforts of the subsidiary or that of the parent.

520.4-2   CONSTRUCTIVE DIVIDENDS

(1) Prepare a schedule of dividends actually paid by the subsidiary since its inception.

(2) Prepare a schedule showing dates and amounts of loans to the parent or controlling interests, and dates and amounts of repayments together with all other pertinent information.

(3) Prepare a schedule comparing, on an annual basis, the parent's payables to the subsidiary at the end of each year with the subsidiary's annual sales and the subsidiary's accumulated earnings at the end of each year.

(4) Prepare a schedule on a monthly basis showing the subsidiary's net quick assets balance and the net working capital balance and compare with loans to and repayments by the parent.

(5) Where the subsidiary is repaying long-outstanding loans, determine if the subsidiary was ever thinly capitalized.

(6) Where there is a long-outstanding payable to an unrelated party on the parent's books, determine if the foreign subsidiary might have paid the debt.

(7) Where there are any sales to or purchases from the subsidiary, resulting in long-term gains to the parent or large losses to the subsidiary, determine if the consideration was a fair price and trace the history of the asset before and after the transaction.

(8) Analyze any dividends from the subsidiary which are allegedly liquidating dividends.

520.4-3   ENGAGED IN TRADE OR BUSINESS

(1) Determine whether the activity in which the foreign corporation engaged constitutes carrying on a trade or business.

(2) Determine if a significant part of the vital business activities are conducted in the United States, such as,

(a) Having an agent in the United States who has authority either expressed or implied, and exercises this authority to negotiate and execute contracts.

(b) Operating property located in the United States.

(c) Having substantial assets, including bank accounts, in the United States.

(d) Having an office or place of business in the United States.

(e) Having officers in the United States who make management decisions.

(f) Deriving a significant part of its income from sources within the United States.

(3) Where applicable, determine whether the foreign corporation has a permanent establishment in the United States within the meaning of the treaty involved.

520.4-4 SOURCES OF INCOME—SALES OF PERSONAL PROPERTY

(1) Secure copies of the distributor agreement between the affiliates.

(2) Secure copies of the sub-distributors' agreements granted by the foreign subsidiary and compare these with the distributor agreements granted by the domestic parent prior to the formation of the subsidiary.

(3) Review the correspondence between the domestic parent and foreign distributors notifying them of the new general foreign distributor.

(4) Schedule the dates on which each foreign sub-distributor's business was first channeled through the foreign subsidiary. Where the change-over was unduly delayed, determine whether the delay was occasioned by negotiating changes in the terms of sale.

(5) Secure the domestic parent's operating manual before and after the creation of the foreign subsidiary. Note changes in instructions regarding terms of sale and routing of shipments.

(6) Secure copies of instructions to the freight forwarders before and after the creation of the foreign subsidiary. Note changes in routing of shipments.

(7) Obtain a full set of all correspondence and documents prepared by the domestic and foreign affiliate, for a representative number of typical sales. Analyze and determine where in form title passed to the foreign customer and whether the form agrees with the substance of the transaction.

(8) Determine whether the trade association for the industry has published trading rules. If affirmative, note if the form of the transactions follows the usages of the trade.

520.4-5 SOURCES OF INCOME—OTHER

Determine that all other income, such as interest, dividends, rents and royalties and gains from sale of real property, derived from sources within and without the United States, were properly treated.

520.4-6 ALLOCATION OF INCOME AND DEDUCTIONS

(1) Determine whether the foreign corporation controls or is controlled by a foreign or domestic corporation.

(2) Determine if they are doing business with each other.

(3) Discuss with the appropriate officer the policy regarding dealings between the related or affiliated entities as compared with unrelated entities.

(4) Secure copies of returns filed by the domestic corporation, if any, and compare gross profit and expenditures with those of the foreign corporation.

(5) Make a tentative computation of the tax consequences of any apparent shifting of income.

(6) If it is necessary to allocate intercompany sales, purchases, commissions, royalties, or servicing income, refer to appropriate techniques.

520.5 WESTERN HEMISPHERE TRADE CORPORATIONS

520.5-1 GENERAL

Discuss with an appropriate official the policy with regards to source of purchases of goods and assets, location of customers, terms of sales and investments.

520.5-2 SOURCE OF INCOME TEST

(1) Secure copies of the distributor agreement between the parent and subsidiary.

(2) Secure copies of sub-distributor agreements granted by the subsidiary and compare these with distributor agreements granted by the parent prior to the creation of the subsidiary.

(3) Review correspondence between the parent and the foreign distributors notifying them of the new general distributor.

(4) Schedule the dates on which each foreign sub-distributor's business was first channeled through the subsidiary. Where the change-over was unduly delayed, determine whether the delay was occasioned by negotiating changes in the terms of sale.

(5) Secure the parent's operating manual before and after the creation of the subsidiary. Note any change in instructions regarding terms of sale and routing of shipment.

(6) Secure instructions to freight forwarders before and after the creation of the subsidiary and note changes in routing of shipments.

(7) Obtain a full set of all correspondence and documents prepared by the parent and subsidiary, for a representative number of typical transactions. Analyze and determine where, in form, title passes to the foreign customer and whether the form agrees with the substance of the transaction.

(8) Determine whether the trade association for the industry has published trading rules. If affirmative, note if the form of the transaction follows the usages of the trade.

(9) Prepare a schedule for the current year and the preceding two years, listing sales made within the United States, and determine the gross income derived therefrom. Add investment income derived from source within the United States. Compare total gross income derived from sources within the United States with total gross income.

520.5-3 BUSINESS TEST

(1) Scrutinize the method of computing gross income from sales to determine that all elements of cost are properly considered in arriving at gross income.

(2) Ascertain that investment income has been properly accrued and reported during the three-year period.

(3) Compare investment income with total gross income.

520.5-4 LOCATION TEST

(1) Analyze the fixed asset accounts and determine the source of each acquisition made during the year. Purchases made through the parent should be traced to supplier.

(2) Scan accounts payable ledger and test-check entries in purchase journal to determine source of goods, materials and supplies purchased during the year.

(3) Determine if purchases made outside the Western Hemisphere were minor, in relation to the business for the year, and non-recurring or unusual.

(4) Compare purchases from sources outside the Western Hemisphere with total gross receipts for the year.

Handbook for Special Agents

Table of Contents

- **100 Statutory Provisions**
- **110 Introduction**
- **120 Criminal Penalties Applicable to Fraud and Miscellaneous Investigations**
- 121 Internal Revenue Code of 1954
- 121.1 Effective Date and Application
- 121.2 IRC 7201—Attempt to Evade or Defeat Tax
- 121.3 IRC 7202—Willful Failure to Collect or Pay Over Tax
- 121.4 IRC 7203—Willful Failure to File Return, Supply Information, or Pay Tax
- 121.5 IRC 7204—Fraudulent Statement or Failure to Make Statement to Employees
- 121.6 IRC 7205—Fraudulent Withholding Exemption Certificate or Failure to Supply Information
- 121.7 IRC 7206—Fraud and False Statements
- 121.8 IRC 7207—Fraudulent Returns, Statements, or Other Documents
- 121.9 IRC 7210—Failure to Obey Summons
- 121.(10) IRC 7212—Attempts to Interfere With Administration of Internal Revenue Laws
- 121.(11) Outline of Other Criminal Penalties
- 121.(12) IRC 7215—Offenses With Respect to Collected Taxes
- 121.(13) IRC 7212—Separate Accounting for Certain Collected Taxes, etc.
- 122 Title 18, United States Code
- 122.1 Introduction
- 122.2 Section 2—Principals
- 122.3 Section 3—Accessory After the Fact
- 122.4 Section 4—Misprision of Felony
- 122.5 Section 111—Assaulting, Resisting, or Impeding Certain Officers or Employees
- 122.6 Section 201—Offer to Officer or Other Person
- 122.7 Section 284—Disqualifications of Former Officers and Employees in Matters Connected With Former Duties
- 122.8 Section 285—Taking or Using Papers Relating to Claims
- 122.9 Section 286—Conspiracy to Defraud Government With Respect to Claims
- 122.(10) Section 287—False, Fictitious or Fraudulent Claims
- 122.(11) Section 371—Conspiracy to Commit Offense or Defraud United States
- 122.(12) Section 372—Conspiracy to Impede or Injure Officer
- 122.(13) Section 494—Contractors' Bonds, Bids, and Public Records
- 122.(14) Section 495—Contracts, Deeds, and Powers of Attorney
- 122.(15) Section 1001—Statements or Entries Generally
- 122.(16) Section 1002—Possession of False Papers to Defraud United States
- 122.(17) Section 1084—Transmission of Wagering Information
- 122.(18) Section 1114—Protection of Officers and Employees of the United States
- 122.(19) Section 1501—Assault on Process Server
- 122.(20) Section 1503—Influencing or Injuring Officer, Juror or Witness Generally
- 122.(21) Section 1510—Obstruction of Criminal Investigations
- 122.(22) Section 1621—Perjury Generally
- 122.(23) Section 1622—Subordination of Perjury
- 122.(24) Section 1623—False Declaration Before a Grand Jury or Court
- 122.(25) Section 1952—Interstate and Foreign Travel or Transportation in Aid of Racketeering Enterprises
- 122.(26) Section 1953—Interstate Transportation of Wagering Paraphernalia
- 122.(27) Section 1955—Prohibition of Illegal Gambling Business
- 122.(28) Section 1962—Prohibited Activities of Racketeer Influenced and Corrupt Organizations
- 122.(29) Section 1963—Criminal Penalties for Racketeer Influenced and Corrupt Organizations
- 122.(30) Section 2071—Concealment, Removal, or Mutilation Generally
- 122.(31) Section 2231—Assault or Resistance
- 122.(32) Section 2232—Destruction or Removal of Property to Prevent Seizure
- 122.(33) Section 2233—Rescue of Seized Property
- **130 Criminal Penalties Applicable to Wagering Tax Investigations**
- 131 IRC 7362—Violation of Occupational Tax Laws Relating to Wagering—Failure to Pay Special Tax
- 132 Other Criminal Penalties
- **140 Periods of Limitation on Criminal Prosecution**
- 141 IRC 6531—Periods of Limitation
- 142 IRC 6513—Time Return Deemed Filed and Tax Considered Paid
- 143 Title 18, United States Code—General Statute of Limitations—Section 3282—Offenses Not Capital
- 144 Title 18, United States Code—Fugitive From Justice
- 144.1 Section 3290—Fugitives From Justice
- 144.2 Section 1073—Flight to Avoid Prosecution or Giving Testimony
- **150 Civil Penalties Applicable to Fraud and Miscellaneous Investigations**
- 151 Introduction
- 152 Internal Revenue Code of 1954, as Amended by Tax Reform Act of 1969
- 152.1 IRC 6651—Failure to File Tax Return or to Pay Tax
- 152.2 IRC 6652—Failure to File Certain Information Returns
- 152.3 IRC 6653—Failure to Pay Tax
- 152.4 IRC 6211—Definition of a Deficiency
- 152.5 Other Civil Penalties
- **200 General Investigative Procedure**
- **210 Planning (Generally)**
- **220 Knowledge of Law and Evidence**
- 221 References
- 222 Law
- 222.1 Definitions of Law
- 222.2 Definitions of Crimes
- 222.3 Parties to Criminal Offenses
- 223 Evidence (General Rules)
- 223.1 Definitions of Evidence
- 223.2 Classifications of Evidence
- 223.3 Relevancy, Materiality, and Competency
- 223.4 Judicial Notice
- 223.5 Presumptions
- 223.6 Burden of Proof
- 223.7 Hearsay
- **230 Sources of Information**
- 231 Introduction
- 232 Confidential Sources of Information
- 232.1 Manual References
- 232.2 Informants
- 232.21 Definition of Informants
- 232.22 Development of Informants
- 232.23 Protection of Informants
- 232.24 Techniques With Informants
- 232.25 Payments to Informants
- 232.3 Social Security Administration
- 232.4 Selective Service Records
- 232.5 United States Customs Service
- 232.6 Department of Labor
- 233 Business Records
- 233.1 Banks
- 233.11 Function and Organization
- 233.12 Bank Records
- 233.121 Classification of Banks
- 233.122 Signature Cards
- 233.123 Bank Deposit Tickets
- 233.124 Customer's Account Records
- 233.125 Certified Check Register

MT 9900–26 (1–29–75) IR Manual

Handbook for Special Agents
Table of Contents—Cont.

233.126	Bank Exchange Records
233.127	Bank Teller's Proof Sheets
233.128	Clearing House Settlement Sheets
233.129	Cash Transit Letters
233.12(10)	Securities Buy and Sell Records
233.12(11)	Collection Records
233.12(12)	Safe Deposit Box Records
233.12(13)	Checks Cashed
233.12(14)	Deposits
233.12(15)	Microfilm
233.12(16)	Forms 4789, Currency Transaction Reports
233.2	Brokers
233.21	Classification
233.22	Broker's Records
233.3	Transfer Agents
233.4	Dividend Disbursing Agents
233.5	Information From Foreign Countries
233.51	Collateral Requests Regarding Foreign Countries
233.52	Information From Canada
233.6	Abstract and Title Company Records
233.7	Agricultural Records
233.8	Automobile Manufacturer and Agency Records
233.9	Bonding Company Records
233.(10)	Credit Agency Records
233.(11)	Department Store Records
233.(12)	Detective Agency Records
233.(13)	Distributors Records
233.(14)	Drug Store Records
233.(15)	Fraternal, Veterans, Labor, Social, Political Organization Records
233.(16)	Hospital Records
233.(17)	Hotel Records
233.(18)	Laundry and Dry Cleaning Records
233.(19)	Insurance Company Records
233.(20)	Newspaper Records
233.(21)	Oil Company Records
233.(22)	Photograph Records
233.(23)	Private Business Records
233.(24)	Publication Records
233.(25)	Public Utility Company Records
233.(26)	Real Estate Agency or Savings and Loan Association Records
233.(27)	Telephone Company Records
233.(28)	Transportation Company Records
233.(29)	Consumer Loan Exchange or Lenders Exchange
233.(30)	Other Business Records
234	Records of Governmental Agencies
234.1	Federal Government Records
234.11	Bureau of Alcohol, Tobacco and Firearms Records
234.12	Bureau of Labor Statistics Records
234.13	Drug Enforcement Agency Records
234.14	Bureau of the Public Debt Records
234.15	Federal Aviation Agency Records
234.16	Secret Service Records
234.17	Department of Defense Records
234.18	Department of State Records
234.19	District Director of Internal Revenue Records
234.1(10)	Examiner of Questioned Documents, Treasury Department
234.1(11)	Federal Bureau of Investigation Records
234.1(12)	Federal Court Records
234.1(13)	Federal Housing Administration Records
234.1(14)	Federal Records Center
234.1(15)	Federal Reserve Bank Records
234.1(16)	Intelligence Division (Internal Revenue Service) Records
234.1(17)	Immigration and Naturalization Service Records
234.1(18)	Interstate Commerce Commission Records
234.1(19)	Post Office Department Records
234.1(20)	Railroad Retirement Board Records
234.1(21)	Securities and Exchange Commission Records
234.1(22)	United States Coast Guard Records
234.1(23)	United States Customs Service Records
234.1(24)	Veterans Administration Records
234.1(25)	Deputy Comptroller of Currency (Bank Examiner's Reports)
234.1(26)	Disbursing Offices of the U. S. Government Records
234.1(27)	Treasurer of the United States Records
234.1(28)	Government Surplus Property Sales
234.2	State, County and Municipal Government Records
240	**Witnesses and Prospective Defendants**
241	Rights and Obligations of Witnesses and Prospective Defendants
241.1	General
241.2	Constitutional Law
241.3	Statutory Provisions
241.31	Introduction
241.32	Misprision of Felony
241.33	Summons
241.34	Unnecessary Examinations
241.4	Legality and Use of Certain Evidence and Equipment
241.41	Admissibility of Evidence
241.42	Use of Investigative Equipment
241.43	Electronic Listening Devices
241.5	Right to Record Interview
242	Prospective Defendants
242.1	Individual as a Prospective Defendant
242.11	Statements of an Individual
242.12	Books and Records of an Individual
242.13	Duty to Inform Individual of His Rights
242.131	General
242.132	Non-Custodial Interviews
242.133	Custodial Interrogations
242.14	Immunity From Prosecution
242.15	Waiver of Constitutional Rights
242.16	Right of Counsel
242.2	Partnership and Other Unincorporated Association Books and Records
242.3	Corporations
242.31	Corporation Books and Records
242.32	Rights of Corporate Officers
243	Third Party Witnesses
243.1	Compelled Testimony or Production of Records of Third Party Witnesses
243.2	Rights of Third Party Witnesses Against Self-Incrimination
243.3	Right of Third Party Witnesses to Counsel
243.31	Court Decisions Regarding Right of Third Party Witnesses to Counsel
243.32	Service Practice Regarding Right of Third Party Witnesses to Counsel
243.4	Right of Third Party Witnesses to Refuse Unreasonable Request
243.5	Witnesses in Foreign Countries
244	Privileged Communications
244.1	Conditions for Privileged Communications
244.2	Attorney-Client Privilege
244.3	Accountant-Client Privilege
244.4	Husband-Wife Privilege
244.5	Clergyman-Penitent Privilege
244.6	Physician-Patient Privilege
244.7	Informant-Government Privilege
244.8	Claim and Waiver of Privilege
245	Admissions and Confessions
245.1	Admissions
245.11	Definition of Admissions
245.12	Judicial Admissions
245.13	Extra-Judicial Admissions
245.14	Implied Admissions
245.15	Corroboration of Admissions
245.151	Corroboration of Admissions Before Offense
245.152	Corroboration of Admissions After Offense
245.16	Post-Indictment Admissions

MT 9900–26   (1–29–75)   IR Manual

Handbook for Special Agents

Table of Contents—Cont.

245.2 Confessions
245.21 Definition of Confession
245.22 Judicial and Extra-Judicial Confessions
245.23 Admissibility of Confessions
245.24 Corroboration of Confessions
246 Techniques of Interviewing
246.1 Definition and Purpose of Interviewing
246.2 Authority for Interviewing
246.3 Preparation and Planning for Interviewing
246.4 Conduct of Interview
246.5 Record of Interview
246.51 Introduction
246.52 Affidavit
246.53 Statement
246.54 Question and Answer Statement
246.541 Elements
246.542 Off-Record Discussions
246.55 Memorandum of Interview
246.56 Informal Notes or Diary Entries of Interview
246.6 Procedure
246.7 Application
247 Circular Form Letters
247.1 General
247.2 Procedure

250 Documentary Evidence

251 Definition of Documentary Evidence
252 Best Evidence Rule
252.1 Definition of Best Evidence Rule
252.2 Application of Best Evidence Rule
252.3 Secondary Evidence
253 Admissibility of Specific Forms of Documentary Evidence
253.1 Statutory Provisions
253.2 Business Records
253.21 Federal Shop Book Rule
253.22 Photographs, Photostats, and Microfilmed Copies
253.23 Transcripts
253.24 Charts, Summaries, and Schedules
253.25 Notes, Diaries, Workpapers, and Memorandums
253.26 Proving Specific Transactions
253.3 Official Records
253.31 Statutory Provisions Regarding Official Records
253.32 Authentication of Official Records
253.33 Proof of Lack of Record
253.34 State and Territorial Statutes and Proceedings
254 Receipt for Records and Documents
255 "Chain of Custody"
255.1 Legal Requirements for "Chain of Custody"
255.2 Identification of Seized Documentary Evidence
256 Questioned Documents
256.1 Use and Application of Questioned Documents
256.2 Definition of Questioned Document
256.3 Standards for Comparison with Questioned Documents
256.4 Handwriting Exemplars
256.5 Typewriting Exemplars
256.6 Other Exemplars
256.7 Identifying Exemplars and Questioned Documents
257 Record Retention Requirements
257.1 General
257.2 Record Requirement Guidelines for ADP Systems

260 Summons

261 Provisions of Law
262 Authority to Issue Summons
263 Considerations Regarding Issuance of Summons
264 Preparation of Summons
265 Service of Summons
266 Time and Place of Examination
267 Examination of Books and Witnesses
267.1 Persons Who May Be Summoned
267.2 Purpose of Examination
267.3 Limitations on Authority of Summons
267.31 Materiality and Relevancy
267.32 Examinations Barred by Statute of Limitations
267.33 Statutory Restriction on Summons
267.34 Constitutional Limitations of Summons
267.35 Privileged Communications and Summons
267.4 Taxpayer—Records and Testimony
267.41 General
267.42 Taxpayer's Records in Possession of Others
267.421 Taxpayer's Records Voluntarily Turned Over to Others
267.422 Taxpayer's Records Involuntarily Turned Over to Others
267.5 Summons on Third Parties—Records and Testimony
267.51 General
267.52 Summons on Banks
267.521 General
267.522 Summons on Foreign Branch Banks
267.523 Summons on Domestic Branches of Foreign Banks
267.53 Summons for Records of Foreign Companies
267.54 Other Third Parties
268 Enforcement of Summons
268.1 General
268.2 Civil Enforcement of Summons
268.21 Procedure for Civil Enforcement of Summons
268.22 Civil and Criminal Contempt Regarding Summons
268.3 Use of Affidavits in Summons Proceedings
268.4 Criminal Enforcement of Summons

270 Scientific Aids and Other Special Equipment

271 Scientific Aids
271.1 Laboratories
271.11 Introduction
271.12 Utilization of Treasury Department and Other Crime Laboratories
271.2 Chemicals
271.21 Anthracene
271.22 Phenolphthalein
272 Special Equipment
272.1 Proper Use and Limitations on Special Equipment
272.2 Radios
272.3 Binoculars and Telescopes
272.4 Microfilm Equipment and Photocopying
272.5 Camera Equipment
272.6 Firearms and Handcuffs
272.7 Specialized Investigative Equipment
272.8 Sirens, Warning Lights and Specialized Automotive Equipment

280 Surveillance, Searches and Seizures, Raids, and Forfeitures

281 Surveillance
282 Undercover Work
283 Searches and Seizures
283.1 Introduction
283.2 Authority and Procedure
283.21 Constitutional Authority
283.22 Statutory Authority
283.3 Unreasonable Searches and Seizures
283.4 Probable Cause and Preparation of Search Warrant
283.5 Preparation for the Search
283.6 The Approach and Search
283.7 Seizures Under Warrant
283.71 Wagering Seizures Under Warrant
283.72 Inventory of Seized Property Under Warrant
283.73 Return of Search Warrant
283.8 Searches and Seizures Without Warrant
283.81 Searches Incident to Arrest
283.82 Searches Made With Consent
283.83 Searches of Vehicles and Vessels
283.9 Seizures of Records
283.(10) Duties of Special Agent After Arrest, Search, and Seizure
284 Forfeiture Procedures
284.1 Introduction

MT 9900–26 (1–29–75) IR Manual

Handbook for Special Agents
Table of Contents—Cont.

284.2 Authority to Seize Property for Forfeiture
284.3 Methods of Forfeiture
284.31 Administrative Forfeiture
284.32 Judicial Forfeiture
284.4 Essential Element to Effect Forfeiture
284.41 Burden of Proof in Forfeitures
284.42 Evidence to Support Forfeitures
284.5 Duties of Special Agent in Seizure and Forfeiture Cases
284.51 Use of Raid Kits
284.52 Custody and Storage of Seized Property
284.53 Preparation of Seizure Forms
284.54 Seizure Report
284.55 Supplemental Investigations and Reports

290 Arrests

291 Definition of Arrest
292 Elements of Arrest
292.1 Authority to Arrest
292.2 Officer's Intent to Arrest
292.3 Offender Must Know He is Being Arrested
292.4 Offender Must Submit
293 Force in Conducting the Arrest
294 Authority to Carry Firearms
295 Proceedings Before the Magistrate
296 Fingerprints
297 Juveniles
2(10)0 Calendar
2(10)1 General
2(11)0 Map
2(11)1 General

300 Tax Cases (Evidence and Procedure)

310 Law and Elements of Offenses

311 Civil and Criminal Sanctions Distinguished
312 Avoidance Distinguished From Evasion
313 Attempted Evasion of Tax or Payment Thereof (IRC 7201)
313.1 Statutory Provisions
313.2 Elements of the Offenses
314 Failure to Collect, Account For, and Pay Over Tax
314.1 Willful Failure to Collect, Account For, and Pay Over Tax (IRC 7202)
314.11 Statutory Provisions
314.12 Elements of Offense
314.2 Failure to Collect and Account For Certain Collected Taxes (Nonwillful Violation) (IRC 7215)
314.21 Statutory Provisions
314.22 Elements of Offense
315 Willful Failure to File Returns, Supply Information, or Pay Tax (IRC 7203)
315.1 Statutory Provisions
315.2 Elements of the Offenses
315.21 Willful Failure to Make a Return
315.22 Willful Failure to Pay Tax
315.23 Willful Failure to Supply Information
315.24 Willful Failure to Keep Records
315.3 Venue and Statute of Limitations
316 Fraudulent Statement or Failure to Make Statement to Employees (IRC 7204)
316.1 Statutory Provisions
316.2 Elements of Offense
317 Fraudulent Withholding Exemption Certificate or Failure to Supply Information (IRC 7205)
317.1 Statutory Provisions
317.2 Elements of Offense
318 False and Fraudulent Statements
318.1 False or Fraudulent Return, Statement or Other Document Made Under Penalty of Perjury (IRC 7206(1))
318.11 Statutory Provisions
318.12 Elements of Offense
318.2 Aid or Assistance in Preparation or Presentation of False or Fraudulent Return, Affidavit, Claim or Other Document (IRC 7206(2))
318.21 Statutory Provisions
318.22 Elements of Offense
318.3 Fraudulent Returns, Statements, or Other Documents (IRC 7207)
318.4 False Statement or Entries Generally (Section 1001, Title 18)
318.41 Statutory Provisions
318.42 Elements of Offense
318.5 False, Fictitious, or Fraudulent Claims (Section 287, Title 18)
318.51 Statutory Provisions
318.52 Elements of Offense
318.6 Removal or Concealment With Intent to Defraud (IRC 7206(4))
318.61 Statutory Provisions
318.62 Elements of Offense
319 Statute of Limitations
319.1 Introduction
319.2 Statute of Limitations Statutory Provisions
319.21 Statute of Limitations on Criminal Prosecutions
319.22 Statute of Limitations on Civil Assessments
319.3 Construction of Statute of Limitations Provisions
319.4 Tolling of the Statute of Limitations
31(10) Conspiracy (Title 18, Section 371)
31(10).1 Statutory Provisions
31(10).2 Elements of Offense of Conspiracy
31(10).3 Application of Conspiracy Statute
31(10).4 Construction of Conspiracy Provisions
31(10).41 Definition
31(10).42 Parties in Conspiracy
31(10).43 Nature of Conspiracy Agreement
31(10).44 Overt Act in Conspiracy
31(10).45 Defraud in Conspiracy
31(10).46 Duration of Conspiracy
31(11) Willfulness
31(11).1 Definition of Willfulness
31(11).2 Proof of Willfulness
31(11).3 Defenses Bearing Upon Willfulness
31(11).31 Common Defenses Bearing Upon Willfulness
31(11).32 Entrapment
31(11).33 Embezzled Funds and Illegally Obtained Income

320 Methods of Proving Income

321 Introduction
322 Distinguishing Between Accounting Systems, Accounting Methods, and Methods of Proving Income
323 Specific Item Method of Proving Income
324 Net Worth Method of Proving Income
324.1 Introduction
324.2 Authority for Net Worth Method
324.3 When and How Net Worth Method Used
324.4 Establishing the Starting Point
324.5 Taxable Source of Income
324.6 Corroboration of Extra-Judicial Admissions
324.7 Investigation of Leads
324.8 Summaries Prepared by Government Agents
324.9 Common Defenses in Net Worth Cases
325 Expenditures Method of Proving Income
325.1 Introduction
325.2 Authority for Using Expenditures Method
325.3 When and How Expenditures Method Used
325.4 Establishing the Starting Point
325.5 Taxable Source of Income—Corroboration of Extra-Judicial Admissions—Investigation of Leads
325.6 Expenditures Summaries Prepared by Government Agents
325.7 Defenses in Expenditures Method Cases
326 Bank Deposits Method of Proving Income
326.1 Formula for Bank Deposits Method
326.11 Introduction

MT 9900–26 (1–29–75) IR Manual

Handbook for Special Agents
Table of Contents—Cont.

326.12 Total Deposits
326.13 Payments Made in Cash
326.14 Nonincome Deposits and Items
326.15 Business Expenses and Costs
326.16 Deductions and Exemptions
326.2 Use of Bank Deposits Method
326.3 Authority for Bank Deposits Method
326.4 Proof of Taxable Income in Bank Deposits Case
326.5 Defenses in Bank Deposits Case
326.6 Schedules and Summaries in Bank Deposits Case
327 Other Methods
327.1 Percentage Method
327.11 Use of Percentage Method
327.12 Application of Percentage Method
327.13 Limitations of Percentage Method
327.14 Examples of Percentage Method
327.2 Unit and Volume Methods

330 Fraud Investigation Assignments

331 Nature of Violations
332 Source of Assignments
333 Types of Investigations
334 Joint Investigations
334.1 Circumstances Determining Joint Investigations
334.2 Responsibilities of Participants in a Joint Investigation
335 Commencing Fraud Investigations
336 Investigations
336.1 Planning and Conducting of Investigations
336.2 Withdrawals
337 Refund Cases
337.1 Introduction
337.2 Investigation of Multiple Claims for Refund
337.3 Investigation of Multiple Fraudulent Returns Prepared by Unscrupulous Returns Preparers

340 Excise Taxes

341 Definition and Purposes
342 Excise and Income Taxes Distinguished
342.1 Base
342.2 Tax Period
342.3 Additional Taxes and Penalties
342.4 Court Appeals
343 Excise Tax Reduction Bill of 1965
343.1 Statutory Provisions
343.2 Excise Taxes Remaining in Effect
344 Occupational Stamps
344.1 Occupations Subject to Tax
344.2 Coin-Operated Gaming Devices
344.21 Definition of Coin-Operated Gaming Devices
344.22 Basis of Coin-Operated Gaming Device Tax
344.23 Liability for Coin-Operated Gaming Tax
344.24 Techniques and Procedures
345 Civil Penalties and Jeopardy Assessments
345.1 Civil Penalties
345.11 Delinquency Penalty (IRC 6651(a))
345.12 Fraud Penalty Applicable to Returns (IRC 6653(b))
345.13 Fraud Penalty Applicable to Documentary Stamps (IRC 6653(e))
345.14 One Hundred Percent Penalty (IRC 6672)
345.15 Other Civil Penalties
345.2 Jeopardy Assessments in Excise Tax Cases
346 Criminal Penalties for Excise Tax Violations
347 Excise Tax Investigations
347.1 Origin of Excise Tax Cases
347.2 Techniques of Excise and Income Tax Investigations Compared

350 Wagering Tax

351 Law Relating to Wagering Tax
351.1 Excise Tax on Wagering
351.11 Statutory Provisions
351.12 Definitions of Wagering Terms
351.121 Wager
351.122 Lottery
351.13 Amount of Wager
351.14 Persons Liable for Wagering Excise Tax
351.15 Exclusions From Wagering Excise Tax
351.16 Territorial Extent of Wagering Excise Tax
351.2 Wagering Occupational Tax
351.21 Statutory Provisions
351.22 Registration
351.3 Record Requirements
351.4 Payment of Special Tax Before Engaging in Wagering Business
351.5 Wagering Excise Tax Returns
351.6 Criminal Violations-Wagering Taxes
352 Elements of Wagering Tax Violations
353 Techniques of Wagering Investigation
354 Venue in Wagering Investigations
355 Statute of Limitations on Wagering Taxes
356 Civil Penalties on Wagering Taxes

360 Interest Equalization Tax

361 Statutory Provisions
361.1 Application of Interest Equalization Tax
361.2 Effective Date and Termination Date of Interest Equalization Tax
361.3 Acquisitions, Limitations, Exclusions, Definitions, Rules and Forms
361.4 Penalty Provisions for Interest Equalization Tax

400 Procedures and Techniques in Other Investigations

410 Interference, Forcible Rescue of Seized Property

411 Interference Cases
411.1 Corrupt or Forcible Interference (IRC 7212(a))
411.2 Assault, Resisting or Impeding Certain Officers and Employees (18 U.S.C. 111)
411.3 Investigative Responsibility
411.4 Investigation of Interference Cases
411.5 Assault or Resistance to Search or Service of Process (18 U.S.C. 1501; 18 U.S.C 2231)
411.6 Obstruction of Criminal Investigations (18 U.S.C. 1510)
412 Forcible Rescue of Seized Property
412.1 Elements of Forcible Rescue Cases
412.11 Forcible Rescue (IRC 7212(b))
412.12 Rescue of Seized Property (18 U.S.C. 2233)
412.2 Investigation of Forcible Rescue Cases

420 Offer of Bribe (18 U.S.C. 201)

421 Reference
422 Elements of Offer of Bribe
423 Jurisdiction in Offer of Bribe
424 Investigation of Offer of Bribe

430 Perjury

431 Reference
432 Elements of Perjury
433 Establishing Elements of Perjury
434 False Declarations Before Grand Jury or Court

440 Anti-Gambling Statutes

441 Transmission of Wagering Information
442 Interstate and Foreign Travel or Transportation in Aid of Racketeering Enterprises
443 Interstate Transportation of Wagering Paraphernalia
444 Prohibition of Illegal Gambling Business
445 Intelligence Division Responsibility

450 Special Investigations

451 Offers in Compromise
451.1 References
451.2 Intelligence Division Responsibility
451.3 Alleged Fraudulent Offers
451.4 Offers in Closed Cases

MT 9900–26   (1–29–75)   IR Manual

Handbook for Special Agents
Table of Contents—Cont.

451.5 Offers in Pending Criminal Cases
451.6 Investigation of Offers in Compromise
451.7 Alleged Fraudulent Offers
451.8 Offers in Closed Cases
451.9 Offers During Criminal Proceedings
452 Jeopardy Assessments
452.1 References
452.2 Intelligence Division Responsibility
452.3 Jeopardy Situations
452.4 Quick Assessments
452.5 Regular Assessments
452.6 Reporting Jeopardy Situations
452.7 Disclosures in Statutory Notices of Deficiency
452.8 Investigation of Jeopardy Assessment Cases
453 Termination of Taxable Periods
453.1 References
453.2 Introduction
453.3 Requirements
453.4 Reporting Termination Situations
453.5 Assessment Procedures at Termination

500 Reports
510 Purpose and Importance of Reports
520 Planning and Writing Reports
521 Essentials of a Good Report
521.1 Introduction
521.2 Fairness
521.3 Accuracy
521.4 Completeness
521.5 Uniformity
521.6 Conciseness
521.7 Logical Presentation
522 Planning the Report
523 Reports on Related Cases
524 Format of Reports
524.1 Address
524.2 Subject
524.3 Case Number and Designation
524.4 Sample Subjects and Designations
524.5 Approval Stamps
524.6 Assembly of a Report
524.7 Identification of Principles, Witnesses, etc.
525 Appendices and Exhibits
525.1 General
525.2 Exhibits-Supplemental Reports
525.3 Documents Submitted with Collateral Reports
526 List of Witnesses
527 Table of Contents
530 Types of Final Reports
531 Introduction
532 Outline for Final Reports on Prosecution Cases
533 Tax Fraud Cases (Prosecution) Reports
533.1 Introduction
533.2 Summary of Cooperating Officer's Findings
533.3 History of Taxpayer
533.4 Evidence
533.41 Evidence in Support of Civil Penalties
533.42 Evidence for Use in Criminal Proceedings
533.5 Explanation and Defense
533.6 Facts Relating to Intent
533.7 Conclusions and Recommendation
533.8 Sample Reports, Tax Fraud Cases
533.9 Optional Format for Final Reports
534 Reports on Wagering Tax, Coin-Operated Gaming Device and Seizure Cases
534.1 Wagering Tax, and Coin-Operated Gaming Device Reports
534.11 Introduction
534.12 Sample Report, Wagering Tax Case
534.13 Sample Short Form Report, Wagering Tax Case
534.14 Coin-Operated Gaming Device Report
534.2 Seizure Report, Form 4008
534.3 Report of Investigation Relating to Petition for Remission or Mitigation of Forfeiture
535 Miscellaneous Criminal Law Violations ("M" Cases)
536 Reports on Nonprosecution Cases
537 Reports on Discontinued Investigations
538 Collateral Reports
539 Chronological Worksheet

600 Federal Court Procedures and Related Matters
610 Law Governing Federal Courts
620 Federal Rules of Criminal Procedures (Pre-Trial)
621 Complaint (Rule 3)
622 Warrant or Summons Upon Complaint (Rule 4)
623 Preliminary Hearing (Rule 5)
624 The Grand Jury (Rule 6)
625 Indictment and Information
625.1 Definitions of Indictment and Information
625.2 Indictment and Information Distinguished (Rule 7a and 7b)
625.3 Bill of Particulars (Rule 7f)
625.4 Joinder of Offenses and Defendants (Rule 8)
626 Arraignment and Preparation for Trial
626.1 Arraignment (Rule 10)
626.2 Please (Rule 11)
626.3 Motions Raising Defenses and Objections (Rule 12)
626.4 Depositions (Rule 15)
626.5 Discovery and Inspection and Subpoenas for Production of Documentary Evidence (Rules 16 and 17(c))
626.6 Motions to Suppress Evidence and for Return of Property (Rule 41(e))
626.7 Other Matters Before Trial
627 Venue
630 Trials and Related Federal Rules of Criminal Procedure
631 Trial by Jury or by Court
631.1 Provisions of the Constitution
631.2 Provisions of Federal Rules (Rule 23)
631.3 Trial by United States Magistrates
632 Trial Jurors (Rule 24)
633 Disability of Judge (Rule 25)
634 Evidence (Rule 26)
635 Opening Statements
636 Presentation of Case
637 Witnesses
637.1 Definition
637.2 Competence
637.3 Credibility
637.4 Impeachment
637.41 Impeachment of Opposing Witness
637.42 Impeachment by a Party of His Own Witness
637.5 Recall
637.6 Refreshing Memory or Recollection
637.61 Introduction
637.62 Past Recollection Recorded
637.63 Present Recollection Revived
637.7 Specific Witnesses
637.71 Expert Witness (Rule 28)
637.72 Special Agent
637.73 Revenue Agent
637.8 Cross-Examination
637.81 General Rules
637.82 Demands for Production of Statements and Reports of Witness
637.9 Redirect Examination
638 Stipulations
639 Motion for Judgement of Acquittal (Rule 29)
63(10) Rebuttal
63(11) Instructions to the Jury (Rule 30)
63(12) Verdict (Rule 31)
63(13) Judgment (Rules 32 through 35)

MT 9900–26 (1–29–75)   IR Manual

383

Handbook for Special Agents

Table of Contents—Cont.

63(13).1 Definition
63(13).2 Presentence Investigation
63(13).3 Withdrawal of Plea of Guilty
63(13).4 Sentence
63(13).5 Probation
63(14) Right of Appeal (Rule 37)

640 Compromise of Criminal Tax Cases

650 Assisting the United States Attorney

651 Planning for Presentation to Grand Jury and for Trial
652 Trial
652.1 Responsibility and Conduct of Special Agent at Trial
652.2 Separation of Witnesses

660 Case Settlement

661 Internal Revenue Service (Joint Investigation)
662 United States Tax Court

14

Mergers—Acquisitions—Takeovers—Divestitures

MANIA FOR GROWTH

American industry has lived through a succession of fads. In the past we have had consolidations, vertical and horizontal integration, mass production, technological revolution, automation, word processing and presently we have "Duke's mixture."

Underneath the furor of these fads we have a powerful trend called growth mania. Corporations acquire, tender and merge in the race to become bigger and better. We have huge syndicates, partnerships, ventures or corporations patched together in a Duke's mixture with borrowed money, Chinese paper, hard sell and investor faith. We merge lawnmowers with grass killers, ball bearings with eye glasses and all sorts of weird combinations. The "in word" is "go" "go" "go" and "grow" "grow" "grow." If a firm does ten million in sales, its goal is one-hundred million. If and when it gets to one-hundred million it is onward and upward to five-hundred million. Sound growth and the industry within which you have operated is no longer an important factor. Firms have special teams of executives who look at and evaluate any firm that is available. The objective is often not to be the most profitable but the largest in all industries except automotive.

THE FINANCIAL ADMINISTRATOR'S ROLE IN MERGERS, ACQUISITIONS, TAKEOVERS AND DIVESTITURES

Dependent upon the size of the firm the financial administrator is most often a key individual in this type of operation. In all cases, the division plays a major role in the planning for growth, the evaluation of prospects and the all-important function of financing the project. In a rapidly growing acquisition-minded firm his is an endless task of reports, studies, conferences and answers to the "What if?" questions that arise. His personal success or failure can ride on the success or failure of the firms which were acquired. If and when a divestiture occurs he occupies the enviable position of being the principal mourner at the wake.

These are the tests that try the financial acumen of financial executives. They have the responsibility for determining if the venture is sound, if it can be profitable and for the most important task of all—providing the wherewithal to make the deal possible. With certainty, the financial administrator is a very important cog in this phase of your firm's growth. You must be quick, competent, confident and right!

EVALUATION OF ACQUISITIONS AND TAKEOVERS—ACQUIRING INFORMATION

If your firm is contemplating faster growth through merger, acquisition or takeover there are some fundamental steps that must be taken in order to insure a greater degree of success through a more scientific approach. You will need to sharpen up your understanding of the basic principles involved in these matters. This is a rather simple outline of the basic factors. It can be expanded to fit your particular requirements. Before you start to acquire information look at these basics:

1. The basic company policy on acquisitions of all types.
    a. What are your objectives?
    b. What do you hope to accomplish—horizontal, vertical, or "Dukes mixture"?
    c. The role to be played by directors, stockholders, president, top management and staff.
    d. Can you afford to use outside consultants? Merger specialists, lawyers, accountants, appraisers, investigators?
    e. What standards have been set for possible acquisitions.

Once you have established the parameters of the problem the task then arises as to how you approach and organize to solve the problem. Interviews indicate that these approaches are used by successful financial executives:

1. Establish ground rules and conduct a search for possible candidates. This depends upon the size of the firm. It can range from examining the small industries in various towns to a detailed analysis of how vulnerable any firm is to a takeover.
2. Use of outside help. There are individuals who specialize in this field for a "finders fee."
3. Utilize your salesmen and other staff personnel to dig up prospects.
4. Utilize or buy out your suppliers.
5. Determine the information and type of reports required for a thorough study and evaluation.
6. Assign responsibility for the various tasks and for policies and acquisitions.

The factors used in evaluating prospects are generally:

1. Responsibility for making the evaluation—Who does what and why?
2. The total factors involved in the merger or acquisition.

Mergers—Acquisitions—Takeovers—Divestitures

3. Investigation of the basic values in plant and equipment.
4. Examination, determination and evaluation of expenses for detailed study, items capitalized, depreciation policies, leased plant and equipment.
5. Evaluate the prospect's "goodwill" and future business potential.
6. Check the value of brand name products, consumer reaction and past promotional efforts.
7. Contact suppliers, customers and others to ascertain the quality of products and their future potential.

It is quite evident that each acquisition prospect must be researched carefully. The main concern in seeking information is not to disclose your intentions. The sources of information are endless. You can start with the annual reports of the firm if they are available. You can examine the 10K SEC reports if the firm is listed. You can start by interviewing the people in the towns in which the firm operates, its employees, its suppliers, the vendors of its products and others. On the financial side there are credit reports, interviews with bankers and others in the financial field. Some firms have even been known to place an employee or two on the prospect's payroll.

PLANNING AND CHECKLISTS FOR ACQUISITIONS

One must realize the fact that in all mergers there is a decided element of risk. Plenty of problems and difficulties lie beneath the surface that will not be encountered until the honeymoon is over. Often you can avoid or lessen these difficulties by some hard-headed analysis prior to starting and completing the negotiations. Everyone should post a sign saying "Approach with Caution!" Too often mergers are sought out as the providential solution to acres of problems, failing profits or to unload a bad situation.

Planning must include the hard questions. What exactly do you wish to accomplish? Can your intentions be concealed? What problems might arise after the merger in products, personnel and customers? Are you certain that the operations are compatible? Combinations of businesses can be magic or pure hell dependent upon how well your joint organizations mesh.

Too often, one finds that the group attempting to sell a firm is intent upon disposing of a problem. It may be a loss operation, a bad union situation, declining product potentials or profits or a bitter disagreement among principals. It can be some unsolvable problem such as too many relatives on the payroll or a sideline operation which is devouring capital borrowed from good results elsewhere.

Just the other day in reading two annual reports this situation arose. One form reported selling an unprofitable part of their business whereas the acquiring firm was reporting to its stockholders that it was successful in buying a real bargain with an extremely high potential. They were both talking about the same firm! In any event whenever a merger comes looking for you it is best to investigate and evaluate it thoroughly.

A friend of mine in the appraisal business talked to me about a firm which would mesh into another business and integrate its supply of raw materials. His analysis of the situation was rather unique. This firm had an annual sales volume of $750,000 with profits before taxes of $75,000. The president of the firm and two members of his family, both daughters, are on the payroll at salaries of $65,000 in total. He has reached the age of sixty-five and is ready to retire. None of his family wishes to continue the business. The asking price for the firm is $650,000. The appraiser states that the sound value of the fixed assets for replacement is $750,000 and the current assets, net of current liabilities, are equivalent to $150,000. He evaluated the situation in this manner. Use 40% of the sound value of the fixed assets as liquidating value. This amounts to $300,000 which when combined with the net current assets equates to $450,000. Since it is a profitable organization the maximum loss risk is $200,000. Salaries and profits before taxes are equivalent to $105,000. This would liquidate your investment in about three years. This is a "buy" situation! Additional volume upon integration into the buying firm would amount to approximately $250,000 annually. It was a successful acquisition!

ACQUISITION CHECKLIST

A simple test to determine if the acquisition is right is to answer the following questions honestly:

1. Does the prospect fall in line with your long-term objectives?
2. Can you properly finance the deal without straining your financial resources?
3. Why is the firm being sold?
4. Is the proposed price right, too high, too low?
5. Will your stockholders be satisfied and will the acquisition add more to your profits and assets than the proposed stock dilution if the purchase is paid by issuing common stock?
6. Do you honestly feel that the combined operations will mesh with a minimum of friction or will it be a "castor oil" proposition?
7. What are the short-term and long-term objectives to be accomplished?
8. Have you overlooked any legal or tax angles?

MERGER CHECKLIST

Any merger or combination of firms is a fateful and nerveracking decision. One holds their fingers crossed and relies on luck or the signs of the Zodiac to assure smooth going and success. Underestimating the problems involved may bring all sorts of headaches out from behind the plush woodwork. In the first few days of living together and meshing operations, tact is required and much frustration is encountered. There are power struggles and other developments which must be watched closely. These are some of the factors involved:

1. Timing the move properly.
2. Clearance from governmental agencies.
3. Centralized or decentralized approach to meshing functions.
4. Integration of key departments and functions. What is to be done?
5. How fast do you integrate?
6. What adverse factors are most likely to be encountered?

Mergers—Acquisitions—Takeovers—Divestitures

7. Personnel problems and reactions.
8. Possible union difficulties. Compatibility of work rules, wages, fringe benefits and other items must be tested. Leadership attitudes will have to be ascertained.
9. Reaction of the sales divisions to a change in company leadership. If substantial changes must be made in sales policies and personnel you may be in for some rude shocks. Sales personnel can be key factors in retaining customers and future profits.
10. Will key sales individuals go along with the change or will they attempt to take key customers over to competitive firms.
11. Watch customer reaction and satisfaction.
12. Compatibility of top management personnel.

In a takeover you may meet considerable resistance and have to fire key personnel. To add to the dilemma the entire operating staff could leave. The cost in time, effort and money in the interim while the gap is being filled could be tremendous. Often older personnel will retire before you can pick their brains of the vital data contained therein.

Often acquisitions are made to obtain a product line. After you acquire it at a bargain and are gleefully rubbing your hands together in joy, the sales manager reports that the product mix is not right or that some items are missing. In order to correct these deficiencies you will have to spend another million or two for additional equipment to round out the product line.

In all mergers, acquisitions and takeovers it is well to proceed slowly, investigate thoroughly and poke and probe for hidden items. Questions on control, key personnel and chain of command, should be explored in detail and agreed upon in writing. Leave as little as possible to chance. In every corporate change someone gets hurt and someone profits. Actions are performed best when they are reduced to written agreements.

WHY ARE FIRMS ACQUIRED?

Interviews and research indicate that the variety of reasons given for acquisitions are legendary and beyond number. They range from having too much money or credit to acquisitions for spite or power. Small firms, in general, merge because they need money to keep the business going or because the family has no competent heirs to continue the line of succession. They team up with other firms to rapidly acquire technical knowledge or research facilities. Reasons listed are as follows:

1. Diversify to fill out product lines.
2. Buy other firms whose products are distributed through the same channels thus increasing volume while cutting costs and strengthening profits through a stronger marketing position.
3. To acquire qualified technical or management personnel. If you cannot hire the personnel—buy the company!
4. To acquire customers and markets.
5. If you are in the automobile rental business you purchase other firms to get additional locations and volume. This also applies to the financing business.

6. You merge ink with crayons to better supply the art markets.
7. If you need a patented product you buy the whole firm.
8. If you store grain you enter the grain merchandising field in order to gain additional sources of grain.

TENDERS

The tender offer is a successful way to gain control of many large publicly held corporations. Often control can be acquired with as little as 10 to 15% of the firm's stock. Once you acquire from 15 to 40% of the outstanding common stock you can place a sufficient number of individuals on the board of directors to control the activities of the firm. Tenders are an interesting development in the struggle for corporate control. Under the merger or acquisition method one was forced to obtain at least 51% of the stock of publicly held firms and had to contend with approval of the directors and from 51% to two-thirds of the stockholders.

Current tender offers generally result in the stockholders being offered an amount in excess of the current market price for their stock. When two or more firms are involved in tenders the prices offered have been revised upward several times. Even if one of the bidders winds up on the low side of the tender he still has an opportunity to reap a handsome profit on his investment. In several instances firms have been outbid and have sold their shares to the winner for a handsome profit. This is particularly true where they started to acquire the stock quietly when the price was depressed. Premiums over market prices prior to the takeover have ranged from 25% to 100%.

Under the present day accounting rules once the buyer acquires 20% of the outstanding common stock it can consolidate sales and earnings under the equity method of accounting. Dependent upon the price it paid for its investment this could result in a favorable increase in consolidated earnings.

Tenders are unusual in that the buyer sets the terms and conditions to suit his requirements. These conditions null the transaction if unfavorable events occur—for example, if the number of shares tendered is insufficient, if the government vetoes the deal, if economic conditions change and the stock market declines, if the SEC rules against them, or if the firm involved issues additional shares of common stock. Often, the target of the tender will cozy up to a company that is favorable to management and have them acquire stock or they will acquire assets for stock in order to thwart the raiders.

Naturally, once you have acquired control through the tender method you have a management and minority stockholder problem which can cause a great deal of trouble. In most cases this has dissipated with time and some lawsuits.

During periods of depressed stock prices many firms become vulnerable to tender offer takeovers. There are firms who specialize in acquiring the stocks of firms whose common stock has an intrinsic value far above its market price. Once they have a substantial number of shares in their portfolio they set out to sell the stocks to anyone who is interested in acquiring control of these businesses. This is a hidden tender offer which could be encountered by some firms. The flow of foreign funds into the United States could increase the tender activity of the future. It would therefore be a part of every financial executive's planning on what steps can be taken to prevent tender takeovers in the future.

JOINT VENTURES

There is a practical and effective way for any industrial firm to get into real estate if it so desires. You acquire a corporation with development capabilities and let that firm enter into joint ventures with any number of successful building firms. This trend has been followed by a number of banks, railroads and other landholding firms. Due to the size and diversity of the parent firm they can bring the financial, management and technical strength needed to be successful in the field. They can coordinate their own financing of the projects with mass production, volume sales, mass advertising and marketing. Several projects are currently under way in the housing field where homes are being produced on a mass production basis. Scheduling is tight, well-controlled and on target. In addition, the ability to finance the sale of their project on variable terms makes sales easy. By covering a nationwide market they can shift their operations from one area to another in conjunction with the ebb and flow of the economy.

The joint-venture route is utilized in many ways. It was used in the late 1920's and early 30's on projects such as building huge dams. Five or six firms pooled their interests to build Hoover Dam adjacent to Las Vegas, Nevada. They are using the same technique on other large projects and often in foreign ventures with foreign firms. The technique is almost limitless in its applications. Here again is an item for study on the financial administrator's list of required knowledge.

PLANNING AND CHECKLISTS FOR DIVESTITURES

Acquisitions must fit very closely into your business plans or they can become a disaster. During the middle 1970's the recession, a depressed stock market, high cost money and the disenchantment with acquisitions for the sake of headlines and publicity caused the pace of acquisitions to slow down to a walk. Many merger consultants hurriedly turned their hats around and became instant experts on divestiture. Organizations in the food business suddenly discovered that there was more to the floor tile and bathtub business than they had bargained for and so they began to phase out the unprofitable parts of their acquisitions or even their own businesses. One firm made over one-hundred fifty tender offers in an eighteen-month period. This could only lead to trouble as there is no way a fast growing firm can be adequately and competently managed when it tries to grow this fast.

During the 1970's a new term appeared in corporate income accounts. It was termed revenues and income from discontinued operations. Most often the income was bracketed into a (loss) figure. Firms were falling all over one another trying to dump unprofitable operations. The financial administrator had two problems. First, he had to provide the split accounting information on the losing division and what could be done with it.

Strangely enough it is often hard to convince the top executive that one of his divisions is in trouble and should be eliminated. It is often felt that this is a temporary situation which will soon correct itself. The ability to recognize stagnation or failure is an art. It requires someone like the financial executive who has his finger in the pulse of the day-to-day activities and who has the ability to spot whether the trend is upward or downward. In order to keep your firm on the most direct path toward the goal line of success, it is necessary to recognize the early symptoms of stagnation, diagnose the problem correctly and take steps to divest your firm of failure or unprofitable activities.

For years a very prominent firm continued to produce and sell a very unprofitable paint line. Due to the excellent profits on other products the failure of the paint line and its losses were concealed. As soon as product profit and loss reports were instituted the problem was apparent and a decision was made to phase out the activity. Strangely enough the operation was sold to a small firm which due to the lack of high-priced personnel and technicians was able to operate it profitably. This illustrates that sometimes operations grow beyond their capacity to produce profits and revenues.

In considering divestiture always remember that personnel are not disturbed by actual things or conditions. If their mental attitude is right there is nothing that is impossible, despite the severity of events. Make certain that the failure is due to things which cannot be corrected by prompt and effective action. These are the items which tip you off to unsatisfactory situations:

1. Lack of increase in sales or decrease in rate of growth without cause.
2. Failure of sales to keep pace with your investment in plant and equipment.
3. Increase in personnel turnover particularly in the top and middle management groups.
4. Inventories keep growing—liquidity decreases.
5. Increases in costs not consistent with sales growth.
6. Lack of equipment additions and failure to change processing methods.
7. Sudden increases in maintenance or other indirect labor costs.
8. Unusually high overtime costs—production problems.
9. Continuing high or increasing marketing costs without a corresponding increase in sales volume.

"GO" OR "NO GO!"

The gauge of business success says "go" or "no go!" Alongside of each machine there is a gauge with two heads on it. Every so often the operator takes an item off of the production line and tries to fit it on the gauge. The top of the gauge carries two instructions—"go" or "no go." Other than a visual inspection for flaws it is comparatively easy to measure whether the machine is producing a quality product. So it is with your business. If one of the divisions fits on the "no go" gauge it is time to divest yourself of it. The problem division or product line is the concern of all industry. Its desperate struggle for success can have an adverse affect on the pricing structure, plant capacities, future planning and profits of your firm and of the entire industry. It represents only one challenge—How to dump it?

Mergers—Acquisitions—Takeovers—Divestitures

The procedures for divestiture are almost identical with those for acquisition. The prospects are often the same firms or your competitors. There is only one difference! You are selling instead of buying. All of your expertise must be expended in doing the job quickly and cleanly with a minimum of lost time.

CHECKLIST FOR DIVESTITURES

1. Are there any legal or tax angles to consider in the divestiture?
2. Does the division or firm have any intangible assets which should be omitted from the sale—patents, etc.?
3. Should the unit be phased out or sold?
4. What adverse effects could arise as a result of the divestiture?
5. Can the firm be sold to a smaller operation which would be able to handle it and be noncompetitive?
6. Will you have to finance the sale or adjust the price based upon future performance?

MODELS AND MEANS OF DETERMINING "WHAT IF?"

The first case study aptly illustrates the type of calculation that goes into the determination of how well the firms can be meshed and what steps can be taken. There are obvious increases in sales, costs, production equipment and personnel that enter into each acquisition and whether they can be fitted into a formula or model for determining the "What ifs?" is a controversial subject. In interviews, we found that certain basic patterns were followed, certain standard questions were utilized and a great deal of secrecy surrounded the whole process.

DYNAMICS OF OPPORTUNITY MODEL

INPUTS

1. Present sales volume
2. Sound replacement cost of plant and equipment
3. Existing capacity to produce
4. Percent utilization of capacity
5. Increase in capacity available through modernization
6. Alternate uses of capacity to produce
7. Anticipated increases in sales volume over time period of x years
8. Costs of modernization of plant and equipment
9. Price elasticity of products—What will the market bear in price increases?
10. Direct costs of production
11. Promotional and distribution costs
12. Hidden cost factor correction—labor rates, pensions, fringe benefits

13. Special equipment and expertise factor
14. Intensity of competition—percent of market
15. Project cost
16. Life of project—x or y years
    x = years required to amortize the initial cost
    y = years of beneficial effect
17. Current cost of capital

"WHAT IF?" QUESTIONS

1. Effect on total sales volume of acquisition?
2. Effect on distribution costs—all lines?
3. Effect on individual product profitability—Will acquisition aid or hurt individual product profitability?
4. If the acquisition has a cash cost of $2,000,000 and a return on investment (ROI) of 15% what would be the effect on ROI of investing an additional $500,000?
5. In the event forecast volumes due to the acquisition are off 5%, 10%, 15% or 20% what would be the projected ROI?

ANALYSIS RATIOS

DATA SHEET	$ YEAR 1	$ YEAR 2	$ YEAR X

CASH AND SECURITIES
ACCOUNTS RECEIVABLE
INVENTORIES
    TOTAL CURRENT ASSETS
CURRENT LIABILITIES
    CURRENT RATIO
LONG-TERM DEBT
    TOTAL DEBT
FIXED ASSETS—GROSS
FIXED ASSETS—NET
STOCKHOLDERS' EQUITY
    RATIO DEBT TO EQUITY
    RATIO DEBT TO CURRENT ASSETS
    RATIO CURRENT LIABILITIES
      TO CASH
NET SALES
COST OF SALES
DEPRECIATION
OPERATING INCOME
FIXED CHARGES
INCOME TAXES
NET INCOME
    CASH FLOW

RATIOS—LIQUIDITY

Current ratio—Receivable turnover—Inventory turnover

RATIOS—EFFICIENCY

Earning power (income to total assets) (income to plant and equipment investment)—Revenues to total assets and plant

RATIOS—PROFITABILITY

Percent of net income to sales—Return on capital—Return on Common Stock—Rate of Cash Flow to Common Stock

RATIOS—VULNERABILITY

Debt as a percentage of total capital—Capital stock as a percentage of total capital—Percentage of stock held by the public

RATIOS—OTHER FINANCIAL

Income taxes as a percentage of income before taxes—Interest coverage (interest costs x "Y" = net income)—Dividend coverage of preferred stock—Earnings per share—Common and preferred

ODDS AND ENDS

Union Camps theory on acquisitions—use three well-situated paper mills instead of scores of small ones—keep product lines simple—avoid the proliferation of new products and new product lines—continue to improve your profitability at a lower percentage of plant capacity.

Use payments in products to acquire firms—not money. If the cost of capital is high pay in stock to increase equity ratio and keep debt ratios down. Don't stretch the financial rubber band too thin! Forget the thrill of growth and its preoccupation. Keep your acquisitions on a fundamentally sound basis.

Diversification spreads risks but can add headaches! Put all of your energies into something you can do something about and not into the solution of someone else's problems. Often you can make more money with a smaller organization that is lean and tough. Generate every dollar you can from within to aid growth and profitability.

Always remember in an acquisition this comment by Mark Twain: "If you pick up a starving dog and make him prosperous, he will not bite you. This is the principal difference between a dog and a man."

In addition, compute the risk of losing all of your investment for the potential profits of the venture? Will your investment require additional funds before it is successful? How long a time period is involved? Are you financially able to withstand a longer period of achievement on the project?

CASTOR OIL!

Despite the fact that firms can use the most sophisticated computer techniques in searching for promising acquisitions they can still make serious mistakes. One large firm spent over a year researching possible acquisition prospects, well over one thousand companies, and finally decided that it had found the ideal prospect. After the acquisition, the recession came along and immediately shot the pot of gold full of holes. Sales declined by one-fifth and profits of approximately 4% dissolved into a loss of 5%. Huge writeoffs occurred in accounts receivables and investments of the new subsidiary. All in all it was a disaster.

To climax the story, the unfortunate investment so depressed the acquiring firm's stock value on the market place that it became the target for a tender offer. While this was being resolved there was a complete management shakeup. In order to strengthen the firm's cash position the new group of managers immediately embarked upon a divestiture program and phased out without mercy any unprofitable portions of the business. The divestitures required cash payments from 50 to 70% and the balance in notes or debentures of varying maturities.

Without doubt, computer models and techniques can aid management in its decision process but a large measure of common sense and investigative effort is still required. Human intelligence and experience has some built-in warning mechanisms that work.

CASE STUDY—MERGER EVALUATION

Dear Ed:

Charlie and I have poured over the copious notes we made following our visit. Our preface was a visualization of what synergism might result from our joining forces.

We started with the operation as it exists today, on the presumed $8,800,000 volume and the $400,000 pretax profits. Based upon our own plant labor distribution and equipment utilization, we guess that it would be possible to double the profit figure on this volume at reasonable costs of layout and automated handling devices over say a three-year period.

In addition, we felt that it was reasonable to predict doubling the present sales volume at say current prices, concentrating on the "X" widget and extrusion-molded "Y" widgets, which offer the better margins and at lower capital costs. Our conservative guess of capital and expenses to do this would be about $1,500,000 "all in," and we thought this business "tail ended" onto present volume might produce an additional $1,200,000 pretax.

Give or take a few dollars, this suggested we might be looking at a volume of say $17,000,000 in five years' time and a net pretax of $2,000,000 on the present fixed capital plus $1,500,000. This was indeed an attractive proposition until we examined all of the probable effects of the merger.

Your labor rates are just over 52% of ours. Our union contracts would require that these rates be equalized in two years or less. We have a pretty generous pension plan, virtually fully funded. We think it would be unrealistic to believe that we could treat one group as "second cousins" and, therefore, presumed we would have to do as well for your people in a relatively short period—say five years.

If we were able to produce the $17,000,000 volume with only 300 hourly employees, the increased costs of our labor rates and pension plan would be at least $1,500,000 per year.

Subtracted from the healthy figure of $2,000,000 this leaves only $500,000 pretax. I'm certain that the number of shares we'd be willing to swap on these prospects would not be interesting to you nor would they reflect the value of your investment as a private company.

I must apologize for not having asked these key labor contract and pay questions earlier, for on them rest the key questions of net profit improvement within our corporate framework.

Many thanks for your splendid cooperation and rest assured that we will maintain the confidence of our meetings.

Cordially,

STUDY NUMBER TWO

Dear Mr. B:

We have just concluded a series of meetings and discussions with the top officials of a nationally known concern on the subject of their expansion and diversification objectives—which they hope to achieve by the acquisition of another company.

Our client is a leading manufacturer of small parts and assemblies, with plants strategically located from coast to coast, and they feel that the ideal candidate would be a company of similar type whose products would complement their own.

From the studies we have since made, your company would appear to closely fit the specifications given us, and it is for this reason that we are addressing this letter to you.

If you and your stockholders have ever considered the possibility of either a sale or merger, this is an affiliation which you most certainly should explore.

As you undoubtedly have received numerous inquiries such as this, I want to assure you that our people are not merely seeking a bargain. On the contrary, they are very hopeful of finding a sound and healthy company such as yours whose growth can be accelerated by the assistance, financial and otherwise, that they are in a position to offer.

I would also like to assure you that any discussions that we might have with you on this subject would be held in the strictest confidence—and entirely without obligation, of course.

Sincerely,

15

Administering and Complying with SEC Financial Reporting Requirements

This is a chapter dealing with reports. It includes internal and external reporting and as such subjects the financial administrator to both internal and external regulation, criticism and control. Throughout the entire reporting structure the financial executive must dramatize the good points as well as emphasizing the weaknesses that require executive attention. Naturally the bias is to paint a favorable picture in the external reports and to sometimes point out serious deficiencies within the privacy of the organization.

Somewhere in between the internal and external requirements is a narrow path for factual representation that maintains the integrity of the firm and its financial administrator, while attempting to satisfy all parties.

The science of reporting has changed so rapidly during the last decade that the old order of hard copy reports has given way to video displays, varied color charts and graphs projected on screens in Command Centers and interactive *on-line* terminals.

The president of one large restaurant firm can now sit in his office and by simply punching a few keys on a video terminal receive an up-to-the-minute report on the number of meals served at each unit, the average check for each patron and, if he so desires, the number of potatoes peeled for the day. If the information is satisfactory, the need for hard copy is nil and the business moves on.

To state it mildly, this has shaken up the financial management of most firms and forced them to reconsider and appraise their reporting systems. Even the smallest firms are now requiring instantaneous reporting of this type.

It is in the area of government and public reporting, however, that the greatest disturbance is occurring. The requirements for new techniques and new data have both disturbed and placed an awesome burden upon the financial executive. He is now required to file timely, inquisitive and interrogative reports with the regulatory authorities. These reports carry a full load of legal responsibilities that were never encountered in the past.

MAJOR AGENCIES

The major agencies involved are:

1. The Securities and Exchange Commission
2. The State Department and other agencies which regulate business with foreign countries and firms.
3. The Department of Commerce
4. Health, Education and Welfare
5. The Internal Revenue Service
6. The Department of Labor

Each of the above agencies has its own reporting requirements and each firm is subject to its particular reporting requests.

For the publicly owned firm or prospective registrants the major source of irritation these days is the SEC. Apparently it is headed on an all-out course of action aimed at dictating and controlling the financial accounting procedures of business.

The most commonly filed forms for this agency are the following:

1. Forms S-1 through S-11. These are registration forms for securities of the various types of firms.
2. Forms 7-K through 11-K. Most common is the 8-K Form—Reports of Non-Scheduled Material Events. The 10-K Form is the Annual Report filed by most firms.
3. Form 10-Q. The Quarterly Reports filed by most firms.

The 10-K Form is now regularly required to be furnished each stockholder upon written request to the firm.

Some of the items that the SEC has required disclosure on over the past few years are:

1. Catastrophic Reserves
2. Inventory Profits
3. Unusual Charges and Credits
4. Interim Financial Reporting

Complying with SEC Financial Reporting Requirements

    5. Income Tax Expense Breakdown
    6. Disclosure of Lease Commitments
    7. Compensating Balances with Banks or Others
    8. Segmented Income Accounts
    9. Replacement Cost Accounting
   10. Changes in Control
   11. Changes in Accountants
   12. Acquisition or Disposition of Assets

Firms that have changed auditing firms have been required to report to the SEC the disagreements that were involved in the change. Among the items listed were the following:

1. Disclosure of Insider Transactions
2. Recording Liabilities or Contingent Liabilities
3. When Revenue or Expense Items Should Appear in the Income Accounts
4. Classification of Assets or Liabilities on the Balance Sheet
6. Internal Control or Auditing Procedures
7. Recoverability of the Costs of Assets

The SEC has also focused on *proxy* statements requiring disclosure of *takeover attempts—legal actions* against *officers* and *directors*—details of *executive compensation plans*—other possible conflicting *directorships* held by *officers* and *directors*.

The SEC in a recent ruling has taken *replacement cost* and made it part of the "law of the land." In taking this action it has brought into sharp focus the impact of inflation upon all firms. In today's economy it can cost two to three times the original value to replace inventories or fixed assets.

While the original SEC directive affects only firms publicly traded with assets exceeding one-hundred million dollars in fixed assets and inventories, it is only a first step toward making all publicly held firms disclose their replacement costs. Ultimately we will have a government directive affecting all firms.

One of the most important factors in this action is the recognition that *historical cost accounting* based upon a sound and steady dollar is gone forever and that the amount of government regulation of business accounting techniques is increasing. In fact, you are now seeing the gradual turnover of accounting procedure regulations from private industry and the CPA associations to a government bureau.

The financial administrator must recognize this trend and prepare to adapt to it as soon as possible. "Forewarned is forearmed!" The major areas under his control that will be affected are:

1. Costing
2. Pricing
3. Return on investment
4. Insurable values

5. Real estate and personal property tax valuations
6. Cash flow projections
7. Strategic planning
8. Cost of money rates

The extent to which the SEC is accelerating its amendments to the various regulations is shown in the recent releases below:

1. Requires insurance firms to disclose unrealized appreciation and gross unrealized depreciation of marketable common and preferred stocks.
2. The basis assigned to securities sold.

This will have the effect of forcing all firms which previously carried their securities at cost to adopt the lower of cost or market pricing. This action will filter down to all firms in due course.

The house cleaning undertaken by industry in disclosing illegal payments both at home and abroad brought forth a veritable flood of questionnaires from the SEC and the IRS. Companies revealed in their 8-K Forms sent in to the SEC some very interesting and complicated deals with foreign governments, taxing authorities, bureaucrats, legal representatives, consultants and other influence peddlers. The responsibility of the financial administrator in ferreting out these items and seeing that they are disclosed in the proper reports filed with the SEC represents a major task and perhaps even a major decision as to whether he will continue to be employed by his present firm.

During the past few years some of the major accounting firms have thrown down the gauntlet to the SEC on the regulation of accounting policies and procedures for public accounting firms. The SEC, in the past five years, has moved aggressively into the field and has spawned some highly controversial changes in accounting, auditing and disclosure. The SEC has traditionally attacked some accounting procedures as misleading and subject to their control. Part of the problem arises from the fact that the "concept of accounting has changed coincident with changes in the tax law!"

The title of one regulation indicates the broadening coverage of SEC regulations; it is: "Promotion of the reliability of financial information, prevention of concealment of questionable or illegal corporate payments and practices and disclosure of the involvement of management in specified types of transactions." This has a direct bearing on the financial administrator in that it increases his responsibility to devise and maintain adequate financial control systems. This could place him in an untenable situation or could result in accounting system restrictions and increased government intervention in the financial affairs of the firm.

The disclosure regulation can conceivably affect the relationship of every publicly owned firm with the investment community. Large firms often hold numerous interviews with financial analysts. Since these interviews involve the financial executive and often disclose more information than is available in the annual reports, 10-K's, 8-K's or 10-Q's, the SEC has taken the position that this favors some investors over others. This will restrict the corporate information disclosed and will force the financial executive to review it thoroughly prior to the meeting. If disclosure is required it will tend to make the projections ultra-conservative or unduly restricted.

The gist of the entire matter is that the financial executive may as well prepare for dramatic changes in financial reporting. One of the most dramatic and drastic changes is the rejection of *historical cost accounting*. The increase in the rate of inflation during the 1970's brought about considerable deliberation and extensive studies of the effect of inflation on accounting and financial reports. Two major solutions were proposed one of which ultimately led to the SEC regulation on *replacement cost accounting*.

1. CVA—Current Value Accounting

   In early 1976 the SEC laid down rules to require the current disclosure of the current cost to replace inventories, plant and equipment and the effect on the cost of sales and depreciation if they were computed on the basis of replacement costs.

   This proved to be a "skunk by the tail" for every financial administrator and the flack that it generated was enormous; however, it was a lost cause and the financial executive has been forced to come to grips with the problem.

Current Value Accounting merely means that the capital requirements are related to a firm's ability to produce goods at the same level at the end of the accounting period as at the beginning. It discards the old historical cost concept by reflecting the specific changes in prices of assets and liabilities on the financial statements. It acts on the premise that an increase in the value of the fixed assets shall be included in the shareholders' equity. The change in the purchasing power of the dollar and the gains and losses arising therefrom are not recognized.

Discussions with top financial executives indicate concern over the failure to recognize monetary gains and losses and the extreme difficulty of implementing it. There is a major problem in obtaining the annual data involved considered reliable enough to measure the replacement costs of the physical plant and equipment. Due to the specialized nature of many facilities problems with highly subjective valuations will arise. As one financial executive of a major copper producing firm stated: "It will be a hell of a job every year! Who will judge whether we are right or wrong?"

2. GPL—General Price Level Accounting

   General Price Level Accounting maintains the historical concept as a base and utilizes a general price level index in order to restate the assets in terms of current purchasing power. Capital requirements are maintained in terms of the constant purchasing power of the dollar by means of a general index of inflation. One of its key working elements is the recognition of gains inherent in long-term debt positions. It provides some substance for the thought that the deeper in debt you are during inflation the better off you are financially. The thought of creating profits through heavy long-term debt is startling to many conservative financial executives.

There are two major objections to the GPL approach. First, the general price index used for inflation cannot apply equally to all firms and could be subject to wide variations. Secondly, monetary gains due to long-term debt are believed to be misleading in nature.

KEY SEC DEFINITIONS

1. *Productive Capacity*—The measurement of your firm's ability to produce and distribute its products. Number of units presently produced within a given time limit.
2. *Current Replacement Cost*—Defined as "replacement cost new" for productive facilities. This is the minimum amount required to replace existing facilities.
3. *Depreciated Replacement Cost*—The minimum cost to replace existing facilities less an amount equal to the depreciation of the replacement cost to reflect the life expiration of the current facilities.
4. *Net Realizable Value*—What you can sell the asset for in the current market less reasonable costs to place it in saleable condition and the costs of selling.
5. *Inventory Valuation*—The lowest cost to acquire or produce the same quantities at the year end. Purchased items would be at prices required to purchase and transport them to the plant at year end and manufactured items would be priced at the year end prices required to reproduce them.

Inventory Indices—To come up with inventory indices one must prepare internal indices of major component costs. The overhead factors must be adjusted to reflect depreciation based upon replacement costs of the producing facilities. External indices can be obtained from trade groups or other sources. Price change classifications, in detail, are useful in preparing and utilizing such indices.

THESE ARE THE QUESTIONS FACING THE FINANCIAL ADMINISTRATOR

How can he improve the quality and credibility of his financial reports?

Should he disclose more raw data?

What should be disclosed and what will satisfy the SEC, the financial community, and the individual investor?

What are the advantages and disadvantages of full disclosure?

What are the dangers inherent in CVA and GPL? Do they really and truthfully solve the information problem?

What affirmative action can be taken to curb the continued intrusion of government agencies into the accounting and financial management of your firm?

The answers can be mighty important to you!

BENEFITS AND PROBLEMS OF DISCLOSURE—REFERENCES

1. AICPA—Corporate financial reporting
2. The Mundheim Paper—"Trends in SEC disclosure for public corporations."
3. The Gray Paper—"The need for disclosure criteria."
4. The Mayo Paper—"The corporate view."
5. The Schoenborn Paper—"Disclosure and the banks: how much is enough?"

Complying with SEC Financial Reporting Requirements

WHAT ARE SOME OF THE IMPORTANT FACTORS IN REPORTS?

1. *Balance Sheet Items*

    a. Accounts Receivable—Status, aging and allowance for losses

    b. Inventories—Components and methods of valuation

    c. Cash—Ratio of cash to accounts payable and current liabilities

    d. Current Ratio—Quick ratio

    e. Categories of Tangible Assets

    f. Market Value of any securities held

    g. Ratio of debt to equity capital

    h. Debt service factors—amounts required to service short-term and long-term debt

    i. Contingent liabilities or commitments

    j. Valuation of amounts invested in subsidiaries, joint ventures, partnerships or other entities

2. *Income Account Items*

    a. Sales and profits by product lines

    b. Dollar values of order backlogs

    c. Costs to complete projects—construction in progress accounts

    d. Provision for bad debts

    e. Depreciation factor in costs

    f. Unusual charges or credits

    g. Sales per dollar of plant

    h. Return on investment—segmented

3. *Other Items*

    a. Changes in accounting methods

    b. Effect of LIFO on profits

    c. Liability on leases—rented equipment or plant

    d. Investments in affiliates—joint ventures—subsidiaries—foreign firms

    e. International currency exposure

    f. Provision for income taxes—amount of deferred income taxes

    g. Reconciliation of retained earnings

    h. Sources and applications of funds

    i. Cash flow projections

    j. Future business projections

These are some of the releases that affect every financial administrator:

1. Replacement cost data must be included in the firm's 10-K Report although it may be labelled "Unaudited."

2. SEC now permits optional filing of forecasts.

3. SEC may allow cash flow forecasts in initial offerings of stocks.
4. SEC acts to thwart accounting changes. It will restrict changes unless the firm's auditors give an opinion that the new principle is "PREFERABLE."

Today there are even more critical issues which must be faced by the financial administrator. At least two congressional committees have filed reports calling for legislation that will directly affect the accounting procedures for all publicly owned firms. The recommendations in these reports require intensive study, analysis and interpretation. Top management must be kept fully informed of the implications contained therein and the regulations proposed for legislation by Congress. It is vitally essential that the financial executive follow the legislative action in Congress. The proposed regulations are broad, wide ranging and impose additional responsibilities on officers and directors.

SEC ACTION CAN AFFECT EARNINGS

In the 1975 Annual Report of the Del E. Webb Corporation the effect of a SEC directive is clearly stated:

". . . the Company deemed it necessary to write off the $2,749,000 of claimed costs. The Company believes that the write-off should have been accorded prior period adjustment treatment since all the criteria for prior period adjustment treatment set forth in Accounting Principles Board Opinion No. 9 were met. This treatment would have reduced previously reported consolidated net earnings by $365,000 ($.04 per share) in 1970 and $1,100,000 ($1.13 per share) in 1971. However, at the insistence of the Securities and Exchange Commission, the $2,749,000 has been charged to operations in the 1974 consolidated statement of earnings resulting in a reduction of consolidated net earnings of $1,475,000 ($.17 per share)."

WORD OF WARNING

In filing SEC reports for any governmental agencies utilize extreme caution, be certain of your position, and do not hesitate to fight for principles that you feel are right. Government regulations can and will inundate you with forms and paperwork. The increased cost to the corporation is currently measured in large sums. The costs have only one way to go . . . *up!*

Those of us who prepare the 8-K's, 10-K's and 10-Q's are well aware of the costs in time, effort and money not to mention the frustrations involved.

LATE DEVELOPMENTS

SEC has moved to widen company disclosures, demanding revenues and profit-and-loss figures by line of business before taxes and extraordinary items. The commission intends to extend such disclosures to foreign operations. At the present time only a general discussion of the risks involved in foreign investments is required. It is also conducting a

Complying with SEC Financial Reporting Requirements

broad review of proxy rules to see if they foster "entrenched management misconduct." It is concerned about the ability of management, through the proxy machinery, to set corporate policies and effectively control the corporation. Items under consideration are:

1. Greater disclosure relative to the "quality" of board nominees, "the process used to select nominees" and the amount of time directors spend on company affairs.
2. Elimination of discretionary proxies held by individuals or management on behalf of shareholders. One of the items targeted is the "street name" proxies held by banks, securities firms and others. The SEC study has found that most "street name" proxies are voted for management.

TIME FACTOR

One company interim report draws attention to the time factor involved in filing the formal SEC reports and the ability to furnish the shareholder with timely reports. This is simply stated in an interim report:

To Our Shareholders:

The time lapse between the end of the Trust's fiscal quarters and the distribution of the Trust's reports to shareholders has increasingly been of concern to the Trustees. In part this has been due to our policy of supplying you much of the information and detail contained in the Form 10-Q which is filed with the Securities and Exchange Commission. In order to provide you with a report that is more timely and perhaps more useful to you, as well as less expensive to produce, we are experimenting this quarter by sending out an abbreviated financial information summary as soon as it is available with some comments on the results. In the effort to minimize costs we will continue to use third class mail except for overseas addresses. Upon request we will be pleased to provide those shareholders who desire more detailed information with a copy of the complete Form 10-Q after it has been filed with the SEC. Your comments on this approach to the timely distribution of information to shareholders will be appreciated. My one comment might be: Reliance on third class mail could be a disaster as far as speedy delivery is concerned. The reference to time factors and costs is of concern to every financial administrator.

16

Macroeconomics and Financial Administration

MAJOR KEY

One of the major keys to financial success is a sound knowledge of economics and the ability to discern future economic trends. No single factor has a greater bearing upon your business growth and profitability. It presents a challenge to every financial administrator to develop a sound financial plan that will meet all the varying economic conditions encountered by his firm. Make no mistake! The lack of realization and understanding that economic conditions are changing has cost firms more money than any other type of action. The real ball game in the business world is the scoreboard reflecting the changes in *gross national product* and your component share of the total.

All of us realize that the level of economic activity will change from month to month and from year to year. These changes will affect your revenues, your production, your profits and your financial requirements. In order to prepare for these changes your best course of action is to prepare quick responses to deal with the upcoming economic surprises. To do this properly you must have a system that will enable you to watch the trends and changes on a disciplined basis. The analysis of business conditions and the forecasting of trends is not too complicated if one is properly organized for the job.

WHY FORECAST?

The answer is money: increased profits for your firm and increased compensation and responsibility for you if you are successful in developing a system that will alert your executives to the economic trends. The rise and fall in the level of business logically prompts the all-important question, "What is the effect of these fluctuations upon our firm?" Financial administrators are not economic illiterates. No one can convince them that their business activity is on a straight-line basis. We all have a sixth sense that tells us when the trend is headed up or down. It becomes apparent in our individual statistics that increasing receivables and inventories forecast declining production and sales. On the other hand, rising order backlogs, shortages and other items forecast problems caused by increasing sales. If you wish to plan and grow successfully you must correlate your planning and financial growth with external business conditions and economic factors. There is a definite time to run with the tide and a time to conserve your assets and strength. The crucial trends of consumer expenditures and capital expansion are vital to growth and profits.

DO NOT UNDERESTIMATE!

Make no mistake about our future potential for growth. People will have both time and money to spend. They will purchase anything that appeals to them with the time and convenience factors becoming increasingly important. We have moved into a rental type economy wherein your status is determined not by what you own but by what you rent or finance. Decreasing supplies of conventional materials and fuels will result in a veritable wealth of new products and trends in technology. Economic changes must be watched for their affect on your business. Avon had to realign its entire selling strategy simply because more wives started working and no longer were home to greet their salespeople at the usual times.

IMPORTANCE OF MACROECONOMICS

You might well ask, "What good are economics and macroeconomics to me?" In my opinion, economics is the whole secret of financial administration. If you know what the present business level is and you are aware of the current trend you have an opportunity to make or save a great deal of money for your firm. You can definitely correlate your firm's revenues and activities with some business indices whether you are in durable goods, non-durables, mining, financing or services.

ADMINISTRATING AND STAFFING THE ECONOMIC FUNCTION

Interviews with executives of various firms indicate that the number of individuals involved in performing economic reporting and analysis varies directly with the type, size and needs of the individual firm. In some larger firms the function is handled by a separate economic section under control of the marketing division. In the majority of instances the responsibility is placed under the financial administrator. In smaller firms the activities are under the direction of the controller or financial executive. Due to the complexities of the extremely sophisticated economic forecasting sections of the large international firms we have concentrated upon an analysis of the administration and staffing of the medium-sized and smaller firms.

Macroeconomics and Financial Administration

Staffs in this category range from ten individuals headed by an economist who was supported by three staff analysts, two statisticians, two chartists and two secretaries to a single individual who prepared reports, economic analyses, charts and maintained the files.

Perhaps the single most important function of the administrator is the orderly collection and reporting of significant economic information. It is vitally important that the administrator be kept informed of the major economic developments on a regular and continuing basis. If this is done, the opportunity to recognize vital economic trends and their resulting effect on your firm's activities are available for immediate action or reaction.

In reviewing your staff requirements you must also consider the need for cooperation and use of the economic knowledge generated within your entire organization. Other members of your firm are constantly traveling about and contacting various segments of the economy. They are in a position to closely observe competitive strategies and the resulting consumer reaction. They are in constant contact with the everyday economy and have a vital knowledge of its current condition and trends.

The major banks have as one of their most important resources, world-wide economic intelligence staffs. The information gathered by these individuals, when fed to responsible analysts, reveals to them the meaningful information behind the ordinary daily news. These are the hard facts they use to transfer funds, buy and sell, borrow or lend and decide which risks to take or avoid. For the cost of a monthly luncheon tab part of this information can be filtered down to you.

This is the "window to business" that each financial executive needs in order to keep in touch with the latest actions and news that can influence company policy decisions. It can give you an arsenal of information on new economic trends, new products and developments—all expertly evaluated—to put you far in advance of the "business as usual" thinking.

Your staff, therefore, could range from one to ten, depending upon how elaborate an economic analysis system you require. Each individual must determine the cost of the operation as contrasted to the benefits received. No matter how large or small your firm is, today's fast-moving economic trends require that some sort of economic analysis program be maintained in order to keep you aware of the economic action. The individuals who staff your economic function should be perceptive, analytical, inquisitive and specialize in figure or chart watching. They must continually ask, "Why did this happen?" and "Where does this trend lead us?" They must have the ability to recognize the value of material in newspaper, magazine and trade journal articles and correlate these items into meaningful economic data.

MACROECONOMICS

Today there is a new and important tool available to keep the financial administrator on top of the changing economic climate: "macroeconomics." The term covers the study of economic aggregates at the national level. It looks at the long- and short-term trends of income and output and at the rate of change in these items. Its primary purpose is to determine the rate of change and to find the underlying factors responsible for these changes. In short, *macroeconomics* is the measurement of economic activity.

As you undoubtedly recognize, the measurement of aggregate economic activity is very complex and difficult. The massive volumes of figures involved in employment, government transactions, credit, money and capital markets, plus other items, is a herculean task. The financial executive must, therefore, simplify the data into certain "target items" which are closely related to his industry and to his individual operation.

After the target items are determined one has the responsibility of establishing or combining them into a base figure. Since all of the items are in different terms a common denominator must be developed. The easiest way to do this is to set one year's average as a base and term this one hundred. Each target item is then based out and assigned a weighted factor based upon its relative importance in the total economy, the industry and the individual firm.

In the event one does not wish to establish target items he can utilize certain indices devised by others and record or chart their action, attempting to correlate them to his own performance. Basic trend indicators are published by the following:

Federal Reserve Board—Industrial production
Business Week—Business activity
Forbes—Business activity

These indices are used by many financial executives as part of their economic watching system. *Business Week*, published weekly, has an excellent set of indicators compiled from various sources which will keep you informed of trends on a weekly, monthly or quarterly basis.

The aggregate total of the production of goods and services in our national economy is expressed as GNP (Gross National Product). This is the basis for all economic forecasting, and every economic forecaster is vitally interested in what this figure currently is and what it is going to be for future months and years. Macroeconomic data combines GNP with NI (National Income) and DI (Disposable Income) into factors which can be readily applied to your company planning and strategies.

Naturally, the question then arises "How does one go about measuring and forecasting business activity and applying it to his own operations?" This is where macroeconomics enters the picture. It is a vital part of financial administration and planning. Even if one only maintains a simple chart book, he is aware of and watching the weekly or monthly changes in the economic picture. The discipline obtained in setting up a macroeconomic system for measuring and forecasting economic trends will benefit you and your firm. Opportunities taken advantage of, and warnings heeded, can be converted into dollars and cents of additional sales or profits. You will learn to refine the general terms into specifics which have a direct relationship to your industry and your firm.

Prior to a good financial plan one needs a good economic forecast. This is broken down into two parts: first a forecast of the various target items or economic variables that have in the past affected the business; second, a forecast of the business action and reaction based upon this past relationship. Although macroeconomics represents the best tool available to quantify a business—economic correlation—its results need to be judged very carefully. Economics does not take into consideration business changes in structure, technology or

Macroeconomics and Financial Administration 413

industry position. One of the major advantages is that it allows you to simulate your business operations and results under various economic assumptions. Properly approached it can be an excellent early warning device.

WHAT IS THE TREND?

If you are watching business conditions closely you can forecast your sales activity within 5% and hit the target nine times out of ten. If the economic conditions in the last three to six months trend downward, unless your situation is exceptional, you must forecast a lower level of activity. To do an excellent job you must carefully analyze your revenues on a month-to-month basis as well as a quarter-by-quarter basis. Do not overlook your seasonal pattern and the effect of adding or dropping or products with substantial volume. Check your correlation with the various indices, product group by product group. Is there a lead or lag factor involved? In this manner the spotting of trends in the indices will enable you to predict the trends in your product revenues.

Always remember you have inflation and price changes to deal with. Remember too, the country is growing and your firm is going to grow with it if you are a good financial executive. The trends and rate of change are important financial factors in your planning and reporting.

SOURCES OF ECONOMIC DATA

Strangely enough, the pages of your local newspaper provide a great deal of economic information. Small items can be most productive if collated, assembled and properly analyzed. All of the major changes in the economy occur quite slowly and the various events reported in the daily newspaper can have a direct bearing on your future. Current economic events will directly or indirectly filter down to your industry and affect your profit-and-loss totals.

Reading the daily financial and economic news will not make one an economic expert overnight. Years of experience, indoctrination and perception are essential for developing a nose for the economic items of importance. First, one must understand the various parts of the economy, and then analyze and correlate them to an understanding of the broad picture which makes up the national economy and its trends. By keeping closely tuned to current events, utilizing a simple or complex micro-target system, skill can be developed in interpreting and forecasting economic trends within reasonable limits.

There are many items in the daily papers which are pertinent and important to any business operation. Large firms clip and circulate news of unusual manufacturing processes, new products, or comments by economists, bankers or other executives. These items can point the way to future changes in markets, processes, financing or strategies. In addition, a close watch on the stock market action of industry groups as detailed in Barrons or comments relative to the action of industries or individual firms by security analysts can also provide important clues to future action and trends in all segments of business.

In order to set a pattern for your base or target figures you must utilize some benchmarks. Many firms use the Federal Reserve Board's indices for the basis of their economic planning and watching. Which indices are used depends upon your product lines. Where, then, does one find the data upon which to prepare his bases? An immense amount of effort has been put into the production of economic statistics. One of the most useful and elaborate sources of material is the "Economic Conditions Digest" available from the Superintendent of Documents. All of the data in this publication are expressed in statistical tables or charts. There are seventy-two indicators, thirty-six lead items, twenty-five coincidental and eleven lagging items. It ties in perfectly with macroeconomics by showing the diffusion indices which show the trend and rate of change in the indicators. While it is a beautiful series, few of us in the field have the time to study all the data in detail. If your staff is large enough, one individual can spend full time on various pertinent items alone. In setting up your target items you may well have to decide which items are most useful.

Another very excellent source of business statistics is the "Survey of Current Business" published by the Office of Business Economics of the Commerce Department and available through the Superintendent of Documents. It has a vast amount of information on production, shipments, orders, inventories and other items. It covers most of the basic industries. The publication is updated weekly by a statistical supplement which contains both weekly data and charts. Frankly, it is considered to be one of the best tools for forecasting individual firm sales and production trends. Much of the data is readily usable in developing your target items and in developing and utilizing financial forecasting models.

Other well-known and often-used sources of economic and business data include Barrons—*The Wall Street Journal—Business Week—U.S. News and World Report*, published daily or weekly. In addition, the Treasury Bulletin and The Federal Reserve Bulletin have valuable information. Many trade publications publish statistics which are directly related to your industry along with comments on trends. For example, the National Association of Home Builders newspaper publishes figures on monthly sales of houses, median sales prices and the inventory of homes currently on hand. The Department of Labor publishes detailed earnings and price statistics which are most useful in economic watching and forecasting.

The accumulation of the normally or desired, required group of economic statistics is quite simple. The basic items include a subscription to Barrons, *Business Week, The Wall Street Journal* and the Survey of Current Business (including the weekly supplement). In order to broaden your national picture of the news it is suggested that you subscribe to about six daily or Sunday editions of newspapers. Daily editions will give you a better cross-analysis of the news; however, the questions of staff, time and costs may be determining factors. As a suggestion, try Chicago, New York, Washington, Los Angeles, Houston and Atlanta or Denver. Canada has an excellent weekly publication titled *The Financial Post* as an additional option. It will alert you to economic and financial trends in Canada plus offering some unbiased opinions of what is going on in the U.S.A. At times it serves as a great ego deflator. Two to ten trade journals should give you ample industry coverage.

As we set up our economic and financial intelligence operation the question normally arises, "What information should be utilized?" In a sample activity study we will abstract the following information from the various sources:

Macroeconomics and Financial Administration

1. Business Activity—Weekly index, chart versus last year, 52 weeks.
2. Production Activity—Charts showing weekly comparison versus one year ago.
   a. Steel production
   b. Automobiles and trucks
   c. Paper and paperboard
   d. Lumber
3. Shipment Activity—Charted versus one year ago.
   a. Rail freight
   b. Intercity truck tonnage
4. Sales Activity—Retail sales charted versus one year ago; may be adjusted for price changes.
5. Prices—Charted versus one year ago; five-year trend.
   a. Industrial raw materials—group or detailed
   b. Foodstuffs
   c. Copper
   d. Scrap iron
   e. Wheat, corn, soybeans—can be expanded to other items such as oil, meal, etc.
6. Finance—Charted versus one year ago.
   a. Interest rates
      1. Treasury bills
      2. Federal funds
      3. Eurodollar rates
      4. Prime rate
      5. Bankers acceptances
      6. Certificates of deposit
   b. Money supply
   c. Currency in circulation
   d. Commercial and agricultural loans
7. Data on Stock and Bond Market Activity
8. Weekly Advances and Declines
   a. New York Exchange
   b. American Exchange
   c. OTC

These items can be accumulated daily or weekly. When all three exchanges are combined it gives an excellent indicator as to the trend of the market and industry in general.

The above thirty or so items represent a "quick" review of the current economic situation for individuals and firms who do not wish to get too deeply involved in economic analysis and forecasting. They will provide excellent, simple reporting and charting material which will show the actual trend of business long before it becomes available at the local level. By accumulating the material weekly, a simple task of from one to three hours' duration, depending on the data utilized, it is possible to keep fully informed on the major economic trends in the country. This is a minute price to pay for such knowledge. Naturally, it takes insight, experience and practice to know just what the action of each item portends.

Once one acquires the feel of it, the game of guessing "What comes next?" is fascinating. One of the most important questions we have to answer is, "Where are we in the business cycle and what is the trend?" These statistics and charts should answer these questions.

If you are interested in commodities the U.S. Department of Agriculture has a series of excellent reports on crop expectations and production. It gives a complete rundown on all types of crops by states. Anyone involved in economic forecasting should secure these reports.

TYPES OF REPORTS AND CHARTS

Interviews with owners and financial administrators of medium and smaller businesses indicate a complete lack of economic reports or charts. Most businessmen rely on the daily newspapers for their economic news. It is only occasionally that one finds a business owner or financial administrator of a smaller firm who is interested enough to systematically accumulate the information and maintain it in disciplined reports or charts. This is a serious deficiency in our management practices for economics is a major factor in our business lives. Many of the individuals follow certain raw material items with some regularity. For example, in the electrical contracting business we find that the prices of copper and aluminum are watched rather closely. The information is utilized to purchase products containing these items for inventory in anticipation of future price increases or to cover needs for contracts bid, which have future completion dates. Actual changes in the prices of the raw materials is not reflected in the cost estimating until such price changes actually occur despite the fact that estimates may cover a period of as long as one year in advance. Placing a price limitation on estimates or limiting the duration of the estimated price to supplies on hand saved over thirty thousand dollars in one three-month period. Charting the prices of certain raw materials and the relationship to product prices would appear to be a valuable tool for the financial executive.

The current trend toward "anticipatory pricing" has made the latter technique an absolute necessity for financial administration. Under this method, the forecast prices of raw materials, labor and other items are fed into a cost estimating computer model and the proposed price for six months to one year in advance is generated. If the traffic will bear it prices are increased to this level. If not, they are gradually raised until the goal is attained. This eliminates the normal pricing lag while the product is flowing through the distribution pipelines. In addition, you have a weekly follow-up of anticipated unusual trends in prices.

Most individuals follow the stock market to some extent but strangely enough few of them watch the bond market or interest rates with any regularity. All of them had outstanding loans whose interest costs floated with the prime rate.

In order to more fully understand the economic forecasting process and the reasons for reporting or watching them we must therefore know more about certain of the more important items and what they consist of. Some basic understanding of the various statistics is necessary to fully interpret the significance of their movement from week to week. Let us review a few of the more important candidates for charting or reporting prior to moving into the depths of macroeconomics.

Macroeconomics and Financial Administration

LEADING, COINCIDENTAL AND LAGGING INDICATORS

The most widely used gauge of future business trends is the Commerce Department's index of leading indicators. It is a composite of twelve statistical series that generally forecasts booms, recessions or trends by a minimum of from two to six months. The diffusion indices covering these items provide the macroeconomic trends required.

The other two indicators, coincident and lagging, tend to confirm a boom or recession and strangely enough can serve as an early warning indicator of future trends. These items alone constitute one of the simplest economic watching systems. The government provides all of the material in concise form for a very reasonable fee.

BUSINESS ACTIVITY

This is a broad spectrum index developed by *Business Week* which shows the current trend of business activity. By closely watching its course you can gauge the direction of the economy. The magazine provides an excellent chart, updated weekly, which can be used without further preparation.

Normal practice is to chart it on an annual chart showing the previous year by weeks versus the current year. This spots any seasonal trends and gives you some relationship between the two years. It also correlates with your financial reports which most often show the figures for the two years on a comparison basis. Weekly comments can be utilized to note any unusual items which affect the statistics. These could include strikes, storms, holidays and other non-normal items. A fifty-two week comparison for two or three years can be used to disclose seasonal trends as follows:

WEEK NO.	YEAR 1	YEAR 2	YEAR 3	CHANGE 2	CHANGE 3
1	121.8*	108.5	124.8	+13.5	−3.0
2	123.0	108.8	124.4	+14.2	−1.4
3	123.0	109.3	124.7	+14.7	−1.7
4	123.2	109.3	125.2	+13.9	−2.0
5	123.4	109.5	125.4	+13.9	−2.0

*Adversely affected by a strike.

Certain of the factors in the index have cycles of light and heavy production.

STOCK PRICES

Next in importance and most fascinating is the current trend in the stock market. Millions of people watch the stock market statistics each day. This index is considered to be a leading indicator which precedes business activity by about six months. One thing is certain, unless you deal in stocks or bonds, no firm correlation can generally be made between your business and the market. It is influenced by many factors, some international in scope, and has ideas of its own totally unrelated to business in general. It is, however, interesting to note that in the 1974–1976 recession and recovery, stock prices in the various industry groups led the decline in sales and production and advanced prior to the announced or apparent recovery.

THE EBB AND FLOW

Business tides are reflected in several items. These can be placed in three categories: first the item of Commercial Loans, then Demand Deposits and finally Government Securities Held. The deposits represent the "quick" assets of industry commonly termed "cash in banks" and the loans represent the "current liabilities" owed by business. Strangely enough, idle funds often mean stagnant activity. This is also indicated by falling business loans. Rising loans and cash shortages often mean business is expanding. The spread between the two items readily shows the corporate liquidity picture and whether ample funds are available or if money is tight. If the difference or spread is slim, corporate liquidity is low, money is tight and interest rates are rising or high.

A rise in commercial loan demand at the banks indicates that the small- and medium-sized firms who do not have access to commercial paper or other sources of funds are borrowing because of increased business. The small firms are the first to borrow as the economy moves up. This indicator is obtained by using the Federal Reserve Board figures. Subtract the loan figures for New York and Chicago to watch the loan picture of the smaller banks.

GOVERNMENT SECURITIES HELD

The level of government securities held indicates the action of the Federal Reserve Board and the banks. Banks liquidate federal securities to participate in the more profitable commercial loans. The Federal Reserve Board controls the money supply by selling or purchasing government securities. The participation of the Federal Reserve in the securities market is often disclosed in news squibs buried on the financial page and needs close watching to observe. It will show up as a line stating, "The Fed entered the market twice today as the Federal Funds rate fell below x.xx."

We also have weekly up-dated figures on the money supply which indicates the federal policy of stimulating or restricting business activity through relaxation or tightening of available credit. The federal funds rate of interest is a "quick" indicator as to the status of the money market.

PAPERBOARD—PAPER

One of the more reliable leading indicators of manufacturing activity is the paperboard production index. This conclusion is based upon the premise that the carton is required while the item is being manufactured and prior to the actual sale. The consumption of paperboard should therefore indicate the future rise or fall of trade. It is also a well-known fact in the

Macroeconomics and Financial Administration

paper industry that when business is bad you produce kraft quality items and when business is good you upgrade into the better papers.

TRUCK ACTIVITY AND RAILROAD CARLOADINGS

These items are closely correlated to the movement of raw materials and finished products. Since future retail activity is preceded by the movement of goods in the distribution channels, we can safely assume that the rise and fall in these figures tells us something about future business trends. A major seasonal bulge occurs in these figures during the annual grain harvest.

RETAIL SALES

The weekly estimate of retail sales is vitally important in measuring the consumer mood. If they are buying, business is stable or expanding. If they tighten up the purse strings, business contracts. This then, subject to inflation, is the most sensitive index we have, indicating each week the consumer's availability of funds or credit and the willingness to spend it. This index is reinforced by the University of Michigan's "Consumer Confidence Index" which indicates current and future attitudes for consumer spending.

These are sample ideas of reports or charts to use in your macroeconomic forecasting system and for target items which can be correlated to your operations. Sample reports and charts actually in use are presented at the end of the chapter. (See pages 422-424.)

COMPUTER MODELS FOR SPOTTING TRENDS

In this world of constant change and new techniques the financial administrator has at his command a modern tool which can help in projecting the many changes of the future. The computer serves as a storehouse for data about past and present operations within and outside of his organization. He has available "models" which will quickly report the results of "What if?" projections. Input/output matrices can be expanded to enhance his insight of current events and sharpen his judgment on the all-important financial decisions.

Interviews have indicated that many firms use models. Strangely enough, they are not confined to the larger firms. We found instances where firms with volume from two million to twenty-five million dollars were successfully using models. In the field of macroeconomic forecasting there were only a few firms utilizing models. The formulas in use were highly confidential and little information could be gleaned as to the extent of the modeling, the items covered, or the success of the projects. The primary use of the economic models is to spot trends and changes in the economy and forecast their future effect on company operations. In addition, in-house models are correlated with external economic trends to reflect changes in consumer demand and its effect on production and sales patterns. In the field of macroeconomics models are utilized to forecast GNP, PI, price levels, employment, interest rates and other changes in the country's economic performance. Measurement of the rate of change is the most important factor. Dependent upon the industry and the individual firm the models for spotting economic trends which will influence their business must be tailormade and based upon the many factors which have a direct relationship to their sales and cost patterns.

PERSONAL INCOME

Since personal income (PI) is one of the major bases for financial forecasting and action, the amount and change can be ascertained, detailed by state, from the government statistics or from an excellent monthly summary published in *Business Week*. These figures and the changes can be correlated with your sales activities by region or state. There is a definite relationship of production to each dollar of spending. For example the materials used in each of the end products are shown below:

AUTOS—TRUCKS	FARM EQUIPMENT	SHOES
Steel	Steel	Steel
Cast Iron	Cast Iron	
Glass	Glass	
Rubber	Rubber	Rubber
Plastics	Plastics	Plastics
Textiles	Textiles	Textiles
Leather	Leather	Leather
Copper	Copper	
Aluminum	Aluminum	
Other	Other	Other

Substituting the number of pounds of each material for each finished unit gives you the interdependence of the various producing and consuming units in our economy. An increase in personal income could mean more automobiles and trucks sold which in turn would flow down through the steel, rubber, copper and other industries. An increase in farm income through higher prices or larger crops would aid the farm equipment manufacturers plus other industries. The flow-through includes related suppliers as well as such service industries as financing, banking or advertising.

Some of the readily available statistics which are sensitive to the changes in the economy are:

Help Wanted Ads—Very sensitive

Labor Statistics—Wages and hours—U.S. Department of Labor

Housing Starts—Dodge Reports

Construction—Dodge Reports

10-Day Auto Sales—Wards Automotive Reports—very sensitive

Wholesale Price Index—U.S. Government—this is a good early warning indicator of inflationary trends

Production Index—   Federal Reserve Board
                          Broad base—covers manufacturing, mining and utilities

Macroeconomics and Financial Administration

	Production Range	*End Use*
	Durable goods	Consumer goods
	Non-durables	Equipment
	Mining	Materials
	Utilities	
Individual Savings—	Correlates with auto purchases	

There are numerous statistics to choose from. Each financial administrator must try each series until he finds the group that moves in relation to his industry and his firm. It requires trial and error to tailormake your own target items and macroeconomic indicators which will do the best job for your firm.

After all of the preliminary work is done and you have fought your way through your financial and economic forecast for the period involved there is still one additional item required to make the task successful. This is the scenario:

"Gentlemen we have completed our financial and economic forecast! Now let us pray!"

WEEKLY CHECKLISTS

FINANCIAL

COMMERCIAL, INDUSTRIAL AND AGRICULTURAL LOANS
U.S. TREASURY SECURITIES—AMOUNT HELD—AMOUNT BOUGHT OUTRIGHT
    DEMAND DEPOSITS—COMMERCIAL BANKS—SAVINGS DEPOSITS—TIME DEPOSITS
    MONEY IN CIRCULATION
    RESERVES—FREE RESERVES—EXCESS BANK RESERVES
    GROSS FEDERAL DEBT
    MONEY SUPPLY—M1 AND M2
    INTEREST RATES
        FEDERAL FUNDS—PRIME RATE—DISCOUNT RATE—90-DAY TREASURY BILLS
        30-DAY BANKERS' ACCEPTANCES—30-DAY COMMERCIAL PAPER—EURODOLLAR RATES
        CERTIFICATES OF DEPOSIT—30 DAYS—120 DAYS—ONE YEAR

ECONOMIC

AUTO—TRUCK PRODUCTION
PAPER—PAPERBOARD PRODUCTION
PETROLEUM REFINING—% OF CAPACITY
STEEL PRODUCTION—TONNAGE—% OF CAPACITY
RAIL AND TRUCK ACTIVITY
RETAIL SALES
CONSTRUCTION—PLANNED BUILDING IN MILLIONS OF DOLLARS

CHECKLISTS

MONTHLY—QUARTERLY—ANNUALLY

ECONOMIC—MONTHLY

DURABLE GOODS—SHIPMENTS—ORDERS—INVENTORIES—BACKLOGS
LEAD INDICATORS
CONSUMER PRICE INDEX—WHOLESALE PRICE INDEX
MACHINE TOOLS—ORDERS—SHIPMENTS—INVENTORIES—BACKLOGS
FEDERAL RESERVE INDEX OF PRODUCTION—BY COMPONENTS
LUMBER—SHIPMENTS—PRODUCTION—INVENTORIES—BACKLOGS
BUILDING CONTRACTS—CONSTRUCTION EXPENDITURES
EMPLOYMENT—UNEMPLOYMENT
MANUFACTURING—BY COMPONENTS—ORDERS—SHIPMENTS—INVENTORIES—BACKLOGS
FARM PRICES—CROP ESTIMATES AND CROP CONDITIONS
HOUSING STARTS

Macroeconomics and Financial Administration

ECONOMIC—QUARTERLY

GROSS NATIONAL PRODUCT—PERSONAL INCOME
MANUFACTURING CAPACITY UTILIZATION
PRODUCTIVITY DATA
CORPORATE PROFITS
HOUSING VACANCIES
BALANCE OF TRADE DATA
STRIKE ACTIVITY
PLANT AND EQUIPMENT INVESTMENT

ECONOMIC—ANNUALLY

CROP FORECASTS
BUDGET FORECASTS
SURVEY OF CURRENT BUSINESS—JULY ISSUE
   CONTAINS DETAILED INFORMATION ON NATIONAL INCOME
CORPORATION INCOME AND PROFITS
FORTUNE 500 LARGEST CORPORATION RATING

SPECIAL

THE WALL STREET JOURNAL HAS A QUARTERLY MICROFICHE CLIPPING SERVICE ON GENERAL NEWS ITEMS ARRANGED ALPHABETICALLY AND CHRONOLOGICALLY BY FIRM

ECONOMIC MONTHLY CHECKLISTS
TIMING CYCLE

1ST WEEK

CONSUMER CREDIT
WHOLESALE PRICE INDEX
CONSTRUCTION EXPENDITURES
MAJOR CROP FORECASTS
EMPLOYMENT—UNEMPLOYMENT

2ND WEEK

RETAIL SALES—ADVANCE DATA
INVENTORIES—MANUFACTURING
INDUSTRIAL PRODUCTION
PERSONAL INCOME STATISTICS
MANUFACTURING—SHIPMENTS

3RD WEEK

CONSUMER PRICE INDEX
DURABLE GOODS STATISTICS
HOUSING STARTS
AVERAGE HOURLY WAGE
STOCK MARKET SHORT INTEREST DATA

4TH WEEK

EXPORTS AND IMPORTS
LEAD INDICATORS
FARM PRICES
LABOR TURNOVER STATISTICS

CHART LIST

1. BUSINESS ACTIVITY—TWO YEARS BY WEEKS
2. STEEL PRODUCTION—TWO YEARS BY WEEKS
3. AUTO PRODUCTION—TWO YEARS BY WEEKS
4. FEDERAL FUNDS RATE—WEEKLY
5. HOUSING STARTS—MONTHLY
6. INDUSTRIAL RAW MATERIALS—TWO YEARS BY WEEKS
7. COPPER PRICES—WEEKLY
8. PRIME COMMERCIAL PAPER INTEREST RATES—WEEKLY

REPORT LIST

1. GENERAL ECONOMIC REPORT—WEEKLY
2. CLIPPING REPORT—RANDOM DATING
3. STOCK MARKET PRICE MOVEMENT—32 INDUSTRY GROUPS
4. COMPUTER PRINTOUT—ECONOMIC AND FINANCIAL EFFECT OF PRICE CHANGES
5. COMPUTER PRINTOUT—TARGET ITEMS—SIGNIFICANT CHANGES

17

Interfacing Financial Administration with Total Company Operation

OPERATION—"CONTROL AND PLAN"

The financial administrator is the hub in a vast formal and informal organization which has evolved in each firm during the years of its existence. Since practically all of the operations require funds, reports and information the financial executive is in the unique position of having access to all of these materials. The informal organization which has developed underneath the formal group saves valuable time, reduces the workload of the top and middle line managers and can be an effective tool in keeping the organization keen and competitive. This is the starting lineup that goes on the playing field every day!

The financial division can serve as the "clearing house" for all types of productive information. Properly applied, it can provide expert advice and help to all areas of the business while performing its normal functions.

PLANNING

The current emphasis on planning has put the financial executive in a "key" position in the interfacing of all of the corporate functions. The ability to assist the operations personnel in preparing their detailed plans calls upon the information and data resources of the division. It can serve as a data base, information gathering, educational, research, informational and counseling group for the entire organization. With competent staff individuals assisting the other segments it can be a real resource or asset to the firm. It can tackle the problems existing between divisions. (We could sell it if they could produce it on time!) It can neutralize the suicidal tendencies to develop a distrustful, adversary relationship between divisions. In determining the various inputs to the plan it can act as an arbitrator in measuring both input and output of each cost or profit center. It can serve as mediator in the event of conflicts and neutralize the tendency to overestimate or underestimate its plans.

There is a tough problem in every organization trying to determine and separate the contribution each unit makes to the final plan. What is its input, brains, attitude, manpower, money, creativity or output per man-hour? What is its output, satisfied customers, new products, product demand, quality products, on-time shipments, reduced costs, additional resources created or profits?

CASE IN POINT

A well thought out tax plan may create as much in dollars of Retained Earnings as five-hundred thousand dollars in profitable sales.

An alert cost reduction program may create before-tax earnings equal to thousands of dollars in sales.

Interfacing and coordinating the efforts of all divisions through planning can help increase the productivity of the entire firm. The plan brings together the fund requirements, manpower requirements, equipment requirements and the ideas and constructive criticism of all the units. These are some of the factors that often must be reconciled:

   a. Personnel wants better, highly motivated people. They cost more money!
   b. Production needs additional capital investments to increase capacity for growth, productivity and cost reduction.
   c. Marketing wants more sales personnel, new warehouses, new products, more advertising and promotional dollars.
   d. Industrial engineering wants additional personnel for better work methods, studies and work measurement.
   e. Research requires additional funds and manpower to develop new products, processes or basic research.
   f. Labor wants wage increases, additional fringe benefits and other items.

In this area the financial division serves as a coordinator and provides impartial research and policy recommendations which are necessary to best allocate the resources of the firm. This takes tact, a great deal of diplomacy and careful study. Interfacing all of these requests to a common, resource-limited target is a masterpiece of financial achievement. If it is an alert organization, it can provide the basic research and information for capital planning, acquisitions or divestitures, innovations in management, marketing or technology without intruding upon the authority of the various division heads.

To assure the success of interfacing the financial executive should insist that its data base provide a repository of knowledge for all units of the firm to turn to for counsel and information. It should have data on how to increase productivity (present or future), capital utilization, cost reduction and ROI. It must have a computerized system to constantly search the input from internal and external sources for new suggestions, new developments, new ideas, new theories and new competitive tactics. It must maintain lines of communication to all operating levels and furnish them with meaningful output as well as receiving meaningful input data.

The adoption of formal planning is one of the most effective ways of assuring interfacing and interaction between all units of your organization. The astute financial executive will arrange to be the central hub of the planning activity and as such contribute to the interfacing of the entire group. Team action and reaction is essential to success.

CONTROL

One of the foremost objectives of every firm is to increase its ROI. The financial executive has a major role in accomplishing this objective through the medium of control techniques. He has the dual responsibility of increasing profits and decreasing capital investment wherever possible. Coordination and interaction is vitally essential to the successful accomplishment of this objective. As the firms become larger and larger the task of coordination and obtaining the cooperation of all units becomes vastly more difficult. While coordination in planning is reasonably easy to obtain—everyone wants to plan for the other fellow—the factor of irritation and resistance rises in applying controls. The resistance is often highest among middle managers. Most of these individuals are strong-willed, aggressive individuals who resent your intrusion into their private bailiwick with control techniques and reports. If the results reported on are adverse, controls can provide some interesting fireworks for the financial administrator. It is here that his tact, personality and training in human relations can be sorely tested. He must then prove his ability as a diplomat and conference leader. If it gets away from him the ability to interface will be lost.

Control techniques, no matter how necessary and valuable they are, are fought by middle managers as restrictive, demeaning and as a loss of authority. Controls have been misused as a punishing device instead of their true function as management tools for measuring and reporting on greater efficiency, productivity and profits and as a guide to future action or reaction.

FINANCIAL CONTROL

As one corporate president states: "I leave my managers strictly alone with their annual plan. If they run out of money they have to come to me. That's when the fireworks start!"

All of us in the financial world recognize and are in agreement that if controls are to be successful in developing cooperation, coordination and interfacing of activities they must be supported by a majority of the top executives. A *planning and control committee* of which the financial administrator is a key member, is an excellent tool for correlating interactive and interrelating responsibilities. In this manner the total executive know-how and resourcefulness of the firm is pooled and the risks of major decisions are known and shared by all members. The team spirit of a highly successful interactive, interfaced corporate team is a sight to behold. It permeates throughout the entire organization.

POINTS TO EMPHASIZE

1. Controls point out good performance as well as performance below plans.
2. Open channels of communication enable one division to relate to the problems of another.
    a. Failure of sales plans can cause overproduction and high inventories—this in turn could affect financial requirements. In addition, additional storage space might be required. Marketing might require additional funds to promote slow-moving items.
3. Most executives do not fully understand the planning function.
4. Interfacing, coordination and cooperation are resisted by autocratic managers.
5. Problems can arise in interfacing if line personnel are not involved in planning and control functions.
6. Objectives are considered to be the exclusive property of each manager.
7. Managers must be *leaders* in order to be effective. To be a leader the team must be aware of the plans, the successes and the failures.
8. *Control* is a nasty word associated with punishment for non-performance.
9. *Persist* in the theory that "top down" is best. Do not utilize the knowledge and experience of your employees. The variations are a summary of individual happenings to every employee and every machine. Interface with every employee for success.
10. Most middle management executives feel that planning is utilized only for control purposes. This induces lack of interfacing and cooperation.
11. *Remember*—Good planning and control can aid in the successful interfacing on the units of a business by creating a team spirit, a common goal, the will to win!

The political infighting and the struggle for power in the modern corporation is a sight to behold, a phenomenon to enjoy, and if you are one of the executives involved—a source of fear or joy—whichever way the ball bounces.

GROWING IMPORTANCE OF INTERFACING

A perusal of the current employee advertisements indicates the increasing emphasis on the ability to interface as a prime consideration for hiring. Such statements are common:

"Demonstrated ability to interface with all levels of management, U.S. subsidiaries and foreign firms."
"Interfacing with the IRS."
"Interface with a wide range of outside managers."
"Heavy interface with senior management, other institutions and third party agencies."

Obviously it is a required and important technique for every financial administrator to master.

18

Case Studies in Successful Financial Administration

As a result of the research, interviews and studies involving the applications of financial administration and its benefits, a series of three case studies were developed. The firms ranged from a small family-owned corporation which suddenly grew up, to a large multinational firm which appeared to be just drifting along aimlessly. Financial planning and control systems involved ranged from none to one reasonably well organized but apparently not fully effective. In each instance the results of corrective action and the strengthening of the financial administrative function resulted in continuing growth and increased profits.

COMPANY A

The subject company is a small electrical contracting firm with an annual volume in excess of two million dollars. It started as an individual proprietorship which was incorporated in 19XX. As a small firm it specialized in commercial construction jobs. Approximately four years after incorporation the business expanded into the residential contracting field. It remains a family-owned enterprise.

OPERATIONS

As previously stated the firm specializes in all types of commercial electrical work. This includes schools, warehouses, commercial buildings, office buildings and other types of construction. It has an excellent reputation in the field. Entrance into the residential construction field was the result of its excellent reputation in the commercial area and pressure by builders to do their work. This area covered electrical work on housing tracts, custom individual residences, townhouses, condominiums and apartments. At the time the study started the dollar volume was about equally divided between the two divisions. Demand is cyclical and dependent upon the activity of the construction industry. Growth during the three years preceding the study was phenomenal.

PROBLEMS—OPERATIONAL

The sudden growth of the firm put a tremendous strain upon the owner and president of the firm. Despite his natural ability and business acumen, the growth from a small organization to a larger one, put the president in the position wherein he was unable or hard-pressed to service the needs of the organization. It had grown so large that he was unable to exercise "fingertip" control with the present operating and accounting methods. The entry into the residential line had created supervisory problems, bidding problems and cost accounting problems. From one or two large jobs with adequately supervised crews, operations had grown to many jobs spread over the entire city or county. The ability to maintain the tight individual control that had made the firm so successful was rapidly drifting away.

In the area of bidding the ability to concentrate on one or two large jobs was totally changed to an almost constant demand for urgent bidding on individual homes, townhouses or condominiums. The multiplicity and complexity of the tasks was consuming more time than one individual could effectively contribute.

FINANCIAL PROBLEMS

The small capitalization and conservative policies of management which had served so well during the slow growth years began to show strains under the demands of rapid expansion. While profits had been high enough to sustain a moderate rate of growth the explosion in business volume was creating some cash problems. In addition, wherein the outside accountant had previously only furnished quarterly statements of the firm's progress there was an urgent need for more frequent statements. In addition, there was a developing requirement for better cost figures and profit-and-loss reports for the individual divisions.

In order to complement the electrical work an affiliated corporation was formed to provide a source for electrical fixtures. This operation was undercapitalized and loans from the larger firm were required to provide the working capital necessary to carry inventories and accounts receivable during the initial stages. This created an additional cash outflow for Company A.

To top off the entire situation, there were also indications that the economy was slowing down and that the cyclical construction industry might be slowing down during the next twelve to eighteen months.

OUTSIDE ASSISTANCE

Realizing that the situation might be beyond the company's capabilities, knowledge and available time, the president sought outside assistance. After a conference with his accountant, he decided to hire someone to handle the financial end of the operation. After a discussion of the various problems with the president and his subordinates it was agreed that a full scale study be made of the entire operation. Difficulties and problems of the various phases of the business were to be explored and solutions presented for executive consideration and action.

Subsequent to this, individual conferences were held with each division head in which they were requested to describe their operations in detail, the problems encountered and the information which they felt was required for effective control.

CONFERENCE RESULTS

The individual conferences indicated a complete lack of formal corporate policies, goals and operating reports. The three most important figures obtained from the records was the check book balance, a monthly aging of the accounts receivable and the total billing for the month. Accounts payable control consisted of looking at the suppliers' statements at the end of the month and seeing if they listed any past-due items. Some cost records were kept on the various jobs wherein the labor and materials charged to a job were posted to a "Job Cost Sheet." To these figures were added an overhead allowance and the total costs compared weekly and monthly to the total billing to date. In the commercial area these reports were reasonably accurate and effective; however, for residential operations they failed to adequately state the cost picture due principally to the failure of recording accurate material costs.

PRELIMINARY REPORT—COMPANY A

The financial administrator spent several weeks reviewing the corporate activities prior to making any recommendations or suggested actions. These were some of the basic recommendations:

1. That the corporation completely revise its financial and accounting procedures.
2. That it commence installing a well-designed planning system.
3. That it design and install an information system.
4. That the corporation secure a minicomputer to implement the planning and information systems. In the interim a sound manual data analyzing and reporting system should be developed which could be converted to computer operation.
5. That effective cost controls be installed and that the financial reports show the true segregated results of the residential and commercial activities. The commercial division felt that it was subsidizing the residential activities.
6. That cost estimating and bidding be computerized as rapidly as possible.
7. That the bidding process be handled by more than one individual and that each of the major executives be capable of bidding a major job in the event of illness or absence of others.
8. That divisional executive compensation be based upon the profit and volume performance of each division.
9. That more individual responsibility and authority be delegated to the various division heads to relieve the mounting pressure on the president.

10. That an annual plan be developed immediately and that a tentative long-range plan be drawn up for a period of three years.
11. That additional personnel be hired to fill the gaps in the operating units of the organization.
12. That an effective capital expenditure program be developed.
13. That a formalized maintenance program be instituted for maintaining all existing equipment.
14. That management meetings be held periodically to discuss common problems and to keep everyone informed of the individual actions and goals as well as the overall corporate actions and goals.
15. To open and strengthen the communications lines and to detail the interfacing action required of each individual.

THE BASIC PROBLEMS ENCOUNTERED

1. Management despite its skills, knowledge and ingenuity was seriously overburdened.
2. Bidding practices were not standardized. Most of them were concentrated in one individual.
3. Material costs were not kept up to date.
4. Labor costs were reasonably accurate and known but seldom compared to the original estimates. There was no way of knowing whether the labor costs on bad performance were being dumped off on the so-called good jobs which could stand the additional costs.
5. Actual performance was seldom compared to estimated results.
6. No credit checks were run on customers. Jobs were accepted from all comers with the result that many slow paying accounts became part of the accounts receivable load. In some instances credit was extended to firms that went bankrupt or were liquidated soon after the work was performed.
7. Fixed assets were acquired with short-term funds.
8. Cash and capital requirements were beyond the ability of the firm's financial status.
9. Expansion was occurring in a period of cyclical decline.
10. Expansion was made by an affiliated firm which drew capital from the main operations at a time when they were experiencing cash flow problems.

SOME OF THE SOLUTIONS

1. Instituted a set of complete financial controls for all phases of the business.
2. Secured an adequate short-term line of credit to provide some working capital for growth and to carry increased accounts receivable during a cyclical decline in activity. The ability of customers to pay promptly declined rapidly in this period.
3. Commenced planning for long-term financing and possible equity capital to provide a stable base for growth.
4. Instituted credit checks, statements and followed up on delinquent accounts more aggressively.
5. Eliminated all no pay, slow pay and non-profitable customers as rapidly as possible.
6. Charged off doubtful items immediately during a period of high profitability rather than

Case Studies in Successful Financial Administration

waiting until the last possible chance of recovery was gone. Losses were recognized as soon as possible.

7. Revised the workload between the commercial and residential divisions. Too often one division might be overworked while the other lacked sufficient work to keep its crews busy. Attempted to smooth out the high and low activity cycles.
8. Beefed up the accounting personnel—numbers and talent.
9. Started on a modified planning program—principally educational in nature.
10. Streamlined the organization prior to a cyclical decline in business.
11. Put the affiliated firm on a "make your own way or fold" basis.
12. Secured a minicomputer. Started training the personnel in its use. To quote one individual: "It scares me!" This is one of the major obstacles to the effective use of a minicomputer.
13. Commenced installation of a data base, computerized inventory, estimating system, job costing, accounts receivable and billing system, designed a model type planning system, contemplated completion date for computerized installation of two years!
14. Some delegation of authority. In a small firm this is a tough nut to crack!
15. Instituted a complete set of new control reports. Details can be found on page 442-464.

CONCLUSIONS

Company A points out the serious deficiencies that exist in smaller corporations that are growing up. The executives are often capable, intelligent and know their business thoroughly; however, as the business grows they are overwhelmed by the sheer volume of tasks that must be performed. They are, in most instances, reluctant to relinquish authority and control to someone else. Often they are good salesmen, technical geniuses or operational wizards but lack the basic concepts of financial administration and control. They realize the problems but somehow fear releasing any of the control to others. This is an admirable trait and is apparent even in some of the larger firms where the top executive rules the roost with an "iron hand" technique. The ability to delegate and control delegated authority is one of the bench marks of successful management. Effective financial administration and control is one of the tools for achieving high marks in this area.

The prompt realization of difficulty existing within and without the firm enabled the president of Company A to take corrective action in time to prevent serious trouble. Despite the extreme cyclical decline in both divisions, operations were controlled promptly with the result that the cash crisis was successfully weathered and profitability restored in a relatively short period of time. While not all of the problems have been solved, nor will they ever be, the new ones will be recognized quicker and acted upon more promptly. With minor changes the control reports will serve to keep management abreast of all of its operations for some time in the future. Financial administration played an important part in the entire rejuvenation process. (Supporting data can be found on pages 442–464.)

COMPANY B

This firm is a medium-sized firm which manufactures glass and plastic containers as well as plastic and metal caps primarily for the food industry. It is a family-owned corporation that is almost one hundred years old. It is still principally owned by heirs of the original founder.

The firm originally commenced operations as a small glass manufacturer with one plant located in the South. As its business grew it realized that it must complement its line with metal closures in order to sell the complete package. As a result of this they acquired a small metal cap manufacturer during the late 1930's. The firm had a highly profitable business even through the depression of the 1930's due to its flexibility, small size and the availability of low-cost, part-time labor. Profits were remarkably stable and provided a good income for the entire family. The firm has never experienced a loss year despite some close calls at various times in the economic cycle. There was no pressure to expand, the markets were stable, and the relationship of costs to prices remained relatively constant.

GROWTH

For over fifty years growth had been sound but slow. Under the impetus of World War II rapid growth and expansion was forced upon the firm. Additional container and cap plants were built or acquired, many of them adjacent to the plants of large customers in order to better serve their market. After the war was over their growth slowed somewhat until the Korean War when once again it accelerated. By the late 1960's their percentage of the glass container and cap market had increased to a large enough percentage of the market to attract the attention of the industry giants. In addition, acquisition-minded firms constantly hounded the family to sell out. Despite this pressure they held on to the firm.

A NEW PRODUCT LINE

During the mid 1960's the firm became aware of the potential markets available in plastic containers and plastic caps. They had some experience with plastics; however, some of the new materials were lighter and less costly so they decided to investigate this market. Accordingly, they assembled a number of plastic research and operational technicians and started an aggressive program to develop plastic containers and plastic caps. After about two years of research they had developed and perfected products that were commercially acceptable. One of the large food processing firms became interested in the project, particularly the cap line, and offered them long-term, large sales contracts if they could successfully develop caps for their new product lines. They were successful and immediately the plastic cap line began a phenomenal growth.

STEALING A MARCH ON INDUSTRY

The new line of plastic closures required raw materials that were less expensive than the materials currently being used. Realizing the competitive advantage this gave them the firm was able to undersell competition by a wide margin. The larger firms were forced to reduce prices on their current product lines while they scrambled to acquire new machinery and perfect their molding techniques. This competitive advantage cost the larger firms millions

Case Studies in Successful Financial Administration

of dollars. Their new product was commercially acceptable, low cost and profitable. Sales immediately ballooned.

OPERATIONAL PROBLEMS

The rapid expansion and profitability of the plastics division had diverted much of the firm's engineering and executive talent from the glass and metal divisions. As a result of this operational production problems started to crop up in these divisions in the early 1970's. Five years later the situation had become critical with deliveries falling behind schedule and repair and maintenance costs skyrocketing.

In addition, the production of new plastic containers had run into problems in the larger sizes. There were both production and quality problems. This necessitated additional research and development costs plus added investments in new equipment to correct production deficiencies.

The rapid expansion of the firm had created a huge deficiency in middle management personnel throughout the entire organization. Troubles were being encountered in manufacturing, engineering, sales, warehousing and financial operations. Top management felt a crisis developing and decided to act immediately.

THE FINANCIAL PROBLEM

While the problems were companywide, we as financial administrators are primarily concerned about the financial aspects of the crisis and confined our analysis to this area of the business. These are some of the problems encountered:

1. The president was seriously concerned about the firm's failure to anticipate the financial requirements of the firm due to the growth in the plastics division.
2. Since there was no formal planning system he requested that some form of planning be recommended.
3. Concern was expressed over the failure of the firm's reporting system to pinpoint areas of stress.
4. He was concerned about his firm's ability to be able to react quickly to these challenges. Timely reaction is required.
5. Extreme concern was expressed about the current cash crisis that was developing and what remedial action should be taken.
6. No figures were available in order to ascertain the profit by product or the profit by customer.
7. Concern was expressed about the allocation of resources among the various divisions and whether the "bread and butter" operations were being neglected.
8. Were all of the capital expenditures going into new products and projects to the detriment of established product lines?
9. What was the firm's ROI and how did it compare with the industry.
10. There was a need to establish goals and objectives for all phases of the business.

436 Case Studies in Successful Financial Administration

11. While the plastics incident indicated their strategy was excellent what could they do to continue to maintain a competitive edge?

SALES PROBLEMS

1. Failure to meet delivery schedules were creating customer complaints and overordering. Customers who required prompt shipments had overordered and requested that these stocks be held for their releases. This in turn had created both inventory and cash flow problems.
2. Reports were inadequate or late in reflecting sales activity by customer, by products and by product lines. In addition, the profit by product and by customer was not ascertainable.
3. Production problems had created difficulties in the plastic container line resulting in order cancellations and a slackening of demand. Communications between divisions was not good.
4. Sales personnel were becoming discouraged and unless prompt action was taken they felt that the firm's growth would suffer. Growth momentum was already slackening.

COST PROBLEMS

1. The firm lacked adequate cost system and cost controls. Although computer time was available the cost system had not been updated.
2. Communication between divisions was lacking. It was felt that each division was operating as a separate firm reporting only to the president. Purchasing was not notifying production or accounting of anticipated cost increases.
3. There were no set purchasing, pricing or production policies.
4. The deterioration of equipment in the metal division had increased costs of almost all of the items. While everyone realized that this was occurring there were no supporting figures to show what the actual costs were. In the plastic container division low unit production rates were increasing costs far beyond estimates. Once again no figures were available.

CREDIT PROBLEMS

1. Accounts receivable were not analyzed in detail on a periodic basis to determine the amount and reasons for delinquencies.
2. Adequate credit checks were not made on new customers. The attitude appeared to be that they will not try to get you on the first order.
3. Special terms were granted by sales to certain customers without notifying the financial division. Requests for immediate payment to these customers resulted in customer irritation.
4. There were no standardized credit policies. Certain product lines were highly seasonal and required special credit terms.

PURCHASING PROBLEMS

1. Purchasing would often arrange for advantageous purchases of raw materials, purchased parts or equipment. It would clear the purchases with the president but never alert the

Case Studies in Successful Financial Administration

financial division. The first notice that they had about the transaction was when they received the invoice.

2. Purchasing would not notify the financial division about actual or anticipated price changes.

PRODUCTION PROBLEMS

1. Production would schedule "down time" without conferring with sales as to the effect on scheduled deliveries. Emergency breakdowns of any magnitude were never reported to other divisions.
2. Adjustment of machine speeds was not reported to the financial division.
3. Failure of equipment to meet anticipated production rates was not reported to the other divisions.
4. Commitments for large machinery purchases were often cleared through the president but never reported to purchasing or the financial division.
5. Overtime was resorted to in order to cover speed delinquencies and machine repairs. Overtime was not cleared with top management.
6. Some customers received preferred treatment in scheduling, timing or overtime. Costs of this special treatment were often buried in the cost records.

NEW PRODUCT PROBLEMS

1. In its haste to introduce the new products—plastic containers—no allowance was made for the technical inexperience in research, sales or production.
2. Was the introduction of the product managed efficiently and carefully?
3. No preliminary cost studies were made to determine what the actual costs might be at slower production rates.
4. No study was made of selling prices to see if the prices set by sales or competition would produce profits at the anticipated level of production. What was the breakeven point?
5. Was a ROI study made and was the investment in equipment justified for the anticipated level of sales?

SOLUTIONS

Since this firm is a well-financed, stable organization the steps necessary to correct the deficiencies did not involve a major reorganization. The firm had a sound basis on which to build and had primarily failed to anticipate the tremendous growth potential in plastics and the resulting effect upon its entire organization.

1. The top organizational structure was realigned into a management committee of four headed by the president. With all major decisions now subject to committee approval, this eliminated the "individual corporation" operation of the various divisions.
2. The financial administrator was placed in charge of planning and strategy operations. All division heads were required to submit annual plans to the management committee detailing their objectives, goals and monetary and personnel requirements.

3. Periodic management committee meetings were set up to review the progress of the planning function. Reports were developed showing actual performance against plan and the variations were carefully analyzed.
4. Company objectives were clearly detailed to all executives together with their role in achieving these objectives.
5. A complete *data base* was developed by the financial division. This consisted of first providing a systematic way of bringing together all of the information about company operations. These data were then integrated into a data base available to all phases of the operation—sales, purchasing, manufacturing and finance, on a standardized basis. Each unit was then dealing with the same set of facts.
6. Long-term financing arrangements and leases were developed to handle the rapid growth of the plastics division. This freed working capital for the increased inventories and receivables that accompany growth.
7. The first annual plan brought forth a formalized statement of the firm's objectives and goals coupled with the divisional and departmental objectives and goals. This brought out in detail the equipment and manpower limitations, the existing production schedules and anticipated levels of production, the production efficiencies and costs, the projected inventory levels of raw materials and finished goods. It detailed the personnel, equipment and monetary requirements of each division and department. As one executive said, "Now we know what it is all about and where we are heading!"
8. Development was started on both economic and financial models in order to keep abreast of external developments and to provide the answers to "What if?" questions in the event of sales or production volume changes, cost or price changes or overall strategy revisions.
9. Probably the most important result of the entire study was improvement in the channels of communication and interfacing between the various units. Each has access to data which will enable them to do a better job within their own operations and at the same time make them aware of what their actions will do to the other units. They will be able to identify the basic cause of certain situations that may or may not be within the realm of their direct control.
10. Based upon ROI studies and other factors each division felt better about the allocation of resources within the firm and that based upon their performance they were getting a "fair shake."
11. The cash flow crisis was short-lived; the growth pattern was quickly resumed and ROI and profitability increased noticeably.
12. Data were now reasonably available for most items. Information is better and more accurate and decisions are made faster with a better sense of confidence. Cost projections are now available for many options and alternates. The use of the computer has been increased immensely without a large increase in cost.
13. Long-term planning and strategy is felt to be on the most cost-effective basis.

Supporting data can be found on pages 465–469.

COMPANY C

Company C is an organized, viable international organization which is publicly owned. No one connected with the founders is currently associated with the business. It is huge.

Case Studies in Successful Financial Administration

Most individuals think of the firm as just a huge mix of people and assets drifting along like the Sargasso Sea without definite goals or purpose. Its financial performance is adequate but dull. It is polished, non-aggressive and non-exciting. As a financial executive I would describe it as a firm that is making money despite itself. Actually it fits a pet theory that I have about some larger corporations which is: "After they reach a certain size, they just drift along on a rudderless course making money despite the actions of the various individuals—if nothing drastic happens to shove them off course into some sort of financial trouble, a slight kick of the prop now and then and a slight adjustment of the rudder will keep them on course for years." Despite the fumbling tactics of top management and their aimless course they plunge in and out of storms, economic upsets and other tribulations. About every ten years a Sir Galahad rescues them, puts them back on the track and spurs the action along. This to my mind is Company C.

PROBLEMS

1. Other than aimless drifting there appeared to be no major problem areas.
2. Management planning and strategy appeared to be very ineffective. In the past fifteen years the firm had jumped from one "hot" product line to another. They directed their efforts to wherever they felt they could make a few million dollars. In their haste to pick up and take advantage of the new technologies and products they were like Company B. They forgot the old "bread and butter" products and let the company drift along at the mercy of the customers and competition. Since many of the products involved rather large investments competition was not a major factor or played the true gentleman.
3. The realization that something was wrong with their operations dawned when a huge investment in a new technology and new products failed to produce anything but losses. As in the case of Company B the production techniques were far from perfect and under normal conditions would not produce either the quality or quantity of product required. The resulting loss in production, productive time, executive effort, and sales produced a sizeable loss which had to be absorbed.

PLAN FOR CHANGE

The tremendous effect on the profits of the huge physical investment failing to produce the required profits during the normal time limits plus the additional costs of millions of dollars required to rescue the process and product line shook the staid firm to its very foundations. This proved to be the *straw that broke the proverbial camel's back*. Top management immediately realized that they had made a major error that could threaten their very existence. It was time to do something!

Management immediately embarked upon a program which enabled it to analyze every division, every phase and every detail of its entire operation. It started off with a tough cost reduction program to conserve funds. It required justification for the total expenditures of each phase of its operations. If the prices were not in line with costs and could not be raised to produce a profit it dropped the product. If the production equipment was not efficient and could not be made so with a reasonable expenditure of funds it was scrapped. Minor operations which were "dead end" or not compatible with the general business objectives and goals were sold off. They cleaned house from foundation to attic and even went underground to eliminate the termites. They had decided to become modern and aggressive!

NEW CORPORATE STRUCTURE

Along with the thorough analysis and cost reduction program the corporation decided to revise its organizational structure. It set up a synergistic, international planning group to guide the corporate policies, strategies and goals. From an unmanageable, unfeeling mix of people and assets it has become a "top down," strategy-oriented, disciplined, aggressive firm. The vital restructuring revised and renewed the spirit of the entire organization. A management committee of five controls all planning and strategy for the firm. It exercises formal, tight control over the entire international operation.

It created a new position of tremendous importance in the corporate hierarchy termed "Director of International Strategy." This individual heads an "intelligence and analytical staff" and is directly responsible to the management committee. This group prepares detailed plans and analyses and aids in the implementation of these plans.

PLANNING—WHAT AND HOW!

The planning function was implemented and strengthened by a completely computerized planning system which has as its goal: "second to none!" The functions of the management committee and planning unit are as follows:

1. Review and projection of any proposed capital expenditure in excess of fifty thousand dollars before it is submitted to the management committee or Board of Directors.
2. Forced review of all corporate plans to make certain that corporate resources are allocated in an optimum manner.
3. Asks the question: "Will this create excess capacity and depress the market?" It forces a review of competitive plans for the same market.
4. Asks the question: "Is the volume in this market sufficient to make it attractive to us?" One large firm insists if they cannot get a volume of fifty to one-hundred million dollars in a market, forget it!
5. Planning forced the development of a huge "data base" to serve as an information center and repository for the entire organization.
6. Increased interest and activity in planning has sharpened management talents, made them more aware of and interested in the future plans of their divisional and departmental executives. They have spent more time discussing their goals and plans with their executives not for just the coming year but well out into the future.
7. Has pointed out markets where large potential profits exist and directed large capital expenditures toward these markets. It replaced the educated hunches of the past—sometimes good! sometimes bad!

Case Studies in Successful Financial Administration

OTHER RESULTS OF PLANNING

1. Earnings per share up 30%. ROI up 3%
2. Increase in enthusiasm and optimism among all executives and line personnel. A new sense of purpose and direction.
3. A more serious and disciplined approach to acquisitions, additions and diversification. "What if?" and "Why?" are answered first.
4. The structural changes increased the firm's executives' ability to function effectively. The communications between former tight and rigid organizational lines has improved immensely.
5. The planning and strategy function has involved everyone. It has given each executive an insight into the tasks and problems of the others. This realization of interdependence and required interfacing has helped reduce old rivalries and internal conflicts.
6. Objectives, plans and responsibilities are nailed down.
7. It has developed and strengthened the profit concept throughout the entire organization—the realization that making a profit is vital to growth and survival. Volume is worthless without profit. Never expand marginal product lines.
8. It has increased the selectivity of the entire business. The central theme is: "We are the best! Do it well or forget it!"
9. While the expansion fiasco produced an immediate cost reduction program, the planning program produced an awareness of controlling costs at all times.
10. It has clearly demonstrated the fact that effective and aggressive planning and strategy are vital elements of the business.
11. Resource allocation is a vital "top management" decision and function.
12. It brought about the realization that financial administration is a vital business operation. The ability to create funds and profits is dependent upon a continuing investment in profitable opportunities.

Supporting data can be found on pages 470–474.

OPERATION SUMMARY

1. *CASH*

    RECEIPTS
    DISBURSEMENTS
    DAILY REPORT
    BANK RECONCILIATION
    SALES TAX REPORTS

2. *ACCOUNTS RECEIVABLE*

    UNPAID FILE
    PAID FILE
    CONTROL REPORTS
    AGING REPORT

3. *ACCOUNTS PAYABLE*

    UNPAID FILE—PACKING SLIPS—STATEMENTS
    PAID INVOICE FILE
    JOB COST FILE—TEMPORARY HOLD
    JOB COST FILE—PERMANENT HOLD
    INVOICE RECORD—DAILY
    INVOICE EXTENSION TESTS—WEEKLY
    CONTROL REPORT—ACCOUNTS PAYABLE
    CONTROL REPORT—MATERIAL COST DISTRIBUTION

4. *SALES*

    INVOICE FILE, CHRONOLOGICAL
    CONTROL REPORT

5. *JOB COSTS*

    JOB COST FILES—INVOICES AND OTHER CHARGES
    JOB COST SHEETS
        WEEKLY CONTROL REPORT BY JOB
        MONTHLY CONTROL REPORT BY JOB
        CLOSED JOB FILES
    CONTROL REPORT—ALL JOBS—BY DIVISION

6. *PAYROLL*

    PAYROLL PREPARATION
    PAYROLL RECORDS
    LABOR DISTRIBUTION—JOB COSTS
    INDIVIDUAL EARNINGS RECORDS
    FEDERAL AND STATE REPORTS
    SPECIAL REPORTS
    TAX DEPOSITS

7. *JOURNAL ENTRIES*

    MONTHLY—STANDARD ENTRIES
    MONTHLY OR VARIABLE—ADJUSTING ENTRIES

8. *GENERAL LEDGER*
    POSTING
    PREPARATION OF TRIAL BALANCE
    PREPARATION OF STATEMENTS
9. *TAXES*
    PREPARATION OF TAX RETURNS
10. *SPECIAL ITEMS*
    CREDIT REPORTS
    BONDING COMPANY AND INSURANCE REPORTS
    BANK REPORTS
    MINUTES

WEEKLY STATUS REPORT

MONTH........................

WEEK ENDING...................

ASSETS			AMOUNT
CASH IN BANK			$_____
ACCOUNTS RECEIVABLE			$_____
INVENTORY	THIS WEEK	THIS MONTH	$_____
PURCHASED	$_____	$_____	
SOLD	$_____	$_____	
TOTAL CURRENT ASSETS			$_____

LIABILITIES

ACCOUNTS PAYABLE			$_____
RATIO - CURRENT ASSETS TO PAYABLES			_____ TO 1

OPERATIONS	THIS WEEK	THIS MONTH	YEAR TO DATE
BILLINGS	$_____	$_____	$_____
COSTS			
PAYROLL	$_____	$_____	$_____
MATERIAL	$_____	$_____	$_____
FREIGHT	$_____	$_____	$_____
COMMISSIONS	$_____	$_____	$_____
OTHER COSTS	$_____	$_____	$_____
TOTAL COSTS	$_____	$_____	$_____
PROFIT OR (LOSS)	$_____	$_____	$_____

Case Studies in Successful Financial Administration 445

WEEKLY STATUS REPORT

MONTH......................

WEEK.......................

ASSETS

CASH IN BANK $_____

ACCOUNTS RECEIVABLE
    RESIDENTIAL $_____
    COMMERCIAL $_____ $_____

INVENTORIES $_____

    TOTAL CURRENT ASSETS $_____

QUICK LIABILITIES
ACCOUNTS PAYABLE $_____

BANK LOAN $_____
    TOTAL QUICK LIABILITIES $_____

OPERATIONAL RESULTS	THIS WEEK	MONTH TO DATE
RESIDENTIAL BILLING	$_____	$_____
RESIDENTIAL COSTS		
LABOR	$_____	$_____
MATERIAL	$_____	$_____
TOTAL	$_____	$_____
INCOME OR (LOSS)	$_____	$_____
COMMERCIAL BILLING	$_____	$_____
COMMERCIAL COSTS		
LABOR	$_____	$_____
MATERIAL	$_____	$_____
TOTAL	$_____	$_____
INCOME OR (LOSS)	$_____	$_____

INCOME ACCOUNT

PERIOD ENDING..............

	COMMERCIAL $ AMOUNT	%	RESIDENTIAL $ AMOUNT	%	UNALLOCATED & ADMINISTRATIVE $ AMOUNT	TOTAL ALL UNITS $ AMOUNT	%
BILLINGS							
COSTS							
Material							
Labor							
Subcontractors							
Truck Expenses							
W/C Insurance							
Union Benefits							
Payroll Taxes							
Sales Taxes							
Warranty Costs							
Shop Supplies-Tools							
Miscellaneous							
TOTAL COSTS							
GROSS PROFIT							
ADMINISTRATION							
Salaries							
Payroll Taxes							
Travel & Enter'mt							
Insurance							
Bad Debts							
Advertising							
Depreciation							
Interest							
Utilities							
Telephone							
Legal & Accounting							
Office Supplies							
Miscellaneous							
TOTAL ADMIN.							
OPERATING INCOME							

INCOME ACCOUNT   MONTH _____

	FORECAST $ AMOUNT	%	ACTUAL $ AMOUNT	%	VARIANCE $ AMOUNT	%
SALES	$ 20,000	100.0				
COST OF SALES						
Material	14,000	70.0				
Labor	3,031	15.2				
Freight	200	1.0				
Truck Expenses	200	1.0				
Payroll Taxes	185	1.0				
Sales Tax	50	.1				
TOTAL COSTS	17,666	88.3				
GROSS PROFIT	2,334	11.7				
ADMINISTRATIVE						
Depreciation	60					
Office Supplies	30					
Legal & Accounting	25					
Advertising	100					
Licenses & Taxes	25					
Telephone	50					
Repairs & Maint.	50					
Rent	300					
Insurance	100					
Misc.	50					
TOTAL	790	4.0				
OPERATING INCOME	1,544	7.7				

DAILY CASH REPORT

MONTH....................

	RECEIPTS		DISBURSEMENTS		
DATE	TODAY	TO DATE	TODAY	TO DATE	CASH BALANCE

ACCOUNTS RECEIVABLE SUMMARY

MONTH......................

DATE	INVOICED TODAY	TO DATE	ACCOUNTS PAID TODAY	TO DATE	BALANCE DUE FROM CUSTOMERS

ACCOUNTS RECEIVABLE SUMMARY

MONTH..........................
WEEK ENDING...................

JOB NO.	CUSTOMER NAME	BALANCE LAST WEEK	INVOICES BILLED	INVOICES PAID	BALANCE THIS WEEK

ACCOUNTS PAYABLE SUMMARY

MONTH..................
WEEK ENDING...........

SUPPLIER NAME & CODE NO.	BALANCE LAST WEEK	INVOICES RECEIVED	INVOICES PAID	BALANCE THIS WEEK

451

ACCOUNTS PAYABLE DETAIL

MONTH..........

DATE	INVOICE NUMBER	SUPPLIER CODE NO.	ACCOUNT NUMBER	$$$$$$ AMOUNT	AVAILABLE DISCOUNT

MATERIAL DISTRIBUTION　　　　　PERIOD..............

WEEK ENDING DATE	INVENTORY A/C NO.	TOOLS A/C	MISC. A/C NO.	COMMERCIAL INVOICED P.O.	RESIDENTIAL INVOICED P.O.	TOTAL AMOUNT INVOICED P.O.'s

MATERIAL DISTRIBUTION

DIVISION....................   MONTH......................
                                      WEEK.......................

JOB NUMBER	INVOICE AMOUNT	LOAD FACTOR	JOB COST AMOUNT

PAYROLL DISTRIBUTION

MONTH..............

WEEK ENDING	COMMERCIAL LABOR	COMMERCIAL SUPERV.	RESIDENTIAL LABOR	RESIDENTIAL SUPERV.	MISC.	TOTAL PAYROLL

DIVISION.............   DIVISION OPERATING SUMMARY   MONTH.............

WEEK ENDING	BILLING	MATERIAL	LABOR	TOTAL COSTS	GROSS PROFIT	GROSS PROFIT TO DATE

JOB COST SUMMARY

JOB NO............
CUSTOMER............

WEEK ENDING	WEEK NO.	LABOR COSTS HOURS	LABOR COSTS $$$$$$	MATERIAL COSTS $$$$$$$	TOTAL COSTS $$$$$$$$$	BILLING $$$$$$$	GROSS PROFIT $$$$$$$$

JOB PROFITABILITY SUMMARY

DIVISION.................. MONTH..................

JOB NO.	CUSTOMER	BILLING	TOTAL COSTS	GROSS PROFIT

MS-1

OP	LABOR EMPL.HOURS ACT$ EST$	MATERIAL ACT$ EST$	TOTAL COST ACT$ EST$	BILLED INV. $$$	PROFIT (LOSS)

REVISED ....

JOB COST ESTIMATING
COST DATA

CODE NO.	DESCRIPTION	PACK CODE	MATERIAL DOLLARS	LABOR UNITS	COMMENTS
01	CEILING	A	2.20	.20	
02	BRACKET	AB	2.40	.20	
03	SP SWITCH	B	2.10	.20	
04	3W SWITCH	BA	3.10	.25	

PACK COST DATA

CODE NO.	DESCRIPTION	UNITS	COST
A.	CEILING OUTLET	1	2.20
17	3/0 BAR HANGER	1	.06
98	R WING NUT	2	.05
100	SPL SLEEVE	1	.14
120	RX STAPLE	2	.03
131	14/3 RX CU	5'	.09
134	14/2 RX CU	15'	.09
239	Y WING NUT	2	.04

(The above information was developed first for manually bringing the cost data up to date. Subsequently a computer program was developed which enabled the computer operator to take the estimator's penciled notes on the attached standardized form and turn out a completed estimate in minutes.)

MATERIAL INVENTORY LISTING
TRIM

Contractor _____ Project _____ Model No. _____ Date _____

DESCRIPTION	MFG.	CAT. NO.	CODE	UNIT PRICE	QUANTITY	CODE	UNIT PRICE	QUANTITY	DESCRIPTION	MFG.	CAT. NO.
Duplex	GE	4077-2B	201								
S. P. Switch	GE	5981-2B	202								
3/W Switch	GE	5983-2B	203								
4/W Switch	GE	5904-2	204								
Cooler SW	BE	RSP326-6T	205								
Duplex PL	GE	72101	206								
Switch PL	GE	72071	207								
2G Com 6 PL	GE	72532	207								
2G SW PL	GE	72072	208								
3G Com 6 PL	GE	72543	209								
3G SW PL	GE	72073	210								
4G Com 6 PL	GE	72554	211								
4G SW PL	GE	72074	212								
TV Jack	SR	TV-1-IV	213								
Coax TV Jack			214								
Tele PL	GE	72181	215								
Blank PL	GE	72121	216								
WP Rec PL	LN	4929	217								
WP SW PL	LN	4925	218								
WP Blank PL	BL	14-2-WP	219								
Power PL	SR	3862-3	220								
30A Dryer Plug F	GE	4132-3	221								
30A Dryer Plug S	GE	41	222								
50A Range Plug F	GE	4152-3	223								
50A Range Plug S	GE		224								
3' Pig Tail	CL	10133-3	225								
5' Pig Tail	CL	10133-5	226								
7' Pig Tail	CL	10133-7	227								
⅜ Rx CN	RL	6623	228								
1" Rx CN	RL	6625	229								
1¼ Rx CN	RL	6626	230								
1½ x 1¼ RE	AN	RW150-125	231								
Handy BLK ½ KO	BR	100K	232								
1" Seal Tite Flex	NA		233								
1" Seal Tite Flex 90 CN	TB	5254	234								
1" Seal Tite Flex ST CN	TB	5234	235								
½ Flex	NA		236								
½ Flex ST. CN	TB	254	237								
Post LT Stub	AC		238								
Y Wing Nut	IL	451	239								
½ Plastic Rx CN	TB		240								
SP Stack SW	LN	5224-I	241								
Chime Kit	CA		242								
Push Button	CA		243								
3/0 Blank	CA		244								
4 x 6 Luminous Ceil	CA		245								
4 x 8 Luminous Ceil	CA		246								
2 x 8 Luminous Ceil	CA		247								
2 Lite 4' Floor Fix & Lamps	CA		248								
2 Lite 8' Floor Fix & Lamps	CA		249								
Smoke Det	CA		250								
Range Cord			251								

RESIDENTIAL COST ESTIMATE DATA

OWNER_____ BUILDER_____ PHONE_____
BUILDING LOCATION_____ DATE_____

ROOM / OUTLET	DINING	LIVING	KITCHEN	BEDROOM	BATH	LAUNDRY STORAGE CLOSET	FAMILY DEN	ENTRY HALL	EXTERIOR	TOTAL	CODE		TOTAL	CODE	SPECIAL FEATURES
Ceiling											A			M	AC Unit — 10 KW Furnace — Roof Mtd
Bracket											AB			MA	15 KW Furnace — Roof Mtd
SP Switch											B			MA-1	15 KW Furnace — inside
3/W Switch											BA			MB	AC Unit — 10 KW Furnace — inside
4/W Switch											BB			N	Post Light
Duplex 15A											C			O	Underground Service
Duplex Split											CA			OA	H. W. Service
Door Operator											CB			P	200A Split Buss RT Panel
Smoke Det											CC			Q	¾ Firred Masonary 1G
Duplex 20A											CD			QA	¾ Firred Masonary 2G
Disposal											CD-1			QB	¾ Firred Masonary 3G
Dishwasher											CD-2			QC	¾ Firred Masonary 4G
Recess Fix											D			QD	¾ Firred Masonary Bracket
TV Jack											E			R	Stud Partition Outlet 2G
Chime											F			RA	Stud Partition Outlet 3G
Electric H. W.											G			RB	Stud Partition Outlet 4G
Dryer F											H			S	Plate 2G Switch
Dryer S											HA			SA	Plate 3G Switch
Range F											I			SB	Plate 4G Switch
Range S											IA			T	Plate 2G Com 6
2 Speed Cooler											J			TA	Plate 3G Com 6
Ex Fan - Hood											K			TB	Plate 4G Com 6
Luminous Clg 4x6											L			U	2" Firring Masonary 1G
Luminous Clg 4x8											LA			UA	2" Firring Masonary 2G
Luminous Clg 2x8											LA-1			UB	2" Firring Masonary 3G
														UC	2" Firring Masonary 4G

SPECIAL ITEMS

Quantity													V	Exposed Masonary (UF) 1G
Code													VA	Exposed Masonary (UF) 2G
													VB	Exposed Masonary (UF) 3G
Quantity													VC	Exposed Masonary (UF) 4G
Code													VD	Exposed Masonary (UF) Bracket
														Each 20A Add 1 Code 142 & 155 Deduct 1 Code 141 & 154

The signing of this instrument by the Buyer shall constitute an aceptance of all its conditions and shall constitute the Contract between the parrties signing the same upon the following terms and conditions. The Seller, sometimes known as the Contractor, submits the following quotation for electrical work set forth in the foregoing schedule:

_____ Dollars ($_____)

payable _____% when roughing in is completed and has passed inspection, if subject thereto, and the balance when the job is completed and has passed final inspection, if subject thereto.

Signed this_____day of_____, 197___

_____ BUYER   _____ SELLER

By_____   By_____

EFFECTIVENESS REPORT
DECEMBER 19XX—FIVE WEEKS

CODE	NAME	LABOR HOURS	$$$$$$	MAT'L	TOTAL COSTS	AMOUNT BILLED	RESULT + OR −
031	CUSTOMER A	319	4,043	839	4,882	9,756	+ 4,874
034							
035							
051							
071	CUSTOMER E	38	427	617	1,044	1,527	+ 483
081							
101							
121	CUSTOMER H	744	8,995	7,160	16,155	17,403	+ 1,248
132							
133							
145							
171	CUSTOMER L	46	564	402	966	862	− 94
200							
201							
231							
232	CUSTOMER W	231	2,789	5,104	7,893	9,750	+ 1,857
261	SHOP	23	301	15	316		− 316
262	WARRANTY	41	500	100	600		− 600
263	MISC.	20	256	772	1,028	500	− 528
OPERATIONS TOTAL		2,193	26,415	23,207	49,612	58,859	+11,237
ADM.—SUPV.			5,283		5,283		− 5,283
MONTH'S TOTAL		2,193	$31,698	$23,207	54,895	58,859	+ 5,954
		TOTAL HOURS	TOTAL $$$$$$	TOTAL MAT'L	TOTAL COSTS	TOTAL BILLED	TOTAL RESULT

CUSTOMER PROFIT CONTRIBUTION REPORT

SUBDIVISION .... PERIOD ....

WEEK ENDING	LABOR HOURS	LABOR DOLLARS	MATERIAL COSTS	TOTAL COSTS	BILLED AMOUNT	GROSS PROFIT OR LOSS
11/5	10	105	230	335	389	64
11/12	29	330	—	330	(358)	(688)
11/19	70	820	470	1,290	703	(587)
11/26	24	295	971	1,266	2,290	1,024
MONTH	133	1,550	1,671	3,221	3,024	(197)

CUSTOMER PROFIT CONTRIBUTION REPORT

COMBINED UNITS .... PERIOD ....

WEEK*** ENDING	LABOR HOURS	LABOR DOLLARS	MATERIAL COSTS	TOTAL COSTS	BILLED AMOUNT	GROSS PROFIT OR LOSS
11/5						
UNIT A	10	105	230	335	389	64
UNIT B	1	12	—	12	—	(12)
UNIT C	4	47	999	1,048	2,447	1,399
UNIT D	14	169	331	500	780	280
TOTAL	29	333	1,560	1,895	3,616	1,731
****						
NOVEMBER						
UNIT A	133	1,555	1,671	3,221	3,024	(197)
UNIT B	31	361	1,291	1,652	3,187	1,535
UNIT C	37	452	462	914	1,106	192
UNIT D	30	358	732	1,100	2,358	1,258
TOTAL	231	2,726	4,156	6,887	9,675	2,988

Company B Organizational Chart

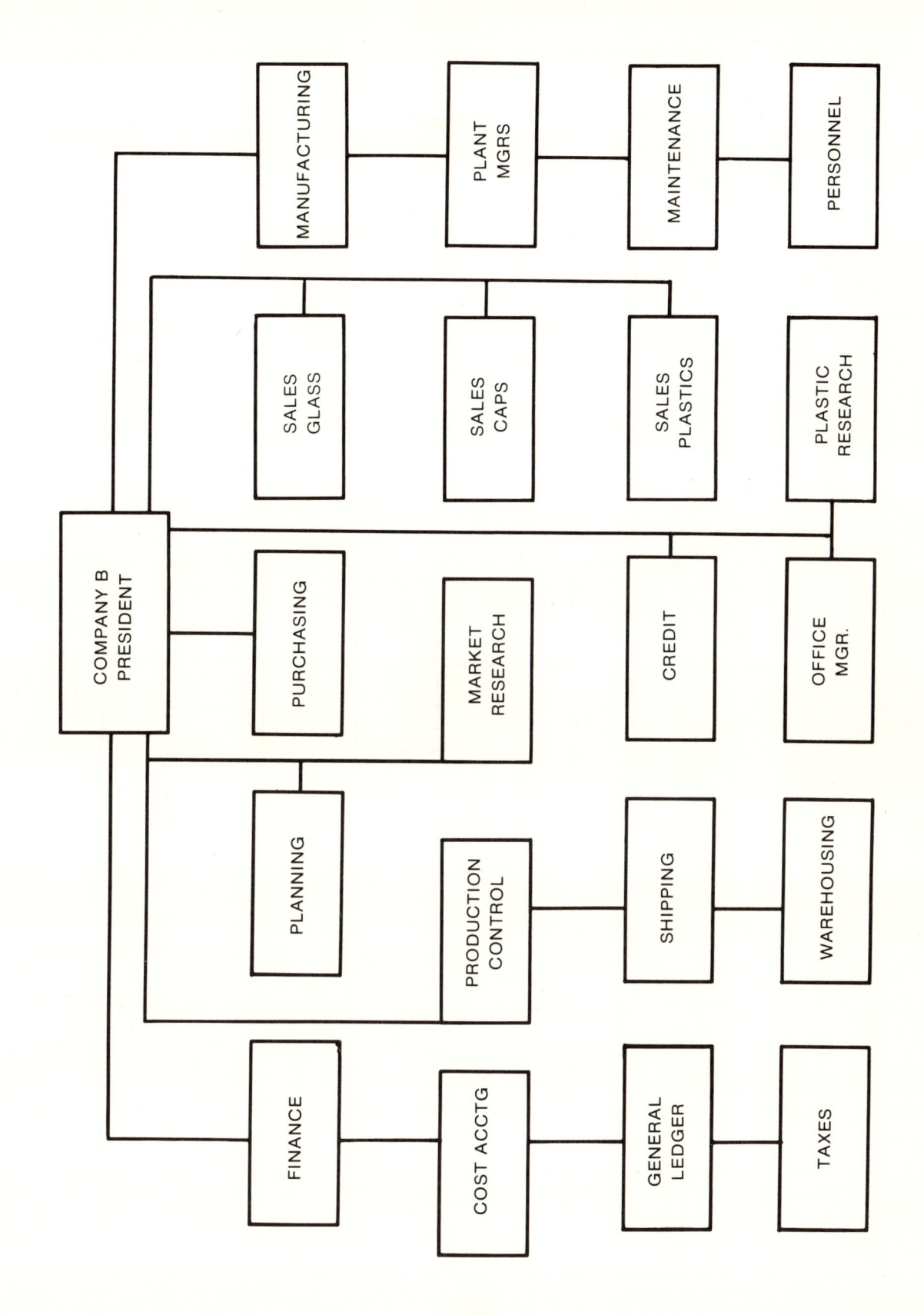

- **COMPANY B PRESIDENT**
  - MANUFACTURING
    - PLANT MGRS
    - MAINTENANCE
    - PERSONNEL
  - SALES GLASS
  - SALES CAPS
  - SALES PLASTICS
    - PLASTIC RESEARCH
  - PURCHASING
    - MARKET RESEARCH
    - CREDIT
    - OFFICE MGR.
  - PLANNING
    - PRODUCTION CONTROL
    - SHIPPING
    - WAREHOUSING
  - FINANCE
    - COST ACCTG
    - GENERAL LEDGER
    - TAXES

465

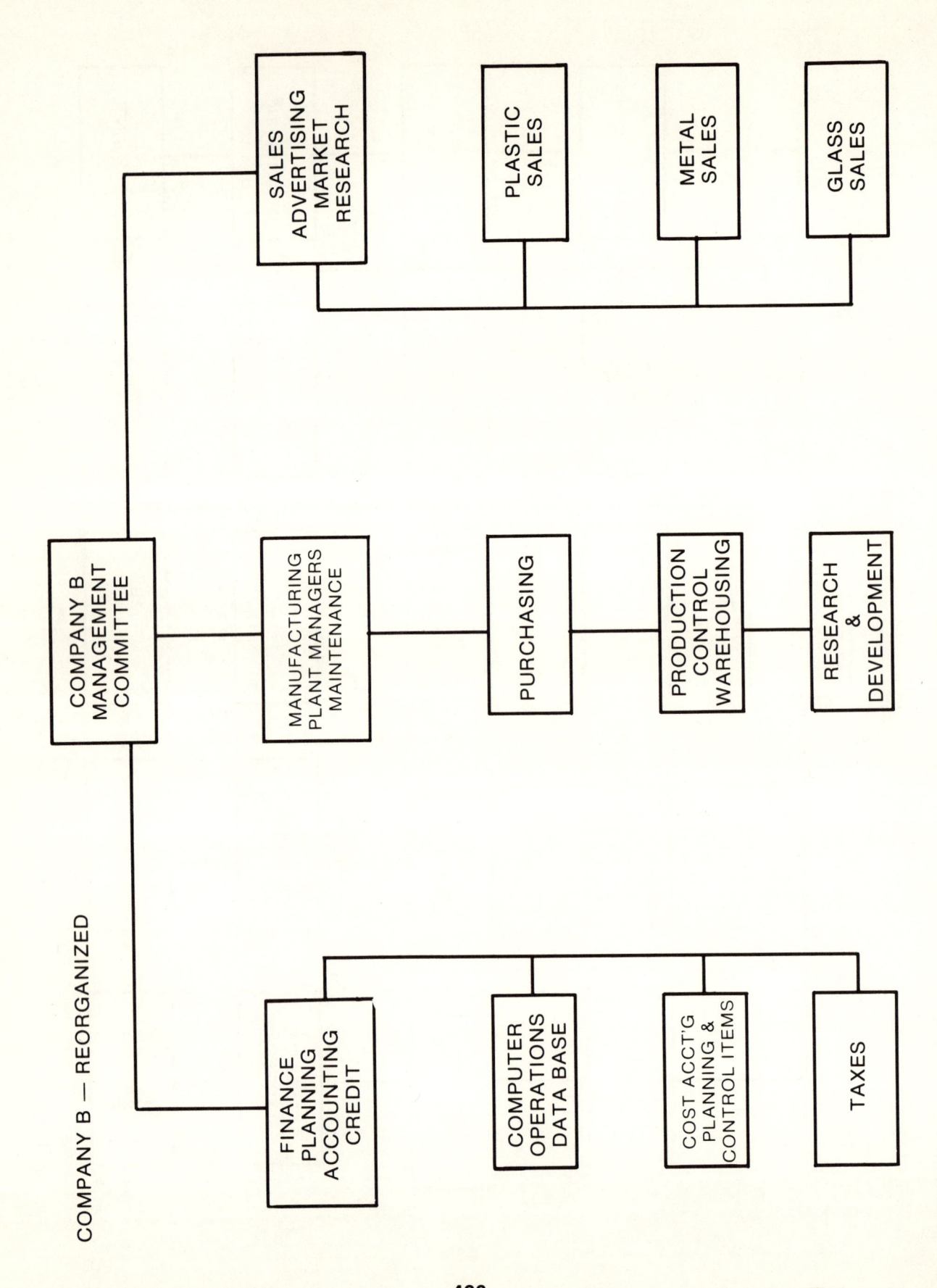

```
                                              ┌──────────────┐
                                              │    SALES     │     ┌─────────┐
                                              │ ADVERTISING  │     │ PLASTIC │
                                              │   MARKET     │─┬───│  SALES  │
                                              │   RESEARCH   │ │   └─────────┘
                                              └──────┬───────┘ │   ┌─────────┐
                                                     │         │   │  METAL  │
                                                     │         ├───│  SALES  │
                                                     │         │   └─────────┘
                                                     │         │   ┌─────────┐
                                                     │         └───│  GLASS  │
                                                     │             │  SALES  │
                                                     │             └─────────┘
  ┌──────────────┐                           ┌──────────────┐   ┌──────────┐   ┌──────────────┐   ┌──────────────┐
  │   COMPANY B  │                           │MANUFACTURING │   │          │   │  PRODUCTION  │   │              │
  │  MANAGEMENT  │───────────────────────────│PLANT MANAGERS│───│PURCHASING│───│   CONTROL    │───│   RESEARCH   │
  │  COMMITTEE   │                           │ MAINTENANCE  │   │          │   │  WAREHOUSING │   │      &       │
  └──────┬───────┘                           └──────────────┘   └──────────┘   └──────────────┘   │ DEVELOPMENT  │
         │                                                                                        └──────────────┘
         │
         │                                    ┌──────────────┐
         │                                    │   FINANCE    │
         │                                    │   PLANNING   │
         └────────────────────────────────────│  ACCOUNTING  │
                                              │    CREDIT    │
                                              └──────┬───────┘
                                                     │
                                          ┌──────────┼──────────┬──────────┐
                                   ┌──────────────┐  │  ┌──────────────┐   │
                                   │   COMPUTER   │  │  │ COST ACCT'G  │   │
                                   │  OPERATIONS  │──┘  │  PLANNING &  │   │
                                   │  DATA BASE   │     │CONTROL ITEMS │   │
                                   └──────────────┘     └──────────────┘   │
                                                                     ┌──────────┐
                                                                     │  TAXES   │
                                                                     └──────────┘

COMPANY B — REORGANIZED
```

MACHINE EFFECTIVENESS
PROFIT CONTRIBUTION

MACHINE BANK A—MACHINE UNITS 1, 2, and 3

DAY NO.	UNITS	SALES VALUE	COSTS	PROFIT CONTRIBUTION
1.	236	$ 236	$166	$ 70
2.	222	222	161	61
3.	234	234	165	69
4.	232	232	172	60
5.	214	214	167	47
TOTALS	1,138	$1,138	$831	$307

DEPARTMENTAL MACHINE EFFECTIVENESS
PROFIT CONTRIBUTION BY MACHINE

DAY NO.	NO. 1	NO. 2	NO. 3	NO. 4	NO. 5	TOTAL
1.	*	*	70	123	90	283
2.	*	*	61	100	95	256
3.	*	*	69	90	115	274
4.	*	*	60	125	100	285
5.	*	*	47	123	120	290

*Machines 1, 2 and 3 were operated as a bank of units during this week.

MAJOR COMPANY OF AMERICA
MONTHLY STATEMENT OF CUSTOMER ACCOUNT
SALES DISTRICT—SAN FRANCISCO

REPORT AS OF 05-31-XX

COMPANY NAME
COMPANY ADDRESS
CUSTOMER CODE NO.

CUST. P.O.	INV. NO.	DATE	TERMS	TYPE	AMOUNT	MATURITY	DAYS PAST DUE
3967	6059	5-31-XX	145	INV.	$538.60	07-15-XX	45-

TOTAL OWING ON ACCOUNT	PAST DUE AMOUNTS					CASH RECEIPTS THIS MONTH
	1–15	16–30	31–60	61–90	91–120	OVER 121	
$539							

TOTAL CURRENT	TOTAL PAST DUE
$539	$0

CUSTOMER CONTRIBUTION REPORT

CUSTOMER NAME ....
CODE NO. .... PERIOD ....

PRODUCT CODE	UNITS SOLD*	SALES $ VALUE	MATERIAL $ COST	LABOR $COSTS	OVERHEAD $COSTS	GROSS PROFIT $	GROSS PROFIT %	CONTRIBUTION $$$$$$	%
122	87	2,883	1,840	87	327	629	22	956	33
217	1,339	14,505	10,752	575	2,182	996	7	3,178	22
388	115	532	296	32	123	81	15	204	38
587	1,588	13,248	7,336	555	2,112	3,245	24	5,357	40
588	151	1,289	709	52	200	328	25	528	41
589	37	336	164	11	44	117	35	161	48
835	48	817	458	28	108	223	27	331	41
854	484	5,491	4,002	237	905	347	6	1,252	23
897	12	260	124	23	63	50	19	113	43
898	5	111	52	9	26	24	22	50	45

*Unit sales in thousands

CUSTOMER CONTRIBUTION REPORT
SUMMARY

MONTH ....

CUSTOMER NAME AND CODE	SALES $ VALUE	MATERIAL $ VALUE	LABOR $ VALUE	OVERHEAD $ VALUE	GROSS PROFIT $$$$$$	%	CONTRIBUTION $$$$$$	%
021—COMPANY A	47,858	31,116	1,974	7,463	7,305	15	14,768	31
034—COMPANY F	11,399	7,260	578	1,670	1,889	17	3,561	31
056—COMPANY L	19,882	12,624	677	2,585	3,996	20	6,581	33
075—COMPANY R	14,441	9,334	1,031	3,919	157	1	4,076	28
089—COMPANY T	32,739	21,162	2,338	8,885	354	1	9,239	28
100—COMPANY X	115,010	70,782	6,104	21,993	16,131	14	38,124	33
COMPANY TOTAL	$241,329	$152,278	$12,702	$46,515	$29,832	12	$76,349	31

(Several of the larger accounts would appear to be very low profit producers; however, when one looks at the overhead absorbed and the total contribution rate they appear to be on a par with those units or customers having a higher gross profit percentage.)

PRODUCTION CONTROL REPORT

DATE .... SHIFT NO ....

START TIME .... STOP TIME ....
ELAPSED TIME—HOURS ....

UNITS PRODUCED   TYPE OF UNIT PRODUCED ....
    ACTUAL ....
    STANDARD ....   VARIATION ....
    EXPLANATION OF VARIANCE
LABOR COSTS
    ACTUAL ....
    STANDARD ....   VARIATION ....
    REASONS FOR VARIATION
MATERIAL COSTS
    ACTUAL ....
    STANDARD ....   VARIATION ....
    EXPLANATION OF VARIANCE
SCRAP REPORT
    SCRAPPED UNITS ....
    STANDARD SCRAP LOSS ....   VARIATION ....
    REASONS FOR SCRAP LOSSES

APPROVED BY ....

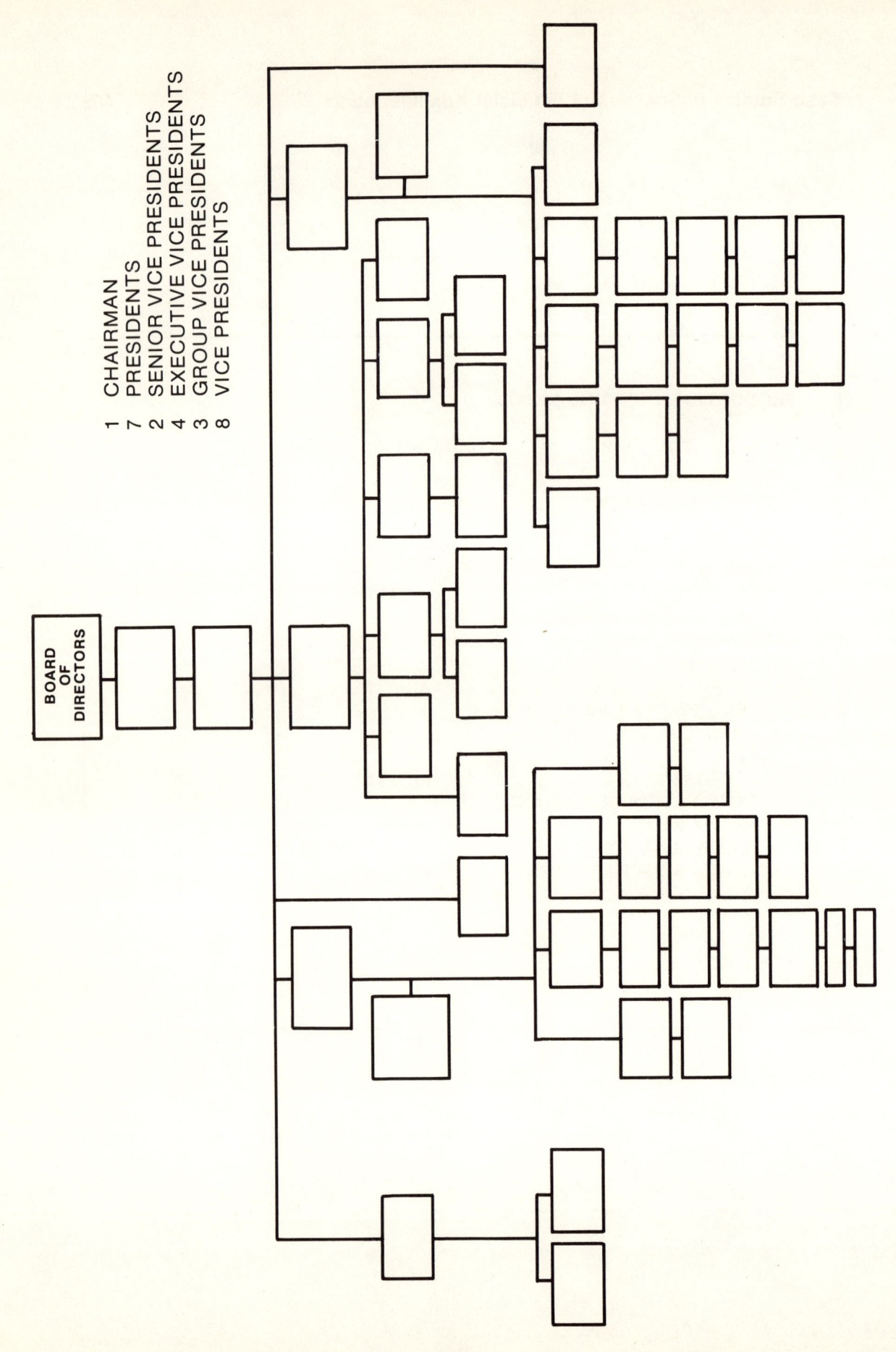

1 CHAIRMAN
7 PRESIDENTS
2 SENIOR VICE PRESIDENTS
4 EXECUTIVE VICE PRESIDENTS
3 GROUP VICE PRESIDENTS
8 VICE PRESIDENTS

BOARD OF DIRECTORS

COMPANY C — REORGANIZED

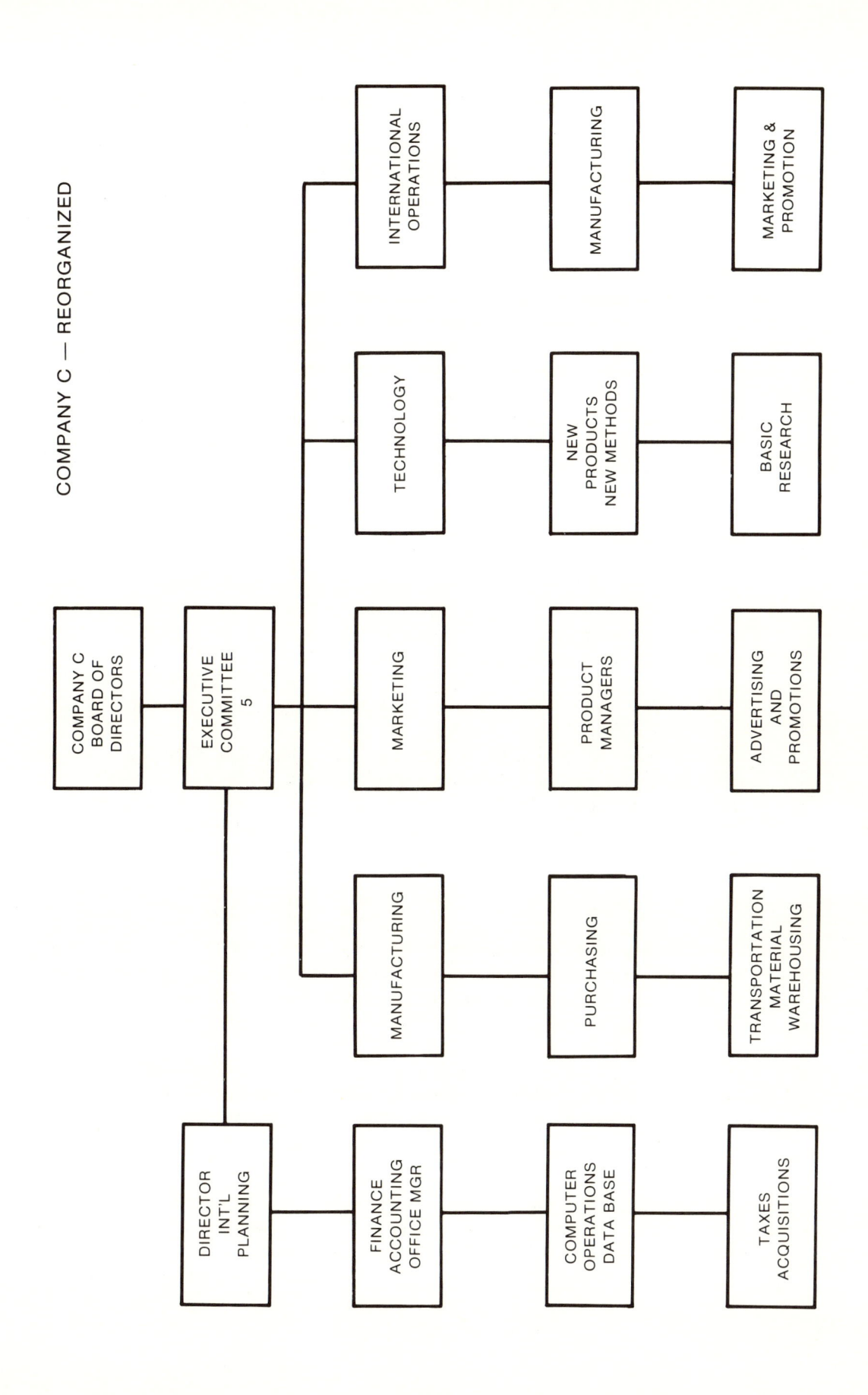

```
COMPANY C                EXECUTIVE
BOARD OF      ─────      COMMITTEE
DIRECTORS                    5
                             │
    ┌────────────────┬───────┼────────────┬──────────────────┐
    │                │       │            │                  │
DIRECTOR         MANUFACTURING MARKETING  TECHNOLOGY    INTERNATIONAL
INT'L                                                    OPERATIONS
PLANNING             │          │            │                │
    │                │          │            │                │
FINANCE          PURCHASING  PRODUCT    NEW PRODUCTS     MANUFACTURING
ACCOUNTING                   MANAGERS   NEW METHODS
OFFICE MGR           │          │            │                │
    │                │          │            │                │
COMPUTER        TRANSPORTATION ADVERTISING  BASIC         MARKETING &
OPERATIONS       MATERIAL      AND          RESEARCH      PROMOTION
DATA BASE        WAREHOUSING   PROMOTIONS
    │
TAXES
ACQUISITIONS
```

471

Case Studies in Successful Financial Administration

Setting Up the Plan

The system operates upon the basic premise that each plant manager is running his or her own business. Four months prior to the start of the next year each manager is given the following data:
1. A detailed projection for each product and product line by marketing area.
2. An economic forecast showing the projections for the various markets, the rate of inflation, the interest rates, the prices of raw materials and other purchased items.

One month prior to the start of the new year the manager must submit for review and consultation a written forecast of operations. This forecast is detailed, month by month, for the coming year. In addition, a plan must be presented in lesser detail for the following three years. Some firms utilize a five-year plan!

Once the manager and the committee agree on the projected plan it then becomes the manager's commitment for the year ahead. There is a final session at which time the annual economic report is discussed and the manager is made aware of the main corporate plans and objectives for growth by expansion or acquisition which may be reflected in their projections.

Plan Approvals

Final plans are approved by the management committee and represent their bench marks for action or reaction during the coming year.

How Are the Plans Monitored? How Are Operations Directed?

The end result of the increased interest in the overall progress of the firm resulted in more face-to-face contact with the individual managers. These sessions were brought about by top management visiting the individual managers on their home grounds. They often resulted in some "knock down" and "drag out" affairs in which no holds were barred.

Points Learned

The percentage contribution by product is not always the true criterion or bench mark of a product. One product may carry a high profit percentage mark-up but be limited in volume due to machine speeds, processing techniques or equipment capacity. For example:

PRODUCT NAME	DAILY PRODUCTION	% OF GROSS PROFIT	$$$$ OF GROSS PROFIT	MACHINE COST EACH MACHINE
A	25,000	30%	$7,500	$100,000
B	50,000	20%	10,000	$200,000

The increased utilization of the computer enabled the firm to control operations and costs in far greater detail. The sales division utilized it to budget the salesmen's time by customer and product. It selected the best itinerary, kept track of his orders, controlled their status in the office and the plant and showed each man's performance rating.

Case Studies in Successful Financial Administration

An increased awareness of the economic situation sharpened the firm's planning operations and tended to increase the conservativeness of their plant expansion plans. The question of where the money was coming from was asked prior to embarking upon every major expansion program.

The firm had leaned down. It had lost its "fat and dumb" attitude with a multitude of management structures. Suddenly it had realized that squeezing cash profits out of an array of different businesses is simply a matter of financial control. Each basic unit had to come to the main group for its cash. This and the review that accompanied the process is one of the greatest for controlling every firm!

The managers were now aware of the entire firm's goals for sales, profits, new products, new customers and possible expansion. Their short term forecasts were followed up promptly, and if they were not meeting their planned program they had to come up with an alternate plan to get back on course in a hurry. If sales were down costs must also be down in order to maintain their profit levels.

The realization dawned upon the organization that they had no control over their customers. If the customer didn't do a good job his sales would fall. If prices were too high the products would not sell. If they raised the prices too high their competition would get the account. Finally, they learned to spread their sales among many customers to reduce their vulnerability and that quality products would always sell if the price was right.

The Reporting System

The entire system of reports was streamlined into one major contribution reporting system which starts with a profit and loss by product beginning at the customer level. This consolidates into a territory report and a regional summary. It then summarizes into a plant total, a division total and finally appears as a company total. This produces a profit contribution by customer, by territory, by region, by plant and by division. This enables you to determine the value contributed by each product to the total operations. Following this we have the plant and divisional contributions to the entire operation. Any weak sisters can be either weeded out or strengthened.

PROFIT CONTRIBUTION

PERIOD........................

COMPANY TOTAL

AMOUNT...$...................

% OF NET SALES ....

NON-ALLOCATED COSTS
AT DIVISION LEVELS

DIVISION A	DIVISION B	DIVISION C
AMOUNT...$..................	AMOUNT...$..................	AMOUNT...$..................
% OF NET SALES	% OF NET SALES	% OF NET SALES ....
NON-ALLOCATED DIVISION COSTS	NON-ALLOCATED DIVISION COSTS	NON-ALLOCATED DIVISION COSTS
COST CENTER A	COST CENTER B	COST CENTER C
PRODUCT 1.	PRODUCT 14.	PRODUCT 20.
PRODUCT 2.	PRODUCT 15.	PRODUCT 21.
PRODUCT 3.	PRODUCT 16.	PRODUCT 22.
PRODUCT 4.	PRODUCT 17.	PRODUCT 23.
PRODUCT 5.	PRODUCT 18.	PRODUCT 24.
PRODUCT 6.	PRODUCT 19.	PRODUCT 25.

INVENTORY STOCK STATUS REPORT

CODE NO.**	REORDER POINT	QTY	OPENING STOCK	VENDOR RECPTS	STOCK ORDERS	SET ASIDE STOCKS	SALES ISSUES	BACK ORDERS	VENDOR REJECTS	STOCK TRF.	CURRENT STOCK
454	5,500	1,000	8,627	6,000	1,000	13,671	13,671				956
458	1,000	500	4,562			2,051	2,051				2,511
470	4,200	1,000	9,555		5,000	7,452	7,452				2,103
490	3,000	1,000	7,439	8,000		11,952	6,452	5,000			3,487
500	5,000	1,000	10,571		3,000	5,782	5,782		2,000		2,789
600	5,000	1,000	18,415		8,000	15,722	15,722			3,000	4,713
700	4,000	1,000	13,455	1,000	3,000	12,456	12,456				1,999
800	1,300	500	3,567		2,000	3,567	3,567				0
900	5,200	500	9,325		7,000	9,316	9,316				7
950	5,500	1,000	8,627	6,000	1,000	13,671	13,671				956

**Detailed description furnished if required in a larger format report.

Financial Administrator's Locatomatic

THE FINANCIAL ADMINISTRATOR

A leader who can operate at and establish his credibility at the highest level of corporate management and who can lead by strength and influence, not dictum.

DEFINITION—VICE PRESIDENT FINANCE AND STAFF—DUTIES, RESPONSIBILITIES AND FUNCTIONS

Vice President Finance

A detailed review of the advertisement covering this position indicates the wide scope of operations covered and knowledge required. The following qualifications are required:

a. Ability to guide the destiny of a substantial multidivisional manufacturing firm. Functions at the corporate policy level but has operating control.
b. Requires a breadth of vision, strong personality and a wealth of tact and diplomacy.
c. Deals with banks, governments, legal firms, accounting firms and investment firms.
d. Ability to prepare stringent and detailed SEC reports.
e. Maintains an up-to-the-day knowledge of the corporate position.
f. Acts to ensure adequate funds to meet outstanding and planned commitments.
g. Can operate at a high level of financial autonomy.
h. Ability to handle pensions and pension funds.
i. Responsible for taxes and tax planning.
j. Handles accounting, finance, data processing, daily, monthly, quarterly and annual reports.
k. Supervises the Treasurer and the Controller
l. Prime objective is the stable financing and well-being of the firm.
m. Top-notch ability in cash and debt management.

The Financial Vice President normally has control over the following operations:

1. Taxes.
2. Budgeting.
3. Short- and long-term planning.
4. International finance.
5. Internal auditing.
6. Financial analysts.
7. Systems analysts.
8. Market analysts.
9. Cost accountants.
10. Controller.
11. Treasurer.

The job requirements for the various jobs are stated below:

Budgeting

1. Long-range budgets.
2. Short-range budgets and budgetary controls.
3. Data processing—installation and operation.
4. Financial reporting.

Director–Taxes

1. Federal and state tax planning and compliance.
2. Tax implications of capital expenditures, mergers, acquisitions and divestitures.
3. Planning for an overall reduction in tax costs.
4. Taxes on foreign operations.
5. Sales, use and property taxes.
6. Tax research.
7. Special assignments.

Manager–International Finance

1. Banking and credit for foreign operations.
2. Structuring financing and financing services to foreign units.
3. Financing foreign marketing.

Internal Auditor

1. Audit supervision.
2. Develop auditing techniques and practices.
3. Management reports.

Marketing Analyst

1. Industrial market research.
2. Statistical analysis techniques.
3. Market locating.
4. Market composition and corporation share studies.
5. Existing products market action.
6. Proposed products market action.
7. Tracking sales and distribution.
8. Developing an on-line marketing *data base*.

Systems Analyst

1. Design business systems for the entire firm.
2. Design systems for order entry, inventory control, credit management, production control and accounts receivable.
3. Install computer systems.
4. Analyze policies, procedures, forms and equipment.
5. Knowledge of computer languages—COBOL, FORTRAN, etc.

Financial Analyst

1. Prepare and design monthly and quarterly operating reports.
2. Monitor budgets and cost center analyses.

Financial Administrator's Locatomatic

3. Prepare capital expenditure budgets.
4. Prepare and interpret reports and management information.
5. Analyze financial impact of decisions on new products, new markets, capital expenditures, pricing and cost reduction programs.
6. Investigate operations and investigate alternatives.
7. Exhibit proven analytical ability and good interpersonal skills.
8. Have financial acumen.
9. Assess the financial consequences of alternative actions.
10. Prepare annual profit plans, updates and forecasts and an analysis of current performance.
11. Analyze and control expenditures.

Treasurer

1. Cash planning and cash flow projections.
2. Bank financing and bank relations.
3. Accounts receivable and credit control.

Controller

1. Supervise and control accounting, budgeting, financial analysis, credits and collection and data processing.
2. Shirt-sleeve operator who can interface with a wide range of outside managers.
3. Install accounting, cost accounting, planning and financial controls and hire and train the staff to operate them.
4. Supervise the office manager.
5. Design and operate all accounting and control systems.
6. Develop a data base.
7. Handle renegotiation.
8. Make pricing decisions.
9. Deliver a reporting system that will keep everyone happy.
10. Provide reports and the financial analysis required to interpret them.

Cost Accountant

1. Handle standard and new product costing.
2. Prepare bills of material and operations analysis for cost estimating.
3. Analysis of cost variations.
4. Provide divisional financial statements.
5. Material and data for planning and budgeting.
6. Provide work measurement information.
7. Operational and material data for the data base.
8. Support for pricing and cost decisions.

Planning Executive

1. Profit planning, forecasting and reporting actual vs. plan results.

2. Prepare budgets and planning reports.
3. Have a working knowledge of quantitative analysis, statistics and economics.
4. Analyze company operations and the various segments of the firm.
5. Analyze financial statement of division and product line performance.
6. Manage and provide leadership for specialists in the following fields—modeling, economic, and general business analysis, and long-range financial planning.
7. Provide financial analysis for short- and intermediate-term financial and strategic decisions.
8. Interpret short-term and long-term plans and objectives in financial terms.
9. Develop standard performance and measurement methods.
10. Provide special analysis projects and reports upon demand.
11. Keep abreast of the latest computer techniques in planning.
12. Provide the future cost of operations or credit.
13. Exhibit solid management experience in MIS.
14. Possess high technical computer knowledge.
15. Show ability to survive heavy interfacing with senior management, other institutions and third party agencies.

To sum it up—the financial administrator must be a genius!

SIZE OF STAFFS

SMALLEST FIRM 3
MEDIAN FIRM 40
LARGEST FIRM 281

PLANNING STAFFS

SMALLEST FIRM 0
MEDIAN FIRM 3
LARGEST FIRM 31

Financial Administrator's Locatomatic

CHAPTER NO.	PAGE	DESCRIPTION
1	25	THE CHALLENGE OF FINANCIAL ADMINISTRATION
	26	IMPACT OF GROWTH ON CAPITAL
	27	NEW TECHNIQUES
	28	PORTABLE DATA TERMINALS
	29	MICROFICHE RECORDS
	30	TELEFAX
	30	GRAPHICS VIDEO DISPLAY
	30	INTERNATIONAL COMMUNICATION LINKS
	31	DATA BASE REQUIREMENTS
	33	CHALLENGES
	33	SOLUTIONS
	34	TOOLS
	35	NEEDS OF MANAGEMENT
2	37	AVAILABLE DATA
	37	TASK ANALYSIS CENTER
	38	ON-LINE OPERATIONS
	39	VIDEO TERMINAL
	40	ON-LINE INVENTORY SYSTEM
	41	ON-LINE DAILY STATUS REPORT
	42	ON-LINE ACCOUNTS RECEIVABLE
	42	ON-LINE MACHINE EFFECTIVENESS
	43	VARIABLE CONTROL TECHNIQUES
	45	THE COMPUTER IN ACTION
	46	ON-LINE DAILY PROFIT AND LOSS STATEMENT
	46	ON-LINE SALES REPORT
	46	TASK ANALYSIS CENTER
	47	INVENTORY STATUS REPORT
	47	ACCOUNTS RECEIVABLE INQUIRY
	48	EXPENSE INQUIRY
	49	TERRITORIAL SALES ANALYSIS
	49	BUSINESS ACTIVITY
	50	DAILY OPERATING REPORT
	51	"BASIC" PROGRAM AND REPORT
	52	DAILY JOB COST SUMMARY
	54	TIRE DEPARTMENT SALES AND CONTROL REPORT
3	55	THE BASIC OBJECTIVE OF PROFIT CENTERS
	56	MATRIX ORGANIZATIONS
	56	COST EQUATION
	57	CONTRIBUTION TO OVERHEAD AND PROFIT
	57	ELEMENTS OF CONTROL
	57	BASIC OBJECTIVES
	58	REQUIREMENTS OF CONTROL
	59	PROFIT CONTROL CENTER
	59	COST CENTERS

	62	"HEAD COUNT" CONTROL
	62	MARKETING HIERARCHY
	63	FUNCTIONAL JOB HIERARCHY
	65	CONTROL REPORTS—BASIC CATEGORIES
	65	SALES CONTROL REPORT
	67	JOB CONTROL REPORT
	67	PRODUCTION CONTROL REPORT
	68	ZERO-BASED BUDGETING FOR CONTROL
	69	ZERO-BASED BUDGETING—CASE STUDY REPORT
	70	WHAT IS A DECISION PACKAGE?
	70	WHAT IS DOCUMENTATION?
	71	ZERO-BASED BUDGETING—THE REAL WORLD—CASE STUDY REFERENCE
	72	THE BASIC CONCEPT OF ZERO-BASED BUDGETING
	73	FIRM EXPERIENCES WITH ZERO-BASED BUDGETING
	82	PLANS, GOALS AND STRATEGIES
	86	THE FOUR BASIC STEPS IN ZERO-BASED BUDGETING—DETERMINING THE DECISION UNITS—DECISION REPORTING PACKAGES
	97	RANKING DECISION PACKAGES
	101	LESSONS LEARNED IN ZERO-BASED BUDGETING
	105	THE PLANNING CALENDAR, ALLOCATION OF RESOURCES, "WHAT IF?" IN ZERO-BASED BUDGETING
	121	MEASURING, ANALYZING AND CORRECTING PERFORMANCE
4	130	STAFFING FOR COST REDUCTION
	131	THE BASIC COST REDUCTION PLAN
	132	CHECKLIST FOR COST REDUCTION
	132	ANALYSIS OF SALES EXPENSES
	133	PRODUCTION COST ANALYSIS
	134	PAYROLL COST ANALYSIS
	135	MISCELLANEOUS COST ANALYSIS
	137	COST CONTROL "WRAP-UP"
	138	THE COST EQUATION—COMPONENTS
5	139	STRATEGIC PLANS
	140	FORECASTS
	141	OBJECTIVES—STRATEGIES
	142	FIVE-YEAR PLAN—GEORGIA—PACIFIC
	143	OBJECTIVE AND FUNCTION INTERFACING
	144	ANNUAL AND LONG-RANGE PLANS
	144	FORMS REQUIRED
	144	MONITORING A PLAN
	145	OFFENSIVE PLANS
	145	DEFENSIVE PLANS
	147	FIVE STEPS IN OBJECTIVE PLANNING
	147	REQUIREMENTS OF OBJECTIVES
	147	KNOWLEDGE SPECIALISTS

Financial Administrator's Locatomatic 483

	148	LONG-RANGE PLAN DEVELOPMENT
	149	DEVELOPING STRATEGIES
	150	MOUSETRAPS IN PLANNING
	150	GENERALITIES IN PLANNING
	151	STRATEGIC BUSINESS FACTORS
	152	TOOLS FOR PLANNING
	153	PLANNING TECHNIQUES
	153	ZERO-BASED BUDGETING
	154	CHECKLIST FOR KEEPING PLANNING AND STRATEGIES ON TARGET
	156	ZERO BUDGETING EXHIBITS
6	166	TYPES OF MODELS
	167	PURPOSE OF MODELS
	168	MODELING TECHNIQUES
	168	MODEL INPUTS AND OUTPUTS
	171	MODEL BASES
	171	TOP DOWN MODELS
	172	STRATEGIC PLANNING MODEL
	174	STRATEGIC MODELS
	174	STANDARD MODELS
	174	CONTROL MODELS
	175	BREAKEVEN POINT MODELS
	175	DO'S AND DON'TS IN MODELING
	176	GAME THEORY
	177	FINANCIAL MODEL
	177	DEFENSIVE CASH MODEL
	178	BASIC GROWTH RATE FORMULA
	180	CHECKLIST FOR EFFECTIVE MODELS
	181	PLANNING CYCLE
	181	AREAS FOR DISCUSSION
	181	PURPOSE OF MODEL
	182	USES OF THE MODEL
	182	DEVELOPMENT OF THE MODEL
	183	BASIC MODEL STRUCTURE
	183	HIGHLIGHTS OF MODEL
	184	OIL COMPANY FINANCIAL MODEL
	185	STRATEGIC PROFIT MODEL
	187	MODEL BASIS
	188	HIERARCHY OF FINANCIAL MODEL
	189	DUPONT ROI MODEL
	190	MILITARY MODEL
7	191	TASK ANALYSIS CENTER
	192	STAFF REQUIREMENTS
	194	STRATEGIC PLANNING FACTORS
	194	FINANCIAL CONTROL FACTORS
	194	MARKETING MANAGEMENT FACTORS
	194	BASIC FACTORS FOR THE DATA BANK
	195	DATA BANK STRATEGIES

	196	TYPES OF INFORMATION REQUIRED
	198	SPECIFIC PRODUCT INFORMATION
	198	THE FAILING PRODUCT
	199	OUTSIDE DATA SOURCES FOR THE DATA BANK
	200	DATA CODING
	201	DATA BASE SYSTEM INFORMATION FLOW
	202	DO'S AND DON'TS FOR DATA BASES
	203	SPECIFIC CUSTOMER COMPETITIVE INFORMATION
	204	THE INQUIRY TERMINAL—GRAPHIC DISPLAY
	205	THE INQUIRY TERMINAL—TEXT DISPLAY
8	207	COMPUTER ORGANIZATION
	209	COMPUTER SURVEY
	209	MINICOMPUTER
	212	MINICOMPUTER JOB LIST
	213	COMPUTER SYSTEM CHECKLIST
	213	COMPUTER SYSTEM BENEFITS
	213	DO'S AND DON'TS FOR MINICOMPUTERS
	214	COMPUTERIZED PRODUCTION CONTROL
	214	COMPUTER EQUIPMENT
	216	TYPE OF REPORTS
	217	SALES AND OPERATING PROFIT REPORTS
	218	BALANCE SHEET
	220	INCOME ACCOUNT
	221	RETAIL INVENTORY MANAGEMENT REPORT
	222	CUSTOMER CONTRIBUTION REPORT
	223	PERIODIC LIABILITY FORECAST
	224	CUSTOMER AGING ANALYSIS
9	230	LEASE OR PURCHASE DECISION
	233	PRESENT VALUE FORMULA
	233	DEPRECIATION METHODS
	234	FINANCIAL REPORTING OF LEASES
	235	REPORTING LEASE COMMITMENTS
	236	WHAT YOU CAN LEASE
	236	TYPES OF LEASES
	237	PITFALLS IN LEASING
	237	ADVANTAGES OF LEASING
	239	LEASE FORM
	243	REQUIREMENTS FOR LEASING
	244	ADVANTAGES AND DISADVANTAGES OF LEASING
	245	PAYBACK AND PRESENT VALUE METHODS
	245	UNCERTAINTIES IN LEASING
	246	EVALUATING LEASES
	246	ALLOCATION CRITERIA
	247	RATING CAPITAL EXPENDITURE PROJECTS
	247	BASIC STEPS IN CAPITAL EXPENDITURE CONTROL
	248	APPROPRIATION CONTROL REPORT
	249	PROJECT CONTROL REPORTS
	250	THE LEASE COMPARISON METHOD

Financial Administrator's Locatomatic

	251	LEASE OR BUY TABLES
10	253	CURRENT ASSETS
	254	ACCOUNTS RECEIVABLE
	254	INVENTORIES
	255	SPEED UP CASH FLOW
	255	CASH ADMINISTRATION
	256	CASH CYCLE
	257	CASH STRATEGY
	257	IDLE CASH TIME CYCLE
	258	CREDIT TIPS
	259	CREDIT PERFORMANCE RATING
	261	CURRENT ASSET REPORTS
	262	FORECASTING ACCOUNTS RECEIVABLE
	263	INVENTORY REPORTING
	265	ZERO BALANCE ACCOUNTS
	266	DRAFTS
	267	CURRENT ASSET COMPARISONS
	268	INVENTORY REPORTS
	269	RECEIVABLES STATUS
	269	INVENTORY STATUS
	271	WEEKLY STATUS REPORTS
11	274	ORGANIZING LIABILITY CONTROL
	275	CURRENT LIABILITIES
	277	STRETCHING PAYMENTS
	280	MINICOMPUTER LIABILITY SCHEDULES
	282	NEW TECHNIQUES IN CURRENT LIABILITY ADMINISTRATION
	283	ACCOUNTS PAYABLE MATURITY SCHEDULE
	284	ACCOUNTS PAYABLE ANALYSIS
	285	CASH FLOW RUN
	285	SHORT-TERM LIABILITY RECORD
	286	ACCOUNTS PAYABLE SCHEDULE
	287	ACCOUNTS PAYABLE LISTING
12	291	CLASSES OF STOCK
	291	PREFERRED STOCK
	295	DEBT POSITION OF VARIOUS FIRMS
	296	LOAN RESTRICTIONS
	297	SPECIAL FINANCING
	298	TRUSTS
	299	LOAN TRAPS
	300	IDEAS PRO AND CON ON VARIOUS TYPES OF FINANCING
	301	FIRM PROFILE
	301	FORECASTS REQUIRED
	301	EXHIBITS AND MODELS
	302	FINANCING EXHIBITS
13	306	TAX DEPARTMENT STRUCTURE
	308	TAX REFERENCE MATERIAL
	309	TAX PLANNING AND PROBLEMS

	311	INTERNATIONAL TAXATION
	312	TAX DODGES
	315	TAX AUDITS
	316	TAX CRACKDOWN
	318	TAX CALENDAR
	318	REQUIREMENTS FOR A "DIRECTOR OF TAXES"
	319	TAX CHECKLISTS
	320	TAXES IN THE ANNUAL REPORT
	323	WHAT THE SPECIAL AGENT LOOKS FOR!
	321	IRS TAX REFERENCES
	322	STATE APPORTIONMENT
	322	SIMPLE TAX CALENDAR
	325	TAX AUDIT PROCEDURES
	326	APPEAL PROCEDURES
14	386	EVALUATION OF ACQUISITIONS
	388	ACQUISITION CHECKLIST
	389	WHY FIRMS ARE ACQUIRED
	392	TIP-OFFS ON UNSATISFACTORY OPERATIONS
	393	CHECKLIST FOR DIVESTITURES
	393	OPPORTUNITY MODEL
	394	WHAT IF?
	394	ANALYSIS RATIOS
	396	MERGER EVALUATION
15	400	MAJOR GOVERNMENT REPORTING AGENCIES
	400	SEC REQUIREMENTS
	401	AREAS UNDER ATTACK
	403	CVA—CURRENT VALUE ACCOUNTING
	403	GPL—GENERAL PRICE LEVEL ACCOUNTING
	404	REPORT QUESTIONS AND ANSWERS
	405	FACTORS IN REPORTS
	406	SEC ACTION
16	412	BASIC INDICATORS
	413	SOURCES OF ECONOMIC DATA
	415	WHAT INFORMATION TO USE
	416	TYPES OF REPORTS AND CHARTS
	417	CHART DATA
	420	PRODUCT END USE
	420	STATISTICS
	422	WEEKLY FINANCIAL AND ECONOMIC CHECKLISTS
	422	CHECKLISTS—MONTHLY, QUARTERLY, ANNUALLY
	423	TIME CYCLE FOR CHECKLISTS
	424	CHART LIST
	424	REPORT LIST
17	426	INTERFACING FACTORS
	428	POINTS TO EMPHASIZE IN INTERFACING
	428	GROWING IMPORTANCE OF INTERFACING
18	431	CASE STUDY—COMPANY A REPORT
	432	PROBLEMS AND SOLUTIONS
	433	CASE STUDY—COMPANY B—SOLUTIONS

Financial Administrator's Locatomatic

- 438 CASE STUDY—COMPANY C—PROBLEMS
- 439 PLANS AND PLANNING
- 441 RESULTS OF PLANNING
- 442 CASE STUDY—COMPANY A—OPERATION SUMMARY
- 444 SAMPLE REPORTS—ORGANIZATION CHARTS—
CASE STUDIES OF COMPANIES A, B, C

Index

A

Ability, 33
Accounting, computerized, 207-228 (*see also* Computerized accounting)
Accounts payable, 275
Accounts receivable, 254, 262-263
Accrued items, 275, 277
Acquisitions:
    checklist, 388
    evaluation, 386-387
    financial administrator's role, 385-386
    planning and checklists, 387-388
    why firms acquired, 389-390
Activity reports, 38
Age, 33
Analytical models, 165
Annual report, 235-236, 320
Appropriation Control Report, 248
Assets, current, 253-272 (*see also* Current assets)

B

Backlog plan, 84
Balloon notes, 296
Billing—prices, 31
Bonds:
    deep discount, 294
    income, 293
    income revenue, 297
    many classes, 293
    revenue, 297
Borrowed funds, 231
Bottom up, 172
Breakeven point models, 175
Budgeting, 477
Bureaucracy, 33
Business activity, 417
Buying, 229

C

Calendar, tax, 307, 318, 322
Capital investments, 229-252 (*see also* Leasing)
Case studies:
    basic problems, 432, 439
    conclusions, 433-434

Case studies (*cont'd.*)
    conference results, 431
    cost problems, 436
    credit problems, 436
    financial problems, 430, 435
    growth, 434
    new corporate structure, 440
    new product line, 434
    new product problems, 437
    operational problems, 430, 435
    operations, 429-430
    outside assistance, 430-431
    plan for change, 439-440
    preliminary report, 431-432
    production problems, 437
    purchasing problems, 436-437
    sales problems, 436
    solutions, 432-433, 437-438
    stealing march on industry, 434-435
Cash, 254-258, 264-265 (*see also* Current assets)
Cash collections, 135
Cash flow techniques, 279
Certificates of Deposit, 257
Charts, 416
City government, 201
Coding, 200
Collateral trust, 293
Commercial Loans, 418
Commercial paper, 257
Common stock, 291
Communication, international, 30-31
Communications center, 191-205 (*see also* Data bank)
Compensation insurance, 134
Competition, 33
Computerized accounting:
    analysis reports, 216
    benefits, 213
    computer users, 209
    do's and don'ts, 213
    equipment, 214-215
    financial administrator, 209-210
    minicomputer, 211-212
    organization, 207-208
    priorities, 210-211
    reports available, 208-209
    routine functions, 216

Computerized accounting *(cont'd.)*
    setting up system, 213
    small business systems, 211
    text editor terminals, 214
Computer models, 419
Conditional sales agreements, 294
Conference results, 431
Consumption tax, 311
Contracts, 275, 276
Control:
    administering, 63
    essential elements, 57
    financial, 427-428
    financial and administrative, 58
    operational, 58
    profit centers, 55-127 (see also Profit centers)
    requirements, 58
    techniques, 427
"Control and Plan," 425
Controller, 479
Control reports, 248
Convertible debentures, 294
Corporate models, 165
Cost Accountant, 479
Cost centers, 59-63
Cost equation—components, 138
Cost estimating, 28-29
Cost problems, 436
Cost reduction:
    action checklist, 132-134
    adverse conditions, 136-137
    cash collections, 135
    charge interest on delinquent accounts, 135
    cost equation—components, 138
    discounts, 135
    examples, 129-130
    obsolete or slow-moving inventory, 135
    order in proper quantities, 135
    payroll and payroll expenses, 134-135
    plan, 131
    promoting purchases, 135
    staffing, 130
    wrap-up, 137-138
Costs:
    determining, 231
    growth challenges, 31, 33
Cost savings, 30
Credit agreements, revolving, 281
Credit function, 258-259
Credit problems, 436
Credit memos, 38
CRT, 40
Current assets:
    accounts receivable, 254, 262
    cash, 254, 255-258, 264-265
        administration, 255-256
        basic rule, 258
        duration of cycle, 256-257

Current assets *(cont'd.)*
    cash *(cont'd.)*
        effectiveness, 258
        emergency balance, 264-265
        idle, time cycle for investments, 257
        speeding up flow, 255
        strategy, 257
    credit function, 258-259
    drafts, 266
    financial administration, 253-255
    inflation and growth, 260-261
    inventories, 254, 259-260, 263-264
    on-line control, 265
    reporting techniques for controlling, 261-262
    zero balance accounts, 265-266
Current liabilities:
    accounts payable, 275-276
        justification of invoice, 275-276
        verification of prices and extensions, 276
    accrued items, 277
    cash flow techniques, 279
    contracts payable, 276
    deferred items, 277
    financial administration, 275
    financial strain, 281
    liquidity, 279
    minicomputer, 280
    mortgages payable, 276
    new methods, new techniques, 282
    notes payable, 276
    organization of control function, 274-275
    pension costs, 277
    plan for progress, 273-274
    revolving credit agreements, 281
    stability, 279
    stretching payments in time of stress, 277-279
    survival tip, 281
    vendor relations, 279
Current replacement cost, 404
Current Value Accounting, 403
Customer information, 38
Customers, 200
Customers' orders, 38

D

Daily inventory report, 38
Daily net income, 43
Daily production reports, 38
Daily profit-and-loss reports, 37-54 (see also On-line reports)
Daily shipment report, 38
Daily status report, 41
Data bank:
    approaches, 195
    central data base, 199-200
    coding, 200
    customer competitive information report, 203

Index

Data bank *(cont'd.)*
   design, 195
   developing, 194-195
   do's and don'ts, 202
   failing product, 198
   financial control, 194
   information, 191-192, 196-198
      competitive, 197-198
      profit, power, success, 191-192
      relative to specific products, 198
      speed of requirements, 196
      types, 196-197
   information flow, 201
   intelligence technology, 198-199
   key-result approach, 196
   marketing management, 194
   paperless office, 199
   role of minicomputer, 193-194
   sample master files, 200
   sources of data, 199, 201-202
      City Government, 201
      Government Agencies, 201
      law service, 199
      libraries, 202
      New York Times Information Bank, 199
      publications, 202
      special information services, 202
      State Agencies, 201
      Wall Street Journal, 199
   staff requirements, 192
   strategic planning, 194, 196
   why important, 193
Data base, 27, 28, 31-32 (*see also* Data bank)
Debentures, 294
Deep discount bonds, 294
Debt and equity capital:
   about financing, 297-298
   acquiring financing, 301
   balloon notes, 296
   bonds, 293
   classes of stock available, 291
   collateral trust—equipment trust certificates, 293
   conditional sales agreements, 294
   convertible debentures, 294
   corporate security and survival, 290
   debentures, 294
   deep discount bonds, 294
   Eurobond, 297, 299
   for or against financing, 300
   income bonds, 293
   income revenue bonds, 297
   increasing your profit, 300
   latest in financing, 300
   leasing, 298
   loan restrictions, 296
   loan traps, 299
   long-term financing, 292, 298
   methods of payment on loans, 298

Debt and equity capital *(cont'd.)*
   mortgage bonds, 293
   multicurrency loans, 297
   overborrowed, 295-296
   preferred stock, 291-292
   project financing, 298
   restructure of debt, 300-301
   revenue bonds, 297
   revolving credit, 297
   short term—convertible to longer term, 296
   short-term financing, 301-302
   special financing, 294
   special projects, 297
   subordinated debentures, 294
   term financing, 301-302
   trust to acquire property, 298-299
   warrants, 292
   what loans are used for, 297
Decision package, 70, 97-100
Decision Package Ranking, 98
Decision units, 87
Defensive cash model, 177-178
Defensive plans, 145
Deferred items, 277
Delinquent accounts, 135
Delphi Theory, 152
Demand Deposits, 418
Depreciated replacement cost, 404
Depreciation, 233
Director—Taxes, 478
Disclosure, 404
Discounted Rate of Return, 245
Discounting Technique, 168
Discounts, utilize, 135
Distributing computers, 36
Diversification, 395
Divestiture model, 171
Divestitures, 385-386, 391-392, 393
Document, leasing, 238-242
Drafts, 266

E

Economic and financial links, 32
Economics, 409-424 (*see also* Macroeconomics)
Energy, 33
Environment, 33
Equilease Forms, 238-242
Equipment, 214-215
Equipment trust certificates, 293
Equity capital (*see* Debt and equity capital)
Eurobonds, 257, 297, 299
Eurodollars, 257
Expansions, reasons, 32

F

Facsimile, 30
Facts, 192-193 (*see also* Data bank)

Fair market value, 243
Files, master, 200
Finance leases, 236
Financial administration, 26
Financial administrator, 209-210
Financial Analyst, 478-479
Financial control, 427-428
Financial management system, 31
Financial model, 168
Financial plan, 85, 147
Financial problems, 430, 435
Financing (*see* Debt and equity capital)
Flexibility, 29, 150
Forecasting models, 165
Forecasts, 140, 409-410
Foreign tax matters, 313-314
Full-service leases, 237
Functional objectives, 142-143

G

Game theory, 176-177
General Price Level Accounting, 403
Goal, 83
Government agencies, 201
Government Securities Held, 418
Graphics video display, 30
Growth, 32, 260-261, 434
Growth rate, 178

H

Historical cost accounting, 403

I

Income bonds, 293
Income revenue bonds, 297
Indicators, 412, 417
Inflation, 33, 260-261
Information, 191-192, 196-198, 308-309 (*see also* Data bank)
Information acquisition and retrieval, 31, 200
Information services, 202
Inputs, model, 168-170
Interest charge, delinquent accounts, 135
Interfacing:
    control, 427
    "Control and Plan," 425
    financial control, 427-428
    growing importance, 428
    planning, 425-426
Interfacing data, 28
Internal Auditor, 478
International communication links, 30-31
Inventories, 40, 200, 254, 259-260, 263-264
Inventory:
    control, 31
    indices, 404

Inventory (*cont'd.*)
    obsolete or slow-moving, 135
    report, 38
    valuation, 404
Investments, capital, 229-252 (*see also* Leasing)
Invoicing, 38

J

Joint ventures, 391

K

Key-result approach, 196

L

Language, on-line reports, 39-40
Law service, 199
Leasing:
    advantages, 237-238
    annual report, 235-236
    control and checkup, 248
    control reports, 248-249
    decision, 248
    determination and allocation, 246-247
    economic climate, 248
    finance, 236
    financial model, 245-246
    financial reporting, 234-235
    full-service, 237
    initiation of projects, 248
    lease or purchase, 230
    leveraged, 237, 243-244
        advantages and disadvantages, 244
        basic requirements, 243
        cost, 244
        what is covered, 243
    long-term finance, 237, 298
    "net," 243
    operating, 236
    payback method, 245
    pitfalls, 237
    presentation, 248
    present value method, 245
    projections, 248
    rating projects, 247
    secured loans, 237
    short-term operating, 237
    should you, 250-252
    "true lease," 243
    typical documents, 238-242
    what can be leased, 236
Leveraged leases, 237, 243-244
Liabilities, current, 273-287 (*see also* Current liabilities)
Libraries, 202
Liquidity, 279
Loans:
    commercial, 418

Index

Loans *(cont'd.)*
    Eurobond, 297, 299
    methods of payment, 298
    multicurrency, 297
    restrictions, 296
    traps, 299
    use, 297
Locatomatic, 475-487
Long range models, 165
Long-term finance leases, 237
Long-term financing, 292, 298

M

Macroeconomics:
    administration and staffing, 410-411
    business activity, 417
    business tides, 418
    checklists, 422-424
    computer models, 419-420
    don't underestimate, 410
    forecasts, 409-410
    government securities held, 418
    gross national product, 409
    importance, 410
    indicators, 417
    paperboard—paper, 418-419
    personal income, 420-421
    reports and charts, 416
    retail sales, 419
    sources of economic data, 413-416
    stock prices, 417-418
    term, 411-413
    trend, 413, 419
    truck activity, railroad carloadings, 419
Management by objective, 143-144
Management communications center, 191-205 (*see also* Data bank)
Management control, 30, 196
Manager—International Finance, 478
Manufacturing Plan, 88
Marketing Analyst, 478
Marketing plan, 83-84, 145-146
Master files, 200
Matrix organizations, 56
Merchandise inquiry, 38
Mergers, 385-386, 388-389, 396-397
Microfiche, 29-30
Minicomputer, 193-194, 211-212, 280
"Mission Control," 30
Mission controller, 27
Models:
    analytical, 165
    answers to interviews, 166-167
    basic growth rate formula, 178-179
    best method, 172
    bottom up, 172
    breakeven point, 175

Models *(cont'd.)*
    check list, 180
    computer, spotting trends, 419
    control, 174
    corporate, 165
    defensive cash, 177-178
    development, 182
    discounting technique, 168
    divestiture, 171
    do's and don'ts, 175-176
    factory control, 174-175
    financial, 168
    flow chart, 184
    forecasting, 165
    game theory, 176
    hierarchy, 188
    highlights of computer program, 183
    inputs and outputs, 168-170
        economic forecasts input, 170
        economic forecasts output, 170
        lease/rent/buy analysis inputs, 170
        lease/rent/buy analysis output, 170
        monthly input—financial operations, 168
        monthly output, 168
        planning inputs, 168-169
        planning outputs, 169
        project analysis inputs, 169
        project analysis outputs, 170
        sales forecasting inputs, 169
        sales forecasting outputs, 169
    long range/short range, 165
    military, 190
    operational, 165
    opportunity, dynamics, 393-395
    practical at every level, 177
    purpose, 167, 181
    return-on-investment, 189
    simulation, 168
    specific types used, 166
    standard, 174
    strategic, 165, 172-174
    strategic profit, 185
    structure, determination, 183
    top down, 171-172
    typical base, 171
    uses, 182
    varied for conditions, 170-171
    who uses, 167
Mortgage bonds, 293
Mortgages payable, 275, 276
Multicurrency loans, 297

N

Net realizable value, 404
New product line, 434
New product problems, 437
New York Times Information Bank, 199
Notes, 275, 276

O

Objectives (*see* Planning)
Offensive plans, 145
On-line challenges, 28
On-line control, 265
On-line reports:
    control techniques for variables, 43
    CRT or VIDEO TERMINAL, 40
    daily inventory, 38
    daily production, 38
    daily profit-and-loss statement, 43
    daily shipment, 38
    daily status, 41-42
    getting on line, 37
    graphic displays, 49
    inventories, 40, 41
    language, 39-40
    on-line editing, 39
    on-line entry, 39
    on-line inquiry, 39
    on-line reporting, 39
    on-line update, 40
    operating on line, 38-39
    order status, 38
    widespread use, 40
Operating leases, 236
Operational control, 196
Operational models, 165
Operational problems, 430, 435
Operations, 429-430
Operations plan, 84-85
Order entry, 31
Ordering, proper quantities, 135
Order inquiries, 38
Orders forecast, 84
Order status report, 38
Organizational objectives, 141-142
Outputs, model, 168-170
Overborrowing, 295-296
Overhead Plan Packages, 88
Overtime, 134

P

Paperboard—paper, 418-419
Paperwork, 199
Payback Method, 245
Payroll and payroll expenses, 134-135
Payrolls, 31
Pension costs, 277
Performance, 121-127
Personal income, 420
Personnel, 200
Planning:
    annual or long-range, 144
    checklist, 154-155

Planning *(cont'd.)*
    defensive plans, 145
    development, 140
    financial—results, 147
    forecasts, 140
    for progress, 33
    long-range, 148
    marketing plan, 145-146
    monitoring plan, 144-145
    objectives, 141-144, 147
        basic requirements, 147
        functional, 142-143
        management by, 143-144
        objective and function interfacing, 143
        organizational, 141-142
    offensive plans, 145
    preparing, 144
    steps, 147
    strategies, 139, 149-155 (*see also* Strategies)
    tax, 305, 309-310
    what it can do for you, 146
Planning calendar, 108
Planning Executive, 479-480
Plans, how evolved, 65
Plant contribution, 66
Portable data terminals, 28
Preferred stock, 291-292
Preliminary orders forecast, 83
Present Value, 233
Present Value Method, 245
"Private placement," 244
Problems, 33-34
Product contribution, 66
Production problems, 437
Production reports, 38
Productive capacity, 404
Products, 200
Profit centers:
    administering with control techniques, 63
    basic activity or cost centers, 59-63
    basic objective, 56
    essential elements of control, 57
    how plans evolve, 65
    matrix organizations, 56
    plant contribution, 66
    product contribution, 66
    reporting, 65
    requirements of control, 58
    what they provide, 59
    what we accomplish, 66
    zero-based budgeting, 68-127 (*see also* zero-based budgeting)
Project Control Report, 249
Project financing, 298
Project/Program Plan, 88
Publications, 202

Index

Purchases, promote, 135
Purchasing, 230, 231
Purchasing problems, 436-437

Q

Quality, 33
Quotations, 38

R

Railroad carloadings, 419
Ranking, 98-100
Rent, 229
Replacement cost accounting, 403
Reporting, 65
Reports:
    computer, 208
    control, 248
    economic, 416
    on-line, 37-54 (*see also* On-line reports)
    preliminary, 431-432
    SEC, 399-407 (*see also* SEC reports)
Repurchase Agreements, 257
Retail sales, 419
Retained earnings, 317
Revenue bonds, 297
Revolving credit agreements, 281, 296

S

Sales, 132
Sales expenses, 132
Sales problems, 436
Sales statistics, 31
Savings, cost, 30
Scheduling order, 38
SEC reports:
    Current Value Accounting, 403
    disclosure, 404
    earnings, 406
    General Price Level Accounting, 403
    important factors, 405-406
    key definitions, 404
    late developments, 406-407
    major agencies, 400
    replacement cost accounting, 403
    time factor, 407
    word of warning, 406
Secured loans, 237
Security, corporate, 290
Shipment plan, 84
Shipment report, 38
Short range models, 165
Short term—convertible to longer term, 296
Short-term financing, 301-302
Short-term operating leases, 237
Simulation, 168

Small business, 211
Solutions, 33-34
Stability, 279
Staff, 192, 306
Staffing, 130, 410-411
State agencies, 201
Statistics, sales, 31
Status report, on-line daily, 41-42
Stock, 291-292
Stock prices, 417-418
Strategic models, 165, 172-174
Strategic planning, 194, 196
Strategies:
    available systems, 152-153
    checklist, 154-155
    Delphi Theory, 152
    development of strategic organizations, 152
    flexibility, 150
    how developed, 149-150
    problems, 150
    strategic factors, 151
    strategic planning here to stay, 153
    tax, 313
    zero-based budgeting, 153-154
Strategy, 30, 83 (*see also* Planning and strategy)
Strategy center profiling, 84
Subordinated debentures, 294
Systems Analyst, 478

T

Takeovers, 385-386
Taxes:
    allocations on state returns, 322
    annual report, 320
    audits, 315-316, 321-384
    calendar, 307, 318, 322
    corporate shelter, 311
    crackdown, 316-317
    dodges, 312-313
    files, 308
    foreign matters, 313-314
    international, 311-312
    manuals, 314
    national sales, 311
    organization and staff, 306-307
    planning, 305, 309-310
    problems encountered, 310
    retained earnings, 317
    skull sessions, 314
    sources of information, 308-309
    state and local, 310-311
    strategies, 313
    tax manager, 318-319
    value added or consumption, 311
    working papers, 308

Tenders, 390-391
Term financing, 301-302
Text editor terminals, 214
Treasury bills, 257
Trends, 412, 413, 419
Trust creation to acquire property, 298

W

Warrants, 292
Working papers, 308

Z

Zero based budgeting, 68